Istanbul 1435 / 2013

© Erkam Publications 2013 / 1435 H
ISBN: 978-9944-83-583-1

Erkam Publications
Ikitelli Organize Sanayi Bölgesi Mah.
Atatürk Bulvarı, Haseyad 1. Kısım No: 60/3-C
Başakşehir, Istanbul, Turkey
Tel: (+90-212) 671-0700 pbx
Fax: (+90-212) 671-0717
E-mail: info@islamicpublishing.net
Web site: http://islamicpublishing.net

The author   : Dr. Murat KAYA
Origina title   : «Efendimiz'den (s.a.v) Hayat Ölçüleri»
                     (İngilizce)
Translator   : Elif ECER
Editor   : İsmail ERİŞ
Graphics   : Râsim ŞAKİROĞLU
Printed by   : Erkam Printhouse

PRINCIPLES FOR LIFE

from the life of

The Prophet Muhammad ﷺ

- 250 Ahadith and Their Commentaries -

Dr. Murat KAYA

ERKAM
PUBLICATIONS

CONTENTS

FOREWORD

اَلْحَمْدُ لِلهِ رَبِّ الْعَالَمِينَ وَالصَّلاَةُ وَالسَّلاَمُ عَلَى

رَسُولِناَ مُحَمَّدٍ وَعَلَى آلِهِ وَصَحْبِهِ أَجْمَعِينَ

Infinite thanks and praises be to our Almighty Lord Allah each one of whose characteristics is almighty, each one of whose names is perfect, and each one of whose artworks is unimaginably beautiful, whose knowledge and wisdom is absolute, whose benediction is abundant, and whose mercy is boundless!

Infinite blessings and greetings be to the Sultan of the worlds, the Prophet Muhammad (pbuh), the cause of our creation, the cure of our life, the eternal light of Islam and faith, the best exemplar who shapes our character, and our interceder in both worlds!

It is known that;

The last divine book is the Noble Qur'an and the last prophet is His Excellency prophet Muhammad Mustafa (pbuh), who is the seal of the Messengers and master of the Prophets.

Qur'an and the Sunnah of the Prophet are the two fundamental sources of Islam, the final religion in the presence of Allah.

If one of them is missing, neither religion nor faith would be complete.

For this reason, in the presence of Allah the Almighty, obeying the Prophet (pbuh) is same as obeying Allah, and He specifically draws attention to this fact in the Noble Qur'an. In the following verses it is stated that:

"He who obeys the Messenger, obeys Allah." (Al-Nisa; 4:80)

"Those who obey Allah and His Messenger will be admitted to Gardens with rivers flowing beneath, to abide therein (forever) and that will be the supreme achievement." (Al-Nisa; 4:13)

These divine statements show that obeying the Prophet (pbuh) is a necessary condition for faith. However, this obedience should not be out of duty but from the heart, out of sincerity and love. This level of obedience is also laid down as a condition by Allah:

"But no, by the Lord, they can have no (real) Faith, until they make you judge in all disputes between them, and find in their souls no resistance against Your decisions, but accept them with the fullest conviction." (Al-Nisa; 4:65)

The same level of delicacy in the rules regarding obeying the Prophet applies when it comes not to revolt against him as well. As a matter of fact, Allah considered disobedience to the Prophet the same as disobedience to Himself and strongly prohibited it. In the noble verses, the warning is clear for those who disobey the Messenger of Allah:

"But those who disobey Allah and His Messenger and transgress His limits will be admitted to a Fire, to abide therein: And they shall have a humiliating punishment." (Al-Nisa; 4:14)

"…let those beware who withstand the Messenger's order, lest some trial befall them, or a grievous penalty be inflicted on them." (Al-Nur; 24:63)

All these divine measures indicate the divine dimension of the sayings of Prophet Muhammad as a source of Islam second only to the Qur'an. This is why obedience to the Prophet (pbuh) means to follow his sayings. And this is also why, just as the Noble Qur'an is a revelation from Allah, Prophet Muhammad's Sunnah and ahadith which explain what the Qur'an concisely means are also considered as revelations from Allah. This is a fact expressed in the Qur'an as follows:

"Nor does he speak of (his own) desire. It is no less than inspiration sent down to him…" (Al-Najm; 53:3-4)

As a matter of fact, since Noble Qur'an is revealed to the heart of the Prophet Muhammad,[1] his every act became the moral of Qur'an. Thus, his sayings (hadith) manifested themselves as the interpretation of the Qur'an. In short, the entire life, sayings, and acts of our Master (pbuh) are the best explanation of the Noble Qur'an.

---

1. Al-Baqarah; 2:97

In this respect, the Noble Qur'an and the Sunnah represent an indivisible unity. Whoever holds on to them does not go astray and earns eternal salvation. Indeed this fact is expressed by the Prophet (pbuh) in his famous Farewell Speech:

"I left with you two things. If you follow them, you will never go astray. One of them is the Book of Allah and the other is the Sunnah of His Prophet." (Ibn Hisham, IV, 276; *Muwatta,* Qadar, 3)

For this reason, the Companions of the Prophet and the righteous scholars who are the inheritors of the prophets have attributed great importance to the Sunnah and to the ahadith which are the written documents of the Sunnah and transmitted them to us with a praiseworthy accuracy. The most important factor in the transmission of the Sunnah to this day is Muslims' learning it from each other and keeping it alive by practicing it in their lives since the time of the Prophet Muhammad (pbuh). So much so that in order to accept someone's reporting of a hadith, some scholars of hadith used to require that the narrator of the hadith practice it in his/her life.

In other words, the issue was not just to report the sayings of the Prophet but also to understand and practice them in the best way. Sunnah of the Prophet is our most valuable and primary source which explain and interpret our sacred book. Ahadith are the channels through which our beloved Prophet Muhammad communicates with us. It is his way of talking to us from centuries ago, and showing us to the straight path. Ahadith are the breaths from the Age of Bliss, the only cure for the problems of the contemporary man who is drowning in the swirls of modern ignorance.

Thus, in order to add our lives a Prophetic cure and love, a Muhammadan blessing and benediction we must always hold tight to the Qur'an and the Sunnah of the Prophet Muhammad (pbuh). In order to achive this, it is our fundamental task to read and understand the ahadith first.

With the encouragement of our esteemed elders, this book that you are holding has been written because of this fundamental duty and out of necessity. First, ahadith about certain topics are selected. We have compiled sayings of our beloved Prophet (pbuh) related to practical side of Islam, faith, worship, avoiding sins, calling to the true path, and serving in the way of Allah. These topics are briefly explained with the help of fundamental sources under the light of verses and other ahadith.

The selected hadith are taken from credible hadith books. Every hadith is compared to its original form by cross checking it with its source. We have paid special attention to their translations as much as we can in terms of being loyal to their originals and expressing the meaning by good usage of the language.

While asking Allah the Almighty to forgive our mistakes and accept our good deeds;

I would like to express my sincere thanks to first of all our honorable teacher Osman Nuri TOPBAŞ who suggested the writing of this work and provided every kind of support and help during the process;

To my honorable teachers Abdullah SERT, Ahmet TAŞGETİREN, Mustafa ERİŞ, Prof. Dr. Ethem CEBECİOĞLU, Ass. Prof. Dr. Ömer ÇELİK, Dr. Âdem ERGÜL and other teachers who put efforts in reviewing and revisions;

To my brothers Harun KIRKIL and Şükrü Mutlu KARAKOÇ;

Especially to asst. prof. Mustafa ÖZTÜRK, Sadettin EKİNCİ and Muhammed Ali EŞMELİ;

Furthermore, I sincerely thank to the directors of Altinoluk Magazine who accurately published and distributed this book to its readers as a gift.[2]*

May Our Lord turn all our efforts into continuous charity that are suitable for His consent. May He grant us the opportunity to live as living Qur'ans by holding on to the Sunnah of our Prophet (pbuh). May Allah bless us with the intercession of His Messenger (pbuh) on the Day of Judgment under his umbrella!

Amen!

Dr. Murat KAYA

June, 2007

Sultantepe – Üsküdar

2. * Turkish version of this book was distributed by Altinoluk as a gift in 2007 to those who subscribed.

A. ACCEPT ISLAM AND FIND SALVATION

١ . عَنِ الشَّعْبِيِّ قَالَ لَمَّا قَدِمَ عَدِيُّ ابْنُ حَاتِمٍ رَضِيَ اللهُ عَنْهُ الْكُوفَةَ أَتَيْنَاهُ فِي نَفَرٍ مِنْ فُقَهَاءِ أَهْلِ الْكُوفَةِ فَقُلْنَا لَهُ: حَدِّثْنَا مَا سَمِعْتَ مِنْ رَسُولِ اللهِ صَلَّى اللهُ عَلَيْهِ وَسَلَّمَ فَقَالَ: أَتَيْتُ النَّبِيَّ صَلَّى اللهُ عَلَيْهِ وَسَلَّمَ فَقَالَ:

«يَا عَدِيَّ ابْنَ حَاتِمٍ، أَسْلِمْ تَسْلَمْ»

قُلْتُ: «وَمَا الْإِسْلَامُ؟» فَقَالَ:

«تَشْهَدُ أَنْ لَا إِلٰهَ إِلَّا اللهُ وَأَنِّي رَسُولُ اللهِ وَتُؤْمِنُ بِالْأَقْدَارِ كُلِّهَا خَيْرِهَا وَشَرِّهَا حُلْوِهَا وَمُرِّهَا».

1. Sha'bi narrates:

When Adi b. Hatim (r.a) came to Kufah, we went to visit him with a group of jurists from Kufah. We said to him:

"Would you mind telling us about the things that you heard from the Prophet?"

Upon this, Adi (r.a.) said:

I went to the Prophet. He told me:

"O Adi b. Hatim, accept Islam and reach salvation!"

I asked him:

"What is Islam?"

The Messenger of Allah (pbuh) said:

" –That you bear witness that there is no god but Allah, and that I am His Messenger, you believe everything in fate, its good, its bad, those which are sweet and those which are bitter." (Ibn Majah, Muqaddimah, 10)

❁

٢. عَنِ الْبَرَاءِ رَضِيَ اللهُ عَنْهُ يَقُولُ: أَتَى النَّبِيَّ صَلَّى اللهُ عَلَيْهِ وَسَلَّمَ رَجُلٌ مُقَنَّعٌ بِالْحَدِيدِ فَقَالَ: ﴿يَا رَسُولَ اللهِ أَقَاتِلُ وَأُسْلِمُ؟﴾ قَالَ:

﴿أَسْلِمْ ثُمَّ قَاتِلْ﴾ فَأَسْلَمَ ثُمَّ قَاتَلَ فَقُتِلَ. فَقَالَ رَسُولُ اللهِ صَلَّى اللهُ عَلَيْهِ وَسَلَّمَ:

﴿عَمِلَ قَلِيلًا وَأُجِرَ كَثِيرًا﴾.

2. It is related that al-Bara' said:

(In the Uhud War) a man who was wearing iron armor came to the Prophet and asked:

"O the Messenger of Allah! Is it all right if I join the war now and convert to Islam when the war is over?"

The Messenger of Allah (pbuh) said:

"First convert to Islam first and then fight!"

After converting to Islam, the man joined the war and was martyred.

Upon that, the Messenger of Allah (pbuh) said:

"His action was little but his reward is great." (Bukhari, Jihad, 13; Ahmad, IV, 293)

❁

٣. عَنِ ابْنِ عُمَرَ رَضِيَ اللهُ عَنْهُمَا قَالَ: قَالَ رَسُولُ اللهِ صَلَّى اللهُ عَلَيْهِ وَسَلَّمَ:

«بُنِيَ الْإِسْلَامُ عَلَى خَمْسٍ: شَهَادَةِ أَنْ لَا إِلهَ إِلاَّ اللهُ وَأَنَّ مُحَمَّداً رَسُولُ اللهِ وَإِقَامِ الصَّلَاةِ وَإِيتَاءِ الزَّكَاةِ وَالْحَجِّ وَصَوْمِ رَمَضَانَ».

3. As narrated by Ibn Umar, Allah's Apostle (pbuh) said:

"*Islam is based on (the following) five (principles): the testifying (shahada) that there is no god except Allah and Muhammad is the Messenger of Allah; establishing the prayer (salat); paying the zakat (wealth-tax), the Hajj and the fast (sawm) of Ramadan.*" (Bukhari, Iman, 2; Tefsir, 2/10; Muslim, Iman, 19-22)

٤. عَنْ عَبْدِ اللهِ بْنِ عَمْرِو بْنِ الْعَاصِ رَضِيَ اللهُ عَنْهُ أَنَّ رَسُولَ اللهِ صَلَّى اللهُ عَلَيْهِ وَسَلَّمَ قَالَ:

«قَدْ أَفْلَحَ مَنْ أَسْلَمَ وَرُزِقَ كَفَافاً وَقَنَّعَهُ اللهُ بِمَا آتَاهُ».

4. Abdullah Amr b. al-As reported Allah's Messenger (pbuh) as saying:

"*He is successful who has accepted Islam, who has been provided with sufficient for his want and been made contented by Allah with what He has given him.*" (Muslim, Zakat, 125. Also see Tirmidhi, Zuhd, 35/2348)

Explanations:

The most important need of human beings who were sent to this world for being tested is to find peace and salvation in the eternal life. Thus, their ultimate goal should be finding peace in this world and reaching eternal happiness in the Hereafter by glorifying the spiritual life in this world. However, due to the impediments of the human inner self and tricks of Satan, it is very difficult for a man to find salvation in the Hereafter by using his intelligence and potential. For this reason, Allah the Almighty showed mercy to His servants and sent His prophets and books. Humanity can find salvation only by following the enlightened teachings of these blessed divine guides.

The real salvation that the humankind needs is giving the last breath in faith, thus entering into the Paradise and avoiding the hellfire. In other words, it is to receive eternal bliss by gaining the consent of Allah. This could only be possible by first accepting Islam and then following a lifestyle in accordance with the limits of the Qur'an and Sunnah; because *"Islam is the beginning of all works."* [3] Going through all kinds of difficulty, trouble, and suffering, the Prophet (pbuh) invited human beings to the straight path. For the salvation of the entire world, he sent messengers to the rulers of the neighboring countries inviting them to *"Accept Islam; Find Salvation."* [4]

Since converting to Islam is the fundamental condition for salvation, the Messenger of Allah (pbuh) strongly wanted for a person to choose Islam and became extremely happy for them if they find the straight path. For example, nothing made him as happy as Abu Bakr's conversion to Islam. (Ibn Kathir, el-Bidaya, III, 80)

Again, when other servants of Allah such as Abu Dharr,[5] Khalid b. Zayd,[6] Hubayb b. Yasaf,[7] and Rayhanah bint-i Amr[8] found salvation by choosing Islam, signs of great happiness, good news, and smiles were seen on his face.

Adi b. Khatim (r.a.) expressed the happiness of our Master as:

"When I became a Muslim, I saw the face of the Messenger of Allah brightened with great happiness." (Ahmad, IV, 378)

Another example regarding the importance of converting to Islam is that the Messenger of Allah (pbuh) asked from a man who came fully equipped to fight at the most difficult moment of a war to convert to Islam before everything else. This is because, in order for our good deeds to mean something in the sight of Allah being Muslim is the necessary condition. Otherwise, good deeds do not benefit us in the Hereafter. For the good deeds done without faith, only some kind of worldly benefits are given due to the justice and mercy of Allah. (Muslim, Munafiqin, 57; Haythami, III, 111)

Islam is the Religion before Allah.[9] If anyone desires a religion other than Islam, it will never be accepted of him; and in the Hereafter he will be among

---

3.   Tirmidhi, Iman, 8/2616; Ibn-i Majah, Fitan, 12; Ahmad, V, 231, 236, 237.
4.   See Bukhari, Bad'ul-vahy, 2; Jihad, 102; Cizye, 6; Ikrah, 2; I'tisam, 18; Muslim, Jihad, 74.
5.   Hakim, *Mustadrak*, III, 385/5459.
6.   Ibn-i Kathir, *Bidaya*, III, 83.
7.   Waqidi, *Maghazi*, I, 47.
8.   Ibn-i Kathir, *Bidaya*, IV, 128.
9.   Al-i Imran; 3:19.

those who are disappointed. [10] This is because Allah has chosen Islam as the religion for His servants. [11] Therefore, the salvation of humans will be only through Islam.

One day, Umar (r.a.) saw Abu Talha sad. When he asked for the reason, Talha (r.a.) said:

"One day the Messenger of Allah (pbuh) said:

"Verily, I know a phrase that whoever says it at the deathbed, it will surely become a divine light for his book of deeds, and his body and soul will gain the consent of Allah, will receive His mercy and find peace."

The Messenger of Allah (pbuh) passed away before I had a chance to ask him what that phrase was. This is why I feel sad."

Upon that, Umar (r.a.) said:

"I know that phrase. It is the phrase of testimony that there is no god but Allah (*La ilaha illallah*) which Allah's (pbuh) Prophet wanted from his uncle (Abu Talib) to utter it on his deathbed. And if there was another phrase better than this phrase, he would ask his uncle to say it." (Ibn Majah, Adab, 54. Also see Ahmad, I, 6)

Conversion to Islam cleanses a human by removing all previous mistakes and sins.[12] For this reason, the Messenger of Allah (pbuh) forgave even his biggest enemies for the sake of saying the words of testimony (*La ilaha illallah*) and cautioned his friends to avoid reminding these newly converts their previous cruel behaviors. [13] For example, just because they uttered the word of testimony (*kalima-i shahada*), Allah's Messenger (pbuh) forgave Habbar b. Aswad who was responsible of the death of Prophet's daughter Zaynab by causing her to fall from her camel; Wahshi who martyred Prophet's beloved uncle Hamza; and Ikrima (r.a.), the son of Abu Jahl who had oppressed believers for many years.

However, saying the word of testimony is not enough for a complete salvation. In other words, after converting to Islam, there are some liabilities that one must fulfill. These can be briefly expressed as obeying the commands of Allah and avoiding His prohibitions.

---

10. Al-i Imran; 3:85.
11. Al-Maidah (The Table); 5:3.
12. See Anfal 8/38; Muslim, Iman, 192; Ahmad, II, 204; Ibn-i Sa'd, I, 299.
13. Waqidi, II, 857-858.

In fact, once Wahb b. Munabbih was asked:

"Isn't "La ilaha illallah" the key to Paradise?"

He replied:

"Yes of course, but there is no key without teeth. If you bring a key which has teeth, it will open for you. If not, it will not open for you." (Bukhari, Janaiz, 1)

In other words, religion is a whole. For this reason, it is necessary for us to accept all of its commands and reflect them in every aspect of our lives. When Abu Bakr (r.a.) became the caliph, he announced that he will declare war against those who does not pay their zakat (obligatory alms). This was done to protect the religion. Otherwise, there would be nothing left but only a system of thought that is separated from worship and practice, just like today's Christianity, and this would mean nothing. Therefore, arguments like historicity which would harm the meaning of religion could not be applied to Islam. Islam presents a complete picture with its belief system (creed), acts of worship, morals, and substantial rules.

Now let's remember some of the rules that resemble the teeth of a key: **The above mentioned third hadith** informs us about the fundamentals upon which Islam is built: These are the testimony of faith, daily prayers, zakat (obligatory alms), Hajj (pilgrimage), and fasting. Islam has brought other commands apart from these five requirements. The following narration of Umar (r.a.) concisely presents some of them:

When a revelation came to the Prophet (pbuh), a sound similar to the sound of buzzing bees used to be heard. One day, he received a revelation. We waited for a while, and after receiving the divine revelation, the Messenger of Allah (pbuh) turned towards Ka'bah and prayed raising his hands up:

"O Allah, increase Your blessings and our numbers; do not decrease. Bless us; do not make us despicable. Bestow upon us; do not deprive us. Prefer us; do not prefer others over us. Make us contented and be content with us!"

Then he said *"I received ten verses of Qur'an. Whoever practices them enters Paradise"* and recited the first ten verses of the chapter al-Muminun:

"The believers must (eventually) win through, those who humble themselves in their prayers; who avoid vain talk; who are active in deeds of charity; who abstain from sex, except with those joined to them in the mar-

riage bond, or (the captives) whom their right hands possess, for (in their case) they are free from blame. But those whose desires exceed those limits are transgressors.

Those who faithfully observe their trusts and their covenants and who (strictly) guard their prayers; these will be the heirs, who will inherit Paradise: they will dwell therein (forever)." (Al-Muminun; 23:1-10) (Tirmidhi, Tafsir, 23/3173; Ahmad, I, 34; Hakim, I, 717/1961)

As a matter of fact, this essentially was the morality of the Prophet. Indeed, when a group of people asked Aisha the mother of believers:

"O the Mother of Believers! What was the character of the Messenger of Allah (pbuh) like?" and she answered:

"His character was the Noble Qur'an."

Then she said to one of them:

"You have read the chapter al-Muminun, haven't you? Recite starting from the verse **"The believers must (eventually) win through…"** and keep reading!"

When the person reciting the verses came to the tenth verse, Aisha (r.a.) said:

"That was the character of the Messenger of Allah (pbuh)." (Hakim, II, 426/3481; Bukhari, Al-Adab al-Mufrad, no: 308)

Indeed, Qur'an formed the character of the Messenger of Allah. Then, those who want salvation must follow all the principles of the Qur'an and the Sunnah. This is the sole condition to be a noble and perfect human being by improving our character. As Qatadah said:

"Qur'an has brought the best of morals that human beings can reach." (Ibn Sa'd, I, 364)

Some of the characteristics mentioned in the Qur'an and the Sunnah about those who found salvation can be listed as:

• To believe in the Unseen, to be steadfast in prayer, to spend out of what is provided for them, and to believe in the Books sent to prophets and the Hereafter, (Al-Baqarah; 2:2-5)

• To invite people what is good and to forbid what is wrong, (Al-i-Imran; 3:104)

• To stay away from interest (*riba*), (Al-i-Imran; 3:130)

• To stay away from traps of Satan such as intoxicants and gambling, and games such as (dedication of) stones, and (divination by) arrows, (Al-Maidah; 5:90)

• To stay away from cruelty and injustice, (Al-An'am; 6:21, 135; Yusuf; 12:23)

• To strive and fight with one's wealth and life in the way of Allah, (Al-Tawbah; 9:88)

• To fulfill one's responsibilities to Allah and to perform good deeds, (Al-Hajj; 22/77)

• To live a modest life and to pledge for one's sins, (Al-Nur; 24:31)

• To purify ourselves from all kinds of spiritual sicknesses such as profanity and insurgency, (Al-A'la; 87:14; (Al-Shams; 91:9)

• To follow the way of Prophet Muhammad, (Ahmad, II, 188)

• To stay away from mischief. (Ahmad, II, 441)

Those who become Muslims by complying with these conditions and those who are provided with sufficient daily bread and who accept it with contentment find salvation and live a peaceful life both in this world and in the Hereafter.

Our fourth hadith expresses that Islam comes before everything else, and the necessity of having sufficient permissible (halal) daily bread and a contented heart for it comes right after that. At this point, regarding daily bread, the issue of being halal is extremely important. That is because the religious and spiritual lives depend on it. Neither worships nor prayers are accepted from those who earn their lives through impermissible (haram) way. Such people deserve to be punished by the fire. It is also extremely important to be satisfied with the earned permissible daily bread once it is sufficient. Those who combine these two aspects will find salvation. Acting greedily, neglecting to worship and to be prepared for the hereafter, collecting money without differentiating between halal and haram, and getting deceived by material goods is the worst disaster which can happen to a human being. Such people's hope for salvation would be very slim. They must pull themselves together immediately and hold on the prescription of "salvation" stated in the above mentioned hadith.

For the believers who are blessed with Islam and live according to the commands of Allah, there is only one important issue left, which is to pass away with faith. Indeed, the Messenger of Allah (pbuh) said:

"Deeds are assessed according to their outcomes." (Bukhari, Riqaq, 33)

Ali (r.a.) said that:

"To attain the whole benediction is to die in the state of Islamic belief." (Baidawi, I, 201, [in the exegesis of Al-Baqarah; 2:150])

For this reason, one must try and pray to die complying with the command of Allah as **"O you who believe! Fear Allah as He should be feared, and die not except in a state of Islam!"**[14] As a matter of fact, since it is unknown in what state someone will die, Muslims always live between fear and hope and pray Allah for good endings. For example, under the tortures of the Pharaoh of Egypt, the magicians who believed after witnessing the miracle of Moses (pbuh) prayed saying:

"Our Lord! Pour out on us patience and constancy, and take our souls unto you as Muslims (who bow to Your will)!"[15]

Joseph (a.s.) prayed as:

"O my Lord! Take my soul (at death) as one submitting to Your will (as a Muslim), and unite me with the righteous."[16]

These are beautiful examples that Allah gives the believers. Our duty is to find salvation by living according to Islam and dying in the state of Islam. Some of the divine statements that guide us on this issue are:

"O you who believe! If you will aid (the cause of) Allah, He will aid you, and plant your feet firmly." (Muhammad; 47:7)

"Do they not then earnestly seek to understand the Qur'an, or are their hearts locked up by them?" (Muhammad; 47:24)

"O you who believe! Obey Allah, and obey the Apostle, and make not vain your deeds!" (Muhammad; 47:33)

---

14. Al-i Imran; 3:102.
15. A'raf; 7:126
16. Yusuf; 12:101.

B. DELIGHTFULNESS OF FAITH

٥. عَنْ أَنَسٍ رَضِيَ اللهُ عَنْهُ عَنِ النَّبِيِّ صَلَّى اللهُ عَلَيْهِ وَسَلَّمَ قَالَ:

«ثَلَاثٌ مَنْ كُنَّ فِيهِ وَجَدَ حَلَاوَةَ الْإِيمَانِ: مَنْ كَانَ اللهُ وَرَسُولُهُ أَحَبَّ إِلَيْهِ مِمَّا سِوَاهُمَا وَمَنْ أَحَبَّ عَبْدًا لَا يُحِبُّهُ إِلَّا لِلّٰهِ وَمَنْ يَكْرَهُ أَنْ يَعُودَ فِي الْكُفْرِ بَعْدَ إِذْ أَنْقَذَهُ اللهُ كَمَا يَكْرَهُ أَنْ يُلْقَى فِي النَّارِ».

5. Anas narrated that Prophet Muhammad (pbuh) said:

"Whoever possesses the following three qualities will have the sweetness (delight) of faith: 1. The one to whom Allah and His Apostle becomes dearer than anything else. 2. Who loves a person and he loves him only for Allah's sake. 3. Who hates to revert to Atheism (disbelief) as he hates to be thrown into the fire."
(Bukhari, Iman, 14; Ikrah, 1; Adab, 42; Muslim, Iman, 67. Also see Tirmidhi, Iman, 10/2624)

❊

٦. عَنْ عَبْدِ اللهِ بْنِ مُعَاوِيَةَ رَضِيَ اللهُ عَنْهُ قَالَ: قَالَ النَّبِيُّ صَلَّى اللهُ عَلَيْهِ وَسَلَّمَ:

«ثَلَاثٌ مَنْ فَعَلَهُنَّ فَقَدْ طَعِمَ طَعْمَ الْإِيمَانِ: مَنْ عَبَدَ اللهَ وَحْدَهُ وَأَنَّهُ لَا إِلَهَ إِلَّا اللهُ وَأَعْطَى زَكَاةَ مَالِهِ طَيِّبَةً بِهَا نَفْسُهُ رَافِدَةً عَلَيْهِ كُلَّ عَامٍ وَلَا يُعْطِي الْهَرِمَةَ وَلَا الدَّرِنَةَ وَلَا الْمَرِيضَةَ وَلَا الشَّرَطَ اللَّئِيمَةَ وَلَكِنْ مِنْ وَسَطِ أَمْوَالِكُمْ فَإِنَّ اللهَ لَمْ يَسْأَلْكُمْ خَيْرَهُ وَلَمْ يَأْمُرْكُمْ بِشَرِّهِ».

6. Abdullah b. Mu'awiyah reported the Prophet (pbuh) as saying:

"There are three things that he who performs them will feel the taste of faith (These are): To worship Allah alone and to believe in that there is no god but Allah; and to pay zakat willingly out of his property every year. Not to choose the aged animals, nor animals suffering from itch or ailing to give as alms, but to choose animals of medium quality, for Allah did not demand from you the best of your animals, nor did He command you to give the animals of worst quality." (Abu Dawud, Kitab al-Zakat, 5/1582)

۷. عَنِ الْعَبَّاسِ بْنِ عَبْدِ الْمُطَّلِبِ رَضِيَ اللهُ عَنْهُ أَنَّهُ سَمِعَ رَسُولَ اللهِ صَلَّى اللهُ عَلَيْهِ وَسَلَّمَ يَقُولُ:

«ذَاقَ طَعْمَ الْإِيمَانِ مَنْ رَضِيَ بِاللهِ رَبًّا وَبِالْإِسْلَامِ دِينًا وَبِمُحَمَّدٍ رَسُولًا».

7. It is narrated on the authority of Abbas b. Abdulmuttalib that he heard the Messenger of Allah saying:

"He relished the flavor of faith (Iman) who became the book of faith pleased with Allah as Lord, with al-Islam as the code of life and with Muhammad as the Messenger (of Allah)." (Muslim, Iman (Faith), 56; Tirmidhi, Iman, 10/2623; Ahmad, I, 208)

۸. عَنْ حُذَيْفَةَ رَضِيَ اللهُ عَنْهُ قَالَ: قَالَ رَسُولُ اللهِ صَلَّى اللهُ عَلَيْهِ وَسَلَّمَ:

«اَلنَّظْرَةُ سَهْمٌ مِنْ سِهَامِ إِبْلِيسَ مَسْمُومَةٌ فَمَنْ تَرَكَهَا مِنْ خَوْفِ اللهِ أَثَابَهُ -جَلَّ وَعَزَّ- إِيمَانًا يَجِدُ حَلَاوَتَهُ فِي قَلْبِهِ».

8. Hudhaifa (r.a.) narrated that he heard the Messenger of Allah (pbuh) saying:

"Looking at haram is one of the poisoned arrows of demon. Whoever quits that out of fear from Allah, Allah the Almighty bestows him/her a delightful faith." (Hakim, IV, 349/7875; Haythami, VIII, 63)

٩ . عَنْ أَبِي هُرَيْرَةَ رَضِيَ اللهُ عَنْهُ... قَالَ رَسُولُ اللهِ صَلَّى اللهُ عَلَيْهِ وَسَلَّمَ:

«جَدِّدُوا إِيمَانَكُمْ» قِيلَ:

«يَا رَسُولَ اللهِ وَكَيْفَ نُجَدِّدُ إِيمَانَنَا؟» قَالَ:

«أَكْثِرُوا مِنْ قَوْلِ (لَا إِلٰهَ إِلاَّ اللهُ)».

9. Narrated from Abu Huraira (r.a.):

The Messenger of Allah (pbuh) said:

"Renew your faith!"

Companions of Prophet Muhammad asked:

"O the Messenger of Allah, how can we renew our faith?"

The Messenger of Allah (pbuh) answered:

"Say the phrase of **'La ilaha Illallah'** a lot." (Ahmad, II, 359; Hakim, IV, 285/7657)

Explanations:

The value of Islam and faith is unquestionable. However, there are levels of them as well. While some people try to perform their duties at a minimum level, others try to perform more than what is required in the best way with sincerity, love, and excitement. Such believers are the ones who feel the delight of Islam and faith in their hearts. Their hearts are satisfied and their faith has got stronger. They take great pleasure and delight from their good deeds. They willingly fulfill all the commands of Allah and His Messenger with love. For the sake of Islam they do not hold back from difficulties. They place the content of Allah and His Messenger before everything else. They do not exchange their religion for worldly benefits. They think of the Hereafter before thinking of this world.

Their excitement primarily comes from their love for Allah and His Messenger more than for their mothers, fathers, children, all humanity, wealth, and even their own lives. As a matter of fact when the Messenger of Allah (pbuh) asked even for a small thing, his Companions, who were at the peak of this excitement, used to respond saying "O Messenger of Allah! My mother, my father, and my life be sacrificed for you". In fact, this is the kind of love preferred by Allah the Almighty.

It is stated in the Qur'an:

"Say: If it be that your fathers, your sons, your brothers, your mates, or your kindred; the wealth that ye have gained; the commerce in which you fear a decline: or the dwellings in which you delight are dearer to you than Allah, or His Messenger, or the striving in His cause; then wait until Allah brings about His decision: and Allah guides not the rebellious." (Al-Tawbah; 9:24)

When a person loves Allah and His Messenger, he loves the things related to them as well, for the lover loves everything about his love. When he feels such love deep inside his heart, doing things for his love becomes easier. The good deeds that make us earn the consent of Allah and His Messenger turn into pleasures and are performed with delight. Other creatures that are loved now become loved only because of Allah. The hatred and anger is now felt only for the sake of Allah. Everything in this world gets measured in terms of earning the consent of Allah.

Muslims who feel the delight of faith consider everything that would take them away from Allah and His Messenger more burning and painful than fire. They become fully aware that having faith leads one to Paradise and disbelief leads to Hell. Hence, they strongly stay away from things that take them away from religion and Allah's consent. They spend all their efforts to quit all the sins and being unawareness. As a matter of fact, every sin means getting a step further away from Paradise. As sins increase, the distance between paradise and the man becomes impassable …

Every believer who realizes these facts holds on tight to the acts that bring him closer to Allah and His Messenger. He becomes sensitive about his worships. With excitement he fulfills his worships such as praying five times a day or fasting which are considered difficult by some. Especially, every year he pays his zakat (almsgiving), which is the hardest act of worship upon our carnal selves. He pays it feeling significance of this worship and thanking the poor. He would not feel any hardship from this; in contrast, he feels contentment. This state makes the believer a traveler to bliss in both worlds with his zakat, alms, and other donations.

As it can be understood from **our second hadith,** a believer who wants to feel the delight of having faith should not act reluctant when giving zakat. It is best if he enthusiastically gives from the best of his wealth, for it is stated in the following verse that

"By no means shall you attain righteousness unless you give (freely) of that which you love; and whatever you give, of a truth Allah knows it well." (Al-i-Imran; 3:92)

If one cannot do this, one should at least give out of his wealth's medium quality instead of the worst part of it. As in everything, a believer should act with piety and deep comprehension and should not put his family in a financially difficult position by spending his money unwisely.

Since a believer sees this world as the field of the hereafter, he must fulfill all of his deeds for the sake of Allah and should realize that this world is temporary and very short. When one has this consciousness, some acts that seem hard to others become very easy for him. By forgiving people, he would not confront with anyone even he is right, he would not act under the control of his desires and do mischievous tricks even under very difficult conditions.

Abdullah b. Mas'ud (r.a.) said that:

"Whoever has the following three characteristics has the delight of faith:

Avoiding confrontation even he is right, not lying even if it is a joke, and knowing that the things that Allah wished for him will surely happen to him and the things that Allah did not wish for him will never happen to him." (Haythami, I, 55. Also see. Ahmad, V, 317)

A believer, who feels the delight of faith in his heart due to his love for Allah, Islam, and His Messenger, would never have a fancy for foreign views, ideas, and ideologies. He does not get carried away with the temporary and worldly winds blowing from right and left. That is because, he knows that his faith is superior to all the other faiths and he lives with confidence and peace that comes from knowing that. His soul is tranquil and his heart is full of love. For this reason, he is not pleased with any view or opinion other than Islam. He practices his faith with no shame, and does not pay attention to anyone's criticism and blaming on this matter.

Even if someone who reaches this level of faith sometimes may act wrong by falling into heedlessness, he immediately pulls himself together and realizes what it takes to be contented from Allah, Islam, and the Prophet and does that. The following incident is a good example of this:

Once Umar (r.a.) came to the Prophet with some pages from Torah in his hands and said:

"O Messenger of Allah! These are some pages from Torah. I got them from a friend of mine who is a member of the Sons of Zuraik."

The color of Prophet's face has suddenly changed. Upon that Abdullah b. Zaid (r.a.) said to Umar:

"Did Allah make you lose your mind? Don't you see how the face of the Messenger of Allah has changed?"

Umar, who understood his mistake, said:

"We are contented with Allah as our Lord, Islam as our religion, Muhammad (pbuh) as our prophet, and Qur'an as our guide."

Upon that, the Messenger of Allah became happy, his sorrow disappeared, and then he said the following:

"I swear to Allah, in whose Hand my soul is, if Moses (pbuh) were with you and you were to leave me and to follow him, you would make a grave mistake. Because you are my destiny among the peoples of the prophets and I am your destiny among the prophets." (Haythami, I, 174)

What a great destiny! It is so great that we are unable to thank for it properly.

The main characteristics of those believers who experienced the delight of faith are mentioned in the chapter al-Anfal as follows:

"For, Believers are those who, when Allah is mentioned, feel a tremor in their hearts, and when they hear His signs rehearsed, find their faith strengthened, and put (all) their trust in their Lord; Who establish regular prayers and spend (freely) out of the gifts We have given them for sustenance." (Al-Anfal; 8:2-3)

Some other characteristics of those servants who experienced serenity and tranquility are listed in chapter al-Furqan as:

"And the servants of (Allah) Most Gracious are those who walk on the earth in humility, and when the ignorant address them, they say, "Peace!"; Those who spend the night in adoration of their Lord prostrate and standing." (Al-Furqan; 25:63-64)

"Those who, when they are admonished with the Signs of their Lord, droop not down at them as if they were deaf or blind." (Al-Furqan; 25:73)

One of the most important conditions of experiencing the delight of faith is turning away from sins. Allah blesses the hearts of those believers who know how to stay away from sins that may seem sweet and nice but in reality are nothing but poison and dirt with such a faith that they experience its indescribable delight in their hearts while they are still in this world. Thus, they would not only protect themselves from the poisonous arrows of devil, but also earn spiritual rewards and beautify and strengthen their faith.

In one of his sayings on this subject, the Messenger of Allah (pbuh) said:

"Whoever notices a beautiful woman and turns his eyes away, Allah blesses him with the spiritual rewards of an act of worship of which gives delight that he feels in his heart." (Ahmad, V, 264; Haythami, VIII, 63)

The following hadith showing Allah's mercy to His servants contains the good news for believers who avoid sins:

"Whoever intends to do an evil deed and does not do it. Allah blesses him with the reward of a good deed." (Bukhari, Riqaq, 31; Muslim, Iman, 207, 259. Also see Bukhari, Tawhid 35; Tirmidhi, Tafsir, 6/3073)

After a Muslim experiences the delight of faith by avoiding sins, continuing his worships, and attaining piety, now he must exert effort to preserve and develop his faith. As the Messenger of Allah advised, this can be possible, apart from the obligatory acts of worship, by performing supererogatory acts of worship, serving in the way of Allah and reciting His names and attributes and remembering Him. As a matter of fact, in our **fifth hadith**, the Messenger of Allah (pbuh) advises to renew and strengthen our faith by saying "*La ilahe il-lallah.*" In the Hereafter, thanks to the intercession of the Prophet (pbuh), the happiest ones will be the ones who sincerely say "*La ilahe illallah.*" (Bukhari, Ilm, 33; Riqaq, 51)

The heart of those who can reflect *Kalima al-Tawhid* (*La ilahe illallah*) in every aspect of their lives will be blessed with closeness to Allah the Almighty.

According to the sayings of the Prophet, the fundamental conditions to reach the delight of faith are affection, compliance, and submission. When we carefully examine them, we can realize that these are also the fundamentals upon which our religion is based. The Messenger of Allah (pbuh) expressed this as:

"*Polytheism is less noticeable than the movements of a black ant in the darkness of a night on the hill of Safa. The least form of polytheism is to love something that is cruel and hating something that is just. Is religion something other than love and hate? As a matter of fact, Allah the Almighty says:*

"Say: "If you do love Allah, Follow me: Allah will love you and forgive you and your sins: For Allah is Oft-Forgiving, Most Merciful." (Al-i-Imran; 3:31), (Hakim, II, 319/3148)

Therefore, in order to experience the delight of faith, one must be careful about whom he loves and hates. In order to reach salvation, a Muslim must know where to use his love and hate. What a nice servanthood it is to love the things that Allah loves and hate the things that Allah hates.

When approached from this angle, for example, it is gravely dangerous and harmful to the heart to have interest in and compliment to a disbeliever because of his human nature to ignore his disbelief and unfaithfulness. When we act in this way, the outcome can turn into approval of the state of the unbeliever and exaltation of his reputation; whereas, without faith, other qualifications have no value whatsoever.

For example, a non-believer may have some qualifications and abilities and therefore may have fulfilled some worldly achievements. He can be an intellectual or a great hero. When we talk about him/her saying "apart from his faith, if we were to speak justly, he is a great hero", hearts may incline towards him/her. This may demean the importance of having faith in the eyes of people and may cause them to be influenced by the wrong behaviors of that disbeliever.

On the other hand, in order to experience the delight of faith, the seeds of faith must spring in our hearts. Drawing our attention to this, Allah the Almighty says:

"…Allah has endeared the Faith to you, and has made it beautiful in your hearts, and He has made hateful to you Unbelief, wickedness, and rebellion: such indeed are those who walk in righteousness." (Al-Hujurat; 49:7)

As it can be understood from the verse, having knowledge is not enough for having faith and for experiencing its delight. Indeed, Allah gives some of the scholars of the sons of Israel as an example and compares them to a "donkey which carries huge tomes." (Al-Jumah; 62:5)

So, one must engrave the knowledge into his heart and shape his acts accordingly. For this in turn training of the heart is a must. At the same time, the heart must be directed towards supreme virtues. When the heart reaches such a state, Allah the Almighty teaches him the things that cannot be learned from the lines of books.

In order for a desire to turn into actions and behaviors, one should have love in addition to having knowledge. For this reason, love is the source of religion and the Messenger of Allah (pbuh) asked for the delight of faith from Allah the Almighty saying:

"O Allah! Make us love the faith, and beautify our hearts with faith. Show us disbelief, sin, and disobedience as evils. Make us among those who have found the truth!" (Ahmad, III, 424)

In the Age of Bliss (Age of Prophet Muhammad), faith and love were merged and rooted in the hearts of the Companions. In this way, they became the best generation of all generations, a golden generation. The friends of Allah who have followed their footsteps felt the delight of faith in their hearts, too. Indeed, Junaid Baghdadi said:

"For the pious people, the joy of praying at night is more delightful than the entertainment of ignorant people."

Ibrahim b. Atham said:

"I swear to God, we are in such a delight that if kings knew about it, they would declare war on us to get it from us."

In summary, in order to experience the delight of faith, one must feel love properly and correctly. This is one of the fundamental principles of Islam.

ℭℜ

C. INTENTION AND SINCERITY

1. Intention

١٠. عَنْ عُمَرَ بْنِ الْخَطَّابِ رَضِيَ اللهُ عَنْهُ قَالَ: قَالَ رَسُولُ اللهِ صَلَّى اللهُ عَلَيْهِ وَسَلَّمَ:

«إِنَّمَا الْأَعْمَالُ بِالنِّيَّةِ وَإِنَّمَا لِامْرِئٍ مَا نَوَى فَمَنْ كَانَتْ هِجْرَتُهُ إِلَى اللهِ وَرَسُولِهِ فَهِجْرَتُهُ إِلَى اللهِ وَرَسُولِهِ وَمَنْ كَانَتْ هِجْرَتُهُ لِدُنْيَا يُصِيبُهَا أَوِ امْرَأَةٍ يَتَزَوَّجُهَا فَهِجْرَتُهُ إِلَى مَا هَاجَرَ إِلَيْهِ».

10. Narrated by Umar b. al-Khattab: Allah's Apostle said:

"The reward of deeds depends upon the intention and every person will get the reward according to what he has intended. So whoever emigrated for Allah and His Apostle, then his emigration was for Allah and His Apostle. And whoever emigrated for worldly benefits or for the woman he will marry, his emigration was for what he emigrated for." (Muslim, al-Imara, 155. Also see Bukhari, Bad'u'l-Wahy, 1; Iman, 41; Abu Dawud, Talaq, 10-11/2201; Tirmidhi, Fazail al-Jihad, 16/1647; Nasai, Taharah, 60/75; Ibn Majah, Zuhd, 26)

❀

١١. عَنْ عَائِشَةَ رَضِيَ اللهُ عَنْهَا قَالَتْ: قَالَ رَسُولُ اللهِ صَلَّى اللهُ عَلَيْهِ وَسَلَّمَ:

«يَغْزُو جَيْشٌ الْكَعْبَةَ فَإِذَا كَانُوا بِبَيْدَاءَ مِنَ الْأَرْضِ يُخْسَفُ بِأَوَّلِهِمْ وَآخِرِهِمْ» قَالَتْ قُلْتُ:

«يَا رَسُولَ اللهِ، كَيْفَ يُخْسَفُ بِأَوَّلِهِمْ وَآخِرِهِمْ وَفِيهِمْ أَسْوَاقُهُمْ وَمَنْ لَيْسَ مِنْهُمْ؟» قَالَ:

«يُخْسَفُ بِأَوَّلِهِمْ وَآخِرِهِمْ ثُمَّ يُبْعَثُونَ عَلَى نِيَّاتِهِمْ».

11. Aisha (r.a.) narrates:

"The Messenger of Allah (pbuh) said,

"An army will invade the Ka'bah. When they are at Bayda' (a desert), the earth will swallow the entire army up from the first to the last of them."

I asked:

"O Messenger of Allah, how will it swallow them up from the first to the last of them when their traders are among them as well as others who are not really part of them?"

The Messenger of Allah (pbuh) said:

"Yes it will swallow them up from the first to the last of them and then each one of them will be resurrected according to their intentions." (Bukhari, Kitab Al-Buyu, 49; Hajj, 49; Muslim, Fitan, 4-8. Also see Tirmidhi, Fitan, 21/2184; Nasai, Manasik, 112/2877; Ibn Majah, Fitan, 30)

❀

١٢. عَنْ أَبِي هُرَيْرَةَ رَضِيَ اللهُ عَنْهُ قَالَ: قَالَ رَسُولُ اللهِ صَلَّى اللهُ عَلَيْهِ وَسَلَّمَ:

«إِنَّ اللهَ لَا يَنْظُرُ إِلَى صُوَرِكُمْ وَأَمْوَالِكُمْ وَلٰكِنْ يَنْظُرُ إِلَى قُلُوبِكُمْ وَأَعْمَالِكُمْ».

12. Abu Huraira reported Allah's Messenger (may peace be upon him) as saying:

"Verily Allah does not look to your faces and your wealth but He looks to your heart and to your deeds." (Muslim, Birr, 34. Also see Ibn Majah, Al-Zuhd, 9)

Explanations

Intention means to be determined and to decide by heart about something and to know why it is done. In other words, intention manifests what the goal of an action is and what is meant by doing it. So, the validity of actions and deeds depends on intentions, and they are valued accordingly.

Since intention is a matter of heart and related to how we feel and think, it is not necessary to say it out loud. On the other hand, the intention is not accepted if the heart does not go along with what the tongue spells out as the intention.

Since Allah knows what is hidden deep in the hearts, the issue of intention closes the doors of finding excuses for those who go after invalid beliefs, harm others, and cheat. Therefore, everybody should be careful about their intentions and should know that they cannot fool Allah.

Intention is so important that sometimes a custom may turn into worship and sometimes worships may become a custom. For example, a Muslim who practices his profession is considered as worshipping at the same time if he thinks to satisfy the needs of his family and raise them with the manners of Islam by earning through permissible means. If someone thinks of protecting his health while eating so that he can better perform his acts of worship, he also earns divine rewards because of his intention. Those who act with good intentions can be compared to a hunter who hunts two birds with one stone. As a matter of fact, it is said in the noble verse that:

"To any that desires the tilth of the Hereafter, We give increase in his tilth, and to anyone that desires the tilth of this world, We grant somewhat thereof, but he has no share or lot in the Hereafter." (Al-Shura; 62:20)

So, whoever performs his religious duties sincerely just to earn divine rewards, Allah not only blesses him with even more divine rewards, but also favors him in this world and bestows blessings to his daily bread. Furthermore, if the wealth that Allah has bestowed is spent in accordance to His will, this can also be turned into benefits in the Hereafter. Those who only work for this world cannot earn benefits for the hereafter and can only get what his predestined share is from this world. This shows how the same action is judged and valued differently according to the actor's intentions.

The Messenger of Allah (pbuh) gave some examples on this subject and said:

"...I shall tell you something which you must remember well. The world exclusively belongs to one of four kinds of people:

There is a servant [of Allah] upon whom Allah the Almighty and Exalted bestowed property and knowledge. He fears Allah because of his knowledge and property, thus he gives charity out of them. By means of them, he seeks to protect himself from His Lord's displeasure and strengthen his family ties, knowing that Allah the Almighty and Exalted has rights over his property and knowledge. This servant is truly at the best of stations.

There is a servant [of Allah] upon whom Allah the Almighty and Exalted has bestowed knowledge but not property, who is truthful in his intention and says: "If I had property, I would do the deeds of so-and-so." His status is according to his intention, and he earns rewards like the one who gives his property as charity.

There is a servant [of Allah] upon whom Allah the Almighty and Exalted bestowed property but not knowledge, who gropes aimlessly with his property without knowledge, not seeking to protect himself from His Lord's displeasure with it, nor strengthening family ties with it, not recognizing that Allah the Almighty and Exalted owns rights over that property. This is truly the worst of stations.

There is a servant [of Allah] upon whom Allah the Almighty and Exalted bestowed neither property nor knowledge, who says: 'If I had property, I would use it to do the [evil] deeds of So-and-so.' His status is according to his intention, and the burden of each of the two is exactly the same." (Tirmidhi, Zuhd, 17/2325; Ahmad, IV, 231; Ibn Majah, Zuhd, 21)

As the mubah acts (the fulfillment or non-fulfillment of which causes no sin) can be turned into worships, acts of worships performed with evil intentions may lead to a sin. For example, acts of worship and good deeds performed for show off or worldly benefits are just burdens upon the performer.

On the other hand, the sincere intention to perform good deeds that come to our heart is in and of itself worship. Since humans are weak, it is impossible to perform every good deed in a perfect manner. Having good intentions comes to our help and may bring us many divine rewards. As a matter of fact, the Messenger of Allah (pbuh) said:

"The intention of a believer is greater than his acts…" (Haythami, I, 61; Suyuti, Jami, II, 194)

Also, it has been reported that the Messenger of Allah (pbuh) said that whoever sought martyrdom with sincerity will be ranked by Allah to be among the martyrs even if he dies in his bed. (Muslim, Kitab al-Imara, 156, 157)

The following story about Amr b. Leys, one of the rulers and heroes of Khorasan is an example on this subject. After Amr b. Leys passed away, a pious man saw him in his dream. The following dialogue took place between them:

"How did Allah treat you?"

"Allah has forgiven me."

"For which of your deeds has Allah forgiven you?"

"One day, I was on top of a hill. When I looked down to my soldiers, I was pleased with the number of soldiers. I thought:

"I wish that I were alive in the time of the Messenger of Allah (pbuh), so I could help him…" Due to my intention and desire, Almighty Allah has forgiven me." (Qadi Iyaz, Shifa, II, 28-29)

This story indicates how important intention and sincerity are.

On the other hand, a believer with good intentions must avoid being with evil people and taking part in their bad acts. That is because evil acts are like contagious diseases. Joining the group ill-natured people and sinners increases their numbers and influences others to join them as well. Some people who see right-minded people with bad people may think that their actions are permissible or righteous.

Even though humans will be treated in the hereafter according to their intentions, the good people close to evildoers will also get affected by their torment. As a matter of fact, in **the second hadith** we are informed about how a group of good people who join a group of bad people in order to do some trade or travel more securely would sink into the ground because of the bad intentions of evil people with whom they travel.

As it can be understood from this hadith, troubles and disasters are not only for the evildoers but also for the heedless who allow evil acts to happen to them. It is natural for helpless people who do not have any mistake to be amongst them. Some believers who are in pain because of others, even though they do not have any sins or mistakes, will receive great rewards from Allah in the Hereafter.

While pointing out the importance of being sincere, the criterion which was presented in **the third hadith** is also a very important principle for us. According to this, when dealing with the servants of Allah, we must treat them in accordance with their intentions and actions rather than their looks, words, and wealth. That is because the heart is at the center of everything. If the heart is not candid and pure, the outward appearance and worldly blessings do not mean anything. It is said in the noble verse that:

"It is not your wealth nor your sons, that will bring you nearer to Us in degree: but only those who believe and work righteousness. These are the ones for whom there is a multiplied Reward for their deeds, while secure they (reside) in the dwellings on high!" (Al-Saba; 34: 37)

In this regard, we must pay attention to the warnings of the Prophet Muhammad (pbuh):

"Shall I inform you about the inmates of Paradise? Every meek person who is considered to be humble and if they were to adjure in the name of Allah, Allah would certainly fulfill it." (Bukhari, Iman (Faith), 9; Tafsir, 68/1; Adab, 61; Muslim, Jannah, 47)

"…There are such innocuous, obedient, pious servants of Allah who keep themselves away from others. These people are the ones that Allah the Almighty really loves. They do not get looked for when they are not present (since they are not attached to importance, their absence does not get noticed), and when they are present, they do not get recognized and invited to meetings. Their hearts are the bright candles of the right path. They can deal with all kinds of difficult conditions and misfortunes."[17] (Ibn Majah, Kitab al-Fitan, 16)

---

17. The last sentence of the noble hadith is also understood as "they are found in every caved in house and ruin." In thise case, the Messenger of Allah (p.b.u.h.) is stating that their residences are simple and plain.

Consequently, we should not look at the outward qualifications of people but rather we should look to their hearts and intentions, and we should also pray to Allah for ourselves by saying:

"O Allah! Compile our intentions with Your honorable consent."

Amen!..

2. Sincerity

١٣. عَنْ أَبِي أُمَامَةَ الْبَاهِلِيِّ قَالَ: قَالَ رَسُولُ اللهِ صَلَّى اللهُ عَلَيْهِ وَسَلَّمَ:

«إِنَّ اللهَ لَا يَقْبَلُ مِنَ الْعَمَلِ إِلَّا مَا كَانَ لَهُ خَالِصًا وَابْتُغِيَ بِهِ وَجْهُهُ».

13. It is narrated by Abu Umamah al-Bahili (r.a.) that the Messenger of Allah (pbuh) said:

"Allah accepts only the deeds that are performed sincerely and for His consent." (Nasai, Jihad, 24/3138)

❁

١٤. عَنْ مُعَاذِ بْنِ أَنَسٍ رَضِيَ اللهُ عَنْهُ أَنَّ رَسُولَ اللهِ صَلَّى اللهُ عَلَيْهِ وَسَلَّمَ قَالَ:

«مَنْ أَعْطَى لِلهِ وَمَنَعَ لِلهِ وَأَحَبَّ لِلهِ وَأَبْغَضَ لِلهِ وَأَنْكَحَ لِلهِ فَقَدِ اسْتَكْمَلَ إِيمَانَهُ».

14. Muadh b. Anas narrated that the Messenger of Allah (pbuh) said:

"Whoever gives for the sake of Allah, forbids for the sake of Allah, loves for the sake of Allah, hates for the sake of Allah, and helps bachelors to get married

for the sake of Allah, will make his faith perfect." (Tirmidhi, Qiyamah, 60/2521; Ahmad, III, 438. Also see Abu-Dawud, Kitab Al-Sunnah, 15/4681)

❀

١٥ . عَنْ ابْنِ عَبَّاسٍ رَضِيَ اللّٰهُ عَنْهُمَا قَالَ: قَالَ رَسُولُ اللّٰهِ صَلَّى اللّٰهُ عَلَيْهِ وَسَلَّمَ:

((مَنْ سَمَّعَ سَمَّعَ اللّٰهُ بِهِ وَمَنْ رَاءَى رَاءَى اللّٰهُ بِهِ)).

15. Ibn Abbas (r.a.) reported Allah's Messenger (pbuh) as saying:

"If anyone wants to have his deeds widely publicized, Allah will publicize (his humiliation). And if anyone makes a hypocritical display (of his deeds) Allah will make a display of him." (Muslim, Al-Zuhd, 47-48. Also see Bukhari, al-Raqaiq, 36; Ahkam, 9; Tirmidhi, al-Zuhd, 48; Ibn Majah, al-Zuhd, 21)

Explanations:

Sincerity (*ikhlas*) means cleansing and purifying the heart, observing Allah's contentedness in all actions and words by protecting oneself from all spiritual illnesses, and staying away from hypocrisy, the act of showing off, and arrogance.[18] Therefore, being sincere is a feeling hidden in our hearts. According to Junayd Al-Baghdadi, sincerity is so secret that an angel cannot record it into the rewards, and Satan cannot mess it up, and the inner selves of human beings cannot be spoiled because of it since they don't know what it is. (Sarraj, *Luma'*, p. 290; Kushayri, *al-Risalah*, p. 446)

Allah the Almighty wants His servants to be sincere.

"Verily it is We Who have revealed the Book to you in Truth: so serve Allah, offering Him sincere devotion." (Al-Zumar (The Troops); 39:2)

"Say: "Verily, I am commanded to serve Allah with sincere devotion." (Al-Zumar; 39:11)

---

18. Hypocrisy (**Riya**): Showing off, doing a deed for humans (not God) to see and appreciate. **Showing off (Sum'a):** Doing a good deed or giving charity so that people would hear. Arrogance ('**Ujub**): Someone's liking and seeing himself better than others (not necessarily displayed to others but felt inside).

Allah the Almighty informs us that He will not accept deeds that are performed without sincerity and not for the sake of Him no matter how plentiful they are. When performed sincerely, even a few good deeds may be enough for us. As a matter of fact, the Messenger of Allah (pbuh) stated this in one of his sayings as:

"Be sincere in your religion! If you do this, even a few good deeds can be enough for your salvation." (Hakim, IV, 341/7844)

Allah's servant should then realize that sincerity is like a soul in his body and should build his life on the basis of being sincere by performing all of his acts only for the sake of Allah. One must give what he gives for the sake of Allah as well as hold what he holds for the sake of Allah; one must love what he loves for the sake of Allah as well as hate what he hates for the sake of Allah; and one must act thinking about the consent of Allah when he performs a good deed or guides others to any good deeds. One should turn this understanding into his natural state and be sincere to Allah, to His book, to His Messenger, to the Qur'an, to the leaders of Muslim believers, and to all Muslims. (Muslim, Kitab Al-Iman, 95)

The faith of a believer who reaches this level of spirituality becomes perfect, and he starts to experience the delight of Islam. With the perfection of faith, sincerity flourishes in his heart, and he finds salvation. (Ahmad, V, 147)

There are many benefits of sincerity:

First of all, it protects us from going astray by the tricks of Satan[19] and it guides us awayfrom the Hell fire.[20]

By summoning the help of our creator, it keeps evil and adultery away.[21] As a matter of fact, Allah's Messenger (pbuh) informed us that Allah helps the followers of Muhammad due to the supplications, prayers, and sincere feelings of the weak. (Nasai, Jihad, 43/3176)

Sincerity elevates the level of acts of worship and makes them more valuable in the sight of Allah. In many narrations, while referring to the divine rewards of worship and supplications,

---

19.   Al-Hijr; 15:39-40
20.   Al-Saffat; 37:40
21.   Yusuf; 12:24

"To do it sincerely from the heart"[22] or

"To believe its divine rewards and ask for the rewards only from Allah, or in other words, to be sincere"[23] are required, which is sufficient to prove the importance of being sincere. As a matter of fact, in one noble hadith:

"When a servant of Allah avoids greater sins (and lives a pious life) and says *La ilahe illallah* with full sincerity, the doors of the sky open up and this phrase ascends to *al-Arsh* (the Highest Sky)." (Tirmidhi, Daawat, 126/3590)

In short, being sincere is the thing that brings us peace in this world and salvation in the Hereafter. When sincerity is absent, humans start to hope help from helpless beings. They can neither benefit anyone nor ward off troubles. In this regard how meaningfull the following story is:

When Mecca was conquered, Ikrimah, the son of Abu Jahl, escaped from Mecca by a ship in fear of his life since he used to be a fierce enemy of Islam. They got caught in a storm in the sea.

People on the ship said:

"Now be sincere and turn towards only to Allah! Here your deities cannot benefit you at all."

Upon this Ikrimah said:

"I swear by Allah, if only sincerity can save me on the sea, it is sincerity again what can save me on the land. O Allah! I swear by You, if You save me from this trouble, I will go to Muhammad (pbuh) and put my hand on his hands and find him to be forgiving and kind."

Ikrimah (r.a.), who was saved from the storm, did what he said and went to the Prophet Muhammad right away and converted to Islam. (Nasai, Tahrim al-Dam, 14/4064)

The Messenger of Allah (pbuh) used to ask for sincerity for himself and his family from Allah and pray saying:

22. See Bukhari, Ilm, 49; Daawat, 2; Muslim, Salah, 12; Abu Dawud, Salah, 36/527; Tirmidhi, Fazail al-jihad, 19/1653; Ahmad, I, 63; IV, 16.
23. Bukhari, Iman, 25, 28, 35, 37, 41; Salah, 45, 46; Hebah, 35; Tibb, 31; Muslim, Imarah, 117.

اَللّٰهُمَّ رَبَّنَا وَرَبَّ كُلِّ شَيْءٍ اجْعَلْنِي مُخْلِصًا لَكَ وَأَهْلِي فِي كُلِّ سَاعَةٍ
فِي الدُّنْيَا وَالْآخِرَةِ يَا ذَا الْجَلَالِ وَالْإِكْرَامِ

"O Allah, the Lord of us and everything else! Make me and my family in this world and in the Hereafter sincere to You, O my Glorious and Kind Lord!" (Abu Dawud, Witr, 25/1508; Ahmad, IV, 369. Also see Tirmidhi, Daawat, 30/3419)

In the Noble Qur'an, we are informed that other prophets were sincere servants of Allah as well.[24] That is because they did not seek anything in their message and mission but did it only for the sake of Allah and refused all proposals made to them to have them give up their cause.

Since sincerity is known only to Allah, Allah is the only one who can compensate it. Allah's compensation is priceless and no one can estimate its value.

Opposite of sincerity, i.e. insincerity (showing-off), is a big disaster for the Hereafter. Associating others to actions that should be done only for the sake of Allah means that you are notsatisfied with Allah's knowing and His contentedness and are hoping to get others' appreciation. This is a sickness of heart and a weakness of faith that wastes the divine rewards of the good acts. As a matter of fact, since Allah knows everything in our hearts, it is impossible to hide any intention and thought from Him. The following saying of the Prophet is significant in terms of explaining the disappointment of insincere people in the hereafter:

"The first of men (whose case) will be decided on the Day of Judgment will be a man who died as a martyr. He shall be brought (before the Judgment Seat). Allah will make him recount His blessings which He had bestowed upon him and he will recount them and admit having enjoyed them in his life.

Allah the Almighty will say:

"What did you do to requite these blessings?"

He will say:

"I fought for You until I died as a martyr."

Allah the Almighty will say:

---

24.   Maryam; 19:51; Yusuf; 12:24; Al-Saad; 38:45-46; Az-Zumar; 39:11.

"You have told a lie. You fought so that you might be called a "brave warrior" and you were called so. Then orders will be passed against him, and he will be dragged with his face downward and cast into Hell.

Then there will be brought forward a man who acquired knowledge and imparted it (to others) and recited the Qur'an. He will be brought forward and Allah will make him recount His blessings and he will recount them and admit having enjoyed them in his lifetime.

Then will Allah ask:

"What did you do (to requite these blessings)?"

He will say:

"I acquired knowledge and disseminated it and recited the Qur'an seeking Your pleasure."

Allah will say:

"You have told a lie! You acquired knowledge so that you might be called "a scholar," and you recited the Qur'an so that it might be said: "He is a Qari (good reader)" and such has been said." Then orders will be passed against him and he shall be dragged with his face downward and cast into the Fire.

Then there will be brought a man whom Allah had made abundantly rich and had granted every kind of wealth. He will be brought and Allah will make him recount His blessings and he will recount them and admit having enjoyed them in his lifetime.

Allah will (then) ask:

"What have you done (to requite these blessings)?"

He will say:

"I spent money in every cause in which You wished that it should be spent."

Allah the Almighty will say:

"You are lying. You did so that it might be said about you "He is a generous fellow" and so it was said." Then Allah will pass orders and he will be dragged with his face downward and thrown into Hell. (Muslim, Kitab Al-Imara, 152)

As it is seen, being insincere drags someone to the foolishness of exchanging the sake of Allah and the divine rewards of the Hereafter with the insincere applauses of people. In the end, neither the contentedness of Allah nor the satisfaction of people will have been earned. This is because, Allah makes the intention of those who act insincerely known to others and disgraces him in front of others by belittling him.[25] When the insincerity of someone becomes known, the hearts turn away from him. On the other hand, by letting others know the act of a person to others, Allah degrades the rewards of the acts done for the worldly benefits also.

The Messenger of Allah (pbuh) said:

"Allah the Most High and Exalted said: "I am the One, the One Who does not stand in need of a partner. If anyone does anything in which he associates anyone else with Me, I shall abandon him with the one whom he associates with Allah." (Muslim, Kitab Al-Zuhd, 46)

In other words, as it is written insincere humans are told to get the rewards of their acts not from Allah but from those to whom they showed off their actions to. However, receiving anything from humans is most of the time impossible. Even if it is possible, it would be next to nothing compared to Allah's rewards.

For this reason, the Companions of the Messenger of Allah used to pay attention to sincerity and be very careful about staying away from insincerity. The following advice of Abu Huraira is enough to prove how far the Companions of the Prophet lived from being insincere:

"When someone fasts, he should tide up himself so that the trace of the fast is not seen on him." (Bukhari, *Al-Adabul Mufrad, no:1303*)

○२

---

25. Also see Ahmad, II, 162.

D. KNOWLEDGE and PRACTICE

1. The Virtue of Knowledge

١٦ . عَنْ أَبِي الدَّرْدَاءِ رَضِيَ اللهُ عَنْهُ قَالَ: سَمِعْتُ رَسُولَ اللهِ صَلَّى اللهُ عَلَيْهِ وَسَلَّمَ يَقُولُ:

«مَنْ سَلَكَ طَرِيقًا يَطْلُبُ فِيهِ عِلْمًا سَلَكَ اللهُ بِهِ طَرِيقًا مِنْ طُرُقِ الْجَنَّةِ وَإِنَّ الْمَلَائِكَةَ لَتَضَعُ أَجْنِحَتَهَا رِضًا لِطَالِبِ الْعِلْمِ وَإِنَّ الْعَالِمَ لَيَسْتَغْفِرُ لَهُ مَنْ فِي السَّمٰوَاتِ وَمَنْ فِي الْأَرْضِ وَالْحِيتَانُ فِي جَوْفِ الْمَاءِ وَإِنَّ فَضْلَ الْعَالِمِ عَلَى الْعَابِدِ كَفَضْلِ الْقَمَرِ لَيْلَةَ الْبَدْرِ عَلَى سَائِرِ الْكَوَاكِبِ وَإِنَّ الْعُلَمَاءَ وَرَثَةُ الْأَنْبِيَاءِ وَإِنَّ الْأَنْبِيَاءَ لَمْ يُوَرِّثُوا دِينَارًا وَلَا دِرْهَمًا وَرَّثُوا الْعِلْمَ فَمَنْ أَخَذَهُ أَخَذَ بِحَظٍّ وَافِرٍ».

16. Abu Darda' (r.a) said: I heard the Messenger of Allah (pbuh) saying:

"If anyone travels on a road in search of knowledge, Allah will lead him to one of the roads of Paradise. The angels will lower their wings on the one who seeks knowledge because they are pleased with him. The inhabitants of the heavens and the Earth and the fish in the deep waters will ask forgiveness for the learned man. The superiority of the learned man over the devout is like that of the moon, on the night when it is full, over the rest of the stars. The learned are the heirs of the Prophets, and the Prophets leave neither dinar nor dirham, leaving only knowledge, and he who takes it takes an abundant portion." (Abu Dawud, Kitab Al-Ilm, 1/3641; Tirmidhi, Ilm, 19/2682. Also see. Bukhari, Ilm, 10; Ibn Majah, Muqaddimah, 17)

45

١٧. عَنْ أَبِي أُمَامَةَ رَضِيَ اللهُ عَنْهُ قَالَ: قَالَ رَسُولُ اللهِ صَلَّى اللهُ عَلَيْهِ وَسَلَّمَ:

«فَضْلُ الْعَالِمِ عَلَى الْعَابِدِ كَفَضْلِي عَلَى أَدْنَاكُمْ» ثُمَّ قَالَ رَسُولُ اللهِ صَلَّى اللهُ عَلَيْهِ وَسَلَّمَ: «إِنَّ اللهَ وَمَلَائِكَتَهُ وَأَهْلَ السَّمَاوَاتِ وَالْأَرَضِينَ حَتَّى النَّمْلَةَ فِي جُحْرِهَا وَحَتَّى الْحُوتَ لَيُصَلُّونَ عَلَى مُعَلِّمِ النَّاسِ الْخَيْرَ».

17. Abu Umamah (r.a.) narrated that the Messenger of Allah (pbuh) said:

"The superiority of the learned man over the devout is like my superiority over the most inferior among you (in good deeds)."

Then the Messenger of Allah (pbuh) added:

"For sure Allah, His angels, and all those in heavens and earths, even the ants in their holes and the fish in the water say blessings on those who instruct people well." (Tirmidhi, Ilm, 19/2685)

❁

١٨. عَنْ أَنَسِ بْنِ مَالِكٍ رَضِيَ اللهُ عَنْهُ قَالَ: كَانَ أَخَوَانِ عَلَى عَهْدِ النَّبِيِّ صَلَّى اللهُ عَلَيْهِ وَسَلَّمَ فَكَانَ أَحَدُهُمَا يَأْتِي النَّبِيَّ صَلَّى اللهُ عَلَيْهِ وَسَلَّمَ وَالْآخَرُ يَحْتَرِفُ فَشَكَا الْمُحْتَرِفُ أَخَاهُ إِلَي النَّبِيِّ صَلَّى اللهُ عَلَيْهِ وَسَلَّمَ فَقَالَ:

«لَعَلَّكَ تُرْزَقُ بِهِ».

18. Anas B. Malik (r.a.) narrates:

"There were two brothers in the time of the Messenger of Allah (pbuh). One of them came to the Prophet in order to acquire knowledge while the

other one was working. One day, the brother who worked came to the Prophet to complain about his brother.

The Messenger of Allah (pbuh) said:

"–*Maybe because of him you are able to find a job and earn your living.*"
(Tirmidhi, Zuhd, 33/2345)

❁

١٩. عَنْ أَبِي سَعِيدٍ الْخُدْرِيِّ رَضِيَ اللهُ عَنْهُ عَنْ رَسُولِ اللهِ صَلَّى اللهُ عَلَيْهِ وَسَلَّمَ قَالَ:

((لَنْ يَشْبَعَ الْمُؤْمِنُ مِنْ خَيْرٍ يَسْمَعُهُ حَتَّى يَكُونَ مُنْتَهَاهُ الْجَنَّةَ)).

19. Abu Said Al-Khudri (r.a) narrated that the Messenger of Allah (pbuh) said:

"*Until the final place that he reaches becomes Paradise, a believer should not get satisfied with hearing the good (knowledge) of any kind.*" (Tirmidhi, Ilm, 19/2686)

Explanations:

Ilm (knowledge) actually is an attribute of Allah the Almighty and is fig-uratively used for human beings. Servants of Allah gain virtue and value as much as they are bestowed with shares from Allah's attribute of knowledge.

There is no other system that gives importance to knowledge as much as Islam does. In the Holy Qur'an, the term "ilm" (knowledge) and related terms are repeated hundreds of times. It is asked from humans to know one's Lord, to learn Qur'an and Sunnah, and to acquire the knowledge which will bring happiness in this world and the Hereafter. Praising those with knowledge, it is stated in the Qur'an that:

"Allah will rise up, to (suitable) ranks (and degrees), those of you who believe and who have been granted (mystic) Knowledge. And Allah is well-acquainted with all ye do." (Al-Mujadilah; 58:11)

"Those truly fear Allah, among His Servants, who have knowledge: for Allah is Exalted in Might, Oft-Forgiving." (Al-Fatir; 35:28)

"And such are the Parables We set forth for mankind, but only those understand them who have knowledge." (Al-Ankabut; 29:43)

Allah has commanded the Prophet Muhammad to pray to advance his knowledge only, and He did not command him to pray to "advance or increase" anything else.

In another noble verse it is expressed that:

$$ وَقُلْ رَبِّ زِدْنِي عِلْمًا $$

"...say, "O my Lord! Advance me in knowledge."" (Al-Taha; 20:114)

In his sayings, the Messenger of Allah (pbuh) gives good tidings for those who sincerely seek knowledge. There are many other sayings about knowledge and those who seek knowledge. Some of them are as follows:

"Those who travel seeking knowledge are on the path of Allah until they return to their homes." (Tirmidhi, Ilm, 2/2647)

"If someone dies while acquiring knowledge to revive Islam and make it practiced, there will be only one degree of difference between him and the prophets in the paradise." (Darimi, Muqaddimah, 32)

"Do not wish to be like anyone except in two cases:

A person, whom Allah has given wealth and he who spends it righteously;

The one whom Allah has given wisdom (the Holy Qur'an) and he who acts in accordance with it and teaches it to others." (Bukhari, Ilm, 15; Zakat 5; Ahkam, 3; Muslim, Musafirin, 268)

"If Allah wants to do good to a person, He makes him comprehend religion." (Tirmidhi, Ilm, 1/2645)

The Messengers of Allah did not bequeath material goods but rather they left knowledge. They used their own wealth for the benefit of their followers. Muslim scholars worked to get this heritage, and even traveled for months in order to hear one saying of the Prophet from its first source. They turned the following saying of the Messenger of Allah into their principle:

"The word of wisdom is the lost property of the believer, so wherever he finds it he has a better right to it."[26] Our scholars who regarded acquiring knowledge and teaching it to others as the most valuable way of charity[27] advanced their knowledge and transmitted it to us by bearing many difficulties.

Those with knowledge are not only useful to themselves but also to others. As humans need food to survive, they need knowledge to practice their religion and find salvation in the hereafter. That is because, the quality of worships and servitude depend on one's knowledge. The spiritually dead hearts can revive with the words of scholars. Allah's Messenger (pbuh) advised believers to join the meetings of scholars and said:

"Luqman Hakim said to his son: "Be in the meetings of scholars (and Gnostics)! Listen to the word of the wise! For, just as Allah the Almighty brings the dead earth to life by rain, He brings the dead heart to life by the divine light of wisdom." (Haythami, I, 125)

When scholars guide people to goodness and good deeds, they also receive divine rewards from the good deeds of those people. Indeed, the Messenger of Allah (pbuh) said:

"Whoever teaches knowledge receives divine rewards when this knowledge is put into practice, and nothing diminishes from the divine rewards of the one who actually performed the deed." (Ibn Majah, Muqaddimah, 20)

Like humans, other creatures also benefit from the knowledge of scholars. As a matter of fact, due to good manners that people learn from scholars, humans act with compassion, mercy, and love towards all creatures. Thanks to this, all creatures find peace, and blessings rain down on the earth. So, all creatures pray for scholars and ask from Allah to forgive them. Even angels show respect, treat them modestly, protect and help those who seek knowledge.

Allah makes the works of those servants who seek knowledge in order to serve Islam and humans easier and bestow their daily bread from unexpected venues. Allah also gives rewards both in this world and in the hereafter to those who help believers seeking knowledge. Maybe people who work for their living get blessed abundantly because of their help to those who seek knowledge for the sake of Allah.

26. Tirmidhi, Ilm, 19/2687; Ibn Majah, Zuhd, 15.
27. Ibn Majah, Muqaddimah, 20.

49

In our fourth hadith, knowledge is defined as a good deed guiding humans to Paradise.

Knowledge is the best goodness since it teaches us the deeds that will bring us closer to Allah the Almighty. Therefore, an intelligent believer would not quit seeking knowledge and putting it into practice until he gets into Paradise. He realizes that this is the path which will take someone to Paradise. He knows that knowledge is a huge blessing needed at all times.

Indeed, Abdullah b. Mes'ud (r.a.) advised:

"Before it goes extinct, cling to knowledge. Its extinction means the disappearance of scholars. Cling to knowledge, because you never know when you might need it…" (Darimi, Muqaddimah, 19)

Ignorance is the beginning of all evil and fouls. Even disbelief and polytheism are caused by ignorance. In this respect, Allah said:

"…so be not you amongst those who are swayed by ignorance (and impatience)!" (Al-An'am; 6:35)

"… turn away from the ignorant." (Al-Araf; 7:199)

However, it is very important to note that the knowledge mentioned in the Qur'an and sayings of the Prophet are primarily the knowledge of Allah, His verses, the religion, and the hereafter and it is the Gnostic knowledge. In other words, it is to understand the truth. This knowledge takes humans from the effect to the cause. Other material sciences such as physics and chemistry also bring us closer to Allah when they are learned and taught in a healthy way. Other sciences that fill our brains but do not help us realize the realities of the universe and that do not cover anything beyond the concrete and tangible beings of this world are not considered knowledge. In other words, knowing is not injecting some information into our brains, but rather trying to solve the secrets and mysteries of the universe.

Allah describes those who know as:

"Is one who worships devoutly during the hour of the night prostrating himself or standing (in adoration), who takes heed of the Hereafter, and who places his hope in the Mercy of his Lord - (like one who does not)? Say: "Are those equal, those who know and those who do not know? It is those who are endued with understanding that receive admonition." (Al-Zumar; 39:9)

According to this verse, "those who know" are the ones who worship at night, who prostrate and stand up, who think about the hereafter, and who hope for the mercy of Allah. Those who do not live as described in this verse are the ones "who do not know" even if they have the knowledge.

2. Beneficial Knowledge (Ilm)

٢٠. عَنْ أَبِي هُرَيْرَةَ رَضِيَ اللهُ عَنْهُ قَالَ: قَالَ رَسُولُ اللهِ صَلَّى اللهُ عَلَيْهِ وَسَلَّمَ:

«اَللّٰهُمَّ انْفَعْنِي بِمَا عَلَّمْتَنِي وَعَلِّمْنِي مَا يَنْفَعُنِي وَزِدْنِي عِلْمًا».

20. Abu Huraira (r.a.) narrated that the Messenger of Allah (pbuh) said that:

"O Allah! Make what You taught me useful for me and teach me knowledge that will be useful to me and advance me in my knowledge." (Tirmidhi, Daawat, 128/3599; Ibn Majah, Muqaddimah, 23; Hakim, I, 690/1879)

❈

٢١. عَنْ زَيْدِ بْنِ أَرْقَمَ رَضِيَ اللهُ عَنْهُ قَالَ: كَانَ رَسُولُ اللهِ صَلَّى اللهُ عَلَيْهِ وَسَلَّمَ يَقُولُ:

«اَللّٰهُمَّ إِنِّي أَعُوذُ بِكَ مِنْ عِلْمٍ لَا يَنْفَعُ وَمِنْ قَلْبٍ لَا يَخْشَعُ وَمِنْ نَفْسٍ لَا تَشْبَعُ وَمِنْ دَعْوَةٍ لَا يُسْتَجَابُ لَهَا».

21. Zaid b. Arkam narrated that the messenger of Allah (pbuh) used to pray as:

"O Allah, I seek refuge in You from the knowledge that does not benefit, from the heart that does not entertain the fear (of Allah), from the soul that does not feel contented and from the supplication that is not responded." (Muslim, Kitab al-Dhikr, 73. Also see. Nesai, Istiazah, 13, 65)

❈

٢٢. عَنْ أَبِي هُرَيْرَةَ رَضِيَ اللهُ عَنْهُ قَالَ: قَالَ رَسُولُ اللهِ صَلَّى اللهُ
عَلَيْهِ وَسَلَّمَ:

«مَثَلُ الَّذِي يَجْلِسُ يَسْمَعُ الْحِكْمَةَ ثُمَّ لَا يُحَدِّثُ عَنْ صَاحِبِهِ إِلَّا
بِشَرِّ مَا يَسْمَعُ كَمَثَلِ رَجُلٍ أَتَى رَاعِيًا فَقَالَ: يَا رَاعِي أَجْزِرْنِي شَاةً مِنْ
غَنَمِكَ قَالَ: اذْهَبْ فَخُذْ بِأُذُنِ خَيْرِهَا فَذَهَبَ فَأَخَذَ بِأُذُنِ كَلْبِ الْغَنَمِ».

22. Abu Huraira (r.a.) narrated that the Messenger of Allah (pbuh) said:

"The similitude of a person who joins a scholarly gathering and listens to words of wisdom, but then narrates the bad parts of what he heard to his friends is the following:

A person comes to a shepherd and says:

«–O shepherd, give a sheep from your herd to me for me to sacrifice».

The shepherd says:

"Go, get the best one and bring it to me!"

The man goes and picks the dog among the huge herd." (Ibn Majah, Zuhd, 15; Ahmad, II, 353, 405, 508; Baihaqi, *Shuab,* II, 268; Haythami, I, 128)

Explanations:

First of all, a Muslim tries to benefit from his knowledge and puts it into practice. Then, he tries to acquire beneficial knowledge that will help him to continue a life which can help him be a good servant of Allah and gain His contentedness. He also prays to Allah to bless him with such knowledge and advance his knowledge.

The best indicator of benefitting from one's knowledge is paying extra attention to commands of religion with devotion. Those who benefit from their knowledge put their knowledge into practice and live a pious life because they are afraid of divine torment.

As a matter of fact, the Messenger of Allah (pbuh) said:

"For sure I am the best in piety (taqwa) to Allah and I know Him the best!" (Bukhari, Iman, 13; Adab, 72)

Therefore, as knowledge increases the level of piety (taqwa) increases as well. Since the Messenger of Allah (pbuh) is the one who knows Allah the best, he is also the one who is best in piety.

As good knowledge benefits people in this world, it is also useful after death as capital in the Hereafter. Indeed, the Messenger of Allah (pbuh) informs us that a believer who leaves beneficial knowledge behind has an unclosed Book of Deeds. Through his students and works will not be closed up, but rather the rewards of this knownledge will continue to be recorded into his book even after he dies. (Muslim, Wasiyyah, 14)

Therefore, we must seek useful knowledge not only to benefit from it but also to put it into service of others, rather than wasting our time with unnecessary things. Indeed, the spiritual state experienced by Ibn Sirin proves this:

He narrates:

"I entered into the praying room and saw that Samir b. Abdurrahman was narrating a story and Humaid was giving a lesson. While I was thinking about which one of them to join, I fell asleep. Someone came to my dream and said:

"You are still thinking about which one to join. If you want, let me show you the place of Gabriel who sits right next to Humaid!" (Darimi, Muqaddimah, 32)

That is to say that even the prominent angels join the gatherings of those who are busy with useful knowledge. This is more than enough to prove the virtue of being busy with useful knowledge.

On the other hand, knowledge is an endless ocean. To get the entire knowledge is outside of human capacity. Therefore, humans should acquire useful knowledge first and turn away from the things that are not beneficial. The Messenger of Allah (pbuh) said:

"Learn your names (your kin) well enough to visit them and give up the rest! Learn Arabic well enough to understand the Holy Book of Allah and give up the rest! Learn astronomy well enough to find your way in the sea darkness of sea or land and give up the rest!" (Baihaqi, *Shuab*, II, 269-270)

Salman al-Farisi (r.a.) advised to Hudhaifa:

"Knowledge is a deep ocean and life is short. In respect to your religion, learn as much as you need and leave the rest behind; don't tire yourself out for nothing!" (Abu Nuaym, *Hilya*, I, 189)

While Salman (r.a.) was taking a walk on the coast of Tigris, his friend bent down and drank some water.

Salman (r.a.) said:

"Go ahead, drink some more!"

His friend answered:

"I am done!"

Salman asked:

"Can you say that anything lessened from the river?"

His friend said:

"No"

This time Salman (r.a.) advised:

"Knowledge is like this river, it does not diminish. Therefore, get the knowledge that will be useful to you!" (Abu Nuaym, *Hilya,* I, 188)

Wasting time with knowledge that is not useful makes one tired for nothing and it is a huge waste in every aspect. For this reason, **in the second hadith** the Messenger of Allah (pbuh) took refuge in Allah from knowledge that does not mature the heart, discipline the self, and beautify manners. That is because knowledge that is not useful will not bring happiness neither in this world nor in the Hereafter.

There are also unfortunate people who do not acquire useful knowledge and also spread the worst part of whatever they learn. Those who act in this way are surely the most unfortunate and deprived ones of all people. Such people get busy with unnecessary and even harmful things by turning away from useful knowledge. In time, they are the ones who will face with the harm of their acts.

Such people look for and find harmful things while they could learn useful knowledge and perform many good deeds. As in the example given in **our third hadith**, it is compared to finding a dog whose meat cannot be eaten while it is possible to pick one of the hundreds of sheep in the herd. That dog will soon bite or even tear him into pieces. In order words, that person picked the hardest and most harmful way.

Another important issue is that the person who acquires useful knowledge must share his knowledge with others. This is because the important thing is to spread the knowledge by explaining and to ensure others have access to it as well. It is a big sin to hide theological information that everyone should know. Those who do this will have to face the divine torment in the Hereafter. It is expressed in the Qur'an that:

"Those who conceal the clear (Signs) We have sent down, and the Guidance, after We have made it clear for the people in the Book, on them shall be Allah's curse, and the curse of those entitled to curse." (Al-Baqarah; 2:159)

The warning of the Prophet on this issue is as follows:

"He who is asked about something he knows and conceals it will have a bridle of fire put on him on the Day of Resurrection." (Abu Dawud, Ilm, 9/3658. Also see Tirmidhi, Ilm, 3/2649; Ibn Majah, Muqaddimah, 24)

On the other hand, man should not acquire knowledge only to gain worldly benefits and satisfy himself. The Messenger of Allah (pbuh) said:

"If anyone acquires knowledge of things by which Allah's contentedness is sought, but acquires it only to get some worldly advantage, he will not experience even the scent of Paradise." (Abu Dawud, Ilm, 12/3664. Also see Ibn Majah, Muqaddimah, 23)

Such a person acts insincerely and anticipates the rewards of his efforts not from Allah but from others. These rewards are given in this world, so he will not receive anything for it in the Hereafter.

The Messenger of Allah (pbuh) said the following about those who acquire knowledge for anything other than Allah's contentedness:

"If anyone acquires knowledge only to discuss it with scholars, to debate with the scoundrels, and to gain people's appreciation, Allah will put him into Hell." (Tirmidhi, Ilm, 6/2654; Ibn Majah, Muqaddimah, 23)

"If anyone acquires knowledge for anything other than Allah, or wants anything else other than Allah with his knowledge, he should prepare for his place in the fire!" (Tirmidhi, Ilm, 6/2655; Ibn Majah, Muqaddimah, 23)

However, a scholar may gain worldly benefits because of his knowledge that he acquired for Allah's pleasure. This is Allah's blessing to him. There is no harm to acquire knowledge which is not obligatory in order to receive honest earnings. However, if one acquires theological knowledge just to earn worldly benefits, he stays away from paradise in the hereafter and will not be among those who enter there first.

3. Putting Knowledge into Practice

٢٣. عَنْ أُسَامَةَ بْنِ زَيْدٍ رَضِيَ اللهُ عَنْهُ قَالَ: سَمِعْتُ رَسُولَ اللهِ صَلَّى اللهُ عَلَيْهِ وَسَلَّمَ يَقُولُ:

«يُؤْتَى بِالرَّجُلِ يَوْمَ الْقِيَامَةِ فَيُلْقَى فِي النَّارِ فَتَنْدَلِقُ أَقْتَابُ بَطْنِهِ فَيَدُورُ بِهَا كَمَا يَدُورُ الْحِمَارُ بِالرَّحَى فَيَجْتَمِعُ إِلَيْهِ أَهْلُ النَّارِ فَيَقُولُونَ: يَا فُلَانُ مَا لَكَ أَلَمْ تَكُنْ تَأْمُرُ بِالْمَعْرُوفِ وَتَنْهَى عَنِ الْمُنْكَرِ فَيَقُولُ: بَلَى قَدْ كُنْتُ آمُرُ بِالْمَعْرُوفِ وَلَا آتِيهِ وَأَنْهَى عَنِ الْمُنْكَرِ وَآتِيهِ».

23. Uthama b. Zaid (r.a.) narrated that he heard the Messenger of Allah (pbuh) saying:

"A man will be brought on the Day of Resurrection and thrown in Hell-Fire and his intestines will pour forth in Hell and he will go round along with them, as an ass goes round the mill stone. The denizens of Hell will gather round him and say:

"O, so and so, what has happened to you? Were you not enjoining us to do what was reputable and forbid us to do what was disreputable?" He will say:

"Of course, it is so; I used to enjoin (upon people) to do what was reputable but did not practice it myself. I had been forbidding people to do what was disreputable, but practiced it myself." (Muslim, Zuhd, 51. Also see Bukhari, Bad' al-khalk, 10; Ahmad, V, 205-209)

٢٤. عَنْ يَزِيدَ بْنِ سَلَمَةَ الْجُعْفِيّ رَضِيَ اللهُ عَنْهُ قَالَ: قَالَ يَزِيدُ بْنُ سَلَمَةَ:

«يَا رَسُولَ اللهِ إِنِّي قَدْ سَمِعْتُ مِنْكَ حَدِيثًا كَثِيرًا أَخَافُ أَنْ يُنْسِيَنِي أَوَّلَهُ آخِرُهُ فَحَدِّثْنِي بِكَلِمَةٍ تَكُونُ جِمَاعًا» قَالَ:

«اِتَّقِ اللهَ فِيمَا تَعْلَمُ».

24. Yazid b. Salman al-Jufi (r.a.) narrated that he told:

"O the Messenger of Allah! I have heard many ahadith from you. However, I am afraid that the new ones will cause me to forgive the previous ones that I heard from you. Will you tell me a word of wisdom that may substitute for all of them?" And he said:

"Fear from Allah concerning the ones that you know (put them into practice!)" (Tirmidhi, Ilm, 19/2683)

٢٥. عَنْ أَبِي بَرْزَةَ الْأَسْلَمِيّ رَضِيَ اللهُ عَنْهُ قَالَ: قَالَ رَسُولُ اللهِ صَلَّى اللهُ عَلَيْهِ وَسَلَّمَ:

«لَا تَزُولُ قَدَمَا عَبْدٍ يَوْمَ الْقِيَامَةِ حَتَّى يُسْأَلَ عَنْ عُمْرِهِ فِيمَا أَفْنَاهُ وَعَنْ عِلْمِهِ فِيمَ فَعَلَ وَعَنْ مَالِهِ مِنْ أَيْنَ اكْتَسَبَهُ وَفِيمَ أَنْفَقَهُ وَعَنْ جِسْمِهِ فِيمَ أَبْلَاهُ».

25. It is reported that Abu Barza al-Aslami (r.a.) narrated that the Messenger of Allah (pbuh) said:

"No one can move on the Day of Judgment until he is asked about his life and how he spent it, about his knowledge and what he did with it, about his wealth

and how he earned it and how he spent it, and about his health and how he wore off his body." (Tirmidhi, Qiyamah, 1/2417)

Explanations:

The knowledge is not a virtue in and of itself, but it is a mean to advance humans to more lofty levels. The real virtue is putting the knowledge into practice. Knowledge that is not practiced in life helps nothing but to be a proof against its owner. As a matter of fact, the Messenger of Allah (pbuh) considered a scholar who does not put his knowledge into practice equal to an ignorant person. (Tirmidhi, Ilm, 5/2653)

In the first hadith, it is presented that the end of those who were beneficial to others with their knowledge but forgot about themselves will be pain and disappointment. All of their knowledge did not benefit them since they did not put it into practice for themselves.

The Messenger of Allah (pbuh) described the miserable situation of those who do not benefit from their own knowledge as:

"The scholar who forgets himself while teaching what is good to others is like a candle exhausts itself while lightening up its surroundings." (Haythami, I, 184)

Whereas one must think of himself first and his knowledge must benefit him first. For this to happen, it is necessary for knowledge to settle in the heart and manifest itself in acts.

How meaningful Ali's following warning is:

"O man of knowledge! Practice your knowledge! The real scholar is the one who puts his knowledge into practice and whose actions are in accordance with his knowledge. There will be a time when people will acquire knowledge but their knowledge will not go beyond their throats and their acts and knowledge and their inside and outside won't be the same. They will sit in circles and be proud of their knowledge and show off to each other. One of them will get mad to his friend just for leaving him and sitting next to another person. Their actions in those meetings don't ascend to Allah." (Darimi, Muqaddimah, 34)

Indeed, these people can not benefit from the knowledge for which they had to bare many difficulties and hardships to acquire. In fact, it is not even appropriate to call them scholars. They are ignorant people who just know many things.

As a matter of fact, Sufyan b. Uyaynah said:

"The most ignorant of all is the one who does not put his knowledge into practice, and the most learned man is the one who practices his knowledge, and the best of all is the one who experience the most reverence towards Allah." (Darimi, Muqaddimah, 32)

The following exemplary story which was narrated by Ammar b. Yasir manifests the miserable state of those who do not benefit from their knowledge to find salvation in the Hereafter:

The Messenger of Allah (pbuh) had sent me to a district of the Qais Clan. I was teaching them the principles of Islam. However, people were like a wild herd of camels. They were very arrogant. All they cared about was their sheep and camels. I came back to the Prophet (pbuh). He asked to me:

"O Ammar! What did you do?"

I explained the state of the clan to him. I informed him about their negligence and deception.

The Messenger of Allah (pbuh) said:

"O Ammar! Would you like me to tell you about people who are more surprising than this clan? They are the ones who know things that this clan does not know but still live in a heedless life such as this clan does." (Haythami, I, 185)

If we think for a moment, we can see how contemporary people fit in the description given this hadith: People who know everything and who can easily obtain any information they need, but see nothing but worldly goods just like those ignorant Bedouins …

People who do not put their knowledge into practice are surely in a worse state and their responsibility is greater than those who do not know.

The knowledge from which is not benefited is like wealth that is not spent in the way of Allah.[28] As the wealth that is not spent in the way of Allah does not benefit its owner, the knowledge that is not put into practice does not bring salvation to its owner neither in this world nor in the Hereafter. Heedless peo-

---

28.   Ahmad, II, 499; Haythami, I, 184.

ple keep both knowledge and wealth for a while before they lose all of them when they die and are held accountable for those blessings that they did not benefit.

As it can be understood from **our second hadith,** one must fear Allah and must put his knowledge into practice. One must stay away from things that Allah has forbidden and fulfill His commands as much as he can. Acting this way forms the basis of piety or "taqwa."

As it is pointed out in this hadith, the purpose of acquiring knowledge is to obtain piety. That is because those with knowledge know better what they have to do and what they have to abstain from and how to live in accordance with these rules.

On the other hand, if a person puts his knowledge into practice and lives a pious life, Allah the Almighty teaches him what he does not know. That is because, the knowledge that is practiced takes its roots in the consciousness and saves the person from the fear of forgetting it and provides a basis for acquiring new knowledge. Since acting this way helps a person to gain the contentedness of Allah, it generates great blessings and advances the person's knowledge of Him. As a matter of fact, the Companions of the Prophet used to put their knowledge into practice as soon as they acquired it. Abu Abdurrahman As-Sulami narrated:

"There was a man from the Companions of the Messenger of Allah who used to teach us the Noble Qur'an. He used to say:

"We would learn ten verses of the Qur'an from the Prophet (pbuh) and would not move on to the next ten verses before we had learned everything in the first ten verses well. The Messenger of Allah (pbuh) taught us both the knowledge and its practice at the same time." (Ahmad, V, 410; Haythami, I, 165)

The Messenger of Allah (pbuh) used to teach knowledge provided that it would be practiced in life and taught to others who would practice it. As an example of that, Abu Huraira (r.a.) narrated:

One day, the Messenger of Allah (pbuh) said to his companions:

"Who will take these words from me and put them into practice and teach others who will also put them into practice?"

I came forward and said:

"I will, O the Messenger of Allah!"

The Messenger of Allah (pbuh) held my hand and counted the following five things:

"If you stay away from the forbidden things (al-haram), you will be the best worshipping servant of Allah.

If you get satisfied with the share that Allah gave you, you will be the richest of all.

Be nice to your neighbor so you will become a perfect believer.

Wish for others the same as what you wish for yourself so you will become a perfect Muslim.

Don't laugh a lot! This is because laughing a lot kills the heart." (Tirmidhi, Zuhd, 2/2305; Ibn Majah, Kitab Al-Zuhd, 24)

In our third hadith presents the first and foremost issues for which humans will be held accountable on the Day of Judgment. They are the life, knowledge, wealth, and health. Allah the Almighty decreed certain rules concerning each one of them and made some requests. **Life** should be spent as it is prescribed by Islam in performing beneficial deeds. One must not acquire **knowledge** as a means for pride, but must put it into practice and also teach others. One must obtain **wealth** through honest earnings and spend it on his family needs and doing good deeds. One must know that **health** is a divine trust and must be used in accordance with Allah's will.

As a matter of fact, one will be held accountable for everything he did with the blessings of Allah. The issues listed in our hadith are the first things that humans will be held accountable for. And one of these is the issue of putting our knowledge into practice. It is impossible for humans to enter into Paradise before being held fully accountable for it first. So, putting our knowledge into practice in this world is the smartest way to ensure both Allah's contentedness and appreciation of others.

E. THE PRACTICE OF WORSHIP

1. Virtues of Ablution (Al-Wudhu)

٢٦. عَنْ أَبِي هُرَيْرَةَ رَضِيَ اللهُ عَنْهُ أَنَّ رَسُولَ اللهِ صَلَّى اللهُ عَلَيْهِ وَسَلَّمَ قَالَ:

«إِذَا تَوَضَّأَ الْعَبْدُ الْمُسْلِمُ -أَوِ الْمُؤْمِنُ- فَغَسَلَ وَجْهَهُ خَرَجَ مِنْ وَجْهِهِ كُلُّ خَطِيئَةٍ نَظَرَ إِلَيْهَا بِعَيْنَيْهِ مَعَ الْمَاءِ أَوْ مَعَ آخِرِ قَطْرِ الْمَاءِ فَإِذَا غَسَلَ يَدَيْهِ خَرَجَ مِنْ يَدَيْهِ كُلُّ خَطِيئَةٍ كَانَ بَطَشْتَهَا يَدَاهُ مَعَ الْمَاءِ أَوْ مَعَ آخِرِ قَطْرِ الْمَاءِ فَإِذَا غَسَلَ رِجْلَيْهِ خَرَجَتْ كُلُّ خَطِيئَةٍ مَشَتْهَا رِجْلَاهُ مَعَ الْمَاءِ أَوْ مَعَ آخِرِ قَطْرِ الْمَاءِ حَتَّى يَخْرُجَ نَقِيًّا مِنَ الذُّنُوبِ».

26. Abu Huraira (r.a.) narrated that he heard the Messenger of Allah (pbuh) saying:

"When a subject of Allah -a Muslim or a believer-washes his face (in the course of ablution), every sin he contemplated with his eyes, will be washed away from his face along with water, or with the last drop of water; when he washes his hands, every sin they wrought will be effaced from his hands with the water, or with the last drop of water; and when he washes his feet, every sin towards which his feet have walked will be washed away with the water or with the last drop of water[29] *with the result that he comes out pure from all sins."* (Muslim, Taharah, 32. Also see Tirmidhi, Taharah, 2/2)

❀

---

29. In the hadith, the dual expressions of *"Muslim or a believer (mumin)"*, *"the water or the last drop of water"* are because of the hesitation of the narrator in order not to make a mistake in wording. This proves how the scholars who study hadith paid attention to accuracy when they were narrating them.

٢٧. عَنْ أَبِي هُرَيْرَةَ رَضِيَ اللهُ عَنْهُ قَالَ: سَمِعْتُ رَسُولَ اللهِ صَلَّى اللهُ عَلَيْهِ وَسَلَّمَ يَقُولُ:

«إِنَّ أُمَّتِي يُدْعَوْنَ يَوْمَ الْقِيَامَةِ غُرًّا مُحَجَّلِينَ مِنْ آثَارِ الْوُضُوءِ فَمَنِ اسْتَطَاعَ مِنْكُمْ أَنْ يُطِيلَ غُرَّتَهُ فَلْيَفْعَلْ».

27. Abu Huraira (r.a.) narrated that he heard our Master the Prophet (pbuh) say:

"For sure my people would come with bright faces and bright hands and feet on account of the marks of ablution, so he who can increase the luster of his forehead (and that of his hands and legs) should do so!" (Bukhari, Wudu, 3; Muslim, Taharah, 35)

❊

٢٨. عَنْ أَبِي هُرَيْرَةَ رَضِيَ اللهُ عَنْهُ أَنَّ رَسُولَ اللهِ صَلَّى اللهُ عَلَيْهِ وَسَلَّمَ أَتَى الْمَقْبَرَةَ فَقَالَ:

«السَّلَامُ عَلَيْكُمْ دَارَ قَوْمٍ مُؤْمِنِينَ وَإِنَّا إِنْ شَاءَ اللهُ بِكُمْ لَاحِقُونَ. وَدِدْتُ أَنَّا قَدْ رَأَيْنَا إِخْوَانَنَا» قَالُوا:

«أَوَلَسْنَا إِخْوَانَكَ يَا رَسُولَ اللهِ؟» قَالَ:

«أَنْتُمْ أَصْحَابِي وَإِخْوَانُنَا الَّذِينَ لَمْ يَأْتُوا بَعْدُ» فَقَالُوا:

«كَيْفَ تَعْرِفُ مَنْ لَمْ يَأْتِ بَعْدُ مِنْ أُمَّتِكَ يَا رَسُولَ اللهِ؟» فَقَالَ:

«أَرَأَيْتَ لَوْ أَنَّ رَجُلًا لَهُ خَيْلٌ غُرٌّ مُحَجَّلَةٌ بَيْنَ ظَهْرَيْ خَيْلٍ دُهْمٍ بُهْمٍ أَلَا يَعْرِفُ خَيْلَهُ؟» قَالُوا:

«بَلَى يَا رَسُولَ اللهِ» قَالَ:

«فَإِنَّهُمْ يَأْتُونَ غُرًّا مُحَجَّلِينَ مِنَ الْوُضُوءِ وَأَنَا فَرَطُهُمْ عَلَى الْحَوْضِ أَلَا لَيُذَادَنَّ رِجَالٌ عَنْ حَوْضِي كَمَا يُذَادُ الْبَعِيرُ الضَّالُّ أُنَادِيهِمْ: أَلَا هَلُمَّ فَيُقَالُ: إِنَّهُمْ قَدْ بَدَّلُوا بَعْدَكَ فَأَقُولُ: سُحْقًا سُحْقًا».

28. Abu Huraira (r.a.) narrated that the Messenger of Allah (pbuh) came to the graveyard and said:

"Peace be upon you! The abode of the believing people and us, if God so wills, are about to join you. I love to see my brothers."

The Noble Companions asked:

"Aren't we your brothers O Messenger of Allah?"

The Noble Messenger (pbuh) said:

"You are my companions, and our brothers are those who have, so far, not come into the world."

Upon that the Noble Companions asked:

"O Messenger of Allah, how would you recognize those persons of your Ummah who have not yet been born?

The Messenger of Allah (pbuh) asked them:

"Supposing a man had horses with white blazes on their foreheads and legs among horses which were all black, tell me, would he not recognize his own horses?

The Noble Companions answered:

"Certainly, O the Messenger of Allah!"

Upon that the Messenger of Allah (pbuh) said:

"They would come with white faces and arms and legs owing to ablution, and I would arrive at the Cistern before them. Some people would be driven away from my Cistern as the stray camel is driven away. I would call out as "Come, come here!" Then it would be said (to me):

"These people changed themselves after you, (they have not followed your Sunnah and they went astray.)" Upon that I would say:

"Be off, be off." (Muslim, Taharah, 39; Fadail, 26. Also see Nasai, Taharah, 110/150; Ibn Majah, Zuhd, 36; *Muwatta,* Taharah, 28; Ahmad, II, 300, 408)

۲۹. عَنْ ثَوْبَانَ رَضِيَ اللهُ عَنْهُ قَالَ: قَالَ رَسُولُ اللهِ صَلَّى اللهُ عَلَيْهِ وَسَلَّمَ:

«اِسْتَقِيمُوا وَلَنْ تُحْصُوا وَاعْلَمُوا أَنَّ خَيْرَ أَعْمَالِكُمُ الصَّلَاةُ وَلَا يُحَافِظُ عَلَى الْوُضُوءِ إِلَّا مُؤْمِنٌ».

29. Thawban (r.a.) narrated that the Messenger of Allah (pbuh) said:

"Stay on the straight path, but know that you cannot perform everything perfectly. Know it well that the best of your deed is your prayer. Only a believer tries to be in a state of ritual purity at all times." (Ibn Majah, Taharah, 4; *Muwatta,* Taharah, 36; Ahmad, V, 276, 282; Darimi, Taharah, 2)

Explanations:

The Messenger of Allah (pbuh) said:

"Allah is pure and loves purity" (Tirmidhi, Adab, 41/2799)

"Being pure is half of faith." (Muslim, Taharah, 1)

For this reason, Islam is known as the religion of purity. Allah the Almighty wants His servants to be purified from both material and moral impurities of all kind. This is the reason why Islam commands a new Muslim-convert to take bath lustration (ghusl)[30] and take ablution (wudu) to those who will perform worship. Thus Muslims pay extra attention to cleanliness as the requirement of their religion, and they covered the topic of cleanliness in detail under the title of "Taharah" (Cleanliness) in the first chapters of the books of Islamic jurisprudence. As a matter of fact, cleanliness is a trait that keeps us

---

30. Abu Dawud, Taharah, 129/355.

away from Satan and makes us closer to the angels and saves us from the torments of the grave.

Also cleanliness helps our soul be exalted and reach the level of benevolence and be closer to Allah. For this reason, it is expressed in the following noble verse that:

"…Allah loves those who keep themselves pure and clean." (Al-Baqarah; 2:222)

As a matter of fact, the material cleanliness influences the spirituality and enlightens one's soul and brings some light to the gloom of the heart caused by sins. This means that good deeds are recorded and mistakes are forgiven. Thus, the virtue of ablution that conduces to both physical and spiritual cleanliness becomes evident.

Since they are the most exposed ones, parts of the body that are washed during ablution are the ones which get more easily dirty. For this reason, washing them five times a day does not just provide material and spiritual health but it also keeps one mentally awake.

Paying attention to all these, a believer must perform his ablution carefully and must put extra effort in order to increase the divine light that he will receive as a reward in the hereafter. The way to accomplish this is to wash three times the body parts required to be washed during ablution and little more than the required limits, to turn towards Ka'bah if possible, to start with reciting the name of Allah (saying *Bismillah*), to make intention (*al-niyyah*), to clean the mouth and nostrils well, to recite the supplications of ablution, and not to waste any water while performing the ablution.

Using a miswaq (tooth-stick, a special wood used to clean the teeth) is also an important Sunnah. The Messenger of Allah (pbuh) expressed the virtue of using miswaq as:

"Miswaq cleanses the mouth and allows one to gain the contentedness of Allah." (Nasai, Taharah, 5/5)

"Were it not that I might over-burden the believers, I would have ordered them to use a tooth-stick at every time of prayer." (Bukhari, Jum'a, 8)

The Messenger of Allah (pbuh) attached importance to the use of miswaq outside of the prayer times as well. When he wakes up for the mid-night prayer, he used to clean his teeth, take ablution, and perform a prayer. (Muslim, Musafirin, 139)

Again, when he came home, the first thing that he did was to clean his teeth. (Muslim, Taharah, 43-44)

On the other hand, ablution cleanses small sins and mistakes unknowingly done other than seizing the rights of the others. The story of Imam Abu Hanifa in this regard is well known: After watching a young man performing ablution, the Prominent Imam told him:

"My son! Stay away from such and such sins!"

The young man shocked by hearing these words asked:

"Sir, how did you know that I committed those sins?"

Abu Hanifa answered:

"From the ablution water that is flowing from parts of your body…"

In the above mentioned sayings of the Prophet, those who are complimented as "my followers" and "my brothers" by the Prophet (pbuh) are the ones who perform ablution and their prayers, and who live an exemplary life by paying attention to their acts of worship. On the Day of Judgment, they will be distinguished by their bright body parts and will be closer to the Prophet (pbuh).

Every believer who is aware of the good news mentioned in these sayings tries to perform his ablution as well as possible and tries to preserve the state of ablution as long as possible. However, being in the state of ablution at all times is a difficult matter to accomplish. For this reason, in the fourth hadith, this practice is conditioned on having a strong faith and its virtue is pointed out. In other words, only those who know the value of having ablution and who really believe its rewards in the hereafter can pay attention to be in a state of ritual purity at all times.

Being in the state of ritual purśty at all times is one of the most important customs of the Messenger of Allah. As a matter of fact, it is narrated that the Messenger of Allah used to make ablution right after using the bathroom. (Ibn-i Sa'd, I, 369)

Preforming a fresh ablution while in the state of ritual purity is a meritorious act, and it is like doubling the divine light. The Messenger of Allah (pbuh) used to perform ablution in each prayer time whether he was in the state of ritual purity or not. In order to encourage his followers to do this, he said:

"Allah records ten rewards for whoever performs ablution even though he was already in the state of ritual purity." (Tirmidhi, Taharah, 44/58, 59)

Due to their importance the Messenger of Allah (pbuh) personally carried out two acts without assigning anyone else to do them on his behalf. One of them was to prepare the water for ablution when he woke up for the midnight prayer, and the second one was to give alms to the poor. He used to prepare his own water for ablution and give alms to the poor personally. (See Ibn Majah, Taharah, 30; Ibn Abi Shayba, I, 178; Ibn Saʾd, I, 369)

The following reports that prove the importance of ablution and preserving ablution at all times will be helpful in understanding this issue better:

One morning, the Messenger of Allah (pbuh) called Bilal next to him and asked:

"O Bilal! What did you do to enter Paradise before me? Whenever I go to Paradise (in my dreams), I hear your footsteps before me. Last night, I went to Paradise and again I heard your footsteps before me…"

Bilal (r.a.) said:

"O Messenger of Allah! Whenever I hear the call to prayer (adhan), I perform two units (rakahs) of prayer. As soon as I break my ablution, I perform another one, and then I think that I am responsible to Allah to perform two units of prayer.

Upon that, the Messenger of Allah said:

"Indeed it is because of these two acts!" (Tirmidhi, Manaqib, 17/3689; Ahmad, V, 354)

Uqba b. Amir (r.a.) reported:

We were entrusted with the task of tending the camels. On my turn when I came back in the evening after grazing them in the pastures, I found Allah's Messenger (pbuh) standing and addressing the people. I heard these words of his:

"If any Muslim performs ablution well, then stands and prays two rakahs (units of ritual prayer) setting about them with his heart as well as his face, Paradise will be guaranteed to him!"

When I heard that, I said:

"What a fine thing this is!"

And someone who was before me said:

"The first one was even better than this."

When I cast a glance, I saw that it was Umar who continued as:

"I see that you have just come. A few minutes ago the Prophet (pbuh) said:

"If anyone amongst you performs the ablution, and then completes the ablution well and then says: I testify that there is no god but Allah and that Muhammad is the servant of Allah and His Messenger, the eight gates of Paradise will be opened for him and he may enter by whichever of them he wishes." (Muslim, Taharah, 17)

2. Being Respectful to Call to Prayer (Adhan)

٣٠. عَنْ عَبْدِ اللهِ بْنِ عَمْرِو بْنِ الْعَاصِ رَضِيَ اللهُ عَنْهُمَا أَنَّهُ سَمِعَ رَسُولَ اللهِ صَلَّى اللهُ عَلَيْهِ وَسَلَّمَ يَقُولُ:

«إِذَا سَمِعْتُمُ الْمُؤَذِّنَ فَقُولُوا مِثْلَ مَا يَقُولُ ثُمَّ صَلُّوا عَلَيَّ فَإِنَّهُ مَنْ صَلَّى عَلَيَّ صَلَاةً صَلَّى اللهُ عَلَيْهِ بِهَا عَشْرًا ثُمَّ سَلُوا اللهَ لِيَ الْوَسِيلَةَ فَإِنَّهَا مَنْزِلَةٌ فِي الْجَنَّةِ لَا تَنْبَغِي إِلَّا لِعَبْدٍ مِنْ عِبَادِ اللهِ وَأَرْجُو أَنْ أَكُونَ أَنَا هُوَ فَمَنْ سَأَلَ لِيَ الْوَسِيلَةَ حَلَّتْ لَهُ الشَّفَاعَةُ».

30. Abdullah b. Amr al-As (r.a.) reported that the Messenger of Allah (pbuh) said:

"When you hear the Muadhdhin, repeat what he says, then invoke a blessing onto me, for everyone who invokes a blessing on me will receive ten blessings from Allah; then beg from Allah al-Wasila for me, which is a rank in Paradise fitting for

69

only one of Allah's servants, and I hope that I may be that one. If anyone who asks that I be given the Wasila, he will be assured of my intercession." (Muslim, Salah, 11)

❈

٣١. عَنْ جَابِرِ بْنِ عَبْدِ اللهِ رَضِيَ اللهُ عَنْهُمَا أَنَّ رَسُولَ اللهِ صَلَّى اللهُ عَلَيْهِ وَسَلَّمَ قَالَ:

«مَنْ قَالَ حِينَ يَسْمَعُ النِّدَاءَ: (اللّٰهُمَّ رَبَّ هٰذِهِ الدَّعْوَةِ التَّامَّةِ وَالصَّلَاةِ الْقَائِمَةِ آتِ مُحَمَّداً الْوَسِيلَةَ وَالْفَضِيلَةَ وَابْعَثْهُ مَقَاماً مَحْمُوداً الَّذِي وَعَدْتَهُ) حَلَّتْ لَهُ شَفَاعَتِي يَوْمَ الْقِيَامَةِ».

31. Jabir b. Abdullah reported that the Messenger of Allah (pbuh) said:

"Whoever after listening to the Adhan says, "Allahumma Rabba hadhihi-d-da'wat it-tammati was-salatil qa'imati, ati Muhammadan al-wasilata wal-fadilata, wab'aththu maqaman mahmudan-il-ladhi wa'adtahu (O Allah! Lord of this perfect call (of not ascribing partners to You) and of the regular prayer which is going to be established! Kindly give Muhammad the right of intercession and superiority and send him (on the Day of Judgment) to the Station of Praise and Glory (the best and the highest place in Paradise) which You promised him)", then intercession for me will be permitted for him on the Day of Resurrection"). (Bukhari, Adhan, 8; Tafsir, 17/11. Also see Abu Dawud, Salah, 37/529; Tirmidhi, Salah, 43/211; Nesai, Adhan, 38/678; Ibn Majah, Adhan, 4)

❈

٣٢. عَنْ سَعْدِ بْنِ أَبِي وَقَّاصٍ رَضِيَ اللهُ عَنْهُ عَنْ رَسُولِ اللهِ صَلَّى اللهُ عَلَيْهِ وَسَلَّمَ أَنَّهُ قَالَ:

«مَنْ قَالَ حِينَ يَسْمَعُ الْمُؤَذِّنَ: (أَشْهَدُ أَنْ لَا إِلٰهَ إِلَّا اللهُ وَحْدَهُ لَا شَرِيكَ لَهُ وَأَنَّ مُحَمَّداً عَبْدُهُ وَرَسُولُهُ، رَضِيتُ بِاللهِ رَبًّا وَبِمُحَمَّدٍ رَسُولاً وَبِالْإِسْلَامِ دِينًا) غُفِرَ لَهُ ذَنْبُهُ».

32. Sa'd b. Abu Waqqas reported that the Messenger of Allah (pbuh) said:

"The Messenger of Allah (pbuh) said: If anyone says on hearing the Muadh-dhin: I testify that there is no god but Allah alone Who has no partner, and that Muhammad is His servant and His Messenger, (and that) I am satisfied with Allah as my Lord, with Muhammad as my Messenger and with Islam as my din (code of life), his sins would be forgiven." (Muslim, Salah, 13. Also see Tirmidhi, Salah, 42/210; Nasai, Adhan, 38/677; Ibn Majah, Adhan, 4)

Explanations:

The essence of being a servant of Allah is being respectful to Him. As our respect gains perfection, so does our servanthood. There are some signs of Allah in this universe and showing our respect and love to them also means to love and honor Allah. Showing disrespect to those signs also means being disrespectful to Allah. Those are the signs and marks that evoke the feeling of being close to Allah, such as the Noble Qur'an, Ka'bah, the Prophet, adhan, prayer, sacrifice, and hills of al-Safa and al-Marwa. Allah commanded that we avoid disrespectful acts towards those signs that He established on the Earth. [31] And it is told that those who honor and show respect to these signs will be rewarded. In the following noble verses, it is stated that:

"Such (is the Pilgrimage): whoever honors the sacred rites of Allah, for him it is good in the Sight of his Lord." (Al-Hajj; 22:30)

"Such (is his state): and whoever holds in honor the symbols of Allah, (in the sacrifice of animals), such (honor) should come truly from piety of heart." (Al-Hajj; 22:32)

Call to prayer (adhan) is one of the important signs of Islam:

Through call to prayer, the principles of Islam are announced loudly five times a day; the unbelievers are being invited to the faith; and the believers are being invited to worship in congregation and to unity and solidarity.

When call to prayer is recited in a place, it means that there are Muslims living there and the land is a land of Islam. In that sense, the call to prayer was the essential part of conquests and victories throughout Islamic history. A newly conquered land turned into the land of Islam with the recitation of the

---

31. Al-Maidah; 5:2

conquest adhan and the Messenger of Allah (pbuh) identified whether a place was the land of Islam or not in accordance with the practice of adhan.[32]

The adhan that is recited in its original language (Arabic) can be easily recognized by the Muslims of the world, no matter what language they speak, and its message can be understood.

The adhan is the continuation of the mission of prophets, because the adhan is a call to the greatest pillar of Islam and to the essence of all acts of worship, i.e. prayer.

Through adhan, Allah the Almighty invites His servants to His presence. For this reason, adhan shows the value that Allah attaches to His servants.

Those kids that adhan is recited into their ears receive the first essence of national and spiritual discipline by this divine invitation.

Therefore, adhan is one of the important signs to which Muslims must show their respect.

The first manifestation of showing respect to adhan is to recite it in the state of ritual purity. (Tirmidhi, Salah, 33/200, 201)

The other indication is to repeat adhan during the recitation of the Muadhdhin. Those Muslims who do that gain the same divine rewards as the Muadhdhin and Allah responds to their prayers.

To repeat adhan with the Muadhdhin is necessary (wajib) according to school of Hanafi law. Hence, upon hearing the adhan, it is also wajib to stop recitation of the Qur'an, saying supplication, greeting others, and talking. Other schools of law view that repeating adhan with the Muadhdhin is recommended but not obligatory. Those views hold same for the call to stand up for the actual start of the ritual prayer (al-Iqamah).

According to some narrations, it is recommended to say "La Hawla wa la quwwata illa billah (There is neither might nor any power except with Allah)" after hearing Hayya 'ala al-Salah and Hayya'ala al-Falah. (Muslim, Salah, 12; Abu Dawud, Salah, 36/527)

---

32. See Bukhari, Adhan, 6; Muslim, Salah, 9; Abu Dawud, Jihad, 91/2635; Ahmad, III, 448-449.

After "Qad qamat al-Salah," is recited, the Messenger of Allah (pbuh) prayed by saying "أَقَامَهَا اللهُ وَأَدَامَهَا" "May Allah establish it and cause it to continue." (Abu Dawud, Salah, 36/528)

Some scholars are of the view that after Muadhdhin says "Assalatu Khayrun min an-nawm" (Prayer is better than sleep), one should say "صَدَقْتَ وَبَرِرْتَ" "You said the truth and you did well."

For those who hear more than one call to prayer at the same prayer period, it is enough to repeat this after one call to prayer.

After the call to prayer ends, one says blessings and praises (salawats) to the Messenger of Allah and recites the supplications that were taught in the sayings of the Prophet. Even though these supplications seem like they are said for the Messenger of Allah (pbuh), in reality, they are for the benefit of the one who recites them. As a matter of fact, when a person says one blessing (salawat), Allah shows mercy on him ten times and forgives his sins. Again, through our prayers for the Messenger of Allah (pbuh) to have high level, he will have the right of intercession for the whole of humanity.

Those who repeat the sentences of adhan which is the sign of Islam and who recite the supplications show that they are loyal Muslims who obey Allah. They emphasize that power and might belong only to Allah and do not get carried away by wrong feelings such as that their worships are based on their personal superiority. They accept the divine invitation with the whole of their hearts.

Another indication of being respectful to the call to prayer is to stop all sermons and speeches.

Terms "al-Wasila" and "Station of Praise and Glory" mentioned in the **first two ahadith** are among the high ranks and levels of being close to Allah and having the right of intercession. Allah the Almighty says:

"And pray in the small watches of the morning: (it would be) an additional prayer (or spiritual profit) for you: soon will your Lord raise you to a Station of Praise and Glory!" (Al-Isra; 17:79)

At the Station of Praise and Glory, the Messenger of Allah (pbuh) will have a right of intercession not only for his followers but also for the entire community of sinners, and will pray Allah to manifest His mercy and grace in the hearts of humans during their hard times.

The Station of Praise and Glory, the best and the highest place in Paradise also refers to the spread and acceptance of Islam by humanity and the repetition of Prophet Muhammad's name continuously trough the call to prayer and other means.

The recommended supplication mentioned **in the third hadith** expresses the fundamentals of faith and Islam. As we mentioned earlier adhan also consists of similar content. Thus, a Muslim refreshes his faith and submission by repeating the fundamentals of his religion five times a day. Because of this consciousness that he keeps alive, he is protected from being carried away by the material world.

The Messenger of Allah (pbuh) informed us that the doors of heaven will be opened while adhan[33] or al-iqamah[34] is being pronounced and during the time between adhan and al-iqamah,[35] and the supplications will be accepted.

Since adhan is so virtuous, those who recite it also take their share from its virtue. As a matter of fact, exegetes of the Qur'an argue that the following verse of Qur'an also refers to the virtues of Muadhdhins:

"Who is better in speech than one who calls (men) to Allah, works righteousness, and says, "I am of those who bow in Islam"?" (Al-Fussilat; 41:33)

Many ahadith are reported about the virtues of Muadhdhins. In one of them, the Messenger of Allah (pbuh) said:

"If the people knew the reward for pronouncing the adhan and for standing in the first row (in congregational prayers) and found no other way to get that privilege except by drawing lots they would draw lots." (Bukhari, Adhan, 9, 32, Shahadah 30; Muslim, Salah 129)

Whoever hears the voice of the Muadhdhin, whether a human being, a jinn or any other creature, will be a witness for him on the Day of Resurrection. (Bukhari, Adhan, 5; Tawhid, 52; Bad' al-khalk 12)

Since muadhdhins strengthen their faith and increase their good deeds through the recitation of adhan, they will be leaders on the Day of Judgment and will have a congregation behind them. (See Muslim, Salah, 14; Ibn Majah, Adhan, 5)

---

33.   Haythami, I, 328.
34.   Ahmad, III, 342.
35.   Abu Dawud, Salah, 35/521; Tirmidhi, Salah, 44/212.

The end of those who do not show the proper respect to adhan is misery. The following story is a clear example to that:

One of the Christians from Medina used to say "Fire to the liar" whenever he heard Muadhdhin saying "I bear witness that Muhammad is the Messenger of Allah."

One night his attendant entered into the house with a fire in his hands. At that time, the Christian man and his family was sitting inside of the house. A spark started up a fire and burned the house and those inside it.

Upon that, the following verse of Qur'an was revealed:

"When you proclaim your call to prayer they take it (but) as mockery and sport; that is because they are a people without understanding." (Al-Maidah; 5:58) (Wahidi, p. 203; Qurtubi, VI, 146)

3. Five Daily Ritual Prayers (Salah)

a. Significance of Salah

٣٣. عَنْ أُمِّ سَلَمَةَ رَضِيَ اللهُ عَنْهَا قَالَتْ: كَانَ مِنْ آخِرِ وَصِيَّةِ رَسُولِ اللهِ صَلَّى اللهُ عَلَيْهِ وَسَلَّمَ:

«الصَّلَاةَ الصَّلَاةَ وَمَا مَلَكَتْ أَيْمَانُكُمْ» حَتَّى جَعَلَ نَبِيُّ اللهِ صَلَّى اللهُ عَلَيْهِ وَسَلَّمَ يُلَجْلِجُهَا فِي صَدْرِهِ وَمَا يَفِيضُ بِهَا لِسَانُهُ.

33. Ummu Salamah (r.a.), the mother of Muslims narrated:

"One of the last wills of the Prophet (pbuh) was:

"Pay attention to your prayers! Pay attention to your prayers! Pay attention to the rights of those who work for you!"

Allah's Messenger (pbuh) repeated these words so many times that when his blessed tongue could not pronounce them any longer, he started to whisper them. (Ahmad, VI, 290, 315. Also see Abu Dawud, Adab, 123-124/5156; Ibn Majah, Wasayah, 1; Baihaqi, *Shuab*, VII, 477)

٣٤. عَنْ أَبِي الدَّرْدَاءِ رَضِيَ اللهُ عَنْهُ قَالَ: أَوْصَانِي خَلِيلِي صَلَّى اللهُ عَلَيْهِ وَسَلَّمَ أَنْ:

«لَا تُشْرِكْ بِاللهِ شَيْئاً وَإِنْ قُطِّعْتَ وَحُرِّقْتَ. وَلَا تَتْرُكْ صَلَاةً مَكْتُوبَةً مُتَعَمِّداً فَمَنْ تَرَكَهَا مُتَعَمِّداً فَقَدْ بَرِئَتْ مِنْهُ الذِّمَّةُ».

34. Abu Darda (r.a.) reported: The Messenger of Allah (pbuh) whom I love more than my soul advised me:

"Even if you are torn apart or even burned, never associate anything as a partner to Allah! And never miss your obligatory (Fard) prayers intentionally! Whoever knowingly misses an obligatory prayer becomes distanced from the protection and trust of Allah." (Ibn Majah, Fitan, 23)

Explanations:

Ritual prayer is the most prominent principle of Islam. It is a distinguishing sign which separates believers from nonbelievers. Therefore, it is necessary to pay attention to prayer and be full of determination to continue performing it. For this reason, one of the last wills of the Messenger of Allah (pbuh) was insistence on prayer.

One of the reports manifesting that the Prophet (pbuh) emphasized prayer in his last wills is as follows:

Anas (r.a.) reported:

We were with the Messenger of Allah in his death bed. He told us three times:

"Fear from Allah about the matter of prayer!" and continued his words:

"Fear from Allah about being unjust to your workers, and fear from Allah about the two weak groups: They are widowed women and children. Fear from Allah about the matter of prayer!"

The Messenger of Allah (pbuh) started to repeat "prayer, prayer…" Even when his blessed tongue couldn't say any longer, he continued to whisper it until his soul ascended to his Divine Companion. (Baihaqi, *Shuab*, VII, 477)

These reports clearly display the significance of prayer which is the foundation and clearest manifestation of being a servant of Allah. In the following verses of the Qur'an emphasizing the importance of prayer Allah the Almighty says:

"And be steadfast in prayer; practice regular charity; and bow down your heads with those who bow down (in worship)." (Al-Baqarah; 2:43)

"Enjoin prayer on thy people, and be constant therein…" (Al-Taha; 20:132)

"But those will prosper who purify themselves, and glorify the name of their Guardian-Lord, and (lift their hearts) in prayer." (Al-A'la; 87:14-15)

Our Almighty Lord wants prayer to be performed with great attention and to be practiced continuously without showing any signs of abatement.[36] He warns with a painful torment His servants who are neglectful of their prayers:

"So woe to the worshippers who are neglectful of their prayers…" (Al-Ma'un; 107:4-5)

"Except the Companions of the Right Hand. (They will be) in Gardens (of Delight): they will question each other, and (ask) of the Sinners: "What led you into Hell Fire?" They will say: "We were not of those who prayed; "Nor were we of those who fed the indigent; "But we used to talk vanities with vain talkers; "And we used to deny the Day of Judgment, "Until there came to us (the Hour) that is certain." (Al-Muddassir; 74:39-47)

The first sin confessed by those who fell into hell was abandoning their prayers. Then, other sins follow. This is an important point to pay attention to.

The Messenger of Allah (pbuh) said the following in order to draw attention to the importance of prayer:

"Your best deed is your prayer…" (Muwatta, Taharah, 6)

"Prayer is the key to the Paradise, and cleanliness is the key to prayer." (Ahmad, III, 340)

The Messenger of Allah (pbuh) said the following to the leader of Saqif Clan who were arguing that practicing prayer would be hard for them:

---

36.   Al-Maarij; 70:23-34.

"There is no good in religion without bowing (prayer)." (Abu Dawud, Haraj, 25-26/3026)

According to what the Prophet (pbuh) informed us:

"The first deed that a person will be asked in the Day of Judgment will be his prayers. If a person had performed the prayers as Allah commanded, he will find salvation. If a person had missed or not performed them with awe, he will lose and be disappointed. If the obligatory prayers are not complete, our Almighty Lord will order:

"Look if My servant has any supererogatory (nafilah) prayers?" The supererogatory prayers will complete the missing obligatory prayers. Then, the person will be questioned for his other deeds." (Tirmidhi, Salah, 188/413; Nasai, Salah, 9/462)

The significance and place of prayer (salah) among other acts of worships is so lofty that it is not allowed to be missed even under extraordinary conditions such as illness or travel, but some compromises are made to ease its performance under such conditions.

In our second hadith, we are informed that those who miss an obligatory prayer without a valid excuse will lose the protection of Allah. Just like they face some dangers in this world, such people will also be condemned to a harsh punishment in the hereafter. The Messenger of Allah (pbuh) explains their bitter end in the Hereafter as:

"Last night two angels came to me (in a dream) and woke me up and said to me, "Proceed!" I set out with them. We came across a man lying down. Another man was standing over his head, holding a big rock. He was throwing the rock at the man's head, smashing it. The rock rolled away and the thrower followed it and took it back. By the time he reached the man, his head returned to the normal state. The thrower then did the same as he had done before.

I said to my two companions:

"Subhan Allah (Glory be to Allah)! Who are these two persons?

They said "We will inform you" and continued:

"As for the first man you came upon whose head was being injured with the rock, he is the symbol of the one who studies the Qur'an and then neither recites it nor acts on its orders, and sleeps, neglecting the enjoined prayers..." (Bukhari, Ta'bir, 48; Jana'iz, 93)

The Prophet (pbuh) saw the harsh punishment that is going to be given to those who dawdle in reciting and practicing the Qur'an, and miss the Dawn and Night Prayer times by falling asleep, and he warned us because of his mercy for his people. Undoubtedly, the prophets' dreams are true and a fact. For this reason, everything they told based on their dreams should be believed as they are.

If the state of those who linger in performance of prayer, one should imagine the state of those who do not perform prayer at all!

It is understood from this hadith that those who abandon the most honorable worship will be punished from their head, which is the most honorable body part.

Due to these kinds of warnings in the verses of the Qur'an and in the sayings of the Prophet (pbuh), his companions paid a lot of attention to their prayers. For example, Umar (r.a.) wrote to his governors as:

"For me your prayers are the most important of your deeds. Whoever performs it well paying attention to its acts and times, he would protect his religion. Whoever neglects his prayers neglects the rest of the commands of the religion more." (*Muwatta*, Wuqutu's-Salah, 6)

Miswar b. Mahrama (r.a.) narrated:

"I went to Umar b. Khattab (when he was stabbed). Covered with a blanket he was unconsciously lying down.

I asked those who were beside him:

"How is his condition?"

"As you see…" they said. And I said:

"Call him to prayer! Nothing else than prayer scares and wakes him up!"

Upon that, they said:

"O the Ruler of Believers, it is the time of prayer!"

At once, Umar (r.a.) said:

"Yes, I swear to Allah, those who abandon prayer do not get any share from Islam" and he stood up and performed his prayer in spite of his bleeding wound." (Haythami, I, 295. Also see *Muwatta*, Taharah, 51; Ibn Sa'd, III, 35)

These examples show how important a place prayer occupies in practicing the religion.

Attaching importance to prayer is parallel to realizing the essence of the religion. When there is a decrease in the religious consciousness, it would immediately have negative effects on our attention and accuracy that we pay to our prayers.

b. The Virtue of Prayer

٣٥. عَنْ أَبِي هُرَيْرَةَ رَضِيَ اللهُ عَنْهُ أَنَّ رَسُولَ اللهِ صَلَّى اللهُ عَلَيْهِ وَسَلَّمَ قَالَ:

«الصَّلَوَاتُ الْخَمْسُ وَالْجُمُعَةُ إِلَى الْجُمُعَةِ وَرَمَضَانُ إِلَى رَمَضَانَ مُكَفِّرَاتٌ مَا بَيْنَهُنَّ إِذَا اجْتُنِبَ الْكَبَائِرَ».

35. Abu Huraira (r.a.) reported that the Messenger of Allah (pbuh) said:

"Five (daily) prayers and from one Friday prayer to the (next) Friday prayer, and from Ramadan to Ramadan are expiations for the (sins) committed in between (their intervals) provided one shuns the major sins." (Muslim, Taharah, 16)

٣٦. عَنْ أَبِي هُرَيْرَةَ رَضِيَ اللهُ عَنْهُ أَنَّهُ سَمِعَ رَسُولَ اللهِ صَلَّى اللهُ عَلَيْهِ وَسَلَّمَ يَقُولُ:

«أَرَأَيْتُمْ لَوْ أَنَّ نَهْرًا بِبَابِ أَحَدِكُمْ يَغْتَسِلُ مِنْهُ كُلَّ يَوْمٍ خَمْسَ مَرَّاتٍ هَلْ يَبْقَى مِنْ دَرَنِهِ شَيْءٌ؟» قَالُوا:

«لَا يَبْقَى مِنْ دَرَنِهِ شَيْءٌ» قَالَ:

«فَذَلِكَ مَثَلُ الصَّلَوَاتِ الْخَمْسِ يَمْحُو اللهُ بِهِنَّ الْخَطَايَا».

36. Abu Huraira (r.a.) heard the Messenger of Allah (pbuh) saying the following to his companions:

"If there was a river at the door of anyone of you and he took a bath in it five times a day would you notice any dirt on him?"

His noble companions said:

"Not a trace of dirt would be left."

The Messenger of Allah (pbuh) said:

"–That is the example of the five prayers with which Allah blots out (annuls) evil deeds." (Muslim, Masajid, 283. Also see Bukhari, Mawaqid, 6; Tirmidhi, Al-Adab, 80/2868; Nasai, Salah, 7/460; Ibn Majah, Iqamat, 193)

Explanations:

After faith, ritual prayer is the most virtuous[37] and perfect act of worship to remember Allah. It is the most important element of Islam after reciting the *Kalimat al-Shahadah*.[38] Prayer is the best medicine for human desires that would refrain one from remembering Allah. There is no other act of worship that makes fear and hope clear and contains the call for help and salvation. Since prayer is repeated in certain times of the day, there is no other act of worship that is more effective on human ego, in restraining worldly desires and ambitions, encourages the truth, and being on the right way in all respects. For this reason, Ali (r.a.) said the following to one of his subordinates:

"Everything depends on your prayer." [39]

First of all the performance of the ritual prayer and then all the other obligatory act of worships become expiation for the minor sins given that one avoids major ones. For those without a sin, it advances their state in the presence of Allah. Allah the Almighty says:

"And establish regular prayers at the two ends of the day and at the approaches of the night: For those things, that are good remove those that

---

37.   Muslim, Al-Iman (Faith), 137-140.
38.   Translator's note: *Kalimah al-Shahadah* or Profession of Faith means believing and saying that there is no god other than the one and only Almighty God, Allah, and His Excellency Muhammad (pbuh) is his subject (servant) and Messenger.
39.   Abdulaziz Çaviş, *Anglikan Kilisesine Cevap*, p. 96.

are evil: Be that the word of remembrance to those who remember (their Lord)" (Hud; 11:114)

"If you (but) eschew the most heinous of the things which you are forbidden to do, We shall expel out of you all the evil in you, and admit you to a gate of great honor." (Al-Nisa; 4:31)

The following narration which shows how prayer elevates the state of a person in the presence of Allah also explains the reason of occurance[40] of the first hadith:

Sa'd b. Abi Waqqas (r.a.) reported:

"There were two brothers. One of them passed away forty days before the other one. The righteousness of the one who passed away earlier had been told to the Messenger of Allah. Upon that the Messenger of Allah (pbuh) asked:

"Was not the other one a Muslim?" They said:

"Yes, O the Messenger of Allah, he was a Muslim and he was not a bad person either!"

The Messenger of Allah (pbuh) said:

"You would not know how much his prayers benefited to him. Prayer is like a river with plenty of fresh water at the door of anyone of you and in which he took a bath five times a day. What do you say, would there be any dirt left on him? You would not know to what levels his prayers elevated him." (Muwatta, Qasr al-Salah, 91)

The brother who passed away later achieved a more elevated state since he had a chance to perform more prayers compared to his brother who had passed away earlier. In other words, the more one performs prayer in awe, the more elevated his state will be. For this reason, we must increase the productivity of our lives and our capital for the Hereafter by performing supererogatory prayers as much as we can after performing the obligatory ones.

---

40. The reason underlying a hadith (*sabab al-wurud*) is why a hadith is occurred (or if it's an act, why it is performed). There is a special branch of science that focuses on this. The reason of occurrence of a hadith is just like the science of studying the underlying reasons of revelation of the verse of the Noble Quran (*Asbab al-Nuzul*). This branch of Islamic science helps us to understand the commands that the hadith contain and if a command is abrogated by a given hadith.

Prayer which nullifies earlier sins also prevents a person from future sins and mistakes.[41] That is because when one knows that his minor sins are forgiven also gets a lesson of self-control for not to commit major sins. A well-performed prayer elevates one to a spiritual maturity and fills his hearth with inner-peace. And a person with inner-peace and awe pays extra attention to stay away from the things that Allah dislikes and therefore gets purified from sins.

In this respect, the Messenger of Allah (pbuh) says *"Prayer is light."*[42] In other words, a prayer prevents humans from rebellious, evil, and impure acts and guides them to the right path just like light brightens its environment. On the other hand, since a servant of Allah turns externally and internally to Allah by removing everything else out of his heart, his prayers cause lights of wisdom to brighten, relieve the hearts, and discover the truths. Also, prayer is a valuable act of worship that enlightens the face of a believer with a divine light both in this world and in the Hereafter.

Since prayer is the key to Paradise[43], the Messenger of Allah (pbuh) advised to perform prayers to those who seek going to Paradise and being next to the Prophet in there.

Rabi'a b. Ka'b (r.a.) said:

I used to spend the nights with the Messenger of Allah (pbuh), bring him water and take care of his other needs. Once he said to me:

"Ask (anything you like)!"

And I said:

"I ask your company in Paradise."

The Prophet (pbuh) said:

"Is it possible that you ask for something else?"

This time I said:

"That is all (that I wish)!

Upon that the Messenger of Allah (pbuh) said:

---

41.   Al-Ankabut; 29:45.
42.   Muslim, Taharah, 1.
43.   Ahmad, III, 340.

"Then help me to achieve this for you by devoting yourself often to prostration!" (Muslim, Salah, 226; Ahmad, III, 500)

When Thawban (r.a.) asked questions similar to the following ones to the Messenger of Allah (pbuh):

"Tell me an act that will help me to enter the Paradise!"

"What is the deed that Allah loves most?"

The Messenger of Allah (pbuh) answered him by saying:

"Perform a lot of prostration to Allah! As a matter of fact, when one performs one prostration to Allah, Allah elevates his level by one and forgives one of his sins." (Muslim, Salah, 225)

The Prophet (pbuh) said to one of his companions:

"If you want to join me (in the hereafter), then increase your prostrations!" (Ahmad, III, 428)

Prostration is also a means to save one from the Fire. This reality is expressed in the following noble hadith:

"...Allah intends mercy on whomever He likes amongst the people of Hell, He will order the angels to take out of Hell those who worshipped none but Him alone. The angels will take them out by recognizing them from the traces of prostrations, for Allah has forbidden the (Hell) fire to eat away those traces. So they will come out of the Fire, it will eat away from the whole of the human body except the marks of the prostrations." (Bukhari, Adhan, 129)

The prostration mostly refers to salah (prayer). In those narrations, prayer is referred to by its most important part, or prostration. Therefore, prayer is an act of worship that will make one enter the Paradise and be next to the Messenger of Allah.

Moreover, prayer will get those believers who entered the Paradise closer to seeing Allah's Face. Jarir (r.a.) reported:

One night, we were sitting with the Messenger of Allah, and he said looking at the full moon:

"As all of you can clearly see the full moon without a hustle, you will see Allah (your Lord) in the same way (in Paradise). Now do your best to perform all prayers between the sunrise and sunset."

Then, the Messenger of Allah (pbuh) recited the following noble verses:

"…and celebrate (constantly) the praises of your Lord, before the rising of the sun, and before its setting; yea, celebrate them for part of the hours of the night, and at the sides of the day: that you may have (spiritual) joy." [44]
(Taha; 20:130) (Bukhari, Mawaqît 16, 26; Tafsir, 50/1; Tawhid, 24; Muslim, Masajid, 211)

As it is seen, the Messenger of Allah (pbuh) mentions the obligatory prayers as the primary requirement of seeing Allah the Almighty.

As prayer is the spiritual nourishment, it is also a healing power for the body. Since it requires the body, clothes, and the place that the prayer is performed to be clean, the prayer is an important protector of health. It is also well-known that prayer keeps the body active by causing some parts of the body to move, some joints to bend, and some muscles to stretch and relax. [45]

Abu Huraira (r.a.) reported that:

"Once, the Messenger of Allah (pbuh) performed a prayer early. Then I performed some more prayer and sat down. The Messenger of Allah (pbuh) turned to me and said:

"Do you have a stomach ache?"

I said:

"Yes, O the Messenger of Allah!"

Upon that the Messenger of Allah (pbuh) advised me:

"Stand up and perform a prayer! Because there is healing in prayer." (Ibn Majah, Tibb, 10; Ahmad, II, 390, 403)

---

44. This Qur'anic verse concisely defines the times of prayer. For detail also see Hud, 11:114; Isra, 17:78; Al-Rum, 30:17-18; M. Kâmil Yaşaroğlu, "Namaz", *Diyanet İslâm Ansiklopedisi*, XXXII, 351.
45. Once paid attention, one can notice that there is a harmony between the movements of the prayer and the human body, as if humans are created to perform prayer or prayer is a worship that fits best for the human nature. Since none of the creatures are created in human form, they cannot perform perfectly the movements in prayer.

Prayer is at the same time a balancing element in a Muslim's life. This act of worship which is performed at certain times of the day makes one's life disciplined and organized.

c. Having Awe in Salah (Prayer)

٣٧. عَنْ أَبِي أَيُّوبَ رَضِيَ اللهُ عَنْهُ قَالَ: جَاءَ رَجُلٌ إِلَى النَّبِيِّ صَلَّى اللهُ عَلَيْهِ وَسَلَّمَ فَقَالَ:

«يَا رَسُولَ اللهِ! عَلِّمْنِي وَأَوْجِزْ» قَالَ:

«إِذَا قُمْتَ فِي صَلَاتِكَ فَصَلِّ صَلَاةَ مُوَدِّعٍ وَلَا تَكَلَّمْ بِكَلَامٍ تَعْتَذِرُ مِنْهُ وَأَجْمِعِ الْيَأْسَ عَمَّا فِي أَيْدِي النَّاسِ».

37. Abu Ayyub (r.a.) reported:

A man came to the Messenger of Allah (pbuh) and said:

"O Messenger of Allah! Teach me (the religion), but let it be brief!"

Upon that the Messenger of Allah (pbuh) said:

"When you intend to pray, perform it like someone who is leaving this world! Do not say a word for which you have to ask forgiveness! Do not raise your hopes for things that others have!" (Ibn Majah, Zuhd, 15; Ahmad, V, 412)

٣٨. عَنِ الْفَضْلِ بْنِ عَبَّاسٍ رَضِيَ اللهُ عَنْهُ قَالَ: قَالَ رَسُولُ اللهِ صَلَّى اللهُ عَلَيْهِ وَسَلَّمَ:

«الصَّلَاةُ مَثْنَى مَثْنَى تَشَهُّدٌ فِي كُلِّ رَكْعَتَيْنِ وَتَخَشُّعٌ وَتَضَرُّعٌ وَتَمَسْكَنٌ وَتَذَرَّعُ وَتُقْنِعُ يَدَيْكَ تَرْفَعُهُمَا إِلَى رَبِّكَ مُسْتَقْبِلًا بِبُطُونِهِمَا وَجْهَكَ وَتَقُولُ يَا رَبِّ يَا رَبِّ وَمَنْ لَمْ يَفْعَلْ ذٰلِكَ فَهُوَ كَذَا وَكَذَا».

38. Fazl b. Abbas (r.a.) reported that the Messenger of Allah (pbuh) said:

"Prayer is performed in two by two by two units. You sit to recite Tashahhud in every two units. You feel deep reverence and say invocation and prayers. You act humbly and modestly. After the completion of a prayer, you say prayers "Dear Lord! Dear Lord!" as the palms of your hand towards your face. Whoever does not do this, his prayer is not complete." (Tirmidhi, Salah, 166/385)

٣٩. عَنْ أَبِي هُرَيْرَةَ رَضِيَ اللهُ عَنْهُ أَنَّ رَسُولَ اللهِ صَلَّى اللهُ عَلَيْهِ وَسَلَّمَ دَخَلَ الْمَسْجِدَ فَدَخَلَ رَجُلٌ فَصَلَّى فَسَلَّمَ عَلَى النَّبِيِّ صَلَّى اللهُ عَلَيْهِ وَسَلَّمَ فَرَدَّ وَقَالَ:

«ارْجِعْ فَصَلِّ فَإِنَّكَ لَمْ تُصَلِّ» فَرَجَعَ يُصَلِّي كَمَا صَلَّى ثُمَّ جَاءَ فَسَلَّمَ عَلَى النَّبِيِّ صَلَّى اللهُ عَلَيْهِ وَسَلَّمَ فَقَالَ:

«ارْجِعْ فَصَلِّ فَإِنَّكَ لَمْ تُصَلِّ» ثَلَاثًا فَقَالَ:

«وَالَّذِي بَعَثَكَ بِالْحَقِّ مَا أُحْسِنُ غَيْرَهُ فَعَلِّمْنِي» فَقَالَ:

«إِذَا قُمْتَ إِلَى الصَّلَاةِ فَكَبِّرْ ثُمَّ اقْرَأْ مَا تَيَسَّرَ مَعَكَ مِنَ الْقُرْآنِ ثُمَّ ارْكَعْ حَتَّى تَطْمَئِنَّ رَاكِعًا ثُمَّ ارْفَعْ حَتَّى تَعْتَدِلَ قَائِمًا ثُمَّ اسْجُدْ حَتَّى تَطْمَئِنَّ سَاجِدًا ثُمَّ ارْفَعْ حَتَّى تَطْمَئِنَّ جَالِسًا وَافْعَلْ ذٰلِكَ فِي صَلَاتِكَ كُلِّهَا».

39. Abu Huraira (r.a.) narrated:

One day the Messenger of Allah (pbuh) came to the mosque. Then, a man came in, offered a prayer, and greeted the Prophet. The Prophet returned his greeting and then said to him:

"Go back and perform your prayer again for you have not prayed!

The man offered the prayer again, came back and greeted the Prophet.

Our Master the Prophet (pbuh) said to him one more time:

"Go back and pray again for you have not prayed!

This happened three times and finally the poor man said:

"By Him Who has sent you with the truth! I do not know a better way of praying. Kindly teach me how to pray."

Upon that Prophet (pbuh) said:

"When you stand for the prayer, say Takbir and then recite from the Qur'an what you know and then bow with calmness till you feel at ease, then rise from bowing till you stand straight. Afterwards prostrate calmly till you feel at ease and then raise (your head) and sit with calmness till you feel at ease and then prostrate with calmness till you feel at ease in prostration and do the same in the whole of your prayer!" (Bukhari, Adhan, 95, 122; Ayman, 15; Isti'dhan, 18; Muslim, Salah, 45. Also see Tirmidhi, Salah, 110/302; Abu Dawud, Salah, 143-144/856; Nasai, Istiftah, 7/882; Ibn Majah, Iqamah, 72)

❀

٤٠. عَنْ عَمَّارِ بْنِ يَاسِرٍ رَضِيَ اللهُ عَنْهُ قَالَ: سَمِعْتُ رَسُولَ اللهِ صَلَّى اللهُ عَلَيْهِ وَسَلَّمَ يَقُولُ:

«إِنَّ الرَّجُلَ لَيَنْصَرِفُ وَمَا كُتِبَ لَهُ إِلَّا عُشْرُ صَلَاتِهِ تُسْعُهَا ثُمْنُهَا سُبْعُهَا سُدُسُهَا خُمُسُهَا رُبْعُهَا ثُلُثُهَا نِصْفُهَا».

40. Ammar b. Yasir heard our master the Messenger of Allah (pbuh) say:

"Verily, a man leaves, and none of his prayer has been recorded for him except a tenth of it, a ninth of it, an eighth of it, a seventh of it, a sixth of it, a fifth of it, a fourth of it, a third of it, or a half of it" (Abu Dawud, Salah, 123-124/796; Ahmad, IV, 321)

❀

٤١. عَنْ أَنَسِ بْنِ مَالِكٍ رَضِيَ اللهُ عَنْهُ أَنَّ رَسُولَ اللهِ صَلَّى اللهُ عَلَيْهِ وَسَلَّمَ كَانَ يَقُولُ:

«اَللّٰهُمَّ إِنِّي أَعُوذُ بِكَ مِنْ صَلَاةٍ لَا تَنْفَعُ».

41. As narrated from Anas b. Malik, the Messenger of Allah (pbuh) used to pray as:

"O Allah, I seek refuge in You from the prayer which is not beneficial!" (Abu Dawud, Witr, 32/1549)

Explanations:

The significance and virtues of *salah* (prayer) mentioned previously refer to a well-performed *salah* that is performed by following the obligatory acts before and during prayer. The best elixir that will accomplish this is having awe in our prayers.

As a result of reverence towards Allah the Almighty, awe (*hushu'*) can be described as tranquility and modesty during the performance of the acts of worship especially during prayer. It is also the reflection of this state in our daily life. Awe is softening the hearts and obeying Allah and being feared from Him due to high respect and love for Him.

When we talk about awe, the first thing that comes to mind is the state of tranquility while performing a prayer. Therefore, one must perform his prayers being aware of that he is the presence of Allah and feeling His Magnificence and Grandeur in his heart. It is expressed in the following verses of Qur'an:

"The believers must (eventually) win through, those who humble themselves in their prayers." (Al-Muminun; 23:1-2)

"Nay, seek (Allah's) help with patient perseverance and prayer: It is indeed hard, except for the humble ones, who bear in mind the certainty that they are to meet their Lord, and that they are to return to Him." (Al-Baqarah; 2:45-46)

That is to say, only a prayer that is performed in awe helps one find salvation. A prayer which is not performed with the feeling of tranquility in the heart and feeling of reverence in the body movements is not considered a true prayer. For this reason, it is said:

$$إِنَّ الْمُصَلِّينَ كَثِيرٌ وَالْمُقِيمِينَ لَهَا قَلِيلٌ$$

"The number of people who perform prayers is a lot but there are very few of them who truly perform it."[46]

The permission for the sick and weak to perform their prayers without doing some of the body movements shows that the essence of prayer is feeling awe in the heart.

The best way to ensure the feeling of awe is to perform the prayer as if it is our last prayer in this world. All the prayers should be performed in a state of a person whose time is up and is spending his last minutes and how he feels being in front of his Lord. Actually, this is what the reality is. As a matter of fact, there is no guarantee that a person will reach to the next prayer time. Accordingly, a person who is performing a prayer should sincerely turn to Allah and stay away from all kinds of material thoughts, think about the meaning of the verses which he is reciting, shed tears, look at the place of prostration, and say prayers. Only a prayer performed in this manner benefits the performer by preventing him from wrongdoings and idle talk which would hurt others. It also protects the believer by turning him towards Allah and the Hereafter away from useless desires such as holding grudge against people and hoping to get something from them.

In the second hadith, the way we should say the supplications is explained by emphasizing the importance of having awe during praying. Allah's servants should acknowledge their weakness, be extremely modest and humble, and pray sincerely to Allah.

A prayer is not complete unless it is performed by feeling such deep awe. For this reason, the Messenger of Allah (pbuh) advised us to stay away from actions which would affect the awe in our prayers such as looking around.[47]

---

46. In Quran, the term "iqamah" is used to refer to the prayers of the believers. In other words, it is informed that they fulfill their prayers well. When it comes to is the prayers of the hypocrites, only the term "musallin" is used. (Al-Maun; 107:4) This shows that there are various types of people who perform their prayers. The number of those who perform a prayer might be a lot but the number of those who give it its real due is few.

47. Bukhari, Adhan, 93; Abu Dawud, Salah, 162-163/912; Tirmidhi, Jum'a, 60/590; Nasai, Sahw, 10/1193-1197; Ahmad, VI, 130, 443.

Muslim scholars also found it contrary to the state of awe playing with one's hair, beard, nose, or something on the floor[48] while praying.

Indeed, Said bin Musayyab said when he saw someone who was playing with his bread while praying:

"If his heart had felt awe, his body parts should also have been in awe." (Abdurrazzak, *Musannaf,* II, 266-267)

The Messenger of Allah (pbuh) did not consider it right to pray when the food is ready[49] or when one has to use the bathroom if there is no issue of expiration of the prayer time.[50] That is because these conditions keep the heart busy and affect the awe.

The Messenger of Allah (pbuh) would perform his prayers in awe as he prescribed in this hadith. During night prayers, he used to experience such a deep awe that he would lengthen his prayers. He used to say that the prayers with long standing are more virtuous than the shorter ones. (Muslim, Musafirin, 165)

Abdullah ibn al-Shikhkhir (r.a.) describes Prophet's (pbuh) state of awe in his prayers:

"I saw the Apostle of Allah (pbuh) praying and a sound was coming from his breast like the rumbling of a mill owing to weeping." (Abu Dawud, Salah, 156-157/904; Ahmad, IV, 25, 26)

The Messenger of Allah would not permit anything that diverts his attention away during his prayers. One day, Abu Jahm (r.a.) gifted a nicely embroidered *khamisa* (a square garment). The Messenger of Allah wore it and performed a prayer. When he finished the prayer he said to the mother of believers Aisha (r.a.):

"Take this khamisa back to Abu Jahm as I looked at its marks and it diverted my attention from the prayer." (Muwatta, Salah, 67; Bukhari, Salah, 14)

The most important requirement for achieving awe is to perform prayer by following the right order. In other words, fulfilling the acts of prayer perfectly; bowing, standing after bowing, prostration, and sitting between the two prostrations, and to perform them very calmly. For this reason, the Messenger

---

48. Nasai, Sahw, 7/1189.
49. Bukhari, Adhan, 42; Muslim, Masajid, 64.
50. Muslim, Masajid, 67; Ahmad, V, 250, 260.

of Allah (pbuh) perfectly explained **in our third hadith** what it means to perform a prayer by following its rules. According to this, while praying, one must keep still for a moment while performing each acts of the prayer, must place all the body parts where they are supposed to be and when someone looks, he should see him staying still. As a matter of fact, it is reported that the amount of time that the Messenger of Allah was spending during bowing, or prostration, or sitting in between the two prostrations, or standing after bowing were almost the same. (Bukhari, Adhan, 121)

The Messenger of Allah (pbuh) warned his companions about performing a prayer in awe and by following its rules saying:

"Do you consider or see that my face is towards the Qibla? By Allah, neither your submissiveness nor your bowing is hidden from me, surely I see you from my back."

"Perform your bowings and prostrations properly!" (Bukhari, Adhan, 88)

He warned about the prayers which are not performed as prescribed:

"Allah does not look at (does not value) prayers of those who do not strengthen their backs in between bowings and prostrations." (Ahmad, II, 525)

That is because, in order for a prayer to be ascended to the divine presence, it should be performed perfectly. Otherwise, it comes back without going to heavens and returns to its owner.

In a hadith, it is said that:

"If a person performs his prayer well by fulfilling the bowings and prostrations right, that prayer says to him:

"As you protected me, may Allah protect you!" The prayer gets glorified and accepted. If a person does not perform his prayer well by fulfilling the bowings and prostrations right, the prayer says to him:

"As you lost me, may Allah lose you!" The prayer is thrown up to his face like a scrap." (Baihaqi, *Shuab,* III, 143; Suyuti, *Jami,* I, 58/364)

Due to such warnings of the Prophet (pbuh), his companions paid extra attention to follow its rules and to achieve awe while praying. One day Hudhaifa (r.a.) entered into a praying room and saw a man praying without paying attention to his bowing and prostrations. After the prayer, he asked the man:

"For how long have you prayed like this?"

The man said:

"For forty years."

Hudhaifa (r.a.) said:

"You have not prayed for forty years. If you die continuing to pray like this, you will not die in a state of Muhammad's (pbuh) nature" and taught him the way he should pray.

Then he said:

"One can perform his prayer lightly, but one must perform the bowings and prostrations properly!" (Ahmad, V, 384; Bukhari, Adhan, 119, 132)

As it can be understood from **our fourth hadith**, the prayer that is performed without paying attention to its acts and without achieving awe eventually gets meaningless and its rewards lessens to one tenth. And the angels record it to the Book of Actions as:

"So and so reduced one fourth of his prayer, or this one omitted half of his prayer..." (Abdurrazzak, *Musannaf*, II, 371)

Prayers performed in such an incomplete manner in time become fruitless. As they do not protect its owner from wrongdoings, they do not advance his level in the sight of Allah. The Messenger of Allah (pbuh) sought refuge in Allah from such prayers that do not benefit. Also, in one of his noble hadith, he said:

"The prayer that does not enjoin its performers goodness and prevent them from wrongdoings does not do anything else than alienating them from Allah." (Haythami, II, 258)

These kinds of sayings of the Prophet are revealed to forbid people from performing prayers unconsciously. That is not to say that "It is better not to perform a prayer at all than performing it deficiently!" As a matter of fact, even it is not complete, its performance is better than not performing it at all. (Abdurrazzak, *Musannaf*, II, 368)

We must express it one more time that, in order to benefit from a prayer, the body should be turned towards Ka'bah and the heart should turned towards Allah the Almighty. As a matter of fact, it is expressed in the noble verse:

"...bow down in adoration, and bring yourself closer (to Allah.)!" (Al-Alaq; 96:19)

The Companions of Allah paid extra attention to perform their prayers in awe. Aisha reported that her mother Ummu Ruman (r.a.) had said:

"I was moving left and right while I was praying. Abu Bakr (r.a.) saw me and he scorned me so bad that I was about to nullify my prayer. Then he said to me:

"The Messenger of Allah (pbuh) said: *"When anyone of you is praying, all his body should be calm and in a state of awe. It should not move to sides like the Jews. As a matter of fact, the calmness of the body parts is one of the essences that complete the prayer."* (Abu Nuaym, *Hilye*, IX, 304; Alusi, *Ruhu'l-Ma'ani*, XVIII, 3)

Abdullah b. Abu Bakr (r.a.) reported the following:

"Abu Talha (r.a.) was performing a prayer in his yard. A bird called *dubsi* wanted to fly away from the yard but could not find a place to fly out and kept flying. Abu Talha liked it and followed it with his eyes for a moment. Then he returned to his prayer but forget how many units (*rak'ahs*) he performed. Later, he informed the Messenger of Allah what had happened in his yard thinking that his wealth caused unrest and affected his awe:

"O Messenger of Allah! I am giving all my wealth as charity, you can spend it as you wish or you can give it to whomever you wish." (*Muwatta,* Salah, 69)

Zainalabidin, one of the grandchildren of the Messenger of Allah, used to grow pale when he prepared to make ablution and his feet used to shiver when he stood up to pray. He answered those who asked why:

"Don't you know to whose presence I am going to?" (Abu Nuaym, Hilya, III, 133)

d. Observing prayer early in its period

٤٢. عَنْ أُمِّ فَرْوَةَ رَضِيَ اللهُ عَنْهَا قَالَتْ:

«سُئِلَ النَّبِيُّ صَلَّى اللهُ عَلَيْهِ وَسَلَّمَ:

«أَيُّ الْأَعْمَالِ أَفْضَلُ؟» قَالَ:

«اَلصَّلَاةُ لِأَوَّلِ وَقْتِهَا».

42. Ummu Farwah (r.a.) reported:

The Messenger of Allah (pbuh) was asked:

"Which of the actions is the most virtuous?"

The Messenger of Allah (pbuh) said:

"–*Observing prayer early in its period.*" (Tirmidhi, Salah, 13/170; Abu Dawud, Salah, 9/426. Also see Bukhari, Mawaqit, 5; Jihad, 1; Muslim, Iman, 137-139)

٤٣ . عَنِ ابْنِ عُمَرَ رَضِيَ اللهُ عَنْهُ قَالَ: قَالَ رَسُولُ اللهِ صَلَّى اللهُ عَلَيْهِ وَسَلَّمَ:

«اَلْوَقْتُ الْأَوَّلُ مِنَ الصَّلَاةِ رِضْوَانُ اللهِ وَالْوَقْتُ الْآخِرُ عَفْوُ اللهِ».

43. Ibn Umar reported that the Messenger of Allah (pbuh) said:

"*There is Allah's contentedness at the early hours of a prayer, and His forgiveness in later hours.*" (Tirmidhi, Salah, 13/172)

Explanations:

The Messenger of Allah (pbuh) responded to a question what the most virtuous act of worship was as "observing prayer early in its period."[51]

---

51. The Messenger of Allah (pbuh) gave different answers at different times when asked about "the most virtuous act." Some of them include "Believing in Allah and His Messenger, a prayer that is performed in time, standing (al-qiyam) more than required while praying, to love and hate for the sake of Allah, Hajj (Pilgrimage) where certain invocations (talbiyah) are recited out loud and many sacrifices are made." There are several reasons for these different answers:
1. The Messenger of Allah (pbuh) answered by taking the time and audience into account.
2. The virtue of an act is parallel to the extent of its benefits to Islam. The Messenger of Allah (pbuh) paid attention to this fact in his answers.
3. The superiority of the acts differs when considered from different angles. The Messenger of Allah (pbuh) always gave the best answer depending on the intention of the question.
4. With his answers, the Messenger of Allah (pbuh) wanted to point out the importance of the mentioned acts.

Allah the Almighty likes the observance of a prayer early in its period more. That is because, in this act are observed the peak of love, obedience, and submission to Allah. These nice traits are the reasons that make the servant of Allah run to a prayer. Therefore, Allah responds with love and contentedness to the prayers performed with these feelings.

On the other hand, a deed is more valuable if it is done on time. As a matter of fact, the most efficient state of something occurs at its scheduled time. If a prayer is performed early in its period, its benefits and wisdom can be better observed.

In order to emphasize the value of earlier parts of a prayer period and hurrying up in performing it, Allah said **"Run"** and **"Race"** in the Qur'an to His servants and praised those who act in this way.[52] This shows that the earlier time of everything is more virtuous and valuable.[53] Therefore believers run to fulfill their acts of worship in early parts of their period in order to be honored with the manifestation of Allah's name **"Al-Awwal" (The First One)**.

Delaying the prayer for a believer who contemplates all these facts cannot be excused unless there is a good reason. As a matter of fact, being reluctant in performing a prayer and delaying it are listed among the signs of hypocrites.

It is mentioned in the noble verse that:

"When they (The Hypocrites) stand up to prayer, they stand without earnestness, to be seen of men, but little do they hold Allah in remembrance." (Al-Nisa; 4:142)

Ala bin Abdurrahman reported the following which has the characteristic to explain the verse above:

We visited Anas ibn Malik after Zuhr (noon). When we reached there, Anas stood up and prayed the late Afternoon Prayer (Salah al-Asr). We mentioned that he performed the prayer early in its time. He explained why he did it this way and said:

"I heard the Messenger of Allah saying:

"That is the prayer of the hypocrites! That is the prayer of the hypocrites! That is the prayer of the hypocrites! The prayer of the hypocrites is that one of

---

52. Ali-Imran; 3:114, 133; Al-Anbiya; 21:90; Al-Muminun; 23:61; Hadid; 57:21.

53. Ibn Arabi, *el-Futuhat al-Makkiyyah*, VI, 73-74.

them sits until the sun becomes yellow and is between the two horns of Satan, and then gets up and rattles off four units just as a bird picks up a food, hardly remembering Allah in them at all." (*Muwatta*, the Qur'an, 46; Muslim, Masajid, 195)

Wherever he was, the Messenger of Allah (pbuh) loved to perform his prayers as soon as it was their time.[54] One can even say that he has performed all of his prayers at earlier parts of their period. As a matter of fact, Aisha, the mother of believers, reported:

"Allah the Almighty has taken the Messenger of Allah (pbuh) to His presence without him postponing two prayers to the last minutes of their period." (Tirmidhi, Salah, 13/174; Ahmad, VI, 92)

In other words, except under extraordinary circumstances, such as war, there was almost no time that the Prophet (pbuh) postponed his prayers to the last parts of its period. Even under the most difficult situations he performed his prayer at its early times. Even most troublesome military expeditions did not prevent this. The following story is one of the best examples of this fact:

In a military expedition, the Messenger of Allah (pbuh) and his companions came to a narrow tunnel. The Messenger of Allah was on his horse. It was heavily raining and the mud under the feet of their horses was preventing them from getting off their horses. It was the prayer time. The Messenger of Allah (pbuh) commanded the muaddhin to call adhan and the muaddhin recited the adhan and *iqamah*. Allah's Messenger (pbuh) came forward on his horse and led the prayer for his companions. They performed their prayer by head gestures. When they were performing the prostration (*al-Sajdah*), they were bending a little more than bowing (*al-Ruku'*). (Ahmad, IV, 173-174)

As the Messenger of Allah (pbuh) paid extra attention to perform his prayers at earlier part of their period, he also taught his companions in this manner. Once, he had to go immediately to somewhere far after he performed the noon prayer. Thinking that they might be late to come back, he told Bilal:

"If I do not return until the late afternoon prayer, tell Abu Bakr to be leader (imam)!"

When it was the time of Salat al-Asr', Bilal (r.a.) asked Abu Bakr:

---

54.   Bukhari, Salah, 48.

"Abu Bakr! The Messenger of Allah (pbuh) did not come back yet. The prayer time has arrived. Would you be our imam and lead us to perform the prayer?"

Abu Bakr said:

"Okay, let's do it" and they started performing the prayer in order to fulfill it in early part of its period. While they were praying, the Messenger of Allah (pbuh) returned.[55]

The Messenger of Allah (pbuh) praised those who perform their prayers at early times of their period, introduced them as examples, and asked Allah's mercy for them. Once he said:

"May Allah show mercy on my brother Abdullah b. Rawaha! Wherever he is, he stops his ride as soon as the prayer time enters and performs it." (Haythami, IX, 316)

Performing a prayer at the last minute saves us from the responsibility but it is an act that needs forgiveness. That is because, it is stated in the second hadith that Allah will forgive those who act this way. Forgiveness is only for wrongdoings or sins.

Thus, prayer is the best act that helps someone to gain the contentedness of Allah when it is performed at its early times, whereas its rewards decrease as time passes and in its last minutes, it only saves one from committing a sin. Therefore, those who perform a prayer at its last minutes miss the chance to earn more divine rewards even if they are saved from the responsibility of the prayer.

e. Praying in Congregation

٤٤. عَنْ عَبْدِ اللهِ بْنِ عُمَرَ رَضِيَ اللهُ عَنْهُ أَنَّ رَسُولَ اللهِ صَلَّى اللهُ عَلَيْهِ وَسَلَّمَ قَالَ:

«صَلَاةُ الْجَمَاعَةِ تَفْضُلُ صَلَاةَ الْفَذِّ بِسَبْعٍ وَعِشْرِينَ دَرَجَةً».

---

55.   See Bukhari, Adhan, 48; Amel fi's-salat, 3, 16; Sahw, 9; Sulh, 1; Ahkam, 36; Muslim, Salah, 102; Abu Dawud, Salah, 168-169/940; Nasai, Imamat, 7/782.

44. Ibn Omar (r.a.) reported that the Messenger of Allah (pbuh) said:

"The prayer in congregation is twenty seven times superior to the prayer offered by person alone." (Bukhari, Adhan, 30; Muslim, Masajid, 249)

❀

٤٥. عَنْ أَبِي هُرَيْرَةَ رَضِيَ اللهُ عَنْهُ أَنَّ رَسُولَ اللهِ صَلَّى اللهُ عَلَيْهِ
وَسَلَّمَ قَالَ:

«أَلَا أَدُلُّكُمْ عَلَى مَا يَمْحُو اللهُ بِهِ الْخَطَايَا وَيَرْفَعُ بِهِ الدَّرَجَاتِ؟»
قَالُوا:

«بَلَى يَا رَسُولَ اللهِ» قَالَ:

«إِسْبَاغُ الْوُضُوءِ عَلَى الْمَكَارِهِ وَكَثْرَةُ الْخُطَا إِلَى الْمَسَاجِدِ وَانْتِظَارُ
الصَّلَاةِ بَعْدَ الصَّلَاةِ فَذٰلِكُمُ الرِّبَاطُ».

45. Abu Huraira (r.a.) reported that the Messenger of Allah (pbuh) say:

"Should I not suggest to you that by which Allah obliterates the sins and elevates the ranks (of a man)?"

His companions said:

"Yes, let us know, the Messenger of Allah!"

The Messenger of Allah (pbuh) said:

"Performing the ablution thoroughly despite odds, steping more towards the mosque, and waiting for the next prayer after observing a prayer, and that is mindfulness." (Muslim, Taharah, 41)

❀

٤٦. عَنْ أَبِي هُرَيْرَةَ رَضِيَ اللهُ عَنْهُ أَنَّ رَسُولَ اللهِ صَلَّى اللهُ عَلَيْهِ وَسَلَّمَ قَالَ:

«إِنَّ الْمَلَائِكَةَ تُصَلِّي عَلَى أَحَدِكُمْ مَا دَامَ فِي مُصَلَّاهُ مَا لَمْ يُحْدِثْ: اَللّٰهُمَّ اغْفِرْ لَهُ اَللّٰهُمَّ ارْحَمْهُ».

Abu Huraira (r.a.) narrated that the Messenger of Allah (pbuh) said:

"The angels keep on asking for Allah's Blessing and Forgiveness for anyone of you as long as he is at his Musalla (praying place) and does not do Hadath (passes wind). The angels say, 'O Allah! Forgive him and be Merciful to him.'" (Bukhari, Adhan, 36)

٤٧. عَنْ أَبِي هُرَيْرَةَ رَضِيَ اللهُ عَنْهُ أَنَّ النَّبِيَّ صَلَّى اللهُ عَلَيْهِ وَسَلَّمَ قَالَ:

«إِذَا أَمَّنَ الْإِمَامُ فَأَمِّنُوا فَإِنَّهُ مَنْ وَافَقَ تَأْمِينُهُ تَأْمِينَ الْمَلَائِكَةِ غُفِرَ لَهُ مَا تَقَدَّمَ مِنْ ذَنْبِهِ».

47. Abu Huraira (r.a.) reported that the Messenger of Allah (pbuh) said:

"Say Amin when the Imam says Amin, for it anyone's utterance of Amin synchronizes with that of the angels, he will be forgiven his past sins." (Bukhari, Adhan, 111; Muslim, Salah, 72)

٤٨. عَنْ أَبِي هُرَيْرَةَ رَضِيَ اللهُ عَنْهُ قَالَ: قَالَ النَّبِيُّ صَلَّى اللهُ عَلَيْهِ وَسَلَّمَ:

«لَيْسَ صَلَاةٌ أَثْقَلَ عَلَى الْمُنَافِقِينَ مِنَ الْفَجْرِ وَالْعِشَاءِ وَلَوْ يَعْلَمُونَ مَا فِيهِمَا لَأَتَوْهُمَا وَلَوْ حَبْوًا».

48. Abu Huraira (r.a.) narrated that the Messenger of Allah (pbuh) said:

"No prayer is harder for the hypocrites than the Fajr and the 'Isha' prayers and if they knew the reward for these prayers at their respective times, they would certainly present themselves (in the mosques) even if they had to crawl." (Bukhari, Adhan, 34; Muslim, Masajid, 252. Also see Ibn Majah, Masajid, 18)

Explanations:

Islam attaches great significance to social solidarity and living in harmony. Allah the Almighty wants His servants to socialize. For this reason, in the Noble Qur'an there are many commands and signs for humans about living in societies. One of them is as follows:

"And hold fast, all together, by the rope which Allah (stretches out for you), and be not divided among yourselves…" (Al-i Imran; 3:102-103)

The Messenger of Allah (pbuh) expressed the importance and virtue of praying in congregation as:

"The hand (help) of Allah is with the congregation. Those who leave the congregation leave for the Hell." (Tirmidhi, Fitan, 7/2167)

"Congregation is mercy and discord is torment." (Ahmad, IV, 278)

"The blessing is with the congregation" (Ibn Majah, At'ima, 17)

"I command you five things that Allah has commanded me: to hear, to obey, jihad, pilgrimage, and congregation. Whoever gets even one step further from the congregation of Islam, he takes down his bonds with Islam until he returns back." (Tirmidhi, Adab, 78/2863)

Attending mosques regularly and going to perform prayers in congregation is the most important act of worship and is the most powerful element which ensures the creation of such spirit. The first thing that the Messenger of Allah did when he arrived at Quba and Madina was to build a prayer room.[56] Later, the number of the prayer rooms/mosques increased quickly. Those who follow the tradition of the Prophet have built prayer rooms in places that they

---

56. Our ancestors paid extra attention to prayer rooms and the first thing that they did when conquering a new land was to build a new mosque. A poet expressed this so well:
Where is Yunus Emre who was walking next to you;
Where is the army spreading gorgeous domes all over?

have conquered throughout history. Today, building a mosque is still considered the best honor and service that one can do and acquire. This is because mosques and congregation are the most important places that Muslims socialize and strengthen the spirit of brotherhood. The following hadith that shows the social solidarity and harmony in mosques is so attention grabbing:

"...If anyone of you leaves congregation and prays by himself, he should not lead anyone else. Whoever does this betrays the congregation." (Ahmad, V, 250, 260)

This hadith shows not only the quality of a congregation that must be achieved but also the importance of praying for the nation of Islam.

As a matter of fact, praying for the followers of Islam (Muslim ummah) was the tradition of the Messenger of Allah (pbuh), which he did after each prayer. One day when Aisha (r.a.) saw that the Prophet was happy asked him:

"O Messenger of Allah, will you pray for me!"

The Messenger of Allah (pbuh) prayed saying:

"O Allah, forgive Aisha's all past, future, hidden, and known sins!"

Aisha, the mother of believers, became so happy that she leaned her head.

The Messenger of Allah (pbuh) asked:

"Did my prayer make you happy?"

She said:

"Why should not your prayer make me happy?"

Upon that the Messenger of Allah (pbuh) said:

"I swear to Allah this is my prayer that I say for my followers in every prayer." (Haythami, IX, 243; Ibn Hibban, *Sahih,* XVI, 47/7111)

In one of his sayings, the Messenger of Allah (pbuh) said:

"In the sight of Allah, there is no better prayer of His servant than this:

اَللّٰهُمَّ ارْحَمْ أُمَّةَ مُحَمَّدٍ رَحْمَةً عَامَّةً

"O My Lord! Show mercy to all the followers of Muhammad!" (Ali al-Muttaqi, no: 3212, 3702)

For this reason, the friends of Allah think about the nation of Islam and pray as:

اَللّٰهُمَّ اغْفِرْ أُمَّةَ مُحَمَّدٍ

اَللّٰهُمَّ ارْحَمْ أُمَّةَ مُحَمَّدٍ

اَللّٰهُمَّ انْصُرْ أُمَّةَ مُحَمَّدٍ

اَللّٰهُمَّ احْفَظْ أُمَّةَ مُحَمَّدٍ

اَللّٰهُمَّ اجْمَعْ أُمَّةَ مُحَمَّدٍ

اَللّٰهُمَّ أَصْلِحْ أُمَّةَ مُحَمَّدٍ

اَللّٰهُمَّ فَرِّجْ عَنْ أُمَّةِ مُحَمَّدٍ

O Allah! Forgive the followers of the Prophet Muhammad!

O Allah! Show mercy to the followers of the Prophet Muhammad!

O Allah! Help and make the followers of the Prophet Muhammad victorious!

O Allah! Protect the followers of the Prophet Muhammad!

O Allah! Bring the followers of the Prophet Muhammad together and unite them!

O Allah! Straighten out the followers of the Prophet Muhammad!

O Allah! Remove the hardships of the followers of the Prophet Muhammad![57]

Muslims should be a strong community interlocked with each other with affection towards one another by praying for their brothers and sisters in Islam.

57. See Abu Nuaym, *Hilya,* VIII, 366; Ibn Asakir, *Tarihu Dimashk,* XXXIX, 402.

The best way to achieve this divine goal is to attend congregations regularly. Performing prayers in mosques with congregation transforms believers into brothers and sisters in Islam who altruistically want and pray for the goodness of each other. Congregation cleanses Muslims from the feelings of egoism and individuality. For this reason, the Messenger of Allah (pbuh) encouraged believers to attend congregations regularly. He mentioned the virtue of praying in congregation and informed us that a prayer performed in congregation is twenty seven times superior to a prayer performed alone. He even expressed that the reward of a prayer is parallel to the number of people in congregation and said:

"A man's prayer performed together with another is purer and more rewarding than his prayer performed alone, and his prayer with two men is purer and more rewarding than his prayer with one, but if there are more people, it is even more pleasing to Allah the Almighty." (Abu Dawud, Salah, 47/554; Nasai, Imamat, 45/841)

He explained the pleasure of Allah with the following example:

"Allah gets pleased and becomes glad by the act of those Muslims who spend time in mosques for prayer and supplication just as a family gets happy when they see their relatives who live abroad." (Ibn Majah, Masajid, 19)

In our second hadith, while we are being informed that prayer in congregation becomes expiation to our mistakes and elevates our level, it is also pointed out that one must be patient for the difficulties that arise during the process. This is because every hardship faced with patience increases the divine rewards of the performed worship.

The end of the second hadith and **the third hadith** give good news for the believers who really love being in mosques and don't want to leave. They inform us about the superiority of acting this way. Those believers who sit after performing a prayer and who look forward to the next prayer earn divine rewards as much as those who keep guard at the borders. And they receive the prayers of the angels. Friends of Allah sincerely considered loving mosques the same as "guarding the borders of the Muslim city from the enemies such as desires of the self and Satan."

However, this is on the condition not to break the ablution which proves the significance of being in the state of ritual purity (or having ablution) at all times.

Being spiritually awake and in a state of awe during the prayer is as important as coming to a mosque with peace and getting used to be there. By getting lost in thoughts, the congregation should not be unaware of what the imam is reciting. For this reason, the congregation should carefully listen to the chapter of the Opening (Al-Fatiha), which is an important invocation, and sincerely say Amin.

The Messenger of Allah (pbuh) also informed us about the harms of neglecting congregations. In several ahadith, he warned those who have difficulties in coming to congregation. This is because showing reluctance in coming to congregation is a sign of being a hypocrite. Joining the congregation is very difficult for them. Especially, the dawn (Salat al-Fajr) and night (Salat al-'Isha) prayers become big issues for those who do not have a strong faith. Therefore, the reward of going to a mosque for these two prayers is more than the rewards for the other prayers.

One day, Uthman b. Affan (r.a.) came for the Night Prayer (Salat al-'Isha). When he saw that there were not many people, he lied down at the back of the mosque and waited for others to come. At that time, Ibn Abi Amr came and sat next to Uthman. Uthman (r.a.) asked him who he was and he introduced himself.

Uthman (r.a.) asked:

"How much do you know from the Qur'an?" He told him how much he knew.

Then, Uthman (r.a.) said:

"O the son of my brother! I heard the Messenger of Allah (pbuh) saying:

"Whoever prays the night prayer (Salat al-'Isha) with congregation, he is like he has spent half of the night praying. Whoever prays the dawn prayer (Salat al-Fajr) with congregation, he is like he has spent the whole night praying." (See Muwatta, Salatu'l-Jama'ah, 7; Muslim, Masajid, 260; Tirmidhi, Salah, 165; Abu Dawud, Salah, 47)

Allah the Almighty attached to prayer in congregation so much value that He not only commanded its performance in normal times but also in extraordinary times such as war, and explained how soldiers should perform it in the Noble Qur'an. (Al-Nisa; 4:102; Bukhari, Salat al-Hawf, 1-4; Tirmidhi, Tafsir, 4/3035; Ahmad, II, 522)

The Messenger of Allah (pbuh) strongly emphasized this issue and wanted that believers should regularly attend the congregation unless they have an important excuse.

As a matter of fact, Abdullah b. Ummi Maktum (r.a.) came and said:

"O the Messenger of Allah! I am blind and my house is far from the mosque. I have a guard but he does not treat me nicely and does not help me a lot. Is there permission for me to pray at home?"

The Prophet (pbuh) asked:

"Do you hear the call (adhan)?"

When he said "Yes", the Messenger of Allah said:

"I cannot find an excuse for you." (Abu Dawud, Salah, 46/552)

Normally, being blind is considered as an accepted excuse for not attending to congregation, but this incidence shows the significance of regularly attending to congregation. However, blind people should also try to attend congregation as much as they can so that they should not be deprived of the virtue and rewards of the congregation.

The Messenger of Allah (pbuh) warned against those who show reluctance in attending congregations:

"Whoever hears the call (adhan) but does not come to the mosque (congregation), his prayer is not accepted (as a perfect prayer) unless he has an acceptable excuse." (Ibn Majah, Masajid, 17)

Once the Companions of the Prophet (pbuh) asked:

"(O Messenger of Allah!) What is an excuse?"

The Prophet (pbuh) answered:

"Fear or illness!" (Abu Dawud, Salah, 46/551)

Based on the hadith, Muslim scholars listed the following "excuses which make it permissible to not attend to a congregation":

- Being too sick to walk,

- Being paralyzed,

- Being very old,

- Being blind,

- Being crippled.

Apart from these, important personal excuses may make not attending to a congregation permissible. For example, taking care of a sick person at home is one of them.

Attaching so much importance to performing prayers in congregation is to direct believers tosalvation. This is because congregation is one of the most important means for eternal salvation. As a matter of fact, praying in congregation is called "*falah*" (salvation) in Arabic since it causes the continuation of goodness and eternal salvation. Thus, believers are invited to mosques with the words of "*Hayya 'ala' al-Falah*" (Hasten to Salvation). (Adil Bebek, "Felah" article, *DIA*, XII, 301)

In shaping the believer's character, there are many benefits of performing prayers in congregation, which ensures the salvation of the individuals and the society. Some of them are:

- The prayer performed in congregation is twenty seven times superior to the prayer performed alone,

- Sins are forgiven and the spiritual levels are elevated,

- The angels pray for the performer to be forgiven and they become witnesses of his performances,

- Getting rid of insincerity in our acts of worship,

- Performing the prayers at the most preferred time: early parts of their time limits.

- Earning divine rewards by being present when *the takbir al-iftitah* (opening takbir) is being recited,

- Being socialized,

- Staying away from Satan,

• Getting our share from the spiritual rewards of prayers and supplications that are said in congregation,

• Establishing friendship among Muslims and its continuation,

• Helping each other in obeying and worshipping Allah,

• Learning how the Chapters of the Qur'an can be better recited by listening to the imam's recitation,

• Performing the prayer perfectly and in a state of awe…

Praying in congregation strengthens the consciousness of being the followers of the same religion by being at the same row in worshipping Allah without discrimination of nation, color, language, position, or rank and by ensuring the social solidarity, cooperation, and accounting. In a social environment where individuals share common thoughts and goals, individual differences can mostly be solved. In such environments, feelings of equality and brotherhood are established in the hearts and religious excitement is experienced.

The exemplary generation that obeyed Allah and His Messenger, the Noble Companions of the Messenger of Allah (pbuh), used to pay extreme attention to praying with the congregation. Abdullah bin Mas'ud (r.a.) expressed this fact saying:

"I swear to Allah, I have not seen anyone of us who missed the congregation except the hypocrites whose insincerities were known to all. I swear to Allah, even sick people who can't stand properly used to come with the help of others and stayed standing up in between two people on his sides and with their helpperformed his prayer." (Muslim, Masajid, 256-257)

Another good example in this topic is the following:

There were two Muslims during the time of the Messenger of Allah (pbuh). One of them was a tradesman and the other one was an ironsmith who made swords. When the tradesman heard the call (adhan), he would put his scale down if he was holding it at the time or just leave it if it was on the floor and run to the Prophet's Mosque.

The ironsmith would leave his hammer if it was on an anvil and if he lifted his hammer to stroke to a sword, he would just drop it to the floor and run to the Prophet's Mosque. In order to praise them and others who are like them, Almighty Allah revealed the following noble verse:

"By men whom neither traffic nor merchandise can divert from the remembrance of Allah, nor from regular prayer, nor from the practice of regular charity: Their (only) fear is for the day when hearts and eyes will be transformed (in a world wholly new)." (Al-Nur; 24:37) (Kurtubi, XII, 184)

One day in the market, Ibn Mas'ud (r.a.) saw a group of people who were running to a prayer by leaving their stuff just like that upon hearing the call to prayer. Upon that, he said:

"Now, these are the kind of people that Allah praised in the (above mentioned) 37th verse of chapter al-Nur (Light)." (Haythami, VII, 83)

4. The Friday Prayer (Salat Al-Jum'a)

٤٩. عَنْ أَبِي هُرَيْرَةَ رَضِيَ اللهُ عَنْهُ أَنَّ رَسُولَ اللهِ صَلَّى اللهُ عَلَيْهِ وَسَلَّمَ قَالَ:

«مَنِ اغْتَسَلَ يَوْمَ الْجُمُعَةِ غُسْلَ الْجَنَابَةِ ثُمَّ رَاحَ فَكَأَنَّمَا قَرَّبَ بَدَنَةً وَمَنْ رَاحَ فِي السَّاعَةِ الثَّانِيَةِ فَكَأَنَّمَا قَرَّبَ بَقَرَةً وَمَنْ رَاحَ فِي السَّاعَةِ الثَّالِثَةِ فَكَأَنَّمَا قَرَّبَ كَبْشاً أَقْرَنَ وَمَنْ رَاحَ فِي السَّاعَةِ الرَّابِعَةِ فَكَأَنَّمَا قَرَّبَ دَجَاجَةً وَمَنْ رَاحَ فِي السَّاعَةِ الْخَامِسَةِ فَكَأَنَّمَا قَرَّبَ بَيْضَةً فَإِذَا خَرَجَ الْإِمَامُ حَضَرَتِ الْمَلَائِكَةُ يَسْتَمِعُونَ الذِّكْرَ».

49. Abu Huraira (r.a.) narrated that the Messenger of Allah (pbuh) said:

"Any person who takes a bath lustration on Friday as if cleansing from major impurities and then goes to mosque for Friday prayer early, he gets rewarded as if he had sacrificed a camel (in Allah's cause); and whoever goes in the second hour it is as if he had sacrificed a cow; and whoever goes in the third hour, then it is as if he had sacrificed a horned ram; and if one goes in the fourth hour, then it is as if he had sacrificed a hen; and whoever goes in the fifth hour then it is as if he had offered an egg. When the Imam ascends the pulpit (i.e. starts delivering the khutba (sermon)), the angels present themselves to listen to the khutba." (Bukhari,

Jum'a, 4; Muslim, Jum'a, 10. Also see Abu Dawud, Taharah, 127/351; Tirmidhi, Jum'a, 6/499; Nasai, Jum'a, 14/1386)

❀

٥٠. عَنْ أَبِي هُرَيْرَةَ رَضِيَ اللهُ عَنْهُ قَالَ: قَالَ رَسُولُ اللهِ صَلَّى اللهُ
عَلَيْهِ وَسَلَّمَ:

«مَنْ تَوَضَّأَ فَأَحْسَنَ الْوُضُوءَ ثُمَّ أَتَى الْجُمُعَةَ فَاسْتَمَعَ وَأَنْصَتَ
غُفِرَ لَهُ مَا بَيْنَهُ وَبَيْنَ الْجُمُعَةِ وَزِيَادَةُ ثَلَاثَةِ أَيَّامٍ وَمَنْ مَسَّ الْحَصَى فَقَدْ
لَغَا».

50. Abu Huraira (r.a.) reported that the Messenger of Allah (pbuh) said:

"He who performs ablution well, then comes to Friday prayer, listens (to the sermon) silently, all his sins between that time and the next Friday will be forgiven with three days extra; and he who touches pebbles, causes an interruption, his rewards will be incomplete." (Muslim, Jum'a, 27. Also see. Abu Dawud, Salah, 202-203/1050; Tirmidhi, Jum'a, 5/498; Ibn Majah, Iqamah, 62, 81)

❀

٥١. عَنْ أَبِي هُرَيْرَةَ رَضِيَ اللهُ عَنْهُ أَنَّ رَسُولَ اللهِ صَلَّى اللهُ عَلَيْهِ
وَسَلَّمَ ذَكَرَ يَوْمَ الْجُمُعَةِ فَقَالَ:

«فِيهِ سَاعَةٌ لَا يُوَافِقُهَا عَبْدٌ مُسْلِمٌ وَهُوَ قَائِمٌ يُصَلِّي يَسْأَلُ اللهَ تَعَالَى
شَيْئًا إِلَّا أَعْطَاهُ إِيَّاهُ» وَأَشَارَ بِيَدِهِ يُقَلِّلُهَا.

51. Abu Huraira (r.a.) narrated that the Messenger of Allah (pbuh) talked about Friday and said:

"There is an hour (opportune time) on Friday and if a Muslim gets it while praying and asks something from Allah, then Allah will definitely meet his demand."

And he (the Prophet) pointed out the shortness of that time with his hands. (Bukhari, Jum'a, 37; Talak, 24; Da'awat, 61; Muslim, Musafirin, 166, 167; Jum'a, 13-15. Also see Tirmidhi, Jum'a, 2/490, 491; Nasai, Jum'a, 45/1428; Ibn Majah, Iqamah, 99)

٥٢. عَنْ عَبْدِ اللهِ بْنِ عُمَرَ وَأَبِي هُرَيْرَةَ رَضِيَ اللهُ عَنْهُمَا أَنَّهُمَا سَمِعَا رَسُولَ اللهِ صَلَّى اللهُ عَلَيْهِ وَسَلَّمَ يَقُولُ عَلَى أَعْوَادِ مِنْبَرِهِ:

«لَيَنْتَهِيَنَّ أَقْوَامٌ عَنْ وَدْعِهِمُ الْجُمُعَاتِ أَوْ لَيَخْتِمَنَّ اللهُ عَلَى قُلُوبِهِمْ ثُمَّ لَيَكُونُنَّ مِنَ الْغَافِلِينَ».

52. Abu Huraira and Ibn Umar (r.a.) reported hearing the Messenger of Allah (pbuh) saying while giving a khutbah (sermon):

"Some people either stop abandoning the Friday Prayer or Allah the Almighty seal their hearts so they join the ignorant ones." (Muslim, Jum'a, 40. Also see Nasai, Jum'a, 2/1368; Ibn Majah, Masajid, 17)

Explanations:

Friday Prayer (*Salat al-Jum'a*) is One of the manifestations of the importance that Islam attached to socialization. As a matter of fact, the word "Jum'a" comes from the root "jama'a" which means "gathering or coming together." Friday is accepted as a holiday for believers[58] and many hadith are reported mentioning its virtues. This is a virtuous day because the Friday Prayer is specific to this day, which is one of the most important acts of worships that gathers all the Muslims together. And it has a moment in it which all supplications are accepted. Many important incidents took place on this day. Allah the Almighty gets pleased to see His servants worshipping together. For this reason, He regards the acts of worship performed in congregation, such as the Friday prayer (*Salat al-Jum'a*), the festivity prayers (*Salat al-Eidain*), and pilgrimage (Hajj) more virtuous than acts of worship performed alone.

Allah says about Friday in a noble verse:

---

58. Ibn Majah, Iqamah, 83.

"O you who believe! When the call is proclaimed to prayer on Friday (the Day of Assembly), hasten earnestly to the Remembrance of Allah, and leave off business (and traffic): That is best for you if you but knew!" (Al-Jum'a; 62:9)

Due to His mercy on His servants, Allah always commanded the things that are good for them. When the call to prayer (adhan) is heard, leaving everything behind and running to the Friday Prayer is one of them. That is because it helps to ensure the eternal salvation.

The divine rewards are more for those who make some preparations before going to the Friday Prayer and go to the mosque as early as possible. The terms used in **the first hadith** such as "the second hour, the third hour" were not used in their literal meanings but rather short time intervals between the time that the congregation begins to assemble and the imam starts delivering his sermon. The goal is to make people pay attention to such an important worship by encouraging them towards it.

To get ready for the Friday Prayer, first of all, one may perform the major ablution (ghusl). The Prophet (pbuh) said:

"If any one of you performs ablution (on Friday) this is all right; and if any of you takes a bath, that is even more virtuous." (Abu Dawud, Taharah, 128/354; Tirmidhi, Jum'a 5/497)

In order not to bother people, one must complete his personal care such as brushing the teeth, grooming the hair and beard, putting on clean clothes, and wearing nice perfumes. (Bukhari, Jum'a, 6, 19; Abu Dawud, Taharah, 128/353)

Mosques should be cleaned and deodorized, and if possible one should recite chapters of *sajdah* and *dahr* in the dawn Prayer, chapters of *jum'a* and *al-munafiqun* (Hypocrites) or *al'a* and *ghashiya* in Friday prayer, *al-kahf*,[59] during the day, and remember and pray Allah and invoke blessings on the Messenger of Allah. As a matter of fact, the Prophet (pbuh) said:

"Friday is among the most excellent of your days...so invoke more blessings on me on that day, because your blessings will be submitted to me." (Abu Dawud, Salah, 201/1047)

---

59. See Hayreddin Karaman, "Cuma" *Diyanet İslâm Ansiklopedisi*, VIII, 85.

A Muslim who gets ready for Friday Prayer should walk to a mosque instead of taking a ride whenever it is possible. That is because acting this way is more suitable for the state of modesty and awe. One must pay attention not to bother anyone while going to a mosque and in the mosque and should not disturb others trying to get to the front rows. If a sermon is given before the prayer, one must listen quietly, and if there is no sermon, one should keep himself busy with remembering Allah and performing supererogatory acts of worship. While the Khutbah is delivered, one must listen carefully to what the imam is saying and listen to him quietly without paying attention to anything else.

In the second hadith, we are informed that a Friday Prayer performed in accordance with its proper rules becomes expiation for minor sins of ten days. In other words, Allah the Almighty responds to a good deed with ten times the rewards and shows his mercy to His servants. In forgiving the sins, the three extra days that is special to Friday Prayer indicates the significance of this particular worship. From this and other similar sayings of the Prophet (pbuh), it is understood that our Lord Almighty wants to forgive us in every chance possible.

In the hadith, it is stated that a person who plays with pebbles would waste his time and be deprived of the rewards of Friday prayer. With this approach, it is intended that Muslims should listen to the sermon carefully and get informed about the issues of the society and pay attention to them together.

In the time of the Messenger of Allah (pbuh), the floor of the mosques and prayer rooms were covered with sand and pebbles. Today, the same thing applies to those who perform their prayers outside a mosque. However, the real object of this hadith is to warn about not listening to the imam and being busy with something else while the sermon is being delivered and also distracting others. The thing that distracts our attention can be a pebble or a cell phone, the design of the rug, or something else. The warning of the Messenger of Allah is for us to get more benefit from the virtues of the Friday Prayer.

According to Hanafi School, the Friday Prayer is composed of, first, a four-unit sunnah prayer,[60] then a two unit fard (obligatory) prayer, followed by a four and two unit sunnah prayers[61].

There is also a four-unit *zuhr akhir* (last noon) prayer performed before the last two units of sunnah, and its performance became a tradition as scholars put forward some requirements for a Friday Prayer to be valid. These are the requirements such as "only one Friday prayer can be performed in one town" or "Friday prayer can be performed only with the permission of the president of the Muslim state." Some scholars viewed that performing four units of *zuhr akhir* prayer after the Friday prayer would be acting cautiously thinking that some of these requirements are not met.

Other scholars said that there is no evidence either in the Qur'an nor in Sunnah that proves requirements such as the permission of the president of the state, however other requirements such as being in a city, a certain number of congregation members, and performing it in a mosque or only one mosque in a city should be sought. Accordingly, Friday prayer should be performed when there is a congregation, regardless of its size, and an imam who can lead the congregation whether in a small or big city.[62]

The moment of time in Friday mentioned in **our third hadith** in which the prayers are accepted is kept short and secret in order to have Muslims alert and enthusiastic. It is possible that this moment of time is in sometime either from the beginning of the sermon to the Friday Prayer[63] or in between the Afternoon Prayer (Salat al-Asr) and sunset. By examining the part of the hadith *"if a Muslim gets it while praying and asks something from Allah"* one may question how a person can ask for something from Allah while performing the ritual prayer. Some of the Noble Companions answered this question saying:

"Whoever sits and waits for the prayer is considered as if he is performing the ritual prayer during this time." (Abu Dawud, Salah, 201/1046)

---

60. Bukhari, Adhan, 14, 16; Muslim, Musafirin, 304; Abu Dawud, Salah, 238; Tirmidhi, Jumu'ah, 24/523.

61. Muslim, Jumu'ah, 67-71; Musafirin, 104; Bukhari, Tahajjud, 25, 29.

62. For details on Jumuah see Hayreddin Karaman, "Cuma" article in *Diyanet İslâm Ansiklopedisi*, VIII, 87; *İslâm'ın Işığında Günün Meseleleri,* I, 14-63.

63. Muslim, Jumu'ah, 16.

Therefore, the reason behind the hadith that prohibits talking or doing something else while the sermon is delivered can better be understood. One must certainly ask from Allah something good and benefitial both in this world and the Hereafter rather than asking for something bad or forbidden.

After the performance of the Friday Prayer, everyone can return to their work, provided that one must never forget Allah in the pace of life…

In the noble verses, it is said that:

"And when the Prayer is finished, then may you disperse through the land, and seek of the Bounty of Allah and celebrate the Praises of Allah often (and without stint): that you may prosper. But when they see some bargain or some amusement, they disperse headlong to it, and leave thee standing. Say: "The (blessing) from the Presence of Allah is better than any amusement or bargain! And Allah is the Best to provide (for all needs).""
(Al-Juma'; 62:10-11)

Therefore, a believer should never prefer worldly benefits over the rewards of Friday Prayer. One must know that the rewards of Allah for those who attend the Friday Prayer are better than everything else. Showing negligence by worrying about earning a livelihood is a sign of forgetting one of the divine attributes of Allah, i.e. al-Razzaq (The Provider). As a matter of fact, all creatures' livelihoods are bestowed upon them by Allah. The forgiveness, mercy, and paradise that Allah will bestow upon them are better than everything in this world combined. Abandoning the Friday Prayer by forgetting all these facts causes the destruction of eternal happiness. This fact expressed in **the fourth hadith** is also expressed in another narration as:

"He who leaves the Friday prayer (continuously) for three Fridays on account of slackness, Allah will print a stamp on his heart." (Abu Dawud, Salah, 203-204/1052; Tirmidhi, Jum'a, 7/500)

Those whose hearts are sealed lose the ability to turn to Allah and to the right path by missing out the blessing and favor of Allah. In order to be saved from this situation, one must pledge not to act wrong anymore, ask for the forgiveness of Allah, and even give alms and do good deeds to show his sincerity. (Abu Dawud, Salah, 203-204/1053-54)

5. Ramadan and Fasting

a. The Virtues of Ramadan and Fasting

٥٣. عَنْ أَبِي هُرَيْرَةَ رَضِيَ اللهُ عَنْهُ يَقُولُ: قَالَ رَسُولُ اللهِ صَلَّى اللهُ
عَلَيْهِ وَسَلَّمَ:

«إِذَا دَخَلَ رَمَضَانُ فُتِّحَتْ أَبْوَابُ الْجَنَّةِ وَغُلِّقَتْ أَبْوَابُ جَهَنَّمَ
وَسُلْسِلَتِ الشَّيَاطِينُ».

53. Abu Huraira (r.a.) reported that the Messenger of Allah (pbuh) saying:

"When the month of Ramadan starts, the gates of Heaven are opened and the gates of Hell are closed and the devils are chained." (Bukhari, Bad' al-khalk, 11; Muslim, Siyam, 1, 2, 4, 5)

❀

٥٤. عَنْ أَبِي هُرَيْرَةَ رَضِيَ اللهُ عَنْهُ يَقُولُ: قَالَ رَسُولُ اللهِ صَلَّى اللهُ
عَلَيْهِ وَسَلَّمَ:

«قَالَ اللهُ: (كُلُّ عَمَلِ ابْنِ آدَمَ لَهُ إِلَّا الصِّيَامَ فَإِنَّهُ لِي وَأَنَا أَجْزِي بِهِ)
وَالصِّيَامُ جُنَّةٌ وَإِذَا كَانَ يَوْمُ صَوْمِ أَحَدِكُمْ فَلَا يَرْفُثْ وَلاَ يَصْخَبْ فَإِنْ
سَابَّهُ أَحَدٌ أَوْ قَاتَلَهُ فَلْيَقُلْ: إِنِّي امْرُؤٌ صَائِمٌ وَالَّذِي نَفْسُ مُحَمَّدٍ بِيَدِهِ
لَخُلُوفُ فَمِ الصَّائِمِ أَطْيَبُ عِنْدَ اللهِ مِنْ رِيحِ الْمِسْكِ. لِلصَّائِمِ فَرْحَتَانِ
يَفْرَحُهُمَا: إِذَا أَفْطَرَ فَرِحَ وَإِذَا لَقِيَ رَبَّهُ فَرِحَ بِصَوْمِهِ».

54. Abu Huraira (r.a.) narrated that the Messenger of Allah (pbuh) said:

"Allah said, "All the deeds of Adam's sons (people) are for them, except fasting which is for Me, and I will give the reward for it." Fasting is a shield or protection

from the fire and from committing sins. If one of you is fasting, he should avoid saying bad words and quarreling, and if somebody should fight or quarrel with him, he should say, "I am fasting." The Prophet added; By Him in Whose Hands my soul is, the unpleasant smell coming out from the mouth of a fasting person is better in the sight of Allah than the smell of musk. There are two pleasures for the fasting person, one at the time of breaking his fast, and the other at the time when he will meet his Lord." (Bukhari, Sawm, 9; Muslim, Siyam, 163)

۵۵. عَنْ أَبِي هُرَيْرَةَ رَضِيَ اللهُ عَنْهُ قَالَ: قَالَ رَسُولُ اللهِ صَلَّى اللهُ عَلَيْهِ وَسَلَّمَ:

«مَنْ لَمْ يَدَعْ قَوْلَ الزُّورِ وَالْعَمَلَ بِهِ فَلَيْسَ لِلّهِ حَاجَةٌ فِي أَنْ يَدَعَ طَعَامَهُ وَشَرَابَهُ».

55. Abu Huraira (r.a.) narrated that the Messenger of Allah (pbuh) said:

"Whoever does not give up forged speech and evil actions, Allah is not in need of his leaving his food and drink (i.e. Allah will not accept his fasting)." (Bukhari, Sawm, 8, Edeb, 51. Also see Abu Dawud, Sawm, 26/2362; Tirmidhi, Sawm, 16/707; Ibn Majah, Siyam, 21)

Explanations:

Ramadan, the Sultan of the 12 months[64], is a blessed[65] time period and a month of worship. In this month, the doors of heaven open up and divine mercy beams everywhere. More rewards are given to worships performed and good deeds done in this month than the rest of the year. Sins are also forgiven in this month. Muslims live through a season of intensive acts of worship in congregation.

The main reasons why the month of Ramadan is so virtuous are:

---

64.   Beyhaki, Sh*uab*, III, 314-315; Haythami, III, 140.
65.   Ahmad, II, 230, 385.

• Our guide to salvation, the Noble Qur'an, started to be revealed in this month. (Al-Baqarah; 2:185)

• The Night of Power[66] (*laylat al-qadr*) that Allah said is "**better than a thousand months**"[67] is in this month.

• The most important reason is that our Almighty Lord made one month of the year a season of worship by blessing it as a favor to His servants. Those believers who take advantage of this opportunity reflect the Noble Qur'an and Sunnah in their lives, and reach to Eid (Festival) by earning many divine rewards free from their sins.

Since the season of Ramadan circles around the year because it's one of the months of the lunar year, Muslims show that they worship Allah under all circumstances with sincerity and with submission.

It is definitely easier to enter Paradise by earning divine rewards and stay away from Hell by defeating Satan in this virtuous month. Since the carnal self, who is the biggest helper of Satan, is being disciplined with fasting, it is easier to stay away from wrongdoings in Ramadan. Then, Muslims should take advantage of the opportunity of Ramadan, and should do their best to give their fasting its due, to recite the Noble Qur'an, to remember Allah, spend the nights worshipping Allah, and to perform many good deeds and help others.

The Companions of the Prophet (pbuh) would live Ramadan with great enthusiasm and excitement and ensured that their children also experienced this spiritual climate. As a matter of fact, Umar (r.a.) said to a person who got drunk in Ramadan:

"Shame on you! Even our children are fasting." (Bukhari, Sawm, 47)

As we spend the days of Ramadan with fasting, it is also necessary to take advantage of the nights of Ramadan with the Tarawih Prayers (*salat al-tarawih*) and midnight Prayers (*salat al-tahajjud*), recitations of Qur'an and remembrance of Allah. The Messenger of Allah gave us the good news:

"*Whoever spends the nights of Ramadan out of sincere faith, and hoping for a reward only from Allah, then all his previous sins will be forgiven.*" (Bukhari, Tarawih, 46)

---

66. *Translator's note:* Some translate the name of this night as "the Night of Worth."
67. Qadr (Power, Fate); 97:3.

One day, the Messenger of Allah (pbuh) came out his house, and he saw a group of people praying at the corner of the mosque. He asked:

"What are they doing?"

"They do not know the Qur'an well, so Ubayy b. Ka'b (r.a.) is leading them in their prayers!"

The Messenger of Allah (pbuh) said:

"They did the right thing and it is good what they did!" (Abu Dawud, Ramadan, 1/1377)

On the other hand, both the obligatory alms (zakat) and supererogatory alms become more important in this month. As a matter of fact, when it is asked to the Messenger of Allah:

"What kind of alms (*sadaqah*) is more virtuous?" He said:

"The one given in Ramadan!" (Tirmidhi, Zakat, 28/663)

The word "*sadaqah*" in this hadith means the obligatory alms (zakat) in Arabic. For this reason, it is better to give zakat in Ramadan. The Companions of the Prophet (pbuh) used to give amply their Sadaqah al-Fitr (alms given during the month of Ramadan) and other charities in this month.[68] That is because the Messenger of Allah (pbuh) informed us that Sadaqah al-Fitr is obligatory for adults and children, males and females, independents and slaves and it is either one sa' from date or barley.[69] (Bukhari, Zakat, 70-78; Muslim, Zakat, 13)

By giving the Sadaqah al-Fitr before the Festival Prayer (*salat al-eid*), it should be ensured that the poor also experience the joy of eid.

In order to take advantage of the blessings of Ramadan, one must increase his generosity. As a matter of fact, the Messenger of Allah (pbuh) used to act this way.

Ibn Abbas (r.a.) narrated:

"The Prophet was the most generous amongst the people, and he used to be more so in the month of Ramadan when Gabriel visited him, and Gabriel used to meet him on every night of Ramadan till the end of the month. The Prophet used to recite the Holy Qur'an to Gabriel, and when Gabriel met him,

---

68. Bukhari, Keffaratul-Ayman, 5.
69. *Sa* is a measure of weight that is equal either to 2,751 kg or 3,328 kg.

he used to be more generous than a fast wind (which causes rain and welfare). (Bukhari, Bad al-Wahy, 5, 6; Sawm, 7; Manaqib, 23; Bad al-Khalk, 6; Fadail al-Qur'an, 7; Adab, 39; Muslim, Fadail, 48, 50)

Fasting comes to mind when Ramadan is mentioned. Fasting is one of the five pillars of Islam. Allah the Almighty made fasting obligatory to the followers of previous religions, too. Fasting is a worship that contains various and deep meanings. Fasting is also the act of worship furthest away from insincerity and showing off. For this reason, Allah said that fasting is performed especially for Him.

For each good deed, divine rewards are given as much as ten to seven hundred times of the deed performed. However, fasting is excluded from this. Allah Himself will give the reward of fasting and will make His servants who perform fasting happy both in this world and in the Hereafter and will host them in His Paradise.

The Messenger of Allah (pbuh) said:

"There is a gate in Paradise called Ar-Raiyan, and those who observe fasts will enter through it on the Day of Resurrection and none except them will enter through it…" (Bukhari, Sawm, 4; Muslim, Siyam, 166)

There are many benefits for His servants in the commands of Allah, and there is much harm in the prohibitions of Allah. Even though human capacity can comprehend some of the wisdom and reasons behind them, most are beyond our capacity. As a matter of fact, in our worships to Allah, the main thing is to perform them sincerely, and therefore, the search for wisdom and reasons is not that important. Muslim scholars say that there are many known and unknown benefits of fasting and mention some of the known benefits that they can understand. Some of them are as follows:

Fasting that keeps humans away from the temptations of the carnal self and teaches us how to be patient advances us to the level of piety by training us in a certain way for self-control and discipline. Due to fasting, one realizes better the value of the blessings that he has. The feelings of mercy and affection in his heart improve and he starts to discern better the needy in the society. He gets filled with the feelings of thanks to Allah and mercy and aid to His servants.

On the other hand, the benefits of fasting to our health are known to all.

In order fasting to be beneficial for the spiritual life, it must be performed by balancing the harmony between the body and soul. In other words, while the body is fasting, the heart, carnal self, and the other body parts should also fast and stay away from all kinds of forbidden (harams) and reproachable acts (makruh). The essence of fasting is to elevate one's spiritual state in the sight of Allah and to gain sensitivity in obeying Allah's commands and prohibitions. For this reason, those who fast should avoid lying, slandering, backbiting, gossiping, using strong language or cursing, fighting, and all the other wrongdoings and sins. Those believers who fast should know how to respond peacefully to those who treat them impolitely. The Messenger of Allah (pbuh) informed us that Allah does not accept the fast of those who do not perform their fasting in this way. When fasting is not performed as it should be, one misses the opportunity to receive the spiritual perfection and virtue of fasting while he only fulfills his responsibility.

One should not forget that the aim of fasting is not to torture or bother the body. For this reason, in the verses that the fasting is commanded, Allah says **"Allah intends every facility for you; He does not want to put to difficulties."**[70] Practices such as Sawm-ı wisal[71] that cause difficulty to humans are prohibited. The Messenger of Allah (pbuh) paid attention to wake up for the Sahur (the meal before dawn during Ramadan) and to be quick in iftar (the breaking of the Ramadan fast), and said that there is a blessing in Sahur meal,[72] and as long as they act quick in breaking their fast, Muslims will continue to live the right path.[73] By improving the individual and the society, the real goal in fasting is to fulfill our responsibility to Allah, to discipline our inner selves and advance our spiritual state to piety, to ensure a peaceful environment with which Allah will be content.

b. The Virtues of The Night of Power (Al-Laylat al-Qadr)

٥٦. عَنْ عَائِشَةَ رَضِيَ اللهُ عَنْهَا قَالَتْ: كَانَ رَسُولُ اللهِ صَلَّى اللهُ عَلَيْهِ وَسَلَّمَ يُجَاوِرُ فِي الْعَشْرِ الْأَوَاخِرِ مِنْ رَمَضَانَ وَيَقُولُ:

---

70. Al-Baqarah; 2/185.
71. **Sawm al-wisal** is fasting for two or three days without breaking it.
72. Tirmidhi, Sawm, 17/708.
73. Bukhari, Sawm, 45; Muslim, Siyam, 48.

«تَحَرَّوْا لَيْلَةَ الْقَدْرِ فِي الْعَشْرِ الْأَوَاخِرِ مِنْ رَمَضَانَ».

56. Aisha (r.a.) narrated:

The Messenger of Allah (pbuh) used to retire in the mosque during the last ten days of Ramadan and devote himself to worship and say:

"*Search for the Night of Qadr in the last ten days of Ramadan.*" (Bukhari, Laylat al-Qadr, 3; Muslim, Siyam, 219; Tirmidhi, Sawm, 72/792)

۞

٥٧. عَنْ أَبِي هُرَيْرَةَ رَضِيَ اللهُ عَنْهُ عَنِ النَّبِيِّ صَلَّى اللهُ عَلَيْهِ وَسَلَّمَ قَالَ:

«مَنْ قَامَ لَيْلَةَ الْقَدْرِ إِيمَاناً وَاحْتِسَاباً غُفِرَ لَهُ مَا تَقَدَّمَ مِنْ ذَنْبِهِ».

57. Abu Huraira (r.a.) narrated that the Messenger of Allah (pbuh) said:

"*Whoever establishes prayers on the night of Qadr out of sincere faith and hoping for a reward only from Allah, then all his previous sins will be forgiven.*" (Bukhari, Sawm, 6; Muslim, Musafirin, 173-176)

۞

٥٨. عَنْ عَائِشَةَ رَضِيَ اللهُ عَنْهَا قَالَتْ: قُلْتُ:

«يَا رَسُولَ اللهِ أَرَأَيْتَ إِنْ عَلِمْتُ أَيَّ لَيْلَةٍ لَيْلَةُ الْقَدْرِ مَا أَقُولُ فِيهَا؟»

قَالَ: قُولِي:

«اَللّٰهُمَّ إِنَّكَ عَفُوٌّ كَرِيمٌ تُحِبُّ الْعَفْوَ فَاعْفُ عَنِّي».

58. Aisha (r.a.) said: I asked the Prophet:

"O the Messenger of Allah! If I get know which night is the Night of Qadr, how should I pray?"

The Messenger of Allah (pbuh) responded:

"Pray saying "O my Lord! You are the most forgiver and generous, You love to forgive; please forgive me!"" (Tirmidhi, Deavat, 84/3513; Ibn Majah, Dua, 5)

Explanations:

One of the manifestations of Allah's endless mercy and blessing is the Night of Power (al-Laylat al-Qadr). This night is the greatest opportunity blessed to us by our Lord who facilitates things for His servants in every chance. That is because this night is better than one thousand months, or in other words better than 83-year and 4-month long life.

The life span of his followers was shown to the Messenger of Allah (pbuh). The Messenger of Allah (pbuh) found it to be too short comparing to the life spans of the previous people. He thought that his followers would miss the opportunity to perform good deeds as much as the previous people. Upon that, Allah blessed him and his followers the Night of Power which is better than one thousand months. (*Muwatta,* Itiqaf 15)

One day, the Messenger of Allah (pbuh) told his companions about a man from Israelites. This man called Shem'un-i Ghazi fought for the sake of Allah for a thousand months and worshipped Him during the nights. Muslims got excited and admired him.

Upon that, Allah revealed the chapter al-Qadr in order to show His blessings and mercy to the followers of Muhammad:

"We have indeed revealed this (Message) in the Night of Power: And what will explain to thee what the night of power is? The Night of Power is better than a thousand months. Therein come down the angels and the Spirit by Allah's permission, on every errand: Peace!... This until the rise of morn!" (Al-Qadr; 97:1-5) (See Wahidi, p. 486)

Allah the Almighty made the night that He appointed our Prophet to the prophethood and started to reveal our Holy Book as the holiest one of all nights. This is enough to express the honor and value of and the Noble Qur'an, and also the Night of Power.

By stating **"We sent it (Qur'an) down during a Blessed Night"**[74] in the chapter al-Duhan, Allah informs us about the blessing and virtue of the Night of Power and abundance of its goodness.

The Messenger of Allah (pbuh) said:

"In Ramadan there is a night that is better than a thousand months. Whoever misses the goodness of this night misses something gravely important." (Ahmad, II, 230, 385)

Acts of worship performed in this night are more rewarding than the ones performed in a thousand months that do not have a Night of Power in them. The things that will take place until the next year are told to angels on this night. In this night, Gabriel (pbuh) and many other angles descend on earth. In this night, people are protected from all kinds of evil; peace and tranquility covers everywhere until the sunrise. Angels descending on Earth greet believers by whom they stop and pray for them and for their forgiveness. They also bear witness to their worship on the Day of Judgment and intercede for that person.

In our first hadith, it is advised that one must search for the Night of Power in the last ten days of Ramadan. In other narrations, it is also advised to search for it in the odd days of the last ten days of Ramadan[75], in the twenty fourth night,[76] and twenty seventh nights.[77] Some of the Noble Companions dreamt that the Night of Power is in the last seven days of Ramadan and told that to the Messenger of Allah. Upon that, the Messenger of Allah (pbuh) said:

"It seems that all your dreams agree that (the Night of Qadr) is in the last seven nights, and whoever wants to search for it (i.e. the Night of Qadr) should search in the last seven (nights of Ramadan)." (Bukhari, Laylat al-Qadr, 2; Ta'bir, 8; Muslim, Siyam, 205-206)

The Messenger of Allah (pbuh) informed us about the signs of this night as:

"In the morning of the Night of Power, the sun rises without brightness, and it looks like a bowl until it gets high." (Muslim, Musafirin, 179; Abu Dawud, Ramadan, 2/1378; Tirmidhi, Sawm, 72/793)

74. Al-Duhan (The Smoke); 44/3.
75. Tirmidhi, Savm, 72/792.
76. Bukhari, Laylat al-Qadr 3.
77. Tabarani, *Kabir*, XIX, 349.

"The Night of Power is bright and it is neither hot nor cold. It is without clouds, rain, and wind. There would not be a falling star in that night either..." (Tabarani, *Kabir*, XXII, 59; Haythami, III, 178-179; Baihaqi, *Shuab*, III, 334)

The reason of hiding the Night of Power is to encourage people to worship and make them worship more and so elevate their spiritual state. A person who searches the Night of Power learns to take advantage of his time by worshipping and practices this same habit in other days as well. In time, being good and worshipping becomes his nature. Also, the value of something depends on the hardship that is gone through to get it. Therefore, in order to take advantage of this virtuous night, one must try hard.

Hiding the Night of Power prevents people to sin by trusting to take advantage of this night. It also saves those who do not respect this night from the responsibility of sinning intentionally for a thousand months. Taking all these reasons into account, wise people said:

"Consider every night as the Night of Power, and every man you see as Hizir.[78]

In the second hadith, the good news is given that the sins of those who take advantage of the Night of Power will be nullified. However, this is conditioned on having faith and being sincere. In other words, one must believe in the words of Allah and His Messenger and acknowledge the virtue of that night and worship by asking the rewards only from Allah. When this happens, that person gets cleansed from all his sins and reaches the morning as pure as a newborn.

Being forgiven is an important privilege. That is because first a thing gets cleaned and then gets enriched with beauties. For this reason, before everything else, one must hold on tight to asking for forgiveness.

The Messenger of Allah (pbuh) would worship more during the month of Ramadan compared to other months, and devote himself to worship especially at the last ten days of Ramadan in order to take advantage of the Night of Power. During these days, he would spend the night worshipping and wake up his family as well. (Bukhari, Laylatu'l-Kadr, 5)

---

78. Translator's Note: A Muslim saint, Hizir is the last-minute rescuer from disaster, a deus ex machina, when all other assistance, natural and supernatural, has failed.

In the third hadith, one of the prayers that can be said in the Night of Power is taught. As other prayers can be said in the Night of Power, this night can also be spent by performing worships such as praying, reciting the Qur'an, asking for forgiveness of sins and promising not to do them again, remembering Allah, saying praises for His messenger, and deeply thinking. Those who have missed prayers should at least make up one day (five) of those missed prayers. Apart from these, one should spend the day of the Night of Power by performing good deeds such as pleasing and helping others, giving charities and cheering up the needy. The least one can do to take advantage of the Night of Power is to join a congregation in the evening prayer (Salat al-Maghrib), the night prayer (Salat al-'Isha), and the dawn prayer (Salat al-Fajr). (See Baihaqi, *Shuab*, III, 340)

To stay up all night might not be possible for everyone. However, in compliance with the Sunnah of the Messenger of Allah, it is quite possible for anyone during the last seven days of Ramadan to decrease the sleeping time and increase the time spend worshipping and to reserve some time from the early and late hours of the night for the acts of worship.

Those who do not benefit from Ramadan, fasting, and the Night of Power and reach the end of Ramadan without receiving forgiveness are miserable people. They insist and resist on staying away from goodness and Allah's mercy. For this reason, the Messenger of Allah (pbuh) said:

"Woe to him who found the blessed month of Ramadan and let it pass by without gaining forgiveness!" (Tirmidhi, Daawat, 100/3545)

c. Utilizing the Festivity (Eid) Days

٥٩. عَنْ أَبِي أُمَامَةَ رَضِيَ اللهُ عَنْهُ عَنِ النَّبِيِّ صَلَّى اللهُ عَلَيْهِ وَسَلَّمَ قَالَ:

((مَنْ قَامَ لَيْلَتَيِ الْعِيدَيْنِ مُحْتَسِبًا لِلَّهِ لَمْ يَمُتْ قَلْبُهُ يَوْمَ تَمُوتُ الْقُلُوبُ)).

59. Abu Umamah (r.a.) reported that the Messenger of Allah (pbuh) said:

"Whoever spends the nights of Eid al-Fitr (the festival day at the completion of the month of Ramadan) and Eid al-Adha (the festival day at the completion of the pilgrimage to Mecca) worshipping and hoping for a reward only from Allah, then his heart will not die on the day when all hearts will." (Ibn Majah, Siyam, 68. Also see Haythami, II, 198)

❁

٦٠. عَنْ نُبَيْشَةَ رَضِيَ اللهُ عَنْهُ قَالَ: ٥ قَالَ رَسُولُ اللهِ صَلَّى اللهُ عَلَيْهِ وَسَلَّمَ:

«إِنَّا كُنَّا نَهَيْنَاكُمْ عَنْ لُحُومِهَا أَنْ تَأْكُلُوهَا فَوْقَ ثَلَاثٍ لِكَيْ تَسَعكُمْ فَقَدْ جَاءَ اللهُ بِالسَّعَةِ فَكُلُوا وَادَّخِرُوا وَاتَّجِرُوا أَلَا وَإِنَّ هٰذِهِ الْأَيَّامُ أَيَّامُ أَكْلٍ وَشُرْبٍ وَذِكْرِ اللهِ عَزَّ وَجَلَّ».

60. Nubayshah (r.a.) reported that the Messenger of Allah (pbuh) said:

"We forbade you to eat the sacrifice meat for more than three days in order that you might have abundance. Now Allah has produced abundance, so you may eat, store up, and seek reward from Allah by distributing some. Beware, the days of Eid are days of eating, drinking and remembrance of Allah, Most High." (Abu Dawud, Al-Dahaya, 9-10/2812, 2813)[79]

Explanations:

At the time when the Messenger of Allah (pbuh) emigrated from Mecca to Medina, there were two festivals in which people of Medina used to perform various plays. The Messenger of Allah (pbuh) saw this and said:

"Corresponding to these two festivals, Allah gave you better ones, Eid al-Fitr and Eid al-Adha" (Ahmad, III, 103, 178, 235, 250; Abu Dawud, Salah, 239/1134; Nasai, I'dain, 1/1554)

---

79. In the time of the Messenger of Allah (pbuh), when it was Eid Al-Adha, there came a group of needy Bedouin people. Upon that, the Messenger of Allah (pbuh) ordered not to keep the meat of the sacrificed animal for more than three days and asked it to be distributed. Later when the prosperity increased, he abrogated this rule while still encouraging Muslims to cooperate and help the poor. (Muslim, Adahi, 28, 34; Abu Dawud, Adahi, 9-10/2812)

Eid days are the signs of Allah's mercy. Eid days are exceptional days where feelings of forgiveness, tolerance, cooperation, conciliation, affection, kindness, and goodness are experienced. Those believers who devote themselves to worship in Ramadan and Hajj and achieve forgiveness and contentment of Allah are the ones who benefit more comfortably from the blessings of Allah in eid days. In a sense, the festivity days represent the believers' reception of the blessings of Paradise by completing the test of this world that is full of hardships and their affection with other believers there without having any negative feelings in their hearts such as envy, jealousy, or hatred. Actually, the real eid is on that day. As a matter of fact, the friends of Allah said:

"The real eid is not for those who put on new clothes but for those who are secure from Allah's torment."

In the first hadith, we are given the good news that the hearts of those believers who spend the nights of eid days worshipping, remembering Allah, supplication, and thinking of Allah will not die. That is because they are the people who experienced the joy of worshipping Allah and can keep their carnal self under control. While all others pursue their carnal desires, they enjoy worshipping by not falling for the temporal joys. Even if they coincide with an era where hearts are dead due to ubiquity of sins, their hearts stay alive, they do not prefer the world over hereafter, and they never fall into disbelief. Also, their aftermath is goodness. Those people do not get surprised and terrified neither at the time of their death or in their grave nor on the Day of Judgment but rather go to their Lord with a peaceful heart. That is because they experience the joy of worshipping. They realize and are conscious of the fact that they are in this world for a test and should take advantage of this world of opportunities until their last minute.

When something is rare and difficult to perform, it means a higher value. While most people forget worshipping with the excitement of eid, performing acts of worship during the nights of the eids shows the strength of faith and love of Allah for those who worship. Even if all hearts die, such hearts that are full of faith and love of Allah never die.

In our second hadith, we are informed that the days of eid are the days of social solidarity and unity, exchanging gifts, cooperation, treating each other with respect and honor, and benefitting from the divine blessings and remembering Allah. Otherwise, eid days are not days of vacation and entertainment.

On the other hand, in order to show happiness, games and entertainment performed without encouraging the carnal self for wrong desires are permitted in weddings and eid days. That is because displaying happiness during eid days is one of the principles of Islam. (Ahmad Naim, *Tecridi Sarih Tercümesi*, III, 157)

As a matter of fact, on an eid day, two young girls together with Aisha were singing songs about the Battle of Buath. The Prophet (pbuh) was resting while his face covered with a cloth. At that moment, Abu Bakr (r.a.) came in and wanted to interrupt.

The Messenger of Allah (pbuh) said, uncovering his head:

"O Abu Bakr! There is an Eid for every nation and this is our Eid!" (Bukhari, I'dain, 3; Muslim, Salat al-I'dain, 16)

In other words, the Messenger of Allah (pbuh) gave permission to Muslims to celebrate eids in this way even though he did not watch it himself. Also on another eid day, a group that came from Ethiopia was playing with shields and spears in the mosque. The Messenger of Allah (pbuh) let Aisha watch this game over his shoulders hiding her behind himself and covering her with his wrap. (Bukhari, I'dain, 2; Salah, 69)

The Messenger of Allah (pbuh) always emphasized the spiritual side of the eids in order for these permissible entertainments and the atmosphere of celebration not to go beyond acceptable limits. The Messenger of Allah (pbuh) who encouraged worshipping, doing well, and remembering Allah in eids said in a hadith:

"The first thing to be done on this day (first day of Eid) is to pray." (Bukhari, I'dain, 3, 10; Muslim, Adahi, 7)

"Beautify your eid days with saying al-Takbir (Allahu Akbar –God is Greatest)!" (Haythami, II, 197)

Indeed, the Companions of the Prophet (pbuh) kept eid days alive with saying Takbirs. Umar used to say Takbirs in his small tent in Mina and people in the mosque used to repeat after him. When people in the market also joined them, the Mina would be reverberated with the sound of Takbirs. Ibn Umar used to say Takbir continuously on eid days. He used to say Takbir after each prayer, when he went to sleep, when he entered his tent, while sitting or walking, in other words, at all times and conditions during these assigned days. (Bukhari, I'dain, 12)

As it can be seen, the happiness of Muslims is displayed by worshipping Allah and exalting His religion. There is no share of the carnal self in their happiness. In the moments of happiness, they never act exorbitant and perform forbidden acts. In these happy days, they run to good deeds that would help them to gain the contentment of Allah and especially treat the needy and the poor nicely and try to please them. They help the poor, helpless, orphan, widow, and people who are tired and exhausted. They make children, especially orphan and poor ones, happy. Eids strengthen the feelings of friendship and kinship by awakening the spirituality of Muslims and carry the good traits such as compassion, mercy, loyalty, and empathy to their peak.

The following is such a good example that shows the cooperation and empathy between Muslims before the eid.

There was a man who did not have anything but a hundred dinars. When eid was approaching, one of his friends wrote him a letter and asked for his help saying:

"Eid is coming, but we do not have anything to satisfy the needs of the children." Upon that, that man put the hundred dinars in a money bag, sealed it, and sent it to his friend. When the man who asked for help got the money, this time he received a letter from one of his friends. The latter also wrote that he did not have enough money and asked for help to get his needs for the eid. So the man sent the money to his friend without even opening it.

The man who initially sent the money bag to his friend also wrote a letter to another one of his friends and asked for help. But this man was last man who got the dinars. Then, this man, too, sent the money to his friend without opening the seal. When the man who initially sent the dinars received the money bag and saw that this was his own sealed money bag, he was surprised. He went to his friend taking the money bag with him and asked:

"What is with this money bag you sent me?"

He explained the situation. Upon the clarification of the situation, he said:

"Let's go to the other friend of us."

They went to the other friend's place and talked about the situation and opened up the money bag and shared the money. (Hatib Bagdadi, *Tarihu Bagdad*, XIV, 282)

On the eid day, first we send our holiday wishes to our relatives who have already passed away and who are waiting for our prayers and rewards of giving alms in their names. Their souls get exalted by reciting the chapter al-Fatiha and giving alms in their names. By taking lessons from their situation, we realize that we need to get ready for the real eid. Then, we need to visit our relatives and friends and inquire after their health. Everybody forgives his rightful dues on each other and those who offended each other reconcile.

There are some things that Islam considers nice to be done on the eid days. Some of them are:

To wake up early on eid days, to perform *ghusl* (bath lustration), to clean the mouth by using a *miswaq*,[80] to wear nice fragrances, to put on clean and nice clothes, to be happy and cheerful to thank the blessings of Allah etc.

It is better to perform the eid prayer in an open and wide space. It is preferred that men, women, and children come to an open and wide place called Musalla.[81] Even women who could not perform the ritual prayer (due to menstruation) are advised to come and join this good deed and prayers of Muslims. That is because having the more people who attend the eid prayers the more it carries the meaning of showing strength of believers and exalting the religion of Allah.

It is sunnah to eat something sweet before going to prayer of Eid al-Fitr. The Messenger of Allah (pbuh) would not go to Eid Prayer without eating a few dates. In addition, he used to pay attention that the number of the dates would be odd such as three or five. (Bukhari, I'dain, 4)

---

80. *Translator's note:* Miswaq is a small stick from a special tree that was used widely to clean the teeth prior to the widespread usage of toothbrushes.

81. **Musalla/ Jamat khana:** An open-air place designated for prayer. Particularly, certain designated places away from residential centers, where eid prayers, prayers for rain (Salat al-Istisqa), and funeral prayers are held. This term is also used for the open-air prayer rooms built next to roadways for travelers to utilize. When the Messenger of Allah went for a long expedition, in places where he rested, a suitable place would be determined and this place would be cleaned and bordered with rocks and announced to be the musalla. In the Tabuk Expedition of the Prophet, fifteen of open-air musallas were made in various places. (Waqidi, III, 999; Ibn Hisham, IV, 179) The Messenger of Allah (pbuh) also established several musallas on the way to Mecca. (Bukhari, Salah, 49) This Sunnah (tradition of the Prophet) continued in the coming eras and sometimes musallahs became places where the army camped. (Nebi Bozkurt, "Namazgah", *Diyanet İslâm Ansiklopedisi*, XXXII, 357-358).

It is considered better not to eat anything until the end of the prayer of Eid al-Adha[82] and eat later from the meat of the sacrificed animal. That is because acting this way shows the importance and respect given to the sacrifice.[83]

Reciting Takbirs silently in Eid al-Fitr and audibly in Eid al-Adha, taking a different way if possible when returning from the Eid Prayer,[84] treating people in a friendly manner and saying nice things to Muslims when coming across them, and give alms as much as possible are among the beauties of the Eid.

Another issue is that the Prophet did not consider appropriate to carry weapons on Eid days in mosques, markets, and where people congregate when there is no danger of enemy. (Bukhari, I'dain, 9; Salah, 66, Fitan, 7; Muslim, Birr, 120-124; Ibn Majah, Iqamah, 168; Abdurrazzak, *Musannaf*, III, 289)

6. Zakat (Obligatory Alms)

٦١. عَنْ أَبِي هُرَيْرَةَ رَضِيَ اللهُ عَنْهُ أَنَّ النَّبِيَّ صَلَّى اللهُ عَلَيْهِ وَسَلَّمَ قَالَ:

«إِذَا أَدَّيْتَ زَكَاةَ مَالِكَ فَقَدْ قَضَيْتَ مَا عَلَيْكَ».

61. Abu Huraira (r.a.) narrated that the Noble Prophet (pbuh) said:

"When you pay the Zakat of your wealth, you would become paid your debt (responsibility)." (Tirmidhi, Zakat, 2/618)

❁

٦٢. عَنْ أَبِي هُرَيْرَةَ رَضِيَ اللهُ عَنْهُ قَالَ: قَالَ رَسُولُ اللهِ صَلَّى اللهُ عَلَيْهِ وَسَلَّمَ:

---

82. Translator's note: The religious festival day marking the completion of Al Hajj when Muslims remember and commemorate the trials and triumphs of the Prophet Abraham.

83. Shah Waliyyullah al-Dahlawi, *Hujjatullah al-baligha*, II, 79.

84. The Messenger of Allah (pbuh) used to use different roads when going to and returning from the Eid Prayers. (Bukhari, I'dain, 24)

«مَنْ آتَاهُ اللهُ مَالًا فَلَمْ يُؤَدِّ زَكَاتَهُ مُثِّلَ لَهُ يَوْمَ الْقِيَامَةِ شُجَاعًا أَقْرَعَ لَهُ زَبِيبَتَانِ يُطَوَّقُهُ يَوْمَ الْقِيَامَةِ ثُمَّ يَأْخُذُ بِلِهْزِمَتَيْهِ يَعْنِي شِدْقَيْهِ ثُمَّ يَقُولُ أَنَا مَالُكَ أَنَا كَنْزُكَ» ثُمَّ تَلَا (وَلَا يَحْسَبَنَّ الَّذِينَ يَبْخَلُونَ) اَلْآيَةَ.

62. Abu Huraira (r.a.) narrated that the Messenger of Allah (pbuh) said:

"If someone is made wealthy by Allah and that person does not pay the Zakat of his wealth, then on the Day of Resurrection his wealth will be made like a poisonous male snake with two black spots over the cheeks (which show the intensity of torment and poison). The snake will encircle the owner's neck and bite his both cheeks and say:

"I am your wealth, I am your treasure (that you loved a lot on Earth)!"

Then the Messenger of Allah (pbuh) recited the following noble verses as evidence to his words:

"And let not those who covetously withhold of the gifts which Allah has given them of His Grace, think that it is good for them: Nay, it will be the worse for them: soon shall the things which they covetously withheld be tied to their necks like a twisted collar, on the Day of Judgment. To Allah belongs the heritage of the heavens and the earth; and Allah is well-acquainted with all that you do." (Al-i-Imran; 3:180) (Bukhari, Zakat, 3)

Explanations:

Allah the Almighty, who provided His servants with various blessings, informed us that there is a share of the poor in our wealth.[85] This amount called zakat is not a charity that the wealthy gives out of their will but it is the right of the poor determined by Allah. Unless one gives this amount to its rightful owner, i.e. the poor, he would become liable. For this reason, in the first hadith, it is expressed that when we pay Zakat, we would pay our debt and be saved from this responsibility.

On the other hand, zakat is an expression of the thanks that the wealthy need to show for Allah's divine blessings that they have. Allah the Almighty

---

85.   Zariyat 51/19; Maarij 70/24-25.

informed us that when thanked He will increase His blessings and in the case of ungratefulness His torment will be harsh. (Ibrahim; 14:7)

While Allah makes us liable for paying the zakat, as always, He did not withhold His mercy from His servants and bestow His favor upon those who paid their zakat.

Above all, the word **"zakat"** means **"to purify"** and **"to increase."** Our Exalted Lord purifies the carnal selves of those who pay their zakat appropriately by obeying Allah's command from undesirable characteristics such as egoism, greediness, love of wealth and worldly goods and place them among His servants who have good moral characters. In addition to that, He increases their wealth by purifying it and deeming it permissible. In the following noble verses of the Qur'an, Allah says:

"Of their goods, take alms,[86] **that so you mightiest purify and sanctify them..."** (Al-Tawbah; 9:103)

"...and nothing do you spend in the least (in His cause) but He replaces it for He is the Best of those who grant Sustenance." (Al-Saba; 34:39)

After explaining who should give sadaqah al-Fitr and how much he should give, the Messenger of Allah (pbuh) said in support of this point:

"...Those of you who are rich will be purified by Allah, and those of you who are poor will have more than they gave returned by Him to them." (Abu Dawud, Zakat, 21/1619)

It is known to everyone that the wealth of the sincere and generous people who give the zakat of their wealth and help the poor increases day by day for unforeseen reasons. It is unquestionable that the happiness of the poor has a great effect in this increase.

Also in one of the ahadith that we mentioned under the title of **"Delightfulness of Faith,"** it is expressed that those who pay zakat out of their wealth with peace of heart and use for this purpose the mid-quality goods instead of

---

86.   The term "Sadaqa" in Quran and hadith sometimes means "Zakat." Since the zakat indicates the sincerity (sadaqat) and maturity of the giver, it is also called "Sadaqa." As a matter of fact:

The hadith of "Sadaqa is evidence" points out this fact. (Muslim, Taharat, 1) However, while sadaqah is used for obligatory (*fard*) and supererogatory (*nafilah*) monetary worships, the term zakat is only used for obligatory ones.

the worst quality ones will experience the delight of faith. (Abu Dawud, Zakat, 5/1582)

As there are many personal benefits of giving zakat, there are also indispensable functions of zakat in terms of social order. Zakat is a bridge between people of the society who are at different financial levels and it ensures social unity. It minimizes the gap between the poor and the rich. By decreasing number of the poor, zakat prevents many unpleasant acts that can take place because of financial distress. It prevents the feelings that may take root in the hearts of the poor against rich people such as jealousy and hatred. Zakat brings people together by fastening the bonds of love, respect, and brotherhood. For this reason, the Messenger of Allah (pbuh) said:

"Zakat is the bridge of Islam." (Baihaqi, *Shuab*, III, 20, 195; Haythami, III, 62)

This hadith also implies that zakat will be a bridge in the Hereafter. As narrated by Qatadah;

"Zakat is a bridge between Hell and Paradise. Whoever pays their zakat crosses the bridge and goes to Paradise." (Abdurrazzak, *Musannaf*, IV, 108)

When zakat is not paid, all these benefits are reversed and big losses take place both for the individual and the society. **In the second hadith**, the sad aftermath is explained. While the example given in this hadith expresses the torment in the Hereafter, it also describes the uneasiness of those who do not perform their responsibility of giving zakat. Those who spare their wealth from Allah which Allah has bestowed upon them and those who as a result get morally corrupted would neither be happy in this world nor in the hereafter. As the illness of greediness that is not cured by giving zakat puts one in a difficult situation in this world, it also leaves him with the poisons of the snakes in the Hereafter.

The Messenger of Allah (pbuh) said the following about this harmful illness:

"Is there a worse illness than greediness?!" (Bukhari, *Al-Adabul Mufrad*, no: 296. Also see Bukhari, Humus, 15, Maghazi, 73; Ahmad, III, 308)

"The most harmful thing that exists in a human is being extremely greedy and intense fear." (Abu Dawud, Jihad, 20/2511)

In another hadith, the Prophet listed greediness among the features that cause destruction. (Munawi, III, 404/3471)

Is it possible to be comfortable and peaceful for those who are struggling in the claws of greediness by not giving their zakat and therefore accumulating the rights and envy of others in their wealth? Those who live distant from love and prayer in this world are of course going to receive the harshest penalty in the Hereafter. As they cannot benefit from their wealth in this world, more than what they could have paid as their zakat will be taken from them due to various causes.

As the number of those who act reluctant in paying their zakat, zakat may start to be seen as a heavy burden in the society and get forgotten all together in time. The Messenger of Allah (pbuh) informed us that the societies that come to this situation would receive some kind of punishment.[87] Once he said:

"Societies that neglect their Zakat will indeed be deprived of rain and if they did not have animals, they would totally be deprived of rain." (Ibn Majah, Fitan, 22; Hakim, IV, 583/8623)

In other words, when zakat is not paid, Allah withholds His blessings from the society. The rain and other blessings are given for the sake of Servants of Allah who bow down to worship, who are innocent, and for animals. As zakat is neglected, deep gaps emerge between the rich and the poor which endangers the social order. This leads many needy people to do wrong things. As a result, neither rich nor poor would live in peace. Drawing our attention to this danger, Allah the Almighty says:

"And spend of your substance in the cause of Allah,[88] and make not your own hands contribute to (your) destruction; but do good; for Allah loves those who do good." (Al-Baqarah; 2:195)

Those mentioned hitherto are the harms of neglecting zakat in respect to this world. On the other hand, as partially mentioned in the hadith, we are informed that the punishment in the Hereafter will be very harsh. Allah the Almighty says:

87. Tirmidhi, Fitan, 38/2210, 2211.
88. The term "infaq" covers the obligatory zakat and all kinds of volunteered good deeds. (Mustafa Çağrıcı, "İnfak", *Diyanet İslâm Ansiklopedisi*, XXII, 289)

"…And there are those who burry gold and silver and spend it not in the way of Allah, announce unto them a most grievous penalty on the Day when heat will be produced out of that (wealth) in the fire of Hell, and with it will be branded their foreheads, their flanks, and their backs: "This is the (treasure) which you buried for yourselves: taste you, then, the (treasures) you buried!"" (Al-Tawbah; 9:34-35)

There are many ahadith on this topic. One of them is:

A woman came to the Messenger of Allah (pbuh) and she was accompanied by her daughter who wore two heavy gold bangles in her hands.

The Messenger of Allah (pbuh) asked to the woman:

Do you pay zakat on them?

She said:

No.

He then said:

"Are you pleased that Allah may put two bangles of fire on your hands?" [89]

Thereupon she took them off and placed them before the Prophet (pbuh) saying:

"They are for Allah and His Apostle." (Abu Dawud, Zakat, 4/1563)

So, a believer should pay his zakat with peace of mind before it is too late and before he regrets it. Otherwise, it will come a time that he would have missed the opportunity and cannot pay his zakat even though he wants to. He will become sorry in regret and yearn. As a matter of fact, Ibn Abbas (r.a.) said:

"Whoever would earn enough money to go to pilgrimage or pay zakat and do not fulfill these obligatory acts would ask to go back the world at the time of their death" and recited the following verses:

"O you who believe! Let not your riches or your children divert you from the remembrance of Allah. If any act thus, the loss is their own and spend something (in charity) out of the substance which We have bestowed on you, before death should come to any of you and he should say, "O my

---

89. There is a disagreement among Muslim scholars regarding zakat on jewelry. It would be more prudent to pay zakat out of jewelry.

Lord! Why did You not give me respite for a little while? I should then have given (largely) in charity, and I should have been one of the doers of good". But to no soul will Allah grant respite when the time appointed (for it) has come; and Allah is well acquainted with (all) that you do." (Al-Munafiqun; 63:9-11) (Tirmidhi, Tafsir, 63/3316)

7. Sadaqah (Charity) and Infaq (Donating)

a. Abundance in Infaq

٦٣. عَنْ أَبِي هُرَيْرَةَ رَضِيَ اللهُ عَنْهُ أَنَّ رَسُولَ اللهِ صَلَّى اللهُ عَلَيْهِ وَسَلَّمَ قَالَ:

«قَالَ اللهُ عَزَّ وَجَلَّ: (أَنْفِقْ أُنْفِقْ عَلَيْكَ) وَقَالَ يَدُ اللهِ مَلْأَى لَا تَغِيضُهَا نَفَقَةٌ سَحَّاءُ اللَّيْلَ وَالنَّهَارَ وَقَالَ أَرَأَيْتُمْ مَا أَنْفَقَ مُنْذُ خَلَقَ السَّمَاءَ وَالْأَرْضَ فَإِنَّهُ لَمْ يَغِضْ مَا فِي يَدِهِ».

63. Abu Huraira (r.a.) narrated that the Messenger of Allah (pbuh) said:

"Allah said, 'Spend (O man), and I shall spend on you.' Allah's hand [treasures] is full, and (its fullness) is not affected by the continuous spending night and day. Do you see what He has spent since He created the Heavens and the Earth? Neverthe-less, what is in His Hand is not decreased." (Bukhari, Tafsir, 11/2; Tawhid, 22)

٦٤. عَنْ أَبِي هُرَيْرَةَ رَضِيَ اللهُ عَنْهُ قَالَ: قَالَ رَسُولُ اللهِ صَلَّى اللهُ عَلَيْهِ وَسَلَّمَ:

«مَنْ تَصَدَّقَ بِعَدْلِ تَمْرَةٍ مِنْ كَسْبٍ طَيِّبٍ وَلَا يَقْبَلُ اللهُ إِلَّا الطَّيِّبَ وَإِنَّ اللهَ يَتَقَبَّلُهَا بِيَمِينِهِ ثُمَّ يُرَبِّيهَا لِصَاحِبِهِ كَمَا يُرَبِّي أَحَدُكُمْ فَلُوَّهُ حَتَّى تَكُونَ مِثْلَ الْجَبَلِ».

64. Abu Huraira (r.a.) narrated that the Messenger of Allah (pbuh) said:

"If one gives in charity what equals one date-fruit from the honestly-earned money --and Allah accepts only the honestly earned money,– then Allah takes it in His right (hand) and then enlarges its reward for that person (who has given it), as anyone of you rears his foal, until it becomes as big as a mountain." (Bukhari, Zakat, 8; Tawhid, 23; Muslim, Zakat, 63, 64. Also see Tirmidhi, Zakat, 28/661, Nasai, Zakat, 48/2523; Ibn Majah, Zakat, 28)

٦٥. عَنْ خُرَيْمِ بْنِ فَاتِكٍ رَضِيَ اللهُ عَنْهُ قَالَ: قَالَ رَسُولُ اللهِ صَلَّى اللهُ عَلَيْهِ وَسَلَّمَ:

«مَنْ أَنْفَقَ نَفَقَةً فِي سَبِيلِ اللهِ كُتِبَتْ لَهُ بِسَبْعِمِائَةِ ضِعْفٍ».

65. Huraym b. Fatiq (r.a.) narrated that the Messenger of Allah (pbuh) said:

"Those who spend his wealth on Allah's cause receive divine rewards as much as seven hundred times of what they spent." (Tirmidhi, Fadail al-Jihad, 4/1625; Nasai, Jihad, 45/3184)

٦٦. عَنْ عَائِشَةَ رَضِيَ اللهُ عَنْهَا: أَنَّهُمْ ذَبَحُوا شَاةً فَقَالَ النَّبِيُّ صَلَّى اللهُ عَلَيْهِ وَسَلَّمَ:

«مَا بَقِيَ مِنْهَا؟» قَالَتْ:

«مَا بَقِيَ مِنْهَا إِلَّا كَتِفُهَا» قَالَ:

«بَقِيَ كُلُّهَا غَيْرَ كَتِفِهَا».

66. Aisha narrated that the family of the Messenger of Allah sacrificed a sheep. The Messenger of Allah (pbuh) asked:

"What is left from it?"

Aisha (r.a.) answered:

"Only its scapula"

Upon that, Prophet (pbuh) said:

"In fact, except the shoulder blade, the whole sheep is here!" (Tirmidhi, Qiyamah, 33/2470)

Explanations:

Allah the Almighty gave us everything that we need[90] and wanted us to let others benefit from these blessings. For this reason, while making to give one fortieth of the wealth obligatory as zakat, He kept the door of Sadaqah (charity) open for those who want to give more and earn more divine rewards. As long as one does not put himself and those who depend on him in a difficult position, he can give alms as much as wants and is encouraged to do so. The Messenger of Allah (pbuh) even said:

"In one's wealth, there are rights other than zakat." (Tirmidhi, Zakat, 27/659-660. Also see Al-Baqarah; 2:177)

One day, the Messenger of Allah (pbuh) told the wisdom and virtues of infaq (giving) and gave the following speech to his companions:

"O people, give charity! O people give charity so that I can be witness to your faith on the Day of Judgment with it. Maybe when one of you and the offspring of his camels are full and comfortable, his nephew might be cringed from hunger. Maybe when the trees of one of you give nice fruits and increase his wealth his neighbor might be a poor person who does not have anything. Isn't there a man who can give one of his camels as charity so it gives milk to poor in the morning and evening and be a blessing to them? Be careful! The reward of this is huge." (Alusi, X, 146, [Al-Tawbah; 9:79]; Ali al-Muttaqi, no: 16181)

---

90. According to Islam, the real owner of the wealth that humans own is Allah. One must give charity from this wealth which He gave it temperorarly to test him. (Al-Nur (Light) 24:33; Hadid (Iron)57:7; Al-Baqara (The Cow) 2:3; Al-Ra'd (The Thunder) 13:22)

In many hadith, we are given the good news that those who give charity will not be deprived of anything and will definitely be compensated by calling the divine mercy and receive blessings. **In the first hadith,** expressing this, the Messenger of Allah (pbuh) encourages and motivates people to give charity by saying that the treasures of our Exalted Lord will never end. In another hadith, he said:

"There are three things that I can swear to:

1. Sadaqah (charity) does not in any way decrease the wealth of a servant.

2. Allah advances the honor of those who are patient to unfairness done to them.

3. Allah opens the door of poverty for those who open the door of begging." (Tirmidhi, Zuhd, 17/2325. Also see Muslim, Birr, 69)

Then, one should absolutely not be afraid of giving charity asking for rewards only from Allah. As a matter of fact, for sure Allah the Almighty, while continuously giving charity at all times to His servants can give more to those who give alms. In a verse, it is stated in the Qur'an that:

"Allah will deprive usury of all blessing, but will give increase for deeds of charity: For He loves not creatures ungrateful and wicked." (Al-Baqarah; 2:276)

Ali's (r.a.) advice deals with the same issue:

"When you get poor, give alms as if you make trade with Allah, so that He will give you more." (Sharif al-Radi', *Nahj al-Balagha,* no: 258)

Pointing out the blessings in charity Abu Mas'ud al-Ansari (r.a.) says:

"When the Messenger of Allah (pbuh) ordered us to give in charity, we used to go to the market and work as porters and get a Mudd[91] and then give it in charity. (Those were the days of poverty) and today some of us have one hundred thousand (dinars)." (Bukhari, Zakat, 10)

Besides the material benefits of giving alms, there are also many spiritual blessings. This issue is clearly explained in **the second hadith.** Even if the thing given as charity is something small, Allah the Almighty increases its divine

91. **Mudd** is a special measurement of weight which is about 687 gr.

rewards, and advances it unimaginably and responds with incomparable blessings. This situation shows that Allah gets very pleased when alms and charities are given. As a matter of fact, in order to express this, it is said that Allah receives the alms with His right hand. The phrase "right hand" is an expression that means Allah accepts alms with pleasure. Otherwise, Allah does not resemble any creature.

Another report that shows how Allah gets pleased with those who give alms is as follows:

"Before the alms are received by poor, they get received by Allah the Exalted. Because of the alms given, apart from the rewards that will be given in the Hereafter for those who give the alms, Allah also closes the doors of seventy disasters in this world. Leprosy, skin discoloration diseases, and some other serious illnesses are among them." (Abu Nuaym, *Hilya*, IV, 81. Also see Haythami, III, 110, 111; Ali al-Muttaqi, VI, 377/16134)

Another hadith that expresses Allah's pleasure when alms are given and informs of its rewards in the Hereafter is as follows:

"If any Muslim clothes a Muslim when he is naked, Allah will clothe him with some green garments of Paradise; if any Muslim feeds a Muslim when he is hungry, Allah will feed him with some of the fruits of Paradise; and if any Muslim gives a Muslim drink when he is thirsty, Allah will give him some of the pure wine which is sealed to drink." (Abu Dawud, Zakat, 41/1682; Tirmidhi, Qiyamah, 18/2449; Ahmad, III, 13)

Once the Messenger of Allah (pbuh) said in order to explain the broad and comprehensive blessings of charity:

"Allah the Exalted puts three people into His paradise in return for a morsel of bread, couple of dates, and other things that the poor can benefit from:

1. The owner of the house and the person who ordered to give these to the poor,

2. The wife who prepares the things that are given,

3. The helper who takes the alms to the poor."

After stating this, the Messenger of Allah (pbuh) completed his words saying:

"Many thanks to Allah who does not forget anyone of us!" (Haythami, III, 112)

On the other hand, giving out of wealth and life strenghtens the spirituality of a person and enriches his character. While people feel overwhelmed by taking something from others, they get elevated by the things that they give. Therefore, giving alms and treating others with respect helps a person to mature his spiritual life.

There is another important issue that must be expressed here. Above all, the Messenger of Allah (pbuh) emphasized that alms should be given out of an income that is rightfully earned. This is because the rightful earning is the essence of happiness both in this world and in the hereafter. In one of his sayings, Allah's Messenger (pbuh) explained this condition as follows:

"...If a person earns an income from a prohibited way (haram) and if he spends it, he does not benefit from it; and if he gives alms from this income, his charity does not get accepted by Allah. The share that he leaves behind only gets him closer to the Fire. That is because Allah does not erase wrongdoings with other wrongdoing, but only with goodness. For sure, something evil does not exterminate another evil thing." (Ahmad, I, 387)

As it can be understood from **our third hadith**, the best charity is the one done in the way of Allah, in other words to glorify His religion and deliver His message to others. The rewards and blessings given to such charity are expressed in the hadith by a term indicating abundance. Or that number shows the minimum level. As a matter of fact, Allah gives much more rewards or even uncountable rewards to those whom He wishes. This is expressed in a noble verse of the Qur'an as:

"The parable of those who spend their substance in the way of Allah is that of a grain of corn: it grows seven ears, and each ear has a hundred grains. Allah gives manifold increase to whom He pleases and Allah cares for all and He knows all things." (Al-Baqarah; 2:261)

Giving charity not only increases the wealth but also saves it from being destroyed by perpetuating it. Wealth is always under the risk of being destroyed in the hands of humans. Even if it stays safe, it might be spent unnecessarily and turn into a sin. Even the wealth spent by the owner himself is considered lost, wasted, or luxury if it does not get spent appropriately. When it comes to wealth that is given as charity, it will be protected in the sight of Allah and turn into a capital for eternal life depending upon the level of sincerity of the donor. Indeed **in our forth hadith**, the Messenger of Allah (pbuh) explained this issue in its best form. In other words, the wealth that is given as charity becomes ours and the wealth spent is lost from us most of the time.

Allah the Almighty says:

"…Whatever of good you give benefits your own souls, and you shall only do so seeking the "Face" of Allah. Whatever good you give, shall be rendered back to you, and you shall not be dealt with unjustly." (Al-Baqarah; 2:272)

On the other hand, sadaqah (charity) prevents many troubles, both material and spiritual. Some of them are stated in various ahadith as follows:

"As the water extinguishes fire, sadaqah extinguishes torment of the sins." (Tirmidhi, Iman, 8/2616. Also see Ibn Majah, Fitan, 12)

"Sadaqah extinguishes the anger of the Lord and protects one from dying in a bad condition." (Tirmidhi, Zakat, 28/664)

"The sadaqah that a Muslim gives lengthens his life time, prevents unfortunate dying, and Allah prevents arrogance, poverty, and pride with it." (Haythami, III, 110)

"Until everyone is judged (on the Day of Judgment), everyone will wait under the shade of the sadaqah that they have given."

Abu'l Hayr, one of the narrators of this hadith, did his best to give a sadaqah every day even if it is a piece of cake, onion, or something small like these… (Ahmad, IV, 147-8; Haythami, III, 110)

In another hadith the Messenger of Allah (pbuh) said:

"Sadaqah extinguishes the heat of the grave for its donor. A believer takes a shade under the sadaqah he has given on the Day of Judgment." (Haythami, III, 110)

"Hurry in giving sadaqah! For trouble cannot pass before sadaqah." (Haythami, III, 110)

According to what the Prophet informed us, a group of people visited Isa (Jesus) (pbuh) and he said to them:

"One of you will die today if Allah wishes."

They went and came back to Jesus (pbuh) in the evening with woodpiles on their shoulders. He said:

"Drop the woodpiles!"

Then he said to the man whom had said that he was going to die:

"Untie the woodpile!"

As soon as the man untied it, a black snake appeared. Jesus (pbuh) asked:

"What good deed have you done today?"

The man said:

"I did not do any good deed today."

Jesus (pbuh) said:

"Think one more time, what did you do?"

Then, the man said:

"I did not do anything, but I had a piece of bread. Then, there came a poor man and asked for something. I shared my bread with him."

Upon this, Jesus (pbuh) said:

"Well, in this way, you had been protected from that trouble." (Haythami, III, 109-110; Ahmad, *Zuhd,* I, 96)

The Companions of the Prophet (pbuh) used to compete with each other in helping others and giving charity. The following story is an exemplary incident speaking to this fact:

Umar (r.a.) narrated:

The Messenger of Allah (pbuh) commanded us to give charity. I was wealthy at the time. I said to myself 'If I ever have a chance to exceed Abu Bakr, this will be the day' and gave half of my wealth to the Messenger of Allah.

The Messenger of Allah (pbuh) asked:

"What did you leave for your family?"

"I left as much as what I brought here" I said.

Abu Bakr (r.a.) brought all of his wealth.

The Messenger of Allah (pbuh) asked:

"Abu Bakr, what did you leave for your children and family?"

Abu Bakr (r.a.) answered:

"Allah and His Messenger."

Then, I said to myself "I swear to Allah that I cannot exceed him in any matter!" (Tirmidhi, Manaqib, 16/3675)

b. To Hurry up in Giving Charity

٦٧. عَنْ أُمِّ سَلَمَةَ قَالَتْ: دَخَلَ عَلَيَّ رَسُولُ اللهِ صَلَّى اللهُ عَلَيْهِ وَسَلَّمَ وَهُوَ سَاهِمُ الْوَجْهِ قَالَتْ فَحَسِبْتُ أَنَّ ذٰلِكَ مِنْ وَجَعٍ فَقُلْتُ:

«يَا نَبِيَّ اللهِ مَا لَكَ سَاهِمُ الْوَجْهِ؟» قَالَ:

«مِنْ أَجْلِ الدَّنَانِيرِ السَّبْعَةِ الَّتِي أَتَتْنَا أَمْسِ. أَمْسَيْنَا وَهِيَ فِي خُصْمِ الْفِرَاشِ».

67. Ummu Salama (r.a.) narrated:

One day, the Messenger of Allah (pbuh) came to me and the color of his face was changed. I thought that he had an ache and asked:

"O Messenger of Allah, what happened, why is you face like that, its color has changed?"

Allah's Messenger (pbuh) said:

"I am in this state because of the seven dinars that we received yesterday. It is almost evening and they are still under the bad (we did not have a chance to donate them yet!)" (Ahmad, VI, 293; Haythami, X, 238)

٦٨. عَنْ عُقْبَةَ رَضِيَ اللهُ عَنْهُ قَالَ: صَلَّيْتُ وَرَاءَ النَّبِيِّ صَلَّى اللهُ عَلَيْهِ وَسَلَّمَ بِالْمَدِينَةِ الْعَصْرَ فَسَلَّمَ ثُمَّ قَامَ مُسْرِعًا فَتَخَطَّى رِقَابَ النَّاسِ إِلَى بَعْضِ حُجَرِ نِسَائِهِ فَفَزِعَ النَّاسُ مِنْ سُرْعَتِهِ فَخَرَجَ عَلَيْهِمْ فَرَأَى أَنَّهُمْ عَجِبُوا مِنْ سُرْعَتِهِ قَالَ:

«ذَكَرْتُ شَيْئًا مِنْ تِبْرٍ عِنْدَنَا فَكَرِهْتُ أَنْ يَحْبِسَنِي فَأَمَرْتُ بِقِسْمَتِهِ».

68. Uqba (r.a.) narrated:

Once in Medina, I prayed the late afternoon prayer led by the Messenger of Allah. When the Messenger of Allah (pbuh) finished the prayer by giving a salutation, he suddenly stood up and went to one of his wives' room. The Companions worried about Prophet's rush. A while later, the Messenger of Allah (pbuh) returned. He recognized that the congregation got worried after him and so he said:

"I remembered that there was some gold - or silver – in our room and that bothered me so I ordered them to be given as charity." (Bukhari, Adhan, 158; al-Amal fi al-Salah, 18; Nasai, Sahw, 104/1363)

❁

٦٩. عَنْ أَبِي هُرَيْرَةَ رَضِيَ اللهُ عَنْهُ قَالَ: جَاءَ رَجُلٌ إِلَى النَّبِيِّ صَلَّى اللهُ عَلَيْهِ وَسَلَّمَ فَقَالَ:

«يَا رَسُولَ اللهِ أَيُّ الصَّدَقَةِ أَعْظَمُ أَجْرًا؟» قَالَ:

«أَنْ تَصَدَّقَ وَأَنْتَ صَحِيحٌ شَحِيحٌ تَخْشَى الْفَقْرَ وَتَأْمُلُ الْغِنَى وَلاَ تُمْهِلْ حَتَّى إِذَا بَلَغَتِ الْحُلْقُومَ قُلْتَ لِفُلاَنٍ كَذَا وَلِفُلاَنٍ كَذَا وَقَدْ كَانَ لِفُلاَنٍ».

69. Abu Huraira (r.a.) said:

A man came to the Prophet and asked:

"O Allah's Apostle! Which charity is the most superior in reward?"

The Messenger of Allah replied:

"The charity which you practice while you are healthy, niggardly and afraid of poverty and wish to become wealthy. Do not delay it to the time of approaching death and then say, "Give so much to such and such, and so much to such and such." And it has already belonged to such and such (as it is too late)." (Bukhari, Zakat, 11; Wasaya, 17; Muslim, Zakat, 92)

❊

٧٠. عَنْ أَبِي سَعِيدٍ الْخُدْرِيّ أَنَّ رَسُولَ اللهِ صَلَّى اللهُ عَلَيْهِ وَسَلَّمَ قَالَ:

«لَأَنْ يَتَصَدَّقَ الْمَرْءُ فِي حَيَاتِهِ بِدِرْهَمٍ خَيْرٌ لَهُ مِنْ أَنْ يَتَصَدَّقَ بِمِائَةِ دِرْهَمٍ عِنْدَ مَوْتِهِ».

70. Abu Sa'id al-Khudri (r.a.) narrated that the Messenger of Allah (pbuh) said the following:

"A man giving a dirham as sadaqah (charity) during his life is better than giving one hundred dirhams as sadaqah (charity) at the moment of his death." (Abu Dawud, Wasaya, 3/2866)

Explanations:

Sadaqah (charity) is considered the best way of doing goodness because of its benefits to individuals and the society. Indeed under the previous title, we have mentioned many narratives concerning the blessings and benefits of sadaqah. Therefore, one must hurry to benefit from such an important act of worship. This was one of the distinguishing attributes of the Messenger of Allah, who was always the leading figure in all good deeds. In **the first and second hadith**, we have seen examples of how the Messenger of Allah used to hurry in giving charity. When the planned charity is postponed, the Messenger of Allah (pbuh) got worried and he got up and went home leaving the congregation right after the prayer even if he did not typically used to act in this way. He explained the reason for this when he returned as:

"I remembered that there were some goods in our room saved to be given as charity, and I hastened to order that they should be distributed among the poor so that it would not prevent me to turn to Allah, and also I should not worry about giving the account of postponing it on the Judgment Day."

One should hurry when he intends to do a good deed.For disasters may ruin the wealth or other obstacles may come up. Most important of all, no one knows when death will come. Therefore, it is not right to postpone performing good deeds and thinking about doing it later. Another point is that everything is better in their times; they would not have any value after their time passes. Because of this, our ancestors said "do not postpone the good deed of the morning to the night!"

In various occasions, the Messenger of Allah (pbuh) forbade walking in hurry in the mosques and stepping on the shoulders of those who are sitting. However, it is understood from the second hadith that he encouraged to hurry in giving charity and performing good deeds. This explains how much one should hurry in performing good deeds and giving charities.

One of the most important benefits of the charity is to beautify human soul by purifying it and to strengthen the donor's faith. One needs this benefit of sadaqah most during his youth and prime years. Young people who are in the best years of their life think that they should earn more to raise their kids. For this reason, they tend to save more and be stingy. Satan also scares one with poverty and discourages giving sadaqah and charity (Al-Baqarah; 2:268)

To be able to give charity by opposing the inner self in such feelings is something hard to accomplish. It is also considered as the best type of sadaqah since it is very influential in disciplining the inner self. On the other hand charity given in this period of life shows that the person prefers the Hereafter over this world and performs his deeds with a tranquil heart and sincerity. The good deeds postponed to a time when all hopes are gone indicate that the person acted selfish and preferred himself over his heirs. Their benefits would be little even if Allah rewards them. That is because they have seen the end of the tunnel and lost their hopes from this world.

If someone gives alms in his young age by overcoming all of the difficulties, he benefits more but if he postpones it to the last minute, he loses. That is because death may catch him before he gets a chance to give alms. After that, even if he wants to give alms, he can not make others listen to him. As a matter of fact, his wealth would already be about to change hands. Now, the wealth that he has not spent due to his greed and love had fallen into hands of others' ambitions and desires. Therefore, a smart person should hurry in performing good deeds when his health is alright and prepare himself for the Hereafter. If a person does not personally do a good deed, he should not expect others to do it on his behalf. What did he do for his ancestors to deserve to expect something from his heirs? One must not forget that wealth spent in the way of Allah is his real wealth and the wealth saved for himself becomes others' at the very end.

The following narration is so meaningful and supports our point:

The Messenger of Allah (pbuh) said:

"Allah the Almighty says:

"O Son of Adam! How would you think that you could incapacitate Me?! As a matter of fact, I have created you from a spit of water and shaped you in a perfect and the most appropriate form in every aspect. You have walked on earth in greed and arrogance within embellished clothing. You have buried your children alive. (In other words, you have committed such major sins) You have saved wealth and did not share it. You say "I give charity" at your last breath. Is this the time to give charity?" (Ahmad, IV, 210. Also see Ibn Majah, Wasaya, 4; Hakim, II, 545/3855)

Since the mystery of testing starts to become clear at the last moments of one's life, the time for some acts ends and the deeds that were very valuable before do not mean a lot anymore. Pointing out to this side of the issue, the Messenger of Allah (pbuh) informed us that the sadaqah given at the death bed is not even as valuable as one hundredth of a charity given on time.

The Messenger of Allah (pbuh) described those who come to their senses at the last minute as follows:

"A man who emancipates a slave (or gives charity) at the time of his death is like a man who gives the remaining food as present after satisfying his appetite." (Abu Dawud, Kitab Al-'Itq, 15/3968; Tirmidhi, Wasaya, 7/2123)

Usage of the term "to give as a present" is to show how ridiculous the situation of such people is. That is because those people think only themselves with selfish feelings, and accept to share things with others only when they are full and satisfied and do not need them anymore.

Another important issue regarding charity ordered to be given at the death bed is that such charity becomes a will. A person who wants to give charity in this state has the right of use only in one third of his wealth. Transactions exceeding this limit require the permission of the heirs. Besides, it is not permissible to give charity just to harm the heirs even if the amount does not exceed one third of the wealth. **The Righteous Predecessors (*Salaf al-Salihin*)** said about those who like to show off and act wastefully:

"They rebel against Allah twice with their wealth. First, they are acting stingily when they have the money in this world. Second, they are wasting their wealth by distributing it on their death bed after they have already lost their right over it." (Ibn Hajar, *Fath al-Bari,* V, 374/2597)

The following noble verse from the Qur'an is so alarming and eye-opening. It expresses the regret of those at the time of death who did not give charity in time and earn rewards for Hereafter:

"And spend something (in charity) out of the substance which We have bestowed on you, before death should come to any of you and he should say, "O my Lord! Why did You not give me respite for a little while? I should then have given (largely) in charity, and I should have been one of the doers of good."" (Al-Munafiqun; 63:10)

Apart from that, if a good heir comes and gives charity on behalf of his ancestors, Allah accepts that as well:

According to the narration of Abdurrahman bin Abi Amra, once his mother had wanted to emancipate a slave and postponed it till the next morning. However, she had passed away before the morning. Abdurrahman came to Qasim b. Muhammad and asked:

"If I emancipate a slave in the name of my mother, would she benefit from it?"

Qasim answered:

"Once Sa'd bin Ubada came to the Messenger of Allah and asked:

"My mother passed away and if I emancipate a slave in her name, would she benefit from it?"

The Messenger of Allah (pbuh) said:

"Yes!" (*Muwatta*, Kitab Al-'Itq, 13)

Aisha (r.anha) narrated that a person came to the Messenger of Allah and asked:

"My mother unexpectedly passed away. I believe that if she could talk she would give charity. Can I give charity in her name?"

The Messenger of Allah (pbuh) said:

"Yes, give charity in her name!" (Bukhari, Wasaya, 19; Abu Dawud, Wasaya, 15/2881)

c. The Manners of Giving Charity

٧١. عَنْ عَوْفِ بْنِ مَالِكٍ قَالَ: دَخَلَ عَلَيْنَا رَسُولُ اللهِ صَلَّى اللهُ عَلَيْهِ وَسَلَّمَ الْمَسْجِدَ وَبِيَدِهِ عَصًا وَقَدْ عَلَّقَ قَنَا حَشَفًا فَطَعَنَ بِالْعَصَا فِي ذٰلِكَ الْقِنْوِ وَقَالَ:

«لَوْ شَاءَ رَبُّ هٰذِهِ الصَّدَقَةِ تَصَدَّقَ بِأَطْيَبَ مِنْهَا» وَقَالَ: «إِنَّ رَبَّ هٰذِهِ الصَّدَقَةِ يَأْكُلُ الْحَشَفَ يَوْمَ الْقِيَامَةِ».

71. Awf ibn Malik narrated: The Messenger of Allah (pbuh) entered the masjid where we were, and he had a stick in his hand. A man had hung there a bunch of low quality dried dates. He probed the bunch with the stick, and said:

"If the owner of this sadaqah (alms) wished to give a better one than this, he could have done it. The owner of this sadaqah will eat low quality dates on the Day of Judgment." (Abu Dawud, Zakat, 17/1608)

٧٢. عَنْ أَبِي ذَرٍّ قَالَ: قُلْتُ:

«يَا نَبِيَّ الله فَأَيُّ الصَّدَقَةِ أَفْضَلُ؟» قَالَ:

«سِرٌّ إِلَى فَقِيرٍ وَجُهْدٌ مِنْ مُقِلٍّ».

72. Abu Dhar (r.a.) narrated:

I asked the Messenger of Allah:

"O the Messenger of Allah! Which sadaqah is more virtuous?"

The Messenger of Allah (pbuh) said:

"The one that is given to the poor secretly and what a man with little property can afford to give" (Ahmad, V, 265, 178-179. Also see Abu Dawud, Zakat, 40/1677)

٧٣. عَنْ أَنَسِ بْنِ مَالِكٍ عَنِ النَّبِيِّ صَلَّى اللهُ عَلَيْهِ وَسَلَّمَ قَالَ:

«لَمَّا خَلَقَ اللهُ الْأَرْضَ جَعَلَتْ تَمِيدُ فَخَلَقَ الْجِبَالَ فَعَادَ بِهَا عَلَيْهَا فَاسْتَقَرَّتْ فَعَجِبَتِ الْمَلَائِكَةُ مِنْ شِدَّةِ الْجِبَالِ قَالُوا: يَا رَبِّ هَلْ مِنْ خَلْقِكَ شَيْءٌ أَشَدُّ مِنَ الْجِبَالِ؟ قَالَ: نَعَمِ الْحَدِيدُ قَالُوا: يَا رَبِّ فَهَلْ مِنْ خَلْقِكَ شَيْءٌ أَشَدُّ مِنَ الْحَدِيدِ؟ قَالَ: نَعَمِ النَّارُ فَقَالُوا: يَا رَبِّ فَهَلْ مِنْ خَلْقِكَ شَيْءٌ أَشَدُّ مِنَ النَّارِ؟ قَالَ: نَعَمِ الْمَاءُ قَالُوا: يَا رَبِّ فَهَلْ مِنْ خَلْقِكَ شَيْءٌ أَشَدُّ مِنَ الْمَاءِ؟ قَالَ: نَعَمِ الرِّيحُ قَالُوا: يَا رَبِّ فَهَلْ مِنْ خَلْقِكَ شَيْءٌ أَشَدُّ مِنَ الرِّيحِ؟ قَالَ: نَعَمِ ابْنُ آدَمَ تَصَدَّقَ بِصَدَقَةٍ بِيَمِينِهِ يُخْفِيهَا مِنْ شِمَالِهِ».

73. Anas bin Malik (r.a.) narrated that the Messenger of Allah (pbuh) said:

153

"When Allah the Exalted has created the Earth, it started to shake. Upon that Allah has created mountains and placed them on earth and stabilized it. Angels were fascinated with the power of the mountains. They asked:

"O our Lord, have You created a more powerful creature than mountains?" Allah said:

"Yes, I have created the iron."

"O our Lord, have You created something more powerful than the iron?" they asked. Allah the Exalted said:

"Yes, I have created the fire." They asked:

"O our Lord, have You created something more powerful than the fire?" Allah the Exalted said:

"Yes, I have created the water!"

"O our Lord, have You created something more powerful than the water?" they asked and He answered:

"Yes, I have created the wind." They asked:

"O our Lord, have You created something that is more powerful than the wind?" Allah said:

"Yes, I have created the humankind. If he gives charity with his right hand and keeps it secret even from his left hand, (he becomes more powerful than all of the mentioned above)." (Tirmidhi, Tafsir, 113-114/3369; Baihaqi, *Shuab*, III, 244)

Explanations:

Since the charity given for the sake of Allah reaches Allah before it reaches to the poor, one must be careful about the quality of the goods saved for zakat and charity. On the other hand, the quality of a person's charity should be as good as he would like it to be if he were the receiver. When one thinks like this, he is expected to give the best of his propert as zakat and sadaqah; however, Allah is so merciful to His servants that He informed us that He accepts our charities from the middle quality of our goods.

The Messenger of Allah (pbuh) said:

"...when paying the zakat, one should not give an aged animal, nor one suffering from itch or ailing, and one most condemned, but one should give animals of medium quality (to have the taste of faith), for Allah did not demand from you the best of your animals, nor did He command you to give the animals of worst quality." (Abu Dawud, Zakat, 5/1582)

When Allah's Messenger (pbuh) sent Muadh to Yemen, he told him to invite them to believe in Allah, perform five-daily prayers, and pay their zakat, and he added:

"Avoid taking the best of their possessions (as zakat)! Be afraid of the curse of an oppressed person because there is no screen between his invocation and Allah." (Bukhari, Zakat, 63; Maghazi, 60; Tawhid, 1; Muslim, Iman, 29, 31)

Allah warned those who save the worst part of their property as zakat and charity ignoring all these blessings and mercy of Allah the Almighty. Bara b. Azib (r.a.) narrated:

Ansar used to hang bunches of dates to a rope tied between two columns of Masjid al-Nabawi during the harvest time and the needy Muslim immigrants used to come and eat from them. Some ansar left dates with poor quality among the others by looking at the abundance of dates and thinking that it would not matter. Allah the Almighty revealed the following verse about those who acted like this:

"O you who believe! Give of the good things which you have (honorably) earned, and of the fruits of the earth which We have produced for you, and do not even aim at getting anything which is bad, in order that out of it you may give away something, when you yourselves would not receive it except with closed eyes. And know that Allah is Free of all wants, and worthy of all praise." (Al-Baqarah; 2:267) (Wahidi, p. 90)

In the first hadith, the Messenger of Allah (pbuh) informed us that those who gave dates with poor quality as charity even if they could afford the better ones will be punished in Hereafter. Since the punishment will be in terms of the sin done, those who bring dates with poor quality will be fed by bad things in the Hereafter. As a matter of fact, even the best blessings of this world would be like pain compared to the unimaginable fruits of Paradise. One must imagine how unfortunate it is to eat dates with poor quality there! Therefore, one must never find it acceptable to give things to the poor which he himself would not like.

One day Aisha (r.anha) wanted to give a piece of meat as sadaqah which smelled a little different.

The Prophet (pbuh) told her:

"Are you going to give something that you are not going to eat yourself?!" (Haythami, III, 113)

Again our mother Aisha asked the following question about a food that the Messenger of Allah did not like:

"O the Messenger of Allah, is it acceptable if we give it to the needy?"

The Noble Prophet (pbuh) said:

"Do not give them something that you would not eat!" (Ahmad, VI, 105, 123; Haythami, III, 113; IV, 37)

Even if giving sadaqah is a good deed under all conditions, it is considered better if it is done secretly. Allah the Almighty says:

"If you disclose (acts of) charity, even so it is well, but if you conceal them, and make them reach those (really) in need, that is best for you: It will remove from you some of your (stains of) evil. And Allah is well acquainted with what you do." (Al-Baqarah; 2:271)

In the following Qur'anic verse, the words "night" and "secret" come before the words "day" and "publicly" to emphasize the importance of giving charity secretly:

"Those who (in charity) spend of their goods by night and by day, in secret and in public, have their reward with their Lord: on them shall be no fear, nor shall they grieve." (Al-Baqarah; 2:274)

The Messenger of Allah (pbuh) put a lot of emphasis upon the importance of giving charity secretly. That is because giving it secretly both protects the donor from the temptations of the carnal-self and also saves the receiver from embarrassment. In order to encourage this, we are informed that those who give charity in such a manner that "the left hand would not know what the right hand gives" will be forgiven and will be under the shade of Heaven in the fearsome moments of the Day of Judgment. (Al-Baqarah; 2:271; Bukhari, Adhan, 36)

The Messenger of Allah (pbuh) said about another benefit of giving sadaqah in secret:

"A sadaqah that is given in secret extinguishes the anger of Allah." (Baihaqi, *Shuab*, III, 244; VI, 255; Haythami, III, 115)

Moreover, those who give sadaqah secretly gain the love of Allah. This is expressed in another hadith:

"...A man comes to a community and asks for something not because he is related to them but only in the name of Allah. They don't give what he asks for. One of them slowly and secretly goes towards the rear of the community and gives something to the man. (He gives so secretly that) only Allah and the man who received the goods knows about it. (Allah loves this person)..." (Tirmidhi, Jannah, 25/2568; Nasai, Zakat, 75/2568)

In our third hadith, it is expressed how much power and strength that a secretly given sadaqah provides humans. As a matter of fact, giving sadaqah secretly requires a strength that is more than what mountains, fire, water, and wind have. That is because acting in this manner requires overcoming greediness and desire to be known by opposing the inner-self and casting Satan down. This indeed is a very difficult thing to do. On the other hand, when a believer gives sadaqah in secret, Allah protects him with the blessing of the sadaqah from disasters that may come from mountains, iron, fire, water, wind, and such.

Also, sadaqah given in secret connects the heart of a believer to Allah with such a strong bond that with this bond the believer becomes more powerful than anything else. The spiritual power of those with strong spiritual lives is an example of this. As a matter of fact, about them is said:

$$ \text{هِمَّةُ الرِّجَالِ تَقْلَعُ الْجِبَالَ} $$

"The favor of the friends of Allah knocks the mountains down."

If no such problematic issues exist, then it is permissible to give sadaqah in public. Furthermore under some circumstance, it may even be better to give sadaqah in public. Under such circumstances, one does not have to give sadaqah in secret. On the other hand, Muslim scholars considered that it is better to give the obligatory zakat in public and supererogatory sadaqah in secret.

There are other manners that must be followed when giving sadaqah. Some of them can be listed as follows:

1. Those who give sadaqah should personally give it to the poor. According to Abdullah bin Abbas's narration, the Messenger of Allah (pbuh) did not have anyone give sadaqah on his behalf, but rather he preferred to give it personally. (Ibn Majah, Taharah, 30)

Companion Harise b. Numan (r.a.) had lost his eyesight. He tied a rope from his prayer room to the door of his living room and placed next to him a basket that had dates and other things in it. When someone poor passed by and saluted him, he would take something from the basket, come to the door holding from the rope and give it to the poor personally.

Whenever his family said:

"We can give it on your behalf," he would respond:

"I heard the Prophet (pbuh) saying:

"Giving sadaqah personally to the poor saves one from dying in an unfortunate way." (Ibn Saʿd, III, 488; Tabarani, *Kabir,* III, 229, 231; Haythami, III, 112)

2. One should not nullify the rewards of his charity by unwanted reminders of his generosity to the receiver and hurting him. Allah strongly forbids acting in such an unpleasant manner. (Al-Baqarah; 2:262-264) (Al-Insan; 76:8-11)

As a matter of fact, the donor should thank the receivers of his zakat or sadaqah. That is because by taking them, the poor ensures that the donor fulfills his responsibility and gain divine rewards.

3. Another important issue is not to return from sadaqah and alms after giving it. Indeed, in order to discourage people from this, the Messenger of Allah (pbuh) said that:

"Those who take their sadaqah back are compared to a dog that eats his vomit." (Muslim, Hibat 5)

Umar (r.a.) narrated:

I had given a horse to a person who fights in the name of Allah. That person did not take good care of the horse and the horse lost weight. Then, I thought that he would sell it for cheap and wanted to buy the horse back from him. I asked this to the Prophet.

The Messenger of Allah (pbuh) said:

"Never buy it! Even if he sells it for one dirham, do not take your sadaqah back! That is because those who take their sadaqah back are like a dog that eats his vomit." (Bukhari, Zakat, 59; Hibat, 29, 37; Jihad, 119, 137; Muslim, Hibat, 1-2; *Muwatta*, Zakat, 49)

4. The most important one is to give sadaqah sincerely and with good intentions, and only for the sake of Allah. The alms that are given to show off or for other worldly benefits would be a waste and do not benefit the donor. (Al-Baqarah; 2:264)

The following are said in the noble verses of Qur'an:

"And they feed, for the love of Allah, the indigent, the orphan, and the captive, (Saying), "We feed you for the sake of Allah alone: no reward do we desire from you, nor thanks." "We only fear a Day of distressful Wrath from the side of our Lord." But Allah will deliver them from the evil of that Day, and will shed over them a Light of Beauty and (blissful) Joy." (Al-Insan; 76:8-11)

In this verse the praised servants of Allah are those who are so sincere and humble in their act of giving that even if they internally say **"…We feed you for the sake of Allah alone…"** they never say this out loud to the face of the poor, and it is as if they reflect this fact in their acts. In order to point out this nuance, the word "saying" is not explicitly mentioned in the verse.

d. Those who can afford to give only a few indeed give from their heart

٧٤. عَنْ عَدِيِّ بْنِ حَاتِمٍ رَضِيَ اللهُ عَنْهُ قَالَ: سَمِعْتُ النَّبِيَّ صَلَّى اللهُ عَلَيْهِ وَسَلَّمَ يَقُولُ:

«اِتَّقُوا النَّارَ وَلَوْ بِشِقِّ تَمْرَةٍ».

159

74. Adi b. Hatim (r.a.) narrated:

I heard the Prophet (pbuh) saying:

"Save yourselves from the Fire (by giving sadaqah) even if it is the half of a date fruit!" (Bukhari, Zakat, 10; Riqaq, 51; Tawhid, 36; Muslim, Zakat, 66-70)

۷٥. عَنْ أَبِي هُرَيْرَةَ رَضِيَ اللهُ عَنْهُ قَالَ: قَالَ رَسُولُ اللهِ صَلَّى اللهُ عَلَيْهِ وَسَلَّمَ:

((سَبَقَ دِرْهَمٌ مِائَةَ أَلْفٍ)) قَالُوا:

((يَا رَسُولَ اللهِ وَكَيْفَ؟)) قَالَ:

((رَجُلٌ لَهُ دِرْهَمَانِ فَأَخَذَ أَحَدُهُمَا فَتَصَدَّقَ بِهِ وَرَجُلٌ لَهُ مَالٌ كَثِيرٌ فَأَخَذَ مِنْ عُرْضِ مَالِهِ مِائَةَ أَلْفٍ فَتَصَدَّقَ بِهَا)).

75. Abu Huraira (r.a.) narrated: The Messenger of Allah (pbuh) said:

"One dirham is more than one hundred thousand dirhams."

The Companions asked:

"O Messenger of Allah, how is that possible?"

The Messenger of Allah (pbuh) answered:

"One man had two dirhams and he gave one of them as sadaqah. Another man was very wealthy but took one hundred thousand dirhams out of his wealth and gave that as sadaqah." (Nasai, Zakat, 49/2526)

Explanations:

In order for zakat to become obligatory upon a believer, one's wealth must exceed a certain level whereas there is no such requirement for sadaqah. Some people have a misconception that "giving sadaqah and alms are for rich people." However, everyone can give in proportion to their means. As a matter of fact, as a proof of His countless blessings, Allah the Almighty made it easy for His servants to gain divine rewards by giving sadaqah.

The Messenger of Allah (pbuh) said:

"A smile to your brother (in Islam) is sadaqah. Enjoining the good and forbidding the evil is sadaqah. Showing the way to someone who lost his way is sadaqah; seeing for the blind is sadaqah (helping him); removing a stone, thorn bush, bone (and such) from the street is sadaqah; emptying water from your bucket to your brother's bucket is sadaqah." (Tirmidhi, Birr, 36/1956)

On the other hand, humans will need the help of even very minor good deeds in the Hereafter. They will strongly wish that they have done any kind of good deed or had given some charity while they were on Earth. They will even ask the help of a glass of water that they had given in this world. The Messenger of Allah (pbuh) explains this situation as:

"On the Day of Judgment, people (or people of heaven according to another narration) will line up. Then one person who will go to Hell comes across someone who will go to Paradise and says:

"O so and so! Did you remember that you wanted a sip of water and I gave it to you?" (and asks for his intercession.) And the believer intercedes for that person.

Another person (who will go to Hell) comes to a person who will go to Paradise and asks for intercession saying:

"Did you remember that one day I gave you water for ablution?" and the person remembers him and intercedes for him.

Again one of the people who will go to Hell says to a person who will go to Paradise:

"O such and such! Do you remember the day that you had sent me for such and such work? And I went that day for you." The person who will go to Paradise intercedes for him." (Ibn Majah, Adab, 8)

In another narration, the Messenger of Allah (pbuh) said:

"There will be none among you but his Lord will talk to him, and there will be no interpreter between him and Allah. He will look to his right and see nothing

but his deeds which he has sent forward, and will look to his left and see nothing but his deeds which he has sent forward, and will look in front of him and see nothing but the (Hell) Fire facing him. So save yourself from the (Hell) Fire even with half a date (given in charity). Those who cannot find this, save yourself even with a good word." (Bukhari, Tawhid, 36; Muslim, Zakat, 97)

Therefore, everyone should take advantage of the benefits of giving charity in both of the worlds even by giving something very small and gain the heart of the needy.

Umm Bujayd (r. anha), one of the female Companions, came to the Messenger of Allah (pbuh) and said:

"O Messenger of Allah, peace and blessings of Allah be upon you! Sometimes, a poor person comes to my door and I cannot find anything to give."

The Messenger of Allah (pbuh) told her:

"Even if you cannot find anything to give him other than a burned nail of a sheep, give that to the poor!" (Abu Dawud, Zakat, 33/1667; Tirmidhi, Zakat, 29/665; Nasai, Zakat, 70/2566; Ahmad, VI, 383)

This saying of the Messenger of Allah is an exaggerated expression to show that sadaqah given to the poor can even be something so small. Therefore, the important thing in giving something is having good intentions, and the importance of the value of the donation is secondary. As a matter of fact, we are informed that a small thing given with difficulty by a relatively poor person is the most valuable type of charity. (Ahmad, V, 265, 178-179)

The Messenger of Allah (pbuh) said to express the value and virtue of such action:

"Three things are among the signs of faith:

1.   Giving charity from the wealth that is not much at all,

2.   Spreading the salutation by saluting everyone,

3.   Being objective in matters about the individual himself. (In other words, being just and not deciding either for or against oneself by being just and measured.)" (Suyuti, *Jami*, I, 117/3441)

One day, a poor person came to Uthman (r.a.) and said:

"O rich men! You took away all the good deeds; you give sadaqah from your wealth, you emancipate slaves, you go to Hajj, and give charity!"

Uthman (r.a.) asked:

"Do you really envy us?" The man said:

"Yes, I swear to Allah we envy you!" Then, Uthman (r.a.) made the following explanation:

"I swear to Allah that one dirham given with difficulty (by someone not so wealthy) is more valuable than ten thousand dirhams given by a wealthy person." (Baihaqi, *Shuab*, III, 251; Ali al-Muttaqi, VI, 612/17098)

That is because those who are not so wealthy are giving out of their own needs rather than giving from what is extra. When this is the case, the chance that it is given only for the sake of Allah is higher. The chance for some humanly desires to interfere with sadaqah given by the rich is higher, and the rich also do not experience any difficulties when giving it.

However, it is not right for a person to give everything and end up needy. In particular, those with weak faith regret for their sadaqah when they become needy by giving too much sadaqah. In such a situation, they lose both their wealth and the divine rewards that they get by giving charity.

The Pride of the Universe (pbuh) told to keep the balance in this matter:

"Some of you bring what they have and say "this is sadaqah!" and then they sit and beg. The most valuable sadaqah is the one that is given from what is more than needed." (Abu Dawud, Zakat, 39/1673)

However, the Messenger of Allah (pbuh) did not object for Abu Bakr to donate all of his wealth as charity. That is because he and some others are among the exceptional characters that have strong faith, and they are exemplary Muslims. They are great characters who know to give charity without hesitation whether they are poor or rich.

How nicely the following story expresses the peak state of Abu Bakr (r.a) in generosity:

One day, after leading the dawn prayer, the Messenger of Allah (pbuh) asked his Companions:

"Is there anyone among you who fed a poor today?" Umar (r.a.) said:

"O Messenger of Allah! We have just performed the dawn prayer and did not leave for anywhere else. How could we feed a poor in this situation?"

Abu Bakr (r.a.) said:

"When I entered into the praying room, I saw someone who was telling about his needs. There was a piece of rye bread that my son Abdurrahman was holding. I immediately took that and gave it to the poor."

Upon this, the Messenger of Allah (pbuh) said:

"*I give you the good news that you will go to Paradise.*" (Haythami, III, 163-164. Also see Abu Dawud, Zakat, 36/1670; Hakim, I, 571/1501)

Another exceptional character who gave a little but from the heart is Zaynap (r.anha), the mother of the faithful. Aisha (r.anha) narrates:

The Messenger of Allah (pbuh) said to his wives:

"*One who has the longest hands amongst you would meet me most immediately (in the hereafter).*"

They (the wives of Allah's Apostle) used to measure their arms as to whose was the longest. It turns out, it was Zainab' arm that was the longest amongst them, for she used to work with her hand and spend (that income) on charity. (Muslim, Kitab al-Fada'il al-Sahabah, 101)

The figurative meaning of having long hands is to give sadaqah and to do good deeds and to be generous. According to the measurement of the mothers of the faithful, the longest arms were those of Sawda (r.anha). However, Zainab (r.anha) was the one who reached the Messenger of Allah the first. Then they understood that what the Messenger of Allah had implied was giving sadaqah, doing good deeds, and being generous.

8. Hajj (Major Pilgrimage to Mecca) and Umra (Minor Pilgrimage)

٧٦. عَنْ أَبِي هُرَيْرَةَ رَضِيَ اللهُ عَنْهُ قَالَ: سَمِعْتُ النَّبِيَّ صَلَّى اللهُ عَلَيْهِ وَسَلَّمَ يَقُولُ:

((مَنْ حَجَّ لِلّٰهِ فَلَمْ يَرْفُثْ وَلَمْ يَفْسُقْ رَجَعَ كَيَوْمِ وَلَدَتْهُ أُمُّهُ)).

76. Abu Huraira (r.a.) narrates: I heard that the Messenger of Allah (pbuh) say:

"Whoever performs Hajj for Allah's pleasure and without pronouncing bad words and committing great sins then he will return (after Hajj free from all sins) as if he were born anew." (Bukhari, Hajj, 4)

٧٧. عَنِ ابْنِ عُمَرَ رَضِيَ اللهُ عَنْهُ عَنِ النَّبِيِّ صَلَّى اللهُ عَلَيْهِ وَسَلَّمَ قَالَ:

«اَلْغَازِي فِي سَبِيلِ اللهِ وَالْحَاجُّ وَالْمُعْتَمِرُ وَفْدُ اللهِ دَعَاهُمْ فَأَجَابُوهُ وَسَأَلُوهُ فَأَعْطَاهُمْ».

77. Ibn Umar (r.a.) narrated that the Noble Prophet (pbuh) said:

"Those who leave their homes to fight in the way of Allah, to perform Hajj or Umra are the delegates of Allah. That is because Allah has invited His servants (to perform these acts) and they have obeyed. In return, they ask something from Allah, and He answers their prayers." (Ibn Majah, Manasik, 5)

٧٨. عَنِ ابْنِ عَبَّاسٍ رَضِيَ اللهُ عَنْهُمَا قَالَ: قَالَ النَّبِيُّ صَلَّى اللهُ عَلَيْهِ وَسَلَّمَ:

«مَنْ أَرَادَ الْحَجَّ فَلْيَتَعَجَّلْ فَإِنَّهُ قَدْ يَمْرَضُ الْمَرِيضُ وَتَضِلُّ الضَّالَّةُ وَتَعْرِضُ الْحَاجَةُ».

78. Ibn Abbas (r.a.) said: The Prophet (pbuh) said:

"Those who want to perform Hajj better hurry! It is possible that they might get sick, or lose their mount for transportation, or another need may come up." (Ahmad, I, 214; Ibn Majah, Manasik, 1)

٧٩. عَنْ عَلِيٍّ رَضِيَ اللهُ عَنْهُ قَالَ: قَالَ رَسُولُ اللهِ صَلَّى اللهُ عَلَيْهِ وَسَلَّمَ:

«مَنْ مَلَكَ زَادًا وَرَاحِلَةً تُبَلِّغُهُ إِلَى بَيْتِ اللهِ وَلَمْ يَحُجَّ فَلَا عَلَيْهِ أَنْ يَمُوتَ يَهُودِيًّا أَوْ نَصْرَانِيًّا وَذٰلِكَ أَنَّ اللهَ يَقُولُ فِي كِتَابِهِ (وَلِلّٰهِ عَلَى النَّاسِ حِجُّ الْبَيْتِ مَنِ اسْتَطَاعَ إِلَيْهِ سَبِيلًا)».

79. Ali (r.a.) narrates: The Messenger of Allah (pbuh) said:

"Whoever owns enough food for the journey and the mount for transportation to the House of Allah (Ka'bah) and does not go to Hajj, there is no difference whether he passes away as Jewish or Christian. That is because Allah the Almighty says in His Book:

"Pilgrimage thereto is a duty men owe to Allah, those who can afford the journey..." (Al-i-Imran; 3:97) (Tirmidhi, Hajj, 3/812)

٨٠. عَنْ أَبِي هُرَيْرَةَ رَضِيَ اللهُ عَنْهُ أَنَّ رَسُولَ اللهِ صَلَّى اللهُ عَلَيْهِ وَسَلَّمَ قَالَ:

«الْعُمْرَةُ إِلَى الْعُمْرَةِ كَفَّارَةٌ لِمَا بَيْنَهُمَا وَالْحَجُّ الْمَبْرُورُ لَيْسَ لَهُ جَزَاءٌ إِلَّا الْجَنَّةُ».

80. Abu Huraira (r.a.) narrated that the Messenger of Allah (pbuh) said:

"(The performance of) the Lesser Pilgrimage (Umra) is expiation for the sins committed (between that one and the previous one). And the reward of Hajj Mabrur (the one accepted by Allah) is nothing except Paradise." (Bukhari, Umra, 1)

Explanations:

Hajj is one of the strongest obligatory (al-fardh) acts of worship based upon the Qur'an, Sunnah, and consensus of the Muslim Scholars. It is obligatory for those Muslims who have the requisites of Hajj.[92] According to Hanafi School, it is necessary (wajib) to perform a woved Hajj or the supererogatory Hajj that has already started but cannot be completed. The Hajj of those who are not obligated to perform or of those who have already performed the obligatory Hajj is considered supererogatory Hajj.

Hajj is the best symbol of faith, submission, and obedience to Allah that Abraham (pbuh) demonstarted with his life, wealth, son, and everything else that he has. This symbol will continue to exist until the Day of Judgment.

Hajj is the assembly of sincere believers who come together at a certain time and place.

Hajj is a comprehensive worship that indicates perfection and maturity in being the servants of Allah that includes some symbolic practices such as *ihram*, *talbiyah*, *tawaf*, *sa'y*, *waqf al-Arafa*, stoning of Satan, sacrifice, and shaving the head or having a haircut. For this reason, Hajj is the last one of the five pillars of Islam which is deemed as obligatory. **In our first Hadith**, our attention is drawn to the virtues of Hajj and we are informed that if Hajj is performed by paying attention to its requisites, it will free us from all sins and some bad traits as if we were born anew.

The Messenger of Allah (pbuh) reminded and said the same thing to Amr b. As who wished that all of his previous sins would be forgiven when he became a Muslim:

"Don't you know that becoming a Muslim purifies one from his previous sins, Immigration (Hijra) nullifies previous sins, and pilgrimage (Hajj) extinguishes the previous sins?" (Muslim, Iman, 192)

The Messenger of Allah (pbuh) was asked:

"Which deed is the most virtuous?"

After mentioning believing in Allah and His Messenger, and Jihad in the cause of Allah, he stated the pilgrimage accepted in the sight of Allah. (Bukhari, Iman, 18; Hajj, 4; Tawhid, 47; Muslim, Iman, 135)

---

92. Muslim, Hajj, 412; Fadail, 130-131; Nasai, Manasik 1/2617.

He we need to remember that the virtue of an act in Islam is parallel to its benefits. From this perspective, Hajj is very important in terms of Islamic consciousness, feeling the excitement of worshipping, experiencing social solidarity and unity and many more.

On the other hand, when the virtues of the deeds are considered from different aspects, this ranking may differ. The purpose of the narration above is to indicate the virtues of exalting the religion of Allah and showing respect to its signs. And this is best done with having faith, doing Jihad, and performing Hajj.

The Messenger of Allah (pbuh) described Hajj and Umra as *"the jihad of the weak"* and *"women's jihad without combat."* (Ibn Majah, Manasik, 8)

One day, Aisha (r. anha), the mother of the faithful, asked:

"O Allah's Apostle! We consider jihad as the best deed. Shouldn't we (women) go to Jihad?"

The Messenger of Allah (pbuh) replied:

"But the best Jihad (for women) is Hajj Mabrur (the one accepted by Allah)." (Bukhari, Hajj, 4; Sayd, 26; Jihad, 1)

In other words, Hajj Mabrur is a deed as virtuous as Jihad. In order Hajj to be Mabrur (to be accepted by Allah), it must be performed without sins and disobedience, cruelty and betrayal, with faith and sincerity, in short in accordance with its rules.

In the second Hadith, the Muslims who go to Jihad, Hajj, or Umra are considered like the delegates who obey Allah, go to visit His House by responding to His invitation, and present their needs. There is no doubt that Allah the Almighty will answer the prayers of such distinguished people and send them back to their homes with many rewards.

Therefore, when the necessary conditions are met, one must not postpone fulfilling such a virtuous worship. As a matter of fact, most of the Muslim scholars agree that those who postpone going to Hajj when they can will commit a sin and if they keep postponing it for years, then their testimony will not be accepted. That is because acting in this way indicates not paying attention to Allah's command. On the other hand, illnesses, lossing the means, and other similar obstacles may come up and prevent a person from fulfilling this obligatory act of worship. Therefore, in the third hadith, it is asked from those who intend to perform Hajj to hurry.

As a matter of fact, Bara b. Ma'rur (r.a.), one of the twelve representatives who joined the Aqabah Pledge, promised the Messenger of Allah (pbuh) that he will come to Mecca next year in Hajj time. However, he fell into death bed before it was time for Hajj. So he said to his family:

"Due to my promise to the Messenger of Allah, turn me towards Ka'bah; because, I told him that I will come" and by this he became the first one who turned towards Ka'bah in his life and after he died.

When the Pride of the Universe (pbuh) visited Madina together with his Companions, he went to the grave of Bara b. Ma'rur and had people line up and led the funeral prayer (Salat al-Janazah.) Then he prayed for him saying:

"O my Lord forgive him! Show mercy to him and be content with him!" (Ibn Abdilbar, I, 153; Ibn Sa'd, III, 619-620)

In our fourth hadith, there is a serious threat for those who postpone going to Hajj while they can afford it. This is because such people neither obey nor thank Allah appropriately for their health and wealth while they are able to do it. They act like non-Muslims. Since they follow a life like Jews and Christians, it is possible that they would die like them. Because of this, Allah the Exalted commands to those whom He has given the means should go to Hajj as His right.

On the other hand, our hadith expresses the importance of Hajj with a striking language and indicates that those who postpone performing Hajj commit a major sin. As a matter of fact, at the end of the verse Allah the Almighty uses the phrase "but if any deny faith", instead of "but if any does not perform Hajj" to indicate how bad it is not to perform Hajj for those who can afford it. (Al-i Imran; 3:97)

Someone inquired about the requirements of going to Hajj and the Prophet (pbuh) said:

"Food and mount for transportation." (Tirmidhi, Hajj, 4/813; Ibn Majah, Manasik, 6, 16)

Therefore, Muslims who can afford the journey and accommodation must humbly set off on the journey without showing off or acting wastefully.

Anas reported that the Messenger of Allah (pbuh) went to pilgrimage just with a camel carrying his food and belongings. (Bukhari, Hajj, 3. Also see Ibn Majah, Manasik 4)

However, believers should avoid being a burden on others by going to Hajj or Umra if they do not have enough wealth. In earlier times, the people of Yemen would not take food along with them and say:

"We put our trust in Allah (tawaqqul)." When they arrived at Mecca, they had to beg for food. Upon that the following noble verse was revealed:

"...And take a provision (with you) for the journey..." (Al-Baqarah; 2:197) (Bukhari, Hajj, 6; Wahidi, p. 63)

The wealth earned with honest work is the most important issue that must be paid attention to. As the Messenger of Allah put it:

"Whoever visits the Noble House of Allah with the money that he has not earned by honest work, he disobeys Allah. If such a person makes intention for Hajj, puts on ihram (the pilgrim's garment), gets on his camel and rides it and says:

"Labbayk Allahumma Labbayk"[93] *a voice from Heaven says:*

"La labbayk wa la sa'dayk (neither labbayk nor sa'deyk for you)!" That is because your wealth, your food, and your mount for transportation are haram (not earned with honest work). Go back without any divine rewards and as sinful! Be sorry that you will face with something that you will not like!"..." (Haythami, III, 209-210)

The pilgrims put their ihrams on in one of the places of Miqat[94] before they reach to Mecca. When they reach Ka'bah, they perform tawaf al-qudum[95] by circumambulating the Ka'bah seven times in order to show how thankful they are to reach to Ka'bah. Pilgrims walk briskly with short steps and somewhat proudly during the first three circuits of *tawaf al-qudum*. This walk is called

---

93. *Translator's note:* Here I am, O Allah, here I am! (The beginning of the traditional Hajj chant).

94. *Translator's note:* Miqat (a stated place) are the stations at which pilgrims on the Hajj put on ihram (the pilgrim's garment). Five of these stations were set up by Muhammad (pbuh), a sixth was added later for the convenience of travelers from India and points further east.

95. *Translator's note:* The initial Tawaf performed by the pilgrim upon entering al-Masjid al-Haram in Mecca pursuant upon his intention for Hajj.

"ramal." Then, a two unit (raqah) prayer is performed next to maqam Ibrahim (Abraham's Station).[96] One performs sa'i[97] between Safa and Marwah[98] with four goings and three comings and perform waqfah in Arafat,[99] and then visits first Muzdalifah and then Mina,[100] followed by stoning Satan, animal sacrifice, shaving, and circumambulation around the Ka'bah. This time pilgrims do not perform *ramal* or *sa'i.*

While Anas (r.a.) was talking about the pilgrimage of the Messenger of Allah, he said:

When the Messenger of Allah (pbuh) reached Mina, he went right away to Jamarat[101] and threw the stones. Then he went to the resting place in Mina and performed his sacrifice. When he was done with all these, he ordered the barber to come and pointed out first the right side of his head and then the left side and said:

"Cut from here!"

Then he gave away his hair to the Companions who were passionately waiting for them. (Bukhari, Wudu', 33; Muslim, Hajj, 323-325)

---

96. *Translator's note:* Maqam-i Ibrahim is the stepping stone used by Prophet Abraham (pbuh) during the original construction of the Ka'bah. The stone carries the imprints of his feet and is housed in a glass enclosure on the north side of the Ka'bah.

97. *Translator's note:* Sa`i is the ritual of walking seven times back and forth between the rocky hillocks of Safa and Marwah. This act retraces the footsteps of Hagar (wife of Prophet Abraham) during her desperate search for water to quench the thirst of her infant son Ismail after they were left in the desert by the Prophet Abraham in response to a divine vision.

98. *Translator's note:* Safa is a small hillock approximately half a mile (0.8 km) from the Ka'bah and Marwah is a rocky hillock located approximately one hundred yards (91 meters) from the Ka'bah and they are both inside al-Masjid al-Haram. The pilgrim performs the devotional rite of Sa`i between the hillocks of Safa and Marwah.

99. *Translator's note:* plane of Arafah is a desert location approximately 14.5 km (9 miles) east of Mecca where the pilgrim spends the 9th of Dhul-Hijjah (the last month of the Islamic calendar) as a rite of Hajj. The waqfah is performed at Arafat which is the ritual of standing before Allah. It is a central rite of Hajj.

100. *Translator's note:* Muzdalifah is a desert location approximately midway between Mina and Arafat. The pilgrim spends the night of the 10th of Dhul-Hijjah there. And Mina is a desert location approximately three miles (4.8 km) east of Mecca where several rites of Hajj are performed.

101. *Translator's note:* The three stone pillars in Mina that symbolically represent the locations where the devil (Satan) tried to tempt Prophet Abraham (pbuh) away from the path of Allah.

In these Holy lands, one must show respect and honor the marks of Islam such as the Magnificent Ka'bah and hillocks of Safa and Marwah. It is not a nice manner to sit or lay down turning one's feet towards Ka'bah, or engaging in idle and useless talk in these Holy lands.

Allah the Almighty informs us that the respect showed to the symbols of Islam comes from piety of heart:

"Such (is his state): and whoever holds in honor the symbols of Allah, (in the sacrifice of animals), such (honor) should come truly from piety of heart." (Al-Hajj; 22:32)

For this reason, when the Messenger of Allah (pbuh) saw the House of Allah in his pilgrimage, he raised his hands and prayed saying:

"O my Lord! Advance the honor, magnificence, grace, and solemnity of Your House. And advance the honor, grace, solemnity, homage, and kindness of those who honor it!" (Ibn Sa'd, II, 173)

One should pay attention to purity, dignity, peacefulness, deliberateness, and avoid impetuousness during the journey and in these Holy lands.

Indeed, the Messenger of Allah (pbuh) was returning from Arafat to Muzdalifah on the day of Arafat. He heard that some people in the back were yelling and whipping their camels in order to speed them up. Upon that, he pointed out to them with his lash and said:

"O people, observe peacefulness! Goodness cannot be earned by walking fast and in a hurry." (Bukhari, Hajj, 94; Muslim, Hajj, 268)

In the same manner, it is not nice to act inappropriately by pushing people around in order to reach some blessed places such as al-Hajar al-Aswad,[102] Maqam Ibrahim, and Rawda-i Mutahhara (the tomb of Muhammad). This is because the Messenger of Allah (pbuh) discouraged us from hurting other servants of Allah.

One day, the Messenger of Allah (pbuh) advised Umar (r.a.) to act politely while circumambulating around Ka'bah and said:

---

102. *Translator's note:* The Black Stone built into the southeast corner of the Ka'bah at a height of approximately four feet. The stone does not belong to the geology of the region and is a piece of the original construction of the Ka'bah by the Prophet Abraham (pbuh). The Prophet Muhammad (pbuh) also kissed it during his Farewell Hajj. Thus, touching and kissing Hajar Al-Aswad during Umrah and Hajj is considered a sunnah.

"O Umar! You are a strong and big man. Do not push people and hurt the weak to touch al-Hajar al-Aswad! Neither be bothered nor bother! If you find it un-crowded, you can touch and kiss al-Hajar al-Aswad. Otherwise, make the gesture of "touching and kissing it" from far, recite al-Kalima al-Tawheed and Takbir, and pass by!" (Ahmad, I, 28; Haythami, III, 241)

There are many benefits and lessons in Hajj. The Messenger of Allah (pbuh) said:

"Join Umra and Hajj! As a matter of fact, they extinguish poverty and sins as bellow cleans the rust from iron, gold, and silver." (Tirmidhi, Hajj, 2/810; Nasai, Manasik, 6/2629; Ibn Majah, Manasik, 3)

"For the expenses made in Hajj, Allah gives divine rewards of one to seven hundred times as if they were spent in the way of Allah." (Ahmad, V, 354-355)

"The day that Allah sets His servants free from Hell most is the Day of Arafat. That day Allah gets closer and takes pride in His servants and says to His angels:

"What are they wishing for?!" (Muslim, Hajj, 436; Nasai, Manasik, 194/3001; Ibn Majah, Manasik, 56)

In other words, Allah accepts the prayers of His servants at that time.

In another hadith, the Messenger of Allah (pbuh) gives the good news that:

"I swear to Allah, Allah resurrects it (or al-Hajar al-Aswad) on the Day of Judgment as a creature having two eyes and a tongue, and it becomes a witness for those who have appropriately touched and kissed it." (Tirmidhi, Hajj, 113/961)

Again, the Messenger of Allah (pbuh) informed us that those who go to Hajj will not be faced with poverty or neediness. (Haythami, III, 208)

During Hajj believers get an intensive training of worship, prayer, and remembrance of Allah. They remember Allah in each of their movements and establish His love in their hearts. In fact the Messenger of Allah (pbuh) said:

"Stoning (Satan) and sa'i between the hillocks of Safa and Marwah are commanded only as the manifestation of remembrance of Allah." (Tirmidhi, Hajj, 64/902)

The real purposes of worship, that is to obey Allah's command and exalt His religion, are fulfilled in Hajj at the level of the entire nation of believers. That is because Hajj is the best example of unity of believers in faith and practice.

Those who go to Hajj engage in deep thinking about the blessings of Allah by remembering the prophets, martyrs, loyals, and those who performed good deeds, and be inspired from the blessed time and place that they are in. They take steps towards moral maturity in this spiritually influencing environment. They attain good traits such as humbleness, feeling of nothingness, patience, submission, cooperation, sincerity, discipline in using the time and performing acts, preparation for death and the Day of Judgment, not hurting any plants or living things, and not to think ill of anybody. That is because Hajj that has some symbolic practices as seen from the outside is really composed of various spiritual practices in different places. Therefore, everyone takes advantage from one or more parts of it.

Muslims in Hajj experience spiritual unity by coming together in the same place at the same time. They listen to each other's problems and issues and send their messages to others who are far away. As a matter of fact, the Messenger of Allah (pbuh) used to deliver the message of Islam and divine truths in the pre-Islamic period festivals done during the pilgrimage season. Of course, while doing this, he used to face with many troubles and difficulties and be patient for the sake of Allah.

Umra (lesser pilgrimage) is also a virtuous act of worship like the Hajj. Umra has some of the benefits and lessons of Hajj. For this reason Umra is also called **"Lesser Hajj."** Indeed, in **our fifth hadith**, we are informed about the virtue of Umra and how it becomes expiation for the previous sins. Thus, those who can perform Umra should take advantage of this act of worship.

For Umra, one goes into ihram by making intention in Miqat,[103] circumambulates around the Ka'bah, performs *sa'i* between Safa and Marwah, and then goes out of ihram by either shaving or shortening his hair.

According to Imam Abu Hanifa, Umra is a sunnah and can be performed at any time of the year. However, it is considered reproachable only when it is

---

103. *Translator's note:* Miqat is an imaginary boundary around Mecca. A prospective pilgrim cannot cross this boundary without first changing into ihram.

done when the pilgrims perform waqfah in Arafat on the day of Arafat and during the four days of the Festival of Sacrifice.

Due to the following verse in the Qur'an **"...complete the Hajj or Umra in the service of Allah,"**[104] it is necessary to complete Hajj or Umra that has already been started.

The Messenger of Allah (pbuh) said:

"Performing Hajj and Umra one after another increases one's wealth and life-time, and extinguishes poverty and sins as bellow cleanses the rust of iron." (Ahmad, III, 446-447)

"Umra in Ramadan is equal to Hajj (in reward) or to Hajj that is performed with me." (Bukhari, Umra, 4; Muslim, Hajj, 221)

The following hadith al-qudsi[105] expressing the importance of Hajj and Umra is also attention grabbing.

The Messenger of Allah (pbuh) narrated from His Almighty Lord:

"Allah the Almighty says:

Those servants of Mine who do not come to me (in other words who do not perform Hajj or Umra) in every four years while I gave them good health and welfare are indeed destitute ones." (Haythami, III, 206)

In another narration, it has been said *"in every five years."* (Haythami, III, 206)

During Hajj and Umra no Muslim can afford to be deprived of visiting the Enlightened city of Madina and receive inspiration from the Messenger of Allah, breathing the spiritual air of his enlightened city and taking lessons from the memories there, which are all multifaceted worships with abundant rewards.

Allah's Messenger (pbuh) said:

"Whoever visits me after my death is like he has visited me in my lifetime!" (Daraqutni, *Sunan*, II, 278)

---

104. Al-Baqara; 2:196.
105. *Translator's note:* Hadith al qudsi are words of Allah as reported by the Prophet, but they are not part of the Quran.

"Whoever performs Hajj and visits my grave is as if he visited me in my lifetime." (Daraqutni, *Sunan,* II, 278; Haythami, IV, 2; Baihaqi, *Shuab*, III, 489)

"My intercession becomes necessary for those who visit my grave." (Haythami, IV, 2; Baihaqi, *Shuab*, III, 488-490)

"A prayer performed in this prayer room is better than one thousand prayers performed elsewhere except al-Masjid al-Haram." (Bukhari, Fadl al-Salat fi Masjidi Makka wa al-Madina, 1; Muslim, Hajj, 505-510)

The Messenger of Allah (pbuh) had told that one was allowed to travel for worship only to three masjids and listed *al-Masjid al-Haram* (Mecca), *al-Masjid al-Rasul* (Medina), and *al-Masjid al-Aqsa* (Jerusalem). (Bukhari, Fadlu al-Salat fi Masjidi Makka wa al-Madina, 1; Muslim, Hajj, 511-513)

Every Muslim has a special love for Madina. That is because the Messenger of Allah (pbuh) loved it. Whenever the Messenger of Allah returned from a journey and saw the walls of Medina, he would speed his camel up. If he was on an animal (e.g., a horse or a mule), he would speed it up because of his love for Medina. (Bukhari, Fadail al-Madina, 10; Umra, 17; Tirmidhi, Daawat, 42/3441)

There are many narrations on the virtues of Enlightened Madina. For details, one can see the chapter of virtues of Madinah (Fadail al-Madina) in Bukhari's *Sahih* .

9. Sacrifice

٨١. عَنْ عَائِشَةَ أَنَّ النَّبِيَّ صَلَّى اللهُ عَلَيْهِ وَسَلَّمَ قَالَ:

((مَا عَمِلَ ابْنُ آدَمَ يَوْمَ النَّحْرِ عَمَلًا أَحَبَّ إِلَى اللهِ عَزَّ وَجَلَّ مِنْ هِرَاقَةِ دَمٍ وَإِنَّهُ لَيَأْتِي يَوْمَ الْقِيَامَةِ بِقُرُونِهَا وَأَظْلَافِهَا وَأَشْعَارِهَا وَإِنَّ الدَّمَ لَيَقَعُ مِنَ اللهِ عَزَّ وَجَلَّ بِمَكَانٍ قَبْلَ أَنْ يَقَعَ عَلَى الْأَرْضِ فَطِيبُوا بِهَا نَفْسًا)).

81. Aisha (r.anha) reported that the Noble Prophet (pbuh) said:

"Among the acts that sons of Adam do on the first day of Festival of Sacrifice (Eid al-Adha) Allah likes best to shed the blood of the sacrificed animal (there is no better act on that day at the sight of Allah). On the Day of Judgment that sacrificed animal comes with its horns, nails, and fur. Before the blood of the animal drops to the ground, the sacrifice gets accepted by Allah and His content is gained. Therefore, sacrifice your animal with ease of heart!" (Ibn Majah, Adahi, 3; Tirmidhi, Adahi, 1/1493)

٨٢. عَنْ أَبِي هُرَيْرَةَ أَنَّ رَسُولَ اللهِ صَلَّى اللهُ عَلَيْهِ وَسَلَّمَ قَالَ:

«مَنْ كَانَ لَهُ سَعَةٌ وَلَمْ يُضَحِّ فَلَا يَقْرَبَنَّ مُصَلَّانَا».

82. Abu Huraira (r.a.) reported that the Messenger of Allah (pbuh) said:

"Whoever does not sacrifice an animal while they can afford it should keep away from our praying rooms!" (Ibn Majah, Adahi, 2; Ahmad, II, 321)

Explanations:

"Qurban" (sacrifice) means something that helps someone to get closer or approach to Allah. Since it carries the meanings of self sacrifice from wealth and life, it is one of the most important means to get closer to Allah.

At the same time, animal sacrifice is the tradition of our forefather Abraham. (Ibn Majah, Adahi, 3)

It is commanded by Allah in the second year of the Hijra (immigration from Mecca to Madina). According to Abu Hanifa, it is necessary to sacrifice on the Festival of Sacrifice (Eid al-Adha) for those who own more than 96 grams of gold or 640 grams of silver. The passage of a year upon the ownership of these minimum limits is not a requirement for offering sacrifice.

Majority of scholars believe that sacrife is a sunnah al-muakkadah.[106]

Some scholars say that the following verses constitute evidence for animal sacrifice:

---

106. *Translator's note:* Sunnah al-Muakkadah (Continuous Tradition) are the traditions (sunnah) that our Prophet would always perform and hardly ever missed.

"To every people did We appoint rites (of sacrifice), that they might celebrate the name of Allah over the sustenance He gave them from animals (fit for food)..." (Al-Hajj; 22:34, 67)

"Therefore to your Lord turn in Prayer and Sacrifice." (Al-Kawthar; 108:2)

"And We ransomed him with a momentous sacrifice." (Al-Saffat; 37:107)

The Messenger of Allah (pbuh) never missed to sacrifice after it is commanded[107] and he even performed it on journey[108] and said:

"O humans! It is necessary to perform sacrifice every year for each household." (Ibn Majah, Adahi, 2; Tirmidhi, Adahi, 18/1518)

The Messenger of Allah (pbuh) said the following for the virtues of the days of Festival of Sacrifice (Eid Al-Adha):

"The greatest day in Allah's sight is the day of sacrifice and next one is the second day of Eid al-Adha (yawm al-qarr)" (Abu Dawud, Kitab al-Manasik al-Umra wa al-Hajj, 18/1765)

Again, Allah's Apostle (pbuh) said:

"The days that good deeds are most liked by Allah are the first ten days of Dhul-hijja!"

Some people in the congregation asked:

"Even from Jihad in the way of Allah?"

The Messenger of Allah (pbuh) said:

"Yes, even from Jihad![109] However, those who go to Jihad with their wealth and lives and do not return with any of them (that is, those who sacrificed their

---

107. Tirmidhi, Adahi, 11/1507. The Messenger of Allah (pbuh) even wished that sacrifices to be offered on his behalf. Hanash (r.a.) saw Ali sacrificing two rams and asked why he was doing this. Ali (r.a.) answered:

"The Messenger of Allah (pbuh) bequested me to sacrifice to his name after his death. One of them are for him and I will never quit doing this!" (Abu Dawud, Adahi, 1-2/2790; Tirmidhi, Adahi, 3/1495; Ahmad, I, 107)

108. Muslim, Hajj, 356-7; Abu Dawud, Adahi, 10-11/2814; Tirmidhi, Adahi, 8/1501. However, due to hardship of sacrificing and distributing the meat during a journey, a permission not to sacrifice is given to travelers. In other words, a traveler may not sacrifice if he wishes to.

109. The "jihad" here is probably a jihaad done during the Hajj time since it prevents one performing Hajj. That is becasue the Messenger of Allah (pbuh) told in several hadiths that the best worship is "making jihaad in the name of Allah."

entire wealth and life and are martyred) are excluded!" (Bukhari, I'dain, 11; Abu Dawud, Sawm, 61/2438; Tirmidhi, Sawm, 52/757)

Therefore, it is necessary to try to get closer to Allah during these virtuous days. **In our first hadith**, it is announced that sacrifice is the best act to be done during these days. That is why the whole animal that is sacrificed will come on the Day of Judgment as a reward.

Sacrifice can be an act of worship that is difficult to perform for human inner-self since it also requires material sacrifice and spending. For this reason, the Messenger of Allah (pbuh) advised Muslims to be at ease by thinking the virtues and rewards of this act of worship.

In our hadith, by choosing the words as *"to shed blood of the sacrificed animal"* or *"before the blood of the animal drops to floor,"* it is shown that the purpose of the sacrifice is to "shed blood." In turn, the purpose of shedding blood is to show the obedience, trust, and call on to Allah. Otherwise, Allah does not need the meat of the animal nor its blood. As a matter of fact, it is said in a noble verse of Qur'an:

"It is not their meat nor their blood that reaches Allah. It is your piety that reaches Him…" (Al-Hajj; 22:37)

When the sacrifice of Abel, the son of Adam, which he had offered unwillingly, was not accepted by Allah, he got jealous of his brother Cain and said "I swear that I will kill you." The response of Cain to his brother is so meaningful:

"…(Allah) does accept of the sacrifice of those who are righteous." (Al-Maidah; 5:27)

Therefore, there is a strong relationship between sacrifice and being righteous. Only righteous people can sacrifice animal with peace of heart. On the other hand, when sacrificing an animal, one must act piously. Due to this sincerity, the sacrificed animal enriches the person who performs the act and gets him closer to Allah. The most valuable person in the sight of Allah is the one who is the most righteous. (Al-Hujurat; 49:13)

On the other hand, Allah only accepts a sacrifice that is performed to fulfill His command and only to gain His content. For this reason, the Messenger of Allah (pbuh) said:

"May Allah curse upon those who sacrifice for other causes than gaining the content of Allah." (Muslim, Adahi, 43-45; Nasai, Dahaya, 34)

In our second hadith, those who do not sacrifice while they can afford are warned with a strong language. In this hadith, it does not mean that prayers are not valid if one does not sacrifice. However, a punishment is given to a person who does not sacrifice, and he gets away from righteous people and is in huge loss. The Prophet (pbuh) wished that all of his followers perform sacrifice and find salvation by gaining divine rewards.

In another noble verse of Qur'an, it is stated that:

"The sacrificial camels we have made for you as among the symbols from Allah." (Al-Hajj; 22:36)

For this reason, one must show respect to the animal sacrifice and to sacrificial animals for the sake of Allah. As in all other acts of worship, the essence of sacrifice is righteousness and exalting Allah. One of the requirements of this act of worship is that the sacrificial animal must be healthy and well-fed. This is expressed in a noble hadith as follows:

"Four (types of animals) should be avoided in sacrifice:

1. *One-eyed animal which has obviously lost the sight of one eye,*

2. *A sick animal which is obviously sick,*

3. *A lame animal which obviously limps and*

4. *A lean animal with dried marrows."* (Abu Dawud, Adahi, 5-6/2802; Tirmidhi, Adahi, 5/1497)

One day Urwa (r.a.) told his children:

"My sons, let none of you sacrifice any animal which he would be ashamed to sacrifice for a noble woman, for surely Allah is the noblest of noble ones, and the most deserving of those for whom things are chosen." (Malik, *Muwatta*, Hajj, 147)

One must be very sensitive in slaughtering the sacrificial animal and cover its eyes tightly and should not sacrifice two animals in one hole. Also, one should pay attention not to sacrifice one animal in front of another. It is not right to hurt the animal while bringing it to the place where it will be sacrificed. If the sacrificial animal is a sheep or goat, it would be nice to carry it gently and tenderly. Cattle should also be gently brought to where it will be sacrificed. The sacrificial animal should be turned towards direction of Ka'bah, the person who will perform the sacrifice should say Bismillah ("in the name of Allah") and then Takbir ("God is Greatest"), and if it is possible whoever fulfills the worship should sacrifice the animal himself.[110] If not, he should find someone to slaughter the animal but try to be present when the sacrificial animal is slaughtered.

The Messenger of Allah (pbuh) said:

"O Fatima! Go and be present in your sacrificial offering, and know it well that with the first drop of blood, your (minor) sins will be forgiven." (Hakim, IV, 247/7524; Haythami, IV, 17; Baihaqi, *Shuab*, V, 483)

The Messenger of Allah (pbuh) ordered to sharpen and hide the knives from the animals and then he advised:

"When you slaughter an animal, do it fast!" (Ibn Majah, Zabaih, 3)

"Verily Allah has enjoined goodness to everything; so when you kill, kill in a good way and when you slaughter, slaughter in a good way. So every one of you should sharpen his knife, and comfort the slaughtered animal." (Muslim, Said, 57; Tirmidhi, Diyat, 14/1409; Abu Dawud, Kitab Al-Dahaya, 11-12/2815)

Here, the meaning of comforting the animal is to pet the animal gently before the sacrifice and slaughter it quickly with a sharp knife.

Once, the Messenger of Allah (pbuh) saw a man slaughtering a sheep. The man was trying to sharpen the knife after he had laid the sacrificial animal down. Upon this harsh and cold-hearted behavior, the Messenger of Allah warned him as follows:

"Are you trying to kill the animal several times? Shouldn't you have sharpened your knife before you lay it down?" (Hakim, IV, 257, 260/7570)

The Messenger of Allah (pbuh) prohibited to cut the throat and some part of the skin of the animal and leave it like that until it dies.[111] It is necessary to cut through the carotids, alimentary, and air tube. When the animal is slaughtered, one should wait for a while until the blood flow stops. One should not start to skin the animal while it is still lingering.

---

110. Muslim, Adahi, 17-18.
111. Abu Dawud, Adaahi, 16-17/2826.

Not to sit and to wait standing up until the blood flow stops is among the acts of righteous ones.

Jabir (r.a.) narrated how the Messenger of Allah (pbuh) sacrificed an animal as follows:

The Messenger of Allah (pbuh) sacrificed two horned white rams with black markings. When he made them face the kiblah, he said:

"For me, I have set my face, firmly and truly, towards Him Who created the heavens and the earth, and never shall I give partners to Allah." (Al-An'am; 6:79)

"Say: "Truly, my prayer and my service of sacrifice, my life and my death, are (all) for Allah, the Cherisher of the Worlds: No partner has He: this am I commanded, and I am the first of those who bow to His will."[112]

"O Lord! (This sacrifice) comes from You and we are sacrificing it for you. I am sacrificing on behalf of Muhammad and his nation. In the name of Allah, and Allah is Most Great." He then made the sacrifice. (Abu Dawud, Adahi, 3-4/2795; Ibn Majah, Al-Dahaya, 1)

Jabir ibn Abdullah also narrated:

"I witnessed sacrificing along with the Messenger of Allah (pbuh) at the place of prayer. When he finished his sermon, he descended from the pulpit, and a ram was brought to him. The Messenger of Allah (pbuh) slaughtered it with his own hands, and said:

"In the name of Allah, Allah is Most Great. This is on behalf of me and those who did not sacrifice from my nation!" (Tirmidhi, Al-Dahaya, 20/1521)

In these narrations, we can also see how much the Messenger of Allah was fond of his followers.

As those who are performing pilgrimage cannot get out of ihram unless they offer their sacrifice and shave, it is also nice for Muslims who offer sacrifice in their home towns to pospone shaving and clipping their nails until after they saw the new moon of the month of Dhulhijja.[113]

---

112. Al-An'am (The Cattle); 6:162-163.
113. Muslim, Adahi, 39-42; Abu Dawud, Adahi, 2-3/2791.

The purpose of this is to transform the unity in faith into a unity in practice all around the world by acting like those who are physically at Hajj as much as possible.

Another lesson in acting this way is to save those who offer sacrifices from the Hellfire with all their cells. That is because for each part of the body of the sacrificed animal, as a reward, Allah saves the corresponding body part of the person who sacrificed it.

After the sacrificial animal is slaughtered and divided appropriately, one should eat from its meat and offer it to others. Allah the Almighty says:

"… then eat you thereof and feed the distressed ones in want." (Al-Hajj; 22:28, 36)

The proper manner is to divide the meat into three parts and leave one part for the family memebers at home, offer one part of it to friends and neighbors, and give the rest as sadaqah (Abu Dawud, Adahi, 9-10/2813)

While it is permissible to use the skin and other useful parts of the sacrificed animal at home, it is not permissible to sell them. If it is sold, then the money should be given as charity. Also, benefiting from the fur or milk of the sacrificial animal (before sacrifice) is considered undesirable and if this is done, it is advised to give charity as much as their value.

While sacrificing the animal, one should pay extreme attention to cleanliness and hygiene. The streets and environment should be kept clean and one should avoid causing bad smells and sights in the streets.

If the lessons and virtues of sacrifice are to be summarized, one can list as follows:

Sacrifice reminds us Abraham's and Ismail's submission and how superior they were as servants of Allah. It physically shows us that Allah offered everything to humans' service and how we should appropriately benefit from them and give charity out of them. Indeed, as it is wrong not to benefit from the blessings of Allah, it is also extremely wrong to waste them. For this reason, Islam ordered sacrifice but also prohibited wasting and torturing animals and even put a minimum age limit for the sacrificial animals.

Sacrifice saves one from being stingy and having love for material goods. Sacrifice develops the feelings of brotherhood, altruism, sharing, and pleasing the needy in the society. Sacrifice builds bonds between people with love and mercy. It ensures that everyone benefits from the blessings of Allah. It helps us to gain the content of Allah and get closer to Him by acts of worship that are performed both individually and socially in the society.

10. Being in the same state as in the Noble Qur'an

a. The Effort to understand the Qur'an

٨٣. عَنْ عُثْمَانَ رَضِيَ اللّٰهُ عَنْهُ عَنِ النَّبِيِّ صَلَّى اللّٰهُ عَلَيْهِ وَسَلَّمَ قَالَ:

«خَيْرُكُمْ مَنْ تَعَلَّمَ الْقُرْآنَ وَعَلَّمَهُ».

83. Uthman (r.a.) narrated that the Noble Prophet (pbuh) said:

"The best among you (Muslims) are those who learn the Qur'an and teach it."
(Bukhari, Virtues of the Qur'an, 21; Abu Dawud, Witr, 14/1452; Tirmidhi, Virtues of the Qur'an, 15/2907)

٨٤. عَنْ أَبِي هُرَيْرَةَ رَضِيَ اللّٰهُ عَنْهُ قَالَ: قَالَ رَسُولُ اللّٰهِ صَلَّى اللّٰهُ عَلَيْهِ وَسَلَّمَ:

«...وَمَا اجْتَمَعَ قَوْمٌ فِي بَيْتٍ مِنْ بُيُوتِ اللّٰهِ يَتْلُونَ كِتَابَ اللّٰهِ وَيَتَدَارَسُونَهُ بَيْنَهُمْ إِلَّا نَزَلَتْ عَلَيْهِمُ السَّكِينَةُ وَغَشِيَتْهُمُ الرَّحْمَةُ وَحَفَّتْهُمُ الْمَلَائِكَةُ وَذَكَرَهُمُ اللّٰهُ فِيمَنْ عِنْدَهُ».

84. Abu Huraira (r.a) narrated: The Messenger of Allah (pbuh) said:

"...If a group of people assemble in a house among the houses of Allah (mosques) and recite the Book of Allah and discuss the Qur'an (among themselves), then tranquility would descend upon them and mercy would cover them

and angels would surround them and Allah the Almighty mentions them in the presence of those near Him." (Muslim, Kitab Al-Dhikr, 38; Abu Dawud, Witr, 14/1455; Tirmidhi, Qiraah, 10/2945; Ibn Majah, Muqaddimah, 17)

Explanations:

Allah the Exalted revealed the Qur'an as a reference book and guide for His servants to enter into Paradise. Therefore, Qur'an guides humans to the most righteous way. (Al-Isra; 17:9-10)

The Noble Qur'an is sent to be understood and practiced. Allah the Almighty explained in the Qur'an all kinds of examples in various ways so that we can benefit from them. (Al-Isra; 17: 41, 89), Al-Zumar; 39:27) (Al-Kahf; 18:54) (Al-Rum; 30:58)

In order for us to understand it, take lessons from it, and put it into practice, He made the Qur'an easy to understand. (Maryam; 19:97) (Al-Duhan; 44:58) (Al-Qamar; 54:17, 22, 32, 40)

Therefore, a believer's duty is to put effort to understand the word of Allah and study the Qur'an. For sure, before trying to understand it, one must learn how to read it correctly. That is because recitation of the Qur'an is necessary for a believer since he will need to recite it five times a day during his prayers. Therefore, knowledge of the recitation of the Qur'an, at least enough to perform five daily prayers, is a *fard al-'ayn*.[114]

Those who learn the Qur'an should strive to teach others. **In the first hadith**, we are informed that the best people are those who participate sincerely in the activities to learn and teach the Qur'an. That is because the book with which they are busying themselves is the word of Allah, the best of all the words.[115]

---

114. *Translator' note:* These are the obligatory acts that each liable Muslim must fulfill individually. For example, praying five times a day and fasting are obligatory on individuals.
115. When learning the Noble Quran, teaching it to others, and studying it, one must show respect, be focused, and follow certain rules of manners. First of all, one must avoid touching it without ablution. (Al-Waqia; 56:79)
It is said in several ahadith that:
"None shall touch (the Qur'an) but those who are clean!" (Hakim, I, 553/1447; *Muwatta*, Qur'an, 1; Kattani, I, 216)
"Neither menstruating woman nor those without the major ablution can read anything from the Quran." (Tirmidhi, Taharah, 98/131)
Also holding the Noble Quran below the waist, laying down towards it, putting other things

The most important and major duty of the Messenger of Allah was to recite the Qur'an[116] and teach it to others. As a matter of fact, one day when Abu Talha (r.a.) arrived where the Prophet (pbuh) was, he saw the Prophet standing up and teaching the Qur'an to the Ashab al-Suffa.[117] And, the Prophet (pbuh), due to his hunger, had tied a stone to his belly in order to be able stand up. (Abu Nuaym, *Hilya,* I, 342)

Companions and righteous people of next generations followed the tradition of the Messenger of Allah on learning and teaching Qur'an.

Abdullah b. Mas'ud (r.a.) used to say when he let someone recite a verse from the Qur'an:

"This verse is better than anything that the sun rises upon or everything exists on this earth."

He used to repeat this sentence for each verse of Qur'an. (Haythami, VII, 166)

Abu Abdurrahman al-Sulami started to teach how to recite the Qur'an at the time of Uthman's Caliphate and continued doing this for a long time. He used to say about the praying room where he used to teach the Qur'an in the city of Kufe:

"The only reason that I am here is my wish to be among those about whom the Messenger of Allah gave the following good news:

"The best among you are those who learn and teach the Qur'an." (Bukhari, Fadail al-Qur'an, 21; Tirmidhi, Fadail al-Qur'an, 15/2907)

However, these services should be done only for the content of Allah. Material benefits and simple calculations should not interfere with it.

Once, Imran b. Husayn (r.a.) came across a person who was reciting the Qur'an. When the man was finished his recitation, he asked for some things from the audience. When Imran (r.a.) saw this, as if he was faced with a disaster, he said:

---

on top of it, taking it to bathroom are among the irrespectful acts towards the Qur'an and indicates the weakness of faith. Showing respect towards the Qur'an is a sign of piety. (al-Hajj; 22:32)

116. Yunus, 61; Zamakhshari, *Kashshaf,* III, 17; Abu al-Suud, *Irshad,* IV, 156.

117. *Translator's note:* Ashab al Suffa are those who stayed in the ante-chamber of the Mosque of the Prophet to advance their Islamic knowledge.

$$اِنَّا اللهِ وَاِنَّا اِلَيْهِ رَاجِعُونَ$$

"Inna lillahi wa inna ilayhi raaciun: To Allah We belong, and to Him is our return."[118]

Then he said:

"One day the Messenger of Allah (pbuh) said:

"Whoever recites the Qur'an, he should ask for it from Allah. That is because there will be a time that people will recite the Qur'an and ask for something from people." (Tirmidhi, Fadail al-Qur'an, 20/2917)

Qur'an is so valuable that it is impossible to compensate the rewards of learning and teaching it. Only Allah the Almighty can give its rewards in the best manner. How terrific the following two stories about those who acknowledged the value of the Qur'an are:

Imam Abu Hanifa gave five hundred dirhams to the teacher of his son Hammad when he taught Hammad the chapter Al-Fatiha. At the time, one could buy a ram for a dirham. The teacher found this generosity too much, for he had only taught the chapter al-Fatiha. Upon that Abu Hanifa said:

"Don't belittle what you have taught to my son! If we had more money with us then this amount, in order to show our respect for the Qur'an, we would give it to you."[119]

While Salahaddin Ayyubi was taking a walk in military quarters, he saw a kid reciting the Qur'an in front of his father. He liked the recitation of the kid and shared his food with him. He also donated part of his field to the kid and his father.[120]

While learning Qur'an and teaching it is so rewarding in the sight of Allah, forgetting it or preventing it from being taught is a major sin. In a hadith the miserable consequences of forgetting the Qur'an are mentioned as follows:

---

118. Al-Baqarah; 2:156. Allah wants us to recite this when we face with a trouble. This is called *"istirja."*
119. Abu Ghudda, *Fathu bab al-inaya*, p. 19; Muhammad Nur surveyed, *Peygamberimizin Sünnetinde Çocuk Eğitimi*, pp. 119-120.
120. Bundari, Abu'l-Feth Ali, *en-Nevadiru's-sultaniye (Siretu Salahuddin)*, p. 9; Muhammad Nur Suveyd, *Raising Children According to the Sunnah of the Prophet (Peygamberimizin Sünnetinde Çocuk Eğitimi)*, p. 120.

"...The sins of my followers are submitted to me. I did not see a worse sin than them forgetting a Chapter or a verse from the Qur'an that they were blessed with." (Abu Dawud, Salah, 16/461; Tirmidhi, Fadail al-Qur'an, 19/2916)

"Those who recite (learn) the Qur'an but then forget it will come to the presence of Allah on the Day of Judgment with empty hands and as deprived of goodness." (Abu Dawud, Witr, 21/1474)

The term "forgetting" here means both literally forgetting the memorized and learned Qur'an and also not reciting the Qur'an regularly, not putting it into practice, and not paying attention to what is permissible (halal) and forbidden (haram.) As a matter of fact the following verses express the same issue:

"But whosoever turns away from My Message, verily for him is a life narrowed down, and We shall raise him up blind on the Day of Judgment."

He will say: "O my Lord! Why have You raised me up blind, while I had sight (before)?" (Allah) will say:

"Thus did you, when Our Signs came unto you, disregard them: so will you, this day, be disregarded." (Taha; 20:124-126)

"He who has nothing of the Holy Qur'an in his heart is like a ruined house." (Tirmidhi, Fadail al-Qur'an, 18/2913; Darimi, Fadail al-Qur'an, 1)

The implied purpose in learning and teaching Qur'an is for sure to put it into practice in every aspect of life. In order to realize this, one must try to understand the content of Qur'an. **Our second hadith** shows how Allah is pleased with the works and efforts in this way. That is because Allah the Exalted descends tranquility upon those who assemble and recite, study, and try to understand the meaning of His Exalted Book and covers them with His mercy, and the angels surround them and Allah makes a mention of them in the presence of those near Him. Thus, those servants who study the Qur'an receive the prayers and love of select angels in the sight of Allah.

Allah's mercy covers such assemblies. All sins and faults of people who are present in such assemblies are forgiven except the sins of violating others' rights. Angels of mercy surround them and protect them from every kind of evil and danger by taking them into a ring that extends from the Earth up to the sky. Angels give acuteness to their intelligence and openness and comfort to their hearts, and they in a sense visit them and shake their hands.

The Companions of the Prophet used to assemble and discuss the Qur'an and the hadith. Abu Nadra narrates:

"When the Companions gathered, they used to study knowledge (noble hadith) and recite a chapter from the Qur'an." (Khatib al-Baghdadi, *al-Faqih wa al-mutafaqqih*, II, 126)

In the same manner, Ashab al-Suffa used to be present at Prophet's Mosque and recite the Qur'an and learn and discuss it among themselves during the night. (Bukhari, Jihad, 9; Muslim, Imarah, 147)

In our hadith, the Messenger of Allah (pbuh) gratified places where the Qur'an is studied as **"the House of Allah."** Here, the intention from the term "the Houses of Allah" is first of all mosques and praying rooms, and then every appropriate and clean place where Qur'an is recited, even our houses.

Getting the "**education**" of the Qur'an means to study deeply by focusing the mind and comprehension on Its verses and chapters one by one and to put them into practice by analyzing the fundamentals of the faith, the rules, the moral principles, and the knowledge covered in them.

The **"tranquility (*sakinah*)"** that is received by the students of the Qur'an purifies the hearts and fills them with the divine light. It also leads hearts to be filled with confidence and inner peace. By acknowledging the power of Allah, the owner of this kind of heart obtains a dignity that fits a believer well. Moreover, the Arabic word "*sakina*" (tranquility) not only means the descent of angels but also the name of the descending angel and angels of mercy.

A concrete example of the descent of "*Sakina*" is as follows:

Once Usaid b. Hudair, who had a nice voice, was reciting the Qur'an at night next to piles of dates and his horse was tied beside him with two long strings. Then, the horse suddenly reared up. When Usaid stopped reciting, the horse calmed down, and the same thing happened two more times. His younger son, Yahya was sleeping close to the horse. Usaid feared that the horse might hurt his kid, and he pulled the boy next to where he is. Then, when he looked towards the sky, he saw something like a cloud containing things that looked like lamps. These things slowly rose in the sky and then disappeared. The next morning he informed the Messenger of Allah (pbuh) what had happened. Allah's Messenger (pbuh) said:

"That was as-Sakina (tranquility) which descended because of (the recitation of) the Qur'an" (Bukhari, Manaqib, 25; Fadail al-Qur'an 11; Muslim, Musafirin 240-241)

In another narration:

"Those were Angels who came near to you for your recitation and if you had kept on reciting till dawn, they would have remained there till the morning when people would have seen them as they would not hide from people." (See Bukhari, Fadail al-Qur'an, 15; Muslim, Musafirin, 242)

The Noble Companions made great sacrifices in order to understand the Qur'an and practice it. For this reason, several companions chose to become a disciple of the Qur'an in Suffa and lead in poor conditions. Maybe they did not receive any material benefits for their sacrifice, but their names will be remembered until the Day of Judgment. Thousands of people who have benefited from the knowledge that they bequeathed pray for them. One of these students, Abdullah b. Mas'ud (r.a.) said:

"By Allah other than Whom none has the right to be worshipped! There is no chapter revealed in the book of Allah but I know at what place it was revealed; and there is no verse revealed in Allah's Book but I know about whom it is. If I hear that someone knows Qur'an better than I do and I know I can go to him with a camel, for sure I would take off right away to reach him." (Bukhari, Fadail al-Qur'an, 8)

Umar (r.a.) recited Qur'an by concentrating on understanding the verses and by deeply thinking through them and putting them into practice. His saying that "I have completed the chapter al-Baqarah in twelve years and to thank Allah, I have sacrificed a camel" proves this fact. (Qurtubi, I, 40)

Imam Malik also reported that Abdullah b. Umar (r.a.) studied the verses of the chapter al-Baqara for eight years in order to learn it. (*Muwatta*, Qur'an, 11)

Al-Baji said:

"This is not due to the weakness of his intelligence or memory, God forbid (we take refuge in Allah from thinking this way.) On the contrary, he was learning the obligatory acts (fards), rules, and other subjects related to them that are mentioned in Qur'an." (Kattani, *Taratib*, II, 191)

A man asked Zaid b. Thabit (r.a.) what he thinks about reciting the entire Noble Qur'an in one week. Zaid b. Thabit said "it would be nice" and continued:

"However, I like reciting the entire Qur'an in fifteen or twenty[121] days better. If you ask why, in this way I can think about the verses and understand them better." (*Muwatta*, Qur'an, 4)

b. Living the Qur'an

٨٥. عَنِ ابْنِ عُمَرَ رَضِيَ اللهُ عَنْهُمَا عَنِ النَّبِيِّ صَلَّى اللهُ عَلَيْهِ وَسَلَّمَ
قَالَ:

«لَا حَسَدَ إِلَّا فِي اثْنَتَيْنِ: رَجُلٌ آتَاهُ اللهُ الْقُرْآنَ فَهُوَ يَقُومُ بِهِ آنَاءَ اللَّيْلِ
وَآنَاءَ النَّهَارِ وَرَجُلٌ آتَاهُ اللهُ مَالًا فَهُوَ يُنْفِقُهُ آنَاءَ اللَّيْلِ وَآنَاءَ النَّهَارِ».

85. Ibn Umar (r.a.) reported that the Prophet (pbuh) said:

"Do not envy, except two kinds of people:

First, a man whom Allah has given the knowledge of the Book and he recites and practices it during the hours of the night and the hours of the day, and, second, a man whom Allah has given wealth, and he spends it in charity during the night and the hours of the day." (Muslim, Musafirin, 266, 267. Also see Bukhari, Tamanni, 5; Tawhid, 45)

٨٦. عَنْ مُعَاذٍ الْجُهَنِيِّ رَضِيَ اللهُ عَنْهُ أَنَّ رَسُولَ اللهِ صَلَّى اللهُ عَلَيْهِ
وَسَلَّمَ قَالَ:

«مَنْ قَرَأَ الْقُرْآنَ وَعَمِلَ بِمَا فِيهِ أُلْبِسَ وَالِدَاهُ تَاجًا يَوْمَ الْقِيَامَةِ ضَوْءُهُ
أَحْسَنُ مِنْ ضَوْءِ الشَّمْسِ فِي بُيُوتِ الدُّنْيَا لَوْ كَانَتْ فِيكُمْ، فَمَا ظَنُّكُمْ
بِالَّذِي عَمِلَ بِهٰذَا».

---

121. Ibn Abdilbar, *Istidhkar*, II, 477.

86. Mu'adh al-Juhani (r.a.) reported that the Messenger of Allah (pbuh) said:

"If anyone recites the Qur'an and acts according to its contents, on the Day of Judgment his parents will be crowned with a crown whose light is better than the light of the sun would be in the dwellings of this world if it were among you. So what do you think of the person himself who acts according to the Qur'an?"
(Abu Dawud, Witr, 14/1453)

Explanations:

The real purpose of reading and understanding the Qur'an is to put it into practice in every aspect of our life. This is stated in the noble verses of the Qur'an as follows:

"(Here is) a Book which We have sent down unto you, full of blessings, that they may mediate on its Signs, and that men of understanding may receive admonition." (Sad; 38:29)

"Those who rehearse the Book of Allah, establish regular Prayer, and spend (in charity) out of what We have provided for them, secretly and openly, hope for a commerce that will never fail." (Al-Fatir; 35:29)

According to such verses of Qur'an, reading and understanding the verses of the Qur'an must be followed by acts that reflect the lessons taken from its commands and prohibitions. For this reason, in the second verse, reading the Qur'an is followed by performing prayers and giving charity openly and secretly from the blessings of Allah. Since a person who reads and understands the Qur'an obeys its rules by thinking about the good news, warnings, and clear verses and explanations of Qur'an and avoids its prohibitions. Satan works hard to keep people away from the Qur'an. Therefore, Allah the Almighty commands to seek His protection especially before reading the Qur'an and says:

"When you do read the Qur'an, seek Allah's protection from Satan the rejected one." (Al-Nahl; 16:98)

With this command of Allah, Satan's interference between the Qur'an and putting it into practice will be prevented.

It is explained in the following saying by the Messenger of Allah (pbuh) what happens to Satan when the believers follow this command of Allah:

"When, the son of Adam recites a verse of prostration and then falls down in prostration, the Satan goes into seclusion and weeps and says:

"Woe unto me, the son of Adam was commanded to prostrate, and he prostrated and Paradise was entitled to him and I was commanded to prostrate, but I refused and am doomed to Hell." (Muslim, Kitab Al-Iman, 133)

The whole point is to read the Qur'an and put it into practice without tripping in front of the obstacles of carnal self and Satan. As a matter of fact, those who do not reflect the Qur'an into their lives are not considered as hafiz (or the person who has memorized the entire Qur'an) no matter how well he recites it from his memory. Indeed Abu Umar (r.a.) described being hafiz of the Qur'an as:

"The real hafiz is the one who knows the commands of it, and what is permissible and forbidden and puts them into practice." (Qurtubi, I, 26)

Abdullah b. Mas'ud pointed out that being a real hafiz of the Qur'an is only possible by living the Qur'an and said:

"Those who memorized the entire Qur'an should be known by:

1. Waking up at night and worshipping,

2. Fasting while others are not fasting,

3. Thinking about their end while others are having fun,

4. Weeping because of their weaknesses in their servitude to Allah while others are laughing,

5. Keeping their silence while others are talking to each other,

6. Being humble while others are arrogant.

Those who have memorized the Qur'an should:

1. Weep,

2. Look sad,

3. Be dignified and knowledgeable,

4. And think a lot and be peaceful.

Those who know the Qur'an should avoid;

1. Being cold hearted,

2. Ignorant,

3. Flattering (i.e. someone who praises others just to get worldly benefits) and,

4. Getting easily upset." (Abu Nuaym, *Hilya*, I, 130)

The Messenger of Allah lived the Qur'an while reading it. When he read the Qur'an, he thought about the meanings of the verses and immediately applied its commands in his life. For instance when he came to the verses about glorifying Allah, he would say the phrases such as "Subhan'Allah" (Glorious is Allah) to glorify the name of Allah. When he read the verses about praying, he would make supplication to Allah. When he read the verses about seeking protection from Allah, he would immediately take refuge in Allah. (Muslim, Musafirin, 203; Nasai, Qiyam al-Layl, 25/1662)

This is the kind of study of the Qur'an which will lead a believer to salvation. As a matter of fact, Muhammad Hadimi, one of the famous Ottoman scholars, said:

The only way to avoid all kinds of hardships, troubles, and disasters is holding onto the Qur'an and putting it into practice. Keep performing acts of worship and services! Especially hold on to reading the Qur'an, which is among the best acts of worship, while thinking about its meaning, pronouncing its verses clearly, and showing respect to it! Indeed, reading the Qur'an in this manner is like directly communicating with Allah. (See Hadimi, *Majmuat al-rasail*, pp. 112, 194, 200)

Allah the Almighty glorifies those who sincerely read the Qur'an and put it into practice, and degrades those who do not practice it even if they read it. (Muslim, Musafirin, 269; Ali al-Qari, *Mirqat,* IV, 620)

In our first hadith, we are told that those who read the Qur'an in the morning and evening and practice it come at the first rank of those whom one can envy. How can someone not wish to be like them?![122] As a matter of fact, it is the greatest wealth to have the knowledge of the Noble Qur'an and then to

---

122. The meaning of the term "*hasad*" mentioned in the Arabic original of the hadith is wishing that someone's wealth be off his hands. Its figurative meaning is *to admire*. There is no doubt that in this hadith the term is used in its figurative meaning. In other words, one should admire those who know the Holy Qur'an and try to be like them.

act in accordance with it. Believers should appreciate the value of this divine blessing and should not turn attention to temporary and deceptive profits.

It is said in a noble hadith:

"Qur'an is a wealth that no poverty can be experienced after it (in other words, those who know the Qur'an obtain the most valuable wealth) and there is no wealth save the Holy Qur'an (in other words, such divine wealth cannot be compared to any material wealth.)" (Haythami, VII, 158)

The following saying of Abdullah b. Mas'ud (r.a.) is really striking in terms of expressing the wealth of those who know the Qur'an:

"Whoever wishes for knowledge should contemplate about the meanings of the verses of the Qur'an, and concentrate their exegesis and recitation! As a matter of fact, it consists of the knowledge of the past and the future generations." (Haythami, VII, 165; Baihaqi, *Shuab*, II, 331)

About this topic, Husayn b. Fadl narrated the following story:

Seven caravans owned by the Jewish tribes of Bani Qurayzah and Bani Nadir arrived at the city of Medina on the same day. The caravans carried various fabrics, perfume glasses, jewelry, and various sea products.

Muslims said:

"We wish that these materials were ours so that we would get stronger and spend it in the way of Allah."

Upon that, Allah the Almighty revealed the following noble verse:

"And We have bestowed upon you the seven oft-repeated (verses) and the Grand Qur'an." (Al-Hijr; 15:87)

In other words, Allah the Almighty meant "I have blessed you with seven verses which are more valuable than those seven caravans."

After this verse, the following verse was revealed:

"Strain not your eyes (wistfully) at what We have bestowed on certain classes of them, nor grieve over them: but lower your wing (in gentleness) to the believers." (Al-Hijr; 15:88) (Wahidi, p. 283)

Aifa b. Abd (r.a.) reported the following incident:

When the tax revenues from Iraq came to Umar, he and his assistant came out. Umar started to count the camels. When he saw that they are more than what they have expected, he said "Alhamdulillah!" His helper said referring to a verse of Qur'an:

"O leader of the believers, I swear to Allah, these are from the blessings and mercy of Allah."

Umar (r.a.) replied:

"No you are wrong. These are not the things that Allah the Almighty referred in the verse **"let them rejoice in the bounty of Allah and in His Mercy..."**[123] Finding the right path, Sunnah, and Qur'an are the real blessings and mercy of Allah. Let all believers rejoice for these. This is the wealth about which the rest of the verse is talking **"The bounty of Allah and His Mercy is better than the (wealth) they hoard"**[124] since such wealth is also among the things that humans collect." (Ibn al-Jawzi, *Manaqib*, p. 229)

In our second hadith is told the merits of those who practice the Qur'an and the divine rewards that will be given to them in hereafter. From a literal perspective, rewards that will be given to parents of those who learn and practice the Qur'an are being told in this hadith. However, the last sentence elequantly shows the virtue and superiority of those who actually practice the Qur'an. If the crown of their parents is so good, then who knows how valuable and superior their reward will be. Therefore, a believer should try to live in accordance with the Qur'an and also give his children a solid education of the Qur'an.

Those who learn, teach, and practice the Qur'an will not only see its rewards in this world but also in their questioning in the grave and in the Hereafter. The Messenger of Allah (pbuh) informs us one of the rewards of those who are acquainted with the Qur'an as:

"When a person who memorized the whole Qur'an and who lived by the commands of the Qur'an, who shaped his manners according to the Qur'an, and who matured himself with the wisdom of the Qur'an passes away, Allah reveals to the earth not to eat (ruin) his body. The earth says:

123. Yunus; 10:58.
124. Yunus; 10:58.

"O My Lord! While Your words are within him, how could I eat his body?"
(Dailami, I, 284/1112; Ali al-Muttaqi, I, 555/2488)

As a matter of fact, sometimes we still see the examples which bodies of the people of the Qur'an do not get decomposed after their death.

A miserable end waits for those who abandon the Qur'an. The state in the hereafter of those whom Allah had given the knowledge of the Qur'an but who had slept all night and had not acted in accordance with it during the day was shown to the Messenger of Allah (pbuh). According to this, the head of those who neglect the Qur'an will be crushed with a big rock until the Day of Resurrection. (Bukhari, al-Jana'iz, 93; Ta'bir, 48)

A noble hadith on this subject presents the following sad scenes:

"A man is brought on the Day of Judgment. The Qur'an is presented to him in human form. In his lifetime, the man had neglected the obligatory acts (fard) of the Qur'an, violated the limits and forbidden acts of the Qur'an. He had not fulfilled the acts of worships that are commanded and opposed to them, and committed acts that are prohibited by the Qur'an. The Qur'an says:

"O My Lord! To what a mean man You have given my verses (taught him and had him memorize!) He violated my limits, neglected my requirements (fard). He did not perform the acts of worships that I have commanded, but he committed the acts that I informed him as prohibited ..."

The Qur'an continued to list the evidences against the man for so long that finally Allah told the Qur'an:

"I am leaving him to you. Do however he deserves!"

The Qur'an holds his hands, and drags the man on his nose and does not leave him until it throws him into the Fire.

Then another man is brought. In his lifetime, this man paid attention to the limits of the Qur'an, fulfilled the requirements (fard), performed the obligatory acts of worship, and avoided from the forbidden acts. The Qur'an stays in front of him and defends him and says:

"O My Lord! To what a nice man You have taught my verses and make him memorize them! He paid attention to my limits, fulfilled my requirements (fard), he followed the acts of worships that I have informed and stayed away from the forbidden acts..."

The Qur'an continued to list the evidences for him for so long that Allah told the Qur'an:

"I am leaving him to you. Do however he deserves!"

Upon that, the Qur'an seen in human form holds the man's hand and does not leave him. He dresses him with white clothes, crowns him like the kings, and offers him water in the bowl of the kings." (Haythami, VII, 160-161; Bazzar, no: 2337)

As the Messenger of Allah (pbuh) complains in this world about those who abandon the recitation and the practice of the Qur'an, he will also complain about them in the Hereafter. What a miserable situation for a believer it is to face with a complaint of the Messenger of Allah at a time when he needs his intercession the most! It is stated in another Qur'anic verse:

"Then the Messenger will say: O my Lord! Truly my people took this Qur'an for just foolish nonsense." (Al-Furqan; 25:30)

This complain contains not only disbelieving the Qur'an and having an attitude against it but also not paying attention to its warnings and good news, and especially abandoning to recite it. In a noble hadith, it is stated:

"Whoever learns the Qur'an and puts the Book away and neither recites it or looks at it, , the Qur'an comes on the Day of Judgment and gets a hold of that person and complains as:

"O the Creator of all! This servant of You abandoned me and stayed away from me. You decide between us!" (Qurtubi, XIII, 27-28; Alusi, *Ruh al-ma'ani*, XIX, 14, [Al-Furqan; 30 (see commentaries)])

There are also people who not only do not learn and practice the Qur'an but also use it to be famous and receive some benefits. The following report of Mu'adh b. Jabal (r.a.) which he very likely heard from the Prophet (pbuh) contains very important warnings and signs. He says:

"For sure there will be some trials in the future. At that time, wealth increases and Qur'an is opened and everyone including believers, hypocrites, man, woman, slave, free, children, and adults read the Qur'an. Such days are close when one of them will say:

"What is wrong with these people that they do not follow me even though I recite the Qur'an? They won't follow me in religion unless I say things against the Qur'an."

Avoid following such innovations (in religion)! As a matter of fact, these kinds of innovations are clearly in error and deviance. I am warning you against the deviation of the wise who are acquainted with knowledge. That is because sometimes Satan tells the false words using the tongues of the scholars, and sometimes, a hypocrite tells a right word."

Someone among them asked:

"May Allah bless you, but how are we going to know that a scholar tells something wrong and a hypocrite tells something right?"

Mu'adh (r.a.) answered as follows:

"Yes, avoid the words of a famous scholar whom everyone's eyes are on, but that sound weird to you and which make you say "What does he mean by that?" However, this temporary deviation of the scholar should not make you stop listening to him all together! That is because it is always possible for him to take his words back. When you hear the right word, take it regardless of who said it! That is because there is divine light on the right thing." (Abu Dawud, Sunnah, 6/4611)

c. Cure with the Qur'an

٨٧. عَنْ عَلِيٍّ رَضِيَ اللّٰهُ عَنْهُ قَالَ: قَالَ رَسُولُ اللّٰهِ صَلَّى اللّٰهُ عَلَيْهِ وَسَلَّمَ:

«خَيْرُ الدَّوَاءِ الْقُرْآنُ».

87. Ali (r.a.) reported the Messenger of Allah (pbuh) say:

"The Qur'an is the best of all cures." (Ibn Majah, Tibb, 28, 41)

٨٨. عَنْ عَبْدِ اللّٰهِ رَضِيَ اللّٰهُ عَنْهُ قَالَ: قَالَ رَسُولُ اللّٰهِ صَلَّى اللّٰهُ عَلَيْهِ وَسَلَّمَ:

«عَلَيْكُمْ بِالشِّفَاءَيْنِ: الْعَسَلِ وَالْقُرْآنِ».

88. Abdullah b. Mas'ud (r.a.) reported that the Messenger of Allah (pbuh) said:

"I recommend you the following two means of cure: Honey and the Qur'an."
(Ibn Majah, Tibb, 7)

Explanations:

Allah the Almighty has given the cure for every affliction that He has created.[125] In order to find them, one has to search for the cures of the illnesses.

When people asked to the Messenger of Allah:

"O Messenger of Allah! Should we make use of medical treatment?" He responded:

"Make use of medical treatment, for Allah has not made a disease without appointing a remedy for it, with the exception of one disease, namely old age."
(Abu Dawud, Tibb, 1/3855; Ibn Majah, Tibb, 1)

However, the Messenger of Allah (pbuh) required a treatment to be done by using permissible materials and said:

"Allah has sent down both the disease and the cure, and He has appointed a cure for every disease, so treat yourselves medically, but use nothing unlawful."
(Abu Dawud, Tibb, 11/3874)

He said to people who said that they are being treated with wine:

"It is not a cure but a trouble" and forbid it. (Tirmidhi, Tibb, 8/2046)

Allah the Almighty, the owner and controller of everything, has related every event to a cause. That is because Allah made this universe *alam al-asbab* or the universe of causes. Therefore, He left the treatment of the illnesses to certain medicines. As a matter of fact, studying illnesses is the topic of the science of medicine. However, the necessity and the benefit of praying to Allah should never be denied as well. Since everything is in Allah's control, as in everything else, praying to Him for the cure of an illness is extremely important. Many supplications that the Messenger of Allah recited for the sick have been reported. The Messenger of Allah (pbuh) not only recited some verses

125. Bukhari, Tibb, 1.

and chapters from the Qur'an in addition to other kinds of supplications but he also approved people who did the same.

Since **our first hadith** informs us that the Qur'an is the best cure, believers should never abandon supplicating for getting well and reciting the Qur'an along with taking the medications. As a matter of fact, the food and vitamins cannot go beyond being a creature of Allah as a mean for the treatment of illnesses. In reality, Allah is the one who provides the cure. Therefore, while one tries all the means of treatment on the one hand, on the other hand he should sincerely pray to Allah for a cure and recite Qur'an.[126]

The Noble Qur'an is a source of guidance and cure. It is the most important cure for the hearts, bodies, and spirits. It combines the worldly science of medicine and the divine medicine, the medicine for the body and the medicine for the soul, and the cure that belongs to this world and the cure of the spiritual world. However, the treatment of the Qur'an is more applicable to spiritual illnesses. With this in mind, the features of the Qur'an treating many carnal illnesses for which the science of medicine cannot find any cure, despite all kinds

---

126. Recently, research has been done on the effects of having faith, praying, and reciting the Quran on human health. We can mention some of them here:

A Muslim scientist Dr. Ahmet al-Qadi who works in the USA researched on **"Quran and Stress"** and presented his works in 1984 in an Islamic Medicine Conference which took place in Istanbul. In his research, this scientist found that the sound of the words of the Quran had positive effects on relieving stress.

(http://www.thehealthnews.org/tr/news/05/11/10/dua.tedavi.iyilesme.html, [23.04.2007])

In the US, according to another study composed of analysis of many different previous researches, religious faith affects life expectancy as much as good nutrition, exercise, regular checkups, and receiving appropriate treatments for the illnesses. The study of Dr. Daniel Hall from the University of Pittsburgh's Center of Medicine indicates that the positive effects of spiritual life on life expectancy are more easily seen than the effects of other variables. Dr. Hall focuses on a particular side of the issue and argues that positive effects of believing is due to the psychology of optimism and social solidarity that are created by the feeling of belonging to a group which in turn decreases the effects of everyday stress. (http://www.ktuvakfi.org.tr/h1.htm, [23.04.2007])

Another study is done on 393 patients between the August of 1982 and May of 1983. In this research, the group divided into two and one is prayed for without their knowledge and the other group is not prayed for again without their knowledge. The statistics of the research show that the group that is prayed for experienced less congestive heart failure, needed less diuretics and antibiotics, experienced fewer pneumonia and intubation cases, and were administered less oxygen. When we look at the statistics, the group that is prayed for, even though they did not know it, drew a better picture in every aspect. The results of this experiment are published in a New York Times article in October 2001. (http://www.benotesi.com/index.php?option=com_content&task=view&id=38&Itemid=56, [23.04.2007])

of research, are being observed by the qualified people all along. (Razi, XXI, 29; Elmalılı, V, 3195, [Al-Isra 17/82 explanation])

It is not right to think that the Qur'an revealed by Allah, the Lord of all the Universes, would not offer treatment for the illnesses, while it is accepted that even some human words can positively affect the course of illnesses. When looked objectively, it can be seen that when recited with full faith in its benefits and blessings, the Qur'an can heal many illnesses.

The Messenger of Allah (pbuh) never abandoned the recitation of the Qur'an for illnesses and troubles. Aisha (r.anha) said:

"Whenever Allah's Apostle went to bed, he would recite Surat al-Ikhlas, Surat al-Falaq and Surat al-Nas and then blow on his palms and pass them over his face and those parts of his body that his hands could reach. And when he fell ill, he used to order me to do like that for him." (Bukhari, Tibb, 39)

Aisha (r.anha) also said:

"During the Prophet's terminal illness, he used to recite the Mu'auwidhat (Surat al-Nas and Surat al-Falaq) and then blow his breath over his body. When his illness was aggravated, I used to recite those two Chapters and blow my breath over him and make him rub his face with his own hand for its blessings." (Bukhari, Tibb, 32)

A man saw a scar on the knee of the Companion Salama b. Aqwa and asked:

"What is this?"

Salama (r.a.) told him his story:

"This scar was afflicted on the Day of Khaibar. Upon that, the people around me screamed saying:

"Salama got hit!" Then the Messenger of Allah (pbuh) came near me and blew on me three times. Finally, one hour later I was completely cured." (Abu Dawud, Tibb, 19/3894)

The Messenger of Allah (pbuh) commanded us to recite supplications for the treatment of evil eye. As a matter of fact, when the Prophet (pbuh) saw in the house of Ummu Salama a girl whose face turned yellow, he said:

"She is under the effect of an evil eye; so treat her with a Ruqya (protective and healing supplications.)" (Bukhari, Tibb, 35)

Abu Sa'id al-Khudri reported.

We were at a military expedition that the Messenger of Allah (pbuh) had sent us. We landed at a place where a maid came to us and said:

"A poisonous snake has bitten the chief of our tribe. The soldiers that can treat him are not with us right now. Is there any incantator (someone who recites Ruqya which means reciting protective and healing supplications) amongst you?"

A person amongst us which we had no idea that he had been a good incantator stood up and went with her. But he practiced incantation and the chief was all right. They gave our friend thirty sheep, and he served us their milk. We said to him:

"Are you a good incantatory?" Thereupon he said:

"No, I only did it by reciting the chapter al-Fatiha."

We said to him [to make sure it is his right]:

"Do not benefit from these sheep until we ask Allah's Messenger about this!"

When we came to Medina and told Allah's Apostle (pbuh) of what happened, he said:

"How did you come to know that this (al-Fatiha) could be used as an incantation? So distribute them (amongst those who had been present there with him) and allocate a share of mine also!"[127] (Muslim, Salam, 66, 65; Bukhari, Fadail al-Qur'an, 9; Ijara, 16; Tibb, 33, 39)

In another hadith, the Messenger of Allah (pbuh) said:

"There is a cure in al-Fatiha for every illness." (Darimi, Fadail al-Qur'an, 12)

---

127. The Messenger of Allah (pbuh) said this in order to make his companions content and ensure that receiving gifts in response to a treatment is permissible. (Ayni, Umdat al-Qari, XXI, 271-272)

Ilaqah b. Sahar came to the Apostle of Allah (pbuh) and embraced Islam. He then returned and on his way stopped by some people who had a lunatic fettered in chains. His people said:

"We are told that your companion (i.e. the Messenger of Allah (pbuh)) has brought some good from Allah. Do you have anything with which you can cure him?

Ilaqah (r.a.) continued his words as:

I then recited al-Fatiha and he was cured. They gave me one hundred sheep. I then came to the Apostle of Allah (pbuh) and informed him of it and asked whether it is permissible for me to take the sheep. He asked:

"Did you say anything other than this (Qur'an)?"

I said:

"No, I have not."

The Messenger of Allah (pbuh) said:

"Take it, for by my life, some accept if for a worthless chain, but you have done so for a genuine one!" (Abu Dawud, Tibb, 19/3896; Buyu, 37/3420; Ahmad, V, 211)

The reason why the Messenger of Allah asked his companion whether or not he has recited something else was to see if some traditions of pre-Islamic Ignorance era are mixed with it. When he saw that this was not the case, he told the man that the reward was permissible (halal).

Jabir (r.a.) narrated as follows:

A scorpion stung one of us while we were sitting with Allah's Messenger (pbuh) and a person said:

"O Allah's Messenger, should I use incantation (for curing the effect of the sting)?

The Messenger of Allah (pbuh) said:

"He who is competent amongst you to benefit his brother should do so!" (Muslim, Salam, 61, 62, 63; Ahmad, III, 302, 304)

Treating with praying and supplications (Ruqya) was a known method of curing in the pre-Islamic Ignorance era as well. However, among the recited words, there were expressions of polytheism. For this reason, the Messenger of

Allah (pbuh) had first forbidden to perform Ruqya, but later said: "Bring your Ruqya to me!" and he gave permission to recite their Ruqya after cleaning up the parts that are not permissible.

The scholars agreed that a Ruqya would be permissible under the following three conditions:

a.   It should be done by reciting the words of Allah, His names or attributes;

b.   It should be done in Arabic or some other language that is clearly understood;

c.   One must believe that the Ruqya is not the cure by itself but it cures only if Allah the Almighty wishes so. (Ibn Hajar, *Fath al-Bari*, X, 206)

In other words, Ruqya is permissible only when it is composed of verses of the Qur'an and sayings of the Prophet (pbuh) in which the names and attributes of Allah are mentioned, and when it is recited in an understandable language. A Ruqya performed by saying unclear words, meaningless sounds, and unknown names is forbidden (haram). Also performing Ruqya by using iron and salt or by knotting a rope is forbidden. A Ruqya performed by praying, seeking refuge, or asking help from something other than Allah is committing polytheism.

The hadith that reports *"those who do not perform Ruqya or do not let Ruqya be done to himself will enter into Paradise without questioning"*[128] refers to the forbidden (haram) kind of Ruqya that is done in pre-Islamic era which contains polytheism.

The most practiced method in treating with Qur'an is reciting the verses that are about healing. Qushayri narrates that his son got sick. His condition got so bad that they lost hopes from his life. Imam Qushayri saw the Messenger of Allah in his dream. He explained the condition of his son to him. The Messenger of Allah (pbuh) reminded him the verses of the Qur'an about healing and advised him to recite them. When Qushayri followed the Prophet's advice, soon his son got well. (See Alusi, XV, 145, [Commentary on al-Isra 17/82])

The verses of Qur'an about healing are as follows:

---

128.   Bukhari, Riqaq, 50; Tibb, 17, 43; Libas, 18; Muslim, Iman, 367, 369, 371, 374.

وَيَشْفِ صُدُورَ قَوْمٍ مُؤْمِنِينَ

"…help you (to victory) over them, heal the breasts of Believers." (Al-Tawbah; 9:14)

وَشِفَآءٌ لِمَا فِي الصُّدُورِ

"… a healing for the (diseases) in your hearts…" (Yunus; 10:57)

يَخْرُجُ مِنْ بُطُونِهَا شَرَابٌ مُخْتَلِفٌ اَلْوَانُهُ فِيهِ شِفَآءٌ لِلنَّاسِ

"…there issues from within their bodies a drink of varying colors, wherein is healing for men." (Al-Nahl; 16:69)

وَنُنَزِّلُ مِنَ الْقُرْاٰنِ مَا هُوَ شِفَآءٌ وَرَحْمَةٌ لِلْمُؤْمِنِينَ

"We send down (stage by stage) in the Qur'an that which is a healing and a mercy to those who believe." (Al-Isra; 17:82)

وَاِذَا مَرِضْتُ فَهُوَ يَشْفِينِ

"And when I am ill, it is He Who cures me." (Al-Shu'ara; 26:80)

قُلْ هُوَ لِلَّذِينَ اٰمَنُوا هُدًى وَشِفَآءٌ

"… Say: "It is a Guide and a Healing to those who believe…" (Al-Fussilat; 41:44)

In seeking cure with the recitation of the Qur'an, it is very important for the heart to be sincere. In order for this method to work, one must act faithfully and sincerely and only for the sake of Allah and must always be acting upon the Qur'an. If the acts of the person do not conflict with his words and with the verses and supplications that he recites, the treatment occurs quicker.

Ibn Qayyim al-Jawziyye explains how Qur'an cures for both physical and spiritual illnesses as follows:

Qur'an is a complete cure for the illnesses of the heart and body which are either related to this world or to the Hereafter. However, not everybody is capable of receiving treatment with it. If a sick person receives a good treatment with the Qur'an, and he puts it in front of his illness with a strong faith, complete trust and righteousness, and by paying attention to its requirements, then the illness cannot resist it. How can illnesses resist to the word of Allah, the creator of the heavens and the earth? If the words of Allah descended onto mountains, they would be disarrayed and if it descended onto the earth, the earth would be destroyed. [129] There is no spiritual and physical illness that its remedy and its prevention cannot be found in the Qur'an! However, only those who are blessed with a special understanding of the Qur'an can benefit from them. [130]

In the second hadith, the Messenger of Allah (pbuh) advised the use of honey next to Qur'an as a treatment.

Allah informs us that there are many cures in honey produced by bees in various colors. (Al-Nahl; 16:69)

For this reason, the Messenger of Allah (pbuh) who liked sweet things and honey[131] said in a hadith:

Healing is in three things:

1.   *A gulp of honey,*

2.   *Bloodletting,* [132]

3.   *Branding with fire (cauterizing). But I forbid my followers to use (cauterization) branding with fire unless it is necessary.* (Bukhari, Tibb, 3)

The Messenger of Allah (pbuh) advised his Companions to drink honey syrup when they got ill. Abu Sa'id al-Khudri reported that a person came to

---

129. In some of the verses of the Quran, it is said that:
    "Had We sent down this Qur'an on a mountain, verily, you would have seen it humble itself and cleave asunder for fear of Allah. Such are the similitudes which We propound to men that they may reflect." (al-Hashr; 59:21)
    "If there were a Qur'an with which mountains were moved, or the earth was cloven asunder, or the dead were made to speak, (this would be the one!)" (al-Ra'd; 13:31)
130. Ibn Qayyim al-Jawziyya, *Zad al-Maad*, IV, 352; Qasimi, *Mahasin al-ta'wil*, X, 3978.
131. Bukhari, Tibb, 4.
132. **Bloodletting:** It is drawing some blood between the shoulders, from the back, from the back of the head, or from some other part of the body for treatment purposes. This method is among the advices of the Messenger of Allah for medical treatment and also a Sunnah that he practiced.

Allah's Messenger (pbuh) and told him that his brother's bowels were loose. Thereupon Allah's Messenger (pbuh) said:

"Give him honey." So he gave him that and then came and said:

"I gave him honey but it has only made his bowels more loose."

He said these three times; and then he came the fourth time, and he (the Holy Prophet) said:

"Give him honey." The man said:

"I did give him, but it has only made his bowels more loose," whereupon Allah's Messenger (pbuh) said:

"Allah has spoken the truth and your brother's bowels are in the wrong." So he made him drink (honey syrup) and he was recovered. (Bukhari, Tibb, 4; Muslim, Salam, 91)

With his last words, the Messenger of Allah (pbuh) expressed that the Qur'anic verse[133] stating there are cures in honey for humans is true and every Muslim should believe in this.[134]

d. The Intercession of the Qur'an

٨٩. عَنْ أَبِي أُمَامَةَ الْبَاهِلِيِّ قَالَ: سَمِعْتُ رَسُولَ اللهِ صَلَّى اللهُ عَلَيْهِ وَسَلَّمَ يَقُولُ:

«اقْرَءُوا الْقُرْآنَ فَإِنَّهُ يَأْتِي يَوْمَ الْقِيَامَةِ شَفِيعًا لِأَصْحَابِهِ».

89. Abu Umame al-Bahili (r.a.) reported: I heard the Messenger of Allah (pbuh) say:

"Recite the Qur'an! That is because, on the Day of Judgment, Qur'an will intercede for those who live by it." (Muslim, Musafirun, 252)

---

133. Nahl; 16:69.

134. For details about the healing power of the Quran see Mustafa Çetin, "Kur'ân'da Şifâ Kavramı", *Dokuzeylül Ünivesitesi İlahiyat Fakültesi Dergisi*, 1992, no. 7, p. 68; Ömer Çelik, *Kur'ân'a Göre Kur'ân-ı Kerim ve Muhatapları*, pp. 182-187; Qasimi, *Mahasin*, X, 3979.

٩٠. عَنِ النَّوَّاسِ بْنِ سَمْعَانَ رَضِيَ اللهُ عَنْهُ يَقُولُ: سَمِعْتُ النَّبِيَّ صَلَّى اللهُ عَلَيْهِ وَسَلَّمَ يَقُولُ:

«يُؤْتَى بِالْقُرْآنِ يَوْمَ الْقِيَامَةِ وَأَهْلِهِ الَّذِينَ كَانُوا يَعْمَلُونَ بِهِ فِي الدُّنْيَا تَقْدُمُهُ سُورَةُ الْبَقَرَةِ وَآلِ عِمْرَانَ» وَضَرَبَ لَهُمَا رَسُولُ اللهِ صَلَّى اللهُ عَلَيْهِ وَسَلَّمَ ثَلَاثَةَ أَمْثَالٍ مَا نَسِيتُهُنَّ بَعْدُ قَالَ:

«كَأَنَّهُمَا غَمَامَتَانِ أَوْ ظُلَّتَانِ سَوْدَاوَانِ بَيْنَهُمَا شَرْقٌ أَوْ كَأَنَّهُمَا حِزْقَانِ مِنْ طَيْرٍ صَوَافَّ تُحَاجَّانِ عَنْ صَاحِبِهِمَا».

90. Nawwas b. Sam'an (r.a.) reported: I heard the Messenger of Allah (pbuh) saying:

"On the Day of Judgment, the Qur'an and the people of the Qur'an who shape their lives according to the Qur'an will be brought forward. At that time, chapters of Al-Baqara and Al-i Imran were in front of the Qur'an."

The Messenger of Allah (pbuh) gave three examples for these chapters of the Qur'an and I still remember them. The Messenger of Allah (pbuh) continued as:

"They are like two clouds or two black shades and there is a bright divine light in between them or they are like two groups of birds on the sky. They intercede for the people who recited them." (Muslim, Musafirin, 253. Also see Tirmidhi, Fadail al-Qur'an, 5/2883)

❁

٩١. عَنْ عَبْدِ اللهِ بْنِ عَمْرٍو قَالَ: قَالَ رَسُولُ اللهِ صَلَّى اللهُ عَلَيْهِ وَسَلَّمَ:

«يُقَالُ لِصَاحِبِ الْقُرْآنِ: اقْرَأْ وَارْتَقِ وَرَتِّلْ كَمَا كُنْتَ تُرَتِّلُ فِي الدُّنْيَا فَإِنَّ مَنْزِلَكَ عِنْدَ آخِرِ آيَةٍ تَقْرَؤُهَا».

91. Narrated Abdullah b. Amr (r.a.) reported that the Apostle of Allah (pbuh) said:

"One who was devoted to the Qur'an will be told in the Hereafter:

"Recite and ascend, and recite carefully as you recited carefully when you were in the world, for the final abode you reach will be the height of the last verse you recite." (Abu Dawud, Witr, 20/1464; Tirmidhi, Fadail al-Qur'an, 18/2914)

Explanations:

The Noble Qur'an was revealed to ensure the happiness of human beings both in this world and the Hereafter. Since the real purpose of being happy in this world is to reach the happiness in the Hereafter, the most important purpose of the Qur'an is to ensure the eternal salvation and happiness of the servants of Allah.

Believers who follow the commands and prohibitions in the Qur'an will reach salvation both in this world and in the Hereafter and their levels will also elevated by the intercession of the Qur'an. **In the first hadith** Allah's Messenger (pbuh) gives the good tidings of this by saying:

"Recite the Qur'an! That is because, on the Day of Judgment, Qur'an will intercede for those who live by it."

In another noble hadith:

"Whoever learns a verse from the Qur'an will happily be met by this verse on the Day of Judgment." (Haythami, VII, 161)

Here the emphasis is that the Qur'an will intercede for those who learn the Qur'an and live in accordance with its rules. **"People of the Qur'an"** or **"Companions of the Qur'an"** are the ones who recite it, follow its instructions, and shape their actions and behaviors accordingly. Otherwise, they are not those who recite it without understanding and contemplating about its meaning and putting them into practice. Ali al-Qari tells that the Qur'an will not intercede for such people but on the contrary it will complain about them. That is because, the Qur'an is not revealed just to be read but also to be practiced in everyday life.

Those who learn, live, and teach the Noble Qur'an are the special servants of Allah. As a matter of fact, one day the Messenger of Allah (pbuh) said:

"For sure there are those who are closer to Allah among His servants!"

The Companions of the Prophet asked:

"O Messenger of Allah! Who are they?"

He (pbuh) said:

"They are the people of Allah, people of the Qur'an, and the exceptional servants of Allah!" (Ibn Majah, Muqaddimah, 16)

According to the good news informed in this hadith, Qur'an will testify on the Day of Judgment for those who recite it and practice its commands and it will intercede for their forgiveness. In turn, Allah the Almighty will treat such servants with His mercy.

Another noble hadith about this topic reads as follows:

"On the Day of Judgment, the Noble Qur'an comes to its reader like a pale man and says:

"I am the one that left you sleepless during the night and thirsty during the day!" (Ibn Majah, Adab, 52)

In other words, the Qur'an will help so much to those Muslims who tried hard and overcame difficulties in order to read and practice the Qur'an in this world that in a sense it will get tired and exhausted. The Messenger of Allah (pbuh) used this expression in order to explain that the Qur'an will help those who practice it on the frightful Day of Judgment, ease their questioning, and relieve the heat and hardship of the Day.

In turn, Allah the Almighty will not punish such servants. As a matter of fact, the Messenger of Allah (pbuh) said:

"Recite the Qur'an... That is because Allah does not punish the heart that has the Qur'an in it..." (Darimi, Fadail al-Qur'an, 1)

In the second hadith, after stating that the Qur'an will intercede for those who live in accordance with its rules, Allah's Messenger also informs us that certain chapters of the Qur'an such as Al-Baqarah and Al-i Imran will come and intercede even more for the people of the Qur'an.

In the rest of the hadith, in order to express the importance and spiritual rewards of these specific chapters of the Qur'an, the Messenger of Allah (pbuh) gave three examples for these chapters.

The superiority of a chapter of the Qur'an over another chapter is something related to their contents and the depth of their meaning. Chapters of al-Baqarah and Al-i Imran almost cover the entire issues of religion.

The following narration shows that the al-Baqara is so rich in terms of its content, and therefore this chapter of the Qur'an is considered more virtuous.

Once, the Messenger of Allah (pbuh) was going to send a military expedition. He made them read the Qur'an. Each of them recited from the verses of Allah as much as they knew. The Messenger of Allah (pbuh) approached the youngest Companions and said:

"O so and so! What do you have in your memory?"

And he said:

"I have such and such chapters in my memory, and I also memorized chapter al-Baqarah!"

The Messenger of Allah (pbuh) asked:

"Do you have in your memory the chapter al-Baqarah?"

The young man said:

"Yes!" Upon this, our Master Pride of the Universe (pbuh) said:

"Now you can go and be the leader (commander) of them! That is because this chapter covers almost the entire religion."

One of the leaders of the congregation said:

"O Messenger of Allah! The fear that I may not be able to practice the content of this chapter prevented me from memorizing it."

Upon that the Messenger of Allah (pbuh) said:

"Know, recite, teach, and practice the Qur'an! That is because, those who learn, teach, and practice the Qur'an are like a leather bag filled with musk whose

scent spreads to everywhere. Those who learn but do not practice it are like a tightly closed leather bag filled with perfume." (Tirmidhi, Fadail al-Qur'an, 2/2876; Haythami, VII, 161)

In our third hadith, it is expressed how the state of those who recite the Qur'an by paying attention to its manners and put it into practice in every aspect of their lives will be advanced in Paradise. Their levels in paradise will be commensurate with their relationship with the Qur'an in this world.

In another hadith, in a way explaining our third hadith, the Messenger of Allah (pbuh) said:

"The Qur'an comes on the Day of Judgment and says for the person who lived by it in the world:

"Dear Lord! Adorn him!"

Upon this, he gets crowned with the crown of honor and divine blessings.

The Qur'an says:

"O my Lord! Bless him with more!"

The person who reads and practices the Qur'an will be dressed with the garment of honor and divine blessings.

The Qur'an says:

"O my Lord! Be content with him!"

Allah becomes content with that person and says to him:

"Recite and ascend!"

So with each verse he recites, his spiritual rewards get increased." (Tirmidhi, Fadail al-Qur'an, 18/2915)

Aisha (r.anha), the mother of believers, said:

"The degrees of Paradise are as many as the number of the verses of the Qur'an. There is no one in Paradise who is more virtuous than those who recite the Qur'an." (Ibn Abi Shaiba, *Musannaf,* VI, 120/29952)

On that Day, whoever recites the whole Qur'an ascends to the highest level of Paradise. Everyone will ascend as much as they recite and will accordingly gain divine rewards.

The recitation of the Qur'an in Paradise of those who know and live the Qur'an will be like the angels' remembrance of Allah so this won't prevent them in any way from experiencing other blessings. In fact, reciting the Qur'an in the best fashion by paying attention to the rules of recitation will be their best pleasure.

The term "best fashion (**tartil**)" mentioned in the hadith essentially means harmony and order, in other words, reciting the Noble Qur'an with measured rhythmic tones and slowly by pronouncing the letters appropriately, namely by giving the Qur'an its due.

The recitation of the Prophet was clear and deliberate, by emphasizing the letters and watching for the measured rhythmic tones, and at the same time by paying attention to the rules of its recitation. (Tirmidhi, Fadail al-Qur'an, 23)

That is because Allah the Almighty commanded him:

$$وَرَتِّلِ الْقُرْاٰنَ تَرْتِيلًا$$

"... recite the Qur'an in slow, measured rhythmic tones." (Al-Muzzammil; 73:4)

What is understood from the usage of Arabic imperative "*rattil*" which is strenghtened with the infinitive "*tartilan*" in this verse is that Allah the Almighty wants us to recite the Qur'an deliberately and in the best fashion. Reciting the Qur'an with measured rhythmic tones is not a matter of music performed with a nice voice and random singing. On the contrary, rhymes should be recited by paying attention to the fluency and rhetoric character of the verses and their relationship with the meaning and by feeling the meaning and making others feel it. So, in the recitation of the Qur'an paying attention to the measured rhythmic tones and the rules of recitation are very important. As a matter of fact, our hadith encourages us to memorize the Qur'an and to recite it in the best fashion and points out that the levels of those who practice the Qur'an will be elevated.

However, there is a benefit to remind the following:

Those who act according to the Book of Allah and contemplate about it are surely better than those who do not put it into practice but just memorizes and nicely recites it. As a matter of fact, among the Companions there were many others who memorized and recited the Qur'an better than Abu Bakr (r.a.). However, there is an agreement that Abu Bakr was the best of the Noble Companions. That is because he was the one who knew Allah and the spirit of the Qur'an best, and the one who shaped his life according to the contents of the Qur'an.

On the other hand, we benefit not only from the Qur'an that we personally recite but also from the Qur'an that we teach to others. So, we gain the honor of its intercession. The Messenger of Allah (pbuh) said:

"The past and the future sins of those who teach their children how to read the Qur'an are forgiven. And whoever makes the child memorize the Qur'an, Allah resurrects him like a full moon on the Day of Judgment and the child will be told:

"Read!"

With each verse the child recites, Allah elevates the level of the father. This continues till the end of the verses that the child remembers." (Haythami, VII, 165-166)

On the Day of Judgment, just as the Qur'an, those who knew the Qur'an will also intercede. The Messenger of Allah (pbuh) informs us of that saying:

"Whoever recites the Qur'an and nicely memorizes it, and accepts its permissions as permissible (halal) and prohibitions as prohibited (haram), Allah places them into His Paradise and gives them permission to intercede for ten people from their family who deserved to be in Hell." (Tirmidhi, Fadail al-Qur'an, 13/2905; Ibn Majah, Muqaddimah, 16; Ahmad, I, 148)

May Allah bless us with learning and reciting the Qur'an in the best fashion by understanding its contents and putting them into practice and benefiting from its intercession on the Day of Judgment! Our Almighty Lord, bless our lives with the services to the Qur'an!

Amin!...

11. Times of Dawn

٩٢ . عَنْ بِلَالٍ رَضِيَ اللهُ عَنْهُ أَنَّ رَسُولَ اللهِ صَلَّى اللهُ عَلَيْهِ وَسَلَّمَ قَالَ:

«عَلَيْكُمْ بِقِيَامِ اللَّيْلِ فَإِنَّهُ دَأْبُ الصَّالِحِينَ قَبْلَكُمْ وَإِنَّ قِيَامَ اللَّيْلِ قُرْبَةٌ إِلَى اللهِ وَمَنْهَاةٌ عَنِ الْإِثْمِ وَتَكْفِيرٌ لِلسَّيِّئَاتِ وَمَطْرَدَةٌ لِلدَّاءِ عَنِ الْجَسَدِ».

92. Bilal (r.a.) reported that the Messenger of Allah (pbuh) saying:

"Try your best to wake up at night, because it was the tradition of the righteous people before you. There is no doubt that waking up at night for worship is the sign of being close to Allah. (This act of worship) prevents from wrongdoings, becomes expiation to sins, and treats the illnesses of the body." (Tirmidhi, Daawat, 101/3549)

✿

٩٣. عَنْ جَابِرٍ رَضِيَ اللهُ عَنْهُ قَالَ: سَمِعْتُ النَّبِيَّ صَلَّى اللهُ عَلَيْهِ وَسَلَّمَ يَقُولُ:

«إِنَّ فِي اللَّيْلِ لَسَاعَةً لَا يُوَافِقُهَا رَجُلٌ مُسْلِمٌ يَسْأَلُ اللهَ خَيْرًا مِنْ أَمْرِ الدُّنْيَا وَالْآخِرَةِ إِلَّا أَعْطَاهُ إِيَّاهُ وَذَلِكَ كُلَّ لَيْلَةٍ».

93. Jabir (r.a.) said: I heard the Prophet saying:

"There is a certain period of time in a night that if a Muslim catches it and asks for something good for this world or the Hereafter, Allah accepts his prayers. This period of time exists in every night." (Muslim, Musafirin, 166)

✿

٩٤. عَنْ أَبِي هُرَيْرَةَ رَضِيَ اللهُ عَنْهُ أَنَّ رَسُولَ اللهِ صَلَّى اللهُ عَلَيْهِ وَسَلَّمَ قَالَ:

«يَتَنَزَّلُ رَبُّنَا تَبَارَكَ وَتَعَالَى كُلَّ لَيْلَةٍ إِلَى السَّمَاءِ الدُّنْيَا حِينَ يَبْقَى ثُلُثُ اللَّيْلِ الْآخِرُ يَقُولُ: مَنْ يَدْعُونِي فَأَسْتَجِيبَ لَهُ مَنْ يَسْأَلُنِي فَأُعْطِيَهُ مَنْ يَسْتَغْفِرُنِي فَأَغْفِرَ لَهُ».

94. It is narrated from Abu Huraira (r.a.) that the Messenger of Allah (pbuh) said:

"Every night when only the last third of the night remains, our Lord descends to the nearest heaven and says:

"Is there anyone to invoke Me that I may respond to his invocation? Is there anyone to ask Me so that I may grant him his request? Is there anyone asking My forgiveness so that I may forgive him?" (Bukhari, Tawhid, 35; Tahajjud, 14; Daawat, 13; Muslim, Musafirin, 166)

٩٥. عَنْ أَبِي هُرَيْرَةَ رَضِيَ اللهُ عَنْهُ أَنَّ رَسُولَ اللهِ صَلَّى اللهُ عَلَيْهِ وَسَلَّمَ قَالَ:

«يَعْقِدُ الشَّيْطَانُ عَلَى قَافِيَةِ رَأْسِ أَحَدِكُمْ إِذَا هُوَ نَامَ ثَلاثَ عُقَدٍ يَضْرِبُ عَلَى كُلِّ عُقْدَةٍ: عَلَيْكَ لَيْلٌ طَوِيلٌ فَارْقُدْ، فَإِنِ اسْتَيْقَظَ فَذَكَرَ اللهَ انْحَلَّتْ عُقْدَةٌ فَإِنْ تَوَضَّأَ انْحَلَّتْ عُقْدَةٌ فَإِنْ صَلَّى انْحَلَّتْ عُقَدُهُ فَأَصْبَحَ نَشِيطاً طَيِّبَ النَّفْسِ وَإِلَّا أَصْبَحَ خَبِيثَ النَّفْسِ كَسْلانَ».

95. It is narrated from Abu Huraira (r.a.) that the Messenger of Allah (pbuh) said:

"Satan puts three knots at the back of the head of any of you when you are asleep. On every knot he reads and exhales the following words, "The night is long, so stay asleep." When one wakes up and remembers Allah, one knot is undone; and when one performs ablution, the second knot is undone, and when one prays, the third knot is undone and one gets up energetic with a good heart in the morning; otherwise one gets up lazy and with a mischievous heart." (Bukhari, Tahajjud, 12; Bad al-khalk, 11; Muslim, Musafirin, 207. Also see Abu Dawud, Tatawwu, 18/1306; Ibn Majah, Iqamah, 174)

Explanations:

The night compared to the day and the hours of early dawn compared to the night are considered better periods of time. So, believers who want to be blessed with Paradise should take the advantage of these valuable periods of time. As a matter of fact, Allah the Almighty advises the following to His servants who do not want to neglect the Hereafter:

"And part of the night, prostrate yourself to Him; and glorify Him a long night through. As to these, they love the fleeting life, and put away behind them a Day (that will be) hard." (Al-Insan; 76:26-27)

The Messenger of Allah (pbuh) said:

"Those who are afraid travel during the night. Someone who travels at night reaches where he wants to go. Know it well that Allah's merchandise is very expensive, and Paradise is Allah's merchandise." (Tirmidhi, Qiyamah, 18/2450)

By this rhetorical narration, Allah's Messenger (pbuh) wants the believers, who are in this world the travelers to the Hereafter, not to lose time. He advises us to take measures and take the advantage of the hour of early dawn to prepare ourselves for the Hereafter just like a person acting cautious during a war time and gains victory as a result of it.

When a period of time is so precious, the acts of worship performed at such periods of time also become very valuable. For this reason, performing a prayer, reciting the Qur'an, remembering Allah, and thinking about His blessings are even more valuable when performed during the early parts of dawn.

The Messenger of Allah (pbuh) said:

"The best prayer after the obligatory prayers is the late night prayer." (Muslim, Siyam, 202, 203)

"Allah does not listen to anything as much as He lsitens to the Qur'an recitation of His servant who performs two units of late night prayer. Allah's mercy descends upon the servant as long as his prayer lasts. The servants of Allah can never get as close to Allah as they do when they recite the Qur'an while praying." (Tirmidhi, Fadail al-Qur'an, 17/2911)

Even the dreams seen in the hour of early dawn are different than the dreams seen at other times. As a matter of fact, the Messenger of Allah (pbuh) said:

"The most truistworthy dream is the one seen in the early parts of dawn." (Tirmidhi, Ru'ya, 3/2274)

In our first hadith, it is mentioned that waking up in the early parts of dawn is the custom of the righteous people. We are informed that this good deed which gets humans closer to Allah mot only becomes expiation for our sins but also treats our physical illnesses. In other words waking up for worship in the early parts of dawn is as good for our physical illnesses as it is for the spiritual ones.

The most prominent custom of the Messenger of Allah was to wake up for worship in the early hours of dawn. Allah the Almighty says:

"And pray in the small watches of the morning: (it would be) an additional prayer (or spiritual profit) for you: soon will your Lord raise you to a Station of Praise and Glory!" (Al-Isra; 17:79)

In other words, the best way to earn this level with which only one person will be blessed in the Hereafter is taking advantage of the early hour of dawn by worshipping Allah.

For this reason, the Messenger of Allah used to pay extra attention to the late night prayers and worshipped a lot without failing to get enough rest. Anas (r.a.) reported:

"If you wanted to see him praying at night, you could see him praying and if you wanted to see him sleeping, you could see him sleeping." (Bukhari, Tahajjud, 11; Sawm, 52, 53; Muslim, Sawm, 178-180)

Allah's Messenger (pbuh) would sometimes wake up for the late night prayer at early parts of the night, and sometimes in the middle of the night, but mostly at the early hours of dawn. The Companions used to be able to see him worshipping or resting in various times rather than a fixed time. However, towards the end of his life, the Messenger of Allah (pbuh) used to wake up for the late night prayer in the last third of the night, in other words, at the early hours of dawn.

Aisha (r.anha) explained the features of Prophet's late night prayers as:

"Allah's Apostle never exceeded eleven cycles (rak'ah) of prayer in Ramadan or in other months; he used to offer four cycles -- do not ask me about their beauty and length, then four cycles, do not ask me about their beauty and length, and then three cycles ..." (Bukhari, Tahajjud, 16; Tarawih, 1; Muslim, Musafirin, 125)

The Messenger of Allah who used to perform indescribably beautiful and long prayers started to perform his prayers while sitting when he became old. He would recite for some time while sitting but when he wanted to perform a bowing, he wound get up, recite some more verses and then perform the bowing. (Bukhari, Tafsir, 48/2)

Allah the Almighty praises His good servants who follow the tradition of the Prophet and benefit from the hour of early dawn as:

"… and who pray for forgiveness in the early hours of the morning." (Al-i Imran; 3:17)

"They were in the habit of sleeping but little by night, And in the hour of early dawn, they (were found) praying for Forgiveness." (Al-Zariyat; 51:17-18)

Let's give some examples from the beautiful states of the righteous people who used to regularly perform night prayers:

The Messenger of Allah (pbuh) said:

"I recognize the Qur'an reciting voices of the soft-hearted tribe of al-Ashariyun when they enter their homes at night. In military expeditions, I recognize their residences at night from their voices when they are reciting the Qur'an although I had not seen where they stay during the day time..." (Bukhari, Al-Maghazi, 38)

Aisha (r.anha) reported:

The Prophet performed the Tahajjud prayer in my house, and then he heard the voice of 'Abbad b. Abdullah who was praying in the Mosque, and said,

"O Aisha! Is this Abbad's voice?" I said,

"Yes," He said,

"O Allah! Be merciful to 'Abbas!" (Bukhari, Shahadat, 11)

For eight or nine nights, the Messenger of Allah (pbuh) performed the obligatory night prayer (*salat al-isha*) until the one third of the night. Upon that Abu Bakr (r.a.) said:

"O the Messenger of Allah! If you lead the salah al-isha a little earlier, it would be easier for us to wake up for the late night prayer!"

From that time on, the Messenger of Allah (pbuh) led the salah al-isha earlier. (Ahmad, V, 47)

When Umar (r.a.) woke up for the late night prayer, he used to pray as follows:

"O Lord! You know where I am and You know what I need! O Lord! Return me from Your presence as a servant whose needs are satisfied, who is safe from all kinds of fears and troubles, who fulfills Your commands right away, whose prayers are answered, whose wrongdoings You forgive and upon whom You have shown Your mercy."

After performing his prayer, he would continue his supplication saying:

"O Lord! I cannot see anything eternal on this world. There is no upright state on it, either. O Lord! Make me among Your servants who speak with knowledge and keep silent with wisdom! O Lord! Do not make me too rich so that I won't go astray, and do not put me in a difficult position so that I won't forget my acts of worships and responsibilities. For sure, wealth that is not much but just the right amount is better than too much wealth that causes one to forget his worships and responsibilities." (Ibn Abi Shayba, *Musannaf*, VII, 82)

The following story is an exemplary one that shows how the late night prayer (*salat al-tahajjud*) makes a believer among the righteous people and leads him to salvation:

Amir b. Rabia who paid extra attention to the late night prayers passed away while he was performing one. When people of his time were faced with an unsolvable disorder, a voice said to Amir in his dream as:

"Wake up! Ask Allah to save you from this unrest from which Allah saves His righteous servants!"

He woke up right away and performed a prayer. He got sick after the prayer and he passed away before going out of his house. (Haythami, IX, 301; Ibn Abi Shayba, Musannaf, VI, 362/32044)

Qatadah said:

Amir b. Abdiqais started to cry in his death bed.

When he was asked why he was crying, he said:

221

"I am neither crying form the fear of death nor from the passion of this world. However, I am crying that I will be deprived of fasting in hot days and **waking up at night to perform a late night prayer.**" (Dhahabi, *Siyar*, IV, 19)

Allah the Almighty mentions the other merits of such righteous people who paid attention to the early hours of dawn as follows:

"Their limbs do forsake their beds of sleep, the while they call on their Lord, in fear and hope: and they spend (in charity) out of the sustenance which We have bestowed on them." (Al-Sajdah; 32:16)

In other words, taking advantage of the early hours of dawn directs them to good services such as charity.

In the rest part of this verse, our Almighty Lord gives the following good news for those who wake up leaving their beds in early dawn and live a life of charity:

"Now no person knows what delights of the eye are kept hidden (in reserve) for them - as a reward for their (good) deeds." (Al-Sajdah; 32:17)

The Messenger of Allah (pbuh) explains this verse as:

"Allah the Almighty said:

"I have prepared for My righteous servants (such excellent things) as no eye has ever seen, nor an ear has ever heard nor a human heart can ever think of!" (Bukhari, Bad' al-khalk, 8; Tafsir, 32/1; Tawhid, 35; Muslim, Jannah, 2-5)

This noble hadith shows that the blessings of the Paradise are far more than the blessings that are mentioned in other verses and ahadith. In some narrations, it is said that those blessings are not known even by the prophets or the angels.

This is the best sign that shows the love of Allah the Almighty for those who wake up for the early dawn worship. The following noble hadith is another proof of this fact:

"There are three types of people that Allah loves most, and there are three types of people the Allah hates most. The three types that Allah loves most are:

1. A man comes into a community and asks for something not because he knows them but only for the sake of Allah. They don't give him what he asks for. One of them slowly and secretly goes towards the back of the community and gives something to the man. (He gives so secretly that) Only Allah and the man to whom he helped know about it.

2. A community is on a trip. They walk the whole night. Then they all feel sleepy and suddenly sleep becomes the most precious thing for them. The caravan stops and everybody falls asleep. One of them wakes up and prays to Me and reads my verses with passion and submission.

3. A person joins to a military expedition. They meet the enemy and lose the war. However, the person moves ahead and fights until he either wins or dies.

The three types of people that Allah hates most include the one who commits adultery in his old age, the haughty poor, and the cruel rich." (Tirmidhi, Jannah, 25/2568; Nasai, Zakat, 75/2568)

The Messenger of Allah (pbuh) likes those who take advantage of the early hour of dawn as well. This is understood from the following hadith:

It is asked to the mother of the believers Aisha (r.anha):

"Who does the Messenger of Allah (pbuh) love the most?"

She replied:

"Fatima!"

"How about from the males?"

Upon this Aisha (r.anha) said:

"Her husband!" and then she pointed out an important fact and continued:

"To the best of my knowledge, he is a person who fasts a lot and performs late night prayers a lot." (Tirmidhi, Manaqib, 60/3874)

The following report is quite important whivh gives the news that those who perform late night prayers will go to Paradise:

The Messenger of Allah (pbuh) said:

"There are some mansions in Paradise. (Due to their transparency and beauty) Their inside is seen from outside and outside is seen from the inside."

A Bedouin who heard this stood up and asked:

"For whom are these mansions O the Messenger of Allah?"

Our Master the Pride of the Universe (pbuh) said:

*"They are for the servants of Allah who say their words nicely, who feed others, who fast regularly, and who **wake up for late night prayer while everyone sleeps!**"*

When the Messenger of Allah (pbuh) explained the way to the Paradise to Ansar[135] and Muhajirin[136] at the first days of the migration (from Mecca to Medina), he pointed out to the same fact and advised them to pray at night while everyone sleeps.

Abdullah bin Salam (r.a.), who had been a prominent Jewish scholar before he embraced Islam, reported this incident as follows:

When the Messenger of Allah (pbuh) came to Medina, people gathered around him.

It was announced as "The Messenger of Allah is here, the Messenger of Allah is here, the Messenger of Allah is here!"

I joined the crowd in order to see him. When I saw the holy face of the Messenger of Allah, I understood that his face cannot be the face of a liar. The first words that I heard from the Prophet were:

يَا أَيُّهَا النَّاسُ! أَفْشُوا السَّلَامَ وَأَطْعِمُوا الطَّعَامَ وَصِلُوا الْأَرْحَامَ وَصَلُّوا بِاللَّيْلِ وَالنَّاسُ نِيَامٌ تَدْخُلُوا الْجَنَّةَ بِسَلَامٍ

*"O humans! Spread the salutation, feed others, keep your connection alive with your relatives and continue to help them! **Pray at night when everyone is at sleeps! In this way, you will safely go to Paradise.**"* (Ibn Majah, At'imah, 1; Iqamah, 174; Tirmidhi, Qiyamah, 42/2485)

The matter in these two reports which draws our attention is to do something different than others by worshipping at night while everyone is at sleep. Something which most people cannot do is surely a thing that is difficult to do. One should acknowledge that waking up for late night prayer while everyone is asleep is a good deed that only exceptional people can perform. For this reason late night prayers hold great value. Another fact that makes this worship im-

---

135. Translator's note: People of Medina who helped to the immigrant Muslims.
136. Translator's note: The immigrant Muslims from Mecca.

portant is that it is an act of worship away from hypocrisy (showing off). Truly, an act of worship performed when everyone is at sleep is not seen by anyone else. Therefore, believers who wake up for prayer at dawn are the sincere servants of Allah who worship only for the sake of Allah.

As a matter of fact, the prayer that is not performed in this manner or the late night prayer performed for other reasons do not have any value. For them, the Messenger of Allah (pbuh) said:

"There are many who wake up for night worship and the only thing they receive from it is the lack of sleep." (Haythami, III, 202)

In our first hadith, we are informed that the night prayers are expiation for our sins. This worship also protects one from committing sins and evil. As a matter of fact, this fact is clearly seen in the following narration:

A man came to the Prophet (pbuh) and said:

"There is a man who prays at night and steals in the morning."

The Messenger of Allah (pbuh) said:

"If he truly performs a prayer, the verses of the Qur'an that he recites in his prayers will take him away from his wrongdoing." (Ahmad, II, 447)

In the second hadith, we are informed of a period of time in every night when all the supplications coinciding with that period will be accepted. This shows that nights are more valuable than days. That is because there is only one period of time during the days, which is in Fridays, when all the prayers get accepted, whereas such a period of time exists in every night. This is a great blessing of Allah the Almighty to His servants. So, in order to find this period of time, believers should wake up at night to turn towards Allah and seek refuge in Him.

When we examine the **third hadith,** we can say that this time period is in the last third of the night, or, in other words, just before dawn. As a matter of fact, we are informed that Allah is closer to His servants who are awake at dawn and pre-dawn time, accepts their prayers, forgives who ask for forgiveness, and blesses them with health.

Amr b. Abasa (r.a.) reported that he asked to the Messenger of Allah (pbuh):

"O Messenger of Allah! Is there a period of time in which performing worship is better in terms of getting closer to Allah?"

The Messenger of Allah (pbuh) said:

"Yes, there is. The time that Allah gets closest to His servants is the middle of the last part of the night. If you are able to join those who worship Allah at that time, be among them! That is because angels came to the prayers performed from that time to sunrise and bear witness…" (Nasai, Mawaqit al-Salat, 35/570. Also see Ibn Majah, Iqamah, 182; Muslim, Salat al-Musafirin, 52)

The friends of Allah consider the dawn time the most precious treasure which the worships hold the utmost value, supplications get accepted, sins get forgiven, and the bodies become healthier. And they say:

Worshipping at night is the true wealth and power that Allah refers to in the Qur'an as **"O Allah. Lord of Power (and Rule), You give power to whom You please…"** (Al-i Imran; 3:26)[137]

In our fourth hadith, it is explained how Satan works to prevent believers to benefit from these rewarding times and hence from eternal salvation. Satan makes sleeping sweeter in the early parts of dawn in order to prevent people from worshipping and whispers into the ears excuses for them, such as "There is still time, go back to sleep," to miss these valuable hours.

In order not to get deceived by such tricks, one should go to sleep with the intention to wake up for worship around dawn time. When one wakes up at night, one should remember Allah and think about His greatness, necessity of fulfilling His commands and the abundance of His rewards, and be filled with the desire of gaining His content. Then one should control his willpower, get up and drive away his sleepiness by performing ablution. And then, he should overcome Satan and perform the late night prayer and try to get closer to Allah.

Taking advantage of the nights like this surely brightens up the days, too. When the nights are lightened up with acts of worship, the days come to life with services to Allah and good deeds. Spending the nights sleeping by getting defeated by Satan also takes away the productivity of the days. When the nights of a person are dark, his days also become dark. The hearts of people who perform worldly duties without receiving the spiritual nourishment get weak.

---

137. Hadimi, *Majmuat al-Rasail* (Risalat al-Wasiyya wa al-Nasiha), p. 194.

Therefore, we must receive strong spiritual nourishment at the early hours of dawn in order to be strong during the day, both physically and spiritually.

The believers who do not benefit from the nights will be empty handed in the Hereafter. The Messenger of Allah (pbuh) did not want this to happen to his followers and warned them by reminding the advice that Solomon's mother gave to his son:

"O my child! Do not sleep much at night! As a matter of fact, sleeping much during the night leaves one poor on the Day of Judgment!" (Ibn Majah, Iqamah, 174)

Again, Messenger of Allah (pbuh) said to his companion Abdullah b. Amr (r.a.):

"O Abdullah! Do not be like so and so who used to pray at night and then stopped the late night prayer." (Bukhari, Tahajjud, 19; Muslim, Siyam, 185)

Allah gives the reward of a late night prayer to those who regularly wake up for the night prayers but oversleep one night and miss the prayer. The sleep that the person gets that night would be considered a blessing from Allah. Since the intention of the person is sincere, even if he misses one night, he wakes up the next night with the help of Allah.

It is stated in a noble hadith that:

"Any person who offers prayer at night regularly but (on a certain night) he is dominated by sleep will be given the reward of praying. His sleep will be a charity (that is, it's a gift from Allah to him)." (*Muwatta'*, Salat al-Layl, 1; Abu Dawud, Salat al-Layl, 20/1314; Nasai, Qiyam al-layl, 61)

Of course, this is the case for the supererogatory acts of worship. The responsibility of obligatory worships does not drop with excuses such as travelling, being ill, or sleep.

There are other ways to compensate not being able to wake up:

When the Messenger of Allah (pbuh) missed his late night prayer for reasons such as pain, ache, or something else, he used to perform twelve units of prayer the next morning. (Muslim, Musafirin, 140)

The Messenger of Allah (pbuh) also said:

"If a person falls asleep before he completes the supplications or the prayers that he used to perform and perform them the following morning between the

dawn prayer and the noon prayer, he receives rewards as if he has performed it at night." (Muslim, Musafirin, 142)

12. Dhikr (Remembrance of Allah)

٩٦. عَنْ أَبِي مُوسَى رَضِيَ اللهُ عَنْهُ قَالَ: قَالَ النَّبِيُّ صَلَّى اللهُ عَلَيْهِ وَسَلَّمَ:

«مَثَلُ الَّذِي يَذْكُرُ رَبَّهُ وَالَّذِي لَا يَذْكُرُ مَثَلُ الْحَيِّ وَالْمَيِّتِ».

96. It is narrated from Abu Musa (r.a.) that the Prophet (pbuh) said:

"The difference between those who remember (performs dhikr) Allah and who don't is like the difference between the living person and the dead one." (Bukhari, Daawat, 66)

❀

٩٧. عَنْ مُعَاذٍ عَنْ رَسُولِ اللهِ صَلَّى اللهُ عَلَيْهِ وَسَلَّمَ أَنَّ رَجُلًا سَأَلَهُ فَقَالَ:

«أَيُّ الْجِهَادِ أَعْظَمُ أَجْرًا؟» قَالَ:

«أَكْثَرُهُمْ لِلّهِ تَبَارَكَ وَتَعَالَى ذِكْرًا» قَالَ:

«فَأَيُّ الصَّائِمِينَ أَعْظَمُ أَجْرًا؟» قَالَ:

«أَكْثَرُهُمْ لِلّهِ تَبَارَكَ وَتَعَالَى ذِكْرًا» ثُمَّ ذَكَرَ لَنَا الصَّلَاةَ وَالزَّكَاةَ وَالْحَجَّ وَالصَّدَقَةَ كُلُّ ذٰلِكَ رَسُولُ اللهِ صَلَّى اللهُ عَلَيْهِ وَسَلَّمَ يَقُولُ:

«أَكْثَرُهُمْ لِلّهِ تَبَارَكَ وَتَعَالَى ذِكْرًا» فَقَالَ أَبُو بَكْرٍ رَضِيَ اللهُ تَعَالَى عَنْهُ

لِعُمَرَ رَضِيَ اللهُ تَعَالَى عَنْهُ:

«يَا أَبَا حَفْصٍ! ذَهَبَ الذَّاكِرُونَ بِكُلِّ خَيْرٍ» فَقَالَ رَسُولُ اللهِ صَلَّى

اللهُ عَلَيْهِ وَسَلَّمَ:

«أَجَلْ».

97. It is narrated from Muadh al-Juhani (r.a.) that a person came to the Prophet and asked:

"Which jihad is rewarded more?"

The Messenger of Allah (pbuh) said:

"The jihad of those who remember (perform dhikr) Allah the most!"

The man asked:

"Which fasting is rewarded more?"

The Messenger of Allah (pbuh) said:

"The fasting of those who remember (perform dhikr) Allah the most!"

After that the Companion repeated the same question for performing prayers, for giving zakat, performing Hajj, and giving charity. The Messenger of Allah (pbuh) gave the same answer for all:

"Those who remember (perform dhikr) Allah the most!"

Upon this, Abu Bakr (r.a.) said to Umar (r.a.):

"O Abu Hafs! Those who remember (perform dhikr) Allah the most carried all of the rewards!"

When the Messenger of Allah (pbuh) heard this, he turned towards them and said:

"Yes, that is right!" (Ahmad, III, 438; Haythami, X, 74)

٩٨. عَنْ مُعَاذِ بْنِ جَبَلٍ أَنَّ النَّبِيَّ صَلَّى اللهُ عَلَيْهِ وَسَلَّمَ أَخَذَ بِيَدِهِ يَوْمًا ثُمَّ قَالَ:

«يَا مُعَاذُ إِنِّي لَأُحِبُّكَ» فَقَالَ لَهُ مُعَاذٌ:

«بِأَبِي أَنْتَ وَأُمِّي يَا رَسُولَ اللهِ وَأَنَا أُحِبُّكَ» قَالَ:

«أُوصِيكَ يَا مُعَاذُ لَا تَدَعَنَّ فِي دُبُرِ كُلِّ صَلَاةٍ أَنْ تَقُولَ:

(اَللّٰهُمَّ أَعِنِّي عَلَى ذِكْرِكَ وَشُكْرِكَ وَحُسْنِ عِبَادَتِكَ)».

98. It is narrated from Mu'adh b. Jabal (r.a.) that one day the Messenger of Allah (pbuh) held his hand and said:

"By Allah, I love you, Mu'adh!"

Mu'adh (r.a.) said:

"May my parents be sacrificed for you[138] O Messenger of Allah! I love you back!"

Then, the Messenger of Allah said:

"I advise you to never leave to recite the folllowing supplication after every (prescribed) prayer:

"O Allah, help me in remembering You, in giving You thanks, and worshiping You well." (Ahmad, V, 244-245; Abu Dawud, Witr, 26/1522; Nasai, Sahw, 60/1301)

❊

٩٩. عَنْ أَبِي هُرَيْرَةَ رَضِيَ اللهُ عَنْهُ قَالَ: قَالَ النَّبِيِّ صَلَّى اللهُ عَلَيْهِ وَسَلَّمَ:

---

138. *Translator's note:* An Arabic expression of respect and love.

«كَلِمَتَانِ خَفِيفَتَانِ عَلَى اللِّسَانِ ثَقِيلَتَانِ فِي الْمِيزَانِ حَبِيبَتَانِ إِلَى الرَّحْمٰنِ:

(سُبْحَانَ اللهِ وَبِحَمْدهِ سُبْحَانَ اللهِ الْعَظِيمِ)».

99. It is narrated from Abu Huraira (r.a.) that the Messenger of Allah (pbuh) said:

"There are two words that are light on the tongue but weigh heavily in the balance, and loved by the Most Merciful Allah:

«Subhan Allahi wa bi Hamdihi, Subhan Allah al-Azim: Allah is free from imperfection and all praise is due to Him. Allah is free from imperfection, the Supreme." (Bukhari, Aiman, 19; Daawat, 65; Tawhid, 58; Muslim, Dhikr, 31. Also see Tirmidhi, Daawat, 59/3467; Ibn Majah, Adab, 56)

١٠٠. عَنِ ابْنِ عُمَرَ قَالَ: قَالَ رَسُولُ اللهِ صَلَّى اللهُ عَلَيْهِ وَسَلَّمَ:

»لَا تُكْثِرُوا الْكَلَامَ بِغَيْرِ ذِكْرِ اللهِ فَإِنَّ كَثْرَةَ الْكَلَامِ بِغَيْرِ ذِكْرِ اللهِ قَسْوَةٌ لِلْقَلْبِ وَإِنَّ أَبْعَدَ النَّاسِ مِنَ اللهِ الْقَلْبُ الْقَاسِي».

100. It is narrated from Ibn Umar (r.a.) that the Messenger of Allah (pbuh) said:

"Do not forget Allah and be lost in vain talk. That is because talking too much by forgetting Allah hardens the heart. The people who are furthest away from Allah are those whose hearts are hardened." (Tirmidhi, Zuhd, 62/2411. Also see Muwatta', Kalam, 8)

Explanations:

The Arabic word *dhikr* means mentioning and remembering. This can be done by tongue or by heart. Allah the Almighty is the One that we should remember the most.

Allah the Almighty wanted His Glorious names to be remembered. For this reason, every being in this universe is in the state of performing His dhikr (remembrance). The order of the beings that remember Allah the most is: first non-living beings, then plants, then animals, and finally humans. In other words, humans are the most heedless among beings. Since the needs and works of humans are more than any other being, forgetfulness of humankind becomes more apparent. On the other hand, in Arabic the word for human, i.e., "*insan*" comes from the same root as the word forgetfulness, (i.e., "nisyan")." "Dhikr" is the only medicine for forgetfulness which costs humans a lot.

Allah the Almighty says:

"The seven heavens and the earth, and all beings therein, declare His glory: there is not a thing but celebrates His praise; and yet you understand not how they declare His glory! Verily He is Oft-Forbear, Most Forgiving!" (Al-Isra; 17:44)

In this verse, Our Almighty Lord encourages us to remember (dhikr) Him by telling us that all beings remember Him.

The following hadith that talks about how much animals remember Allah is very exemplary:

The Messenger of Allah (pbuh) came across to a group of people on his way. They were chatting while they are on their rides.

The Messenger of Allah (pbuh) commanded them as follows:

*"When you ride your animals treat them nicely without exhausting them and when you are not using them leave them to relax. Do not treat them like your benches for your chats on the streets (do not chat while sitting on your rides). **There are many animals that are better than their riders and remember Allah the Almighty more than their riders do.**"* (Ahmad, III, 439)

What is honorable and proper for humans is to obey their Lord and remember Him a lot and exalt Him to a level appropriate for Him. As a matter of fact, being lower than animals and non-living creatures in remembrance of Allah does not suit human nobility.

Allah the Almighty commands His servants as:

"And do you (O reader!) Bring your Lord to remembrance in your (very) soul, with humility and in reverence, without loudness in words, in

the mornings and evenings; and do not be of those who are unheedful." (Al-Araf; 7:205)

"O you who believe! Celebrate the praises of Allah, and do this often; and glorify Him morning and evening." (Al-Ahzab; 33:41-42)

This noble verse does not set limits for the worship of remembering Allah as set for the other acts of worships. So, it is asked from humans to remember Allah in all circumstances and never to forget Him.

Since it can easily be done and it is very rewarding, there is no excuse for not fulfilling this worship. Possible excuses for other worships such as being ill, travelling, or working conditions are not considered as valid excuses for remembering Allah and as a matter of fact, they might even be good opportunities to fulfill this act of worship. We may find better chances to remember Allah in such conditions.

The goal of *dhikr* is to remember Allah in the heart and shape our acts accordingly. Otherwise, the goal is not just repeating the noble name of Allah without being aware what we are doing. Therefore the best *dhikr* is to remember Allah the Almighty at all times and in every act, or in other words to try not to forget Him at all. Nothing can prevent remembering Allah in the heart.

Those who remember Allah all the time not only earn abundant spiritual rewards but also embrace other acts of worships with aspiration and perform them easily.

Abdullah b. Busr (r.a.) narrated:

Two Bedouins came to the Messenger of Allah (pbuh) to ask a question. One of them asked:

"O Messenger of Allah! Who is the best kind of all humans?"

The Messenger of Allah (pbuh) said:

"Those whose life is long and deeds are righteous."

The other one said:

"O Messenger of Allah! The rules of Islam increased, tell me such an act that I can strongly adhere to it."

The Messenger of Allah (pbuh) said:

"Let your tongue always be wet for mentioning the name of Allah (always remember Allah)!" (Ahmad, IV, 188; Tirmidhi, Daawat, 4/3375)

As it can be understood from the above narration, those who always remember Allah obey the commands of Allah more and show submission to His commands and prohibitions by freeing themselves from negligence and forgetfulness. On the other hand, this hadith also shows us that remembering Allah is one of the easiest and most rewarding supererogatory acts of worships.

If people forget their Lord who provides with all kinds of blessings, they would commit a huge disloyalty. In this respect Allah's Messenger (pbuh) said that:

"If people gather in a meeting but do not mention the name of Allah, they would do something imperfect, they would commit a sin. Whoever walks on the street and does not remember Allah the Almighty would do something imperfect and would commit a sin. Whoever goes to his bed and does not remember Allah again would do something imperfect and would commit a sin." (Ahmad, II, 432; Abu Dawud, Adab, 25/4855, 97-98/5059)

In the Hereafter, people will feel strongly the regret for the time that they wasted in this world due to their negligence. They will long for and regret the times that they wasted by not remembering Allah.

The Messenger of Allah (pbuh) said:

"The people of Paradise will regret most for nothing but the times that they have wasted without remembering Allah in this world!" (Haythami, X, 73-74)

Therefore, a believer must try to mention the name of Allah under all circumstances. As a matter of fact, according to the report of Aisha (r.anha), our beloved example the Messenger of Allah (pbuh) would remember Allah under all circumstances. (Muslim, Hayd, 117; Abu Dawud, Taharah, 9/18; Tirmidhi, Daawat, 9/3384; Ibn Majah, Taharah, 11)

Hussein (r.a.) asked his father Ali about the general behavior and morals of the Messenger of Allah, and his father explained them in detail. The following sentence that he mentioned in his speech shows how much importance the Messenger of Allah attached to remembering Allah:

"The Messenger of Allah (pbuh) would neither sit nor stand without mentioning the name of Allah…" (Ibn Sa'd, I, 424)

In other words, he used to remember Allah under all circumstances and in every one of his actions, pray to Him and seek refuge in Him.

Our first hadith explains the influence of *dhikr* upon our spiritual life. Human heart is something alive and finds peace and tranquility as much as it remembers Allah. By remembering Him, it becomes extremely aware of the eternal life. The beauty of heart influences the other parts of the body. And such a person's actions become nicer, and he attains the perfect morality. That is because when a person frequently repeats a certain *dhikr*, his carnal self gets colored by the meaning of that dhikr.

In another saying the Messenger of Allah (pbuh) described the difference between those who perform dhikr and those who do not as:

"The person who remembers Allah among the heedless people is like a person who fights in a war behind the others. The person who remembers Allah among the heedless people is like a lamp in the dark house. The person who remembers Allah among the heedless people is like a green tree among the deadwood. Before he dies, Allah shows his place in Paradise to this person who remembers Allah among the heedless. Allah forgives the sins of those who remember Allah among the heedless as many as the number of all humans and animals." (Abu Nuaym, *Hilya*, VI, 181)

Therefore, reviving the heart and finding peace is only possible through dhikr. As a matter of fact, Allah the Almighty says in a noble verse:

"... for without doubt in the remembrance of Allah do hearts find satisfaction." (Al-Ra'd; 13:28)

When the heart is not busy with dhikr, it lives under the tyranny of the carnal self. It is impossible for this kind of a heart to find peace.

Once, the Messenger of Allah (pbuh) said the following about the virtues of those who remember Allah:

"The mufarridun have surpassed all!"

The Noble Companions asked:

"O Messenger of Allah! Who are the *mufarridun*?"

He replied:

235

"Those men and women who remember Allah abundantly"[139] and then he made the following explanation:

"Mufarridun are those who are devoted themselves to remember Allah. They resurrect weightless on the Day of Judgment since dhikr takes the weight of their sins away from their shoulders." (Tirmidhi, Daawat, 128/3596)

The following story is very important in terms of expressing the situation of those who remember Allah in the Hereafter:

One day the Messenger of Allah (pbuh) said:

"Allah the Almighty resurrects a group of people on the Day of Judgment. Their faces shine from divine light, they sit on pulpits made out of pearls and everyone envies them. They are neither prophets nor martyrs!"

One Bedouin bent on his knees and said:

"O Messenger of Allah! Please let us know about them so we know!"

Our Master the Pride of the Universe (pbuh) explained as:

"They are from different tribes and places but love each other for the sake of Allah and get together in order to remember Allah." (Haythami, X, 77)

Those who do not remember Allah incur huge losses both in this world and in the Hereafter. The sad situation of those is told in the noble verses as:

"But whosoever turns away from My Message, verily for him is a life narrowed down, and We shall raise him up blind on the Day of Judgment." (Taha; 20:124)

"If anyone withdraws himself from remembrance of (Allah) Most Gracious, We appoint for him an evil one, to be an intimate companion to him." (Al-Zukhruf; 43:36)

"O you who believe! Let not your riches or your children divert you from the remembrance of Allah. If any act thus, the loss is their own." (Al-Munafiqun; 63:9)

The Messenger of Allah (pbuh) said:

"...Allah the Almighty loves every heart that is full of awe, sadness and mercy, and that teaches goodness to people and invite them to obey Allah. Allah

---

139. Muslim, Dhikr 4. Also see Tirmidhi, Daawat, 128/3596.

dislikes the hearts that are harsh, busy with idle work, and that spend the whole night sleeping without being sure that their souls will be returned to them, and that remember Allah rarely." (Dailami, I, 158)

Our Almighty Lord has warned us many times in order to protect us from the harms and dangers of not remembering Allah. For example, in one those warnings Allah the Almighty says:

"Has not the time arrived for the believers that their hearts in all humility should engage in the remembrance of Allah and of the Truth which has been revealed (to them)?" (Al-Hadid; 57:16)

This verse was revealed about some of the Companions of the Messenger of Allah who had somewhat been overcome with languor after the migration despite the fact that they had been living in difficulties while they were in Mecca. (Suyuti, *Lubab*, p. 227)

Even if they were prophets, Allah the Exalted said to Moses (r.a.) and Aaron (r.a.) when He sent them to Pharoah:

"Go, you and your brother, with My Signs, and slacken not, either of you, in keeping Me in remembrance." (Taha; 20:42)

As we can infer from this verse, remembrance of Allah should not be abandoned even under very difficult and dangerous circumstances. Also, remembrance of Allah gives a person strength to overcome the difficulties of life.

The difference between those who remember Allah and those who are heedless, which is mentioned **in our first hadith,** can be applied to our homes as well. The Messenger of Allah (pbuh) said:

"The difference between a house in which Allah is remembered and the house in which Allah is not remembered is comparable to the difference between the alive and dead." (Muslim, Musafirin, 211)

The way to save our houses from being places like graves or arid fields is to perform the acts of worships and prayers, recite the Qur'an, and remember Allah in them. As a matter of, the Messenger of Allah (pbuh) said:

"When you perform an obligatory prayer in a mosque, leave performing some of (the sunnah) parts of the prayer to your homes. As a matter of fact, Allah creates goodness to your house for that performed prayer." (Muslim, Musafirin, 210. Also see Ibn Majah, Iqamah, 186)

The Prophet also said about recitation of the Qur'an in our homes:

"Do not turn your houses into graves. For sure, Satan runs away from a house in which the chapter al-Baqarah is recited!" (Muslim, Musafirin, 212)

As dhikr (remembrance) revives the hearts and spiritual life, it also adds another dimension to the worship. Acts done in remembrance of Allah are superior to and are more rewarding than the acts that are not done in this way. That is because acts done in remembrance of Allah are perfectly performed with sincerity. Those who fill their lives with the remembrance of Allah would attain several goodnesses.

The following event is so meaningful in expressing how continuously remembering Allah adds a deep meaning to our lives:

Three people from the Bani Uzra Tribe had come to the Messenger of Allah and converted to Islam. The Messenger of Allah (pbuh) asked:

"Who will take the responsibility of taking care of these people?"

Talha (r.a.) said:

"I can take care of them, O Messenger of Allah!"

While they were with Talha, the Messenger of Allah (pbuh) had sent a *sariyya*[140] (minor military expedition.) One of the three people joined this expedition and became a martyr. After that, the Messenger of Allah (pbuh) sent another minor expedition. In this expedition, the second man became a martyr. A while later, the third man passed away in his bed.

Talha (r.a.) reported the rest of the narration as:

"I saw those three people who stayed with me in my dream that they were in Paradise. The one who passed away in his bed was at the front and the person who became a martyr in the second expedition was following him. The person who became martyr in the first expedition was behind them. I got surprised and a little disappointed. I immediately went to the Prophet (pbuh) and told him what I saw in my dream.

The Messenger of Allah (pbuh) said:

---

140. "Sariyyah" is a political and military expedition of our Prophet in which he did not take part, instead he consigned one of his Companions as the leader of such military units.

"There is nothing to be surprised about this! There is no better person in the sight of Allah than a believer who lives a life praising Allah, uttering His Greatness, and His Oneness (La ilaha illallah)." (Ahmad, I, 163)

Therefore remembrance of Allah is one of the best preparations for the Hereafter. The Messenger of Allah (pbuh) used to wake up after one third of the night and warned us as follows about the necessity of getting prepared for the Hereafter by remembering Allah:

"O people! Remember Allah! Remember Allah! The first trumpet, which will shake the earth, will be blown. Then the second one will follow. Death will come with all its agony! Death will come will all its agony!..." (Tirmidhi, Qiyamah, 23/2457)

In the third hadith, the Messenger of Allah (pbuh) teaches us to ask help from Allah in remembering Him. The Prophet taught a supplication to recite after prayers to Muadh whom he said that he loved him by taking an oath. This is enough to prove the worth and value of the remembrance of Allah.

The Messenger of Allah (pbuh) taught other supplications which can be recited after the prayers as well. As a matter of fact, in one of such noble ahadith, he said:

"Those who recite the following supplications done after the obligatory prayers never incur losses. Those are the recitation of tasbih (Subhan Allah) thirty-three times, tahmid (al-Hamdu li-Allah) thirty-three times, and takbir (Allah-o-Akbar) thirty-three times." (Muslim, Masajid, 144, 145. Also see Tirmidhi, Daawat, 25/3412; Nasai, Sahw, 92/1347)

In our fourth hadith, we are informed that Allah the Exalted shows mercy on His servants and gives many divine rewards even for very little and easy efforts. That is because dhikr that is easy on the tongue will weigh heavy on the divine scale and will make our Merciful Lord pleased.

The dhikr "Subhan Allah" mentioned in the hadith means "I absolve Allah the Most High and Exalted from all imperfections that do not fit to the state of being God. I do not let any evil to be associated with Him nor be close to Him. I praise Him with the most high and perfect attributes," and it is a dhikr that Allah taught to the angels. (Al-Baqarah; 2:30)

Allah desires that the hearts always be with Him. For this reason, He made dhikr easy on tongues and said:

"(men of understanding) **Men who celebrate the praises of Allah, standing, sitting, and lying down on their sides…**" (Al-i Imran; 3:191)

Therefore, one must not take a back seat by only performing some of the practical dhikrs such as the ones taught in the hadith. The reason that we are informed that those dhikrs will be greatly awarded is to express their importance. Therefore, a believer should not limit the remembrance of Allah only to those dhikrs, but should try to be in a state of remembrance of Allah at all times. As a matter of fact, filling life with idle talk by forgetting Allah hardens the heart, and people who are in this situation eventually get further away from Allah.

It is said in a noble verse:

"Woe to those whose hearts are hardened against celebrating the praises of Allah…" (Al-Zumar; 39:22)

Even if someone has to speak for a long time, he should not continue with his speech without remembering Allah, and instead he should often remember his Lord.

Our words may not always be necessary and appropriate. People many times put themselves in difficult positions and commit sins with their tongues. For this reason, Islam has brought a discipline to our words and commanded Muslims to be extremely careful about this issue. That is because we'll be held accountable for our words as well.

The Messenger of Allah (pbuh) said:

"All of the words except the ones that enjoin the good and forbid the evil or the ones that are said to remember Allah the Exalted work against the son of Adam not for him." (Tirmidhi, Zuhd 63/2412)

Thus, a Muslim should pay attention to say good and beneficial words and should know when to prefer silence over talking. By acting this way, he would gain both the rewards for the talk, for the dhikr and for the contemplation when he keeps his silence. The following word of the wise is so meaningful and significant:

"One should not waste his time and instead should things beneficial to Islam and the Muslims! The smallest good deed is more valuable than saying the greatest right word since talking is easy."

A Muslim should reach to such a maturity level by continuously remembering Allah that those who see him should too remember Allah.

One day the Messenger of Allah (pbuh) asked:

"Pay attention! Should I let you know the best amongst you?"

Noble Companions said:

"Yes, O Messenger of Allah! Let us know"

The Prophet (pbuh) said:

"The best among you are the ones who remind Allah when they are seen!"
(Ibn Majah, Zuhd, 4; Ahmad, VI, 409)

Another time, the Messenger of Allah (pbuh) said:

"Among people there are keys to the remembrance of Allah. When people see them, they remember Allah." (Haythami, X, 78)

Another day, when the Noble Companions asked:

"Who are the friends of Allah?" the Messenger of Allah (pbuh) said:

اَلَّذِينَ اِذَا رُئُوا ذُكِرَ اللّٰهُ عَزَّ وَجَلَّ

"Those are the people who remind Allah when their faces are seen!" (Haythami, X, 78; Ibn Majah, Zuhd, 4)

As it can be seen, the best people are those who remember Allah a lot and as a result their spiritual states get elevated and therefore their faces and actions help reminding Allah the Exalted. This is because they continuously remember Allah wherever they are. They turn their faces away from idle talk and acts, and they always guide and advise others to righteousness and goodness.

O my Lord! Make us among Your servants who are keys to Your remembrance! Make us one of Your servants who reminds You when seen!..

Ameen!..

13. Praising and Thanking Allah

١٠١. عَنْ أَبِي هُرَيْرَةَ رَضِيَ اللّٰهُ عَنْهُ قَالَ: قَالَ رَسُولُ اللّٰهِ صَلَّى اللّٰهُ عَلَيْهِ وَسَلَّمَ:

«كُلُّ أَمْرٍ ذِي بَالٍ لَا يُبْدَأُ فِيهِ بِالْحَمْدِ أَقْطَعُ».

101. It is narrated from Abu Huraira (r.a.) that the Messenger of Allah (pbuh) said:

"Every important matter which is not begun by an expression of praise to Allah turns out unproductive." (Ibn Majah, Nikah, 19. Also see Abu Dawud, Adab, 18/4840)

❖

١٠٢. عَنْ أَنَسِ بْنِ مَالِكٍ رَضِيَ اللهُ عَنْهُ قَالَ: قَالَ رَسُولُ اللهِ صَلَّى اللهُ عَلَيْهِ وَسَلَّمَ:

«إِنَّ اللهَ لَيَرْضَى عَنِ الْعَبْدِ أَنْ يَأْكُلَ الْاَكْلَةَ فَيَحْمَدَهُ عَلَيْهَا أَوْ يَشْرَبَ الشَّرْبَةَ فَيَحْمَدَهُ عَلَيْهَا».

102. It is narrated from Anas bin Malik that the Messenger of Allah (pbuh) said:

"Allah becomes pleased when His servant eats or drinks something and praises and thanks Him for them." (Muslim, Dhikr, 89. Also see Tirmidhi, At'ima, 18/1816)

❖

١٠٣. عَنْ أَبِي مُوسَى الْأَشْعَرِيّ رَضِيَ اللهُ عَنْهُ أَنَّ رَسُولَ اللهِ صَلَّى اللهُ عَلَيْهِ وَسَلَّمَ قَالَ:

«إِذَا مَاتَ وَلَدُ الْعَبْدِ قَالَ اللهُ لِمَلَائِكَتِهِ: قَبَضْتُمْ وَلَدَ عَبْدِي فَيَقُولُونَ: نَعَمْ فَيَقُولُ: قَبَضْتُمْ ثَمَرَةَ فُؤَادِهِ فَيَقُولُونَ: نَعَمْ فَيَقُولُ: مَاذَا قَالَ عَبْدِي فَيَقُولُونَ: حَمِدَكَ وَاسْتَرْجَعَ فَيَقُولُ اللهُ: ابْنُوا لِعَبْدِي بَيْتاً فِي الْجَنَّةِ وَسَمُّوهُ بَيْتَ الْحَمْدِ».

103. It is narrated from Abu Musa al-Ash'ari (r.a.) that the Messenger of Allah (pbuh) said:

"When a child of a person dies, Allah the Exalted says to His angels:

"Did you take the soul of the child of my servant?"

Angels say:

"Yes."

Allah the Exalted says:

"Did you get the fruit of his heart (his beloved)?"

Angels say:

"Yes."

Allah the Exalted says:

"Then, what did my servant say?"

Angels say:

"He praised you and performed istirja[141] *by saying* **"Inna lillah wa inna ilayhi rajiun (To Allah We belong, and to Him is our return)"**

Upon that Allah the Almighty says:

"Then build a house in Paradise for my servant and name it "The House of Praise"!" (Tirmidhi, Janaiz, 36/1021)

۱۰٤. عَنْ جَابِرِ بْنِ عَبْدِ اللهِ رَضِيَ اللهُ عَنْهُمَا يَقُولُ: سَمِعْتُ رَسُولَ اللهِ صَلَّى اللهُ عَلَيْهِ وَسَلَّمَ يَقُولُ:

---

141. The word "istirja" used in the hadith is remembering Allah and the Hereafter by saying:

اِنَّا لِلهِ وَاِنَّآ اِلَيْهِ رَاجِعُونَ

"To Allah We belong, and to Him is our return" when faced with unexpected bad situations or when sad news are given and find consolation. This situation is expressed in a noble verse of the Quran as: **"Who say, when afflicted with calamity: "To Allah We belong, and to Him is our return." They are those on whom (Descend) blessings from Allah, and Mercy, and they are the ones that receive guidance.** (Al-Baqarah; 2:156-157)

«أَفْضَلُ الذِّكْرِ لَا إِلٰهَ إِلَّا اللهُ وَأَفْضَلُ الدُّعَاءِ اَلْحَمْدُ لِلهِ».

104. Jabir b. Abdullah (r.a.) reported: I heard the Messenger of Allah (pbuh) say:

"The best dhikr is "La ilahe illallah" (There is no god but God), and the best prayer is "al-Hamdu lillah." (Praise be to Allah)" (Tirmidhi, Daawat, 9/3383)

⊛

١٠٥. عَنْ عَائِشَةَ رَضِيَ اللهُ عَنْهَا أَنَّ نَبِيَّ اللهِ صَلَّى اللهُ عَلَيْهِ وَسَلَّمَ كَانَ يَقُومُ مِنَ اللَّيْلِ حَتَّى تَتَفَطَّرَ قَدَمَاهُ فَقَالَتْ عَائِشَةُ:

«لِمَ تَصْنَعُ هٰذَا يَا رَسُولَ اللهِ وَقَدْ غَفَرَ اللهُ لَكَ مَا تَقَدَّمَ مِنْ ذَنْبِكَ وَمَا تَأَخَّرَ؟» قَالَ:

«أَفَلَا أُحِبُّ أَنْ أَكُونَ عَبْدًا شَكُورًا».

105. As narrated from the mother of believers Aisha (r.anha), the Prophet of Allah (pbuh) used to offer prayer at night for such a long time that his feet used to crack.

Aisha (r.anha) said:

"O Allah's Apostle! Why do you do this (endure such hardship) since Allah has forgiven you your faults of the past and those to follow?" [142]

The Messenger of Allah (pbuh) said:

"Shouldn't I want to be a thankful servant of Allah?" (Bukhari, Tafsir, 48/2; Muslim, Munafikin, 81. Also see Bukhari, Tahajjud, 6; Riqaq, 20; Muslim, Munafikin, 79-80; Tirmidhi, Salah, 187/412; Nasai, Qiyam al-layl, 17/1642; Ibn Majah, Iqamah, 200)

⊛

---

142. A note about Aisha's statement: "Allah has forgiven you, your faults of the past and those to follow:" As a matter of fact, prophets do not commit a sin on purpose. Their mistakes consist of either not performing the better act or some minor lapses. And there are various wisdoms for these acts to happen. However, Allah does not leave the mistakes of the Prophets as is and corrects them right away.

١٠٦. عَنْ صُهَيْبٍ رَضِيَ اللهُ عَنْهُ قَالَ: قَالَ رَسُولُ اللهِ صَلَّى اللهُ عَلَيْهِ وَسَلَّمَ:

«عَجَبًا لِأَمْرِ الْمُؤْمِنِ إِنَّ أَمْرَهُ كُلَّهُ خَيْرٌ وَلَيْسَ ذَاكَ لِأَحَدٍ إِلَّا لِلْمُؤْمِنِ إِنْ أَصَابَتْهُ سَرَّاءُ شَكَرَ فَكَانَ خَيْرًا لَهُ وَإِنْ أَصَابَتْهُ ضَرَّاءُ صَبَرَ فَكَانَ خَيْرًا لَهُ».

106. According to a narration from Suhaib b. Sinan the Messenger of Allah (pbuh) said:

"Strange are the ways of a believer for there is good in every affair of his and this is not the case with anyone else except in the case of a believer for if he has an occasion to feel delight, he thanks (God), thus there is a good for him in it, and if he gets into trouble and shows resignation (and endures it patiently), there is also a good for him in it." (Muslim, Zuhd, 64)

Explanations:

Hamd (praise) is the way of expressing gratefulness for someone's beneficence, kindness, and goodness.

Shukr (thanking) is to acknowledge a favor which is done to a person and respond to it by praising the beneficiary and letting others know about it. Therefore, hamd (praise) is a more general than the concept of shukr.

There is no other word than *hamd* that expresses the respect, love, and gratefulness which we feel towards Allah, because a believer who says "Alhamdulillah" means that all praises are due to Allah and Allah is the only One who is worthy of *hamd*.

There is no superior spiritual rank than **"The Rank of Hamd"** for the good servants of Allah, because:

• The Messenger of Allah (pbuh) is the one who praised Allah most among all people in this world and the Hereafter. For this reason he was named as "*Ahmad.*"

245

• *"Hamd"* is the name of the flag that the Messenger of Allah will carry in Paradise. All prophets from Adam to the Day of Judgment will gather under this *"The Flag of Hamd"* or *"Liwa al-Hamd."*

• **"Maqam-i Mahmud"** is the name of the highest rank of intercession, which Allah will give only one of His servants, i.e. His Messenger Muhammad (pbuh).

• When the Messenger of Allah (pbuh) performs prostration at the most terrifying moment of the Day of Judgment to intercede for the entire humanity, Allah will inspire him the best *"hamd"* that He did not inspire anyone before. So the Messenger of Allah (pbuh) will intercede after saying this special *hamd*. Those who are saved because of his intercession will praise this exalted Ahmad. And this way, his other names Mahmud and Muhammad will gain their meanings.

• One of the characteristics of the followers of Muhammad, who are praised in previous Scriptures as well, is that they are called **"Hammadun"** which means "the ones who praise Allah a lot." As a matter of fact, Allah especially blessed the followers of Muhammad (pbuh) with **"chapter of Hamd"** (al-Fatiha) in the Qur'an and they recite this chapter in every unit of their prayers.[143]

• The only duty of the angels, the special creatures who are closest to Allah, is to praise Allah. This is expressed in the noble verses of the Qur'an as follows:

"And you will see the angels surrounding the Throne (Divine) on all sides, singing Glory and Praise to their Lord." (Al-Zumar; 39:75)

"Those who sustain the Throne (of Allah) and those around it sing Glory and Praise to their Lord." (Al-Mu'min; 40:7)

• All of the creatures glorify and praise Allah, however humans cannot understand their way of exalting. (Al-Isra; 17:44)

Even thunders loudly join this praising. Allah informs us about this as:

"Nay, thunder repeats His praises, and so do the angels, with awe." (Al-Ra'd; 13:13)

---

143. See Tirmidhi, Tafsir, 17/3148; Ahmad, I, 281; Ibn Hajar, *Fath al-Bari*, VI, 555; Elmalılı, I, 506.

• Allah is the most Gracious, Merciful, and Benevolent. He bestows His blessings to His creation day and night. Therefore everything is grateful to Allah for everything they have. For this reason, living a life glorifying Allah for His blessings shows our loyalty. Since Abraham (pbuh) was a loyal servant of Allah, he gained the praise of our Almighty Lord. He earned this attribute by praising Allah a lot.

One day the Messenger of Allah (pbuh) asked:

"Dou you want me to tell you why Allah said **"Very loyal Abraham"**[144] *for His beloved servant Abraham?" and continued*:

That is because, every morning and every evening he used to say:

$$\text{فَسُبْحَانَ الله حِينَ تُمْسُونَ وَحِينَ تُصْبِحُونَ.}$$

$$\text{وَلَهُ الْحَمْدُ فِي السَّمٰوَاتِ وَالْاَرْضِ وَعَشِيًّا وَحِينَ تُظْهِرُونَ}$$

"So (give) glory to Allah, when you reach eventide and when you rise in the morning; Yea, to Him be praise, in the heavens and on earth; and in the late afternoon and when the day begins to decline." (Al-Rum; 30:17-18) (Ahmad, III, 439)

• Allah begins the Noble Qur'an with **"All praise be to Allah, the Lord of all the worlds"** in order to emphasize the importance of praising Him (hamd) and repeated this fact several times.

Allah the Almighty says the following addressing to each one of His servants:

"Say: Praise be to Allah…" (Al-Isra; 17:111)

Therefore praising Allah is a very important act of worship and a big honor for us. A smart believer who wants to get closer to Allah should praise Allah by referring to what *Hamd* really means by saying "O my Lord! I praise You as what *hamd* really means on Your sight" without restricting the meaning of *hamd* to his limited comprehension. One should enrich his life with *hamd* and it should be expressed at the beginning of every act. One must begin his every

---

144. Al-Najm; 53:37

word and act with *hamd*. As mentioned **in our first hadith**, it is impossible to hope from an act which does not start with *hamd* to be blessed and fruitful.

As we are told **in the second hadith,** Allah becomes pleased when His servants praise and thank Him after they eat or drink something. The Prophet (pbuh) gave the good news that the sins of those who praise and thank Allah after they eat will be forgiven:

"If anyone eats food and then says: "Praise be to Allah Who has fed me with this food and provided me with it through no might and power on my part," he will be forgiven his former and later sins." (Abu Dawud, Libas, 1/4023; Tirmidhi, Daawat, 55/3458. Also see Ibn Majah, At'ima, 16)

Eating and drinking is one of the most important blessings since they are necessary for survival. It is harder for those who do not appreciate these blessings to realize and thank for lesser blessings.

Shaqiq b. Abraham said:

There are three conditions to thank Allah for His blessings properly and in the best manner. These are:

1.   To know from whom it comes when Allah the Almighty bestows upon you something,

2.   To be satisfied with the blessings of Allah no matter how much they are,

3.   Not to disobey Allah as long as you have the energy in your body which you obtained from the blessings of Allah. (Qurtubi, I, 134)

It is necessary to praise and thank Allah not only after eating or drinking something but under any circumstances. The following story is so exemplary in expressing how Aisha used to express her gratefulness:

Qasir b. Ubayd narrated:

"When someone in her family had a newborn baby, Aisha would not ask:

"Is it a boy or a girl?" rather she would ask:

"Is the baby all right?"

When she is told:

"Yes, the baby is all right" she would then say:

"Alhamdu lillahi Rabbi'l-alemin" (Bukhari, *al-Adab al-mufrad*, no: 1256)

In order to appreciate the significance of the given blessings and thank them accordingly, we need to be fair and look at those who are less fortunate than us. If we do not act this way and look at those who are richer than us, it becomes harder to feel grateful to Allah.

The Messenger of Allah (pbuh) warned his followers on this issue by saying:

"Whoever looks up to those who are better in spiritual life and follow him, and looks at those who are less fortunate in worldly blessings and thanks Allah for the blessings that he has, Allah records him as a thankful and patient servant. Whoever looks at those who are worse than himself in their spiritual life and looks up to those who are better off in terms of worldly goods, and gets sad for those worldly goods that he does not have, Allah does not record him as thankful and patient servant." (Tirmidhi, Qiyamah, 58/2512)

In our third hadith, we are told that how superior and praiseworthy those who do not react against Allah in the face of an unfortunate happening, like losing one's child, but rather act patiently and praise Allah are in the sight of Allah.

Since being patient when facing the death of a loved one is a rank or state that is very hard to reach, the reward of acting patiently will be a castle in Paradise. As a matter of fact, when faced with such unfortunate incidents, reacting in such a way other than praising Allah does not change anything. Those who passed away do not come back. Therefore, a believer should act patiently, praise Allah and try to earn eternal happiness through worldly losses.

Even though Allah is All-knowing, in order to show the importance of being patient in the face of a misfortune, He asks His angels how His servant reacted in such a case. When the angels tell that His servant acted patiently, Allah orders a house to be built in Paradise called "The House of Hamd" as a reward of acting this way which not everyone can do. Thus, this hadith also gives the good news that such a patient servant will surely go to Paradise.

In another hadith on this subject, the Messenger of Allah (pbuh) said:

"When someone is ill, Allah sends two angels to him and says:

"Look at what he says to his visitors."

If he praises Allah and lauds Him when the visitors come, angles take that up to Allah, the Mighty, the Majestic, and All Knowing, and He says:

"If I make my slave die, I will make him enter the Garden. If I heal him, I will replace his flesh with better flesh and his blood with better blood and I will efface his evil actions." (Muwatta, Ayn, 5)

In the fourth hadith, we are told that the best prayer is to say "All praises are due to Allah." Allah advances His blessings to those who praise Him and who are grateful to His blessings before they even wish for anything. So, first we must acknowledge the value of the blessings that we have and be loyal to Allah by praising and thanking Him appropriately before asking for new blessings. Only when we can achieve this, we would have prayed Allah in the best manner and His blessings would increase before we ask.

Allah informs us of this:

"If you are grateful, I will add more (favors) unto you." (Ibrahim; 14:7)

Since *hamd* includes the term *shukr* or being grateful as mentioned in the verse above, it is the best type of prayer that ensures what is asked for. For this reason, we start our prayer by praising Allah. As a matter of fact, the Messenger of Allah (pbuh) gave the good news that Allah responds to supplications that begin with exaltation and praising Him and then invoking blessings on His Messenger (pbuh). He also advised to those who are in a hurry to begin their supplications with praising Allah and invoke blessings to the Prophet (pbuh). (Tirmidhi, Daawat, 64/3476; Abu Dawud, Witr, 23/1481)

On the other hand, there are levels in praising Allah. The Messenger of Allah (pbuh) informed us about one of the best ways of praising Allah:

"One of the servants of Allah said:

$$ يَا رَبِّ! لَكَ الْحَمْدُ كَمَا يَنْبَغِي لِجَلَالِ وَجْهِكَ وَلِعَظِيمِ سُلْطَانِكَ $$

"O my Lord! All praises which are proper to Your Majesty and Greatness of Your Power be to You!"

This praising incapacitated the two angels that were appointed to record the deeds of the servant since they did not know how many rewards they should write in return for this hamd. They ascended to the Heavens and said:

"O our Lord! Your servant said such a word for which we do not know how many rewards to record." Even though All-knowing Allah already knew well what the servant had said, He asked:

"What did my servant say?"

The angels responded:

"O our Lord! That servant praised You as: "O my Lord! All praises which are proper to Your Majesty and Greatness of Your Power be to You"

Upon this, Allah orders to those two angels:

"Record these words as my servant had said it until he reaches Me and I give him the rewards of these words!" (Ibn Majah, Adab, 55)

Praising Allah is one of the good deeds that saves one from the Hell and ensures him to enter the Paradise. The following story reported by Abu Huraira (r.a.) is one of the proofs of this fact:

One day the Messenger of Allah (pbuh) said:

"Get your shields!"

We asked:

"Is there an enemy approaching so you ordered us to get our shields?"

The Messenger of Allah (pbuh) said:

"No, get your shields that will save you from the Hell:

$$\text{سُبْحَانَ اللهِ وَالْحَمْدُ لِلهِ وَلَا اِلٰهَ اِلَّا اللهُ وَاللهُ أَكْبَرُ}$$

Say "Subhanallahi Walhamdulillahi wa La ilaha illallahu wallahu Akbar: Glory be to Allah and All praise be to Allah and there is no god but Him and He is the greatest!" These words come to save and greet you on the Day of Judgment. These words are one of the good deeds which will stay till eternity." (Hakim, I, 725/1985)

Our fifth hadith explains how significant praising Allah and thanking Him was in our beloved Prophet's life.

As the servant who knows Allah best, the Messenger of Allah (pbuh) exemplified with his actions that no matter what we do, it can not be enough to thank Allah.

As understood from this hadith, being grateful to Allah is also necessary for the forgiveness of our sins.

The Messenger of Allah (pbuh) also expresses in this hadith that worships and thanking Allah should not be performed in return for worldly rewards and benefits but rather they are expressions of servitude out of love for Allah.

As can be inferred from the answer that the Messenger of Allah gave to Aisha, he would have endless pleasure from thanking Allah. So, he loved to feel thankful to Allah and reflect his gratitude in his actions. In spite of his heavy responsibilities such as conducting the affairs of Muslims, preaching the religion, protecting his followers, fighting in the name of Allah, protecting the borders of the country, there was no one else who worshipped and obeyed Allah more to express his gratitude than he did.

On top of that, our Master the Pride of Universe (pbuh) used to ask Allah to help him to thank Him more:

*"O my Lord! I pray to You to keep me on the right religion and help me to stay on the straight path, and **to be able to thank Your blessings appropriately and be a good servant of You.** I ask from You a tranquil heart and a truthful tongue. I ask for Your forgiveness of my sins that You know of (but I don't). I wish for every goodness that You know of (but I don't), and I seek refuge in You from all such evil."* (Ahmad, IV, 125)

Our sixth hadith praises and informs about those who live a calm and peaceful life since they feel grateful to Allah and act patiently due to their strong faith.

Life is full of happy and sad moments. Those moments visit our hearts by turns. It is not possible for anyone to avoid them. For this reason, Allah informs us that we should not go to extremes when we are sad for the things that we lost and also when are happy for the things that we gain. (Al-i Imran; 3:153) (Al-Hadid; 57:23)

Then, we must know how to benefit from our happy moments by showing our gratitude and from the sad moments of our lives by being patient. One must not forget that being grateful to blessings increases them and being patient to unfortunate events transforms them into goodness. That is how a believer follows an exemplary and peaceful life by continuously taking advantage of these two good traits.

As a matter of fact, believers should be grateful to Allah under any circumstances. Otherwise, they would be ungrateful and punishment of ingratitude is very harsh. As a matter of fact, it is expressed in several verses of the Qur'an:

"Then remember Me; I will remember you. Be grateful to Me, and reject not Faith." (Al-Baqarah; 2:152)

"… if you show ingratitude, truly My punishment is terrible indeed." (Ibrahim; 14:7)

In order for a person to express properly his gratefulness to Allah, he should also thank people from whom he received goodness. As a matter of fact, Allah's Messenger (pbuh) said:

"He who does not thank people does not thank Allah!" (Abu Dawud, Adab, 11/4811; Tirmidhi, Birr, 31/1955)

The believers who express their gratitude in this life also will continue to be busy with *hamd* in Paradise:

"Their prayers end with:

"Praise be to Allah, the Cherisher and Sustainer of the worlds!" (Yunus; 10:10)

14. Saying Blessings for the Prophet Muhammad

١٠٧. عَنْ أَبِي هُرَيْرَةَ رَضِيَ اللهُ عنهُ: أَنَّ رسُولَ اللهِ صَلَّى اللهُ عَلَيْهِ وَسَلَّمَ قَالَ:

((مَا مِنْ أَحَدٍ يُسَلِّمُ عَلَيَّ إلَّا رَدَّ اللهُ عَلَيَّ رُوحِي حَتَى أَرُدَّ عَلَيْهِ السَّلاَمَ)).

107. Abu Huraira (r.a.) narrated that the Messenger of Allah (pbuh) said:

"If any one of you greets me, Allah returns my soul to me and I respond to the greeting." (Abu Dawud, Menasik, 96/2041. Also see Ahmad, II, 527)

۱۰۸. عَنْ أَبِي هُرَيْرَةَ قَالَ: قَالَ رَسُولُ اللهِ صَلَّى اللهُ عَلَيْهِ وَسَلَّمَ:

((مَنْ صَلَّى عَلَيَّ صَلَاةً صَلَّى اللهُ عَلَيْهِ بِهَا عَشْرًا)).

108. Abu Huraira (r.a.) narrated that the Messenger of Allah (pbuh) said:

"If anyone invokes blessings on me once, Allah the Almighty will bless him ten times." (Tirmidhi, Witr, 21/485. Also see Muslim, Salah, 70; Abu Dawud, Witr, 26/1530; Nasai, Adhan, 37/676; Sahw, 55/1294)

۱۰۹. عَنْ عَبْدِ اللهِ ابْنِ مَسْعُودٍ رَضِيَ اللهُ عَنْهُ أَنَّ رَسُولَ اللهِ صَلَّى اللهُ عَلَيْهِ وَسَلَّمَ قَالَ:

((أَوْلَى النَّاسِ بِي يَوْمَ الْقِيَامَةِ أَكْثَرُهُمْ عَلَيَّ صَلَاةً)).

109. It was narrated from Abdullah b. Mas'ud (r.a.) that the Messenger of Allah (pbuh) said:

"Among the people the closest one to me on the Day of Judgment is the one who invokes blessings on me most." (Tirmidhi, Witr, 21/484)

۱۱۰. عَنْ عَلِيِّ بْنِ أَبِي طَالِبٍ رَضِيَ اللهُ عَنْهُ قَالَ: قَالَ رَسُولُ اللهِ صَلَّى اللهُ عَلَيْهِ وَسَلَّمَ:

((الْبَخِيلُ الَّذِي مَنْ ذُكِرْتُ عِنْدَهُ فَلَمْ يُصَلِّ عَلَيَّ)).

110. It was narrated from Ali b. Abi Talib (r.a.) that the Messenger of Allah (pbuh) said:

"The true miser is the one in whose presence I am mentioned but he does not invoke blessings for me." (Tirmidhi, Daawat, 100/3546. Also see Ahmad, I, 201)

❀

١١١. عَنْ أَبِي هُرَيْرَةَ رَضِيَ اللهُ عَنْهُ قَالَ: قَالَ رَسُولُ اللهِ صَلَّى اللهُ عَلَيْهِ وَسَلَّمَ:

«رَغِمَ أَنْفُ رَجُلٍ ذُكِرْتُ عِنْدَهُ فَلَمْ يُصَلِّ عَلَيَّ وَرَغِمَ أَنْفُ رَجُلٍ دَخَلَ عَلَيْهِ رَمَضَانُ ثُمَّ انْسَلَخَ قَبْلَ أَنْ يُغْفَرَ لَهُ وَرَغِمَ أَنْفُ رَجُلٍ أَدْرَكَ عِنْدَهُ أَبَوَاهُ الْكِبَرَ (أَوْ أَحَدُهُمَا) فَلَمْ يُدْخِلَاهُ الْجَنَّةَ».

111. It was narrated from Abu Huraira (r.a.) that the Messenger of Allah (pbuh) said:

"May those who do not invoke blessing on me upon hearing my name become miserable! May those who reach the month of Ramadan and pass it without receiving forgiveness become miserable! May those whose parents live their elderly years with them and the children cannot enter into Paradise by pleasing their parents become miserable!" (Tirmidhi, Daawat, 100/3545)

Explanations:

It is impossible for the followers of the Muhammad Mustafa (pbuh) to thank enough for having the honor of being his followers. That is because the Messenger of Allah (pbuh) is the most beloved servant of Allah and the most eminent among His prophets. Allah the Almighty has commanded His servants who love Allah to follow the Messenger of Allah as an indication of their love. Allah tells us that He will love us back and that He will forgive our sins if we act in this way. (Al-i Imran; 3:31)

One of the verses of the Qur'an related to Allah's love for His messenger is as follows:

اِنَّ اللهَ وَمَلٰئِكَتَهُ يُصَلُّونَ عَلَى النَّبِيّ يَٓا اَيُّهَا الَّذينَ
اٰمَنُوا صَلُّوا عَلَيْهِ وَسَلّمُوا تَسْليمًا

"Allah and His angels send blessings on the Prophet: O you who believe! Send you blessings on him, and salute him with all respect." (Al-Ahzab; 33:56)

In this verse, after our Almighty Lord expresses His love, blessings, and compassion towards the Prophet, He then commands us to invoke blessings on him, salute him with all respect, and obey his orders.

Salat has several meanings such as asking for forgiveness and mercy, supplication, blessings, praising, celebrating, and honoring. Muslim scholars made various interpretations of this word depending on who is saying it:

- **"The meaning of Allah's invocation of *salat* upon one of His servants"** is that He shows mercy on that servant, purifies him by exalting his name and honor, bestows upon him divine rewards, and protects him by making him successful.

- **"The meaning of angels' invocation of *salat* upon a servant of Allah"** is that they ask for his forgiveness, pray for him to realize the blessings of Allah, to elevate his spirituality, and to help him in any cases.

- **"The meaning of Muslims' invocation of *salat* upon the Messenger of Allah"** is that they pray for his goodness, show their respect to him, and exalt his reputation.

The meaning of **"Salam"** mentioned in the above mentioned verse refers to salvation, soundness, peace, and safety. **Salam** also means submission, obedience, and be in peace.

In this case, when we invoke blessings upon the Messenger of Allah (pbuh), as if we pray to Allah the Almighty as follows:

"O my Lord! Exalt the reputation and honor of the Prophet both in this world and Hereafter! Spread the religion Islam that he brought to the whole world and protect this religion as long as the world exists! In the hereafter, give him the right to intercede for his followers and give him countless divine rewards! Bless him with salvation, peace, and safety!"

Muslim scholars have differing views about the ruling of invocation of blessings upon the Messenger of Allah:

Some of them argued that it is obligatory (fard) to invoke blessings upon the Messenger of Allah (pbuh) both upon a person who mentions the name of the Messenger of Allah and upon those who hear it. Others maintained that it is necessary (wajib) to invoke blessings on the Messenger of Allah (pbuh) a lot without limiting it with a certain number. Some others view that no matter how many times the honorable name of the Messenger of Allah (pbuh) gets mentioned in a given gathering, it is enough to invoke blessing upon him just once. In order to be on the safe side, it is better to invoke blessings upon the Messenger of Allah (pbuh) each time his name is mentioned or he is remembered.

The Messenger of Allah (pbuh) informs us that he personally receives our blessings. That is because prophets are alive in a life form that is special to them. [145]

In one of his sayings, the Messenger of Allah (pbuh) stated that:

"There are Allah's angels wandering on earth. They bring the greetings of my followers to me." (Nasai, Sahw, 46/1280)

How would we feel if we were truly aware that the Messenger of Allah (pbuh) knows about our greetings thanks to the angels who transmit them, receives our humble gifts and accepts them graciously, and even responds to

---

145. See Abu Dawud, Salat, 201/1047; Witr, 26/1531; Nasai, Jum'a, 5; Ibn Majah, Iqamah, 79; Janaiz, 65. Also Allah informs us that martyrs do not die:
"And say not of those who are slain in the way of Allah "They are dead." Nay, they are living, though you perceive (it) not." (Al-Baqarah; 2:154)
"Think not of those who are slain in Allah's way as dead. Nay, they live, finding their sustenance in the presence of their Lord; They rejoice in the bounty provided by Allah. And with regard to those left behind, who have not yet joined them (in their bliss), the (Martyrs) glory in the fact that on them is no fear, nor have they (cause to) grieve." (Al-i Imran; 3:169-170)
Since those who die in the way of Allah are not dead, it makes even more sense for prophets to be alive. On the other hand, the Messenger of Allah (pbuh) is also a martyr. He passed away due to the effect of the poisoned meat that he was served in Khaibar. Therefore, Allah blessed him with the rank of being martyr apart from prophethood. (Ibn Hisham, III, 390; Waqidi, II, 678-679; Haythami, VI, 153)
As a matter of fact, during his ailment in which he died, the Prophet (pbuh) used to say:
"O Aisha! "I still feel the pain caused by the food I ate at Khaibar, and at this time, I feel as if my aorta is being cut from that poison." (Bukhari, Al-Maghazi)

them? Probably our psychology would change, and we would try to invoke *salat* on the Messenger of Allah all the time. Indeed, this is very honorable and an important blessing for a believer. By invoking *salats* upon the Messenger of Allah, one can both communicate with the Endless Pride of the Worlds (pbuh) and also gain many divine rewards.

It is a blessing of Allah that He bestows so many rewards so easily upon His servants. When we think about this, would we consider invocation of blessings as a difficulty? It is just a matter of uncovering from the veil of heedlessness.

On the other hand, there is no precondition that one must fulfill before invoking blessings upon the Messenger of Allah (pbuh) either. One can invoke blessings on the Messenger of Allah anytime, anywhere and under any circumstances. As a matter of fact, the Pride of the Universe (pbuh) said:

"…invoke blessings on me, for your blessings reach me wherever you may be." (Abu Dawud, Manasik, 96-97/2042)

While it is possible to invoke blessings on the Messenger of Allah (pbuh) anytime, it is especially virtuous to continue doing it on Fridays. One day, the Messenger of Allah (pbuh) said:

"The best of your days is Friday; so invoke blessings upon me frequently on that day, for your invocations will be presented to me"

The Noble Companions asked:

"O Messenger of Allah! How will our blessings be presented to you when your decayed body will have mixed with the earth?"

Upon that, the Prophet (pbuh) said:

"Allah has prohibited the earth from consuming the bodies of the Prophets." (Abu Dawud, Salah, 201/1047. Also see. Nasai, Jum'a, 5; Ibn Majah, Iqamah, 79)

Ali (r.a.) said about the virtues of invoking blessings on the Prophet on Fridays:

"Whoever invokes blessings on the Messenger of Allah a hundred times on Fridays, he appears on the Day of Judgment with his face very beautiful and shining with the divine light. Everyone envies him and asks each other:

"What good deed did this man perform?" (Baihaqi, *Shuab*, III, 212)

Allah gives ten times the divine rewards and elevates the spiritual level of those who invoke blessings on the Messenger of Allah. It is said in a noble hadith:

"Whoever invokes blessings on me ten times, Allah sends ten blessings upon him, erases his ten mistakes, and advances his spiritual level ten levels." (Nasai, Sahw, 55/1290)

Again the Messenger of Allah (pbuh) said to one of his Companions who said that he will invoke lots of blessings on the Prophet in his supplications:

"If you do so, Allah removes all of your difficulties and forgives your sins." (Tirmidhi, Qiyamah, 23/2457)

In addition, Gabriel (pbuh) also responds with many times more to those who invoke blessings on the Prophet:

One day, the Messenger of Allah (pbuh) came to his followers with a smiling face and let them know that Gabriel (pbuh) gave him the following good news:

"O the Messenger of Allah! Would you not be happy if I pray to Allah ten times for the forgiveness of the sins of one of your followers when he invokes blessings on you once, and if I respond to one of your follower's greetings ten times when he greets you?" (Nasai, Sahw, 55/1293)

This shows the degree of the Messenger of Allah (pbuh) in the sight of Allah and His angels.

The greetings we sent to the Prophet (pbuh) are to our benefit before anyone else. By invoking blessings on the Messenger of Allah (pbuh), we obtain significant rewards such as mercy of Allah, His forgiveness, prayers and supplications of Angels for our forgiveness, and enrichment of the spiritual life. Most importantly, because of our invocations for the Messenger of Allah (pbuh), we will be closer to him in the hereafter. As believers recite the Noble Qur'an and advance their levels in the Paradise, they also get closer to the Endless Pride of the Worlds (pbuh) in Paradise as they invoke blessings on him. **Allahumma salli ala sayyidina Muhammadin wa ala alihi wa sahbihi wa barik wa sallim!**

Only when the crowded Day of Judgment comes, one can realize the importance of being closer to the Messenger of Allah (pbuh), the loved one of

Allah and the sunshine of this world and the hereafter. It is extremely easy to gain this reward which not everybody is blessed with.

By keeping our tongues busy with invoking blessings on the Messenger of Allah all the time…

Those who act reluctant in performing this much rewarding act of invoking blessings on the Messenger of Allah for their own happiness in hereafter are the ones who caught the worst and evil spiritual illness, such as "misery." As a matter of fact, the Messenger of Allah (pbuh) informed us that the real miser is the one in whose presence the holy honorable name of the Prophet is mentioned but he does not supplicate for the Prophet.

The miser person thinks that his wealth will vanish or it will cost him a lot when he gives something. He thinks that he will profit and be better when he does not give anything to anyone. As a matter of fact, all of these thoughts are wrong. Giving alms increases the wealth. Just like this, those who do not invoke blessings on the Messenger of Allah are making a big mistake. Since invoking blessings on the Messenger of Allah does not require any compensation or anything to give, those kinds of people are the real misers and they are the ones who will be inflicted more losses. As a matter of fact, a simple effort will benefit them a lot in hereafter.[146]

So, those who act reluctant and become miser in invoking blessings on the Messenger of Allah (pbuh) are inflicted with losses without even realizing them. Since our Master the Pride of Universe (pbuh) could not stand this, he

---

146. As bad traits such as being miser are harmful and undesirable in material subjects, they are also harmful in terms of spirituality. The Messenger of Allah (pbuh) said that those who abandon the chance of enhancing their own spiritual development are the real miser people.
A person came to the Noble Prophet and asked for:
"O the Messenger of Allah! So and so has a date tree in my garden. Would you tell him to sell or donate that tree to me!"
The man did not accept this offer.
The Messenger of Allah (pbuh) said:
"Do what we say and you will receive a date tree in the Paradise!"
The man still did not accept the offer. Upon that, the Messenger of Allah (pbuh) said:
"This man is the most miser of all humans." (Ahmad, V, 364)
That person would have not only gained a date tree in hereafter but also ensured his entrance to the paradise. However, due to his misery, he lost unimaginable benefits. Those who do not invoke blessings on the Messenger of Allah waste an opportunity of easily gaining many divine rewards. Such people are for sure the most miser people on earth and the real misery is the one shown in spiritual matters.

warned with a strong language those who do not invoke blessings on him upon hearing his name.

As a matter of fact, one of the requirements of having strong faith is to love the Messenger of Allah (pbuh). We would not have had faith in Allah if we do not love His Messenger more than our parents, children, and even more than our own selves. (Bukhari, Iman, 8; Ayman, 3; Muslim, Iman, 69-70)

One must ensure such love so that his faith would gain perfection, and he would be happy both in this world and the hereafter, because it is the Messenger of Allah (pbuh) who announces and delivers the message of Islam, which ensures the happiness in this world and in the hereafter. Therefore those who do not love the Messenger of Allah can neither ensure happiness in this world nor in the hereafter. One of the most important acts that can help us to achieve such love is to invoke blessings upon the Messenger of Allah (pbuh) when his name is mentioned.

Despite all these benefits, one who abandons invoking blessings on the Messenger of Allah (pbuh) deserves to be miserable, to deflate, and to fall from both Allah's and men's favor and bring shame on himself. As a matter of fact, the Messenger of Allah (pbuh) said:

"Whoever neglects and forgets to invoke blessings on me gets confused on the way to Paradise." (Ibn Majah, Iqamah, 25)

Gabriel (pbuh) came to the Messenger of Allah (pbuh) and prayed saying:

"Those who do not invoke blessings on you when your name is mentioned be away from the mercy of Allah!" and the Prophet said "Amin!" (Hakim, IV, 170/7256; Tirmidhi, Daawat, 100/3545)

The reason that our beloved Prophet (pbuh) wanted us to invoke blessings on him and warned those who abandon it is not a personal demand but rather to ensure the respect the rank of prophethood and the spiritual link between the servant of Allah and this rank. As a matter of fact, accepting the existence and oneness of Allah is not enough for a person to be Muslim, one must aslo believe in that the Prophet Muhammad is His Messenger.

Another reason of attaching this much importance to invoking blessings on the Messenger of Allah is the following:

Our Almighty Lord who is so merciful towards His servants wants to forgive them. Therefore, He made invoking blessings on the Messenger of Allah (pbuh) an opportunity for His servants.

On the other hand, wishing for the Prophet to be elevated to Maqam-i Mahmud[147] in our supplications after performing our prayers or invoking blessings on him is something that will benefit us at the end; because, in this rank, the Messenger of Allah (pbuh) will intercede for the entire humanity.

Invoking blessings on the Messenger of Allah is something that the whole humanity should perform. Humanity that had been struggling with injustices relieved by the religion that he brought. Even those who do not believe in his prophecy benefitted from the divine light of the truth that he brought. He opened up the true path not only for Muslims but for the entire humanity. Mawlana Jalaladdin Rumi expresses this fact in his work called *Fihi Ma Fih* as:

"The way to Truth was very frightening, closed, and covered with snow. First, the Messenger of Allah (pbuh) took the burden, rode his horse, and opened up the path. Whoever can go through this path can do so due to his guidance and protection. He opened up the path, put signs on every corner and built columns, and told which ways to go and which ways to avoid."

Muslims' debt to the Prophet is even greater, because by bearing unimaginable troubles throughout his life, he saved them from eternal darkness and unbelievable deviations. Mawlana who wants to awaken our feelings of gratitude addresses the Muslims as follows with his style, full of wisdom:

"O today's Muslims! If it weren't for Ahmad's (pbuh) efforts and zeal and his help to crush the idols, you would be worshiping idols today as your ancestors did."

For this reason, may our Almighty Lord reward our Prophet as appropriate for his name, and in the most beautiful and good fashion!..

Then, how should we invoke blessings on the Messenger of Allah?

Qa'b b. Ujra (r.a.) narrated:

One day the Messenger of Allah (pbuh) had come to our circle and we asked him:

---

147. Translator's note: "Maqam-i Mahmud" is the name of the highest rank of intercession (shafaat) that Allah will give only to the Messenger of Allah.

"O Allah's Apostle! We know how to greet you; but how can we send 'Sala-wat' (invoking blessings) upon you?

He said:

اَللّٰهُمَّ صَلِّ عَلَى مُحَمَّدٍ وَعَلَى اٰلِ مُحَمَّدٍ كَمَا صَلَّيْتَ عَلَى (اِبْرٰهِيمَ وَعَلَى) اٰلِ اِبْرٰهِيمَ اِنَّكَ حَمِيدٌ مَجِيدٌ. اَللّٰهُمَّ بَارِكْ عَلَى مُحَمَّدٍ وَعَلَى اٰلِ مُحَمَّدٍ كَمَا بَارَكْتَ عَلَى (اِبْرٰهِيمَ وَعَلَى) اٰلِ اِبْرٰهِيمَ اِنَّكَ حَمِيدٌ مَجِيدٌ.

Allahumma Salli ala Muhammadin wa 'ala Ali Muhammadin, kama sallaita 'ala al-i Ibrahima innaka Hamidun Majid. Allahumma barik 'ala Muhammadin wa 'ala al-i Muhammadin, kama barakta 'ala al-i Ibrahima, innaka Hamidun Majid.

"O Allah! Let Your mercy come upon Muhammad and the family of Muhammad as You let it come upon Abraham and the family of Abraham! Truly You are Praiseworthy and Glorious. O Allah! Bless Muhammad and the family of Muhammad as You blessed Abraham and the family of Abraham. Truly You are Praiseworthy and Glorious." (Bukhari, Daawat, 32; Tirmidhi, Witr, 20/483; Ibn Majah, Iqamah, 25)

Also, when the honorable name of the Prophet is heard, either one of the following blessings can be said:

اَللّٰهُمَّ صَلِّ عَلَى سَيِّدِنَا مُحَمَّدٍ

اَللّٰهُمَّ صَلِّ عَلَى سَيِّدِنَا مُحَمَّدٍ وَعَلَى اٰلِ سَيِّدِنَا مُحَمَّدٍ

اَللّٰهُمَّ صَلِّ عَلَى مُحَمَّدٍ وَعَلَى اٰلِهِ وَصَحْبِهِ وَبَارِكْ وَسَلِّمْ

Allahuma Salli 'ala Sayyidina Muhammadin

Allahuma Salli 'ala Sayyidina Muhammadin wa 'ala al-i Sayyidina Muhammadin

Allahuma Salli 'ala Muhammadin wa 'ala alihi wa sahbihi wa barik wa sallim

Also we should keep saying short versions of the "salawats" such as "Sallal-lahu alayhi wa sallam," "alaihissalatu wa al-salam," or "Alaihissalam."

The word "barik" stated in salats means "abundance." Abundance refers to increase goodness, kindness, and favor, and to purify from mistakes and improve.

The Family of Muhammad, i.e. "al-i Muhammad" refers to the wives, children, and other relatives of the Prophet. Scholars like Imam Malik have said that the entire followers of the Prophet Muhammad are included in the term *al-i Muhammad*. On the other hand, some scholars limited this term with God-consciousness and said that the term "al-i Muhammad" includes only God-conscious and pious followers of Prophet Muhammad. As a matter of fact, the Messenger of Allah (pbuh) said:

أَلَا إِنَّ آلَ أَبِي لَيْسُوا لِي بِأَوْلِيَاءَ إِنَّمَا وَلِيِّيَ اللهُ وَصَالِحُ الْمُؤْمِنِينَ

"Notice that my friends are not the family of my father. My real friends are Allah the Almighty and righteous believers." (Muslim, Iman, 366; Bukhari, Adab, 14)

According to another narration, the Messenger of Allah (pbuh) gathered the tribe of Quraish and said:

"My friends among you are the ones who are pious." (Hakim, II, 358/3266)

15. Supplication (du'a)

١١٢. عَنْ أَنَسِ بْنِ مَالِكٍ رَضِيَ اللهُ عَنْهُ عَنِ النَّبِيِّ صَلَّى اللهُ عَلَيْهِ وَسَلَّمَ قَالَ:

«الدُّعَاءُ مُخُّ الْعِبَادَةِ».

112. Anas bin Malik (r.a.) narrated that the Prophet (pbuh) said:

"Supplication (du'a) is the essence of being the servant of Allah." (Tirmidhi, Daawat, 1/3371)

١١٣. عَنْ عَائِشَةَ رَضِيَ اللهُ عَنْهَا قَالَتْ:

«كَانَ رَسُولُ اللهِ صَلَّى اللهُ عَلَيْهِ وَسَلَّمَ يَسْتَحِبُّ الْجَوَامِعَ مِنَ الدُّعَاءِ
وَيَدَعُ مَا سِوَى ذٰلِكَ».

113. Aisha (r.anha) said:

"The Messenger of Allah (pbuh) liked comprehensive supplications and abandoned the other kinds." (Abu Dawud, Witr, 23/1482)

❀

١١٤. عَنْ فَضَالَةَ بْنِ عُبَيْدٍ رَضِيَ اللهُ عَنْهُ يَقُولُ: سَمِعَ رَسُولُ اللهِ
صَلَّى اللهُ عَلَيْهِ وَسَلَّمَ رَجُلًا يَدْعُو فِي صَلَاتِهِ لَمْ يُمَجِّدِ اللهَ تَعَالَى وَلَمْ
يُصَلِّ عَلَى النَّبِيِّ صَلَّى اللهُ عَلَيْهِ وَسَلَّمَ فَقَالَ رَسُولُ اللهِ صَلَّى اللهُ عَلَيْهِ
وَسَلَّمَ:

«عَجِلَ هٰذَا» ثُمَّ دَعَاهُ فَقَالَ لَهُ أَوْ لِغَيْرِهِ:

«إِذَا صَلَّى أَحَدُكُمْ فَلْيَبْدَأْ بِتَمْجِيدِ رَبِّهِ جَلَّ وَعَزَّ وَالثَّنَاءِ عَلَيْهِ ثُمَّ
يُصَلِّي عَلَى النَّبِيِّ صَلَّى اللهُ عَلَيْهِ وَسَلَّمَ ثُمَّ يَدْعُو بَعْدُ بِمَا شَاءَ».

114. It is narrated that Fadala b. Ubaid (r.a.) said the following:

The Messenger of Allah (pbuh) heard a person supplicating during prayer. He did not mention the greatness of Allah, nor did he invoke blessings on the Prophet. The Messenger of Allah (pbuh):

"He made haste!"

He then called him and said either to him or to any other person:

"If any of you prays, he should mention the exaltation of his Lord in the beginning and praise Him; he should then invoke blessings on the Prophet (pbuh);

265

thereafter he should supplicate Allah for anything he wishes." (Abu Dawud, Witr, 23/1481)

❀

١١٥. عَنْ أُبَيِّ بْنِ كَعْبٍ رَضِيَ اللهُ عَنْهُ أَنَّ رَسُولَ اللهِ صَلَّى اللهُ عَلَيْهِ وَسَلَّمَ كَانَ إِذَا ذَكَرَ أَحَدًا فَدَعَا لَهُ بَدَأَ بِنَفْسِهِ.

115. Ubai b. Qa'b (r.a.) narrated that when the Messenger of Allah (pbuh) would mention someone and pray for him, he used to start his supplication first by saying prayers for himself. (Tirmidhi, Daawat, 10/3385)

❀

١١٦. عَنْ أَبِي هُرَيْرَةَ رَضِيَ اللهُ عَنْهُ أَنَّ رَسُولَ اللهِ صَلَّى اللهُ عَلَيْهِ وَسَلَّمَ قَالَ:

«يُسْتَجَابُ لِأَحَدِكُمْ مَا لَمْ يَعْجَلْ، يَقُولُ: دَعَوْتُ رَبِّي فَلَمْ يُسْتَجَبْ لِي».

116. It is narrated from Abu Huraira (r.a.) that the Messenger of Allah (pbuh) said:

"One of you is granted an answer to his supplication provided he does not say: "I prayed but I was not granted an answer." (Bukhari, Daawat, 22; Muslim, Dhikr, 90, 91. Also see Abu Dawud, Witr, 23; Tirmidhi, Daawat, 12; Ibn Majah, Du'a, 7)

❀

١١٧. عَنْ أَبِي الدَّرْدَاءِ رَضِيَ اللهُ عَنْهُ قَالَ: قَالَ رَسُولُ اللهِ صَلَّى اللهُ عَلَيْهِ وَسَلَّمَ:

«مَا مِنْ عَبْدٍ مُسْلِمٍ يَدْعُو لِأَخِيهِ بِظَهْرِ الْغَيْبِ إِلَّا قَالَ الْمَلَكُ: وَلَكَ بِمِثْلٍ».

117. Abu al-Darda (r.a.) narrated that the Messenger of Allah (pbuh) said:

"He who supplicates for his brother behind his back (in his absence), the Angel commissioned (for carrying supplication to his Lord) says: Amin, and may you receive the like." (Muslim, Dhikr, 86. Also see Abu Dawud, Witr, 1534)

Explanations:

In a noble verse Allah the Almighty says:

"And your Lord says: "Call on Me; I will answer your (Prayer): but those who are too arrogant to serve Me will surely find themselves in Hell - in humiliation,"[148] and declares that prayer is one of the fundamentals of being servants of Allah.

Supplication (*du'a*), which means to call, to invoke, to ask, and to appeal for help, is "for a servant of Allah to turn towards Allah with all his consciousness" or "as a mortal being whose power is limited and finite, to accept his impotence before the omnipotent Allah and to ask for help." Supplication is to turn to Allah and humbly and modestly express our own individual needs to Him. In fact with our supplications, we want to express our respect and trust in Allah and that we expect everything only from Him rather than asking the realization of our personal wishes.

If a person prays to Allah with all his heart and takes refuge in Him, then he expresses his respect to Allah Who is closer to him more than anything.

According to the Qur'an, offering a supplication is the easiest way to get closer to Allah. As a matter of fact, Allah is closer to us than our carotid and He is omniscient and All Hearing… Even a single thought that passes our minds cannot be secret to Allah. In order to show the right path to His servants by eliminating their doubts on this matter, Allah the Almighty says:

"When My servants ask you concerning Me, I am indeed close (to them): I listen to the prayer of every suppliant when he calls on Me. Let them also, with a will, listen to My call, and believe in Me that they may walk in the right way." (Al-Baqarah; 2:186)

---

148. Al-Mu'min; 40:60.

A person can gain value before Allah only as he gains consciousness of the servanthood of Allah. For this reason, we must turn to Allah and ask His forgiveness for our mistakes and ask help only from Him.

Supplication, compressed only to the end of five daily prayers or some other acts of worship these days, actually covers the whole life and constitutes its axis. It is impossible to imagine a life in this world without supplication. Our lives are all about supplication. If we pay attention, we can see that those who do not take saying supplications seriously are the ones who do not take the acts of worship seriously. Such people neglect invoking to Allah but feel grateful to the courtesies of the creation. In contrast, the Messenger of Allah (pbuh) informed us that prayer is the essence of worship.

In one of his sayings, he stated:

"Supplication (du'a) is itself the worship." (Abu Dawud, Witr, 23/1479; Tirmidhi, Tafsir, 2/2969)

This statement draws our attention to the importance of supplication in being the servants of Allah. Otherwise, even though supplication is a kind of worship, there are many other kinds of worship as well. The importance of supplication comes from the state of begging Allah humbly for help whenever we are in need and are destitute.

There are Prophet's other sayings which are similar in terms of the logic of the saying *"Supplication (du'a) is itself the worship."* For example, the hadith *"Hajj is Arafat"*[149] is one of them. Everyone knows that Hajj is not an act of worship performed only on the Day of Arafah in the plain of Arafat in Mecca. There are many other rituals of Hajj and Tawaf (circumambulation of Ka'bah) is one of them. However, those who do not stay in the plain of Arafat for a while on the Day of Arafah cannot fulfill the requirement of Hajj. Thus, just like staying in Arafat on the Day of Arafah is the most important ritual of Hajj, supplication is the most important essence and fundamental of worship, in other words, being a good servant of Allah.

Therefore, saying supplication is an act of worship whether it is granted or not. That is because by saying a supplication, one expresses that he has acknowledged his weakness and fully comprehended that only his omnipotent Lord can answer his prayers and that is why he seeks refugee in Him.

---

149. Tirmidhi, Tafsir, 2/2975; Abu Dawud, Kitab al-Manasik wa al-Hajj, 68/1949.

The Messenger of Allah explained the following verse **"Say (O Muham-mad, unto the disbelievers): My Lord would not concern Himself with you but for your prayer. But now ye have denied (the Truth), therefore there will be judgment"**[150] saying *"There is nothing before Allah that is more valuable than du'a."*[151] The Prophet also encouraged us to pray continuously to Allah by saying:

"Ask from the graciousness of Allah! As a matter of fact, Allah likes when He is being asked."[152]

According to a noble hadith that is narrated from Abu Huraira (r.a.), the Messenger of Allah (pbuh) said:

"Ask Allah for everything, even if it is only a shoelace, because if Allah does not make it easy, then even that will not be possible!"[153] and he integrated the lives of Muslims with du'a.

Abdullah b. Umar (r.a.), who held tight on every advice of the Messenger of Allah, said:

"I pray to Allah in everything even to give ease to the walk of my animals… I have witnessed good things that made me happy due to this." (Bukhari, *al-Adab al-mufrad,* no: 628)

Aisha (r.anha), the mother of the believers, told that the Messenger of Allah (pbuh) loved concise prayers. Allah gave our Prophet (pbuh) the trait of *"jawami' al-kalim*: expressing a lot with a few words."[154] For this reason, as his speeches, he used to say his prayers concise.

Believers should also be concise in their prayers while they express their needs and wishes to Allah. When a person prays, he should keep in mind that he is in the presence of Allah and pay attention to his words. Since prayer is a way to express wishes to Allah, one must ask from Him good things both in this world and in the Hereafter.

The son of Sa'd b. Abi Waqqas said:

---

150. Al-Furqan; 25: 77.
151. Tirmidhi, Daawat, 1/3370.
152. Tirmidhi, Daawat, 115/3571.
153. Baihaki, *Shuab,* II, 41/1118.
154. Bukhari, Jihad, 122; Muslim, Masajid, 5-8.

My father heard me say; "O Allah, I ask You for Paradise, its blessings, its pleasure and such-and-such, and such-and-such; I seek refuge in You from Hell, from its chains, from its collars, and from such-and-such, and from such-and-such." Upon this, he said:

"I heard the Apostle of Allah (pbuh) say "There will be people who will exaggerate in supplication." You should not be one of them. If you are granted Paradise, you will be granted all what is good therein; if you are protected from Hell, you will be protected from what is evil therein." (Abu Dawud, Witr, 23/1480; Taharah, 45/96; Ahmad, I, 172, 183, 269)

Exaggerating a supplication is interpreted in three ways:

a. As in the above mentioned hadith, listing the details of what is already asked for,

b. Asking for things that are not normal such as "rising to sky without a vehicle," "transforming a mountain into gold," or "resurrecting someone from death,"

c. Trying to make it poetic by repeating the similar words (in other words praying as if reciting a poem) and shouting while praying. As a matter of fact, pointing out this fact, Ibn Abbas (r.a.) said:

"Avoid using a poetic language when praying. As a matter of fact, I lived in the time of the Messenger of Allah (pbuh) and his noble companions and they haven't done so." (Bukhari, Daawat, 20)

The situation of those who pray loudly as if they are commanding or who repeat what they already said with different words as if they do not know and have not heard of the noble verse of Qur'an saying **"Call on your Lord with humility and in private: for Allah loves not those who trespass beyond bounds"**[155] is really saddening. Allah who commanded us to pray Him and promised that He will answer our prayers explained how we should pray and His messenger the Prophet (pbuh) established many examples of it. The befitting act of a servant of Allah is to pray in remembrance of being in the presence of Him, with a supplicant manner, careful voice, and concise expressions.

The Prophet (pbuh) who was the best example in every aspect explained the manners and fine points that we have to pay attention while praying.

---

155. Al-A'raf; 7:55.

One has to start his prayer by praising and thanking Allah and invoking blessings on the Messenger of Allah. We have already mentioned that praying is a way of remembering and praising Allah in addition to expressing our wishes and needs. In the prayers of the prophets mentioned in the Qur'an our Lord is exalted together with His characteristics. The Prophet (pbuh) indicated that a prayer that does not start by praising and thanking Allah and invoking blessings on the Messenger of Allah is a prayer performed in haste. When praying, one must distant himself from everything else except Allah. Then, in order to perfectly acknowledge his impotency, he must praise and thank Allah by turning towards Him. After that he should express his gratitude to the Messenger of Allah for delivering the message of Islam by invoking blessings on him, and finally he must continue on with his prayer. This is like greeting the one who is holding the keys to the door at which you are knocking. On the other hand, the meaning of invoking blessings on the Messenger of Allah (pbuh) is to ask that he be given the same blessings that were given to Abraham and his family and be blessed with the same kind of respect that Abraham had in the hearts of people. In a way, following this process in sayng supplications guarantees that requests followed by these two acceptable forms of prayers will be granted.

One day, when the Messenger of Allah (pbuh) was sitting at the prayer room, a man came in. After the prayer, the man supplicated saying "O Allah, forgive me and show mercy on me!" Upon this the Messenger of Allah (pbuh) said:

"O performer of the prayer! You made haste. When you pray and then sit, you should mention the exaltation of your Lord in the beginning and praise Him; then you should invoke blessings on me; thereafter you should supplicate Allah for anything you wish."

Then another person performed a prayer. After the prayer, the man mentioned the greatness of Allah and invoked blessings on the Prophet (pbuh). The Messenger of Allah (pbuh) said to this man:

"O the man who performed a prayer! Make du'a (supplication), you will be answered." (Tirmidhi, Daawat, 64/3476; Abu Dawud, Witr, 23/1481)

Another manner of praying is to begin from oneself and then praying for others starting from the closer people to the further ones. As a matter of fact, the same order is recommended when spending money or donating it (sadaqah). This order should not be confused with being selfish. Above all, a person is responsible to save himself. And it is obvious that everyone would make mistakes to ask for forgiveness or needs to express. The act of skipping himself and praying for others may mean that the person is spoilt and does not need help. Therefore, a believer should act humbly and think that he is the one who needs forgiveness and mercy of Allah before everyone else, and then pray for others.

After we express our wishes and needs to our Lord by a prayer that started by praising Him and invoking blessings on His Messenger, we must not hurry for our wishes to come true. This is because, in the **fifth hadith:**

We are given the good news that our prayers will be answered sooner or later as long as we do not hurry and say *"I prayed but I was not granted an answer."* As expressed in a qudsi hadith[156] *"Allah the Almighty says: I am just as My slave thinks I am (i.e. I am able to do for him what he thinks I can do for him),"*[157] Allah will show mercy to those who pray with no hurry. So, praying by paying attention to its manners is an important blessing for the servants of Allah. The Messenger of Allah (pbuh) said:

"When the door of prayer opens up to a person, the door of mercy opens up for him as well. Allah loves when He is being asked for wellness. Prayer is good for existing and future troubles. For this reason, O servants of Allah, hold on tight to prayer." (Tirmidhi, Daawat, 101/3548)

If a person says "I have prayed but it was not accepted" when his wish did not come true or happened some other way, it implies that the person became hopeless and his faith is in danger. As a matter of fact, it is said in a noble verse:

"… and never give up hope of Allah's Soothing Mercy: truly no one despairs of Allah's Soothing Mercy, except those who have no faith." (Yusuf; 12:87)

When someone sees that his wish did not come true, he may think that his prayer is not accepted. In reality, the acceptance of a prayer may be in three ways. As a matter of fact, the Messenger of Allah (pbuh) said:

"When a Muslim asks Allah for something other than asking for something forbidden or getting disconnected from his relatives, then Allah accepts his prayer

---

156. Translator's note: Not part of the Quran but words of God reported by the Messenger.
157. Bukhari, Tawhid ,15, 35; Muslim, Tawba, 1; Dhikr 2, 19.

for sure or prevents a bad thing happening to him as big in value as the person has asked for.

Upon these words of the Prophet (pbuh), someone present there said:

"In this case, we would ask Allah for many things." Then the Messenger of Allah (pbuh) said:

"The blessings of Allah are more than what you ask for." (Tirmidhi, Daawat, 115/3573; 9/3381)

Zaid b. Aslam (r.a.) said:

"Every person who prays obtains one of these three things: Either his prayer gets accepted, or it will be kept for him for the hereafter, or the prayer becomes expiation for his sins." (*Muwatta*, Qur'an, 36)

In narrations about the virtues of praying, it is said that:

"Accidents can be prevented only by prayer and lifetime can be extended only by good deeds" (Tirmidhi, Qadar, 6; Ibn Majah, Muqaddimah, 10; Ahmad, II, 316, 350; V, 277, 280)

"Should I say something that will save you from your enemies and make your bread abundant? Pray to Allah at night and during the day. That is because prayer is the weapon of a believer." (Haythami, X, 147)

While we pray with absolute submission, we also must pay attention to certain conditions for our prayers to be accepted. A person who says that his prayer did not get accepted even if he fulfilled all the requirements is for sure mistaken. There is either a fault with him or his prayer. Otherwise, his prayer will be accepted in one of the three ways that we have mentioned before.

For our prayers to be accepted, one of the most important requirements is being fed by permissible food that is earned by honest work. The Messenger of Allah (pbuh) said:

"A person who travels widely, his hair disheveled and covered with dust lifts his hands towards the sky (and thus makes the supplication): "O Lord, O Lord," whereas his diet is unlawful, his drink is unlawful, and his nourishment is unlawful. How can then his supplication be accepted?" (Muslim, Zakat, 65; Tirmidhi, Tafsir al-Qur'an, 3)

Ibn Ata said that there are elements, wings, facilitators, and times of a prayer and continued: "If the elements of a prayer are complete the prayer gets stronger, if the wings fit, it ascends to Heavens, if the time is caught it wins, and if its facilitators are found, it reaches its goal. The elements of a prayer are peace in heart, compassion, obedience and awe; its wings are righteousness; its time is dawn, and its facilitator is invoking blessings on the Messenger of Allah (pbuh)" (N. Yeniel-H. Kayapınar, *Sünen-i Ebû Dâvûd Terceme ve Şerhi*, V, 479)

In several of his sayings, the Messenger of Allah (pbuh) said that the time of a prayer is also important. He informed us that the prayers said in certain times are acceptable such as while the call to prayer (adhan) is being recited, when facing with the enemy in a war,[158] between the call for prayer and call for actual start of the prayer (al-Iqamah),[159] in a short period of time hidden on Fridays,[160] during the last hours of the night, after the obligatory prayers,[161] and while it's raining.[162]

The Messenger of Allah (pbuh) said:

"Extol in bowing (ruk'u) the Great and Glorious Lord, and while prostrating yourselves be earnest in supplication, for it is fitting that your supplications should be answered." (Muslim, Salat, 207; Abu Dawud, Salat, 148/876; Nasai, Tatbiq, 8, 62)

"The time when the servant of Allah gets closest to Allah is the time of prostration. For this reason, try to pray Allah a lot in prostration!" (Muslim, Salat, 215; Abu Dawud, Salat, 148/875; Nasai, Tatbiq, 78)

Our Lord sent Islam as a life system and He announced believers to be brothers and sisters, and advised them to love each other, wish each other's goodness, and pray for each other.

As the Messenger of Allah (pbuh) always prayed for other Muslim brothers and sisters in Islam, he advised us to do the same. **In our sixth hadith**, by saying:

"He who supplicates for his brother behind his back (in his absence), the Angel commissioned (for carrying supplication to his Lord) says: Amin, and may

---

158. Abu Dawud, Jihad, 39/2540; Ahmad, III, 342.
159. Tirmidhi, Daawat, 79/3594-95; Abi Dawud, Tatawwu, 10/521; Nasai, Mawaqit, 35, 40.
160. Bukhari, Jum'a, 37; Talaq, 24; Daavat, 61; Muslim, Musafirin, 166, 167; Jum'a, 13-15.
161. Tirmidhi, Daawat, 78/3498-99; Abu Dawud, Tatawwu' 10; Nasai, Mawaqit, 35, 40.
162. Abu Dawud, Jihad, 39/2540; Muwatta, Salat, 7.

you receive the like", he drew our attention to another point that we should be careful about in our prayers.

One day, when Umar (r.a.) asked for permission to go to Umrah, the Messenger of Allah (pbuh) said:

"My beloved brother, do not forget us in your prayers!"

With the expression "my beloved brother," the Messenger of Allah gained the love of Umar and became an example to us how to ask for a prayer from each other.

Upon such a compliment, Umar (r.a.) said:

"This compliment of the Messenger is worth the whole world to me. I would not be happier if they have given the world to me" and expressed what it meant for the Noble Companions to receive the compliment of the Messenger. (Also see Abu Dawud, Witr, 23/1498; Tirmidhi, Daawat, 109/3562; Ibn Majah, Manasik, 5)

In this hadith, it is told that when Muslims pray for each other in their absence, their prayers get accepted and an angel prays for them in order the same things that they wish for their brothers to be given to them as well.

When it is said "**in his absence**," the first thing comes to mind is "in somewhere far from him, or not in his appearance." The intended meaning of "**in his absence**" in this hadith is that the prayer is not heard by the person who is prayed for. In other words, he does not know about the prayer that is made for him. As this can be by being physically away from the person one is praying for, it can also be by praying next to him from his mind or so quietly that he does not hear the prayer.

The prayers done for Muslims in their absence are so important since they indicate real sincerity and are free from hypocrisy or two-facedness. Also, this indicates the noble-heartedness of the person who prays, and it distances him from bad traits such as greed and jealousy. He would experience the noble feeling as mentioned in the hadith of *"You would not have the perfect faith unless you pray for the same things (that you pray for yourself) for your brother in Islam."*[163] Praying for the other Muslims makes believers get used to altruism.

---

163. Bukhari, Iman, 7; Muslim, Iman, 71-72; Tirmidhi, Qiyamah, 59; Nasai, Iman, 19, 33; Ibn Majah, Muqaddimah, 9.

The verses of Qur'an that command Muslims to pray for each other and teach how they can do this prove the importance of the subject:

"O our Lord! Cover (us) with Your Forgiveness - me, my parents, and (all) Believers, on the Day that the Reckoning will be established!" (Ibrahim; 14:41)

"... and ask forgiveness for your fault, and for the men and women who believe." (Muhammad; 47:19)

"And those who came after them say: "Our Lord! Forgive us, and our brethren who came before us into the Faith..." (Al-Hashr; 59:10)

As humanity gained economic freedom, people started to see themselves as not in need of anything and in time got further away from praying to their Lord. This situation is harmful for them both in this world and in the hereafter. Hence, believers should get back to practice praying as soon as possible, which is the essence of being servants of Allah and try to live a life filled with prayers.

16. Steadfastness in Supererogatory Deeds

١١٨. عَنْ عَائِشَةَ رَضِيَ اللهُ عَنْهَا قَالَتْ: قَالَ رَسُولُ اللهِ صَلَّى اللهُ عَلَيْهِ وَسَلَّمَ:

«أَحَبُّ الْأَعْمَالِ إِلَى اللهِ تَعَالَى أَدْوَمُهَا وَإِنْ قَلَّ».

118. Aisha (r.anha) narrated: The Messenger of Allah (pbuh) said:

"The most beloved deed to Allah is the most regular and constant even though it is little." (Muslim, Musafirin, 218. Also see Bukhari, Riqaq, 18)

١١٩. عَنْ عَلْقَمَةَ قُلْتُ لِعَائِشَةَ رَضِيَ اللهُ تَعَالَى عَنْهَا:

«هَلْ كَانَ رَسُولُ اللهِ صَلَّى اللهُ عَلَيْهِ وَسَلَّم يَخْتَصُّ مِنَ الْأَيَّامِ شَيْئًا؟» قَالَتْ:

«لَا، كَانَ عَمَلُهُ دِيمَةً وَأَيُّكُمْ يُطِيقُ مَا كَانَ رَسُولُ اللهِ صَلَّى اللهُ عَلَيْهِ وَسَلَّمَ يُطِيقُ».

119. Alqama (r.a.) narrated: I asked Aisha, the mother of the believers:

"Did the Messenger of Allah (pbuh) use to allocate any day to a certain kind of worship?

Aisha answered:

"No. His deeds were like a light and constant rain. Who among you is able to do what the Messenger of Allah (pbuh) was able to do in worshipping Allah?!" (Bukhari, Sawm, 64; Riqaq, 18; Muslim, Musafirin, 217)

❁

١٢٠. عَنْ أَبِي سَعِيدٍ رَضِيَ اللهُ عَنْهُ عَنْ رَسُولِ اللهِ صَلَّى اللهُ عَلَيْهِ وَسَلَّمَ أَنَّهُ قَالَ:

«الشِّتَاءُ رَبِيعُ الْمُؤْمِنِ».

120. According to a narration from Abu Said al-Hudri (r.a.) the Messenger of Allah (pbuh) said:

"Winter is the spring of the believers." (Ahmad, III, 75)

❁

١٢١. عَنْ أَبِي هُرَيْرَةَ رَضِيَ اللهُ عَنْهُ قَالَ: قَالَ رَسُولُ اللهِ صَلَّى اللهُ عَلَيْهِ وَسَلَّمَ:

«إِنَّ اللهَ قَالَ: مَنْ عَادَى لِي وَلِيًّا فَقَدْ آذَنْتُهُ بِالْحَرْبِ وَمَا تَقَرَّبَ إِلَيَّ عَبْدِي بِشَيْءٍ أَحَبَّ إِلَيَّ مِمَّا افْتَرَضْتُ عَلَيْهِ وَمَا يَزَالُ عَبْدِي يَتَقَرَّبُ إِلَيَّ بِالنَّوَافِلِ حَتَّى أُحِبَّهُ فَإِذَا أَحْبَبْتُهُ كُنْتُ سَمْعَهُ الَّذِي يَسْمَعُ بِهِ وَبَصَرَهُ

الَّذِي يُبْصِرُ بِهِ وَيَدَهُ الَّتِي يَبْطِشُ بِهَا وَرِجْلَهُ الَّتِي يَمْشِي بِهَا وَلَئِنْ سَأَلَنِي
لَأُعْطِيَنَّهُ وَلَئِنِ اسْتَعَاذَنِي لَأُعِيذَنَّهُ وَمَا تَرَدَّدْتُ عَنْ شَيْءٍ أَنَا فَاعِلُهُ تَرَدُّدِي
عَنْ نَفْسِ الْمُؤْمِنِ يَكْرَهُ الْمَوْتَ وَأَنَا أَكْرَهُ مَسَاءَتَهُ)).

121. Abu Huraira (r.a.) narrated that the Messenger of Allah (pbuh) said:

"Allah said, "I will declare war against him who shows hostility to a pious worshipper of Mine. And the most beloved things with which My slave comes nearer to Me, is what I have enjoined upon him; and My slave keeps on coming closer to Me through performing Nawafil (praying or doing supererogatory deeds besides what is obligatory) till I love him, so I become his sense of hearing with which he hears, and his sense of sight with which he sees, and his hand with which he grips, and his leg with which he walks; and if he asks Me, I will give him, and if he asks My protection (Refuge), I will protect him; (i.e. give him My Refuge) and I do not hesitate to do anything as I hesitate to take the soul of the believer, [164] *for he hates death, and I hate to disappoint him."* (Bukhari, Ar-Riqaq, 38. Also see. Ahmad, VI, 256; Ibn Hibban, *Sahih*, II, 58/347)

❁

١٢٢. عَنْ عُتْبَةَ بْنِ عَبْدٍ رَضِيَ اللهُ عَنْهُ قَالَ: إِنَّ رَسُولَ اللهِ صَلَّى اللهُ
عَلَيْهِ وَسَلَّمَ قَالَ:

((لَوْ أَنَّ رَجُلًا يُجَرُّ عَلَى وَجْهِهِ مِنْ يَوْمِ وُلِدَ إِلَى يَوْمٍ يَمُوتُ هَرَمًا
فِي مَرْضَاةِ اللهِ عَزَّ وَجَلَّ لَحَقَّرَهُ يَوْمَ الْقِيَامَةِ)).

122. Utba b. Abd (r.a.) narrated that the Messenger of Allah (pbuh) said:

"If a person spends every minute of his life from his birth to his death for the sake of Allah's content by worshipping, obeying Allah and serving in His way, on the Day of Judgment, he would not see this enough and wish that he would have done more." (Ahmad, IV, 185; Baihaqi, *Shuab*, I, 479; Haythami, I, 51; X, 225, 358)

---

164. Allah is excluded from humanly traits such as hesitating. The expressions used in this hadith are for us to understand the great care and diligence that Allah shows to His beloved servants.

Explanations:

The Prophet informed us that supererogatory acts of worship are very important in getting us closer to Allah and encouraged us to perform them regularly. Few but regular deeds are considered more virtuous than the deeds that are more but performed irregularly.

Supererogatory acts of worship should be done without forcing it on people and tiring them out. There is no limit or end for being a servant of Allah. If a person gets further from moderation, he may exhaust himself by too much worship and may feel bored. However, no matter how many acts of worship we perform, it would not be enough. As Allah does not get bored from bestowing His blessings upon His servants, His treasure does not get reduced by His generosity.

Another version of this hadith mentioned in Bukhari explains its meaning better:

Once the Prophet came home while a woman was sitting with Aisha (r.anha) and asked:

"Who is this lady?"

Aisha (r.anha), the mother of believers, said:

"She is so and so"[165] and told him about her (excessive) praying.

Upon this, the Messenger of Allah (pbuh) said disapprovingly:

"Do not mention this; Doing (good) deeds within your capacity (without being overtaxed) is enough. I swear to Allah, unless you are tired of asking, Allah does not get tired (of giving rewards) but (surely) you will get tired."

At the end of the narration, it is said:

The best kind of good deeds that the Messenger of Allah liked the most were the deeds of the Companions which are done regularly. (Bukhari, Iman, 32; Tahajjud, 18; Muslim, Musafirin, 221)

The Messenger of Allah (pbuh) advised us to be moderate in our deeds. Another point that draws our attention in this hadith is that the Messenger of Allah did not approve to mention and praise someone's deeds and acts of wor-

---

165. In Muslim's report, it is told that this lady was Hawla bint Tuwait. (Muslim, Musafirin, 200)

ship when introducing him/her. Introducing him/her in such a way may lead to pride and hypocrisy. Also, encouraging people to compete in their supererogatory acts of worship may lead some unintended negative consequences. For this reason, the Messenger of Allah (pbuh) used the term "within your capacity" when defining their limits.

It is true that the power and the capacity of people are limited. Before this power is gone, it should be spent in the best way. Our Lord has pointed out that we must not take the responsibility of things that we cannot do by teaching us how to pray for not laying upon ourselves a burden greater than we have strength to bear,[166] and He referred to us as "justly balanced nation."[167] Allah's Messenger (pbuh) did not perform some of the deeds and worships regularly thinking that his followers would not be able to perform them regularly and he encouraged us to do easier deeds which we can perform regularly. As a matter of fact, when Companion Abdullah b. Amr b. As (r.a.) wanted to perform excessive supererogatory acts of worship in his youth, the Messenger of Allah (pbuh) did not give him permission to do that.

Abdullah (r.a.) reported this exemplary story as:

"Allah's Apostle was informed that I had taken an oath to fast daily and to pray (every night) all the night throughout my life.

Upon that the Messenger of Allah (pbuh) came to me and asked whether it was correct:

"Are you the one who said that?"

I replied:

"Let my parents be sacrificed for you! I said so."

He said:

"You cannot do that. Fast (for some days) and give up fasting (for some days); pray and sleep, for your eyes have a right on you, and your body and your family (i.e. wife) has a right on you. Your children have a right on you as well. Fast three days a month as the reward of good deeds is multiplied ten times and that will be equal to one year of fasting."

---

166. Al-Baqara; 2:286.
167. Al-Baqara; 2:143.

I replied:

"I can do better than that."

The Messenger of Allah (pbuh) said:

"Fast one day and give up fasting for a day!"

I replied:

"I can do better than that" and the Messenger of Allah (pbuh) said:

"Fast one day and give up fasting for a day and that is the fasting of Prophet David and that is the best fasting. The best prayer on the sight of Allah is the prayer of Prophet David. He used to sleep half of the night and wake up to pray one third of the night and then again go to sleep for the one sixth of the night. He used to fast one day and give up fasting for a day and he used not to flee on meeting the enemy."

I replied:

"I can do better than this." The Messenger of Allah (pbuh) said:

"There is no better fasting than that." He then said:

"Whoever fasts daily throughout his life is just as the one who does not fast at all" and he repeated this three times.

I realized that it would have been better for me if I had accepted the permission of the Prophet (i.e. to fast only three days a month).

Then the Messenger of Allah (pbuh) asked me:

"How do you recite the whole Qur'an?"

I replied:

"I recite it every night."

The Messenger of Allah (pbuh) said:

"Recite the whole Qur'an once a month!"

I replied:

"O the Messenger of Allah! I could do more than this."

The Prophet said:

"Then recite the whole Qur'an once every twenty days!"

I again said:

"O the Messenger of Allah! I could do more than this."

He said:

"Then recite the whole Qur'an every ten days!"

I insisted and said one more time:

"I could do more than this, o the Messenger of Allah!"

"Then recite the whole Qur'an every seven days but do not exceed this!"

As I increased, it was for my disadvantage. The Messenger of Allah (pbuh) said:

"You do not know, maybe your life will be long?"

At the end it happened as the Messenger of Allah said. Afterwards, when I became old, I wished that I had accepted the permission of the Prophet."

When Abdullah (r.a.) got old, he used to say "I wish I had accepted the permission of the Prophet!" To sleep better every night he used to recite one seventh of the Qur'an to his family members during the day and made them listen. When he wanted to be strong and energetic, he skipped fasting for a couple of days. Then he would fast for the days that he hasn't in order to keep his promise to the Messenger of Allah. (See. Bukhari, Sawm, 55, 56, 57; Tahajjud, 7; Anbiya, 37; Nikah, 89; Muslim, Siyam, 181-193)

People should take the responsibility of the things within their capacity and shouldn't skip performing the things that they have started for the sake of Allah unless there is a valid excuse. Even if one cannot perform this kind of worship on time, he should perform it at another time. The following story describes an easier way on this subject:

One night, Umar (r.a.) couldn't recite the Noble Qur'an. The next day, the Messenger of Allah (pbuh) said to him:

"O the son of Hattab, Allah has revealed a verse about you" and recited:

"And it is He Who made the Night and the Day to follow each other: for such as have the will to celebrate His praises or to show their gratitude."[168]

Then he said:

"Perform the deeds that you could not perform at night during the day, and perform the deeds that you could not do during the day at night." (Razi, XXIV, 93, [In the interpretation of Al-Furqan; 25:62)

In supererogatory acts of worship, Allah has bestowed upon us various blessings. One of them is this: When a person cannot perform a good deed which he used to perform regularly due to a valid excuse, Allah rewards him as if he did perform the deed.

It is expressed in another hadith that:

"When someone falls ill or travels (for jihad or another good cause), then he will get the same rewards to that he gets for good deeds practiced at home when in good health." (Bukhari, Jihad, 134; Ahmad, IV, 410, 418)

The following verse of the Qur'an points out the same meaning:

"Except such as believe and do righteous deeds: For they shall have a reward unfailing." (Al-Tin; 95:6)

Scholars who study and interpret the Qur'an explained the meaning of this verse as:

If a believer regularly performs good deeds, our Almighty Lord blesses him with the same rewards as if he had performed them when he cannot perform them in difficult times such as during travel, illness, or in old age. When he is in such a condition that he is unable to perform any physical deeds or even after his death, the rewards will continue forever.

In our second hadith, the fact that the Messenger of Allah (pbuh) regularly performed the deeds that he had started to do is concisely explained. His deeds are compared to the blessed spring rains that keep raining. The spring rains, also known as "forty later afternoon rains" since it lasts for forty days, became the symbol of abundance and mercy with its soft touching and regularity since it brings life to earth and ensures the fruitfulness of the seeds.

---

168. Al-Furqan; 25:62.

Performing few but regular good deeds may seem easy and not a big deal at first, however when it is performed patiently, it builds up an important richness in time. This is the abundance of regularity.

In the hadith, it is expressed that the Messenger of Allah did not save any one of his days for a special worship. However, one shouldn't infer from this sentence that he never appointed some of his worships to certain times. There are strong reports that the Messenger of Allah fasted on certain days. We know from various reports that he fasted on Mondays and Thursdays, three days in every month, and on the day of Ashura in the month of Muharram, and increased his obedience and worships on holy days and nights. The hadith expresses that the Messenger of Allah did not limit his deeds to these special days but rather performed good deeds on other days as much as he could, and he was tolerant on this subject.

Performing acts of worship only for a couple of hours during the holy days and nights and not practicing any of them on other days would not be consistent with the spirit of the hadith. Everyone knows the fact that the deeds that are not performed on a regular basis cannot be fruitful and productive.

The Messenger of Allah (pbuh), sent to humanity to save it from the darkness, has enlightened the humanity in the extent that has never seen before and brought it back to life. He sometimes used the symbols of revival and mercy such as "rain" and "spring" in his sayings that brought life to humanity, which will last until the Day of Judgment. **In our third hadith,** the Messenger of Allah (pbuh) compared winter with spring for Muslims. Spring is a cheerful, blessed and an anticipated season since it brings life and blessings to earth. It gives the good news that the summer is approaching in which farmers harvest their crops. In the same manner, by comparing winter with *"the spring of a believer,"* the hadith points out that days and nights of winter can be utilized by performing good deeds and can be conducive towards the life of a believer in order to be spiritually alive and fruitful. During this time period where most of the animals go on hibernation and most of our activities are limited, believers' spiritual energy will surely make him experience a new spring. As a matter of fact, one of the reports of Baihaqi reads as follows:

"Winter is the spring of a believer. Its days get shorter so he fasts during them; its nights are longer so he revives them with acts of worship." (Baihaqi, Shuab, III, 416)

In another saying of the Prophet (pbuh):

"Fasting during winter is like spoils that are earned comfortably without pain." (Tirmidhi, Sawm, 74/797; Ahmad, IV, 335)

Winter's characteristic to be the spring of a believer is explained by the suitability of its days for fasting and of its nights for other acts of worship. The important thing is to be aware of the opportunities that winter has. A believer should not waste these opportunities by being busy with unnecessary things but rather he should try to earn some rewards for the Hereafter.[169]

In the fourth hadith, it is explained why the supererogatory acts of worship which are encouraged this much are so important. A servant of Allah gets closest to Allah through obligatory (fard) acts of worships. However, since this is the responsibility of all responsible believers, one is in need of supererogatory deeds to reach a special closeness to Almighty Lord and be one of his beloved friends. The journey of the ultimate union which starts with the obligatory acts can continue with voluntary acts of worship. As a matter of fact, Allah loves His servant who gets closer to Him by supererogatory acts of worship and in a sense He becomes his hearing ears, seeing eyes, working hands, and walking feet. In other words, Allah helps him in everything. He provides anything that he wishes and protects him if he takes refuge in Him. Our Almighty Lord loves so much this kind of servants that He does not like the things that they do not like, either. So much so that, since they do not like death, Allah does not want to take their souls. And Allah declares war on those who are hostile to them.

This great happiness is the result of regular performance of supererogatory acts of worship.

The declaration "I will be their hearing ears, seeing eyes..." does not mean that Allah the Almighty enters into their bodies. This is a strong and nice metaphoric explanation of how divine help will take place in various aspects of life.

In the fifth hadith, it is pointed out that the real value of the supererogatory deeds will be realized in the Hereafter. If a person spends his whole life with worship and in the service of Allah and bears many troubles on this way, then he will surely gain many divine rewards. However, in the hereafter, when the truth becomes visible to everyone and when everyone sees the rewards and the blessings of Allah given for the supererogatory acts of worship, believers

---

169. For a detailed explanation of this hadith, see İsmail L. Çakan, *Hadislerle Gerçekler,* p. 174.

will realize how little they have worshipped in this world and wish that they had done more. Even if a believer spent his whole long life with worship, what he had done would look too little then. As Muhammad b. Abi Umayra said:

"...they'll wish to return to earth to increase their deeds and rewards." (Ahmad, IV, 185; Haythami, I, 51; X, 225)

Abu Hazim said:

"Abu Huraira and I visited a newly buried grave. Abu Huraira said:

"For me, even a two cycle of prayer that you think of as a simple act of worship is more valuable and sweeter in here (grave) than this world." (Ibn Abi Shayba, Musannaf, VII, 126/34702)

Then, before we die, while the opportunity is in our hands, let's increase our supererogatory deeds so that our regrets will be less in the Hereafter. In this respect, one shouldn't belittle even the smallest effort. As Abu Huraira said, even a two cycle prayer performed with the recitation of short chapters from the Qur'an will be more valuable in the grave and in the hereafter than the worlds.

17. Worshiping during the period of widespread turmoil

١٢٣. عَنْ مَعْقِلِ بْنِ يَسَارٍ رَضِيَ اللهُ عَنْهُ أَنَّ رَسُولَ اللهِ صَلَّى اللهُ عَلَيْهِ وَسَلَّمَ قَالَ:

«الْعِبَادَةُ فِي الْهَرْجِ كَهِجْرَةٍ إِلَيَّ».

123. Ma'qil b. Yasar narrated that Allah's Apostle (pbuh) said:

"Worshiping during the period of widespread turmoil is like emigration to-wards me." (Muslim, Fitan, 130. Also see. Tirmidhi, Fitan, 31/2201; Ibn Majah, Fitan, 14)

❁

١٢٤. عَنْ أَبِي هُرَيْرَةَ رَضِيَ اللهُ عَنْهُ قَالَ: قَالَ رَسُولُ اللهِ صَلَّى اللهُ عَلَيْهِ وَسَلَّمَ:

«وَيْلٌ لِلْعَرَبِ مِنْ شَرٍّ قَدِ اقْتَرَبَ فِتَنًا كَقِطَعِ اللَّيْلِ الْمُظْلِمِ يُصْبِحُ الرَّجُلُ مُؤْمِنًا وَيُمْسِي كَافِرًا يَبِيعُ قَوْمٌ دِينَهُمْ بِعَرَضٍ مِنَ الدُّنْيَا قَلِيلٍ. الْمُتَمَسِّكُ يَوْمَئِذٍ بِدِينِهِ كَالْقَابِضِ عَلَى الْجَمْرِ».

124. Abu Huraira (r.a.) narrated that the Messenger of Allah (pbuh) said:

"Woe to the situation of Arab (humanity) due to widespread turmoil that is coming soon! A person reaches the morning as a believer but becomes nonbeliever in the evening. People will change their religions in exchange for a little bit of worldly benefit. Those who stick to their religion in such a difficult time will be like holding a fire ball with bare hands." (Ahmad, II, 390; Also see Muslim, Iman, 186; Tirmidhi, Fitan, 30/2196)

Explanations:

Fasad means turmoil, chaos, disorder and going astray. It refers to all kinds of rebellious behavior starting with disbelief. We can also describe *fasad* as the act of separating humans from the Qur'an and the Sunnah. The most dangerous kind of *fasad* is to appear like someone in favor of the religion but to be someone spreading views causing confusion in the minds about the religion.

Those who rebel against Allah and who encourage others to do so as well are the ones who cause disorder in this world. As a matter of fact, the improvement of the heavens and the earth can be achieved through obedience to Allah.

Those people who listen to their carnal soul and Satan cause corruption in this world under the influence of their bad traits such as greed, desires, and naughtiness. Allah the Almighty says:

"… and do no evil or mischief on the (face of the) earth." (Al-Baqarah; 2:60)

After commanding Muslims to obey Him by being pious, He says:

"And follow not the bidding of those who are extravagant, who make mischief in the land, and mend not (their ways)." (Ash-Su'ara; 26:151-152)

As it can be seen Allah the Almighty does not like mischief and those who cause it. (Al-Baqarah; 2:205) (Al-Maidah; 5:64)

That is because the trouble that they cause for Muslims is huge. For this reason Allah the Exalted taught us to pray as Prophet Lot (pbuh) did:

$$رَبِّ انْصُرْنِي عَلَى الْقَوْمِ الْمُفْسِدِينَ$$

"O my Lord! Help me against people who do mischief!" (Al-Ankabut; 29:30)

Those who cause mischief on earth do not like religion and religious people. Therefore, it becomes very difficult to practice the religion of Allah in a society in disorder caused by them. In such an environment, as acts of worship, belief is also wanted to be under control. People who are placed under such pressure retire into themselves in time and be afraid of worshipping.

On the other hand, since the religious and moral values of people get weak, everyone starts to follow values of this world. Some people try to benefit from chaos and obtain some temporary gains from the situation. The number of those who are interested in spirituality decreases. In conclusion, Muslims find themselves in a lonely situation as they were in the first days of Islam.

Trying to practice the religion of Allah and worship Him under such difficult circumstances becomes as valuable as the extent of their difficulty. As a matter of fact, **in our first hadith,** we are told that worshipping during the periods of widespread turmoil is like emigration towards the Messenger of Allah, in other words, it is like a travel towards his world.

As it is known, until the conquest of Mecca, emigration (hijrah) was a very virtuous and desirable act. Those who emigrated at that time are praised and showed as an example in various places of the Noble Qur'an. Worshiping during the periods of widespread turmoil is a must and praiseworthy deed just like emigration. Distancing oneself from the turmoil and experiencing the climate of peace through worshipping, evaluating the situation from the point of Islam and acting accordingly is like a moral and spiritual emigration to blessed city of Medina, the city of the Messenger of Allah. As it was possible to save oneself from the darkness of infidelity by immigrating to Medina, it is possible to save oneself from the darkness of mischief by practicing Islam and immigrating to Sunnah.

As a matter of fact, the reason for emigration was to get away from the evil and practice the commands of Allah. The Messenger of Allah (pbuh) said:

"A real Muhajir (emigrant) is the one who gives up (abandons) all what Allah has forbidden." (Bukhari, Iman, 4; Riqaq, 26)

Muslims should avoid sins in periods of mischief and seek refuge in Allah from their evil environments, and should gain strength against chaos and disorder by practicing the acts of worship commanded by Allah. Worshipping Allah in good days but showing weakness in this respect and inclining to objectionable acts in difficult times is not a desirable approach for the servants of Allah. The real servanthood is to practice the commands of Allah during the hard times as well. Therefore, a conscious believer should save his eternal life by protecting his religion and obeying the commands of Allah in periods of mischief as well.

In our second hadith, Muslims are warned about the future mischiefs and informed that practicing the religion at those times will be as difficult as holding a fire ball in their bare hands. As a matter of fact, in such times people may change their religions in return for a small worldly benefit and become a nonbeliever in the evening while they were believers in the morning. And during such times everything will become measured by its worldly benefits. No more respect is paid to faith. Believers will feel themselves not wanted in the society since people who cause mischiefs will worry that believers will cause trouble to their life styles. It will be very difficult for believers to live in such a society where no one knows who is who. There is no doubt that its rewards will be in the extent of its difficulty.

The Messenger of Allah (pbuh) said:

"In the period when my followers are subjected to mischief, those who practice my sunnah are given the rewards of being a martyr." (Haythami, I, 172; Abu Nuaym, *Hilya*, VIII, 200; Suyuti, *al-Jami*, no: 9171)

In the reports of Baihaqi, this hadith is recorded as *"the rewards of a hundred martyrs."* (Baihaqi, al-*Zuhd al-kabir*, s. 151/209)

As a matter of fact, it is very difficult to find people who practice the Sunnah in periods of *fasad*. On the contrary, there will be many people who belittle the Sunnah and try to destroy it during such periods of time. Those who want to practice Islam will be persecuted and face with troubles. Since such believers practice the Sunnah no matter what kind of persecutions they face with, they will be elevated to the levels of martyrs.

289

In another hadith, the Messenger of Allah (pbuh) gave the good news to those believers who worship in the period of *fasad* as:

"Islam began as something strange, and it shall return to being strange as it were, so give glad tidings to the strangers! They are the ones who correct my sunnah which has been corrupted by the people after me." (Tirmidhi, Iman, 13/2630. Also see. Muslim, Iman, 232-233; Ahmad, I, 184; IV, 73)

The meaning of correction here is tha they try to practice the sunnah of our Prophet and teach others as much as they can at a time when the number of Muslims decreases and they are seen as stranger by others. As a matter of fact, in Baihaqi's narration, when he was asked:

"Who are those strangers, O Messenger of Allah?" he replied:

"Those who practice my sunnah and teach it to others." (Baihaqi, *al-Zuhd al-Kabir*, p. 150/207)

Therefore, the strangers who were praised by the Prophet (pbuh) are the ones who protect their religion by sticking to the commands of Islam in periods of mischief and try to direct others to the straight path as well. (See. Ahmad, I, 184; IV, 73)

Another day the Messenger of Allah (pbuh) said:

"Give glad tidings to strangers! Give glad tidings to strangers! Give glad tidings to strangers!"

It was asked "O the Messenger of Allah, who are those strangers?"

Our Master the Prophet (pbuh) said:

"They are a small group of people among a large population of evil people. Those who oppose them are more than those who follow them." (Ahmad, II, 222, 177)

In periods of turmoil, great rewards are given even to small deeds. Even if they are few in numbers, good deeds performed in a corrupt society and despite the obstacles of the evil and dark-spirited people of the society are very valuable. Thus, ultimate salvation for Muslims becomes easier during such periods of time.

For this reason, one should serve even more in the way of Islam in difficult times for believers. As a matter of fact, it is very profitable to utilize such periods od time when Allah the Almighty gives many rewards to even few good deeds.

With that being said, one should stay away from the evil things that take place in such times of mischief. In such a period of time, a person who sits is better than who stands up, who stands up is better than who walks, and who walks is better than who runs.[170] In other words, one must prefer to be inactive, show effort only on the issues that are possible to be corrected but stay away from the evil in other matters and spend time with worship.

That is because people then would abandon the right path all together. They would not listen to those who warn and call them to the right path. When Muslims who fight for the ultimate wisdom during such times think that they cannot influence anyone, they should at least try to protect themselves and their families from the mischief and disorder.

Therefore, a Muslim should fight against the evil in the society as much as he can and try to correct them. That is because this is the only way to practice all the commands of Allah. However, if one sees that the evil in the society is growing and will eventually influence him and his family, then he should retire from active life and practice the religion with his family. As a matter of fact, the Messenger of Allah (pbuh) advised believers to go aside and worship Allah and protect their religion from the evil things. (See Bukhari, Iman, 12; Jihad, 2; Bad' al-khalk, 15; Riqaq, 34; Muslim, Imara, 122-123)

Sa'd b. Abi Waqqas (r.a.) is a nice example for this subject:

Umar (r.a.) appointed Sa'd b. Abi Waqqas (r.a.), who was one of the first Muslims, to the six-men-committee to elect the caliph after him. When there were disagreements choosing the next or the following caliphs, Sa'd (r.a.) got very sad. He found the solution to retire to his barn outside Medina. When Abi Waqqas was taking care of his camels and sheep, he saw his son Umar was coming. Sa'd understood the intention of his son and said:

"I seek refuge in Allah from the mischief of this rider."

And when his son got down and said:

---

170. Tirmidhi, Fitan, 29/2194

"Father, are you busy with your camels and your sheep while people are contending with each another to get the political power?" Sa'd (r.a.) struck his chest and said:

"Be quiet! I heard Allah's Messenger (pbuh) as saying:

"Allah loves the servant who is God-conscious and is free from want and is hidden (from the view of people)." (Muslim, Zuhd, 11)

Because of this and other similar sayings of the Prophet, Sa'd b. Abi Waqqas (r.a.) retired from the active life completely and stayed away from the complicated things when Uthman (r.a.) was martyred and disorder emerged in the society.

18. I'tikaf

١٢٥. عَنْ أَبِي هُرَيْرَةَ رَضِيَ اللهُ عَنْهُ قَالَ: كَانَ النَّبِيُّ صَلَّى اللهُ عَلَيْهِ وَسَلَّمَ يَعْتَكِفُ فِي كُلِّ رَمَضَانَ عَشَرَةَ أَيَّامٍ فَلَمَّا كَانَ الْعَامُ الَّذِي قُبِضَ فِيهِ اعْتَكَفَ عِشْرِينَ يَوْماً».

125. Abu Huraira (r.a.) narrated:

"The Prophet used to perform I'tikaf for ten days every year in the month of Ramadan, and when it was the year of his death, he stayed in I'tikaf for twenty days." (Bukhari, I'tikaf, 17. Also see Abu Dawud, Sawm, 78; Ibn Majah, Siyam, 58)

❀

١٢٦. عَنْ عَائِشَةَ رَضِيَ اللهُ عَنْهَا قَالَتْ: كَانَ النَّبِيُّ صَلَّى اللهُ عَلَيْهِ وَسَلَّمَ إِذَا دَخَلَ الْعَشْرُ شَدَّ مِئْزَرَهُ وَأَحْيَا لَيْلَهُ وَأَيْقَظَ أَهْلَهُ».

126. Aisha (r.anha) said:

"When the last ten days of Ramadan came, the Prophet (pbuh) kept vigil and prayed during the whole night, and awakened his family (to pray during the night)." (Bukhari, Laylat al-Qadr, 5; Muslim, I'tikaf, 7. Also see Abu Dawud, Ramadan, 1; Nasai, Qiyam al-Layl, 17; Ibn Majah, Siyam, 57)

Explanations:

The term i'tikaf literally means to imprison, to detain, to settle down in a place and to put down roots there, and to prevent oneself from doing regular and mundane activities. In technical terms, it means to retreat in a mosque for a certain period time to improve spiritually and to get closer to Allah through acts of worship. Those who are in i'tikaf are called "*mu'takif*" or "*akif.*"

Keeping oneself away from all kinds of the human acts and desires, even if they are permissible, and keeping oneself busy with acts of worship is one of the most important means of spiritual development. For this reason, I'tikaf used as an important acts of worship performed with some variations by the previous prophets as well. As a matter of fact, the following verse of the Qur'an refers to this matter:

"… **We covenanted with Abraham and Isma'il, that they should sanctify My House for those who compass it round, or use it as a retreat, or bow, or prostrate themselves (therein in prayer).**" (Al-Baqarah; 2:125)

Our beloved Prophet (pbuh) used to retreat in the Cave of Hira even before he had chosen as a prophet and keep himself busy with meditation. When it got closer to the times of his prophethood, he increased his meditations. On the first days of his prophethood, Allah commanded him to perform night prayers (tahajjud.) Since he was going to be busy with delivering his message of calling people to the right path during the day, he needed to gain spiritual power by being with his Lord during the quiet early hours of dawn. When the message of Islam reached to a certain point and fasting was declared to be obligatory in Medina, the Messenger of Allah (pbuh) increased his acts of worship and good deeds during the month of Ramadan which is the most virtuous of all months and is like the early hours of dawn compared to the rest of the day. He even started to spend the second ten days of Ramadan only with acts of worshipping. When the possibility of the Night of Qadr being in the last ten nights of the month Ramadan increased, the Messenger of Allah started to perform his i'tikaf on these days. (Bukhari, I'tikaf, 1)

He used to perform i'tikaf in a small in a Turkish tent with a mat hanging at its door. (Muslim, Siyam, 215; Ibn Majah, Siyam, 62)

Aisha (r.anha) said:

"The Messenger of Allah (pbuh) used to practice i'tikaf in the last ten days of Ramadan. I used to pitch a tent for him, and after offering the dawn prayer he used to enter the tent for i'tikaf."

Once, some of the wives of the Prophet pitched tents for themselves in the mosque. When the Messenger of Allah (pbuh) saw the tents, he asked:

"What are those?"

When he was told of the whole situation, he said:

"Do you think that they intended to do righteousness by doing this?" and he therefore abandoned the i'tikaf in that month and practiced i'tikaf for the first ten days in the month of Shawwal. (Bukhari, I'tikaf, 6, 7, 14; Muslim, I'tikaf, 6; Abu Dawud, Sawm, 77; Tirmidhi, Siyam, 71)

Based on this hadith, it is seen more appropriate for women to retire for i'tikaf in a part of their house instead of going to mosques.

When the Messenger of Allah (pbuh) intended for i'tikaf, his bed was placed in Masjid al-Nabawi next to the Column of Penitence towards the direction of Mecca. The Prophet (pbuh) used to lean on that column. (Ibn Majah, Siyam, 61; Tabarani, *Kabir,* XII, 385/13424; Baihaqi, *Kubra,* V, 247)

As expressed **in our first hadith,** the Messenger of Allah (pbuh) increased the days of his i'tikaf to twenty in his year of passing. By this, he indicated that one must increase worship and obedience even more towards the end of his life. As a matter of fact, in his last year, the Messenger of Allah (pbuh) recited the entire Qur'an to Gabriel twice as he used to do once in the previous Ramadans.

The Messenger of Allah (pbuh) could not observe i'tikaf in the year when he was in the military expedition for the conquest of Mecca. He observed i'tikaf for twenty days in the following year in order not to be devoid of the virtue of this worship. (Abu Dawud, Sawm, 77/2463; Ibn Majah, Siyam, 58)

Then, no matter how much a person worships, he cannot reach the perfection in faith if he doesn't retire into seclusion at least once in a while and think about his actions and deeply contemplate about the divine signs of the Creator in this universe. For, retreating in a mosque is a good opportunity for someone to collect his thoughts, to keep the heart away from the daily life, to concentrate on obedience, and to get closer to Allah.

The Messenger of Allah (pbuh) said about the virtue of those who perform i'tikaf:

"He stays away from the sinful acts and evils. Divine rewards are given to him as he has performed all kinds of good deeds." (Ibn Majah, Siyam, 67)

In another noble hadith:

"Whoever performs i'tikaf for ten days in Ramadan, he is like he has performed two major pilgrimages and two lesser pilgrimages to Mecca as well." (Tabarani, *Kabir*, III, 128/2888; Baihaqi, *Shuab*, III, 425)

A believer who goes to a mosque and starts i'tikaf is like a person who is in prayer at all times. In this state, he is like a person who takes refuge into the protection of a strong castle. Ata, one of the prominent figures of Islam, said:

"The similitude of a person who in i'tikaf is a person who knocks the door of an important person and says "I will not leave without getting what I need." That is because he is the one who entered one of the houses of Allah and says "I will not leave before You forgive me."

As expressed **in our second hadith,** just like the Messenger of Allah (pbuh) himself concentrated on worshipping in the last ten days and nights of Noble Ramadan, he encouraged his family to do so as well, and they together reduced their sleep times. The mothers of the believers who used to practice i'tikaf continued to perform it even after the death of the Prophet. (Bukhari, I'tikaf, 1; Muslim, I'tikaf, 5. Also see Abu Dawud, Sawm, 77)

Those who are in i'tikaf spend their time by performing prayers as much as they can, by reciting the Noble Qur'an, pledging, praying and supplicating, reciting the Kalimah Al-Tawheed and Taqbir, and sending invovations for the Messenger of Allah, thinking about the existence of Allah, His Oneness and His signs of power in this universe, reading books about the life of the Messenger of Allah (pbuh) and other Islamic books. At this time, he stays away from all kinds of unnecessary things.

The Hanafi scholars examine i'tikaf under three categories and state that each of them has different rulings. According to this:

1. Performing i'tikaf in the last ten days of Ramadan is considered Sunnah al-Muakkadah (regular tradition of the Prophet) by comparing to similar cases.

2. It is necessary (wajib) to perform i'tikaf if it is vowed. All the schools of Islamic law agree in this ruling. If a person feels that he will die before he get the chance to perform his vowed i'tikaf, he should make a will for a certain amount of monetary compensation (fidyah) given to the poor for each day of the vowed i'tikaf.

3. Other types of i'tikaf are Mustahab (i.e. liked and recommended).

Scholars had differing views on the minimum duration of i'tikaf as well. According to the Shafi school, even a moment as short as one can say "Subha-nallah" (Glory be to God) is enough for i'tikaf. This is also the well-known view of Ahmad bin Hanbel. However, it is the appropriate way of acting to stay in i'tikaf at least one day just to be on the safe side.

Ata b. Abi Rabah said:

"If a person goes and sits in a mosque with some good intentions, he will be in i'tikaf during the time that he spends in the mosque."

For this reason, our forefathers used to hang a sign reading "I intend to perform i'tikaf" on the entrance of the mosques so that people remember to intend for i'tikaf and gain its rewards even if they stay for fifteen minutes or so.

According to the Hanafis, one must fast during the necessary (wajib) i'tikafs. In mustahab (liked, recommended) i'tikafs, since there is no classified time period, fasting is not required.

One who is in i'tikaf should not passionately touch his wife, or have sexual intercourse or go out for anything but necessary purposes. (Abu Dawud, Sawm, 80/2473)

This is because Allah the Almighty says:

"…but do not associate with your wives while you are in retreat in the mosques." (Al-Baqarah; 2:187)

While i'tikaf is one of the most virtuous worships, it should not hinder more important social acts of worship. A Muslim should use his time wisely by spending time on both performing good deeds for the benefit of the society and performing personal worships. When one has to make a decision between the two, the most beneficial one should be chosen. One of the exemplary hadith on this subject is as follows:

One day, when Abdullah b. Abbas (r.a.) was in i'tikaf in the masjid of the Messenger Allah, someone approached him and sat after saluting him.

Ibn Abbas (r.a.) said:

"My friend, I see you worried and sad" and their conversation continued as:

"Yes, O the son of the Prophet's uncle! I borrowed some money from so and so, but I swear to the owner of this tomb (the Messenger of Allah), I cannot repay my debt."

"Should I talk to him for you?"

"If you don't mind."

Ibn Abbas (r.a.) put his shoes on and go out of the mosque.

The man called:

"Did you forget that you were in i'tikaf, why did you go out of the masjid?"

Ibn Abbas (r.a.) said:

"No, I didn't. I have heard from the noble person in this tomb who recently left us, (with tears in his eyes while speaking):

"Whoever tries to help his brother in Islam and acts on it, this is better for him than staying in i'tikaf for ten years. As a matter of fact, if a person stays in i'tikaf for three days, Allah creates three trenches between that person and the Hell, and the distance within each trench is as much as the distance between the east and west."[171] (Baihaqi, *Shuab*, III, 424-425. Also see Haythami, VIII, 192)

❀

---

171. For more details about i'tikaf see. Mehmed Şener, "İtikâf" *Diyanet İslâm Ansiklopedisi*, XXIII, 457-459.

F. AVOIDING SINFUL ACTS

1. Allah has a sense of jealousy so He doesn't like when His servants perform sinful acts

١٢٧. عَنْ أَبِي هُرَيْرَةَ رَضِيَ اللهُ عَنْهُ عَنِ النَّبِيِّ صَلَّى اللهُ عَلَيْهِ وَسَلَّمَ أَنَّهُ قَالَ:

«إِنَّ اللهَ يَغَارُ وَغَيْرَةُ اللهِ أَنْ يَأْتِيَ الْمُؤْمِنُ مَا حَرَّمَ اللهُ».

127. It is narrated from Abu Huraira (r.a.) that the Messenger of Allah (pbuh) said:

"Allah has a sense of ghira (jealousy), and Allah's sense of ghira is provoked when a believer does something which Allah has prohibited." (Bukhari, Nikah, 107; Muslim, Tawbah, 36. Also see Tirmidhi, Rada, 14/1168; Ahmad, II, 519, 536, 539)

❊

١٢٨. عَنْ عَبْدِ اللهِ رَضِيَ اللهُ عَنْهُ قَالَ: قَالَ رَسُولُ اللهِ صَلَّى اللهُ عَلَيْهِ وَسَلَّمَ:

«لَا أَحَدٌ أَغْيَرُ مِنَ اللهِ وَلِذٰلِكَ حَرَّمَ الْفَوَاحِشَ مَا ظَهَرَ مِنْهَا وَمَا بَطَنَ».

128. Abdullah bin Mas'ud reported that the Messenger of Allah (pbuh) said:

"No being has more sense of ghaira (jealousy) than Allah. Therefore, He prohibits shameful sins whether committed openly or secretly..." (Muslim, Tawbah, 33, 32-35. Also see Bukhari, Tafsir, 6/7; Tawhid, 15)

❊

١٢٩. عَنْ ثَوْبَانَ رَضِيَ اللهُ عَنْهُ قَالَ: قَالَ رَسُولُ اللهِ صَلَّى اللهُ عَلَيْهِ
وَسَلَّمَ:

«إِنَّ الرَّجُلَ لَيُحْرَمُ الرِّزْقَ بِالذَّنْبِ يُصِيبُهُ وَلَا يَرُدُّ الْقَدَرَ إِلَّا الدُّعَاءُ
وَلَا يَزِيدُ فِي الْعُمُرِ إِلَّا الْبِرُّ».

129. Thawban reported that the Messenger of Allah (pbuh) said:

"A person can be destitute of his livelihood due to a sin that he committed. Only prayer can change destiny. Only good deeds, manners, and being virtues can extend life time." (Ahmad, V, 277, 280, 282; Ibn Majah, Muqaddimah, 10; Fitan, 22; Hakim, I, 670/1814)

Explanations:

Sinful acts include beliefs, words, acts, and behaviors that are against the divine commands and the religion. The Messenger of Allah (pbuh) defined sin in his noble hadith as:

"(Sin) is the thing that scratches your heart and the thing that you do not want others to know." (Muslim, Birr, 14, 15. Also see Tirmidhi, Zuhd, 52)

"Sin is the thing that you fret about and the thing that questions and bothers you even others give permission (religious ruling) for you to do it." (Ahmad, IV, 227-228; Darimi, Buyu', 2)

Humans, who have been sent to this world to be tested, are able to perform both good and bad deeds. The inclination in human character towards sinful acts is due to their desires originating from their carnal self. That is because the carnal soul is the enemy inside of us which is **"certainly prone to evil"**[172] and makes dark suggestions to us by whispering all the time in order to lead us to commit sins.[173]

Another motivation that leads humans to sinful acts is the desire for an everlasting life in this world and forgetting about the life in the hereafter.[174] Those

---

172. Yusuf; 12:53.
173. Qaf; 50:16; Al-Najm; 53:23.
174. Al-Baqara; 2:95-96.

who follow these poisonous desires act without thinking about the hereafter and fall into a trap by committing a sin in order to satisfy their desires.

Also, there are other factors that drag man into committing sins such as having been created weak,[175] and being fond of wealth, possession, and children.[176]

There are external causes of sinful acts as well. The appeal of this world,[177] ubiquity of bad examples,[178] and the pledge of Satan to deviate men by sitting on the True Path [179] are some of the examples.

In order to fight with all of these distracting temptations, one must be busy with purifying the human soul and heart. Therefore, one must learn to follow a life without being unwary of Allah and remembering Him at all times. As a matter of fact, all of such sinful acts start to step in when men forget Allah.

Quitting sinful acts and staying away from them come before performing the commands of Allah. First, the heart should be purified from all kinds of evil, and then it should be filled with the divine light by performing the obligatory acts. That is because sinful and forbidden acts are like poisons which destroy spirituality. However, in appearance they seem like sweet honey to the people. Those who believe them waste their spiritual lives in the end.

One must not forget that every blessing necessitates some effort. Believers who wish to be in Paradise and to see God's Face should bear some difficulties in order not to be trapped by the sins that seem sweet to human soul. This situation is one of the secrets of the divine test.

Since Allah loves His servants a lot, He always wants the best for them and treats them with His mercy. Therefore, Allah does not want His servants to fail in this test by committing sins and He never likes this. **As expressed in our first hadith,** Allah has a sense of *ghira* (jealousy) so He doesn't like when His servants commit sins. Omnipotent Allah never wishes His servants to deviate from the true path and the path to Paradise by committing sins due to being carried away by the carnal soul and Satan. He wishes that His servants improve their spirituality by coming towards Him and enter into Paradise. He advises

---

175. An-Nisa; 4:28.
176. Al-Baqara; 2:155; Al-i Imran; 3:14.
177. Al-i Imran; 3:14, 185; Yunus; 10:23; Ar-Rad; 13:26.
178. An'am; 6:116; Al-Furqan; 25:27-29.
179. Al-A'raf; 7:14-18; Al-Hijr; 15:36-42.

His servants not to forget His Exalted Being and gain the consciousness of being close to Him at all times, because this is the approach which benefits the human beings.

When it is used in respect to Allah, the word "*ghira*" in the hadith, which we translated from Arabic as "jealousy," refers to His discontentedness with "His servants' performances of prohibited and illegitimate acts, their utterances of illegal words, and going astray from the straight path." Rather He wants them to be on the true path and be happy due to His mercy for them. Otherwise, it is not imaginable to think of jealousy for Allah as it reveals itself in some people as abrupt and abnormal reactions.

Allah expresses that He does not want His servants to be in a difficult position as:

"If you reject (Allah), Truly Allah has no need of you; but He likes not ingratitude from His servants" (Az-Zumar; 39:7)

As a matter of fact the term "jealousy" is generally used for a feeling between wife and husband whereby they guard each other from others due to their feelings of love and protection towards each other and sometimes it is expressed by passion and reproach. As in this example, Allah wants to protect His servants and does not want them to get further away from Him. For this reason, He prohibits committing sins and punishes those who commit sins in order to keep them away from sinful acts and purify them. In such situations, it is said that "this action provokes the *ghira* of Allah."

Our Almighty Lord does not like His servants to decline spiritually and be miserable in the hereafter. Sins transform spiritual feelings into bestial feelings and prevent souls to advance towards perfection and drag it to the lowest level (*asfal al-safilin*). Sins eventually darken the heart and cause it lose its purity. This means the exhaustion of blessed human beings who is created in the best form. Therefore, in order to protect the purity of the heart, one must be extremely careful to avoid sins and negative inspirations.

Allah made everything clear and easy to protect His servants from sins. The following noble hadith clearly presents how merciful Allah the Almighty is:

The Messenger of Allah (pbuh) said:

"Allah the Almighty commands to His angels:

301

"If My slave intends to do a bad deed then (O Angels) do not write it unless he does it; if he does it, then write it as it is, but if he refrains from doing it for My Sake, then write it as a good deed (in his account). (On the other hand) if he intends to go to a good deed, but does not do it, then write a good deed (in his account), and if he does it, then write it for him (in his account) as ten good deeds up to seven-hundred times." (Bukhari, Tawhid, 35; Muslim, Iman, 203, 205)

Apart from this, Allah the Almighty always wishes to forgive His servants by leaving many doors of opportunities open for them.

In our second hadith, it is expressed that none has more sense of *ghira* (jealousy) than Allah, so He prohibits shameful sins whether they are committed openly or secretly.

This means that there is no one who is more merciful to the servants of Allah than Allah Himself. Since Omniscient Allah knows how sins are dangerous for His servants, He prohibits sins whether committed openly or secretly. There cannot be anyone who is against shameful sins as much as Allah is and who prohibits them as strictly as He does. Therefore, one must not be surprised at the punishment that Allah gives to those who disobey. Our Almighty Lord wishes to scare His servants away from shameful sins and protect them from their harms.

Allah the Exalted has sent prophets and books and informed His servants about His commands in order to protect them from sins and evil. He also informed them in advance that He will be angry at those who violate His limits. All of these are because He wishes to protect His servants from shameful sins.

While Allah has a sense of jealousy towards His servants about committing sins, He reacts wisely, justly, and in the best form if this happens. He never treats them with cruelty and injustice. The following report related to our hadith clarifies the subject even more:

One day, Sa'd b. Ubada (r.a.) said in the presence of the Messenger of Allah that:

"If I see a man next to my wife, I would strike him with the sharp edge of my sword and kill him."

Upon that, the Messenger of Allah (pbuh) said to people around him:

"Are you surprised with this sense of jealousy and sense of honor of Sa'd? I have even more sense of jealousy than Sa'd. Allah has even more sense of jealousy than me." (Bukhari, Nikah, 36, 107)

Of course, the discontent of Allah and His Messenger when one of Allah's commands is violated is much more than the feeling of jealousy between the couples. Despite this, Allah had prohibited to make rushed decisions and to act impulsively. He restricted the approach how to react against sins with firm and fundamental principles. Therefore, it is not right for someone to give judgments on one's own and punish sinners accordingly. One must acknowledge that there are many virtues in Allah's commands and should obey them.

The term *"fawahish"* mentioned **in our second hadith** means all kinds of shameful deeds whether committed in actions or in words. All of the shameful deeds that are prohibited by Allah are included in this term.

The statement *"He prohibits shameful sins whether committed openly or secretly"* in this hadith refers to the following Qur'anic verse:

"Say: "Come, I will rehearse what Allah has (really) prohibited you from": Join not anything as equal with Him; be good to your parents; kill not your children on a plea of want; We provide sustenance for you and for them; <u>come not nigh to shameful deeds whether open or secret; take not life</u>, which Allah has made sacred, except by way of justice and law: thus does He command you, that you may learn wisdom." (Al-An'am; 6:151)

Our Almighty Lord says "do not come near to shameful deeds whether open or secret" instead of "do not perform shameful deeds whether open or secret." In other words, let alone performing them, He does not even want us come near them. This is one of the wise remarks that show how much Allah is jealous of His servants from shameful deeds.

Allah permitted in the Qur'an benefiting from the permissible, nice, and clean blessings and warned those who want to prohibit them. Then, He said the following to explain that He did not prohibit beneficial things to humans but only prohibited things that are harmful to them:

"Say: the things that my Lord has indeed forbidden are: <u>shameful deeds, whether open or secret</u>; sins and trespasses against truth or reason; assigning of partners to Allah, for which He has given no authority; and saying things about Allah of which you have no knowledge." (Al-Araf; 7:33)

303

Even though Allah the Almighty has a sense of strong jealousy towards His servants from sins, He does not punish them immediately. He gives them time to repent, ask for forgiveness and to turn back to the right path. To be deceived by this and be caught up in sins would be utmost foolishness and causes misery.

It is expressed in another verse:

"If Allah were to punish men according to what they deserve, He would not leave on the back of the (earth) a single living creature: but He gives them respite for a stated term: when their term expires, verily Allah has in His sight all His Servants." (Al-Fatir; 35:45)

However, in order sinners to wake up from being negligent or to ease their punishment in the Hereafter, Allah may inflict various troubles upon them.[180] These may not be the same for everyone, and they may appear as a variety of warnings. For example, one of them is to decrease in one's daily bread.

In our third hadith, the Messenger of Allah (pbuh) informed us that one may be deprived of some livelihood due to his sins.[181] Even the livelihood pre-destined for him reaches him, it may somehow get off his hands, and he can-not benefit from it due to his sins. As a matter of fact, when the owners of the garden mentioned in the Chapter the Qalam wanted to secretly harvest their crops to avoid giving some to the poor, their garden faced with a disaster and turned into pitch black. Almighty Allah explains this event in detail[182] for us to learn our lesson and concludes the story as:

---

180. Ibn Majah, Fitan, 22; Hakim, IV, 583/8623.
181. At the end of the third hadith, we are informed that good deeds may extend one's lifetime. The scholars of hadith mention having good relations with the relatives at the top of the list. These scholars also argue that the meaning of **extending one's lifetime** is to make it fruitful and blessed with good deeds. Those who perform good deeds benefit from their lifetime a lot even if it is short. For sure, this blessed and spiritual benefaction is very important in terms of eternal happiness. On the other hand, there are those who also believe that the lifetime written in our destiny and known by the angel can actually change. That is because Allah may delete the things that He wishes from The Protected Book (*Lawh Mahfuz*) and keeps the things that He does not want to change as they are. (Al-Ra'd; 13:38) **Prayers effect of changing destiny** is also understood in the same manner. Praying prevents bad happenings to take place and calls attention to divine mercy. This is also a part of destiny (See. Haydar Hatipoğlu, Sünen-i Ibn Majah Tercemesi ve Şerhi, I, 159-160)
182. Al-Qalam; 68:17-33.

"Such is the punishment (in this life); but greater is the punishment in the Hereafter, if only they knew!" (Al-Qalam; 68:33)

Ali (r.a.) told a story as an example to an immediate warning of a sin:

During the time of the Messenger of Allah (pbuh), a man walking in the streets of Medina looked at a woman who was walking as well. Satan cast upon them some doubts, and they thought that they have looked at each other with affection. While they were looking each other like this, a wall appeared in front of the man. The man hit his nose to the wall, and his nose started to bleed. The man realized that he did something wrong and said:

"I swear to Allah I won't treat my nose and wipe off this bleeding before I go and tell what happened to the Messenger of Allah."

Then he told the Prophet (pbuh) what happened.

The Messenger of Allah (pbuh) said:

"This is the punishment of the sin that you have committed."

Upon this incident, Almighty Allah revealed the following noble verse:

"Say to the believing men that they should lower their gaze and guard their modesty: that will make for greater purity for them: And Allah is well acquainted with all that they do." (Al-Nur; 24:30) (Alusi, XVIII, 138)

Therefore, it is necessary to pay extra attention to stay away from shameful deeds and take refuge in Allah. The Messenger of Allah (pbuh) became an example to his followers in this respect by praying as:

اَللّٰهُمَّ إِنَّا نَسْأَلُكَ مُوجِبَاتِ رَحْمَتِكَ وَعَزَائِمَ مَغْفِرَتِكَ وَالسَّلَامَةَ مِنْ كُلِّ إِثْمٍ وَالْغَنِيمَةَ مِنْ كُلِّ بِرٍّ وَالْفَوْزَ بِالْجَنَّةِ وَالنَّجَاةَ بِعَوْنِكَ مِنَ النَّارِ

"O My Lord! I ask to perform good deeds that make me gain your mercy and forgiveness, and I ask to be safe from all evil deeds, to perform all good deeds and Your commands, to reach Paradise and be safe from the Hell with Your help!"
(Hakim, I, 706/1925. Also see Tirmidhi, Witr, 17/479; Ibn Majah, Iqamah, 189)

2. Major Sins

a. Ascribing Partners to Allah and Disobedience to Parents

١٣٠. عَنْ أَبِي بَكْرَةَ رَضِيَ اللهُ عَنْهُ قَالَ: قَالَ النَّبِيُّ صَلَّى اللهُ عَلَيْهِ وَسَلَّمَ:

«أَلاَ أُنَبِّئُكُمْ بِأَكْبَرِ الْكَبَائِرِ؟» -ثَلاَثًا- قَالُوا:

«بَلَى يَا رَسُولَ اللهِ» قَالَ:

«الْإِشْرَاكُ بِاللهِ وَعُقُوقُ الْوَالِدَيْنِ» وَجَلَسَ وَكَانَ مُتَّكِئًا فَقَالَ:

«أَلاَ وَقَوْلُ الزُّورِ» قَالَ فَمَا زَالَ يُكَرِّرُهَا حَتَّى قُلْنَا: «لَيْتَهُ سَكَتَ».

103. Abu Bakr (r.a.) narrated that the Prophet (pbuh) asked three times:

"Shall I inform you of the biggest of the great sins?"

His Companions said:

"Yes, O the Messenger of Allah!"

The Messenger of Allah (pbuh) said:

"To ascribe partners in worship with Allah, to be undutiful to one's parents." Then he sat up from where he had been reclining and added:

"And listen well as I warn you against giving forged statement and a false witness; I warn you against giving a forged statement and a false witness."

The Prophet kept on saying that warning till we thought that he would not stop (and wished that he would do so that he wouldn't be sorry any more).

(Bukhari, Shahadah, 10; Al-Adab, 6; Isti'zan, 35; Istitabe, 1; Muslim, Iman, 143. Also see Tirmidhi, Shahadah, 3; Birr, 4; Tafsir, 4/5)

١٣١. عَنْ شَدَّادِ بْنِ أَوْسٍ رَضِيَ اللهُ عَنْهُ قَالَ: قَالَ رَسُولُ اللهِ صَلَّى اللهُ عَلَيْهِ وَسَلَّمَ:

«إِنَّ أَخْوَفَ مَا أَتَخَوَّفُ عَلَى أُمَّتِي الْإِشْرَاكُ بِاللهِ أَمَا إِنِّي لَسْتُ أَقُولُ يَعْبُدُونَ شَمْسًا وَلَا قَمَرًا وَلَا وَثَنًا وَلٰكِنْ أَعْمَالًا لِغَيْرِ اللهِ وَشَهْوَةً خَفِيَّةً».

131. Shaddad b. Aws narrated that the Messenger of Allah (pbuh) said:

"I am most worried about my followers that they may ascribe partners to Al-lah. With these words, I do not mean worshipping to the moon, sun, or idols. The thing that worries me is their deeds which are performed for someone other than Allah and their hidden desires (their feeling of showing-off)." (Ibn Majah, Zuhd, 21)

❁

١٣٢. عَنِ الْمُغِيرَةِ بْنِ شُعْبَةَ رَضِيَ اللهُ عَنْهُ عَنِ النَّبِيِّ صَلَّى اللهُ عَلَيْهِ وَسَلَّمَ قَالَ:

«إِنَّ اللهَ حَرَّمَ عَلَيْكُمْ عُقُوقَ الْأُمَّهَاتِ وَمَنْعَ وَهَاتِ وَوَأْدَ الْبَنَاتِ وَكَرِهَ لَكُمْ قِيلَ وَقَالَ وَكَثْرَةَ السُّؤَالِ وَإِضَاعَةَ الْمَالِ».

132. Al-Mughira b. Shu'ba (r.a.) narrated that the Messenger of Allah (pbuh) said:

"Allah has forbidden you to be undutiful to your mothers to withhold (what you should give) or demand (what you do not deserve), and to bury your daugh-ters alive. And Allah has disliked that you talk too much about others (gossip), ask too many questions (in religion), or waste your property." (Bukhari, Al-Adab, 6; Istiqrad, 19; Zakat, 53; Muslim, Aqdiya, 10-14)

❁

١٣٣. عَنْ عَبْدِ اللهِ بْنِ عَمْرٍو رَضِيَ اللهُ عَنْهُ عَنِ النَّبِيِّ صَلَّى اللهُ عَلَيْهِ وَسَلَّمَ قَالَ:

«رِضَى الرَّبِّ فِي رِضَى الْوَالِدِ وَسَخَطُ الرَّبِّ فِي سَخَطِ الْوَالِدِ».

133. Abdullah b. Amr narrated that the Messenger of Allah (pbuh) said:

"The contentedness of Allah can be gained by pleasing the parents. The anger of Allah can be atracted by angering the parents." (Tirmidhi, Birr, 3/1899; Hakim, IV, 168/7249)

❁

١٣٤. عَنْ أَبِي هُرَيْرَةَ رَضِيَ اللهُ عَنْهُ عَنِ النَّبِيِّ صَلَّى اللهُ عَلَيْهِ وَسَلَّمَ قَالَ:

«رَغِمَ اَنْفُ ثُمَّ رَغِمَ اَنْفُ ثُمَّ رَغِمَ اَنْفُ» قِيلَ:

«مَنْ يَا رَسُولَ اللهِ؟» قَالَ:

«مَنْ اَدْرَكَ اَبَوَيْهِ عِنْدَ الْكِبَرِ اَحَدَهُمَا اَوْ كِلَيْهِمَا فَلَمْ يَدْخُلِ الْجَنَّةَ».

134. Abu Huraira (r.a.) narrated that the Messenger of Allah (pbuh) said:

"Let him be humbled (on his nose), let him be humbled (on his nose)!" It was asked:

"O the Messenger of Allah! Who is he?"

The Prophet (pbuh) answered:

"He who finds his parents in old age, either one or both of them, and does not enter Paradise." (Muslim, Birr, 9, 10)

Explanations:

In fact, one must stay away all kinds of shameful deeds that Allah has forbidden, no matter how great or little they are. That is because why and for whom the act has been done is more important than the act itself. Therefore, even the smallest mistake done to Allah without an excuse is a shame for a believer. However, considering mistakes that can easily be fallen into due to human nature can be divided into two sub-categories as the minor ones and the major ones according to their consequences.

The major sins are the ones cursed and severely threatened mistakes in the Qur'an and the sayings of the Prophet. They are also the ones whose performers are called sinners and deserve to be punished. Such sins necessitate torments in the tombs and in the hereafter. Also, it is clear that the deeds cursed by Allah, referred to as away from His mercy, and end with misery are the ones that are considered the forbidden (haram) deeds or one of the major sins.

Major sins contain very serious dangers for humans. As a matter of fact, the pervasiveness of insurgency and major sins and inability to prevent them may cause total destruction of humanity.

Those who do not avoid major sins provoke Allah's anger and receive punishment even for their minor sins and would not benefit from their good deeds a lot. As a matter of fact, in previous subjects, we have seen that some of the good deeds and acts of worship can be expiation for our minor sins. However this is conditioned on "avoiding major sins."[183]

In other words, only if the servant avoids major sins then their good deeds can be expiation for the minor sins. Allah says:

"If you (but) eschew the most heinous of the things which you are forbidden to do, We shall expel out of you all the evil in you, and admit you to a gate of great honor." (Al-Nisa; 4:31. Also see Al-Najm; 53:32)

In our first hadith, due to the importance of the subject, the Messenger of Allah (pbuh) used an attention grabbing style by first asking "Shall I inform you of the biggest of the great sins?" before he talked about them. Then he listed ascribing partners to Allah, disobeying the parents, and lying.

---

183. For example see Bukhari, Hajj, 4; Muhsar, 9, 10; Muslim, Taharah, 14, 16; Hajj, 438; Tirmidhi, Mawaqit, 46; Hajj, 2; Nasai, Hajj, 4; Ibn Majah, Iqamah, 79; Manasik, 3.

The biggest of the major sins is not to acknowledge the existence of Allah and to ascribe partners to Him in His being, attributes, and deeds. This is called "*akbar al-kabair.*" Allah the Almighty explained ascribing partners to Him as **"the highest wrong-doing"**[184] and **"devise a sin most heinous indeed."**[185] That is because ascribing partners to Allah is the most wrongful approach in the face of the truth. Those who ascribe partners to Allah would be doing wrong to themselves and do injustice by not giving Allah His due. The result of this is to be strayed far, far away (from the true path).[186]

Ascribing partners to Allah who created man and the whole universe is a very disrespectful and misbehaved way of acting. As a matter of fact, when Abdullah b. Mas'ud asked the following question to the Prophet (pbuh):

"Which offense is the most grievous in the eye of Allah?" the Messenger of Allah (pbuh) said:

"That you associate a partner with Allah (despite the fact) that He created you." (Muslim, Iman, 141)

If attention is paid, it can be seen that the same thing applies to when one disobeys to his parents. As a matter of fact, Allah appointed them as a means for a person to come to this world and gain existence. Parents gladly do all kinds of sacrifices to raise their children until they grow up and take care of themselves. Therefore, we must give the right due to Allah and to our parents to whom we owe our existence.

Ascribing partners to Allah does not harm Allah in any way. All harm of ascribing partners to Allah is for people. Since Almighty Allah has a sense of jealousy towards His servants from sins and mistakes, He strictly prohibits ascribing partners to Him.

Almighty Allah explained how bad ascribing partners to Allah is and how harmful it is to humans as:

"Being true in faith to Allah, and never assigning partners to Him: if anyone assigns partners to Allah, is as if he had fallen from heaven and been snatched up by birds, or the wind had swooped (like a bird on its prey) and thrown him into a far- distant place." (Al-Hajj; 22:31)

---

184. Luqman; 31:13.
185. Al-Nisa; 4:48.
186. Al-Nisa; 4:116.

While believing Allah elevates people and makes them spread their wings to everlasting spirituality, ascribing partners to Him causes them to fall from heavens and get shattered. Ascribing partners to Allah is such a destructive sin and it breaks one's heart into pieces and throws it down from cliffs and drags it to places where all sorts of danger are present. As a matter of fact, when one is trapped into the sin of ascribing partners to Allah, each one of the fanciful desires of the carnal soul drags him to different ways and Satan, who is the wind of destruction, throws him to the furthest corners of the valleys of Hell. This destruction of the heart is much worse than the destruction of the body. For this reason, the Messenger of Allah (pbuh) said:

"Even if you are cut into pieces or burned in fire, never ascribe partners to Allah!.." (Ibn Majah, Fiten, 23)

There is no stability and peace in the hearts of those who ascribe partners to Allah. They never know whom or what they want to please. How nicely their confused situation is expressed in the following Qur'anic verse:

"Allah puts forth a Parable a man belonging to many partners at variance with each other, and a man belonging entirely to one master: are those two equal in comparison? Praise be to Allah, but most of them have no knowledge." (Al-Zumar; 39:29)

Think about a servant and some partners who disagree with each other. Each partner wants the servant to obey only his commands and gets angry when the servant obeys other partners. Anyone in this situation would not know what to do and angers one partner while trying to please the other one since while the servant thinks about performing the command of one, other partners give different commands. As a result, this servant would be worthless in the eyes of each of the partner and his life would be wasted with never-ending troubles and exhaustion.

On the other hand, think about a servant who is devoted only to one master and who is in peace. He would please his master each time and earns rewards. In turn, his master helps him with his works and needs and grants his wishes. Could the situation of these two servants be the same?

As the state of those who ascribe partners to Allah is dishonorable and miserable in this world, it is also very frightening in the Hereafter. Allah the Almighty does not forgive those who ascribe partners to Him while He forgives anything else if He pleases. (Al-Nisa; 4:48, 116)

Those are the ones who waste the eternal life. It is said in a noble verse of the Qur'an:

"Those who reject (Truth), among the people of the Book and among the Polytheists, will be in Hell-Fire, to dwell therein. They are the worst of creatures." (Al-Bayyinah; 98:6)

Each prophet surely explained the truth about ascribing partners to Allah. They have warned their followers to acknowledge Allah, the Cause of all causations, without getting fooled by the perceptible causes. We can list the acts that the Prophets explained as acts of ascribing partners to Allah:

• Prostrating to something or someone other than Allah,[187]

• Presenting the needs to someone other than Allah and expecting the results (which should be expected only from Allah) from other powers and persons,

• Naming some creatures as "the daughters of Allah" or "the sons of Allah,"

• Adopting rulers as Lord who make things permissible (halal) or forbidden (haram). That is because the power to make things permissible or forbidden for people is unique to Allah.

• Sacrificing an animal for the name of someone other than Allah,

• Swearing in the name of someone other than Allah,

• Visiting places special to beings ascribed as partners to Allah,

• Naming children after the beings that remind ascribing partners to Allah...[188]

---

187. It is said in the Noble Quran that:
"Among His Signs are the night and the day, and the Sun and the Moon. Adore not the sun and the moon, but adore Allah, Who created them, if it is Him you wish to serve." (Al-Fussilat; 41:37)

188. See Shah Waliyyullah al-Dihlawi, *Hujjatullah al-Baligha*, I, 183-188.
In our first hadith, lying is listed among the major sins after ascribing partners to Allah and disobeying one's parents. We will cover the subject of lying in the next chapter. For now it suffices to express this: in order to show how important the issue is, the Messenger of Allah (pbuh) sat up from where he had been reclining and said "And listen well as I warn you

In our second hadith, the dangers of showing off, being insincere, and performing some deeds for something other than Allah's contentedness which is also known as "implicitly (secretly) ascribing partners to Allah" are being drawn attention to. Performing the things that should be done for the contentment of Allah for others to see, admire, and for some worldly benefits is a situation that the Messenger of Allah was worried about his followers. That is because acting this way is among the major sins and is also something very easy to be trapped into since it is not obvious. On the other hand, the greater shirk, i.e., ascribing partners to Allah openly (explicitly), is evident. The Messenger of Allah (pbuh) explained this with all its aspects to his followers. After that, it is not possible for a sane believer to worship creatures such as moon or sun. However, the desires of the carnal self and sense of showing-off is not like that so one must be aware of them at all times. For example, the Messenger of Allah (pbuh) considered trying to perform a prayer better knowing that it is being observed by others as a manifestation of ascribing partners to Allah implicitly. (Ibn Majah, Zuhd, 21)

The result of the implicitly ascribing partners to Allah is a surprise misery. While the person expects divine rewards from the worships that he has performed as showing-off, he will face with a punishment in the Hereafter and realize that he gained nothing.

One day, the Prophet (pbuh) said:

"The thing that worries me the most about you is the lesser (implicit ascription of partners to Allah."

The people around him asked:

"What is the lesser ascription of partners to Allah, O the Messenger of Allah?"

The Messenger of Allah (pbuh) answered:

"It is hypocrisy, or, in other words, it is showing-off. On the Day of Judgment, while people receive what corresponds to their deeds, Allah will tell the hypocrites:

---

against giving forged statement and a false witness" and he kept on saying that warning so many times that the Noble Companions of the Messenger who love him more than anything else wanted him to stop since they did not want the Messenger to get tired.

"Go to those whom you wanted to see your deeds! See if you can find any rewards with them?" (Ahmad, V, 428, 429)

Therefore, a Muslim should sincerely perform his acts of worships and good deeds, and avoid anything other than the content of Allah such as hypocrisy, showing-off, and similar senses of benefits.

It is said in the Noble Qur'an:

"… whoever expects to meet his Lord, let him work righteousness, and, in the worship of his Lord, admit no one as partner." (Al-Kahf; 18:110)

In our third hadith, we are informed that Allah the Exalted prohibits disobedience to parents and to break off relations with them. Even if "mothers" is used in the original text of the hadith, it is clear that both of parents are implied. The reason why "mothers" are specifically mentioned in the hadith is the fact that they are mistreated and abused more often than fathers since they are more merciful, gentler, and weaker.

The Prophet (pbuh) informs us that, on the Day of Judgment, He will not look at the faces of those who disobey their parents. (Nasai, Zakat, 69/2560)

Almighty Allah says:

"Serve Allah, and join not any partners with Him; and do good to parents, kinsfolk, orphans, those in need, neighbors who are near, neighbors who are strangers, the companion by your side, the wayfarer (ye meet), and what your right hands possess: For Allah loves not the arrogant, the vainglorious…" (Al-Nisa; 4:36)

In this verse, our Exalted Lord prohibits ascribing partners to Him and, right after that, commands being nice to parents. This is enough to prove the importance of being nice to parents and how bad it is to disobey them.[189]

---

189. In the rest of **our third hadith**, our Almighty Lord also prohibits not helping the poor and asking for alms from others, not paying one's debt back and asking for more loans, being miser and begging while one is not in need, in short, not performing one's duties and asking for the things that one does not deserve.

The command of not to bury baby girls alive follows this. The scholars of exegesis of the Quran tell that the most scary and alarming Noble verse of the Quran is **"When the female (infant), buried alive, is questioned for what crime she was killed;"** (Al-Taqwir; 81:8-9) This killing was one of the worst practices of the Era of Ignorance (the era before Islam). In those days, the parents were committing a grave sin by killing their baby girls while the eternal life of the babies killed were being saved since they pass away in childhood. In today's world, the same kind of crime takes place by dragging pure and innocent generations

For this reason, the way of gaining the consent of Allah passes through gaining the consent of parents. Angering the parents attracts the wrath of Allah.

Someone came to the Messenger of Allah (pbuh) and asked:

"O Messenger of Allah! What is the right of parents upon their children?"

The Messenger of Allah (pbuh) said:

"They are either your Paradise or your Hell." (Ibn Majah, Adab, 1/3662)

In other words, parents are two big opportunities presented to everyone. A Muslim can make it easy to gain Paradise for himself by pleasing his parents. If one does not act in this way and displeases his parents, this time, he makes the ways of Paradise difficult for himself. As a matter of fact, Almighty Allah lets us know that the Paradise lies under the feet of our mothers.

Aisha, the mother of believers, told a story about an act of a Companion who gained Paradise by being nice to his mother:

One day, the Messenger of Allah (pbuh) said:

"I fall asleep and saw myself in Paradise. I heard someone reciting the Qur'an.

"Who is this?" I asked.

They said "This is Haritha b. Nu'man."

The Messenger (pbuh) continued saying:

"Doing goodness should be like this, doing goodness should be like this!"

At the end of the narration, it is told that Haritha advanced his spiritual level by acting nicely towards his mother and said:

"He was one of the Noble Companions who treated his mother in the best fashion." (Ahmad, VI, 151-152; Hakim, IV, 167)

that are entrusted to parents into a moral breakdown and both of their worlds are wasted. Therefore, as being His creation, reviving the hearts of our kids by raising them with Islamic moral values and ensure their happiness in both worlds is our duty to Allah.

In the second part of the hadith, we are also informed that Allah does not like gossip, asking too many questions, and wasting one's money by spending it in a way that Islam does not permit.

Our Master the Pride of the Universe (pbuh) prayed for those who are nice to their parents as:

"How happy those who treat their parents well are! May Allah lengthen their lives!" (Haythami, VIII, 137)

While one must treat his parents well all the time, it is an important duty to serve them nicely especially in their old age.

It is said in a noble verse:

"Your Lord has decreed that you worship none but Him, and that you be kind to parents. Whether one or both of them attain old age in your life, say not to them a word of contempt, nor repel them, but address them in terms of honor. And, out of kindness, lower to them the wing of humility, and say: "My Lord! Bestow on them your Mercy even as they cherished me in childhood." (Al-Isra; 17:23-24)

That is because; humans need kindness, help and service most in their old ages. And there is no one else who could do this better than one's own child. Those children who take advantage of this can easily gain Paradise. The Messenger of Allah (pbuh) harshly warned those who reach the old age of their parents and lose the chance of earning Paradise since they avoid serving them and treating them nicely.

There is only one exception for not obeying one's parents: A child should not obey his parents if they ask to ascribe partners to Allah. However, he should still continue to keep his relations with his parents and treat them nicely. (Luqman; 31:14, Al-Ankabut; 29:8)

b. Killing someone or Committing Suicide

١٣٥. عَنْ أَنَسٍ رَضِيَ اللهُ عَنْهُ قَالَ: سُئِلَ النَّبِيُّ صَلَّى اللهُ عَلَيْهِ وَسَلَّمَ عَنِ الْكَبَائِرِ قَالَ:

«الْإِشْرَاكُ بِاللهِ وَعُقُوقُ الْوَالِدَيْنِ وَقَتْلُ النَّفْسِ وَشَهَادَةُ الزُّورِ».

135. Anas (r.a.) said: When it was asked about the major sins to the Messenger of Allah:

"Ascribing partners to Allah, disobeying one's parents, killing someone, and false witnessing." (Bukhari, Shahadah, 10)

۱۳٦. عَنِ ابْنِ عُمَرَ رَضِيَ اللهُ عَنْهُمَا قَالَ: قَالَ رَسُولُ اللهِ صَلَّى اللهُ عَلَيْهِ وَسَلَّمَ:

«لَنْ يَزَالَ الْمُؤْمِنُ فِي فُسْحَةٍ مِنْ دِينِهِ مَا لَمْ يُصِبْ دَمًا حَرَامًا».

136. Abdullah b. Umar (r.a.) said that the Messenger of Allah (pbuh) said:

"A faithful believer remains at liberty regarding his religion (hoping for Allah's mercy) unless he kills somebody unlawfully." (Bukhari, Ad-Diyat)

۱۳۷. عَنْ عَبْدِ اللهِ بْنِ عَمْرِو بْنِ الْعَاصِ رَضِيَ اللهُ عَنْهُ قَالَ: قَالَ رَسُولُ اللهِ صَلَّى اللهُ عَلَيْهِ وَسَلَّمَ:

«وَالَّذِي نَفْسِي بِيَدِهِ لَقَتْلُ مُؤْمِنٍ أَعْظَمُ عِنْدَ اللهِ مِنْ زَوَالِ الدُّنْيَا».

137. Abdullah b. Amr b. As (r.a.) narrated: The Messenger of Allah (pbuh) said:

"I swear to Allah who holds my life in His power, killing a believer is worse in the sight of Allah than the destruction of the Earth." (Nasai, Tahrimu'd-Dem, 2/3984. Also see. Tirmidhi, Diyat, 7/1398; Ibn Majah, Diyat, 1)

۱۳۸. عَنْ عَبْدِ اللهِ رَضِيَ اللهُ عَنْهُ قَالَ: قَالَ النَّبِيُّ صَلَّى اللهُ عَلَيْهِ وَسَلَّمَ:

«أَوَّلُ مَا يُقْضَى بَيْنَ النَّاسِ فِي الدِّمَاءِ».

138. Abdullah b. Mas'ud narrated that the Messenger of Allah said:

"The first (thing) that will be decided among people on the Day of Judgment will pertain to bloodshed." (Bukhari, Diyat, 1; Muslim, Qasama, 28)

❁

١٣٩. عَنْ أَبِي الْحَكَمِ الْبَجَلِيِّ قَالَ: سَمِعْتُ أَبَا سَعِيدٍ الْخُدْرِيَّ وَأَبَا هُرَيْرَةَ رَضِيَ اللهُ عَنْهُمَا يَذْكُرَانِ عَنْ رَسُولِ اللهِ صَلَّى اللهُ عَلَيْهِ وَسَلَّمَ قَالَ:

«لَوْ أَنَّ أَهْلَ السَّمَاءِ وَأَهْلَ الْأَرْضِ اشْتَرَكُوا فِي دَمِ مُؤْمِنٍ لَأَكَبَّهُمُ اللهُ فِي النَّارِ».

139. Abu al-Hakim al-Bajali said: I heard Abu Said al-Hudri and Abu Huraira narrating the sayings of the Messenger of Allah (pbuh) as:

"If the dwellers of heaven and earth participated in committing the sin of killing a believer unjustly, Allah would send all of them to Hell." (Tirmidhi, Diyat, 8/1398)

❁

١٤٠. عَنْ أَبِي هُرَيْرَةَ رَضِيَ اللهُ عَنْهُ عَنِ النَّبِيِّ صَلَّى اللهُ عَلَيْهِ وَسَلَّمَ قَالَ:

«مَنْ تَرَدَّى مِنْ جَبَلٍ فَقَتَلَ نَفْسَهُ فَهُوَ فِي نَارِ جَهَنَّمَ يَتَرَدَّى فِيهِ خَالِدًا مُخَلَّدًا فِيهَا أَبَدًا وَمَنْ تَحَسَّى سُمًّا فَقَتَلَ نَفْسَهُ فَسُمُّهُ فِي يَدِهِ يَتَحَسَّاهُ فِي نَارِ جَهَنَّمَ خَالِدًا مُخَلَّدًا فِيهَا أَبَدًا وَمَنْ قَتَلَ نَفْسَهُ بِحَدِيدَةٍ فَحَدِيدَتُهُ فِي يَدِهِ يَجَأُ بِهَا فِي بَطْنِهِ فِي نَارِ جَهَنَّمَ خَالِدًا مُخَلَّدًا فِيهَا أَبَدًا».

140. Abu Huraira (r.a.) narrated that the Prophet (pbuh) said:

"He who killed himself by falling from (the top of) a mountain would con-stantly fall in the Fire of Hell and would live there forever and ever. He who drank poison and killed himself would sip that in the Fire of Hell where he is doomed forever and ever; and He who killed himself with steel (weapon) would be the eternal denizen of the Fire of Hell and he would have that weapon in his hand and would be thrusting that in his stomach forever and ever." (Bukhari, Tibb, 56; Muslim, Iman, 175; Tirmidhi, Tibb, 7/2044-2045; Nasai, Janaiz, 68; Abu Dawud, Tibb, 11/3872)

Explanations:

The Messenger of Allah (pbuh) listed killing someone among the greatest sins. In various reports, it is listed among the sins right after ascribing partners to Allah.[190]

Ibn Umar (r.a.) described killing someone unjustly as a very dangerous and dead-end cliff. (Bukhari, Diyat, 1)

According to Imam Shafi, the second biggest sin after ascribing partners to Allah is to kill someone.

As stated **in our second hadith,** as long as a believer does not kill anyone, he can hope for the mercy and forgiveness of Allah. In other words, all sins can be forgiven but when it comes to killing someone, one has to stop there. One has to be careful about that.

On the other hand, Muslim scholars who agree that all the sins can be forgiven except ascribing partners to Allah state that this hadith aims to dis-courage us strongly from killing someone. Here, homicide is described as one of the greatest sins and is very difficult to be forgiven.

In Islam, reviving someone is considered as great and as important deed as bringing the whole humanity into life. Also, killing someone is as bad as kill-ing the whole humanity.

On the other hand, in the sight of Allah, killing a believer is as bad as de-struction of the Earth. In other words, destruction of the whole world is lighter according to Allah than slaying of a believer other than for a valid reason.

---

190. For example see Bukhari, Diyat, 2; Nasai, Tahrim al-Dam, 3/4007.

Adam's son, Cain, had killed his brother Abel by obeying his carnal self due to his jealousy towards Abel. He acted this way regardless of his brother's warnings, and this shows that he has forgotten Allah and was not afraid of Him due to his heedlessness. In the end, by killing someone, he took upon hşs shoulders both his own sins and the sins of the person whom he killed and became one of the dwellers of the Hell. This grave sin that he had committed by obeying his carnal self dragged him into a complete misery. Finally, he had realized his weakness and mistake and started to burn in the fire of great regret. This is because the sin that he had burdened himself with was a very heavy one. As a matter of fact, the Messenger of Allah informed us that Cain will receive his share of the sin from all of the killings in the world after that.[191] That is because he is the one who opened the path to this bad act.

Almighty Allah says the following after telling about the story of Cain and Abel in the Noble Qur'an:

"… if any one slew a person - unless it be for murder or for spreading mischief in the land - it would be as if he slew the whole people: and if any one saved a life, it would be as if he saved the life of the whole people." (Al-Maidah; 5:32)

Therefore, killing someone destroys one's both material and spiritual world and brings sadness to both of the worlds. It distances the person from Allah's mercy and makes him subject to the anger of Allah.

The punishment in the Hereafter for killing someone is very harsh too. **In our fourth hadith,** we are told that the first thing which will be decided among people on the Day of Judgment will pertain to bloodshed. In other words, the first sin that was committed on Earth will be the first one that will be accounted for in the Hereafter.

When it comes to issues between the servant and Allah, the first deed that will be asked is the ritual prayer. The first thing that will be asked on the issue of others' rights will be about unjust bloodshed. This is enough to prove how great a sin killing someone is.

---

191. *"No human being is killed unjustly, but a part of responsibility for the crime is laid on the first son of Adam who invented the tradition of killing (murdering) on the earth. (It is said that he was Qabil (Cain))"* (Bukhari, Al-Janaiz, 33; Enbiya, 1; Ad-Diyat, 2; I'tisam, 15; Muslim, Qasama, 27. Also see. Tirmidhi, Ilm, 4; Nasai, Tahrim, 1; Ibn Majah, Ad-Diyat, 1)

Therefore, the punishment of this sin in this world is to be executed according to the principle of "an eye for an eye." Even if many people participate in a killing of one person, all of them receive the same punishment.[192] **In our fifth hadith,** this situation is expressed with a more striking style. It says that, if all humans participate in killing one believer, Allah the Almighty can punish all of them with the Fire in return for the death of that one soul. This way of thinking shows the best value that can be given to human life. Therefore, one must not participate or help the unjust killing of a believer. It is said in a noble hadith:

"If a person helps the killing of a believer even with a half of a word, he reaches Allah with a note written in between his eyes "This person lost his hope from the mercy of Allah"." (Suyuti, *al-Fath al-kabir,* III, 164)

One of the most frightening verses of the Qur'an about the punishment for bloodshed is:

"If a man kills a believer intentionally, his recompense is Hell, to abide therein (For ever): And the wrath and the curse of Allah are upon him, and a dreadful penalty is prepared for him." (Al-Nisa; 4:93)

The scholars of the Qur'anic exegesis say that such a threatening language is used in this verse in order to strongly discourage people from intentionally killing someone. As a matter of fact, Allah informed us that He could forgive all kinds of sins except ascribing partners to Him. A believer who kills someone will sure face a great punishment even if he does not stay in Hell forever. Therefore this verse is interpreted as forbidding Muslims from killing someone on purpose or unjustly with a strong and frightening language.

However, there is no doubt that those who kill a believer just because he is a believer will stay in Hell forever.

No one has the right to take away a life that Allah has entrusted to us. Allah has given the life to humans and He is the One who will take it back. Interference in this matter angers Almighty Allah. Committing suicide, not to mention homicide, is strictly forbidden and considered among the major sins. As a matter of fact, **in our sixth hadith** it is seen that the punishment of committing suicide is sharply expressed. In this hadith, we are told, three times, that those who commit a suicide will be punished in the same manner they

---

192. Bukhari, Ad-Diyat, 21.

kill themselves, and this punishment will repeat forever and ever. It is attention drawing that in the hadith the words "khuld" and "abad" which express eternity are repeated three times after mentioning each punishment. This style refers to a very rarely used threat.

Those who kill themselves in this world will torture themselves in the Hereafter as well. Their punishment in the Hereafter will be exactly the same as they killed themselves. The Messenger of Allah (pbuh) said in another hadith:

"Whoever commits suicide in a certain manner will be punished with the same method on the Day of Judgment." (Bukhari, Al-Janaa'iz, 84; Adab, 44, 73; Iman, 7; Muslim, Iman, 176, 177)

Abu Huraira (r.a.) narrates:

We were in the company of the Messenger of Allah (pbuh) in the Khaibar Military Expedition. The Prophet (pbuh) remarked about a man who claimed to be a Muslim as:

"This (man) is from the people of the (Hell) Fire!"

When the battle started, the man fought violently until he got wounded. Some among the Companions said:

"O Allah's Apostle! The man whom you described as being from the people of the (Hell) Fire fought severely today and died!"

The Messenger of Allah (pbuh) said again:

"He will go to the (Hell) Fire."

Some people were on the verge of doubting (the truth of what the Prophet had said) when suddenly someone said that he was still alive but severely wounded.

When night fell, the wounded man lost patience due to the pain of his wound and committed suicide by leaning on the sharp side of his sword. When the Prophet (pbuh) was informed of that, he said:

"Allah is Greater! I testify that I am Allah's Slave and His Apostle!"

Then he ordered Bilal to announce amongst the people:

"None will enter Paradise but a Muslim, and Allah may support this religion (i.e. Islam) even with a disobedient man." (Bukhari, Jihad, 182; Maghazi, 38; Qadar, 5; Muslim, Iman, 178)

c. Lying and False Oath (Perjury)

١٤١. عَنْ صَفْوَانَ بْنِ سُلَيْمٍ رَضِيَ اللهُ عَنْهُ أَنَّهُ قَالَ: قِيلَ لِرَسُولِ اللهِ صَلَّى اللهُ عَلَيْهِ وَسَلَّمَ:

«أَيَكُونُ الْمُؤْمِنُ جَبَانًا؟» فَقَالَ:

«نَعَمْ» فَقِيلَ لَهُ:

«أَيَكُونُ الْمُؤْمِنُ بَخِيلًا؟» فَقَالَ:

«نَعَمْ» فَقِيلَ لَهُ:

«أَيَكُونُ الْمُؤْمِنُ كَذَّابًا؟» فَقَالَ:

«لَا!».

141. Safwan b. Sulaim (r.a.) narrates:

It is asked the Messenger of Allah (pbuh):

"Can a believer be coward?"

"Yes, he can be!" he said.

"Can a believer be a miser person?" it is asked.

The Messenger of Allah (pbuh) said again:

"Yes, he can be!"

"Can a believer be a liar?" it is asked.

This time, the Messenger of Allah (pbuh) said:

"No, never!" (*Muwatta'*, Kalam, 19; Baihaqi, *Shuab*, IV, 207)

❈

١٤٢. عَنْ مَعَاوِيَةَ بْنِ جَيْدَةَ رَضِيَ اللهُ عَنْهُ قَالَ: سَمِعْتُ رَسُولَ اللهِ
صَلَّى اللهُ عَلَيْهِ وَسَلَّمَ يَقُولُ:

«وَيْلٌ لِلَّذِي يُحَدِّثُ فَيَكْذِبُ لِيُضْحِكَ بِهِ الْقَوْمَ وَيْلٌ لَهُ وَيْلٌ لَهُ».

142. Mu'awiyah b. Jaidah (r.a.) narrated: I heard the Messenger of Allah (pbuh) saying:

"Woe to him who tells things, speaking falsely, to make people laugh thereby. Woe to him! Woe to him!" (Abu Dawud, Kitab Al-Adab, 80/4990; Tirmidhi, Zuhd, 10/2315)

❈

١٤٣. عَنْ أَبِي أُمَامَةَ رَضِيَ اللهُ عَنْهُ قَالَ: قَالَ رَسُولُ اللهِ صَلَّى اللهُ
عَلَيْهِ وَسَلَّمَ:

«أَنَا زَعِيمٌ بِبَيْتٍ فِي رَبَضِ الْجَنَّةِ لِمَنْ تَرَكَ الْمِرَاءَ وَإِنْ كَانَ مُحِقًّا
وَبِبَيْتٍ فِي وَسَطِ الْجَنَّةِ لِمَنْ تَرَكَ الْكَذِبَ وَإِنْ كَانَ مَازِحًا وَبِبَيْتٍ فِي
أَعْلَى الْجَنَّةِ لِمَنْ حَسَّنَ خُلُقَهُ».

143. Abu Umamah (r.a.) narrated: I heard the Messenger of Allah (pbuh) say:

"I guarantee a house in the surroundings of Paradise for a man who avoids quarrelling even if he were in the right, a house in the middle of Paradise for a man who avoids lying even if he were joking, and a house in the upper part of Paradise for a man who made his character good." (Abu Dawud, Kitab Al-Adab, 7/4800. Also see Tirmidhi, Birr, 58/1993; Ibn Majah, Muqaddimah, 7)

❈

١٤٤. عَنِ ابْنِ عَبَّاسٍ رَضِيَ اللهُ عَنْهُ عَنِ النَّبِيِّ صَلَّى اللهُ عَلَيْهِ وَسَلَّمَ قَالَ:

«مَنْ تَحَلَّمَ بِحُلْمٍ لَمْ يَرَهُ كُلِّفَ أَنْ يَعْقِدَ بَيْنَ شَعِيرَتَيْنِ وَلَنْ يَفْعَلَ».

144. As narrated by Ibn Abbas (r.a.), the Messenger of Allah (pbuh) said:

"Whoever claims to have seen a dream which he did not see, will be ordered to make a knot between two barley grains[193] *which he will not be able to do."*
(Bukhari, Ta'bir, 45. Also see Abu Dawud, Kitab Al-Adab, 88/5024; Tirmidhi, Ruya, 8; Ibn Majah, Ruya, 8)

⚜

١٤٥. عَنْ عَبْدِ اللهِ بْنِ عَمْرٍو رَضِيَ اللهُ عَنْهُمَا قَالَ: جَاءَ أَعْرَابِيٌّ إِلَى النَّبِيِّ صَلَّى اللهُ عَلَيْهِ وَسَلَّمَ فَقَالَ:

«يَا رَسُولَ اللهِ مَا الْكَبَائِرُ؟» قَالَ:

«اَلْإِشْرَاكُ بِاللهِ» قَالَ:

«ثُمَّ مَاذَا؟» قَالَ:

«ثُمَّ عُقُوقُ الْوَالِدَيْنِ» قَالَ:

«ثُمَّ مَاذَا؟» قَالَ:

«اَلْيَمِينُ الْغَمُوسُ» قُلْتُ:

---

193. *In the report of Abu Dawud, the punishment is described as "to make a knot between two barley grains" which aims to order something that is not possible to do to increase the punishment of a liar."*

«وَمَا الْيَمِينُ الْغَمُوسُ» قَالَ:

«الَّذِي يَقْتَطِعُ مَالَ امْرِئٍ مُسْلِمٍ هُوَ فِيهَا كَاذِبٌ».

145. Abdullah b. Amr (r.a.) narrated: A Bedouin came and asked the Messenger of Allah:

"O Messenger of Allah! What are the biggest of all sins?"

Our Prophet said:

"To associate partners with Allah!"

"Then what?" asked the man.

"To be undutiful to one's parents!"

"Than what?" asked the man.

"To take an oath al-Ghamus!"

I asked:

"What is an oath al-Ghamus?"

The Messenger of Allah (pbuh) said:

"It is a false oath in order to grab the property of a Muslim." (Bukhari, Aiman, 1; Iman, 16; Ad-Diyat, 2. Also see Tirmidhi, Tafsir, 4/3020; Nasai, Tahrim al-Dam, 3/4009; Qasama, 48)

Explanations:

Lying is one of the most harmful sins for the humanity. It is an illness that rots the soul. It will be one of the major evidences against humans on the Day of Judgment.

People often lie in order to avoid embarrassment. A person can deceive others by lying but he should think about what to say to Almighty Allah who knows everything. In fact, the lie that people tell in order not to be embarrassed in this life will embarrass them even worse in the Hereafter. What will those who avoid being embarrassed in front of a few people in this world do in the hereafter in front of the whole humanity? In that crowd, there will be their most beloved ones as well as their biggest enemies. As a matter of fact, a person never wants to show his weaknesses to both of these groups. Those who tell a lie in order to save themselves from a little trouble will face even more troublesome difficulties in the eternal life. That is because each and every word of humans is recorded. This is stated in the following Qur'anic verse:

"Not a word does he utter but there is a sentinel by him, ready (to note it)." (Qaf; 50:18)

For this reason, Almighty Allah, the Most Merciful, warns His servants from the beginning:

"And pursue not that of which you have no knowledge." (Al-Isra; 17:36)

According to this command of our Exalted Lord, believers should be very careful about their talks and should not tell anything that they are not sure of or express their view about the issues that they are not well informed. (Bukhari, I'tisam, 7)

As a matter of fact *"telling everything that he hears is enough for a person as a lie."* (Muslim, Muqaddimah, 5; Abu Dawud, Adab, 80/4992)

Those who lie would harm themselves not others. The lies of a liar are always against him. (Al-Mu'min; 40:28)

Before everything else, angels keep away from the liars. The Messenger of Allah (pbuh) said:

"When a person lies, due to the bad smell of the wrong deed that he has done, the angels go one mile away from him." (Tirmidhi, Birr, 46/1972)

On the other hand, lies drag people first to sinful acts and then to Hell. As a matter of fact, it is said in a noble hadith:

"Falsehood leads to al-Fujur (i.e. wickedness, evil-doing), and al-Fujur (wickedness) leads to the (Hell) Fire, and as a man keeps on telling he ends up being recorded before Allah as 'a liar.'" (Bukhari, Al-Adab, 69; Muslim, Birr, 103-105)[194]

---

194. Also see Abu Dawud, Adab 80; Tirmidhi, Birr, 46; Ibn Majah, Muqaddimah, 7; Dua, 5. Abdullah b. Mas'ud (r.a.) says on this:
   "Pay attention to tell the truth at all times! That is because telling the truth makes one perform good deeds and good deeds bring one to the Paradise. Stay away from lying! That is because lying leads one to wrong deeds and sinful acts. These evil deeds drag one to the Hell. Don't you realize that why it is said "One did good by telling the truth; one committed sin by lying." (Muwatta', Kalam, 16)

Telling a lie darkens the heart and constitutes a great hurdle to finding the right path. In this subject, the Messenger of Allah (pbuh) said:

"When a person keeps lying, a black dot is stricken to his heart. Then the black dot becomes bigger and covers the whole heart. This person finally gets recorded as a 'liar' before Allah." (*Muwatta*, Kalam, 18)

Allah the Almighty does not help those liars whose hearts are darkened find the true path. (Al-Zumar; 39:3; (Al-Mu'min; 40:28)

For this reason, **in our first hadith,** it is told that telling a lie and having faith never go hand in hand and turning away from the truth does not befit a believer under any circumstances. A believer temporarily may have some undesirable traits such as being a coward or a miser but telling a lie should not come close to him in any case. That is because telling a lie is not one of the characteristics that a believer can have. As a matter of fact, a believer should be neither coward nor miserly since these are undesirable characteristics. However compared to being a liar, even these characteristics become light. The Prophet (pbuh) used this style to express the magnitude of lying and how far believers should keep away from it; otherwise, none of these can be the characteristics of a perfect believer. As a matter of fact, the Messenger of Allah (pbuh) said:

"You would never find me miserly, liar, or coward!" (Bukhari, Jihad, 24; Nasai, Hiba, 1)

Umar (r.a.) explained that there is no relationship between believers and lying by saying "you will not find a believer as a liar."[195]

As lying is a bad trait that does not befit to a believer, it does not befit to the Paradise, either. As the liar gets away from the Paradise, there is never a place for a lie in the Paradise as well. As a matter of fact, it is told in a noble verse of the Qur'an:

"No vanity shall they hear therein, nor untruth." (Naba; 78:35)

As the Qur'an associated lying to disbelievers, the Messenger of Allah (pbuh) associated it with hypocrites:

In a noble verse of the Qur'an:

---

195. Baihaqi, *Shuab*, IV, 230.

"It is those who believe not in the Signs of Allah that forge falsehood: it is they who lie!" (Al-Nahl; 16:105)

The Messenger of Allah (pbuh) said:

"The signs of a hypocrite are three; whenever he speaks, he tells a lie; whenever he promises, he always breaks it (his promise); if you trust him, he proves to be dishonest. (If you keep something as a trust with him, he will not return it.)" (Bukhari, Iman, 24; Muslim, Iman, 107)

In spite of the mischief and many harms of lying, unfortunately people descend on lies as moths descend on fire and do not take it seriously. In contrast, the exemplary generation of the Noble Companions of the Messenger of Allah was the one which stayed away from lies the most. The following two narrations are the best examples to prove how much they stayed away from lying:

When the Messenger of Allah (pbuh) distributed more of the war booty of the Hunain War among those who were likely to embrace Islam, the youth of Ansar were disturbed and said:

"This is so strange! While our swords are dripping with their blood (of the Quraish), our war booty have been given to them."

This (remark) reached the Messenger of Allah (pbuh), and so he gathered them and said:

"What is this that has been conveyed to me about you?"

Even though they were so embarrassed, they said with their heads down that:

"Yes, it happened exactly as you heard."

That is because they were not (the people) to speak lie. (Muslim, Zakat, 134)

The last sentence in this report proves that the Noble Companions of Allah never lied no matter how difficult their situation was.

Another example of this can be seen in the following statement of Anas (r.a.):

"I swear to Allah that not all our reports that we narrate are heard directly from the Messenger of Allah (we were learning the hadith of the Messenger from each other.) **However, we never told a lie to each other."** (Haythami, I, 153)

Hypocrites who did not join the Tabuk Military Expedition thought that they saved themselves by lying, but Qa'b b. Malik (r.a.) told the truth no matter what. Due to telling the truth, he faced with many troubles and life became unbearable for him. However, the reward that he gained in the end was irreplaceable: He was saved from the anger of Allah and the scorn that is expressed in a Qur'anic verse related to the topic and he was blessed with the mercy of Allah. He narrated as:

"I swear to Allah that the biggest blessing that I have received after being blessed with Islam is telling the truth (about the reason why I have not joined the Tabuk Expedition) to the Prophet and saving myself from going astray with the liars. That is because Allah revealed the noble verse scorching those who did not join the Tabuk Expedition and who lied about it with a style that is not used for anyone else in the Noble Qur'an before:

"They will swear to you by Allah, when you return to them, that you may leave them alone. So leave them alone: For they are an abomination, and Hell is their dwelling-place,-a fitting recompense for the (evil) that they did. They will swear unto you, that you may be pleased with them but if you are pleased with them, Allah is not pleased with those who disobey." (Al-Tawbah; 9:95-96) (Bukhari, Maghazi, 79)

As telling the truth saves people from going astray, it is the first requirement to be a wise person:

When asked to Luqman Hakim, referring to his wisdom:

"What is the secret that made you obtain this high level that we observe?" He answered:

"Telling the truth, protecting the things that are entrusted to me, and quitting the things that do not concern me." (*Muvatta*, Kalam, 17)

In our second hadith, there is a strong warning even for those who lie in order to be funny and make people laugh. People do not take these kinds of lies seriously. After a while, they get used to telling lies, and they start lying easily in other occasions. Due to this and similar dangers of lying as a joke, it is forbidden and strongly warned against. As a matter of fact, the hadith indicates that the punishment of this kind of lying is even bigger than the other kinds. That is because the term "*wayl*" which means "*Woe to him*" is used for those whose ends are extremely scary. And this term is repeated three times in the hadith.

In what a pitiful situation those who put themselves in danger just to make others laugh are! That is because they are addressed with the term *"wayl"* not only by the Prophet but also by Almighty Allah.

$$\text{وَيْلٌ لِكُلِّ اَفَّاكٍ اَثِيمٍ}$$

"Woe to each sinful dealer in Falsehoods." (Al-Jasiyah; 45:7)

The three praiseworthy characteristics of a believer are pointed out **In our third hadith**. Since it is difficult to achieve them, the Prophet (pbuh) has promised many good rewards in turn.

The first one is to avoid unnecessary quarreling and argument even if the person is in the right side. The human soul likes debates and arguments.[196] It takes please from winning the debate. The reward of those who discipline their carnal soul and overcome their temptations is a house in the surroundings of Paradise.

The second characteristic of a believer is avoiding lying even if it is a joke. Humans are tempted to make jokes to others and have fun. They usually fall back on lying when doing these. Eventually, it becomes very hard to quit this harmless looking habit. Therefore, the reward of quitting it is a house in the middle of Paradise.

The third one is saving oneself from all the bad traits and moving towards a perfect moral character. Acquiring a good character by acquittal of the human soul requires a serious effort. The reward of this bliss which not many can achieve is a house in the upper part of Paradise.

It is expressed in another noble hadith:

"A person would not have perfect faith until he quits lying even if he is joking and avoids quarrelling even if he is right." (Ahmad, II, 352, 364; Haythami, I, 92)

As it can be understood from our hadith, a believer should not take lying lightly. As a matter of fact, there are many words that the speaker would not think of as lying but they are recorded in his book of deeds as a lie. Abdullah b. Amir (r.a.) narrated as follows:

---

196. Al-Kahf ; 18:54; Al-Zukhruf; 43:58.

One day when the Messenger of Allah (pbuh) was sitting in our house, my mother called me and said:

"Come here and I shall give you something."

The Messenger of Allah (pbuh) asked her:

"What did you intend to give him?

My mother replied:

"I intended to give him some dates." The Messenger of Allah (pbuh) said:

"If you were not to give him anything, a lie would be recorded against you."
(Abu Dawud, Kitab Al-Adab, 80/4991; Ahmad, III, 447; II, 452)

Therefore one should pay attention to stay away from lying even for disciplining the kids and should avoid telling them lies in order to make them happy or scare them.

In our fourth hadith, a different type of lie is mentioned. This hadith talks about how big a sin it is to tell that one has dreamt about something even he has not. That is because this is one of the lies that can be told most easily, and it is impossible to disprove it. Therefore, it causes more damage compared to the other kinds of lies. By this way, many people can be deceived and various benefits may be obtained from them, which violate their rights.

On the other hand, those who lie about their dreams first belie Allah and slander against Him. This slander, in turn, is a greater sin than lying about other people and vilifying. Therefore the Messenger of Allah (pbuh) gave an example to express that there is an unending punishment for those who resort to this type of lying.

In our fifth hadith, taking a false oath in order to grab the property of others is mentioned as one of the major sins. Since this kind of lie makes forbidden things appear to be permissible and wrong thins seem to be right, it means changing the rules of Islam, which drags people into sin in this world and then to Hell in the Hereafter. For this reason, a false oath is called "An oath of ghamus" which means "the oath that drags to sin and Hell!"

Since those who take false oaths try to deceive people by showing Allah as witness, they exploit the name of Allah and, as such, vilify Him. For this reason, the Messenger of Allah (pbuh) mentioned taking false oath as one of the greatest sins.

The Prophet (pbuh) said:

"Those who take false oaths in order to grab some wealth of a Muslim will be brought to Allah as a person who was subject to the anger of Almighty Allah." Then he recited a noble verse of the Qur'an:

"As for those who sell the faith they owe to Allah and their own plighted word for a small price, they shall have no portion in the Hereafter: Nor will Allah (Deign to) speak to them or look at them on the Day of Judgment, nor will He cleans them (of sin): They shall have a grievous penalty." (Al-i Imran; 3:77) (Bukhari, Ayman, 11, 17; Muslim, Iman, 220, 222)

One day, the Messenger of Allah (pbuh) said:

"Allah made the Hell necessary and the Paradise forbidden for those who violate the right of a Muslim by taking false oaths."

Someone asked:

"What if the right that is being violated is something not of importance, is it still the same O the Messenger of Allah?"

The Messenger of Allah (pbuh) said:

"This rule applies even it is a spring from a miswaq tree." (Muslim, Iman, 218. Also see Nasai, Adab al-Qudat, 30; Ibn Majah, Ahkam, 8, 9)

Taking false oaths in trading drives off the blessings of the goods and causes their waste. (Bukhari, Kitab Al-Buyu, 44, 26; Muslim, Kitab Al-Buyu, 47)

The Messenger of Allah (pbuh) advised merchants who mistakenly involve with untrue speech and swearing in business dealings to compensate this with sadaqah (alms) to purify themselves from these sins. (Abu Dawud, Kitab Al-Buyu, 1/3326-7; Tirmidhi, Kitab Al-Buyu, 4/1208)

One of the proofs that show that taking false oaths is one of the major sins is this:

When a person breaks his promise, he can save himself from its burden by paying monetary compensation. However, taking false oaths is such a great sin that even paying monetary compensation cannot decrease its punishment, so there is no expiation for false oaths. If someone violates others' rights by taking false oaths, he commits a second sin. Unless he returns the thing that he obtained unjustly to its rightful owner, it is not possible for him to be forgiven by repenting Allah not to do it again (i.e., repenting).[197]

Being a false witness is also regarded among the major sins just like taking false oaths. It even makes sense to consider them the same thing. One day, after performing the dawn prayer, the Messenger of Allah (pbuh) stood up and said:

"False witnessing is considered the same as ascribing partners to Allah" and he repeated this three times. Then he recited the following verse from the Qur'an:

"…but shun the abomination of idols, and shun the word that is false."
(Al-Hajj; 22:30) (Abu Dawud, Kitab Al-Aqdiyah, 15/3599; Tirmidhi, Shahadah, 3/2300; Ibn Majah, Ahkam, 32)

Allah praised those servants who stay away from committing this sin saying:

"Those who witness no falsehood…" (Al-Furqan; 25:72)

d. Interest

١٤٦. عَنْ جَابِرٍ رَضِيَ اللهُ عَنْهُ قَالَ: لَعَنَ رَسُولُ اللهِ صَلَّى اللهُ عَلَيْهِ
وَسَلَّمَ آكِلَ الرِّبَا وَمُوكِلَهُ وَكَاتِبَهُ وَشَاهِدَيْهِ وَقَالَ:

﴿﴾«هُمْ سَوَاءٌ».

146. Jabir (r.a.) narrates:

"The Messenger of Allah (pbuh) cursed the receiver of interest and its payer, and the one who records it, and its witnesses, and he said:

---

197. As a matter of fact, even taking oaths, let alone taking false ones, is not considered something nice. Muslims stay away from taking oaths as much as possible since the Messenger of Allah (pbuh) said:
"Taking oaths leads either to commit a sin or to be sorry (in the end)." (Ibn Majah, Kaffarat, 5)

"They are all equal..." (Muslim, Musakat, 105-106. Also see Bukhari, Buyu', 24, 25, 113; Abu Dawud, Buyu, 4/3333; Tirmidhi, Buyu, 2/1206; Ibn Majah, Ticarat, 58)

۱٤۷. عَنِ ابْنِ مَسْعُودٍ رَضِيَ اللهُ عَنْهُ عَنِ النَّبِيِّ صَلَّى اللهُ عَلَيْهِ وَسَلَّمَ قَالَ:

«مَا أَحَدٌ أَكْثَرَ مِنَ الرِّبَا إِلَّا كَانَ عَاقِبَةُ أَمْرِهِ إِلَى قِلَّةٍ».

147. As narrated by Abdullah b. Mas'ud, the Messenger of Allah (pbuh) said:

"The end of everyone who increases their wealth through interest is to inflicted with poverty by the decrease in their wealth." (Ibn Majah, Trade, 58; Hakim, IV, 353/7892; Baihaqi, *Shuab,* IV, 392/5512; Taberani, *Kabir,* X, 223/10539)

۱٤۸. عَنْ أَبِي هُرَيْرَةَ رَضِيَ اللهُ عَنْهُ أَنَّ رَسُولَ اللهِ صَلَّى اللهُ عَلَيْهِ وَسَلَّمَ قَالَ:

«لَيَأْتِيَنَّ عَلَى النَّاسِ زَمَانٌ لَا يَبْقَى أَحَدٌ إِلَّا أَكَلَ الرِّبَا فَإِنْ لَمْ يَأْكُلْهُ أَصَابَهُ مِنْ غُبَارِهِ».

148. Abu Huraira (r.a.) narrated that the Messenger of Allah (pbuh) said:

"There will be a time when there will be no one who does not receive interest. Even if a person does not receive it directly, its dust[198] will reach him." (Abu Dawud, Kitab Al-Buyu, 3/3331. Also see. Nasai, Kitab Al-Buyu, 2/4452; Ibn Majah, Tijarah, 58)

Explanations:

For the Messenger of Allah, the worst of all earnings is the one earned through interest.[199] Interes, which is based on obtaining profit with no underly-

---

198. In another versions of this hadith recorded by Abu Dawud, the phrase "its vapor" is used.
199. Ibn Abi Shayba, *Musannaf,* VII, 106/34552; Waqidi, III, 1016; ; Ibn Kathir, *Bidayah,* V, 13-14.

ing trade, is a great violation of people's rights. Even if it seems in appearance like a help and an aid to the people in need, in reality it is a disaster nothing more than taking advantage of others' misfortune. It is a malignant tumor which is a death-warrant to morality and destroys the economy from inside. By increasing inflation, it makes the rich more powerful and the poor even poorer. Thus, it worsens the income inequality. As a matter of fact, as per the definitions of famous economists the best countries in terms of economic state are the ones whose inflation and interest rates are close to zero.

Besides, there are many harms of interest such as increasing unemployment rates, causing artificial price increases. It fuels greed for money and influence by stirring up egoism and selfishness and debilitates moral values such as altruism, generosity, social solidarity, affection, mercy, and compassion.

Interest keeps humans away from honest earning by working and being busy with production. Those who get used to do transactions with interest quit fundamental ways of earning such as agriculture, artisanship, and trade. Then there remains only one option left for livelihood, which is earning money from money. Soon everyone realizes that it is not enough for living.

Interest earning causes major competitions and ongoing hostilities. There is no other thing that causes hostility and enmity between the transactors than interest.

The worst part of interest is that humans can get addicted to it and can't quit it no matter what. Even though some people may like earning money by money, it is neither in favor of individuals nor the society. As a matter of fact, in the long run, since it alters the relationship between labor and capital, even those who earn interest will be harmed by it in the end.

Interest is a sin that is prohibited in all religions since its harms are so clear. In some verses of Qur'an, it is stated that interest is forbidden in Judaism as well. (Al-Nisa; 4:160-161)

In the Era of Ignorance, the people of Quraish Tribe, were aware of its harms and knew that it was forbidden even if they were deep in interest. As a matter of fact, five years before the emergence of Islam, when Meccan people were planning to fix Ka'bah, Abu Wahb b. Amr, one of the prominent figures of Mecca, stood up and said:

"O people of Quraish! Donate from the honest earning of your money for the construction of Ka'bah! Do not mix any money that is earned through illegitimate ways such as adultery, interest, or seized money by oppression. (Ibn Hisham, I, 210; Ibn Kasir, *al-Bidaya*, II, 305)

The people of Quraish had a difficult time to find honest earning and had to leave the *hatim* section of the Ka'bah unfinished.[200] In other words, even if the polytheists of that era knew that interest earning is too wrong to be used in the construction of the House of Allah, they still could not save themselves from it.

Islam came a while later and advised people to increase their wealth by building partnerships instead of through interest. That is because it is the best way of earning for everyone. Apart from this, Islam encourages "*qard hasan*" or "giving loans without interest, just for the sake of Allah, as much as one can" and regarded the loans given to the needy better than the charity. The Messenger of Allah (pbuh) informed us about this as:

"*In the night of ascension, I saw that it was written on the door of the Paradise as:*

"*Sadaqahs (alms) will be rewarded by ten times, and loans will be rewarded by eighteen times.*"

I asked:

"*O Gabriel! Why is loan better than sadaqah (alms)?*"

Gabriel (pbuh) answered:

"*That is because a beggar (most of the time) asks for money in spite of he has some with him. However, those who ask for a loan ask due to their need.*" (Ibn Majah, Sadaqah, 19)

In addition to these, by ordering zakat (obligatory alms) and sadaqah (alms), Islam has ensured economic stability and order of the Muslim society.[201]

---

200. Translator's Note: The area enclosed by a half-moon shaped wall beside the Ka'bah called hatim.
201. Our ancestors had reached to the peak of being nice and kind when giving alms to needy. In order not to embarrass those who could not want anything from anyone due to their honor and modesty, they placed " alms stones" in various locations. Those who are wealthy would leave their alms in the hole on top of these stones. Then the modest and honorable needy of

Interest, which was seen as a normal way of transaction by the people of the Era of Ignorance, was gradually prohibited by the Noble Qur'an for it was deeply rooted in the society. That is because it is very hard to deter people from their deep rooted traditions and beliefs. For this reason, first the prophets and then all other reformers have faced many troubles and gone through many difficulties in order to deter people from their wrong ideas and false traditions. In order to be successful, they employed the method of gradualism.

Almighty Allah reproached interest in a noble verse of Qur'an revealed in Mecca saying **"That which you lay out for increase through the property of (other) people will have no increase with Allah"**[202] and pointed out that it was going to be forbidden in the future.

In the following verse of the Qur'an, revealed during the first years of Medinan era, counts interest among the sins that led the punishment of the Jews:

"For the iniquity of the Jews We made unlawful for them certain (foods) good and wholesome which had been lawful for them; in that they hindered many from Allah's Way that they took usury, though they were forbidden; and that they devoured men's substance wrongfully; We have prepared for those among them who reject faith a grievous punishment." (Al-Nisa; 4:160-161)

In these verses, there is not a clear command forbidding interest for Muslims. They just point out that interest is a major sin from which a believer has to stay away.

Through other verses which were revealed in later periods, interest is prohibited for Muslims:

"O you who believe! Devour not usury, doubled and multiplied; but fear Allah that you may (really) prosper. Fear the Fire, which is repaired for those who reject Faith: And obey Allah and the Messenger that you may obtain mercy." (Al-i Imran; 3:130-132)

the neighborhood would come and take as much as they need from these alms and would leave the rest. A French traveler who wrote about the 17th century Istanbul stated that he had observed a stone with money on top of it but had not seen anyone to come and get the money.

202. Al-Rum; 30:39.

In the practice called **"interest of the Era of Ignorance"** the increase was based on postponing the payment of the loan. The creditor would ask for extra payment either at the beginning of the agreement knowing that the debt will be paid back at a later time or to postpone the payment when the debt is unpaid on the due date. Usually, since the debts would not get paid on time, the interest would multiply. The above mentioned verse points out this fact by saying **"doubled and multiplied"** and expresses that this is a heartbreaking brutality. Therefore, it is not possible to understand from these expressions that small amounts of interest which do not double the principal are not forbidden. As a matter of fact, the aim of this verse is not to put a limit on the prohibition but to remind the miserable end that interest eventually reaches and the fact that it is harmful to people.

For this reason, whether the rate is small or big, all kinds of interest are prohibited. As a matter of fact, interest is absolutely prohibited with the following later noble verse of the Qur'an that was revealed without mentioning the expression **"doubled and multiplied"** and some questions that can be raised is answered:

"Those who devour usury will not stand except as stand one whom the Evil one by his touch has driven to madness. That is because they say: "Trade is like usury,"[203] but Allah has permitted trade and forbidden usury. Those who after receiving direction from their Lord, desist, shall be pardoned for the past; their case is for Allah (to judge); but those who repeat

---

203. Interest is to take more than what is given in transactions of goods that are same in measurements, weight or kind. It does not matter whether the transaction is in full payment or installments. If a person lends some gold, silver, wheat, or date, and then receives gold for the gold, silver for the silver, wheat for the wheat, and date for the date but more than what he has given in terms of measurement or kind, this extra is the interest prohibited in the noble verses; the command does not change even if the payment happens at a later time. There is no problem by taking gold for gold, silver for silver or wheat for wheat as long as attention is paid to the kind, measurements, and weights are the same. If a person gives gold to someone and receives silver in turn, gives barley and receives date in turn, or gives barley and receives wheat in turn, the extra money that he makes is permissible (halal) even if the measurements or the kinds are not the same because it is the profit that he makes. That is because the work he has done is trade whether it is done in full payment or in installments.

Charging for a higher amount in transactions of exchanging different goods is the compensation for the cost of effort, time, the good, and the business. However, receiving extra in transactions of the same goods with the same kinds and measurements is earning something for free. (Izzet Derveze, et-Tefsiru'l-hadis, V, 309-310)

(the offence) are companions of the Fire: They will abide therein (for ever)." (Al-Baqarah; 2:275)

Ibn Abbas (r.a.) said referring to these verses:

"One of the last noble verses of the Qur'an that is revealed to the Prophet (pbuh) was the one about interest." (Bukhari, Tafsir, 2/53)

This verse continues as:

"O you who believe! Fear Allah, and give up what remains of your demand for usury, if you are indeed believers. If you do it not, take notice of war from Allah and His Messenger. But if you turn back, you shall have your capital sums: Deal not unjustly, and you shall not be dealt with unjustly." (Al-Baqarah; 2:278-279)

In the Noble Qur'an, Almighty Allah did not declare war against any disobedient and sinner other than who gain from interest and threaten anyone so severely.[204] This is enough to prove how big a sin taking interest is. We see the miserable ends of those who continue to take interest by being deaf and blind to such divine warnings in various examples in our daily life.

In his farewell sermon, the Messenger of Allah (pbuh) announced that interest is forbidden to everyone and said:

"All claims to usury of the pre-Islamic period have been abolished. **"You shall have your capital sums, deal not unjustly and you shall not be dealt with unjustly."**[205] *The first of those I remit is the interest of my uncle Abbas ibn AbdulMuttalib. His interest is remitted completely."* (See Muslim, Hajj, 147-8; Abu Dawud, Kitab Al-Buyu, 5/3334; Tirmidhi, Tafsir, 9/3087)

In another hadith, the Messenger of Allah (pbuh) informs us that interest is one of the seven things that drag humans to misery. (Bukhari, Wasaya, 23; Tibb, 48; Hudud, 44; Muslim, Iman, 145. Also see Abu Dawud, Wasaya, 10/2874; Nasai, Wasaya, 12)

There are also other strong statements that exemplify how big a sin interest is. In one of them, the Messenger of Allah (pbuh) talks about seventy kinds of sins due to interest and says:

---

204. The Messenger of Allah (pbuh) mentions one more case where Allah declares war against which is against those who show hostility to the friends of Allah. (Bukhari, al-Riqaq, 38)
205. Al-Baqara; 2:279.

"The lightest of them would be like getting married to one's own mother." (Ibn Majah, Ticarat, 58; Hakim, II, 43/2259; Baihaqi, *Shuab,* IV, 392-395)

Here the number seventy is not mentioned to limit the harms of interest but rather to show the magnitude of its harms. As a matter fact, in various narrations different numbers, such as seventy two or seventy three, are used. Therefore, interest leads to many other sins and all of them cause major harms. Even the least harmful of them would be similar to the worst and most undesirable situation.

In another hadith stating the punishments of the interest receivers, the Prophet (pbuh) said:

"In the night of Ascension, I saw some people whose bellies were as big as a house. Their bellies were full of snakes and they were visible from the outside. I asked:

"O Gabriel! Who are they?" He answered:

"Those are the interest receivers!" (Ibn Majah, Trade, 58)

There are other reports that inform us about the miserable end in the grave and in the Hereafter of those who receive interest. The Messenger of Allah (pbuh) warned his followers in many occasions for them not to fall into such miserable situation. For example, as we are told **in our first hadith,** in order to keep his followers away from this major sin, he cursed those who receive interest, who give interest, who record the transactions of interest, and the witnesses of these kinds of agreements and told that they are all the same in terms committing this sin.

The term "receiver (literally consumer)" is used to indicate those who take the interest earning. It does not make any difference whether he personally consumes the interest (money) or not. Since one of the most important and known ways of benefiting from wealth is expressed as "consuming," these terms are generally used to mean to benefit from interest.

The Prophet cursed everyone who takes part in interest bearing transactions in order to show that there is no place for it in Muslim societies. His cursing also clearly explains that everyone should stay away from it, and closes the doors to all the wrong deeds and evils that interest causes. The Messenger of Allah (pbuh) has been so careful about the issue of interest that he did not leave any loopholes and made the criteria very clear and accurate. For example, let's look at the following noble hadith:

"Whoever mediates for another and receives a gift in turn, if he accepts the gift, he opens one of the great doors of interest (and loses the reward of his good deed.)" (Abu Dawud, Kitab Al-Buyu, 82/3541)

"If one of you lends some money to another and the receiver gives a gift to the lender, the lender should not accept the gift or if the receiver offers the lender a ride with his animal, he should not use it unless it is customary between them to give and receive gifts or help from each other before the loan." (Ibn Majah, Sadaqah, 19)

Hence, one should be very careful about interest and avoid even the suspicious acts. As a matter of fact, Umar (r.a.) said:

"One of the last noble verses of Qur'an is about interest. Therefore, you should quit interest and anything related that is suspicious." (Ibn Majah, Trade, 58)

Here, Umar's object is to express that interest is one of the things prohibited lastly and it is not possible that this command was abrogated. In other words, the prohibition of interest is clear and for this reason, one must pay extra attention and avoid even the suspicious things in order to protect oneself from it. As a matter of fact, the Companions of the Prophet (r. anhum) used to act in this way. Umar (r.a.) expressed how much attention they paid to this matter saying:

"We have abandoned nine out of the ten permissible (halal) things due to the fear of getting into interest." (Ali al-Muttaqi, IV, 187/10087)

While Muslim scholars agree that it is liked (*mandub*) to stay away from suspicious things, they agree that when it comes to interest, it is required (*wajib*) to avoid them.

The Messenger of Allah (pbuh) used to pay so much attention to the issue of interest that he said when he made an agreement with the people of Najran: *"There is no more transaction of interest. Those who receive interest from now on are not under my protection."* (See Abu Dawud, Kitab al-Kharaj, 29-30/3041; Baihaqi, *al-Sunan al-Kubra*, IX, 202; Ibn Abi Shayba, *Musannaf*, VII, 426/37015)

In the *Musannaf* of Ibn Ebi Shaybah, the following expression is recorded

"If you receive interest, there is no more peace between us" in the section about the peace agreement with the people of Najran. Then, it is written that the Prophet did not do any peace or agreement with those who receive interest. (Ibn Abi Shayba, Musannaf, IV, 448/22006)

While many people may agree that interest is bad for the society, sometimes people may wrongly consider it to be beneficial for individuals. However, as expressed **in our second hadith,** the happiness of a person who thinks that his wealth has increased with the interest would not last long. His calculations would turn upside down and he will face misery. The bounty of his wealth would be lost from the beginning and he would not benefit from it. Then, for various reasons his wealth will decrease and he will even go bankrupt. At the end, he will be condemned to misery both in this world and in the hereafter.

It is told in other noble verses of the Qur'an:

"That which you lay out for increase through the property of (other) people, will have no increase with Allah, but that which you lay out for charity, seeking the Countenance of Allah, (will increase): it is these who will get a recompense multiplied." (Ar-Rum; 30:39)

"Allah will deprive usury of all blessing, but will give increase for deeds of charity: For He loves not creatures ungrateful and wicked." (Al-Baqarah; 2:276)

Although interest is such a harmful and painful sin, many people get biased by how it externally looks and get stuck in interest. As a matter of fact, as **our third hadith** informs us that there will be a time when there will be no one who does not receive interest, even if a person tries to avoid interest, he will get from its dust. That is because a person who lives in a society will have relations with others, visit each other, exchange gifts, and join in weddings and holidays. He will have to receive his salary from a bank, and as such it will be impossible to stay away from interest.

People living in such society will eventually start not even to worry about what is permissible (halal) or what is forbidden. That is because their souls and hearts will be completely bankrupt. The Messenger of Allah (pbuh) said:

"There will be a time when a person will not care whether his earnings are coming through permissible or prohibited means." (Nasai, Buyu, 2/4451)

From these statements, it is not right to conclude that "it is not possible to imagine a society without interest in today's world." If this were the case, Allah the Almighty would not prohibit interest. For sure there could be a life without interest, and it would be much better than it is thought. As a matter of fact, there are societies who achieved that. It is necessary for Muslims to face the struggle of getting interest out of their lives when interest is widespread and build a clean society free from interest. As a matter of fact, it is possible to take the words of the Prophet *"There will be a time when there will be no one who does not receive interest. Even if a person does not directly earn from interest, its dust will reach him"* as a warning in these terms. In other words, the time will be so bad that Muslims will have to be extra careful about this issue. Otherwise, even if they directly do not receive interest, its dust will reach them.

May our Almighty Lord protect the followers of the Muhammed from all kinds of sins and bless us with a peaceful society free of all sins!

Amin!..[206]

e. Alcohol Consumption

١٤٩. عَنِ ابْنِ عُمَرَ رَضِيَ اللهُ عَنْهُ قَالَ: قَالَ رَسُولُ اللهِ صَلَّى اللهُ عَلَيْهِ وَسَلَّمَ:

«كُلُّ مُسْكِرٍ خَمْرٌ وَكُلُّ مُسْكِرٍ حَرَامٌ وَمَنْ شَرِبَ الْخَمْرَ فِي الدُّنْيَا فَمَاتَ وَهُوَ يُدْمِنُهَا لَمْ يَتُبْ لَمْ يَشْرَبْهَا فِي الْآخِرَةِ».

149. Ibn Umar (r.a.) narrated: The Messenger of Allah (pbuh) said:

"Every intoxicant is khamr (wine) and every intoxicant is forbidden. He who drinks wine in this world and dies while he is continuing its consumption and not having repented from it will not be given the wine (of Paradise) in the Hereafter." (Muslim, Kitab Al-Ashriba, 73, 77. Also see Bukhari, Kitab Al-Ashriba, 1; Abu Dawud, Kitab Al-Ashriba, 5)

---

206. For more details about interest see İsmail Özsoy, "Faiz" *Diyanet İslâm Ansiklopedisi*, XII, 110-126; ibid, *Faiz ve Problemleri*, İzmir 1993.

١٥٠. عَنْ جَابِرِ بْنِ عَبْدِ اللهِ رَضِيَ اللهُ عَنْهُ قَالَ: قَالَ رَسُولُ اللهِ
صَلَّى اللهُ عَلَيْهِ وَسَلَّمَ:

«مَا أَسْكَرَ كَثِيرُهُ فَقَلِيلُهُ حَرَامٌ».

150. Jabir b. Abdullah (r.a.) narrated that the Messenger of Allah (pbuh) said:

"Every intoxicant is forbidden; if a lot of anything causes intoxication, a handful of it is forbidden as well." (Abu Dawud, Kitab Al-Ashribah, 5/3681; Tirmidhi, Kitab Al-Ashribah, 3/1865)

١٥١. عَنْ أَبِي الدَّرْدَاءِ رَضِيَ اللهُ عَنْهُ قَالَ: أَوْصَانِي خَلِيلِي صَلَّى
اللهُ عَلَيْهِ وَسَلَّمَ:

«لَا تَشْرَبِ الْخَمْرَ فَإِنَّهَا مِفْتَاحُ كُلِّ شَرٍّ».

151. Abu al-Darfa (r.a.) said: The Messenger of Allah (pbuh) whom I love more than anything advised me:

"Never consume alcohol because it is the key of all wrong doing and evils." (Ibn Majah, Kitab Al-Ashribah, 1)

١٥٢. عَنِ ابْنِ عُمَرَ رَضِيَ اللهُ عَنْهُ يَقُولُ: قَالَ رَسُولُ اللهِ صَلَّى اللهُ
عَلَيْهِ وَسَلَّمَ:

«لَعَنَ اللهُ الْخَمْرَ وَشَارِبَهَا وَسَاقِيهَا وَبَائِعَهَا وَمُبْتَاعَهَا وَعَاصِرَهَا
وَمُعْتَصِرَهَا وَحَامِلَهَا وَالْمَحْمُولَةَ إِلَيْهِ».

152. Ibn Umar (r.a.) narrated that the Messenger of Allah (pbuh) said:

"It is for sure that Allah has cursed alcohol, its drinker, its server, its seller, its buyer, its presser, the one for whom it is pressed, the one who conveys it, and the one to whom it is conveyed." (Abu Dawud, Kitab Al-Ashribah, 2/3674)

٭

١٥٣. عَنْ جَابِرٍ رَضِيَ اللهُ عَنْهُ أَنَّ النَّبِيَّ صَلَّى اللهُ عَلَيْهِ وَسَلَّمَ قَالَ:

«...وَمَنْ كَانَ يُؤْمِنُ بِاللهِ وَالْيَوْمِ الْآخِرِ فَلَا يَجْلِسْ عَلَى مَائِدَةٍ يُدَارُ عَلَيْهَا بِالْخَمْرِ».

153. Jabir (r.a.) narrated that the Noble Prophet (pbuh) said:

"...Those who believe in Allah and the Hereafter should not sit on a table where alcohol is consumed (even if he does not drink)!" (Tirmidhi, Kitab Al-Adab, 43/2801)

٭

١٥٤. عَنْ جَابِرٍ رَضِيَ اللهُ عَنْهُ أَنَّ رَجُلًا قَدِمَ مِنْ جَيْشَانَ وَجَيْشَانُ مِنَ الْيَمَنِ فَسَأَلَ النَّبِيَّ صَلَّى اللهُ عَلَيْهِ وَسَلَّمَ عَنْ شَرَابٍ يَشْرَبُونَهُ بِأَرْضِهِمْ مِنَ الذُّرَةِ يُقَالُ لَهُ الْمِزْرُ فَقَالَ النَّبِيُّ صَلَّى اللهُ عَلَيْهِ وَسَلَّمَ:

«أَوَ مُسْكِرٌ هُوَ؟» قَالَ:

«نَعَمْ» قَالَ رَسُولُ اللهِ صَلَّى اللهُ عَلَيْهِ وَسَلَّمَ:

«كُلُّ مُسْكِرٍ حَرَامٌ إِنَّ عَلَى اللهِ عَزَّ وَجَلَّ عَهْدًا لِمَنْ يَشْرَبُ الْمُسْكِرَ أَنْ يَسْقِيَهُ مِنْ طِينَةِ الْخَبَالِ» قَالُوا:

«يَا رَسُولَ اللهِ وَمَا طِينَةُ الْخَبَالِ؟» قَالَ:

«عَرَقُ أَهْلِ النَّارِ أَوْ عُصَارَةُ أَهْلِ النَّارِ».

154. Jabir (r.a.) narrated:

A person came from Jaishan, a town in Yemen, and he asked Allah's Apostle (pbuh) about a beverage which was drunk in their land and which was prepared from millet and was called Mizr.

Allah's Messenger (pbuh) asked:

"Is it intoxicating?"

The man said:

"Yes."

Thereupon Allah's Messenger (pbuh) said:

"Every intoxicant is forbidden. Verily Allah the Exalted and Majestic made a covenant to those who drank intoxicants to make their drink "Tinat al-Khabal."

They said:

"O Allah's Messenger, what is *tinat al-khabal*?"

The Messenger of Allah (pbuh) said:

"It is the sweat of the denizens of Hell or the pus of the denizens of Hell."
(Muslim, Kitab Al-Ashribah, 72; Abu Dawud, Kitab Al-Ashribah, 5)

Explanations:

Almighty Allah loves His servants and wants them to enter Paradise. For this reason, He is jealous of His servants from sins and prohibited whether it is open or secret. For the same reason, all kinds of intoxicating drinks which are causes of many other sins are strictly prohibited whether they are consumed a little or a lot.

Intoxicants are harmful drinks that are completely contrary to the human nature. As a matter of fact, in the Night Journey, when two cups of drinks with one containing wine and the other containing milk was offered to the Prophet, the Messenger of Allah (pbuh) looked at both of them, and he took the one containing milk. (As a matter of fact, the wine that was offered to him was not the wine that we know of but it was a drink from Paradise. At the time, drinking wine had not been prohibited, yet.)

Upon this, Gabriel (pbuh) said:

"Praise Allah Who guided you to the true nature; had you taken the one containing wine, Your Umma (followers) would have gone astray."[207] (Muslim, Iman, 272; Kitab Al-Ashriba, 92. Also see Bukhari, Tafsir, 17/3; Kitab Al-Ashriba, 1, 12; Nasai, Kitab Al-Ashriba, 41)

As can be understood from the story, the important thing is to be conscious and serious. It is not pleasant to be unconscious and relaxed by the taste of wine. The end of being unconscious usually results in falling into deviation. Therefore, for those who internalize drinking by considering it normal, it is inevitable to fall into deviation.

For this reason, the Messenger of Allah (pbuh) had never come close to drinking before Islam, too. One day, when it was asked to him:

"O the Messenger of Allah! Have you drink wine before Islam?" He said:

"No! Even when I did not know what the Book and faith is, I knew that the things that people in the period of Jahiliyya (ignorance) did were disbelief." (Diyarbekri, I, 254-255; Ali al-Muttaqi, no: 35439)

In the Era of Ignorance, smart people such as Abdulmuttalib, Abu Talib, Abu Bakr, and Uthman who realized that drinking did not fit with the human nature had not touched intoxicating drinks.[208] There were even those who prohibited them to their families and children.

Since people were addicted to alcoholic beverages at that time, Allah the Almighty did not prohibit this wicked habit suddenly but did it step by step.

---

207. The Messenger of Allah (pbuh) preferred the one that is suitable for the true human nature, in other words the one that is right and good for the characteristics with which humans are born. Milk is the first nutrient of humans. Babies are fed by milk when they are born and start to build their characters with it. Allah the Almighty implanted the "love of milk" in human character. If the Messenger of Allah (pbuh) had chosen the wine, his followers, even though the wines (the one in this world and the one offered to the Prophet) are only same by their names, would be inclined to drink wine on earth and to do the wrong deeds that it causes. As a matter of fact, the followers act upon the behaviors and paths of their leaders.

208. See Abu Dawud, Kitab Al-Diyat, 3/4502; Ahmad, I, 163; Halabi, I, 184.

In fact, if it had been suddenly forbidden, most of the people would have disagreed with that. As a matter of fact, Aisha (r.anha), the mother of Muslims said:

"…The Verses regarding legal and illegal things were revealed only after the people embraced Islam. If the first thing to be revealed had been:

"Do not drink alcoholic drinks" people would have said:

"We will never leave alcoholic drinks!"

Again, if there had been revealed:

"Do not commit adultery!" they would have said:

"We will never give up adultery…" (Bukhari, Fadail al-Qur'an, 6)

By taking the human nature into account, the prohibition of drinking was commanded gradually as follows:

First the noble verse **"And from the fruit of the date-palm and the vine, you get out wholesome drink and food: behold, in this also is a sign for those who are wise"**[209] got revealed in Mecca.

In this noble verse, by saying that people make intoxicating drinks from the fruit of date and vine apart from healthy drinks and foods, it is implied that the intoxicating drinks are not considered nice and good and indicated that it will be prohibited in the future.

After the migration from Mecca to Medina, as an answer to the questions asked by the people of Medina, Allah the Almighty revealed:

"They ask you concerning wine and gambling. Say: "In them is great sin, and some profit, for men; but the sin is greater than the profit." (Al-Baqarah; 2:219)

After the revelation of this noble verse, majority of the Muslims quit drinking.

Then some time passed. One day, one of the Companions of the Messenger misread a noble verse in a way that changed its meaning while performing the Evening Prayer. Upon this, the following noble verse got revealed:

---

209. Al-Nahl; 16:67.

"O you who believe! Approach not prayers with a mind befogged, until you can understand all that you say"[210]

After this, the number of Muslims who drink wine considerably decreased. When it is time to pray, a person appointed by the Prophet (pbuh) used to announce:

"Those who are drunk should not come close to prayer!" Muslims understood that drinking will be forbidden soon and got ready for it.

A while after that, almost all of the Muslims abandoned drinking. Some of them, on the other hand, were still in embarrassing situations due to their drinking.

Umar (r.a.) used to pray as:

"O my Lord! Reveal a clear command about drinking to us!" Finally, after a fight that took place between drunken people, the wickedness of drinking became more evident. By then, prohibition of drinking became something that everyone can easily appreciate. Upon this, Allah the Almighty revealed these noble verses of the Qur'an:

"O you who believe! Intoxicants and gambling, (dedication of) stones, and (divination by) arrows, are an abomination of Satan's handwork: eschew such (abomination), that you may prosper. Satan's plan is (but) to excite enmity and hatred between you, with intoxicants and gambling, and hinder you from the remembrance of Allah, and from prayer: will you not then abstain?" (Al-Maidah; 5:90-91)

The Messenger of Allah (pbuh) called Umar (r.a.) and recited these noble verses. When the Prophet recited the part **"Will you not then abstain?"** Umar said:

"We have abstained! We have abstained O our Lord!" Other Muslims joined Umar and said:

"We have abstained from drinking and gambling O our Lord!"

When these noble verses of Qur'an revealed, the Prophet appointed someone to announce:

---

210. Al-Nisa; 4:43.

"Know that from now on drinking alcoholic beverages have been prohibited!"

The alcoholic drinks whose barrels were broken and emptied were seen flowing through the streets of Medina!..

Anas (r.a.) narrated:

I used to offer alcoholic drinks to the people at the residence of Abu Talha. Then the order of prohibiting alcoholic drinks was revealed, and the Prophet ordered somebody to announce that: Abu Talha said to me:

"Go out and see what this voice (this announcement) is."

I went out and (on coming back) said:

"This is somebody announcing that "Alcoholic beverages have been prohibited!" Abu Talha said to me:

"Go and spill it."

Then it (alcoholic drinks) was seen flowing through the streets of Medina. (Bukhari, Tafsir, 5/11)

After that, Muslims who used to drink alcoholic beverages destroyed the wine they had. They never drank it again. They have considered drinking as an act of deviation from the religion. For example, Abu Musa (r.a.) used to say:

"In my opinion, there is no difference whether I drink alcohol or abandon Allah and worship this column (both of them are among the major sins.)" (Nasai, Kitab Al-Ashriba, 42/5661)

Therefore, one must stay away from all kinds of intoxicating drinks. As a matter of fact, the Messenger of Allah (pbuh) informed us **in the first hadith** that every intoxicating drink is like wine, and it is forbidden (haram). In other words, the difference in their names is not important. It does not make sense for some people to say that "the forbidden drink is wine and since the name of what we consume is not wine, it is not forbidden." The Messenger of Allah (pbuh) miraculously pointed out to this fact and said:

"Some of my followers will drink wine by changing its name." (Nasai, Kitab Al-Ashriba, 41/5656. Also see. Bukhari, Adahi, 3; Ibn Majah, Fitan, 22)

Thus, those who try to find a juristic opinion that permits drinking with some excuses only deceive themselves.

On the other hand, the Messenger of Allah (pbuh) informed us that those who are addicted to alcoholic drinks and die before they repent will not get the chance to drink from the divine wine of the Paradise. In another hadith, he said that those addicted to alcohol will not even enter into the Paradise. (Nasai, Zakat, 69/2560)

Having a positive attitude towards drinking wine in this world by thinking that there will also be wine in the Paradise is not a right way of thinking. There is no similarity between the wine of this world and Paradise other than their names. While the wine of this world leads people to all kinds of wrong deeds by intoxicating them, the wine of the Paradise will not have the quality of intoxicating people and leading them to disgracefulness.

Prohibition of drinking is not based on its level of consumption either. **In our second hadith**, it is told that a little of something is also forbidden if much of it is intoxicating. For this reason, one must not be deceived by those who say "it is okay to drink a little as long as it won't make you get drunk." The criterion is very clear that if much of something is intoxicating, a little bit of it is also prohibited (haram). Our religion aims to prevent sins by tightly closing the doors which lead to wrong deeds. It does not take theoretic solutions that do not fit with the practical life. It commands discouraging rules wisely and punishes harshly those who do not obey. This is not due to being inconsiderate of humans but on the contrary our religion covers the whole humanity with everlasting mercy and affection.

According to the Islamic law, the punishment of drinking alcohol is to inflict 40 to 80 lashes. The goal of this punishment is to discourage drinking and making those who drink embarrassed and quit drinking. (Abu Dawud, Kitab al-Hudud, 35/4478)

One day, a man who had drunk alcohol was brought to the Messenger of Allah. The Messenger of Allah (pbuh) told people to inflict the prescribed punishment on him. A while passed and a man among the people said:

"May Allah dishonor and curse you!"

Upon this, the Messenger of Allah (pbuh) said:

"Do not curse him, do not help Satan by saying things against him!" (Bukhari, Kitab Al-Hudud, 4; Abu Dawud, Kitab Al-Hudud, 35, 36)

After his punishment was inflicted, in order for him to pull himself together, the Noble Companions of the Prophet set him free after giving him a talk:

"Were you not ashamed from Allah? Don't you fear from Allah? Were you not ashamed from the Prophet?" The Prophet who was like an ocean of mercy said to his companions:

"Pray for him as "O my Lord, forgive him, O my Lord, show mercy and grace on him..." (Abu Dawud, Kitab Al-Hudud, 35/4478)

Here, we can observe the mercy of the Messenger of Allah towards his followers. Is it not also out of his mercy that he commands us not to commit prohibited (haram) acts?

The Messenger of Allah (pbuh) expresses the wisdom in prohibition of drinking **in our third hadith** as:

"Never drink alcohol because it is the key of all evils."

The Prophet (pbuh) said as part of his long speech at Tabuk:

"Drinking brings all kinds of sins together." (Waqidi, III, 1016)

Drinking is a cause of mischief both for the individual and the society. Drinking affects mental abilities negatively. As a matter of fact, all the beneficial deeds for this world and hereafter take place with intelligence. Without intelligence, humans dive into unimaginable sins.

When one looks into the committed sins, he can see that they are always performed in moments of negligence. If even negligence is so effective in getting into sinful acts, it is not difficult to imagine what kind of major sins being drunk can cause to.

Things that cause material and spiritual intoxication such as drinking, gambling, and games of chances are the most influential weapons of Satan, the constant enemy of humans. Unless man stays away from them, his salvation is not possible. Satan employs drinking and gambling to start hatred, hostility, and enmity among people and set them against each other. By withholding them from the remembrance of Allah, prayer, and worshiping, Satan turns them into poor people of the hereafter. In short, Satan ruins their lives both in this world and in the hereafter. Thus, the way to save oneself from misery in both of the worlds passes through abandoning the sins forbidden by Allah theAlmighty. (Al-Maidah; 5:90-91)

According to the recent report of the World Health Organization covering thirty countries including Turkey, alcohol is the underlying cause for 85% of homicides (60-70% of them are homicides within the family), 50% of rapes, 50% of violent acts, 70% of domestic violence, 60% of unemployment, and 40-50% of mental disorders.

The children of those who consume alcohol are also harmed and endangered because of this. 90% of the children of the alcoholics are born with brain damages. The risk for an alcoholic mother to have a disabled child is a high ratio of 35%. This risk is due to the fact that the unborn child gets affected by the alcohol that his mother consumes. That is because alcohol prevents the growth of the unborn child and the development after birth; it causes retardation, short stature, and behavioral disorders.

Since children of alcoholic people live in a family where always arguments take place, the risk of seeing depression and behavioral disorders in them is high. Thus, most of these kids become unsuccessful in their schools and social lives.[211]

Traffic accidents, suicides, abetting, breaking families apart, failures in business life and professions, and various economic losses are among the harms that drinking usually causes. Drinking which causes a decrease in human intelligence seduces people's thoughts and wastes their wealth. Apart from these, it breaks families apart, corrupts generations, disarrays social dignity and status. That is because it is the mother of all wrong doings and evils.

Uthman (r.a.) expressed with an example that drinking is the mother of all evils as follows:

"Stay away from drinking because it is the mother of all evils. Before your time, there was a pious man who had devoted himself to worshipping. A bad natured woman got obsessed with him. She had sent her servant to him and made her say:

---

211. Musa Tosun, "İçki" *Diyanet İslâm Ansiklopedisi*, XXI, 463.

"We are calling for you to testify."

The devoted man (in order not run away from testifying) went with the servant. When they have arrived, the servant locked all the doors that the man has entered. At the end, the man came to next to a beautiful woman. There was a child and a bottle of wine next to the woman. The woman told him:

"I swear to God I did not call you to testify. I called you to be with me or to drink from this wine or kill this child." The desperate man thinking that he had picked the least harmful one said:

"Give me a cup from the wine."

The woman gave him a cup of wine. The man said:

"Give me some more!"

When the man drunk from the wine, he soon fornicated with the woman and (being scared from everyone will know what he had done) killed the child. For this reason, please stay away from drinking! I swear to Allah, having faith and addiction to drinking can't be present together. Soon one drives off the other one." (Nasai, Kitab Al-Ashriba, 44/5664)

In other words, being addicted to drinking harms one's faith unless he repents. When he repents, he achieves perfection in faith and such faith keeps him from the illness of drinking. That is because drinking is inappropriate for a true believer. Being carried away with this wicked job of Satan is shameful for those who believe in Allah. It does not make sense to both believe in Allah and disobey His commands. This is expressed in a noble hadith as:

"An adulterer, at the time he is committing adultery is not a believer; and a person, at the time of drinking an alcoholic drink is not a believer; and a thief, at the time of stealing, is not a believer…" (Bukhari, Mazalim, 30; Tirmidhi, Iman, 11/2625; Nasai, Kitab Al-Ashriba, 42/5657)

Another noble hadith expresses other harms of drinking reads as follows:

"Alcohol is the mother of all evil and shameful things, the biggest of the major sins. Whoever drinks it may even commit adultery with his mother, maternal aunt, or paternal aunt." (Haythami, V, 67)

For this reason, the Messenger of Allah (pbuh) used harsh expressions in order to keep his followers away from drinking and prohibited everything related to it. **In our fourth hadith,** we are informed that Allah cursed wine, the person who drinks it, who sells it, who buys it, who makes it, who orders it to be made, who transports it, and who gets it. In other reports, we are told that the place where the wine is made, those who donate it or gift it, and those who receive its value and profit are also cursed.[212]

Thus, in order to seek protection from the evils of drinking, it is necessary to close all the doors and stay away from anything that is related to it. This is the most important duty for the happiness of both individuals and societies.

Drinking also endangers the worships of those who are cursed because of drinking. The Messenger of Allah (pbuh) warned those and said:

"Allah does not accept the prayers for seven days of someone who drinks alcohol. If he dies during this period, he dies as unbeliever. If the alcohol he drinks makes him intoxicated and detains him from performing obligatory acts, Allah does not accept his prayers for forty days and if he dies during this period, he dies as unbeliever." (Nasai, Kitab Al-Ashriba, 44/5667; Darimi, Kitab Al-Ashriba, 3; Ibn Majah, Kitab Al-Ashriba, 4)

Worships have two sides. The first one is that the worshipper pays the debt of nature by worshipping and the second one he gains divine rewards. In the hadith above, it is meant that those who drink alcohol would not gain divine rewards from their prayers or other worships.

Thus, a believer who believes in Allah and the Day of Judgment should strictly stay away from drinking. One should not sit the tables of those who drink alcohol and should not organize weddings or other celebrations that does not fit with Islam by serving alcohol and should not attend such organizations. One should tell the reason why he is not sitting the drinking tables or meetings without worrying to offend their owners; so that those who disobey the rules of Allah may understand their faults. Otherwise he would be the object of Allah's curse and anger for just not to offend a sinner and this is the biggest foolishness.

The result of disobeying Allah's commands is getting into various troubles and losses in this world and incurring a miserable punishment in the Hereafter. **In our sixth hadith,** a harsh punishment that will be given to those who drink

---

212. See Abu Dawud, Kitab Al-Ashriba, 2/3674; Tirmidhi, Kitab Al-Buyu, 59/1295; Nasai, Kitab al-Ashriba, 1-2; Ibn Majah, Kitab al-Ashriba, 6; Ahmad, I, 53; II, 351; Hakim, II, 305/3101.

alcohol is described. Those who see themselves fit to drink impure beverages will be punished by drinking the most impure drinks in the Hereafter. That is because punishment is given in accordance with the type of the crime. The punishment of those who drink alcohol will be making them drink the things that are even hard to look at such as the sweat, blood, and pus of the burned skins of denizens of Hell.

f. Fornication and Adultery

١٥٥. عَنْ عَائِشَةَ رَضِيَ اللهُ عَنْهَا أَنَّ رَسُولَ اللهِ صَلَّى اللهُ عَلَيْهِ وَسَلَّمَ قَالَ:

«يَا أُمَّةَ مُحَمَّدٍ مَا أَحَدٌ أَغْيَرَ مِنَ اللهِ أَنْ يَرَى عَبْدَهُ أَوْ أَمَتَهُ يَزْنِي! يَا أُمَّةَ مُحَمَّدٍ لَوْ تَعْلَمُونَ مَا أَعْلَمُ لَضَحِكْتُمْ قَلِيلًا وَلَبَكَيْتُمْ كَثِيرًا».

155. Aisha (r.anha), the mother of Muslims, narrated that the Messenger of Allah (pbuh) said:

"O followers of Muhammad! There is none, who has a greater sense of ghira (jealousy) than Allah (causing His dislike and hatred), so He has forbidden that His slave commits illegal sexual intercourse. O followers of Muhammad![213] If you but knew what I know, you would laugh less and weep more." (Bukhari, Nikah, 107)

✿

١٥٦. عَنْ بُرَيْدَةَ رَضِيَ اللهُ عَنْهُ قَالَ: قَالَ رَسُولُ اللهِ صَلَّى اللهُ عَلَيْهِ وَسَلَّمَ لِعَلِيٍّ:

«يَا عَلِيُّ لَا تُتْبِعِ النَّظْرَةَ النَّظْرَةَ فَإِنَّ لَكَ الْأُولَى وَلَيْسَتْ لَكَ الْآخِرَةُ».

---

213. Our Master the Prophet addressed twice as "O the Ummah (followers) of Muhammad!" to make his affection and mercy towards his followers felt. The Messenger of Allah (pbuh) cherished his followers and warned them insistently to save them from falling into such wicked sins.

357

156. Buraida (r.a.) said: The Messenger of Allah said to Ali:

"O Ali, if you suddenly see something that is forbidden to look at, do not turn and look back! As a matter of fact, the first look is forgiven, but the second one is against you (as a sin.)" (Abu Dawud, Nikah, 42-43/2149; Tirmidhi, Adab, 28/2777; Haythami, VIII, 63)

۱۵۷. عَنْ أَبِي أُمَامَةَ رَضِيَ اللهُ عَنْهُ عَنِ النَّبِيِّ صَلَّى اللهُ عَلَيْهِ وَسَلَّمَ قَالَ:

((مَا مِنْ مُسْلِمٍ يَنْظُرُ إِلَى مَحَاسِنِ امْرَأَةٍ أَوَّلَ مَرَّةٍ ثُمَّ يَغُضُّ بَصَرَهُ إِلَّا أَحْدَثَ اللهُ لَهُ عِبَادَةً يَجِدُ حَلَاوَتَهَا)).

157. Abu Umana (r.a.) narrated that the Noble Prophet (pbuh) said:

"Whoever sees a beautiful woman and takes his look away from her, Allah rewards him with the reward of worship that he will feel its delight from the heart." (Ahmad, V, 264; Haythami, VIII, 63)

۱۵۸. عَنِ ابْنِ عَبَّاسٍ رَضِيَ اللهُ عَنْهُمَا أَنَّهُ سَمِعَ النَّبِيَّ صَلَّى اللهُ عَلَيْهِ وَسَلَّمَ يَقُولُ:

((لَا يَخْلُوَنَّ رَجُلٌ بِامْرَأَةٍ وَلَا تُسَافِرَنَّ امْرَأَةٌ إِلَّا وَمَعَهَا مَحْرَمٌ)) فَقَامَ رَجُلٌ فَقَالَ:

((يَا رَسُولَ اللهِ اكْتُتِبْتُ فِي غَزْوَةِ كَذَا وَكَذَا وَخَرَجَتِ امْرَأَتِي حَاجَّةً؟)) قَالَ:

((اذْهَبْ فَحُجَّ مَعَ امْرَأَتِكَ)).

158. Ibn Abbas (r.anhuma) narrated that the Noble Prophet (pbuh) said:

"It is not permissible for a man to be alone with a woman, and no lady should travel except with a mahram (i.e. her husband or a person whom she cannot marry in any case for ever; e.g. her father, brother, etc.)"

Then a man got up and said:

"O Apostle of Allah! I have enlisted in the army for such and such *ghazwa* and my wife is proceeding for Hajj."

The Messenger of Allah (pbuh) said to him:

"Go, and perform the Hajj with your wife." (Bukhari, Jihad, 140; Nikah, 111; Muslim, Hajj, 424; Ahmad, I, 222. Also see Tirmidhi, Rada, 15-17; Fitan, 7)

Explanations:

Adultery has been considered as wrong and immoral all along by human intelligence, by moral and legal systems, and by the Abrahamic religions. And it is one of the major sins in Islam.

Allah loves His servants a lot and does not want them to fall into this wicked situation. As expressed in our **first hadith**, there is no one else angrier than Allah when someone commits adultery. As anyone does not like and becomes sad when someone from his relatives commits adultery, Allah the Almighty wishes even more to protect His servants from falling into wrong deeds. He does not want His servants to become distant from Him by getting into sins. For this reason, He strictly prohibited these acts and threatened those who commit them and informed that they will be punished severely. Due to His mercy, Almighty Allah informs us about the sins and their punishments in advance in order for us to get preventive actions and do not to fall into them.

Adultery is such a wicked sin that Allah the Almighty prohibited even to get close to it not to mention committing it.

It is commanded in the noble verses of Qur'an as:

$$\text{وَلَا تَقْرَبُوا الْفَوَاحِشَ مَا ظَهَرَ مِنْهَا وَمَا بَطَنَ}$$

"... come not close to shameful deeds whether open or secret." (Al-An'am; 6:151)

وَلَا تَقْرَبُوا الزِّنٰى اِنَّهُ كَانَ فَاحِشَةً وَسَآءَ سَبِيلًا

"Nor come close to adultery: for it is a shameful (deed) and an evil, opening the road (to other evils)." (Al-Isra; 17:32)

In other words, one must stay away all kinds of things that may lead to adultery.[214]

The Messenger of Allah (pbuh) said *"If you but knew what I know, you would laugh less and weep more"* after informing us how angry Allah the Almighty gets in case of adultery. The Messenger of Allah (pbuh) meant that "If you knew the wisdom and reasons behind the commands of Allah and the punishments in case of disobedience and the worries of the Day of Judgment, you would laugh less and weep more thinking about these grand matters all the time."

Allah the Almighty Who is jealous of His servants from sins wants them to be chaste and modest. There are many noble verses of Qur'an pointing out this fact.[215] Preserving the chastity and modesty is listed among the most important characteristics of Muslim men and women. (Al-Mu'minun; 23:5, Al-Nur; 24:30-31; Al-Furqan; 25:68; (Al-Ahzab; 33:35)

---

214. In order to prevent sins Islam pays attention to amelioration of feelings, circumstances, and means that may lead people to sinful acts. For this reason, first of all it takes some measures at the primary stages such as for men and women to cover certain parts of their bodies, to avoid suggestive acts, for stranger men and women (who are legally allowed to get married) to avoid being alone, to prevent nastiness and suggestiveness in the society. This is the reason why Islam criticizes suggestive words, looks, and close relations as they may lead to adultery. Apart from these, Islam assigns families and societies with the duties of raising and nurturing kids, not postponing the age of marriage unless it is necessary, easing marriage process, and keeping the moral and religious values of the society alive.

As it can be understood from these, the goal of Islam is not to punish criminals but to ensure secure and peaceful living environment for people by preventing the suitable circumstances for crimes to take place. Islam is based on the principle of "preventing sins" rather than "punishing sins." For this reason, throughout the Islamic history, the punishment for adultery has been seen rarely.

In spite of all these preventive measures taken by Islam, the punishment of those who commit sinful acts is real justice and mercy for both the individual and the society. (Al-Nur; 24:2) Due to the punishment, the sinner saves himself from wasting his eternal life by getting used to commit sinful acts and receiving even harsher punishment in the Hereafter. The other members of the society get discouraged from sinning by learning some lessons from the punishment of the sinner.

215. For example See An-Nisa; 4:25; Al-Maida; 5:5; Al-Anbiya; 21:91; An-Nur; 24;4, 23; Al-Tahrim; 66:12.

The Messenger of Allah (pbuh), who used to seek refuge in Allah from his body parts gravitating towards evil and committing a sin because of them,[216] gave the following good news to his followers:

"Whoever can guarantee (the chastity of) what is between his two jaw-bones and what is between his two legs (i.e. his tongue and his private parts), I guarantee Paradise for him." (Bukhari, Ar-Riqaq, 23)

The following is an exemplary one, in which the Prophet reasonably explained why one should keep his chastity to a young person who was about to commit a sin:

Abu Umama (r.a.) narrated:

"A young person came approached to the Prophet and asked:

"O the Messenger of Allah! Will you give me permission for adultery?"

People around him advanced on him and scorned him saying "Be quiet, be quiet!"

The Prophet said:

"Come closer!"

The young man came closer to Prophet and sat down.

The Messenger of Allah (pbuh) asked him:

"Would you like this to happen to your mother?"

The young man said:

"May Allah sacrifice me on your way the Messenger of Allah, I swear to Allah I would not want this to happen to her!"

The Messenger of Allah (pbuh) said:

"Others would not like this to happen to their mothers either."

Then, the Messenger of Allah (pbuh) asked the same question regarding his daughter, sister, maternal aunt, and paternal aunt. The young man answered to all:

---

216. Abu Dawud, Witr, 32/1551; Tirmidhi, Daawat, 74/3492. Also see Muslim, Dhikr, 72; Nasai, Istiadha, 4, 10, 11, 28. Since it is not possible for our Prophet (pbuh) to commit sinful acts, here his aim is to teach his followers how to say prayers.

"May Allah sacrifice me on your way the Messenger of Allah, I swear to Allah I would not want this to happen to her!"

The Messenger of Allah (pbuh) reminded him that *"others would not like this to happen her either"* after each question. At the end of the talk, he put his blessed hands on him and prayed as:

"O my Lord! Please forgive his sins and purify his heart and protect his chastity!"

Henceforth, the young man never inclined to do that action." (Ahmad, V, 256-257; Haythami, I, 129)

On the other hand, the Messenger of Allah (pbuh) used to take a vow of obedience from people to stay away from adultery and the deeds that may lead to adultery and to protect their chastity. Aisha (r.anha) narrated:

The Messenger of Allah (pbuh) used to take a vow of obedience just in words (not by shaking hands) and ask them to comply with the conditions given in the following verse:

"O Prophet! When believing women come to you to take the oath of allegiance to you, that they will not associate in worship any other thing whatever with Allah, that they will not steal, that they will not commit adultery (or fornication), that they will not kill their children, that they will not utter slander, intentionally forging falsehood, and that they will not disobey thee in any just matter, then do you receive their allegiance, and pray to Allah for the forgiveness (of their sins): for Allah is Oft-Forgiving, Most Merciful." (Al-Mumtahinah; 60:12)

To the women who accept these conditions, the Messenger of Allah (pbuh) used to say:

"Now I took your vow." I swear to Allah, his hands never touched the hands of a woman when taking their vows. The Messenger of Allah (pbuh) only took the vows in words as:

"I took your vow based on the conditions stated in this noble verse." (Bukhari, Tafsir al-Nabi, 60/2; Ahmad, VI, 270)[217]

---

217. The Messenger of Allah (pbuh) strictly avoided shaking hands with women when taking their vows (Bukhari, Talaq, 20) and said:
"I do not shake hands with women!" (Ibn Majah, Jihad, 43)

Abu Shahm (r.a.) narrated an exemplary memory about this topic:

In Medina, a young girl passed by me. I hold from her collar and then let her go. The next morning, the Messenger of Allah (pbuh) was taking vows of obedience. I went him too. He did not take my vow and said:

"Did the one who held and pulled the collar come?"

I said:

"I swear to Allah that I will not do it again."

Upon this the Messenger of Allah (pbuh) took my vow. (Ahmad, V, 294)

As another preventive measure for adultery, the Messenger of Allah (pbuh) also prohibited earning money from it.[218] Money paid or taken for fornication, as a corresponding value of modesty and chastity of humans, the most honorable of all creatures, is prohibited (haram). As expressed in a hadith, the money earned in this way is *"wicked and all evil."* (Muslim, Musakat, 41; Abu Dawud, Kitab Al-Buyu, 38; Tirmidhi, Kitab Al-Buyu, 46)

On the other hand, the Messenger of Allah (pbuh) discouraged his followers from adultery by explaining its spiritual and material dangers. In one of his noble sayings, it is expressed that adultery endangers the most valuable blessing, namely faith:

"Whoever commits adultery, faith exits him, stays on him like a cloud. When he repents from it and quits it completely, faith returns him again." (Abu Dawud, Kitab Al-Sunnah, 15/4690; Tirmidhi, Iman, 11/2625; Hakim, I, 72/56)

In another hadith, the Messenger of Allah (pbuh) explained the material dangers of adultery and said:

"When adultery and prostitution become widespread and finally begin to be committed publicly in a nation, plague or other illnesses that never happened before spread in that nation." (Ibn Majah, Fiten, 22; Hakim, IV, 583/8623)

It is narrated from Ibn Abbas (r.anhuma) as:

"…If adultery becomes widespread in a society, deaths will increase in that society…" (*Muwatta,* Jihad, 26; Ibn Majah, Fitan, 22)

---

218. Bukhari, Buyu, 25, 113; Ijara, 20; Talaq, 51; Tibb, 46; Libas, 86, 96; Muslim, Musaqat, 40. Also see Abu Dawud, Buyu, 26, 63; Tirmidhi, Buyu, 46, 49, 50; Nikah, 37; Tibb, 23; Nasai, Sayd, 15; Buyu, 91, 92, 94; Ibn Majah, Tijarah, 9.

Adultery causes bloodline to mix up, families, relations with relatives, neighbors, and friends to break up and moral and spiritual values to be shaken to the foundation. It disregards the honor and dignity of people by making them slaves of their carnal pleasures.

There are also many dangers of adultery to one's health. Illnesses such as syphilitic and gonorrhea are among the transmissible illnesses usually seen in those who fell into the marsh of adultery. The deadly illness AIDS, to which today's medical world could not find a cure, is usually transmitted by adultery.

Those who commit adultery are so wicked and evil people that Allah the Almighty will call the Day of Judgment on them. As the Prophet (pbuh) informed us, towards the end of the world, those Muslims who protect themselves from the instigations of antichrist (Dajjal) and gog and magog and who live a happy life will all die as a result of a divine fate. *"...would take the life of every Muslim and only the wicked would survive who would commit adultery like asses and the Last Hour would come to them."* (Muslim, Fitan, 110. Also see Tirmidhi, Fitan, 59/2240; Ibn Majah, Fitan, 33)

Thus, one must stay away from every word, act, thought, and means that brings him closer to adultery in order to be saved from the anger of Almighty Allah and from being afflicted with such harms. As a matter of fact, words and acts are considered according to their consequences, the things that lead to forbidden acts are also forbidden (haram) and the things that lead to necessary acts (wajib) are also necessary. For this reason, the acts that may lead to adultery such as evil gazing, listening, speaking, reading, and smelling are also forbidden. In this case, when one unintentionally sees something forbidden, one must turn his eyes away and should not be carried away with the attraction of the sin. Indeed, **in our second hadith,** the Messenger of Allah (pbuh) commands that when one sets his eyes on something forbidden, he must turn away his eyes immediately and should not look back again. Almighty Allah forgives the unintended and sudden first seeing, but considers the second look which is done intentionally as sin.

Jarir b. Abdullah (r.a.) reported:

I asked the Prophet about the sudden glance (that is cast) on the face (of a stranger woman). He commanded me:

"You should turn away your eyes immediately!" (Muslim, Kitab Al-Adab 45. Also see Abu Dawud, Kitab Al-Nikah, 43; Tirmidhi, Adab, 28)

That is because to look (at something which is sinful to look at) is the misconduct (adultery) of the eye and it is a sin. In the same manner, the adultery of the ear is to listen, the adultery of the tongue is to utter (what it is unlawful to utter), the adultery of the hand is to touch, the adultery of feet are to go to adultery, and the adultery of the heart and soul is to wish and long for (adultery). (Bukhari, Isti'dhan 12, Al-Qadar, 9; Muslim, Al-Qadar 20-21. Also see Abu Dawud, Kitab Al-Nikah, 43)

By forbidding these acts, Islam prevents major sins from happening. In Islamic Law, this is called "Sad al-Dharia" or "the principle of closing the door to evil."

The Messenger of Allah (pbuh) said:

"Every eye commits adultery when it looks (at something which is sinful to look at). When a woman wears a perfume and passes through a place where men are gathered, she too is considered as committed adultery."[219] (Tirmidhi, Adab, 35/2786; Abu Dawud, Kitab Al-Tarajjul, 7/4173; Nasai, Kitab Al-Libas wa al-Zinah, 35)

Almighty Allah said:

"Say to the believing men that they should lower their gaze and guard their modesty: that will make for greater purity for them: And Allah is well acquainted with all that they do. And say to the believing women that they should lower their gaze and guard their modesty..." (Al-Nur; 24:30-31)

The Messenger of Allah (pbuh) expresses the harm of unnecessary looks for the heart as:

---

219. Women should avoid walking, wearing perfume, and talking to men in a provocative way. They should not draw the attention of men by striking their feet when walking. Allah prohibits these kinds of acts and says:
"...and that they should not strike their feet in order to draw attention to their hidden ornaments." (An-Nur; 24:31) (Ornaments such as feet rings).
"...if you do fear (Allah), be not too complacent of speech, lest one in whose heart is a disease should be moved with desire: but speak you a speech (that is) just. And stay quietly in your houses, and make not a dazzling display, like that of the former times of ignorance; and establish regular Prayer, and give regular charity; and obey Allah and His Messenger..." (al-Ahzab; 33:32-33)

"Looking at what is forbidden is one of the poisonous arrows of demon. Whoever quits this for the sake of Allah, Allah blesses him with such a faith that he will experience its sweetness in his heart." (Hakim, IV, 349/7875; Haythami, VIII, 63)

Eyes are the windows of the heart. When eyes look at wrong things, the brain gets negatively influenced by it and becomes busy with sinful acts. Thus, it causes heart to darken and to be spirituality ruined.

Thus, saving oneself from the poisonous arrows of demon by controlling his inner soul is a great gain for a believer. **In our third hadith**, we are given the good news that this will be rewarded with the reward of a worship that gives peace to heart. In other words, Almighty Allah considers this simple act as a worship since it is important in terms of preventing a major sin. This is one of the manifestations of His mercy and affection towards His subjects.

In another noble hadith, the virtue of the eye that avoids looking at forbidden things is expressed as:

"There are three kinds of people whose eyes will never see the Hell. The eye that is on guard duty in the way of Allah; the eye that cries because of the fear of Allah; and the eye that avoids looking at the forbidden." (Haythami, V, 288)

Our forth hadith puts believers under protection by prohibiting another wrong deed that opens the door of adultery. It is to be alone with a woman who is not a close relative and with whom there is nothing preventing a person from getting married to her. One must strictly avoid being alone or staying with women whose close relatives such as her husband, mother, father, son, siblings, aunt, or milk-sibling are not with her. If there are close relatives of a man such as his sister, daughter, aunt, or maternal aunt are with him, it is also considered as if the stranger woman has her close relatives with her. In the same manner, women should pay extra attention not to be alone with stranger men. That is because as the Messenger of Allah (pbuh) said:

"When a man is left in private with a stranger woman, for sure the third one there is Satan." (Tirmidhi, Rada, 16/1171; Fitan, 7/2165; Ahmad, I, 18, 26)

When the wives of the Prophet (pbuh) needed to ask something from strange men or needed to tell them something, they had to do this from behind a curtain or a wall. (Al-Ahzab; 33:53) Even though this was an order for the wives of the Prophet, it can also be followed by the rest of the Muslim women as much as possible.

One important fact that is overlooked today is this: One should not be alone with his brother's wife (sister-in-law). The close relatives of the husband such as the children of the siblings, uncle and the children of the uncle are the same in terms of this rule.

One day the Messenger of Allah (pbuh) said:

"Avoid going next to women (whose intimate relatives are not with her!)"

Upon this, one person from Ansar asked:

"O the Messenger of Allah! What would you say about the male relatives of the husband (*al-hamwu*)?"

The Messenger of Allah (pbuh) said:

"Being alone with them is like death." (Bukhari, Nikah, 111; Muslim, Salam, 20; Tirmidhi, Rada, 16/1171)

The word "*al-hamwu*" means husband's close relatives such as his brother, cousins, uncles, and the children of his uncles.

Since these kinds of close relatives always have the opportunity of easily visiting one's house, they face with more dangers in this respect. For this reason, they have to be extra careful about this matter and should avoid being alone with them. These people may have very good intentions. However, Islam tightly closes the doors of possible dangers so that people do not get harmed and face with troubles after all. As a matter of fact, the situations of the families who did not pay attention to this fact and became miserable in the end are known to all. On the other hand, it is impossible to stop the bad-mouthing of others.

In the second part of our hadith, it is commanded for women not to travel unless they have a close relative with them. The Prophet had sent one of his noble companions to go to Hajj with his wife instead of going for a military expedition (jihad), and this is enough to show the importance of the principle.

g. Betrayal, being disloyal

١٥٩ . عَنْ أَنَسٍ رَضِيَ اللهُ عَنْهُ قَالَ: قَلَّمَا خَطَبَنَا رَسُولُ اللهِ صَلَّى اللهُ عَلَيْهِ وَسَلَّمَ إِلَّا قَالَ:

«لَا إِيمَانَ لِمَنْ لَا أَمَانَةَ لَهُ وَلَا دِينَ لِمَنْ لَا عَهْدَ لَهُ».

159. Anas bin Maliq (r.a.) narrated:

The Prophet (pbuh) used to say in most of the speeches he made to us:

"One who can not be trusted has no faith, and one who does not fulfill his promises has no religion." (Ahmad, III, 154, 135)

۱٦۰. عَنْ أَبِي هُرَيْرَةَ رَضِيَ اللهُ عَنْهُ عَنِ النَّبِيِّ صَلَّى اللهُ عَلَيْهِ وَسَلَّمَ قَالَ:

«آيَةُ الْمُنَافِقِ ثَلَاثٌ إِذَا حَدَّثَ كَذَبَ وَإِذَا وَعَدَ أَخْلَفَ وَإِذَا اؤْتُمِنَ خَانَ» وَفِي رِوَايَةٍ: «وَإِنْ صَامَ وَصَلَّى وَزَعَمَ أَنَّهُ مُسْلِمٌ».

160. It is narrated from Abu Huraira (r.a.) that the Noble Prophet (pbuh) said:

"The signs of a hypocrite are three:

1. Whenever he speaks, he tells a lie.

2. Whenever he promises, he always breaks it (his promise).

3. If you trust him, he proves to be dishonest. (If you keep something as a trust with him, he will not return it.)" (Bukhari, Iman, 24; Muslim, Iman, 107-108. Also see. Tirmidhi, Iman, 14/2631-2633)

In other reports, the following is added to this narration:

"Even if he observed fast and prayed and asserted that he was a Muslim!" (Muslim Iman, 109)

۱٦۱. عَنْ أَبِي هُرَيْرَةَ رَضِيَ اللهُ عَنْهُ قَالَ: قَالَ رَسُولُ اللهِ صَلَّى اللهُ عَلَيْهِ وَسَلَّمَ:

«أَدِّ الْأَمَانَةَ إِلَى مَنِ ائْتَمَنَكَ وَلَا تَخُنْ مَنْ خَانَكَ».

161. It is narrated from Abu Huraira (r.a.) that the Messenger of Allah (pbuh) said:

"When you are entrusted with something, return it to its owner! Do not betray those who betrayed you!" (Abu Dawud, Kitab Al-Buyu, 79/3535; Tirmidhi, Kitab Al-Buyu, 38/1264)

۱٦۲. عَنْ عَدِيِّ بْنِ عَمِيرَةَ رَضِيَ اللهُ عَنْهُ قَالَ: سَمِعْتُ رَسُولَ اللهِ صَلَّى اللهُ عَلَيْهِ وَسَلَّمَ يَقُولُ:

«مَنِ اسْتَعْمَلْنَاهُ مِنْكُمْ عَلَى عَمَلٍ فَكَتَمَنَا مِخْيَطًا فَمَا فَوْقَهُ كَانَ غُلُولًا يَأْتِي بِهِ يَوْمَ الْقِيَامَةِ» قَالَ فَقَامَ إِلَيْهِ رَجُلٌ أَسْوَدُ مِنَ الْأَنْصَارِ كَأَنِّي أَنْظُرُ إِلَيْهِ فَقَالَ:

«يَا رَسُولَ اللهِ، اقْبَلْ عَنِّي عَمَلَكَ» قَالَ:

«وَمَا لَكَ» قَالَ:

«سَمِعْتُكَ تَقُولُ كَذَا وَكَذَا» قَالَ:

«وَأَنَا أَقُولُهُ الْآنَ مَنِ اسْتَعْمَلْنَاهُ مِنْكُمْ عَلَى عَمَلٍ فَلْيَجِئْ بِقَلِيلِهِ وَكَثِيرِهِ فَمَا أُوتِيَ مِنْهُ أَخَذَ وَمَا نُهِيَ عَنْهُ انْتَهَى».

162. Adi b. Amira (r.a.) narrated that:

I heard the Messenger of Allah (pbuh) say:

"Whoso from you is appointed by us to a position of authority and he con-ceals from us a needle or something smaller than that, it would be misappropria-tion (of public funds) and will (have to) produce it on the Day of Judgment."

Upon this, a dark-complexioned man from the Ansar stood up - I can still visualize him - and said:

"O Messenger of Allah, take back from me your assignment."

The Messenger of Allah (pbuh) asked:

"What has happened to you?"

The man answered:

"I have heard you say so and so."

The Messenger of Allah (pbuh) said:

"I say that (even) now: Whoso from you is appointed as to a position of (fis-cal) authority, he should bring everything, big of small, and whatever he is given therefrom he should take, and he should restrain himself from taking that which is forbidden." (Muslim, Kitab Al-Imara, 30. Also see Abu Dawud, Aqdiya, 5/3581)

❋

١٦٣. عَنْ أَبِي هُرَيْرَةَ قَالَ: كَانَ رَسُولُ اللهِ صَلَّى اللهُ عَلَيْهِ وَسَلَّمَ يَقُولُ:

«اَللّهُمَّ إِنِّي أَعُوذُ بِكَ مِنَ الْجُوعِ فَإِنَّهُ بِئْسَ الضَّجِيعُ وَأَعُوذُ بِكَ مِنَ الْخِيَانَةِ فَإِنَّهَا بِئْسَتِ الْبِطَانَةُ».

163. Abu Huraira (r.a.) narrated:

"The Messenger of Allah used to pray as:

"O Allah, I seek refuge in You from hunger, for it is an evil state; and I seek refuge in You from treachery, for it is an evil hidden trait." (Abu Dawud, Witr, 32/1547. Also see Nasai, Istiadha, 19, 20; Ibn Majah, At'ima, 53)

Explanations:

Since the word "mu'min" (believer) comes from the same root of the words "amniyyah" (safety) and "amanat" (trust), Muslims who have faith in Allah should be the most trustworthy people on earth. Almighty Allah wants believers to be "trustworthy." As a matter of fact, "amanat" was one of the most important characteristics of the prophets. Our Prophet was the symbol of being trustworthiness and the word "*amin*" (trustworthy) became like his second name. Thus, nothing is more natural for believers as the followers of the Muhammad al-Amin to be trusted ones. Those who deviate from this and be disloyal eventually lose their tie with being a believer and being a follower of Muhammad al-Amin.

As one of the signs of hypocrisy, disloyalty means treating something entrusted in contradiction with Islam, being unjust, and not giving the feeling of trustworthiness. As this is true in regards to the material issues, it also holds in moral matters as well. If a person changes or abandons the commands of the Book and the Sunnah, he becomes disloyal to the things that are entrusted him by Allah and His Messenger.

On the other hand, since a secret given to a friend is also a thing that should be kept safe, revealing a secret is also being disloyal.

Our Almighty Lord does not like the treacherous. (Al-Hajj; 22:38) (Al-Anfal; 8:58)

The snare of the false ones will never be successful. (Yusuf; 12:52)

Allah commands His Prophet to stay away from disloyalty and say:

"... so be not (used) as an advocate by those who betray their trust." (Al-Nisa; 4:105)

"Contend not on behalf of such as betray their own souls; for Allah loves not one given to perfidy and crime." (Al-Nisa; 4:107)

Those who became disloyal would not be saved in the hereafter even if they are the closest relatives of the Prophet.

It is said in a noble verse of the Qur'an:

"Allah sets forth, for an example to the unbelievers, the wife of Noah and the wife of Lot: they were (respectively) under two of our righteous

servants, but they were false to their (husbands), and they profited nothing before Allah on their account, but were told: "Enter you the Fire along with (others) that enter!" (Al-Tahrim; 66:10)

When the Messenger of Allah was listing the inmates of Hell, he said:

"…And dishonest ones whose greed cannot be concealed even in the case of minor things.

…those who betray you morning and evening, in regard to your family and your property." (Muslim, Jannat, 63)

In order to save one self from the Hell and enter into Paradise, one must be a believer. Faith cannot exist together with treachery. As a matter of fact, **in our first hadith,** we are told that there is no faith for the one who has no trust, and there is no religion for the one who does not fulfill his promises. Both of these issues are related to being trustworthy. This hadith proves how great the sin disloyalty is.

In some narrations, it is told that a believer can sometimes fall into sinful acts but being disloyal and lying are the things that a believer never commits. (Ahmad, V, 252; Baihaqi, *Shuab,* IV, 207)

The aim of this hadith is to emphasize the greatness of the sin of being disloyal and lying. Otherwise it does not aim to open the door of other sins to the believers. A believer should avoid all kinds of sins however disloyalty and lying are the things that should never seen in a believer. That is because these bad characters do not befit to a believer and do not comply with having faith.

The Messenger of Allah (pbuh) described a Muslim as:

"Muslim is a brother to a Muslim. He would not be disloyal to him, lie to him, and withhold his help to him. The chastity, wealth, and blood of Muslims are forbidden (haram) to each other." (Tirmidhi, Birr, 18/1927)

It is not possible to hide anything from Almighty Allah. He knows the evil looks of disloyal people and their bad intentions and records them as evidence against them in their book of deeds. It is said in the noble Qur'an:

"(Allah) knows of (the tricks) that deceive with the eyes, and all that the hearts (of men) conceal." (Al-Mu'min; 40:19)

Thus, it is impossible for a person who believes in Allah and the Hereafter to be disloyal. As a matter of fact, in our second hadith, it is told that being disloyal is a sign of hypocrisy. The hadith continues listing the signs of hypocrisy as lying and breaking promises which are also various manifestations of treachery. In other words, those who are not trustworthy in their words and actions and give the impression of disloyalty eventually get away from being a believer and get closer to hypocrisy. Even if this person performs his acts of worship such as fasting and praying and thinks that he is a believer, the last situation would be the case in reality. For this reason, believers should pay extra attention to being trustworthy and having a high moral character.

In another hadith, the Messenger of Allah (pbuh) said that Allah the Exalted said:

"I will be the enemy of three persons on the Day of Resurrection" and mentioned people who don't keep promises among them. (Bukhari, Buyu, 106)

In another hadith, he gave us the scaring news of:

"On the Day of Judgment, a flag will be planted for each disloyal people and it will be announced that the flags are the signs of their disloyalty." (Bukhari, Jizya, 22; Adab, 99; Hiyal, 99; Muslim, Jihad, 11-17)

In our third hadith, the Messenger of Allah (pbuh) advised us to be trustworthy (*amin*) people and not to react with disloyalty to those who were disloyal to us.

These two issues are so important that they are the foundations of social order and morality.

The first article commands us to fulfill the commands of Allah and also give other people their dues. In other words, as one pay attention to be loyal and honest in material goods, one must also do the same in moral issues.

The trust of Almighty Allah to His subjects is composed of all of His commands and revelations as it is expressed in the following verse:

"We did indeed offer the Trust to the heavens and the earth and the mountains; but they refused to undertake it, being afraid thereof..."[220] A believer who fulfills these commands becomes loyal to the trust. Those who do not obey the rules of Islam become disloyal to Allah and His Messenger. He

220. Al-Ahzab; 33:72.

but no one else would be the one who faces the burdens of acting this way. As a matter of fact, **"On account of their arrogance in the land and their plotting of evil, but the plotting of evil will surround only the authors thereof."** (Al-Fatir; 35:43)

This fact is more clearly told us in another noble verse:

"O you who believe! Betray not the trust of Allah and the Messenger, nor misappropriate knowingly things entrusted to you." (Al-Anfal; 8:27)

If one thinks his own benefit, he should avoid being disrespectful and dishonest to the divine commands and the Sunnah of the Prophet and should extend our endless gratitude to Allah for His commands that make us alive. Performing our religious duties seriously and sincerely by not deviating from being loyal and obedient to them guarantees our happiness and salvation. If a person does not act this way and becomes disloyal to Allah and His Messenger, he becomes even more disloyal to the trusts of other people. If a person loses his character and self-respect and start being disloyal to Allah and His Messenger, that person becomes disloyal to others' wealth, life, chastity, modesty, rights, laws, and his country, and national duties.

When they are dealt with from the perspective of entrusted things to humans, every right and responsibility, no matter how small they are, is a trust. Doing people injustice and deceiving them intentionally is treachery. If a promised work is not carefully done on time, it is also an example to disloyalty. Not being at work on time, doing late or incomplete job by ignoring the work is also being disloyal and the wage earned unfairly in turn is forbidden (haram.)

In our hadith, as being disloyal is forbidden, to react to disloyalty with disloyalty is also forbidden. However, those who started it are always more oppressive and their punishment is worse.

Since Our Exalted and Just Lord knows what everyone is doing the best, He will prove who has how much to give and how much to take and judge accordingly. This following story is one of the examplary examples of this fact:

Someone sat before Allah's Messenger (pbuh) and asked:

"O Messenger of Allah! I have some slaves. They are disloyal and they always lie to me and disobey me. Thus, I scorn and strike them. What will be my situation because of them?"

The Messenger of Allah (pbuh) answered:

"The punishment that you enforce on them will be measured against their disloyalty, disobedience, and lies, and if the punishment that you give them is equal to their wrong deeds, it is neither to your advantage or disadvantage. If the punishment that you give is less than what they have deserved, it is to your advantage. If the punishment that you give exceeds what they have deserved, you have to pay for the extra punishment and that will be taken from you by the method of eye for an eye."

The man went to corner and started to cry his eyes out. Upon this, the Messenger of Allah (pbuh) asked:

"Don't you recite Almighty Allah's following verse: **"We shall set up scales of justice for the Day of Judgment, so that not a soul will be dealt with unjustly in the least, and if there be (no more than) the weight of a mustard seed, We will bring it (to account): and enough are We to take account."**[221]

Upon this, the man said:

"O the Messenger of Allah! I swear to Allah, both for my goodness and theirs, there is no other option left than freeing them. You are my witness that they are all free." (Tirmidhi, Tafsir, 21/3165)

In our forth hadith, a matter that most frequently causes the carnal-self to fall into disloyalty is mentioned. No matter how small, being disloyal to state and public goods is among the major sins that Allah informed us that He will not forgive and may cause one to go to Hell. That is because everybody in a country has a right in them. Thus, its punishment will be accordingly. Those who commit such major sins will come to terms with those they have deceived in the Hereafter in the sight of Allah unless they ask for their forgiveness in this world and promise Allah not to commit this kind of sin again. For the disloyal people, if there are rights of others on them, their good deeds will be distributed among the deceived innocents and when the good deeds are all finished, they will take the sins of those who have rights on them and thus they will go completely bankrupt.

221. Al-Anbiya; 21:47.

Those who are disloyal cannot find anyone to help them in the difficult times of the doomsday. Abu Huraira (r.a.) narrated the important warning of the Prophet (pbuh) on this fact:

Once the Prophet (pbuh) got up amongst us and made a speech out misappropriation of war spoils and the state funds (*ghulul*). He emphasized that such disloyalty is a great evil, declared that it was a great sin, and explained that hence it is strictly prohibited. He said:

"Don't commit ghulul for I should not like to see anyone amongst you on the Day of Resurrection, carrying over his neck a sheep that will be bleating, or carrying over his neck a horse that will be neighing and beg:

"O Allah's Apostle! Intercede with Allah for me!" or I will reply:

"I can't help you, for I have conveyed Allah's Message to you on earth!"

Nor should I like to see a man carrying over his neck, a camel that will be grunting and say:

"O Allah's Apostle! Intercede with Allah for me!" I will say to him:

"I can't help you for I have conveyed Allah's Message to you on earth!"

Nor should I like to see a man carrying over his neck gold and silver and saying:

"O Allah's Apostle! Intercede with Allah for me!" I will say to him:

"I can't help you for I have conveyed Allah's Message to you on earth!"

Nor should I like to see a man one carrying clothes that will be fluttering and saying:

"O Allah's Apostle! Intercede with Allah for me!" I will say to him:

"I can't help you for I have conveyed Allah's Message to you on earth!"
(Bukhari, Jihad, 189; Muslim, Imarat, 24)

The fact that those who are disloyal will come on doomsday with the things that they have obtained unjustly is a strong threat and indicates that they deserve to go to Hell.

❁

Umar b. Khattab (r.a.) narrated that:

It was the day of Khaibar Military Expedition. A party of Companions of the Apostle of Allah (pbuh) came and said:

"So and so is a martyr."

Then, they happened to pass by a man and said:

"So and so is a martyr too."

Upon this, the Messenger of Allah (pbuh) remarked:

"Nay, not so verily I have seen him in the Fire for the garment or cloak that he had stolen from the booty."

Then the Messenger of Allah (pbuh) ordered:

"Umar the son of Khattab, go and announce to the people that none but the believers shall enter Paradise!"

I (Umar bin Khattab) went out and proclaimed:

"Verily none but the believers would be able to enter Paradise." (Muslim, Iman (Faith), 182)

Unjustly getting others' rightful shares is such an important matter that even martyrdom, which is one of the highest ranks, did not help for its forgiveness. For this reason, one must strictly stay away from undeserved gain and disloyalty.

The fact that the Prophet ordered to be announced that only believers will go to Paradise is to show that disloyalty and faith cannot be together under any circumstances.

On the other hand, aiding disloyal ones is also disloyalty. The Prophet (pbuh) said:

"Anyone who conceals one who has been disloyal to a trust is like him." (Abu Dawud, Jihad, 135/2716)

As it can be understood from our **forth hadith,** one must not go after the duties involving the rights of the public. However, if duty is given, one must try to do it in the best manner. A person who accepts this kind of responsibility does not have a right to take anything more than what is designated for him. Also, it is not considered nice of him to accept gifts while he is in that position.

That is because those who give gifts to people in positions of responsibility may be after their own benefits that are against the benefits of the society. This may cause various disloyalties and corruptions.

The Noble Companions of the Prophet used to be extra careful about this issue:

Abu Bakr (r.a.) appointed Muadh b. Jabal as the zakat collector. Muadh (r.a.) returned with some stuff and said to Abu Bakr:

"These are yours and there are the gifts given to me."

Umar (r.a.) said:

"Deliver all of them to Abu Bakr."

Muadh (r.a.) acted slowly in returning the gifts that were given to him. When he went to sleep, he saw a dream. He saw himself as if he was at the edge of a huge fire. He was afraid of falling into it. At that moment, Umar (r.a.) came and saved him by pulling from his belt.

Muadh (r.a.) went to Abu Bakr in the morning and told him about his dream and returned all the stuff that was with him.

Abu Bakr said:

"Since you are doing this, I give the gifts back to you sincerely."

Upon this Umar (r.a.) said:

"Now they became permissible (halal) for you." (Ibn al-Jawzi, *Manaqib*, p. 261)

The Messenger of Allah (pbuh) praised people who are loyal to public goods and showed that this is something to be proud of. One day, he said:

"What nice tribes are the tribes of Asad and Ash'ari; they do not run away from fighting and they are not disloyal to war booty. They are for my side, and I am for their side." (Tirmidhi, Manaqib, 74/3947)

Almighty Allah is also with those who are trustworthy. In a noble hadith, this fact is told as:

"Allah, Most High, says: "I make a third with two partners as long as one of them does not cheat the other, but when he cheats him, I depart from them." (Abu Dawud, Buyu, 26-27/3383)

There is no doubt that when Allah departs from the two partners, Satan will immediately interfere and drag them to miserable ends.

Another issue related to being disloyal is misguiding a friend who asks for advice. Those who misguide to the wrong path in spite of knowing the right one would be disloyal to their friends who trusted them and asked for their advice.

It is said in a noble hadith:

"If anyone advises his brother, knowing that guidance lies in another direction, he has deceived him." (Abu Dawud, Ilm, 8/3657)

It is impossible to think of a worse betrayal than lying to a friend who trusts and listens to he liar. That is because people can be very deceivable and incautious to people that they think they would never lie. Thus, the damage they would get in such situations would be much more compared to other cases.

The Messenger of Allah (pbuh) said:

"It is great treachery that you tell your brother something and have him believe you when you are lying!" (Abu Dawud, Kitab Al-Adab, 71/4971; Ahmad, IV, 183; Bukhari, *al-Adab al-mufrad*, no: 393)

The Messenger of Allah (pbuh) who explained the dangers of disloyalty and treachery sought refuge in Allah in his prayers in order to be an example for his followers. As it can be seen in our **fifth hadith**:

He used to pray saying *"O Allah, I seek refuge in You from treachery, for it is an evil hidden trait"* and showed us how to pray. By this, he wanted to show that disloyalty is a bad characteristic that brings shame on people and degrades them to the lowest degrees and advised his followers to seek refuge in Allah from it.

h. Backbiting and Being a Talebearer

١٦٤. عَنْ أَبِي هُرَيْرَةَ رَضِيَ اللهُ عَنْهُ أَنَّ رَسُولَ اللهِ صَلَّى اللهُ عَلَيْهِ وَسَلَّمَ قَالَ:

«أَتَدْرُونَ مَا الْغِيبَةُ؟» قَالُوا:

«اللهُ وَرَسُولُهُ أَعْلَمُ» قَالَ:

«ذِكْرُكَ أَخَاكَ بِمَا يَكْرَهُ» قِيلَ:

«أَفَرَأَيْتَ إِنْ كَانَ فِي أَخِي مَا أَقُولُ؟» قَالَ:

«إِنْ كَانَ فِيهِ مَا تَقُولُ فَقَدِ اغْتَبْتَهُ وَإِنْ لَمْ يَكُنْ فِيهِ فَقَدْ بَهَتَّهُ».

164. It is narrated from Abu Huraira (r.a.) that one day the Messenger of Allah (pbuh) asked:

"Do you know what is backbiting?"

The Noble Companions answered:

"Allah and His Messenger know better."

Prophet (pbuh) said:

"Backbiting is your mention of your brother in a manner which he does not like."

One of them asked:

"What is your opinion about that the situation that I actually find (that failing) in my brother which I made a mention of?

The Messenger of Allah (pbuh) said:

"If (that failing) is actually found (in him) what you assert, you in fact back-bit him, and if that is not in him, it is a slander." (Muslim, Birr, 70; Abu Dawud, Adab, 40/4874)

❀

١٦٥. عَنْ عَائِشَةَ رَضِيَ اللهُ عَنْهَا قَالَتْ: قُلْتُ لِلنَّبِيِّ صَلَّى اللهُ عَلَيْهِ وَسَلَّمَ:

«حَسْبُكَ مِنْ صَفِيَّةَ كَذَا وَكَذَا» قَالَ غَيْرُ مُسَدَّدٍ تَعْنِي قَصِيرَةً فَقَالَ:

«لَقَدْ قُلْتِ كَلِمَةً لَوْ مُزِجَتْ بِمَاءِ الْبَحْرِ لَمَزَجَتْهُ» قَالَتْ:

وَحَكَيْتُ لَهُ إِنْسَانًا فَقَالَ:

«مَا أُحِبُّ أَنِّي حَكَيْتُ إِنْسَانًا وَأَنَّ لِي كَذَا وَكَذَا».

165. Aisha (r.anha) narrated: I said to the Noble Prophet (pbuh):

"It is enough for you that Safiyyah is short-statured."

The Messenger of Allah (pbuh) said:

"O Aisha! You have said such a word that it would pollute the sea if it were mixed in it."

In another day, I have imitated someone before him.[222]

The Messenger of Allah (pbuh) said:

"Even if I should get the most valuable things on earth, I would never like to imitate and mention anyone in a way that they would not like." (Abu Dawud, Adab, 35/4875; Tirmidhi, Qiyamah, 51/2502; Ahmad, VI, 189)

١٦٦. عَنْ أَبِي بَرْزَةَ رَضِيَ اللهُ عَنْهُ قَالَ: قَالَ رَسُولُ اللهِ صَلَّى اللهُ عَلَيْهِ وَسَلَّمَ:

«يَا مَعْشَرَ مَنْ آمَنَ بِلِسَانِهِ وَلَمْ يَدْخُلِ الْإِيمَانُ قَلْبَهُ! لَا تَغْتَابُوا الْمُسْلِمِينَ وَلَا تَتَّبِعُوا عَوْرَاتِهِمْ فَإِنَّهُ مَنِ اتَّبَعَ عَوْرَاتِهِمْ يَتَّبِعِ اللهُ عَوْرَتَهُ وَمَنْ يَتَّبِعِ اللهُ عَوْرَتَهُ يَفْضَحْهُ فِي بَيْتِهِ».

---

222. Aisha (r.anha) and other mothers of Muslims were humans in spite of their many good virtues. Thus, it is very natural for them to make mistakes from time to time. They used to quit their mistakes as soon as they understand their mistakes. On the other hand, the mistakes of those who lived with the Messenger of Allah (pbuh) helped some important principles to be learned.

166. It is narrated from Abu Barza (r.a.) that the Messenger of Allah (pbuh) said:

"O community of people, who believed by their tongue, and belief did not enter their hearts, do not back-bite Muslims, and do not search for their faults, for if anyone searches for their faults, Allah will search for his faults, and if Allah searches for the fault of anyone, He disgraces him even in his house." (Abu Dawud, Adab, 35/4880; Tirmidhi, Birr, 85/2032; Ibn Kathir, Tafsir, IV, 229)

❀

١٦٧. عَنْ جَابِرِ بْنِ عَبْدِ اللهِ رَضِيَ اللهُ عَنْهُ قَالَ: كُنَّا مَعَ النَّبِيِّ صَلَّى اللهُ عَلَيْهِ وَسَلَّمَ فَارْتَفَعَتْ رِيحُ جِيفَةٍ مُنْتِنَةٍ فَقَالَ رَسُولُ اللهِ صَلَّى اللهُ عَلَيْهِ وَسَلَّمَ:

﴿﴿أَتَدْرُونَ مَا هٰذِهِ الرِّيحُ؟ هٰذِهِ رِيحُ الَّذِينَ يَغْتَابُونَ الْمُؤْمِنِينَ﴾﴾.

167. Jabir (r.a.) narrated:

"I was next to the Messenger of Allah (pbuh). Then suddenly the smell of carcass was felt.

The Messenger of Allah (pbuh) said:

"Do you know what that smell is? This is the smell of those who backbite about believers." (Ahmad, III, 351)

❀

١٦٨. عَنْ أَنَسِ بْنِ مَالِكٍ رَضِيَ اللهُ عَنْهُ قَالَ: قَالَ رَسُولُ اللهِ صَلَّى اللهُ عَلَيْهِ وَسَلَّمَ:

﴿﴿لَمَّا عُرِجَ بِي مَرَرْتُ بِقَوْمٍ لَهُمْ أَظْفَارٌ مِنْ نُحَاسٍ يَخْمِشُونَ وُجُوهَهُمْ وَصُدُورَهُمْ فَقُلْتُ:

﴿﴿مَنْ هٰؤُلَاءِ يَا جِبْرِيلُ؟﴾﴾ قَالَ:

«هٰؤُلَاءِ الَّذِينَ يَأْكُلُونَ لُحُومَ النَّاسِ وَيَقَعُونَ فِي أَعْرَاضِهِمْ».

168. It is narrated from Anas b. Malik (r.a.) that the Messenger of Allah (pbuh) said:

"When I was taken up to heavens, I passed by people who had nails made of copper and who were scratching their faces and their breasts. I asked:

"O Gabriel! Who are these people?" He replied:

"They are those who were given to backbiting and who aspersed people's honor and chastity." (Abu Dawud, Adab, 35/4878; Ahmad, III, 224)

❁

١٦٩. عَنِ ابْنِ عَبَّاسٍ رَضِيَ اللّٰهُ عَنْهُ قَالَ: خَرَجَ النَّبِيُّ صَلَّى اللّٰهُ عَلَيْهِ وَسَلَّمَ مِنْ بَعْضِ حِيطَانِ الْمَدِينَةِ فَسَمِعَ صَوْتَ إِنْسَانَيْنِ يُعَذَّبَانِ فِي قُبُورِهِمَا فَقَالَ:

«يُعَذَّبَانِ وَمَا يُعَذَّبَانِ فِي كَبِيرٍ وَإِنَّهُ لَكَبِيرٌ كَانَ أَحَدُهُمَا لَا يَسْتَتِرُ مِنَ الْبَوْلِ وَكَانَ الْآخَرُ يَمْشِي بِالنَّمِيمَةِ» ثُمَّ دَعَا بِجَرِيدَةٍ فَكَسَرَهَا بِكِسْرَتَيْنِ أَوْ ثِنْتَيْنِ فَجَعَلَ كِسْرَةً فِي قَبْرِ هٰذَا وَكِسْرَةً فِي قَبْرِ هٰذَا فَقَالَ:

«لَعَلَّهُ يُخَفَّفُ عَنْهُمَا مَا لَمْ يَيْبَسَا».

169. Ibn Abbas (r.a.) narrated:

Once the Prophet went through the grave-yards of Medina and heard the voices of two humans who were being tortured in their graves. The Prophet (pbuh) said:

"They are being punished because of a major sin that they did not think of it as a major sin, yet their sins are great. One of them used not to save himself from (being soiled with) the urine, and the other used to go about with calumnies."

Then the Prophet asked for a green palm tree leaf and split it into two pieces and placed one piece on each grave, saying:

"I hope that their punishment may be abated as long as these pieces of the leaf have not dried." (Bukhari, Adab, 49; Wudu, 55, 56; Janaiz, 82. Also see Muslim, Taharah, 111; Abu Dawud, Taharah, 11; Tirmidhi, Taharah, 53; Nasai, Taharah, 26; naiz, 116; Ibn Majah, Taharah, 26)

❁

١٧٠. عَنْ هَمَّامِ بْنِ الْحَارِثِ قَالَ: كُنَّا جُلُوسًا مَعَ حُذَيْفَةَ رَضِيَ اللّٰهُ عَنْهُ فِي الْمَسْجِدِ فَجَاءَ رَجُلٌ حَتّٰى جَلَسَ إِلَيْنَا فَقِيلَ لِحُذَيْفَةَ رَضِيَ اللّٰهُ عَنْهُ: إِنَّ هٰذَا يَرْفَعُ إِلَى السُّلْطَانِ أَشْيَاءَ فَقَالَ حُذَيْفَةُ رَضِيَ اللّٰهُ عَنْهُ إِرَادَةَ أَنْ يُسْمِعَهُ: سَمِعْتُ رَسُولَ اللّٰهِ صَلَّى اللّٰهُ عَلَيْهِ وَسَلَّمَ يَقُولُ:

«لَا يَدْخُلُ الْجَنَّةَ قَتَّاتٌ».

170. Hammam b. al-Harith (r.a.) narrated:

We were sitting with Hudhaifa (r.a.) in the mosque. A man came and sat along with us. It was said to Hudhaifa:

"This was the man who carried tales to the ruler."

Hudhaifa remarked with the intention of conveying to him:

"I have heard the Messenger of Allah (pbuh) saying:

"The tale-bearer will not enter Paradise." (Muslim, Iman, 170, 168, 169; Bukhari, Adab, 50; Also see Abu Dawud, Adab, 33; Tirmidhi, Birr, 79)

Explanations:

Since Almighty Allah loves His servants a lot, especially the believers, He protects them in every way such as their lives, wealth, and chastity. He announced backbiting as one of the major sins and prohibited it for this reason. By prohibiting backbiting, Almighty Allah protects even the hearts of His sinful subjects from getting hurt. This shows us how valuable the heart, the sacred place for the sight of Allah is. Even a more important reason for the prohibition of backbiting is that it destroys the friendship between people, and it endangers and destroys the most important foundations of social life such as peace and tranquility and feelings of friendship.

Our Almighty Lord tells with a blood-tingling expression that backbiting is an act that is harmful for one's intelligence, heart, conscience, and religion:

"O you who believe! Avoid suspicion as much (as possible): for suspicion in some cases is a sin: And spy not on each other behind their backs. Would any of you like to eat the flesh of his dead brother? Nay, you would abhor it...But fear Allah. For Allah is Oft-Returning, Most Merciful." (Al-Hujurat; 49:12)

Since backbiting is a sin that one can easily fall into, the preventions and punishments are discouraging and serious. For this reason, Almighty Allah gives one of the striking examples in the noble verse about backbiting.

Since those who are talked about are absent, they are defenseless and helpless just like the dead. When it comes to the position of those who perform the backbiting, it is same as disloyalty since he attacks his brother from the back in such a helpless position.

In the noble verse, by saying "Would any of you like?" attention is drawn to the fact that backbiting is something as distasteful as eating the flesh of one's dead brother, not to mention that eating live human flesh is itself impure and of course forbidden. What a mental, spiritual, and moral corruption it is to eat the rotten and wormy flesh of one's dead brother.

Backbiting is the name of the foolishness of transferring as one's own capital the sinful acts of those who one does not like. Sadi-i Shirazi says the following:

"When a sinner's goblet is full, the sins of this unfortunate person, whose book of deeds is dark, drag him to Hell. However, another one who does not want him to be alone there runs after him because of backbiting." (*Bostan*, p. 236)

Since backbiting people includes some of the worst spiritual illnesses such as self-importance, two-facedness, envy, and belittling the subjects of Allah, it arises the anger of Allah and causes damages to people in all directions. Sheyh Sadi also told about this fact:

"O generous and smart people; do not backbite anyone, be they evil or good! That is because if the person you have backbitten is really a bad person, you would make him your enemy. If the person you have backbitten is a good person, you would have done something bad.

If someone comes to you and says "so and so is a bad person," know that he is telling you his own fault. That is because when he only says "the act of so and so is this," he would need a proof. Just telling is not enough. He is not proving his words. His words are only backbiting. Thus, his backbiting is for sure. Backbiting is a major sin. Thus, his own words become evidence against him.

Should I tell you the right word: when you backbite, you are the evil one even if you tell the truth!..

Once, a person had backbitten someone. A scholar there told him:

"Do not bad mouth anyone with me! Do not make me think badly about you! That is because if you bad mouth someone, I would know you as the evil one. Also, I do not understand what good there will be from this bad mouthing. **Let's assume that you caused a decrease in his reputation by backbiting him, this reduction will not be added to your reputation!**" (*Bostan*, pp. 234-235)

Thus, a believer should control his tongue and watch his words. The criteria put by the Prophet (pbuh) are so wise:

"Talk what is good or keep quiet!" (Bukhari, Adab, 31, 85; Riqaq, 23; Muslim, Iman, 74; Luqata, 14)

"Those who keep quiet found salvation!" (Tirmidhi, Qiyamah, 50/2501; Darimi, Riqaq, 5)

The Messenger of Allah (pbuh) establishes how bad backbiting is **in our first hadith.** In order to teach the Noble Companions what backbiting is, the Messenger of Allah (pbuh) first asked a striking question to them and then drew the strict limits of backbiting:

"...talking about your brother in a manner which he would not like."

The things that are told may not be necessarily bad but if the person does not like these things to be said about him, then that is backbiting. Backbiting is based on whether the person likes the things that are said about him or not rather than the things that are said.

There is another issue that most people confuse, and the Prophet (pbuh) clearly explained it as:

"If (that failing) is actually found (in him) what you assert, you in fact backbit him, and if that is not in him it is a slander."

Thus, saying things such as "I am telling the truth", "I am saying what is substantial" or "I would say the same things to his face" cannot save one from backbiting.

The definition of backbiting (ghibah) is very wide. Expressing verbally or in writing, explaining with symbols, mimics or body language, imitating or even implying things about someone who is not present such as his physical structure, moral values, worships, wealth, children, relatives, his stuff, the way he walks or talks, or about his habits in such a way that he does not like are considered as backbiting. In other words, any word or act that is done in an absence of a Muslim that may hurt his heart is backbiting.

❁

A man who used to sit next to the Messenger of Allah (pbuh) stood up and left. However, he had difficulty when he was trying to stand up. After he left, some people said:

"So and so is very weak."

The Messenger of Allah (pbuh) said:

"You have eaten the flesh of your brother, you have backbit." (Haythami, VIII, 94)

❁

Abdullah b. Mas'ud (r.a.) narrated:

We were sitting with the Prophet (pbuh). A man stood up and left. After he left, someone bad mouthed him. Upon this, the Messenger of Allah (pbuh) said:

"Go and wash your mouth really well and clean the left pieces between your teeth!"

The man asked:

"What should I clean in between my teeth O the Messenger of Allah, as if I have eaten meat?!"

The Messenger of Allah (pbuh) replied:

"You have eaten the flesh of your brother." (Haythami, VIII, 94)

❀

Sheikh Sadi gives a wise example on this topic:

I had a duty at the Nizamiya Madrasa I used to attend conferences day and night. One day, I told to my master:

"My friend so and so envies me. When I explain the meaning of a hadith nicely, his heart fills with darkness!.."

My master, who had high moral values, got very angry when he heard this:

"This is very bad" he said and added "I did not like your friend to envy you. **However! Who told you that backbiting is something good? If he is on the way to Hell due to his jealousy, you will reach him from another way!.."** (*Bostan,* pp. 235-236)

❀

People should talk about others in their absence in such a way that they should be able to say the same things to their faces without hesitation and without breaking their hearts. If one abstains from the eyes looking at him and speaks differently to others' faces and from their backs, he should not forget that Omniscient Allah is present everywhere and at all times. He should pull himself together and abstain from Allah the Almighty at least as much as he abstains from the looks of others.

If what one is saying about the other person is not actually found in him, as our hadith expressed it, it is a slander and its punishment is ever greater. It is stated in a verse:

"And those who annoy believing men and women undeservedly bear (on themselves) a calumny and a glaring sin." (Al-Ahzab; 33:58)

Since backbiting and slandering are attacking others' rightful dues, asking Allah for forgiveness is not enough for getting forgiven. The Messenger of Allah (pbuh) said:

"Unless those who are backbitten forgive those who backbit them, the backbiter cannot be forgiven." (Haythami, VIII, 92)

Thus, one has to ask for forgiveness from Allah first by asking forgiveness from the person whom he backbit. Then, one has to pay expiation for the backbiting done and Mujahid, one of the scholars of Tabiin, expressed this fact saying:

"The expiation of eating the flesh of your brother is to praise him and pray good things for him."

On the other hand, it is not backbiting to talk about the faults of mischievous people who go beyond the limits of modesty and commit sins openly, oppressor administrators, and those who want to corrupt religion by mixing some innovations. Also, it is not backbiting to give directly relevant information about others to those who needs this information for reasons such as affinity, partnership, vicinity, conducting business, or entrusting something. That is because when the relevant information is not given in such cases, the other party would be harmed.

However, one must not fall into the traps of the carnal self on these matters. As a matter of fact, the carnal self always runs after some excuses that may make him look right.

In our second hadith, we are informed that backbiting by even one word is enough to pollute a sea. In the rest of the hadith, we are informed that the sin of talking about someone in a manner that he would not like it cannot be compensated.

Since the Prophet (pbuh) interrupted Aisha (r.anha), the Mother of Believers, we understand that as a believer we should not only avoid backbiting, but also should prevent others to commit this sin. One must not listen to backbiting that is being done in his presence and should interfere as much as he can.

It is said in a Noble verse that:

"And when they hear vain talk, they turn away therefrom and say: "To us our deeds, and to you yours; peace be to you: we seek not the ignorant."
(Qasas; 28:55, Al-Muminun; 23:3)

That is because no goodness comes from a backbiter. A wise man put it nicely:

"If someone comes to you and talks about another person, do not think that he will thank you and acknowledge your goodness!"

Thus, the one who prevents others from backbiting saves from getting harmed both himself, and the person who wants to backbite, and also the one who was going to be talked about.

The Messenger of Allah (pbuh) said:

"If anyone guards a believer from a hypocrite, Allah will send an angel who will guard his flesh on the Day of Resurrection from Hellfire; but if anyone attacks a Muslim saying something by which he wishes to disgrace him, he will be restrained by Allah on the bridge over Hell till he is acquitted of what he said." (Abu Dawud, Adab, 36/4883)

In our third hadith, by addressing as *"O community of people, who say their belief by their tongue but belief did not enter their hearts!"*, the Messenger of Allah (pbuh) pointed out that backbiting and searching for others' faults cannot be seen in a believer and this spiritual illness is a sign of hypocrisy.

Those who backbite about believers and search for their faults take the risk of facing opposition of Allah, the Lord of all universes. In this case, Allah will uncover their faults and bring shame on them even if they are in the middle of their houses.

According to what we have learned from other narrations, after the Messenger of Allah (pbuh) led the Noon Prayer, he turned towards the congregation in an angry fashion and even went up to a pulpit and loudly announced the hadith about backbiting and ensure that everyone heard the divine message about backbiting. (Tirmidhi, Birr, 85/2032; Haythami, VIII, 92)

The Messenger of Allah (pbuh) said in another hadith:

"Whoever blames his brother for his fault, he himself would not die before making the same fault." (Tirmidhi, Qiyama, 53/2505)

Our ancestors who experienced this hadith many times said "Don't laugh to your neighbor for you'll be in the same position."

In our forth hadith, the Messenger of Allah (pbuh) talked to the believers about the offensive odor of backbiting. According to some noble hadith, there are very bad smells, tastes, and shapes of sins.[223] If people could feel them, they would never come close to sinful acts. However, for the purpose of the test of Allah, these bad smells, tastes, and shapes are hidden from people. The Prophet (pbuh) informed us about them. Thus, what falls upon Muslims is fully trust the words of the Messenger of Allah and stay away from sinful acts.

Some people replied as follows to the question of "Why don't we smell the offensive odor of backbiting today?"

"In the Era of Happiness people used to pay extra attention to stay away from backbiting. If someone backbit from time to time, an offensive odor used to be felt. Since the sin of backbiting is being committed all the time in today's world, our senses got used this offensive odor, and so we do not feel it anymore."

In our fifth hadith, the punishment of backbiting in the hereafter is symbolically explained for us to realize better.

The act of scratching one's face and breast is a sign of extreme regret and sorrow due to a major trouble that he knowingly got himself into. In other words, those who backbite harm no one else but themselves, and prepare their own punishments. Thus, the punishment that they will be given in the Hereafter is shown as scratching their faces and their breasts with copper nails.

On the other hand, when the backbiting is heard by the brother who was backbiten, it brings shame on the backbiter and makes him blush by dishonoring him in the society. Thus, as backbiting does not befit Islam, it does not befit chivalry either.

Sadi-i Shirazi expressed this saying:

One day, someone said:

"Robbery is better than backbiting!.."

I thought that he made this analogy as a joke. I asked him:

---

223. See Bukhari, Ta'bir, 48; Abu Dawud, Adab, 35/4875; Tirmidhi, Birr, 46/1972; Qiyamat, 51/2502; Ahmad, III, 351; VI, 189; Haythami, II, 322, 324.

"You talked nonsense my friend. I think what you have said is weird. What good have you seen in robbery that you prefer it over backbiting?"

He replied:

"Those who commit robbery are brave people. When they see a caravan, they attack it with fury and they fight, struggle, and capture the caravan. They win and get their booty. They fill their pockets by earning money and stuff and live a prosperous life at least in this world. However, what shapeless, monkey-like, and sneaky backbiters do is to darken their book of deeds with backbiting and do not gain anything in return." *(Bostan, p. 235)*

The goal in this talk is not to belittle robbery but to explain the magnitude of wickedness and harms of backbiting in a sarcastic way.

Thus, when the backbiters realize that they did not gain anything in neither this world nor the hereafter, and see the punishment that they will receive, they will punish themselves with extreme remorse.

Another important matter about backbiting is that the person who became the subject of the backbiting should show the virtuousness of forgiving the backbiter. When the person who became the subject of backbiting forgives the backbiter, he will receive great divine rewards in the hereafter for being virtuous.

Encouraging this, one day the Messenger of Allah (pbuh) said:

"Can't anyone of you be like Abu Damdam?"

The Companions asked:

"Who is Abu Damdam?"

Our Noble Prophet replied:

"He was a member of a clan before your time. He used to say "I forgive those who abuse or backbite me." (Abu Dawud, Adab, 36/4887)

This is certainly the manifestation of the principle of "Tolerating the creatures due to the love for their Creator." In other words, mature believers who love Allah can forgive His subjects easily for the sake of Allah.

One of the magnanimous examples of virtue in this respect is Ulba b. Zaid (r.a.), a poor companion of the Prophet. When the Messenger of Allah (pbuh) called the help of Muslims in Tabuk Military Expedition, Ulba woke up for the night prayer and prayed and begged Allah. The next morning, he took the single piece of stuff that he owned and went to the Prophet. In a great spirit, he showed an example of virtue and altruism and said:

"O the Messenger of Allah! There is nothing that I can give as a sadaqah (alm). I donate this one piece of stuff that I have. I also forgive those who make me sad or talk behind me or make fun of me due to this!" (Ibn Hajar, *el-Isaba*, II, 500; Ibn Kathir, *es-Sire*, IV, 9; Waqidi, III, 994)

There are also people who make self-sacrifice to protect their neighbors from the sin of backbiting. One pious man said:

"I know people who do not put on new clothes thinking that his neighbors may get jealous and commit the sin of backbiting!"

In our sixth hadith, a major sin is mentioned that is similar to backbiting but worse than that. That sin is to cause mischief and disorder by being a talebearer between people. This sin which is also known in popular language as "to make mischief" or "to disunite" differs from backbiting since the intention is to destroy the friendship between two people.

The talebearers are called "*nammam*" and "*kattat*" in the hadith. Both of these words almost mean the same thing but with a nuance. In this case, ***nammam*** refers to those who tell the things that are spoken in an assembly that he was present as well. ***Kattat*** on the other hand refers to those who listen to others secretly and then tell what is being told to others.

As can be understood from the hadith, people take this wicked sin lightly and consider it unimportant. However, since being a talebearer causes mischief and disorder, it is a major sin. That is because it is told in the Nobel Qur'an that causing mischief and disorder is worse than killing someone.[224] For this reason, being a talebearer leads to severe punishment in the Hereafter and causes one to go to Hell.[225]

---

224. Al-Baqarah; 2:191, 217.
225. In the sixth hadith, apart from tale-bearing, the Messenger of Allah (pbuh) also talked about not saving oneself from (being soiled with) the urine. Some people urinate standing up and not pay attention to their hygiene, and take this issue lightly. Especially, in today's restrooms where the base is covered with concrete or porcelain, the urine splashes on them. As a matter of fact, this filth does not befit a Muslim who appears before his Lord five times a day and who is the symbol of purity. A Muslim should respond to either call of the nature nicely and in a sitting position and then should clean himself without getting a drop of filth to his

As a matter of fact, **in our seventh hadith,** we are informed that talebearers will not enter into Paradise.

As it can be understood from the hadith, those who commit the sin of talebearing among the Muslims will not go to Paradise at first. If they are forgiven, they will first go to Hell and receive punishment for their sins and then will enter the Paradise. That is because sinner Muslims will not be deprived of Paradise forever as the disbelievers will be.

On the other hand, those who inform the administrators about what the general public is saying with the intention of causing disorder are also included in the definition of tale bearing.

i. Oppression

١٧١ . عَنْ أَبِي ذَرٍّ رَضِيَ اللهُ عَنْهُ عَنِ النَّبِيِّ صَلَّى اللهُ عَلَيْهِ وَسَلَّمَ فِيمَا رَوَى عَنِ اللهِ تَبَارَكَ وَتَعَالَى أَنَّهُ قَالَ:

«يَا عِبَادِي إِنِّي حَرَّمْتُ الظُّلْمَ عَلَى نَفْسِي وَجَعَلْتُهُ بَيْنكُمْ مُحَرَّمًا فَلَا تَظَالَمُوا».

171. Abu Dhar (r.a.) reported Allah's Messenger (pbuh) as saying that Allah, the Exalted and Glorious, said:

"My servants! I have made oppression unlawful for Me and unlawful for you, so do not commit oppression against one another!..." (Muslim, Birr, 55)

---

cloths. Otherwise, when one's clothes get filthy, one endangers the validity of his worships. The Messenger of Allah (pbuh) said the following in order to discourage from this:
"The majority of the suffering in grave will be the result of not avoiding impurity properly." (Ibn Majah, Taharat, 26)
The fact that the Prophet (pbuh) placed a green palm tree leaf on a grave and hoped for their punishment to be abated is a sign of his profound mercy and affection for his followers. By doing this, our Master the Prophet also encouraged us to plant and keep the grave yards green.

١٧٢. عَنْ أَبِي مُوسَى رَضِيَ اللهُ تَعَالَى عَنْهُ قَالَ: قَالَ رَسُولُ اللهِ صَلَّى اللهُ عَلَيْهِ وَسَلَّمَ:

«إِنَّ اللهَ لَيُمْلِي لِلظَّالِمِ حَتَّى إِذَا أَخَذَهُ لَمْ يُفْلِتْهُ» قَالَ ثُمَّ قَرَأَ:

(وَكَذٰلِكَ اَخْذُ رَبِّكَ اِذَا اَخَذَ الْقُرٰى وَهِيَ ظَالِمَةٌ اِنَّ اَخْذَهُ اَلِيمٌ شَدِيدٌ).

172. Abu Musa (r.a.) narrated: The Messenger of Allah (pbuh) said:

"Allah gives respite to the oppressor, but when He takes him over, He never releases him."

Then he recited the following verse:

"Such is the seizure of your Lord when He seizes (population of) towns in the midst of their wrong: Painful indeed, and severe is His seizure!" (Al-Hud; 11:102) (Bukhari, Tafsir, 11/5; Muslim, Birr, 61. Also see Tirmidhi Tafsir, 11; Ibn Majah, Fitan, 22)

❦

١٧٣. عَنْ جَابِرِ بْنِ عَبْدِ اللهِ رَضِيَ اللهُ عَنْهُ أَنَّ رَسُولَ اللهِ صَلَّى اللهُ عَلَيْهِ وَسَلَّمَ قَالَ:

«اتَّقُوا الظُّلْمَ فَإِنَّ الظُّلْمَ ظُلُمَاتٌ يَوْمَ الْقِيَامَةِ وَاتَّقُوا الشُّحَّ فَإِنَّ الشُّحَّ أَهْلَكَ مَنْ كَانَ قَبْلَكُمْ حَمَلَهُمْ عَلَى أَنْ سَفَكُوا دِمَاءَهُمْ وَاسْتَحَلُّوا مَحَارِمَهُمْ».

173. Jabir (r.a.) narrated that the Messenger of Allah (pbuh) said:

"Be on your guard against committing oppression, for oppression is darkness on the Day of Resurrection, and be on your guard against miserliness for miserliness destroyed those who were before you, as it incited them to shed blood

and make lawful what was unlawful for them." (Muslim, Birr, 56; Bukhari, *al-Adab al-mufrad*, no: 483. Also see Ahmad, II, 92, 136; Hakim, I, 55/26)

﷽

١٧٤. عَنْ أَبِي سَلَمَةَ رَضِيَ اللهُ عَنْهُ أَنَّهُ كَانَتْ بَيْنَهُ وَبَيْنَ أُنَاسٍ خُصُومَةٌ فَذَكَرَ لِعَائِشَةَ رَضِيَ اللهُ عَنْهَا فَقَالَتْ لَهُ:

«يَا أَبَا سَلَمَةَ! اجْتَنِبِ الْأَرْضَ فَإِنَّ النَّبِيَّ صَلَّى اللهُ عَلَيْهِ وَسَلَّمَ قَالَ:

«مَنْ ظَلَمَ قِيدَ شِبْرٍ مِنَ الْأَرْضِ طُوِّقَهُ مِنْ سَبْعِ أَرَضِينَ».

174. It is narrated from Abu Salama b. Abdurrahman that there was a dispute between him and some people from his tribe (about a piece of land). When he told Aisha, the Mother of Believers, about it, she said:

"O Abu Salama! Avoid taking the land unjustly! I heard the Prophet saying:

"Whoever usurps even one span of the land of somebody, his neck will be encircled with it down the seven earths." (Bukhari, Mazalim, 13; Bad' al-khalk, 2; Muslim, Musaqat, 139-142. Also see. Tirmidhi, Diyat, 21)

﷽

١٧٥. عَنْ أَبِي هُرَيْرَةَ رَضِيَ اللهُ عَنْهُ أَنَّ رَسُولَ اللهِ صَلَّى اللهُ عَلَيْهِ وَسَلَّمَ قَالَ:

«لَتُؤَدُّنَّ الْحُقُوقَ إِلَى أَهْلِهَا يَوْمَ الْقِيَامَةِ حَتَّى يُقَادَ لِلشَّاةِ الْجَلْحَاءِ مِنَ الشَّاةِ الْقَرْنَاءِ».

175. It is narrated from Abu Huraira (r.a.) that the Messenger of Allah (pbuh) said:

"The claimants would get their claims on the Day of Resurrection so much so that the hornless sheep would get its (eye-to-eye kind of) claim from the horned sheep." (Muslim, Birr, 60. Also see Tirmidhi, Qiyamah, 2/2420; Ahmad, II, 235, 302, 372, 411)

Explanations:

Oppression is the opposite of justice and it means not doing something as it is supposed to be done and not paying its right due. Oppression also refers to acting unjustly, or disposing of others' rights unjustly and exceeding one's boundaries.

In many of the noble verses of the Qur'an, Almighty Allah called those who do not believe in Him, who do not acknowledge His messengers, who do not abide by the Qur'an and do not obey its commands and commit sins oppressors. (See Al-Baqarah; 2:229, 254; Al-Maidah; 5:45; Al-Furqan; 25:8)

Every unjust conduct is a kind of oppression. Seizing others' wealth or attacking their honor and chastity are also oppression. Getting the rights of others by false oaths or with any other method that is forbidden is also oppression. Committing sins or hostility is oppression. Disputing in order to make oneself look right and others wrong or trying to belittle others are oppression. Blocking the streets by sitting or placing objects and making it difficult for others to pass is definitely oppression. *"It is oppression for the rich to postpone paying off their debt."*[226] Not taking lessons from experiences is also a kind of oppression. Causing or facilitating oppression is also oppression.

In our first hadith, we are told that oppression is prohibited (haram) by Almighty Allah.

Allah the Exalted informs us that He is exempt and away from oppression. As a matter of fact, He is Just and "al-Adl" (The just one) is one of His divine attribues. (Tirmidhi, Daawat, 82/3507)

In other words, He is the source of justice and all of His works are based on full justice.

Since Almighty Lord does not like and approve oppression, He informed us that He will never be unjust or oppress His subjects. It is said in the Nobel Qur'an:

---

226. Bukhari, Hawalah, 1, 2; Istiqraz, 12; Muslim, Musaqat, 33; Abu Dawud, Buyu', 10; Tirmidhi, Buyu', 68; Nasai, Buyu', 100, 101; Ibn Majah, Sadaqat, 8.

"Say: "Short is the enjoyment of this world: the Hereafter is the best for those who do right: Never will you be dealt with unjustly in the very least!" (An-Nisa; 4:77)

"But how (will they fare) when we gather them together against a day about which there is no doubt, and each soul will be paid out just what it has earned, without (favor or) injustice?" (Al-i Imran; 3:25)

"This is because of the (unrighteous deeds) which your hands sent on before you: For Allah never harms those who serve Him." (Al-i Imran; 3:182) (Al-Hajj; 22:10) (Al-Anfal; 8:51)

"If any do deeds of righteousness, - be they male or female - and have faith, they will enter Heaven, and not the least injustice will be done to them." (Al-Nisa; 4:124)

Since Almighty Allah is the Lord of all the universes and there is no other Creator than Him, oppression is not even a matter of discussion for Allah. In other words, Almighty Allah is free from all kinds of oppression and injustice at all times.

Almighty Allah does not want His subjects to be cruel to each other. As a matter of fact, He informs us in the Noble Qur'an that He does not like oppressors and will not direct them to the right path. (Al-i Imran; 3:86, 140)

Thus, a Muslim should be just when he is judging, measuring, or testifying, be the other party is his relative or a stranger, his friend or an enemy, a wealthy person or a poor one, no matter if he is angry or relaxed, in other words, at all times and under all circumstances, a Muslim shouldn't make concessions about justice by being overpowered by his feelings. (An-Nisa; 4:135; Al-Maidah; 5:8; Haythami, I, 90)

If a Muslim becomes just and acts justly in everything, he gains the love of Almighty Allah. (Al-Hujurat; 49:9)

On the other hand, one must not be deceived by seeing the oppressors in comfort in this world for a short period of time. As a matter of fact, Allah gives them some time to repent, to ask for forgiveness, and to quit being cruel. As expressed **in our second hadith**, Allah will severely seize them at the end of this period if they do not start behaving wiser. Then, it is not possible for them to run away. That is because the seizure of our Almighty Lord is very painful and severe.

Almighty Allah does not hurry in implementing the punishments of His subjects due to His mercy towards them. He gives them time to ask for forgiveness for their oppression and wrong deeds. He even leaves most of their punishments to the Hereafter. Oppressors should never be deceived by this. They should not think that they will get away with what they have done and they should come to their senses as soon as possible. They should know that "Allah delays but He never neglects". In other words, He gives them some extra time but implements the punishment that should be done when the time comes. Then, oppressors should know that they have no rights to raise an objection or make excuses.

This is expressed in several noble verses as:

"And to how many populations did I give respite, which was given to wrong-doing? In the end I punished them. To me is the destination (of all)." (Al-Hajj; 22:48)

"Think not that Allah does not heed the deeds of those who do wrong! He but gives them respite against a Day when the eyes will fixedly stare in horror." (Ibrahim; 14:42)

Oppression cannot go forever; it ends with misery. No matter who does the oppression, he will receive its punishment. While it is not even a matter of discussion about prophets to be oppressors, even they would have received their punishments if they had oppressed. The following incident, which expresses this fact and shows how the Prophet used to avoid oppression, is so exemplary:

Suhail b. Amr was the speaker of the people of Quraish. In a time period when literature was at its peak and when people would start or end wars depending on speeches of their speakers, Suhail spoke out against Islam in every chance he got and provoked people. This person was taken as a prisoner in the Battle of Badr.

Umar (r.a.) said:

"O Messenger of Allah! Let me pull Suhail's front teeth off so that his tongue will roll out! Thus he will not be able to speak against you and Islam anytime and anywhere from now on!"

The Messenger of Allah (pbuh) said:

"O Umar! Leave him alone. I cannot cause this kind of harm to his body parts. If I did, even if I am a Prophet, Allah would punish me with the same thing. Don't hasten for there would come a time when he would give a speech in a place where you would admire him and be happy." (Ibn Hisham, II, 293)[227]

Let's say, even if a prophet would receive a punishment for oppression, it is impossible to understand in what people trust when they are found in oppression! As a matter of fact, our Almighty Lord clearly says:

"Certain it is that the wrong-doers will not prosper." (Qasas; 28:37)

The end of cruel people is misery. History is like a graveyard of people and societies who were ruined due to their oppressions. As a matter of fact, most of such people's sad end is told in the Noble Qur'an for us to take a lesson.

Almighty Allah says:

"…will any be destroyed except those who do wrong?" (Al-An'am; 6:47)

The Prophet informs us that oppression will definitely be punished by saying:

"There is no sin more fitted to have punishment meted out by Allah to its perpetrator in advance in this world along with what He stores up for him in the

---

227. When the time came, Suhail (r.a.) made that admirable speech that our Master the Prophet miraculously foresaw. Upon the passing of our Master the Pride of the Universe, at a time when conversion out of Islam were being seen in some localities, Mecca was in turmoil and its young governor Attab b. Asid was scared and hiding, Suhayl (ra) stood up beside the Ka'bah and gave a speech and said:
"Whoever accepted Muhammad (pbuh) as his deity should know that he passed away. Allah, on the other hand, is al-Hayy (The Living) and never passes away. O the community of Quraish! You have been the last of those embracing Islam, at least don't be the first of apostates. I swear to God I know well that this religion will stay standing up so long as the rise and setting of the moon continues. Don't let this person who is one of you deceive you. For sure, he also knows what I know in this matter, but his jealousy towards the Sons of Hashim hardens his heart.
O People! I am the wealthiest of the people of Quraish. You should respect your ruler! Pay your zakat to him. If Islam does not prevail until the end, I guarantee to pay back the mandatory alms you have paid." And could not handle himself and started crying.
When Suhayl finished his speech, people had calmed down.
When Umar (r.a.) heard this speech that Suhail gave, he recalled the words of our Master the Messenger of Allah, his eyes got wet and said: "Once again, I testify that you are the Messenger of Allah, O Messenger of Allah!" (Ibn Hisham, IV, 346; Waqidi, I, 107; Balazuri, I, 303-304; Ibn Abd al-Barr, II, 669-671; Hakim, III, 318/5228)

next world than oppression and severing ties of relationship." (Abu Dawud, Adab, 43/4902; Tirmidhi, Qiyamah, 57; Ibn Majah, Zuhd, 23)

The real sad ends of the oppressors will be in the afterlife. The noble verse informs us that oppressors will be left in Hell:

"But We shall save those who guarded against evil, and We shall leave the wrong-doers therein, (humbled) to their knees." (Maryam; 19:72)

Thus, one must immediately quit being an oppressor and ask for forgiveness from the oppressed ones. There is no other way for salvation. The Messenger of Allah (pbuh) warns his followers before the Day of Judgment when justice will be complete and says:

"Whoever has oppressed another person concerning his reputation or chastity or wealth, he should beg him to forgive him before the Day of Resurrection when there will be no money (to compensate for wrong deeds), but if he has good deeds, those good deeds will be taken from him according to his oppression which he has done, and if he has no good deeds, the sins of the oppressed person will be loaded on him." (Bukhari, Mazalim, 10; Riqaq, 48)

Indeed, this is a real failure. It means that the eternal darkness has begun for those in this situation. As a matter of fact, **in our third hadith**, we are told that oppression will be darkness upon darkness on the oppressor in the Day of Judgment. That is because oppressors had darkened the lives of those that they oppressed and made their lives miserable. The oppressors did not know that they were darkening their own lives by acting in such a way! They are indeed in such a wrong way!

As a matter of fact, Almighty Allah has warned them in this world but they didn't get the advice. While the following verses of the Qur'an were being recited, they did not want to listen:

"…it is not Allah that hath wronged them, but they wrong themselves." (Al-i Imran; 3:117)

"… but the Transgressors are in manifest error." (Luqman; 31:11)

On the Day of Judgment, it will be too late for anything and there won't be anything to hold on to. That day:

"No intimate friend nor intercessor will the wrong-doers have, who could be listened to." (Al-Mu'min; 40:18)

That day;

"…but the wrong-doers have no helpers." (Al-Baqarah; 2:270, Al-Hajj; 22:71)

In the second part of our hadith, stinginess is also prohibited. That is because being stingy and miserly is among the causes of oppression. Oppression and being stingy are among the primary causes of major sins such as killing someone, regarding the things that Allah forbids as permissible, and deviation from the religion.

Our forth hadith tells us the afterlife punishment for an oppression related to a land issue. Just like in the case of other kinds of oppressions, the punishment of getting someone's land by force is also severe and harsh.

The size of the land seized by force is not important. Even if it is as small as a hand span, it is enough to regard that person as an oppressor and cause him to get severe punishment. Even if it seems like the size of a hand span, there are seven layers under that land. Our hadith draws the best example to express what oppression is. A negligible oppression in the eyes of an oppressor could actually be very important and may cause a deep harm. As oppression causes people to be in deep sorrow in this world and drags them to utter darkness in the hereafter.

Being unjust about the land issues is a common type of oppression. Many lives are taken and families are shattered because of a small piece of land. For this reason the Messenger of Allah (pbuh) drew our attention to this fact and stated that its punishment will be severe.

In our fifth hadith, we are told that none of the acts of oppression will be unreciprocated no matter how small they are, and all the rights will be returned to their rightful owners. The Messenger of Allah (pbuh) gave an example for us to understand this fact well by saying that even the hornless sheep would get its claim from the horned sheep which hit it.

Even the animals that are not liable from their actions would pay for their unjust acts, one should think about how just and fair the treatment of humans who are liable for all of their acts will be.

These noble sayings of the Prophet (pbuh) which warn the oppressors also provide consolation for the oppressed. While being patient in despair in this world, they seek refuge in Allah and wait for the day that scales of justice will be set. The following event is a good example of this:

Jafar al-Tayyar (r.a.) was one of the earliest Muslims. He immigrated to Ethiopia with his wife running away from the oppression of the idolaters in Mecca. He lived there for years. However, he returned to Medina in the 7th year of Hijra. One day, when the Messenger of Allah asked him to narrate some of the attention grabbing moments that he had witnessed in Ethiopia, he told the following memory:

"One day we were sitting when an old nun passed by. There was a big water jug on her head. A young man pushed this poor woman from her back. The woman fell on her knees and the water jug got broken. The nun stood up and said looking at the young man:

"O poor oppressor! You will see how this matter between us will be taken care of when Allah sets forth the Throne, when everyone ever lived gathers, when hands and feet start to confess everything they did, and when the claim of the oppressed gets taken away from the oppressor!"

When the Prophet heard this, he smiled meaningfully and said:

"The woman had told the truth. Yes, she had told the truth. How could Allah purify a society where the claims of the weak are not taken from the oppressors?" (Ibn Majah, Fitan, 20; Abu Ya'la, *Musnad,* IV, 7-8; Ibn Hibban, XI, 443-444)

Our ancestors pointed probably out this fact when they said "If the oppressor has his oppression, the oppressed has his Allah."

In short, the oppressor is actually in a pitiful situation as opposed to how he may seem in this world. It is due to human dignity to help them. The best way to help them is to stop their oppression.

One day, the Messenger of Allah (pbuh) said:

"Help your brother, whether he is an oppressor or he is an oppressed one!"

Someone asked:

"O Messenger of Allah! It is all right to help him if he is the oppressed, but how should we help him if he is the oppressor?"

The Messenger of Allah (pbuh) said:

"By preventing him from oppressing others. For sure this is being helpful to him." (Bukhari, Mazalim, 4; Iqrah, 6. Also see Tirmidhi, Fitan, 68)

j. Arrogance and continuously reminding favors

١٧٦. عَنْ أَبِي ذَرٍّ رَضِيَ اللهُ عَنْهُ عَنِ النَّبِيِّ صَلَّى اللهُ عَلَيْهِ وَسَلَّمَ قَالَ:

«ثَلَاثَةٌ لَا يُكَلِّمُهُمُ اللهُ يَوْمَ الْقِيَامَةِ وَلَا يَنْظُرُ إِلَيْهِمْ وَلَا يُزَكِّيهِمْ وَلَهُمْ عَذَابٌ أَلِيمٌ» قَالَ: فَقَرَأَهَا رَسُولُ اللهِ صَلَّى اللهُ عَلَيْهِ وَسَلَّمَ ثَلَاثَ مَرَّاتٍ. قَالَ أَبُو ذَرٍّ:

«خَابُوا وَخَسِرُوا، مَنْ هُمْ يَا رَسُولَ اللهِ؟» قَالَ:

«الْمُسْبِلُ وَالْمَنَّانُ وَالْمُنَفِّقُ سِلْعَتَهُ بِالْحَلِفِ الْكَاذِبِ».

176. Abu Dhar (r.a.) narrated that the Messenger of Allah (pbuh) said:

"There are three types of (persons) with whom Allah would neither speak on the Day of Resurrection, nor would look at them nor would absolve them and there is a painful chastisement for them."

The narrator said:

The Messenger of Allah (pbuh) repeated this sentence three times. Then Abu Dharr (r.a.) asked:

"Then, they completely failed and lost; who are these persons, O Messenger of Allah?

The Noble Prophet (pbuh) answered:

"They are the dragger of lower garment, the bestower of gift who does not give anything but by laying obligation on him, and the seller of goods by taking false oath." (Muslim, Iman, 171. Also see Abu Dawud, Libas, 25/4087; Tirmidhi, Buyu, 5/1211; Nasai, Zakat, 69; Buyu, 5; Zinet, 103; Ibn Majah, Ticarat, 30)

❁

١٧٧. عَنْ سَلَمَةَ بْنِ الْأَكْوَعِ رَضِيَ اللهُ عَنْهُ قَالَ: قَالَ رَسُولُ اللهِ
صَلَّى اللهُ عَلَيْهِ وَسَلَّمَ:

«لَا يَزَالُ الرَّجُلُ يَذْهَبُ بِنَفْسِهِ حَتَّى يُكْتَبَ فِي الْجَبَّارِينَ فَيُصِيبُهُ
مَا أَصَابَهُمْ».

177. Salama b. Aqwa' (r.a.) narrated that the Messenger of Allah (pbuh) said:

"A person who keeps being arrogant finally gets listed among the oppressors and tyrants. Thus the punishment of those would be given to him as well." (Tirmidhi, Birr, 61/2000)

❀

١٧٨. عَنْ حَارِثَةَ بْنِ وَهْبِ الْخُزَاعِيِّ رَضِيَ اللهُ عَنْهُ عَنِ النَّبِيِّ
صَلَّى اللهُ عَلَيْهِ وَسَلَّمَ قَالَ:

«أَلَا أُخْبِرُكُمْ بِأَهْلِ الْجَنَّةِ: كُلُّ ضَعِيفٍ مُتَضَاعِفٍ لَوْ أَقْسَمَ عَلَى اللهِ
لَأَبَرَّهُ، أَلَا أُخْبِرُكُمْ بِأَهْلِ النَّارِ كُلُّ عُتُلٍّ جَوَّاظٍ مُسْتَكْبِرٍ».

178. It is narrated from Haritha b. Wahb al-Khuzai (r.a.) that the Messenger of Allah (pbuh) said:

"Shall I inform you about the people of Paradise? They comprise every obscure unimportant humble person, and if he takes Allah's Oath that he will do that thing, Allah will fulfill his oath (by doing that).

Shall I inform you about the people of the Fire? They comprise every cruel, violent, proud and conceited person." (Bukhari, Adab, 61; Ayman, 9; Tafsir, 68/1; Muslim, Janna, 47. Also see Tirmidhi, Jahannam, 13; Ibn Majah, Zuhd, 4)

❀

١٧٩. عَنْ عَمْرِو بْنِ شُعَيْبٍ عَنْ أَبِيهِ عَنْ جَدِّهِ عَنِ النَّبِيِّ صَلَّى اللهُ
عَلَيْهِ وَسَلَّمَ قَالَ:

«يُحْشَرُ الْمُتَكَبِّرُونَ يَوْمَ الْقِيَامَةِ أَمْثَالَ الذَّرِّ فِي صُوَرِ الرِّجَالِ يَغْشَاهُمُ
الذُّلُّ مِنْ كُلِّ مَكَانٍ فَيُسَاقُونَ إِلَى سِجْنٍ فِي جَهَنَّمَ يُسَمَّى بُولَسَ تَعْلُوهُمْ
نَارُ الْأَنْيَارِ يُسْقَوْنَ مِنْ عُصَارَةِ أَهْلِ النَّارِ طِينَةَ الْخَبَالِ».

179. It was narrated from 'Amr ibn Shu'ayb via his father and grandfather that the Noble Prophet (pbuh) said:

"On the Day of Resurrection, the arrogant will be resurrected in the form of men with the size of small red ants. Humiliation will overwhelm them from all sides. They will be driven to a prison in Hell called Bawlas, with the hottest fire rising over them, and they will be given to drink of the juice of the inhabitants of Hell, which is blood, pus, and other discharges which are called tinat al-khabaal."
(Tirmidhi, Qiyamah, 47/2492; Ahmad, II, 179; Bukhari, *al-Adab al-mufrad*, no: 557)

Explanations:

There are certain major sins that on the Day of Judgment, Almighty Allah will not speak to those who commit them, neither look at their faces, nor will acquit them.

Indeed, the unfortunate who fell into this situation are, just like Abu Dhar explained, in complete loss and disappointment and had been severely punished. As a result, such people receive the anger of Allah and the severe punishment in Hell.

That Almighty Allah will not speak to a person means that He will not favor that person and will not receive and be pleased with that person as His righteous subjects, and He will not tell him things that will benefit or please that person.

Almighty Allah's not looking at someone and not facing him means that He will not treat them with His favor and mercy.

Also, Almighty Allah's not acquitting someone means that He will not purify that person from the dirt of the sins and evil that will lead him to be punished.

Losers who will be punished so severely are the ones who are arrogant bestowers of gift who do not give anything but by laying obligation on others, and who try to sell commercial goods at a good price by taking false oaths.

Arrogance is one of major sins that Allah fully disliked and strictly prohibited. Almighty Allah commands as follows:

"And swell not your cheek (for pride) at men, nor walk in insolence through the earth; for Allah loves not any arrogant boaster." (Luqman; 31:18)

"Nor walk on the earth with insolence!" (Al-Isra; 17:37)

Greatness is an attribute that is unique to Allah. Arrogance of a person is trying to see in himself a characteristic that belongs only to Allah, and as such, it is extremely wrong and shows that the person does not know his limits. Indeed, the following characteristics of humans, which are so obvious that they cannot be denied, keep presenting human imperfections: incapability, weakness, erring, forgetfulness, ignorance, oppression and cruelty, hurrying, miserliness, selfishness, and ingratitude… There is nothing that humans can be proud of per the phases of creation and the way their lives end. So, arrogance is not a behavior that befits them.

If Allah the Exalted gives some material and spiritual bounties to someone, that person should not fall into pride and arrogance but should rather thank Almighty Allah. Indeed, humbleness and gratitude are what befit to being a creation and subject of Allah. A servant's scorn and contempt of persons that were subjected to less blessings than he had would be disrespectful towards Almighty Allah before anything else.

Arrogance is one of the biggest calamities of the carnal self. A person who is caught by arrogance and fell in love with fame would commit many cruelties and oppression but would not even become aware of these. As a result, he lowers himself and falls into embarrassing situations and becomes one of the oppressors. Indeed, in the second noble hadith it is said that:

"A person who keeps being arrogant finally gets listed among the oppressors and tyrants."

The arrogance of a person and seeing himself as superior to others, his admiration of himself, and strengthening his carnal self into believing that he is better than everybody else leads him to a sad end. If a person advances in this state of arrogance and vanity, at the end he is recorded in the circle of oppressors and arrogants and falls to the lower of lows with them. The punishment given to Pharaoh, Qarun, and Haman is also given to that person.

The arrogant people are denounced in many verses of the Noble Qur'an. Arrogance is generally used to express disbelief and rebellion to Allah. People turn away from worship because of their arrogance and do not obey His commands and listen to His prophets. On the other hand, arrogance is the distinguishing characteristics of Satan. When the term arrogance is mentioned Satan comes to mind, who rebelled Allah by being arrogant and unable to overcome his pride and not prostrating to Adam (pbuh).

"...for Allah loves not the arrogant, the vainglorious." (An-Nisa; 4:36) (Al-Nahl; 16:23) (Al-Hadid; 57:23)

As a matter of fact, since Qarun trusted and boasted about his fortune whose keys could be carried only by a group of very strong people, and performed various wrong and mischievous deeds, Allah caused the earth to swallow him up and his fortune. (Qasas; 28:79-82)

Arrogance originates from ignorance and true scholars are never conceited. In fact, arrogant people can neither receive knowledge[228] nor can serve any good.

Almighty Allah says:

"Those who behave arrogantly on the earth in defiance of right - them will I turn away from My signs." (Al-Araf; 7:146)

Mawlana Jalaladdin Rumi says

"Would a stone turn green in spring? Be humble like the soil so that colorful roses and flowers grow up from you!"

Arrogance and being conceited not only become apparent in one's feelings and thoughts but also in his attitudes, behaviors, and dresses. If it is done with such intention, wearing a long dress that its skirt touches the ground can be a manifestation of arrogance.

---

228. Bukhari, al-'Ilm, 50.

It is said in a noble hadith that:

"Allah will not look, on the Day of Resurrection at the person who drags his garment (behind him) out of conceit." (Bukhari, Libas, 1, 2, 5; Fadail al-Sahaba, 5; Muslim, Libas, 42-48)

However, there is no harm in wearing nice dresses and shoes without falling into the feeling of arrogance. If wearing beautiful dresses cause one to be arrogant or conceited, then they become harmful. A person should wear nice dresses not to be arrogant, or make everyone feel that he is different, or to swagger but rather to make sure that bounties given by Allah are shown on him and to than thank His blessings. When someone wears a nice and new dress, he should praise the Lord per our Master's advice and donate the extra clothes to the needy. (Tirmidhi, Daawat, 107/3560)

Muslim scholars say that the way to dress in compliance with the traditions of the Prophet (pbuh) is to wear the dress down to one's legs, and they also find it acceptable if it stretches down to heels. However, even if there is no thought of arrogance, they find it reproachable (makruh) if the clothes fall below the heels because that would be against the prohibition of the Messenger of Allah.

Our third hadith informs us that the conceited people will go to Hell. This is because arrogance causes many bad attributes and evil acts. Then the end of this road is undoubtedly Hell. For this reason in order to discourage from arrogance the Messenger of Allah (pbuh) said:

"He who has in his heart the weight of a mustard seed of pride shall not enter Paradise." (Muslim, Iman, 147-149; Tirmidhi, Birr, 61/1998)

Also, in another the Messenger of Allah informed us that Hell boasts to Paradise by saying:

"The haughty and the proud would find abode in me." (Muslim, Jannah, 34; Bukhari, Tafsir, 50/1; Tawhid, 25; Tirmidhi, Jannah, 22)

This is because the bounties of the land of the Hereafter are favored upon those who conduct their servanthood in humility not those who are conceited.

Almighty Allah commands as follows:

"That home of the Hereafter We shall give to those who intend not high- handedness or mischief on earth: and the end is (best) for the righteous." (Qasas; 28:83)

In our fourth hadith, the Messenger of Allah (pbuh) describes the state of the conceited people in the Hereafter. Since they unjustly boasted in the world, the arrogant people will receive **"a fitting recompense"**[229] in the Hereafter. Just as it is necessary to bend it in the reverse direction to straighten a curved stick, in order to purify the arrogant people from this evil characteristic, it is necessary to humiliate and lower them. So, the arrogant people in the world will be as small as ants in the Hereafter even though they look like humans in form and stature. They will be turned into extremely servile and contemptible beings, and since Allah did not value them at all, people will step over them and move on and will continue to crush them until the rights of all of the people of the Day of Judgment are accounted for. (Haythami, X, 334)

The fire that surrounds them at last, "the mother of all fires," is so hot that it burns other fires just like normal fire burns wood. When explaining this fire, the commentators point out the following noble verse:

"Who will enter the Great Fire, in which they will then neither die nor live." (Al-A'la; 87:12-13)

Some scholars say that the rhetoric in these sayings of the Prophet (pbuh) is figurative.

One of the greater sins is to taunt someone by reminding a favor done to him. On the Day of Judgment, the people who will be second in loss only to oppressors are the people who taunt others by reminding the favors that they did and burdening people with indebtedness. The person to whom a favor is granted is already squashed in his heart. İn addition to this, taunting him by reminding the favor is the worst spiritual torment that he can be subjected to. So, being in such behavior is one of the great sins that Allah the Almighty would never be content with.

On the other hand, the ugliness of taunting someone by reminding a previously done favor is so obvious that it does not require an explanation and it is accepted by everyone.

---

229. An-Naba'; 78/26.

God Almighty states as follows that taunting someone by reminding a previous favor does not befit a Muslim and is a sign of hypocrisy and completely nullifies the performed good deed:

"O you who believe! Cancel not your charity by reminders of your generosity or by injury, like those who spend their substance to be seen of men, but believe neither in Allah nor in the Last Day. They are in parable like a hard, barren rock, on which is a little soil: on it falls heavy rain, which leaves it (Just) a bare stone. They will be able to do nothing with aught they have earned. And Allah guide not those who reject faith." (Al-Baqarah; 2:264)

With this example, our Exalted Lord beautifully described the inner worlds of such cold-hearted people who taunt others by reminding their previous favors.

In another noble verse, this situation is explained as follows:

"Those who spend their substance in the cause of Allah, and follow not up their gifts with reminders of their generosity or with injury, for them their reward is with their Lord: on them shall be no fear, nor shall they grieve." (Al-Baqarah; 2:262)

The Messenger of Allah (pbuh) informed us that the people who taunt others by reminding their previous favors will not enter paradise. (Nasai, Zakat, 69/2560)

Of course, these expressions are to discourage from such sins. If the arrogant person or those who taunt people for whom they did favors by reminding them die upon faith, then they will first go to hell and will return to paradise upon completing their punishment unless they are forgiven.

The third group of people informed in our third hadith that will face grave loss and disappointment are the ones who show a higher cost or quality by taking oath in order to be able to sell merchandise that they posses in return for a higher price than it is worth. We had previously covered this topic in detail under the title "Lies and False Oaths."

Taking false oaths is always prohibited not just when selling merchandise. However, people are more likely to lie in commercial transactions. On the other hand, trading relationships is the first among the areas where rights of other slaves of Allah are at issue. This is because all people have to trade in order to survive.

k. Practicing Sorcery and Other Sins

١٨٠. عَنْ أَبِي هُرَيْرَةَ رَضِيَ اللهُ عَنْهُ عَنِ النَّبِيِّ صَلَّى اللهُ عَلَيْهِ وَسَلَّمَ قَالَ:

«اِجْتَنِبُوا السَّبْعَ الْمُوبِقَاتِ» قَالُوا:

«يَا رَسُولَ اللهِ وَمَا هُنَّ؟» قَالَ:

«اَلشِّرْكُ بِاللهِ وَالسِّحْرُ وَقَتْلُ النَّفْسِ الَّتِي حَرَّمَ اللهُ إِلَّا بِالْحَقِّ وَأَكْلُ الرِّبَا وَأَكْلُ مَالِ الْيَتِيمِ وَالتَّوَلِّي يَوْمَ الزَّحْفِ وَقَذْفُ الْمُحْصَنَاتِ الْمُؤْمِنَاتِ الْغَافِلَاتِ».

180. Abu Huraira (r.a.) narrated that the Prophet (pbuh) said:

"Avoid the seven great destructive sins!"

The Companions asked:

"O Allah's Apostle! What are they?"

The Messenger of Allah (pbuh) answered:

"To join others in worship along with Allah, to practice sorcery, to kill the life which Allah has forbidden except for a just cause, (according to Islamic law), to eat up riba (usury), to eat up an orphan's wealth, to give back to the enemy and fleeing from the battlefield at the time of fighting, and to accuse, chaste women, who never even think of anything touching chastity and are good believers." (Bukhari, Kitab Al-Wasiyya, 23; Tibb, 48; Hudud, 44; Muslim, Iman, 145. Also see. Abu Dawud, Kitab Al-Wasiyya, 10/2874; Nasai, Kitab Al-Wasiyya, 12)

❀

١٨١. عَنْ أَبِي هُرَيْرَةَ رَضِيَ اللهُ عَنْهُ قَالَ: قَالَ رَسُولُ اللهِ صَلَّى اللهُ عَلَيْهِ وَسَلَّمَ:

«مَنْ عَقَدَ عُقْدَةً ثُمَّ نَفَثَ فِيهَا فَقَدْ سَحَرَ وَمَنْ سَحَرَ فَقَدْ أَشْرَكَ وَمَنْ تَعَلَّقَ شَيْئًا وُكِلَ إِلَيْهِ».

181. Abu Huraira (r.a.) narrated: The Messenger of Allah (pbuh) said:

"Whoever binds something and blows to it will have practiced sorcery. Whoever practices sorcery falls into polytheism. Who wears something on his neck (things from the traditions of the Era of Ignorance like an animal's nail, an amulet) will be referred to that thing (will be deprived of Allah's help)." (Nasai, Tahrim al-Dam, 19/4076)

❁

١٨٢. عَنْ عَبْدِ اللهِ بْنِ عُمَرَ رَضِيَ اللهُ عَنْهُ قَالَ: أَقْبَلَ عَلَيْنَا رَسُولُ اللهِ صَلَّى اللهُ عَلَيْهِ وَسَلَّمَ فَقَالَ:

«يَا مَعْشَرَ الْمُهَاجِرِينَ! خَمْسٌ إِذَا ابْتُلِيتُمْ بِهِنَّ وَأَعُوذُ بِاللهِ أَنْ تُدْرِكُوهُنَّ، لَمْ تَظْهَرِ الْفَاحِشَةُ فِي قَوْمٍ قَطُّ حَتَّى يُعْلِنُوا بِهَا إِلَّا فَشَا فِيهِمُ الطَّاعُونُ وَالْأَوْجَاعُ الَّتِي لَمْ تَكُنْ مَضَتْ فِي أَسْلَافِهِمُ الَّذِينَ مَضَوْا وَلَمْ يَنْقُصُوا الْمِكْيَالَ وَالْمِيزَانَ إِلَّا أُخِذُوا بِالسِّنِينَ وَشِدَّةِ الْمَئُونَةِ وَجَوْرِ السُّلْطَانِ عَلَيْهِمْ وَلَمْ يَمْنَعُوا زَكَاةَ أَمْوَالِهِمْ إِلَّا مُنِعُوا الْقَطْرَ مِنَ السَّمَاءِ وَلَوْلَا الْبَهَائِمُ لَمْ يُمْطَرُوا وَلَمْ يَنْقُضُوا عَهْدَ اللهِ وَعَهْدَ رَسُولِهِ إِلَّا سَلَّطَ اللهُ عَلَيْهِمْ عَدُوًّا مِنْ غَيْرِهِمْ فَأَخَذُوا بَعْضَ مَا فِي أَيْدِيهِمْ وَمَا لَمْ تَحْكُمْ أَئِمَّتُهُمْ بِكِتَابِ اللهِ وَيَتَخَيَّرُوا مِمَّا أَنْزَلَ اللهُ إِلَّا جَعَلَ اللهُ بَأْسَهُمْ بَيْنَهُمْ».

182. Abdullah b. Umar (r.anhuma) narrated:

The Messenger of Allah (pbuh) turned to us and said: *"O the people of Muhajirin! There are five things that I seek refuge in Allah for you not to reach them. They are:*

1. If adultery and indecency emerges in a nation and finally that nation starts to commit it openly, for sure plague and illnesses that are unseen in previous nations that lived before them spread in them.

2. Every nation that misconducts in measuring and weighing will be punished by famine, poverty, and oppression by their rulers.

3. Every nation that avoids giving the mandatory alms from their wealth surely will be deprived of rain (will be punished by drought) and if it weren't for their animals, it would not rain on them.

4. Every nation that left Allah's pledge (commands) and the Messenger's pledge (his agreements and traditions) is surely burdened with an enemy that is not from them and that enemy takes some of what they have.

5. As long as their rulers do not act upon the Book of Allah and pick and choose among the rules Allah decreed according to what they prefer, Allah accounts for them among themselves (they would be inflicted with the troubles of mischief, corruption, and anarchy). (Ibn Majah, Fitan, 22; Hakim, IV, 583/8623; Baihaqi, Shuab, III, 197)

۱۸۳ . قَالَتْ زَيْنَبُ ابْنَةُ جَحْشٍ رَضِيَ اللهُ عَنْهَا: فَقُلْتُ:

«يَا رَسُولَ اللهِ، أَنَهْلِكُ وَفِينَا الصَّالِحُونَ؟» قَالَ:

«نَعَمْ إِذَا كَثُرَ الْخَبَثُ».

183. Zainab bint Jahsh (r.anha) narrated:

I asked the Messenger of Allah:

"O Allah's Apostle! Shall we be destroyed even though there are pious persons among us?"

The Messenger of Allah (pbuh) said:

"Yes, when the evil people (sinking in sin) increases!" (Bukhari, Anbiya, 7)

Explanations:

In our first hadith, we're informed that the major sins are destructive and seven of these are counted. We had covered the topic of polytheism before. Sorcery, which comes next, is also among the major sins. Our covering of magic and sorcery here is not because it is lighter compared to the earlier topics. This is because it is counted among the other sins that we cover it here. Actually, enumerating major sins completely is quite difficult. When we look at the narrations we see that each one is worse and more harmful than the other. The best way is to keep away from all knowing that each of them will destroy humans.

The lexical meaning of the term sihr (magic) is something that is covered and secret. The terminological meaning is to turn something from its true nature to something else. In traditional context, magic is understood as an influence, directing, deceiving, or making one fall into certain negative conclusions without sufficient evidence. In this sense, things like illusion and deception which are secret and causing untrue images are magic.

The majority of Muslim scholars accepted the existence and impact of magic. The 102th verse of Chapter Al Baqarah shows this.

Since it causes great harm to people in their absence and at unexpected instances by influencing them, magic is an extremely sinful act and its punishment is severe. Only people who are not afraid of God and whose faith are weak engage with it.

In the noble worse, instead of saying "Soloman never conducted magic" it is said that **"the blasphemers were, not Solomon, but the evil ones."**[230] This expression equates magic to blasphemy, which is sufficient to show the evilness and ugliness or magic and sorcery. Harut and Marut's warning of "We are only for trial; so do not blaspheme (by conducting magic)" also shows that magic is among the main reasons that lead one to blasphemy and unbelief. (Al-Baqarah; 2:102-103)

This is because in magic lies the claim to perform acts beyond Allah's control and power. On the other hand, since the thought of selfishness belies under magic and sorcery, the people who engage in these do not acknowledge religion or sacred.

---

230. Al-Baqarah; 2:102-103

In the Noble Qur'an, Allah declared His prophets and the revelations that we revealed to them were the truth and have nothing to do with sorcery or sorcerers, mentioned the opposition and slanders of sorcerers against the prophets and informed us that they are liars and deceitful people who will never achieve salvation. (Al-Araf; 7:116; Al-Taha; 20:69 (Yunus; 10:76-77) (Al-Zariyat; 51:52) (Al-Zukhruf; 43:30)

In our second hadith, it is told that acts such as tying a knot and blowing on the knot that carry the meaning of magic have been prohibited and that sorcery is a sin close to associating partners with God.

One of the usual acts of sorcerers is to take a piece of string and tie a knot and blow to the knot by uttering some magical words. Whoever does such a thing would commit a work of the people of sorcery. This act is among those of the people of idolatry. It leads the person to idolatry step by step. At the very least, it causes hidden idolatry since one leaves trusting in Allah and destiny (after doing the best one can), i.e., tawaqqul, and relies on sorcery.[231]

Based on this and other similar rulings, Muslim scholars have put forth miscellaneous opinions on learning and practicing sorcery. According to Abu Hanifa, Imam Malik, and Ahmad ibn Hanbal learning and practicing sorcery is unbelief. According to some of the authorities of the Hanafi school, sorcery can be learned to be protected from its evil and this is not considered as disbelief. However, it leads to unbelief to believe that practicing sorcery is allowed or that it provides benefits. The Islamic punishment of those who perform magic and sorcery is explained in detail in our books of Islamic jurisprudence. (See Hamdi Yazır, *Hak Dini Kur'ân Dili*, I, 441-451; Kâmil Miras, *Tecrîd Tercümesi*, VIII, 224-235) Muslim Scholars have expressed that magicians and sorcerers can hurt no one except by the Will of Allah and that it is prohibited for Muslims to engage with sorcery or have someone perform sorcery. It is not right for people who have been subjected to sorcery to apply in order to be free of its influence to insincere people who have assumed this a profession. Before all, it is necessary to seek refuge in Allah, worship and pray, and donate to poor. If a trustworthy,

---

231. **In our second hadith,** it is also forbidden to wear on the neck things like musqa (written supplications), evil eye deterrent (nazar), animal nail, or bone hoping that it can be beneficial or protect from harm. Allah deprives people who do such things from His mercy by referring them to those things that they trusted. Hanging expressions from the Quran and holy names to show respect to them is considered an exception from this ruling, But again, it is not considered right to believe that these will bring benefits and deter harm. This is because it is only Allah the Almighty who provides cure and deters evil.

pious, and knowledgeable person is helping people then it is also possible to benefit from that person.

Almighty God commands as follows in the Chapter of Daybreak desiring that we seek refuge in Him from the evil of sorcerers. (Al-Falaq; 113:

"Say: I seek refuge with the Lord of the Dawn from the mischief of created things; from the mischief of Darkness as it overspreads; from the mischief of those who practice secret arts; and from the mischief of the envious one as he practices envy." (Al-Falaq; 113:1-5)

When it comes to other great sins, violating the **property rights of orphans** is counted among these. An orphan refers here to a young child whose father has passed away. According to what is understood from the noble verses and hadith, orphans are God's trusts to the Muslim society. Namely, it is necessary to protect the orphans and their property as a society.

Citing the violation of the property rights of orphans among the destructive sins shows how severe a crime and responsibility it is.

Allah the Almighty says:

"To orphans restore their property (when they reach their age), nor substitute (your) worthless things for (their) good ones; and devour not their substance (by mixing it up) with your own. For this is indeed a great sin." (An-Nisa; 4:2)

Ibn Abbas (r.a.) narrates the following about how careful the noble companions were in respect to the orphans' property:

"When the following verses were revealed,

"And come not near to the orphan's property, except to improve it, until he attains the age of full strength; give measure and weight with (full) justice…"[232]

"Those who unjustly eat up the property of orphans, eat up a Fire into their own bodies: They will soon be enduring a Blazing Fire!"[233] the noble companions who had orphans in their care immediately left and separated their food and drinks from their own. When something was left from the food

---

232. An'am; 6:162
233. Al-Nisa; 4:10

and drinks of the orphans, companions would not touch them, and they would keep them until the orphan ate them or they would spoil.

This placed a heavy burden on them. They brought the matter to the attention of the Prophet (pbuh). Upon this, the Almighty and Exalted Allah revealed the following noble verse:

"…They ask you concerning orphans. Say: "The best thing to do is what is for their good; if you mix their affairs with yours, they are your brethren; but Allah knows the man who means mischief from the man who means good. And if Allah had wished, He could have put you into difficulties: He is indeed Exalted in Power, Wise." (Al-Baqarah; 2:220)

After the revelation of this verse, the noble companions mixed the food and drinks of the orphans with theirs. (Abu Dawud, Wasaya, 7/2871; Nasai, Wasaya, 11)

If someone taking care of an orphan is poor and needy, he is allowed to benefit from the property of the orphan without going to excess and waste. If he is rich, he should be content with the property Allah gave him and stay away from the orphan's property. In the noble verse, it is reminded that Almighty Allah knows the people who watch for the orphans versus people with evil intentions who want to utilize their property by abusing their weakness and wanted people who deal with orphans to control the feelings in their hearts.

One of the greater sins is to **run away from the fight with the enemy**. Jihad is one of the most important duties performed in order to to protect the religion, life, property, and modesty and chastity. Running away from doing jihad means first endangering his personal security and then the life of the Muslim society. So, unless it is a battle tactic, running away from the battle ground is among the greatest sins that are never forgiven.

Allah the Almighty commands:

"O you who believe! When you meet the unbelievers in hostile array, never turn your backs to them. If any do turn his back to them on such a day - unless it be in a stratagem of war, or to retreat to a troop (of his own) - he draws on himself the wrath of Allah, and his abode is Hell, - an evil refuge (indeed)!" (Al-Anfal; 8:15-16)

On the other hand, launching a charge against chaste Muslim women and trying to blemish their honor and dignity, i.e. **slandering with adultery,** is one of the destructive great sins. The slander against chaste Muslim men has the same ruling. The people who violate this prohibition are extremely wicked transgressors. For this reason they are flogged with eighty stripes in this world. (Al-Nur; 24:4)

On the other hand, Almighty Allah states the spiritual punishment in the Hereafter as follows:

"Those who slander chaste women, indiscreet but believing, are cursed in this life and in the Hereafter: for them is a grievous penalty, On the Day when their tongues, their hands, and their feet will bear witness against them as to their actions." (Al-Nur; 24:23-24)

There are other great sins than the ones that we hitherto counted. For this reason, it is not right to limit the great sins with a certain number or to consider them limited with the lists given in a hadith. The restrictions in the hadith are meant to say "these seven acts are among the great sins." The seven, four, or three sins in miscellaneous narrations are brought forward because they are the most prominent, most disconcerting, and most frequent.

Some of the great sins apart from the ones we have studied are as follows:

- Contempt and scorn a Muslim, belittling and putting him down

- Deceiving people

- Calling a Muslim unbeliever and believing that he is like that

- To neglect the duty of enjoining the good and forbidding the evil

- A person's negligence of his duties against the individuals whose sustenance he assumed

- Leaving the ritual prayer

In the noble verse, it is said that:

"But after them there followed a posterity who missed prayers and followed after lusts soon, then, will they face Destruction." (Maryam; 19:59)

- Telling the private things that one shared with his wife to others

- Committing a forbidden act in the Masjid al Haram (Mecca) (Abu Dawud, Kitab Al-Wasaya, 10/2875)

- Researching and trying to keep a custom from the Era of Ignorance alive in the Muslim community (Muslim, Iman, 165)

- Stealing (Tirmidhi, Tafsir, 17/3144)

- Gambling

- Dying without leaving sufficient property to pay off one's debt even though one owes a debt.[234]

The punishment for such sins is extremely severe and painful.

The following narration which informs us about certain sins and their respective punishments in the grave is extremely important for our subject.

Samura b. Jundub (r.a.) narrated:

The Messenger of Allah would very often ask his companions:

"Did anyone of you see a dream?" So dreams would be narrated to him by those whom Allah wished to tell. One morning the Prophet said:

"Last night two persons (Gabriel and Mikhail) came to me (in a dream) and woke me up and said to me, "Proceed!" I set out with them and we came across a man lying down, and behold, another man was standing over his head, holding a big rock. Behold, he was throwing the rock at the man's head, injuring it. The rock rolled away and the thrower followed it and took it back. By the time he reached the man, his head returned to the normal state. The thrower then did the same as he had done before. I said to the angels:

"Subhan Allah! Who are these two persons?"

They said, "Proceed!" So we proceeded and came to a man lying flat on his back and another man standing over his head with an iron hook, and behold, he would put the hook in one side of the man's mouth and tear off that side of his face to the back (of the neck) and similarly tear his nose from front to back and his eye from front to back. Then he turned to the other side of the man's face and did just as he had done with the other side. He hardly completed this side when the other side returned to its normal state. Then he returned to it to repeat what he had done before. I said:

"Subhan Allah! Who are these two persons?"

---

234. Abu Dawud, Buyu, 9/3342; Ahmad, IV, 392.

They said to me, 'Proceed!' So we proceeded and came across something like a Tannur (a kind of baking oven, a pit usually clay-lined for baking bread). In that oven there was much noise and voices. We looked into it and found naked men and women, and behold, a flame of fire was reaching to them from underneath, and when it reached them, they cried loudly.

I asked them:

"Who are these?"

They said to me, 'Proceed!' And so we proceeded and came across a river red like blood. And behold, in the river there was a man swimming, and on the bank there was a man who had collected many stones. While the other man was swimming, he went near him. The former opened his mouth and the latter (on the bank) threw a stone into his mouth whereupon he went swimming again. He returned and every time the performance was repeated, I asked my two companions:

"Who are these (two) persons?"

They replied, 'Proceed! Proceed!' And we proceeded till we came to a man with a repulsive appearance, the most repulsive appearance you ever saw a man having! Beside him there was a fire and he was kindling it and running around it. I asked my companions:

"Who is this man?"

They said to me, 'Proceed! Proceed!' So we proceeded till we reached a garden of deep green dense vegetation, having all sorts of spring colors. In the midst of the garden there was a very tall man and I could hardly see his head because of his great height, and around him there were children in such a large number as I have never seen. I said:

"Whose are this man and the children?"

"Proceed! Proceed!" So we proceeded till we came to a majestic huge garden, greater and better than I have ever seen! My two companions said to me, 'Go up and I went up!' So we ascended till we reached a city built of gold and silver bricks and we went to its gate and asked (the gatekeeper) to open the gate, and it was opened and we entered the city and found in it, men with one side of their bodies as handsome as the handsomest person you have ever seen, and the other side as

ugly as the ugliest person you have ever seen. My two companions ordered those men:

"Throw yourselves into the river!" Behold, there was a river flowing across (the city), and its water was like milk in whiteness. Those men went and threw themselves in it and then returned to us after the ugliness (of their bodies) had disappeared and they became in the best shape.

My two companions (angels) said to me:

"This place is the Eden Paradise, and that is your place." I rose up my sight, and behold, there I saw a palace like a white cloud! My two companions said to me:

"That (palace) is your place." I said to them:

"Allah bless you both! Let me enter it." They replied:

"As for now, you will not enter it, but you shall enter it (one day)." I said to them:

"I have seen many wonders tonight. What does all that mean which I have seen?" They replied:

"We will inform you."

"As for the first man you came upon whose head was being injured with the rock, he is the symbol of the one who studies the Qur'an and then neither recites it nor acts on its orders, and sleeps, neglecting the enjoined prayers.

As for the man you came upon whose sides of mouth, nostrils and eyes were torn off from front to back, he is the symbol of the man who goes out of his house in the morning and tells so many lies that it spreads all over the world.

(In another report, it is narrated as:

"He was a liar and always used to lie when he was on earth. The lies he spread used to cover the horizon.") so this punishment will go on till the Day of Resurrection.

And those naked men and women whom you saw in a construction resembling an oven, they are the adulterers and the adulteresses.

The man whom you saw swimming in the river and given a stone to swallow, is the eater of usury (Riba).

The bad looking man whom you saw near the fire kindling it and going round it, is Malik, the gatekeeper of Hell.

The tall man whom you saw in the garden, is Abraham and the children around him are those children who die with Al-Fitra (the Islamic Faith)."

Some Muslims asked the Prophet:

"O Allah's Apostle! What about the children of pagans?"

The Messenger of Allah (pbuh) replied:

"And also the children of pagans." The Prophet added:

"The men you saw half handsome and half ugly were those persons who had mixed an act that was good with another that was bad, but Allah forgave them." (Bukhari, Ta'bir, 48; Al-Jana'iz, 93; Tahajjud, 12; Buyu, 2; Jihad, 4; Bad' al-khalk, 6; Anbiya, 8; Tafsir, 9/15; Adab, 69; Tirmidhi, Ru'ya, 10/2295)

The kinds of punishment shown to the Prophet are the ones that are going to continue until the Day of Judgment. There are no mentions here of the kinds of punishments that are going to be given after the accounting.

Another matter is that the dreams of prophets are not like ours. Their dreams are trusted ones. There are examples of this in the Noble Qur'an. For this reason, what the Messenger of Allah told us "I saw in my dream" is an expression of truth. The Messenger of Allah (pbuh) has warned his nation by informing them about the future and has wished to save them from loss both in this world and in the hereafter.

This is because the punishment for the sins is not just given in the grave or the Hereafter but sometimes also given in this world. Indeed, **in our third hadith**, certain punishments to be given in this world for bad acts like adultery, betrayal, not giving the zakat, and disobeying Allah's commands is given.

On the other hand, **in our fourth hadith**, we are informed that once the sins increase in a society people can face total destruction. This ruling will not change even though there are pious people among them,

If Almighty Allah wishes, He sends a calamity that hits everyone – both good and bad – in the society in which sins increase,[235] and He demolishes

235. See Tirmidhi, Fitan, 38/2210-2211; Ibn-i Majah, Fitan, 20, 22; Hakim, IV, 583/8623.

places. However, people will be raised based on their intentions and conditions in life and receives compensation accordingly.[236]

Almighty Allah warns as follows:

"And fear mischief or oppression, which affects not in particular (only) those of you who do wrong: and know that Allah is strict in punishment." (Al-Anfal; 8:25)

In this case, what is required upon us is to fulfill our duty to enjoin the good and forbid the evil and try to decrease sins.

3. Not to belittle sins

١٨٤. عَنْ عَمْرِو بْنِ الْأَحْوَصِ رَضِيَ اللهُ عَنْهُ قَالَ: سَمِعْتُ رَسُولَ اللهِ صَلَّى اللهُ عَلَيْهِ وَسَلَّمَ يَقُولُ فِي حَجَّةِ الْوَدَاعِ لِلنَّاسِ:

«...أَلَا وَإِنَّ الشَّيْطَانَ قَدْ أَيِسَ مِنْ أَنْ يُعْبَدَ فِي بِلَادِكُم هٰذِهِ أَبَدًا وَلٰكِنْ سَتَكُونُ لَهُ طَاعَةٌ فِيمَا تَحْتَقِرُونَ مِنْ أَعْمَالِكُمْ فَسَيَرْضَى بِهِ...».

184. Amr bin Ahvas (r.a.) says: I heard the Messenger of Allah saying to people when he was giving his sermon in his Farewell Pilgrimage:

"…Pay attention! Satan has forever lost his hope that in these lands he will never be worshipped. However, obeying him will be possible in acts (sins) that you see as minor, and he will be pleased with this…" (Tirmidhi, Fitan, 2/2159; Ibn Majah, Manasik, 76; Nasai, *al-Sunan al-kubra,* II, 444/4100. Also see Hakim, II, 32/2221; Baihaqi, *Shuab,* V, 454)

❁

١٨٥. عَنْ عَبْدِ اللهِ بْنِ مَسْعُودٍ رَضِيَ اللهُ عَنْهُ أَنَّ رَسُولَ اللهِ صَلَّى اللهُ عَلَيْهِ وَسَلَّمَ قَالَ:

---

236. Bukhari, Fitan, 19; Muslim, Jannah, 84. We had touched upon this subject previously under the heading "Intentions."

«إِيَّاكُمْ وَمُحَقَّرَاتِ الذُّنُوبِ فَإِنَّهُنَّ يَجْتَمِعْنَ عَلَى الرَّجُلِ حَتَّى يُهْلِكْنَهُ»

وَإِنَّ رَسُولَ اللهِ صَلَّى اللهُ عَلَيْهِ وَسَلَّمَ ضَرَبَ لَهُنَّ مَثَلًا كَمَثَلِ قَوْمٍ نَزَلُوا أَرْضَ فَلَاةٍ فَحَضَرَ صَنِيعُ الْقَوْمِ فَجَعَلَ الرَّجُلُ يَنْطَلِقُ فَيَجِيءُ بِالْعُودِ وَالرَّجُلُ يَجِيءُ بِالْعُودِ حَتَّى جَمَعُوا سَوَادًا فَأَجَّجُوا نَارًا وَأَنْضَجُوا مَا قَذَفُوا فِيهَا.

185. It was narrated from Abdullah b. Mesud (r.a.) that the Messenger of Allah (pbuh) spoke as follows:

"Avoid sins that are seen as minor because they accumulate in an individual and eventually destroy that person."

Then, the Messenger of Allah (pbuh) gave an example as follows about sins.

A group stops to rest in a desert. When the time comes for eating, each one brings a tree branch, then they put those together, and this way they construct a bonfire and cook their food by placing their food on it. (Ahmad, I, 402-403; V, 331)

⚜

١٨٦. عَنْ عَائِشَةَ رَضِيَ اللهُ عَنْهَا قَالَتْ: قَالَ لِي رَسُولُ اللهِ صَلَّى اللهُ عَلَيْهِ وَسَلَّمَ:

«يَا عَائِشَةُ إِيَّاكِ وَمُحَقَّرَاتِ الْأَعْمَالِ فَإِنَّ لَهَا مِنَ اللهِ طَالِبًا».

186. Aisha (r.anha) says: The Messenger of Allah told me the following:

"O Aisha! Stay away the acts that are belittled (even from the smallest of sins that are not paid attention to). This is because there is someone (an angel) in the

sight of Allah who watches and records them." (Ibn Majah, Zuhd, 29; Darimi, Riqaq, 17; Ahmad, VI, 70, 151)

❊

١٨٧. عَنْ أَبِي هُرَيْرَةَ رَضِيَ اللهُ عَنْهُ عَنْ رَسُولِ اللهِ صَلَّى اللهُ عَلَيْهِ وَسَلَّمَ قَالَ:

»إِنَّ الْعَبْدَ إِذَا أَخْطَأَ خَطِيئَةً نُكِتَتْ فِي قَلْبِهِ نُكْتَةٌ سَوْدَاءُ فَإِذَا هُوَ نَزَعَ وَاسْتَغْفَرَ وَتَابَ صُقِلَ قَلْبُهُ وَإِنْ عَادَ زِيدَ فِيهَا حَتَّى تَعْلُو قَلْبَهُ وَهُوَ الرَّانُ الَّذِي ذَكَرَ اللهُ:

(كَلَّا بَلْ رَانَ عَلَى قُلُوبِهِمْ مَا كَانُوا يَكْسِبُونَ)«.

187. *According to the narration from Abu Huraira (r.a.), the Messenger of Allah said the following:*

"When a slave of Allah commits a wrongdoing, a black spot is stamped on his heart. If he manages to keep his carnal self from doing this, repents, and returns from sin, his heart is purified from this spot and polished. If he returns to sins, this stamp enlarges and in the end covers his whole heart. And this is the rusting of hearts that Allah the Exalted mentions in the following noble verse:

"By no means! But on their hearts is the stain of the (ill) which they do!" (Al-Mutaffifin; 83:14) (Tirmidhi, Tafsir, 83/3334; Ibn Majah, Zuhd, 29. Also see Ahmad, II, 297)

Explanations:

Since all sins carry the meaning of disobeying Allah's rules whether great or minor, they cause Him to be displeased and even attract His anger. For this reason, Bilal b. Sa'd, who is famous for his piety, said:

"Pay attention not the size of the sins but to whom you are rebelling!" (Abu Nuaym, *Hilyah*, V, 223; Ahmad, *Zuhd*, p. 460)

On the other hand, sins prevent knowing Allah and obeying Him truly ad appropriately by hanging like a thick curtain between Allah and the slave. Thus, just like the great sins, minor sins also contain dangers for one's spirituality. For this reason they should never be belittled.

Sins move us away from Allah's consent and please our eternal enemy, Satan. **In our first hadith,** we are informed that even the minor sins mean obedience to Satan and would please him. This is because Satan is trying to move mankind away from our Lord's mercy and compassion as he has been casted away from divine mercy. In fact, he devoted his life to this. This is because when humans were first created, Satan was jealous of them and disobeyed Allah's orders by being consumed with arrogance. Namely, mankind has a role in his being sent off from Paradise and mercy. For this reason, it is quite natural for Satan to sit on the way to Heaven and try to turn humans into travelers destined for Hell by using all kinds of deceptions and tricks. What is really strange is the humans' falling for their eternal enemy and following him.

The only thing Satan does in order to reach his goal is to move him away from his religion. For this reason, after warning his nation in the Farewell Sermon with the expression in our hadith the Messenger of Allah (pbuh) says:

"Be very protective of your religion by staying away from the acts (sins) that you call minor and contempt." (Haythami, III, 267)

In our second hadith, the Prophet explained as follows why minor sins should not be belittled:

"...because they accumulate in an individual and eventually destroy that person."

The Messenger of Allah (pbuh) also gives an example to this, and explains in the best fashion. Just like the cooking of food by the fire of small pieces of bush and branches, the minor sins accumulate and cause someone to fall into Hell.

Sometimes people don't notice and they think that the sins that they committed are minor matters. In fact, it is a great crime in the sight of Allah. In respect to the incident of slandering our mother Aisha (r.anha), the mistake of humans' seeing their sins as minor amtters is alluded to in the Noble Qur'an as follows:

427

"Were it not for the grace and mercy of Allah on you, in this world and the Hereafter, a grievous penalty would have seized you in that you rushed glibly into this affair. Behold, you received it on your tongues, and said out of your mouths things of which you had no knowledge; and you thought it to be a light matter, while it was most serious in the sight of Allah." (Al-Nur; 24:14-15)

Also, a person says a careless word and sees it as trivial. In fact, the crime he committed is great enough to destroy him but he does not know it. Indeed, the Messenger of Allah (pbuh) said the following:

"Allah's slave happens to say something without properly thinking and he ends up falling to the part of Hell that is further than the distance between the East and West." (Bukhari, Riqaq, 23)

On the other hand, minor sins turn into the way that takes people to great sins. They gradually turn a person and throw him into the claws of great sins. Indeed Ibn Abbas said the following:

"If one repents from a great sin it does not stay as it is, it is forgiven. The minor sin on the other hand does not remain minor if one insists and becomes a great sin." (Baihaqi, *Shuab*, V, 456)

A person who does not place importance to sins does not stay where he is, God forbid, knowingly or unknowingly, advances. For this reason, Muslim scholars warned us saying:

"Minor sins take a person to great sin, and, in turn, great sins take him to unbelief." (Ajluni, *Kashf al-Khafa,* number: 2317)

In this matter, Abu Hafs (r.a.) says:

"As malaria is the bearer of the news of death, sins are the bearers of the news of unbelief." (Baihaqi, *Shuab*, V, 447)

Thus, the disease of seeing the wrongdoings and sins as minor should not be a characteristic of a believer. A believer should take all types of sins seriously and try to stay away from them. Abdullah b. Masud (r.a.) describes the spiritual state of believers in the face of sins:

"A believing person increases his sins in his imagination so much that it is as if he is sitting in the skirts of a mountain and the mountain will collapse on him. On the other hand, a mischievous person sees his sins as a fly that landed on his nose." (Bukhari, Daawat, 4)

The Companions lived in this very spiritual state against the sins. Indeed, one of the great scholars of the generation following the Noble Companions, Hasan al-Basri, narrates his observations about this exemplary generation as follows:

"The companions of the Prophet (pbuh) used to perform even a small act if they see it as nice. On the contrary, they used to stay away even from a small thing if they see it inappropriate." (Ibn Dunya, *Mawsua*, I, 89)

Anas (r.a.) warned some people who later lost their sensitivity in this matter:

"You people do (bad) deeds (commit sins) which seem in your eyes as tiny (minute) than hair while we used to consider those (very deeds) during the life-time of the Prophet as destructive sins." (Bukhari, Ar-Riqaq)

In this regard, Musa Topbaş, may he rest in peace and mercy, says in his letters to his students:

"The state and perfection of the heart of a believer is displayed in his acts. Some among the most prominent of these beautiful acts are as follows:

Being humble all the time, not wasting his time knowing the value of his time and that his number of breaths are limited, loving the slaves of Allah and not struggling with them, treating others according to their religious levels, having the habit of covering others' wrongdoings, being careful about haram and halal, and seeing as great even the matters everyone else considers as minor. This is because whoever sees his sin as minor – God forbid – sees the command of Almighty Allah as minor."

In our third hadith, the Messenger of Allah (pbuh) desired that believers reach the state of sincerity and control and avoid even the minor sins. Whether minor or major, all acts of humans are being recorded. There are angels recording the actions of a person without leaving them even for a moment. Our Exalted Lord informs us as follows:

"Not a word does he utter but there is a sentinel by him, ready (to note it)." (Qaf; 50:18)

Before all, God Almighty already hears, sees, and knows everything.

One day these records will be opened and the individual will find everything he committed in front of him. Anyone who has done well in the size of an atom will see that and the same for any evil doings.[237] The astonishment of the sinners is described as follows by Allah the Exalted:

"And the book (of deeds) will be placed (before you); and you will see the sinful in great terror because of what is (recorded) therein; they will say, "Ah! Woe to us! What a book is this! It leaves out nothing small or great, but takes account thereof!" They will find all that they did is placed before them: And not one will your Lord treat with injustice." (Al-Kahf; 18:49)

The criminals were not paying attention to minor sins when they were in this world, and they used to see their wrongdoings as minor issues. When they continued with this mentality, in time, they fell into major sins, and they even did not place importance to them. In the end, they found themselves in the bosom of horrifying fear,

How wise the following words of Abu Ayyub al-Ansari are:

"A person performs a good act, and then commits minor sins by relying on the good act, and he faces Allah together with the great dangers that these sins caused. On the other hand, another person commits a sin. However, he lives in fear (by thinking the compensation for that sin) and finally goes to the sight of Allah in peace." (Baihaqi, *Shuab*, V, 456; Ibn Hajar, *Fath al-Bari,* XI, 330)

Thus, a believer should always be alert, keep away even from the minor wrongdoings that people do not place importance to, and live in a state of complete check and control.

A believer should be so sensitive in the matter of sin that he should even control the thoughts in his heart.

Umar (r.a.) said the following:

"Avoid the wish and desire that come to your heart prior to sin because that is the beginning of sin! If you do not avoid this desire, your hearts fall into heedlessness from Allah." (Baihaqi, *Shuab*, V, 458)

So, feelings, thoughts, and dreams are of great importance in the matter of leading a person to sin or goodness."[238]

---

237. Al-Zilzal; 99:7-8.

238. It is pointed out in some ahadith that the thoughts and wishes that cross one's heart have a directing influence and are regarded as prayer:

It is also possible to understand the following from our third hadith: in respect to worshipping Allah and avoiding sins, a man should warn his wife and should try to endow her with the consciousness of responsibility. Essentially, to be a pious Muslim in a family, both husband and wife must warn each other, forbid the evil, and encourage goodness and beautiful things.[239]

The influence and effects of sins on heart are told **in our fourth hadith**. Each sin is like a black spot stamped to the heart, just like a drop of black ink on a pure white paper... If the person leaves the sin and embraces repentance, then his heart gets cleaned. If he does not repent and continue, then these spots mount and cover the whole heart. After this, the heart is no longer sharp, its light goes away, its wise vision is blocked, and its surface is covered with dirt just like the rusting and steaming of a mirror. In time it hardens and stops recognizing the good. Afterwards, the person can commit even the greatest sins that scatter their poison into the soul without even feeling them. How nicely, the following words of Omar bin Abdulaziz express this fact:

"Prohibitions are a kind of fire. Only those whose hearts are dead reach out to them. If those who reach out to the prohibited things were alive, they would feel the pain of that fire."

Therefore, those who commit major sins came to this state because of the darkening in their hearts due to the minor sins that they neglected.

Abu Turab an-Nahshabi says:

"There are three signs of a darkened heart:

1. *The person's not feeling any fear because of committing sins*

2. *Not feeling any joy out of obedience and worship*

3. *Advices having no influence on him."*

According to the narration, the Black Stone in the Ka'bah (Hajar al Aswad), which was whiter than milk or snow when it came down from the Heav-

---

"When one of you wishes something, he should be careful as to what he is thinking of. This is because he can't know what is recorded for him due to this wish." (Ahmad, II, 357, 387; Baihaqi, *Shuab*, V, 457)
"When one of you wishes something, he should think big! This is because in this situation he is asking from his Exalted Lord and praying to Him." (Ahmad, II, 357, 387; Baihaqi, *Shuab*, V, 457)
239. Zekeriya Güler, *40 Hadiste Kadın ve Aile*, Konya 2004, p. 338.

en, darkened in time due to the sins of people who touched it.[240] Indeed it is said that the blackness is only in the visible part of the Black Stone and the part buried in the Ka'bah wall is still white.[241]

If sins can even darken a stone like this, what would it do to a heart, which is such an elegant being?

Those who do not pay attention to sins and who can even commit them while laughing deserve to cry tomorrow in the Hereafter. Indeed Abdullah b. Abbas (r.a.) says:

"Someone committing a sin while laughing enters Hell while crying." (Ghazali, *Ihya*, III, 273)

Let us conclude our subject by citing some of the harms of sins:

• Sins call for Allah's anger and cause the rewards to be wasted. How nice a lesson and warning the following narration provides:

According to Thawban's narration, the Messenger of Allah told that:

"I know some people from my nation who come on the Day of Judgment with pure white good deeds like the Tihama Mountains. Allah the Magnificent and Exalted turns those rewards into scattered dust, makes them as if they did not exist."

Thawban (r.a.) said:

"O Messenger of Allah! Please explain their state for us so that we do not unintentionally become one of them.

Upon this the Prophet (pbuh) said:

"They are your brothers in Islam. They are humans like you. They too gain rewards from the night (worship). However, when they are alone with the prohibitions of Allah, they violate and commit those prohibitions." (Ibn Majah, Zuhd, 29)

• Sins prevent provisions. Allah removes His blessings and favors from the sinner.

---

240. See Tirmidhi, Hajj, 49/877; Ahmad, I, 307.
241. See Said Bektaş, *Fadlu al-Hajar al-Aswad wa Maqam Ibrahim*, p. 36-38; Muhammed Ilyas Abdulghani, *Tarihu Makka al-Mukarramah Qadiman wa Hadithan*, p. 43.

- Sins spoil the spirituality of the perpetrator, darken his heart, and cause to move away from the original nature of human beings. The sinner stays away from repentance cold-heartedly, unconscientiously, and without fear, rids of the feelings of shame and morality that make a person human.

- Sins and rebellious actions cause to get subjected to Allah's torment. By attracting the troubles and problems, they harm the past, current, and future generations.

- Sin harms not only the perpetrator but also the others. If the person who sees the sinner expresses that he finds this act shameful, he may experience the same evil state in the future; if he backbites, he also commits a sin; and if he finds acceptable what the sinner does, he becomes a partner in that sin.

- Every sin leads to another and weakens the belief.

- Since Almighty Allah does not give the treasure of knowledge to a rebellious heart, sinners are deprived of true knowledge. Ibn Qayyim al-Jazviyyah says:

"There are such bad influences of sins that no one other than Allah knows them. One of these influences is to be deprived of knowledge because knowledge is light and is given to the heart, but sin puts it out." (Munawi, *Fayz*, I, 155/113)

- Sins cause people to be deprived of angels' repentance and asking for forgiveness and from the intercession of our Mater the Prophet.

- The sinner alienated from his self, relatives, and society is bound to be alone.

4. Staying away from suspicious things

١٨٨ . عَنِ الْحَسَنِ بْنِ عَلِيٍّ رَضِيَ اللهُ عَنْهُ قَالَ: حَفِظْتُ مِنْ رَسُولِ اللهِ صَلَّى اللهُ عَلَيْهِ وَسَلَّمَ:

«دَعْ مَا يُرِيبُكَ إِلَى مَا لَا يُرِيبُكَ فَإِنَّ الصِّدْقَ طُمَأْنِينَةٌ وَإِنَّ الْكَذِبَ رِيبَةٌ».

433

188. Hassan b. Ali (r.anhuma) says the following:

I memorized the following words from (my grandfather) the Messenger of Allah:

"Stay away from the suspicious thins, be busy with the certain one. Because, honesty is a source of serenity whereas lying is a source of doubt." (Tirmidhi, Qiyamah 60/2518. See Bukhari, Buyu, 3; Nasai, Qada, 11; Ahmad, I, 200)

❁

١٨٩. عَنِ النُّعْمَانِ بنِ بَشِيرٍ رَضِيَ اللهُ عَنْهُ قَالَ: سَمِعْتُ رَسُولَ اللهِ صَلَّى اللهُ عَلَيْهِ وَسَلَّمَ يقُولُ:

«إِنَّ الْحَلَالَ بَيِّنٌ وَإِنَّ الْحَرَامَ بَيِّنٌ وَبَيْنَهُمَا مُشْتَبَهَاتٌ لاَ يَعْلَمُهُنَّ كَثِيرٌ مِنَ النَّاسِ فَمَنِ اتَّقَى الشُّبُهَاتِ اِسْتَبْرَأَ لِدِينِهِ وعِرْضِهِ وَمَنْ وَقَعَ فِي الشُّبُهَاتِ وَقَعَ فِي الْحَرَامِ كَالرَّاعِي يَرْعَى حَوْلَ الْحِمَى يُوشِكُ أَنْ يَرْتَعَ فِيهِ، أَلَا وَإِنَّ لِكُلِّ مَلِكٍ حِمًى، أَلَا وَإِنَّ حِمَى اللهِ مَحَارِمُهُ، أَلَا وَإِنَّ فِي الْجَسَدِ مُضْغَةً إِذَا صَلَحَتْ صَلَحَ الْجَسَدُ كُلُّهُ وَإِذَا فَسَدَتْ فَسَدَ الْجَسَدُ كُلُّهُ، أَلَا وَهِيَ الْقَلْبُ».

189. Nu'man b. Bashir (r.a.) reported: I heard Allah's Messenger (pbuh) as having said this:

"What is lawful is evident and what is unlawful is evident, and in between them are the things doubtful which many people do not know.

So he who guards against doubtful things keeps his religion and honor blameless, and he who indulges in doubtful things indulges in fact in unlawful things, just as a shepherd who pastures his animals round a preserve will soon pasture them in it.

Beware, every king has a preserve, and the things God his declared unlawful are His preserves.

Beware, in the body there is a piece of flesh; if it is sound, the whole body is sound and if it is corrupt the whole body is corrupt, and hearken it is the heart." (Muslim, Musaqat, 107, 108. Also see Bukhari, Iman, 39; Kitab al-Buyu, 2; Abu Dawud, Kitab al-Buyu, 3/3329; Tirmidhi, Kitab al-Buyu, 1/1205; Nasai, Kitab al-Buyu, 2; Qudat, 11; Ibn Majah, Fitan 14)

❁

١٩٠. عَنِ النَّوَّاسِ بْنِ سَمْعَانَ رَضِيَ اللهُ عَنْهُ قَالَ: سَأَلْتُ رَسُولَ اللهِ صَلَّى اللهُ عَلَيْهِ وَسَلَّمَ عَنِ الْبِرِّ وَالْإِثْمِ فَقَالَ:

«الْبِرُّ حُسْنُ الْخُلُقِ وَالْإِثْمُ مَا حَاكَ فِي صَدْرِكَ وَكَرِهْتَ أَنْ يَطَّلِعَ عَلَيْهِ النَّاسُ».

190. Nawwas b. Sim'an al-Ansari reported:

I asked Allah's Messenger (pbuh) about virtue and vice.

He answered:

"Virtue is a kind disposition and vice is what rankles in your heart and that you disapprove if people should come to know of it." (Muslim, Birr, 14, 15. Also see. Tirmidhi, Zuhd, 52/2389)

❁

١٩١. عَنْ أَنَسٍ رَضِيَ اللهُ عَنْهُ قَالَ: مَرَّ النَّبِيُّ صَلَّى اللهُ عَلَيْهِ وَسَلَّمَ بِتَمْرَةٍ مَسْقُوطَةٍ فَقَالَ:

«لَوْلَا أَنْ تَكُونَ مِنْ صَدَقَةٍ لَأَكَلْتُهَا».

191. Anas (r.a.) narrated:

The Prophet passed by a fallen date and said:

"Were it not for my doubt that this might have been given in charity, I would have eaten it." (Bukhari, Buyu, 4; Lukata, 6; Muslim, Zakat, 164-166. Also see. Abu Dawud, Zakat, 29)

Explanations:

An individual faces clearly permissible things, clearly prohibited things, and also some doubtful ones due to some uncertainties and probabilities. It is easy to recognize permissible and prohibited things that are obvious. However, it is difficult to decide about the things that are doubtful. If they are considered permissible, there is the possibility to fall into prohibited. This possibility, in turn, disturbs one's heart. The Messenger of Allah (pbuh) who wanted to save his followers from this trouble recommends to stay away from doubtful things and to focus on the clear certain ones **in our first hadith.** This is because things that are certainly permissible give serenity to the heart and doubtful ones bother and annoy. Once the doubtful ones are left, it is easier to judge and act appropriately in other matters. Indeed, once Muslims questioned Ibn Mas'ud (r.a.) on many issues. Ibn Mas'ud (r.a.) provided the following explanation for them:

"If any one of you faces an issue, let him judge with the Book of Allah! If he faces an issue whose solution is not in the Book of Allah, let him take care of the matter by following the judgments that the Noble Prophet gave.

If one cannot find a solution in the Book of Allah or in the rulings of the Prophet, then he should respond to the question by utilizing the rulings issued by pious scholars.

If he faces a matter that is not responded in the Qur'an, Sunnah, and rulings of the pious, then he should opine by using his intellect. He should not say "I fear to put forth my opinion" because what is permissible and prohibited is clear. There are doubtful and unclear matters between permissible and prohibited. Then, leave aside options that cause you to doubt and focus on the certain." (Nasai, Qada, 11)

As it is understood from the recommendations of Ibn Mas'ud, life is really easy for those who stay away from doubtful things. Then, paying attention to things that are clearly permissible or prohibited and staying away from the doubtful will lead one to salvation.

In our second hadith, it is expressed that most people do not know the doubtful things, so in this case the importance of staying away from doubtful things increases.

Giving an example here, the Messenger of Allah (pbuh) expresses that the shepherd who allows his flock to graze next to the prohibited land is face to face with the danger of violating the prohibition. Most of the times the shepherd does not enter the prohibited field himself and cause harm but cannot control the animals he is shepherding and becomes responsibile because of them. Similarly, an individual who comes close to the border of the prohibited action may fall into sin because of his carnal self, body parts, and individuals who are under his jurisdiction by being unable to control them. This is because people follow the path of their leaders and elders.

Staying away from doubtful matters protects one from violating prohibitions or falling into major sins and saves that person from many troubles right away and provides peace and tranquility. Also, consciousness of what is permissible and what is not gets strengthened as a result of being extra careful against the doubtful matters. On the other hand, a person who does not pay attention to doubtful issues starts seeing the abnormal situation that he is in as normal in time, and without noticing gets used to sinning and faces the danger of violating prohibitions and falling into major sins.

Everything that a human has depends on his heart. If he corrects his hear, then all his body parts will act well. Then, that person acts with sincerity and honestly and does not hold on to excuses on doubtful matters. In time, his heart becomes more sensitive and reaches a state where he starts to notice doubtful matters immediately. He, in turn, stays away from them with his whole mind. On the other hand, the person whose heart is spoiled sees every doubtful thing as permissible and does not hesitate performing such acts by putting forth excuses.

Then, in respct to doubtful matters the heart needs to be pious and tranquil in order to achieve an attitude that would please Allah. In time, the heart occupied with the prohibited loses its purity and becomes dirty. It even starts to darken after a time. At the end, it completely loses its sensitivity towards the prohibited.

For the salvation of the heart it is a must to hold on to the obligatory and supererogatory acts of worship and to the remembrance of Allah. The following is the advice of the Almighty Allah to His subjects:

"...for without doubt in the remembrance of Allah do hearts find satisfaction." (Al-Raʿd; 13:28)

Here the term remembrance also means the Qur'an. Namely, the attempt of living the entire rules of Islam will revive the heart and will increase its sensitivity against dangers.

In another noble verse it is said that:

"Is one whose heart Allah has opened to Islam, so that he has received Enlightenment from Allah, (no better than one hard-hearted)? Woe to those whose hearts are hardened against celebrating the praises of Allah. They are manifestly wandering (in error)!" (Al-Zumar; 39:22)

Umar (r.a.) expressed the sensitivity of the Noble Companions on suspicious things as follows:

"We deserted nine permissible things out of ten in order not to fall into interest (usury)." (Ali al-Muttaqi, IV, 187/10087)

In our third hadith, another criterion is provided to understand whether something is permissible.

When someone attempts to do something, if a question mark arises in his heart, or his heart does not feel that it is right, or if he is in doubt and afraid that it would be a sin, then he needs to stop there. Indeed, this is a warning of the clean heart and conscience, one needs to listen to it.

Wabisa b. Mabad (r.a.) says:

I had approached the Prophet. He told me:

"Did you come to ask what virtue is?"

I said "Yes."

Then, the Messenger of Allah (pbuh) said:

"Ask your heart. Virtue is what your soul finds appropriate and your heart approves. Sin, on the other hand, is something that bothers you from inside even though others issue many legal opinions in order for you to do it and raises doubt and hesitation." (Ahmad, IV, 227-228; Darimi, Buyu, 2)

The role of conscience in the matter of finding the truth is very big. A person who sincerely listens to his heart is generally not mistaken.

Once, someone from the Noble Companions had come to the Prophet (pbuh) and asked:

"How can I understand whether something causes doubt in me?"

The Messenger of Allah (pbuh) responded with the following advice:

"Put your hand on your heart because the heart gets scared from the prohibited and finds peace and tranquility in the permissible." (Haythami, X, 294)

Another criterion is the following: when a person feels ashamed from others' hearing about what he did, and hence does not want them to hear about it, that act is definitely inappropriate and sinful. Allah the Almighty does not approve such actions. This is a matter related to heart and conscience. A person knows in his conscience what people see as good or evil and acts accordingly. This situation is like a forced confession of those who try to interpret the voice of their hearts in one way or another. When a person attempts to do something, he may silence the voices in his heart and conscience with various excuses. However, his approach to the same action changes when he knows that it will be heard by other people. Because he knows that when people hear it, his misdeed will become apparent, he does not want others to know about it. Whereas, he was giving permission for himself to do it at the beginning! And so this is another sound criterion. This shows that the act in question is a sin.

A person should not forget that all feelings in the heart are known to Allah. He is All Knowing, All Seeing, and All Hearing. Therefore, everybody should understand that they can't deceive anyone but themselves.

On the other hand, feeling doubts about an act is enough to be a reason to stay away from it.

However, while trying to stay away from doubtful things, it is not right to part from the path of moderation and stay away from permissible things or raising unnecessary questions by falling into baseless suspicions about permissible blessings and causing trouble for Muslims. Because of the significance of this issue, Imam Bukhari included a special section in his *Sahih* and gave some examples related to it. (Bukhari, Buyu', 5)

In our fourth hadith, we are seeing an example of the Prophet's sensitivity about doubtful matters. He saw a date on the ground but did not eat it for it might be a charity or zakat. As it is known, the Messenger of Allah (pbuh), his family, and his descendants could not accept and consume zakat or charity (sadaqah). Almighty Allah has forbidden zakat and charity for the Prophet's family.[242]

However, this rule only applies to the Messenger of Allah (pbuh) and his family. Except them, it is not permissible for someone in need to refuse zakat or charity based on the prohibition of zakat for the Prophet and his family and to cause his family to fall into financially difficult situation. This is because the needy among the Noble Companions and friends of Allah have accepted zakat.

Moreover, even though the Messenger of Allah (pbuh) did not accept zakat and charity he had accepted the gifts of those who had received zakat or charity.[243]

The Prophet's thinking of picking up and eating a date on the ground shows that he does not like wasting and that he does not want even one date to go to waste. This incident also shows that the Messenger of Allah (pbuh) was so humble that he would pick up a date from the ground and eat.

By such characteristics the Messenger of Allah gives his nation such nice lessons. Accordingly, one should avoid doubtful things, nothing of value should be wasted, even a small thing should be utilized, and one should be humble.

242. Some of the wisdom behind this prohibition could be as follows:
• Almighty Allah did not want them to tend towards the material goods of this world.
• He wished that they protect their dignity.
• If there had been no such prohibition, Muslims might have started to give all their zakat to the Prophet's family and deprived others.
• Some people may have thought that our Master the Prophet had claimed prophethood for the purpose of obtaining wealth. By prohibiting zakat to the Messenger of Allah (pbuh) and his family Almighty Allah has removed this doubt all together.

243. Some meat was presented to the Messenger of Allah (pbuh) from the meat donated as charity to Barira, the servant of our mother Aisha. The Messenger of Allah (pbuh), who learned from where the meat had come, said:
"This is charity (sadaqah) to her but gift to us." (Bukhari, Zakat, 62; Hiba, 5; Muslim, Zakat, 170)
Again, the Pride of Universe (pbuh) had donated to Nusaibah al-Ansari a sheep from the zakat collwctions. She sent some meat from that sheep to Aisha. At that time the Messenger of Allah (pbuh) had asked to Aisha (r.anha) if she had with her something to eat. Aisha responded:
"No, except some meat from the sheep that you donated to Nusaybah."
The Messenger of Allah (pbuh) said:
"You can bring it, that sheep has found its appropriate place (It came to her as zakat but as gift to us)" (Bukhari, Zakat, 31, 62; Hibah, 5; Muslim, Zakat, 174)

The following incident that shows the sensitivity of the Companions in the face of doubtful and prohibited things is full of wisdom.

Abu Bakr (r.a.) had a slave who used to give him some of his earnings, and he used to eat from it. One day he brought something and Abu Bakr (r.a.) ate from it. The slave said to him:

"You used to ask about the source of my earning, but you didn't ask to-night, why?

Abu Bakr (r.a.) said:

"I was so hungry that I forgot to ask, so tell me how did you earn it?"

The slave said:

"Once, in the pre-Islamic period I foretold somebody's future though I did not know the knowledge of foretelling, namely I had cheated him. I met him today. He gave me something for that service, and that is what you have eaten from." Then Abu Bakr put his hand in his mouth and vomited whatever was in his stomach (even though it was tormenting).

"Shame on you! You were about to ruin me."

When it is said to him:

"Was it worth to torment yourself so much just because of a small bite?" Abu Bakr (r.a.) said:

"If I knew that I would even die, I would still take it out. That is because I heard from the Messenger of Allah (pbuh):

"The body fed by forbidden earning deserves more to be in the Hell." (Abu Nuaym, *Hilya*, I, 31; Bukhari, Fadail al-Ansar, 26; Ahmad b. Abdullah al-Tabari, *al-Riyad al-Nad-ra*, II, 140-141)

5. Repentance and Asking for Forgiveness

١٩٢. عَنِ ابْنِ عُمَرَ رَضِيَ اللهُ عَنْهُ قَالَ: قَالَ رَسُولُ اللهِ صَلَّى اللهُ
عَلَيْهِ وَسَلَّمَ:

«يَا أَيُّهَا النَّاسُ تُوبُوا إِلَى اللهِ فَإِنِّي أَتُوبُ فِي الْيَوْمِ إِلَيْهِ مِائَةَ مَرَّةٍ».

192. It is narrated from Ibn 'Umar (r.anhuma) that Allah's Messenger (pbuh) said:

"O people, seek repentance from Allah. Verily, I seek repentance from Him a hundred times a day." (Muslim, Kitab Al-Dhikr, 42. Also see. Abu Dawud, Witr, 26; Ibn Majah, Adab, 57)

❀

١٩٣. عَنْ أَبِي مُوسَى الْأَشْعَرِيّ رَضِيَ اللهُ عَنْهُ عَنِ النَّبِيِّ صَلَّى اللهُ عَلَيْهِ وَسَلَّمَ قَالَ:

«إِنَّ اللهَ عَزَّ وَجَلَّ يَبْسُطُ يَدَهُ بِاللَّيْلِ لِيَتُوبَ مُسِيءُ النَّهَارِ وَيَبْسُطُ يَدَهُ بِالنَّهَارِ لِيَتُوبَ مُسِيءُ اللَّيْلِ حَتَّى تَطْلُعَ الشَّمْسُ مِنْ مَغْرِبِهَا».

193. Abu Mu'sa al-Ash'ari (r.a.) narrated that Allah's Messenger (pbuh) said:

"Allah, the Exalted and Glorious, Stretches out His Hand during the night so that the people repent for the fault committed from dawn till dusk and He stretches out His Hand during the day so that the people may repent for the fault committed from dusk to dawn. (He would accept repentance) before the sun rises in the west (before the Day of Resurrection)." (Muslim, Kitab Al-Tawba, 31; Ahmad, IV, 395, 404)

❀

١٩٤. عَنْ أَبِي هُرَيْرَةَ رَضِيَ اللهُ عَنْهُ قَالَ: قَالَ رَسُولُ اللهِ صَلَّى اللهُ عَلَيْهِ وَسَلَّمَ:

«مَنْ تَابَ قَبْلَ أَنْ تَطْلُعَ الشَّمْسُ مِنْ مَغْرِبِهَا تَابَ اللهُ عَلَيْهِ».

194. Abu Huraira (r.a.) narrated that Allah's Messenger (pbuh) said:

"He who seeks repentance (from the Lord) before the rising of the sun from the west (before the Day of Resurrection), Allah turns to him with Mercy." (Muslim, Dhikr, 43)

❁

١٩٥. عَنِ ابْنِ عُمَرَ رَضِيَ اللهُ عَنْهُ عَنِ النَّبِيِّ صَلَّى اللهُ عَلَيْهِ وَسَلَّمَ قَالَ:

«إِنَّ اللهَ يَقْبَلُ تَوْبَةَ الْعَبْدِ مَا لَمْ يُغَرْغِرْ».

195. According to a narration from Ibn Umar, the Prophet (pbuh) said:

"Allah the Exalted accepts his servant's repentance so long as he does not show signs of dying." (Tirmidhi, Daawat, 98/3537. Also see Ibn Majah, Zuhd, 30)

❁

١٩٦. عَنِ ابْنِ عَبَّاسٍ رَضِيَ اللهُ عَنْهُ قَالَ: قَالَ رَسُولُ اللهِ صَلَّى اللهُ عَلَيْهِ وَسَلَّمَ:

«مَنْ لَزِمَ الْاِسْتِغْفَارَ جَعَلَ اللهُ لَهُ مِنْ كُلِّ ضِيقٍ مَخْرَجًا وَمِنْ كُلِّ هَمٍّ فَرَجًا وَرَزَقَهُ مِنْ حَيْثُ لَا يَحْتَسِبُ».

196. Abdullah ibn Abbas (r.anhuma) narrated that the Messenger of Allah (pbuh) said:

"If anyone continually asks pardon, Allah will appoint for him a way out of every distress, and a relief from every anxiety, and will provide for him from where he did not reckon." (Abu Dawud, Witr, 26/1518; Ibn Majah, Adab, 57. Also see. Ahmad, I, 248; Hakim, IV, 291/7677)

❁

١٩٧. عَنْ أَبِي مُوسَى رَضِيَ اللهُ عَنْهُ قَالَ: قَالَ رَسُولُ اللهِ صَلَّى اللهُ عَلَيْهِ وَسَلَّمَ:

«أَنْزَلَ اللهُ عَلَيَّ أَمَانَيْنِ لِأُمَّتِي:

(وَمَا كَانَ الله لِيُعَذِّبَهُمْ وَأَنْتَ فِيهِمْ، وَمَا كَانَ الله مُعَذِّبَهُمْ وَهُمْ يَسْتَغْفِرُونَ)

فَإِذَا مَضَيْتُ تَرَكْتُ فِيهِمُ الْاسْتِغْفَارَ إِلَى يَوْمِ الْقِيَامَةِ».

197. Abu Musa (r.a.) narrates that the Messenger of Allah (pbuh) said:

Allah the Exalted revealed two trusts to me for my nation.

"But Allah was not going to send them a penalty whilst you were amongst them; nor was He going to send it whilst they could ask for pardon." (Al-Anfal; 8:33)

When I leave them I leave asking for forgiveness (which is the second trust that will prevent Allah's torment) with them until the Day of Judgment." (Tirmidhi, Tafsir, 8/3082)

❁

١٩٨. عَنْ عَبْدِ اللهِ بْنِ بُسْرٍ رَضِيَ اللهُ عَنْهُ يَقُولُ: قَالَ النَّبِيُّ صَلَّى اللهُ عَلَيْهِ وَسَلَّمَ:

«طُوبَى لِمَنْ وَجَدَ فِي صَحِيفَتِهِ اسْتِغْفَارًا كَثِيرًا».

198. According to a narration from Abdullah bin Boushr (r.a.) the Noble Prophet (pbuh) said:

"Glad tidings to those who find many repentences in their book of deeds on the Day of Judgment." (Ibn Majah, Adab, 57)

❁

١٩٩. عَنْ شَدَّادِ بْنِ أَوْسٍ رَضِيَ اللهُ عَنْهُ عَنِ النَّبِيِّ صَلَّى اللهُ عَلَيْهِ وَسَلَّمَ قَالَ:

«سَيِّدُ الْاسْتِغْفَارِ أَنْ تَقُولَ: (اللَّهُمَّ أَنْتَ رَبِّي لَا إِلَهَ إِلَّا أَنْتَ خَلَقْتَنِي وَأَنَا عَبْدُكَ وَأَنَا عَلَى عَهْدِكَ وَوَعْدِكَ مَا اسْتَطَعْتُ أَعُوذُ بِكَ مِنْ شَرِّ مَا صَنَعْتُ أَبُوءُ لَكَ بِنِعْمَتِكَ عَلَيَّ وَأَبُوءُ بِذَنْبِي فَاغْفِرْ لِي فَإِنَّهُ لَا يَغْفِرُ الذُّنُوبَ إِلَّا أَنْتَ)» قَالَ:

«وَمَنْ قَالَهَا مِنَ النَّهَارِ مُوقِنًا بِهَا فَمَاتَ مِنْ يَوْمِهِ قَبْلَ أَنْ يُمْسِيَ فَهُوَ مِنْ أَهْلِ الْجَنَّةِ وَمَنْ قَالَهَا مِنَ اللَّيْلِ وَهُوَ مُوقِنٌ بِهَا فَمَاتَ قَبْلَ أَنْ يُصْبِحَ فَهُوَ مِنْ أَهْلِ الْجَنَّةِ».

199. It is narrated from Shaddad bin Aws that the Messenger of Allah (pbuh) said:

"The most superior way of asking for forgiveness from Allah is:

"Allahumma anta Rabbi la ilaha illa anta, Anta Khalaqtani wa ana abduka, wa ana 'ala ahdika wa wa'dika mastata'tu, A'udhu bika min Sharri ma sana'tu, abu'u Laka bini'matika 'alaiya, wa abuu laka bi dhanbi faghfirli innahu la yagh-firu adh-dhunuba illa anta."

"O my Allah! You are my Lord. There is no god worthy of worship other than You. You created me. I am your servant. I am still keeping as much as I can my promise and wow that I gave you in the beginning of time. I seek refuge in You from the evil of my wrongdoings. I cite the favors that You granted upon me with thankfulness and confess my sin. Please forgive me, there is no doubt that there is no one else other than you who will forgive sins."

The Messenger of Allah (pbuh) continued as follows:

"If somebody recites it during the day with firm faith in it, and dies on the same day before the evening, he will be from the people of Paradise; and if somebody recites it at night with firm faith in it, and dies before the morning, he will be

from the people of Paradise." (Bukhari, Daawat, 2, 16. Also see. Abu Dawud, Adab, 100-101; Nasai, Istiadha, 57/5519; Tirmidhi, Daawat, 15/3393)

Explanations:

There is no question that people may commit sins. It is natural for mankind to err or fall into sin, knowingly or unknowingly. However, it can never be approved to continue to be in that state. It is necessary for a smart believer to immediately accept and confess his mistake and turn away from sin and turn to Allah. Indeed, the Messenger of Allah (pbuh) said:

"Every person can err. However, the best of those who err are the ones who repent a lot." (Tirmidhi, Qiyamah, 49/2499; Ibn Majah, Zuhd, 30)

Since Allah the Almighty desires that His servants hold on to repentance, He says:

"…And O Believers! Turn all together towards Allah, so that you may attain Bliss." (Al-Nur; 24:31)

"O you who believe! Turn to Allah with sincere repentance…" (Al-Tahrim; 66:8)

Before everybody else, the Messenger of Allah (pbuh) himself obeyed this divine command of God Almighty and has repented and asked for forgiveness every day. He did this not because he had committed sins but rather to obey Allah's command, to remember him, and to be an example to his followers and to show them how to repent and ask for forgiveness. He felt more than satisfied by confessing his weakness with great humility to our Exalted Lord and wrapping himself in a deep consciousness of being a subject of Allah. By recommending this state to his nation in **our first hadith**, he said *"O people! Repent to Allah! I repent to Him one hundred times a day."*

As we mentioned before in similar cases, the number "one hundred" here is not meant to limit the amount of repentance and asking for forgiveness with that specific number but to express that it needs to be done many times. In fact, there would be times when the Prophet repented one hundred times only in one gathering.

Ibn Umar (r.anhuma) narrated:

"We counted that the Apostle of Allah (pbuh) said a hundred times during a meeting:

$$\text{رَبِّ اغْفِرْ لِي وَتُبْ عَلَيَّ إِنَّكَ أَنْتَ التَّوَّابُ الرَّحِيمُ}$$

"My Lord, forgive me and pardon me; You are the Pardoning and Forgiving One." (Abu Dawud, Witr, 26/1516; Tirmidhi, Daawat, 38/3434)

One should repent as much as he is able to do, for this state would elevate the servant to the contentment of God Almighty.

It is expressed in a noble verse:

"...For Allah loves those who turn to Him constantly and He loves those who keep themselves pure and clean." (Al-Baqarah; 2:222)

The following noble hadith, which helps us understand how happy God Almighty becomes when one of His servants repents, should lead everyone to repent without losing time.

"Allah is more pleased with the repentance of a servant as he turns towards Him for repentance than this that one amongst you is upon the camel in a water-less desert and there is upon (that camel) his provision of food and drink also and it is lost by him, and he having lost all hope (to get that) lies down in the shadow (waiting for the death) and is disappointed about his camel and there he finds that camel standing before him. He takes hold of his nose string and then out of boundless joy says: O Lord, You are my servant and I am Your Lord. He commits this mistake out of extreme delight. (Muslim, Kitab Al-Tawba, 7; Tirmidhi, Qiyamat, 49; Daawat, 99)

Can anyone describe a happier moment than someone finding all his sustenance right beside him while he was hungry and thirsty and waiting for his death after losing everything? Then, Almighty God is much happier because His servant who was lost in the deserts of sin and was drifting towards destruction has returned and reached the shore of salvation. That means He loves His servant so much.

In our second hadith, we are told that repentance should not be delayed and that Allah accepts repentance all the time. Almighty Allah expects that His servant who errs should immediately realize his mistake and turn back. He expects that someone who commits a sin during the day should repent before the day passes on it. Similarly, someone who commits a sin during the night should hug repentance during the day. Allah mentions in the Noble Qur'an those who hasten in repentance with praise:

"And those who, having done something to be ashamed of, or wronged their own souls, earnestly bring Allah to mind, and ask for forgiveness for their sins, and - who can forgive sins except Allah - and are never obstinate in persisting knowingly in (the wrong) they have done." (Al-i Imran; 3:135)

Another aspect of the noble verse is the following: Only Allah the Exalted can forgive sins. Since sins carry the meaning of disobeying Allah, no one other than Allah can pardon from the punishment that will be given. (Al-i Imran; 3:129, al-Araf; 7:149)

While it is always possible to repent and ask for forgiveness, there is a special place for pre-dawn time in this respect. There are signs in certain noble verses and sayings of the Prophet indicating that it is better to repent and ask for forgiveness at times just before the morning.

We are informed that Allah's contentment, Paradise, and bounties will be bestowed upon the pious servants who repent during pre-dawn time.

In another verse, it is also said that:

"They were in the habit of sleeping but little by night, and in the hour of early dawn, they (were found) praying for forgiveness." (Al-Zariyat; 51:17-18)

For this reason, the time of pre-dawn and dawn are known as "the time for asking for forgiveness and prayer" among the salaf al salihun (the righteous predecessors) and paid attention accordingly. (Haythami, VII, 47; Mubarakfuri, *Tuhfat al-ahwazi*, II, 473-474; Ibn Hajar, *Talkhis al-Khabir*, IV, 206)

As stated in **our third hadith**, Allah the Exalted continues to accept repentances until "the rise of the sun from the West," which is one of the major indicators of the Day of Judgment. On the other hand, He does not forgive those who repent after seeing the rise of the sun from the West. This is because there remains no one who does not believe in Allah after seeing this major event. Thus, the test has ended. The essential matter is to repent while the test is ongoing.

Allah the Exalted says:

"...The day that certain of the signs of your Lord do come, no good will it do to a soul to believe in them then if it believed not before nor earned righteousness through its faith." (Al-An'am; 6:158)

The Messenger of Allah (pbuh) spoke of a gate located in the West and that its width is seventy years measured by the speed of a horse rider.

One of the scholars of hadith from Damascus, Sufyan b. Uyayna, said while talkin about this gate:

"Allah created this gate open when He created the Heavens and the Earth. This door will not be shut until the Sun rises from where it sets." (Tirmidhi, Daa-wat, 98/3535; Taharat, 71; Also see Nasai, Taharat, 97, 113; Ibn Majah, Fitan, 32)

"True, the "Door of Repentance" will remain open until the Day of Judgment, but not everyone is guaranteed to live until the Day of Judgment. Each person's Day of Judgment is his death. For this reason, **in our fourth hadith,** the arrival of the moment of death is compared to the rise of the Sun from West. When a person realizes that he will die for sure, there is no point of repentance and also no benefit will occur.

Allah the Exalted says:

"Of no effect is the repentance of those who continue to do evil, until death faces one of them, and he says, "Now have I repented indeed;" nor of those who die rejecting Faith…" (Al-Nisa; 4:18)

It is mentioned many times in the Noble Qur'an that no extra time will be given to those whose determined terms are reached. (Al-Muminun; 23: 43, Al-Araf; 7:34, Al-Munafiqun; 63:11, Al-Hijr; 15:5, Yunus; 10:49, Al-Nahl; 16:61)

On the other hand, no one knows his appointed time of death. The most curious conundrum that all the people want to solve is when they will meet the Angel of Death. In general, death suddenly seizes a person. Then, one should never delay repentance. One should hold on to repentance and asking for forgiveness immediately after wrongdoing. It is very wrong to think like "I am worried that I will nullify my repentance (i.e., return to sin), therefore I will repent in the future." No matter how many times one nullifies his repentance, one should still hold on to repentance. However, one should try to be sincere in this respect. Indeed, there is no point of repentance while having in mind the intention to sin. One should repent after each sin with the intention to never nullify it again. The following conditions for an acceptable repentance also indicate this point:

1. To part from the committed sin.

2. To regret for having committed it.

3. To strongly intend not to do it again.

4. If one has violated the rights of someone else, to pay it and make it up.

If someone falls prey to his carnal self and sins afterwards, what needs to be done is to again tend sincerely towards repentance. This is because our Exalted Lord is very merciful to us His subjects. Truly no one despairs of Allah's Soothing Mercy, except those who have no faith." (Yusuf; 12:87)

Inviting his subjects who oppressed themselves by sinning to immediately repent Allah the Exalted says:

"Say: "O my Servants who have transgressed against their souls! Despair not of the Mercy of Allah! For Allah forgives all sins: for He is Oft-Forgiving, Most Merciful. "Turn to our Lord (in repentance) and bow to His (Will), before the Penalty comes on you: after that you shall not be helped." (Al-Zumar; 39:53-54)

It is not right to continue sinning recklessly by giving up hope of Allah's Soothing Mercy or being sure of Allah's torment and not caring about sins. No matter how much a believer sins, he should stay between hope and fear, never turn away from his Lord, and immediately tend toward repentance. Indeed:

"For Allah does not love creatures ungrateful and wicked!..." (Al-Baqarah; 2:275-276)

As Allah the Exalted forgives those who rightfully repent before its time passes, He also turns its sins to rewards.

This good news is given as follows in a noble verse:

"Unless he repents, believes, and works righteous deeds, for Allah will change the evil of such persons into good, and Allah is Oft-Forgiving, Most Merciful." (Al-Furqan; 25:70)

However, it also understood from this verse that repentance and asking for forgiveness should not remain in the hearts and should be approved and supported by righteous deeds. This is because such righteous deeds performed after sins help remove the negative influence of sins. (Al-Hud; 11:114)

Indeed the Messenger of Allah (pbuh) advised a person who wants to repent from his sins to do good to his mother. When he learned that his mother was not alive, he told him to do good to his maternal aunt indicating that she is also at the same status of his mother. (Tirmidhi, Birr, 6; Ahmad, II, 13-14)

In the same fashion, expiation, which is a way to purify from certain sins, also aims to purify the carnal self from the dirt of sins by feeding and clothing the poor, sacrificing, or fasting. (Al-Maidah; 5:89, 95; Al-Mujadilah; 58:3-4)

The benefits and virtues of keeping on repenting are stated **in our fifth hadith**.

Since when one asks for forgiveness a lot the sins will be forgiven, Almighty Allah will start showering His purified subjects with His mercy, will save them from all sorts of trouble and problems and favor them with abundant blessings.

❀

At the time of Umar (r.a.), there was a drought and people were suffering from famine. They proposed the Caliph to go for a supplication for rain. When everyone gathered, Umar (r.a.) went up the pulpit to pray for rain. He started to ask for forgiveness. He was only asking for forgiveness and saying nothing else. After continuing in this fashion for a while, he came down the pulpit. The people there said in a perplexed fashion:

"O the Ruler of Believers, you went up to pray for rain but we never heard you pray. You only asked for forgiveness and came down?"

Umar (r.a.) said:

"I asked the mercy that you want by using the keys of heaven from which rain is descended" and as evidence to his word put forth the following noble verses:

"Saying: Ask forgiveness from your Lord; for He is Oft-Forgiving; He will send rain to you in abundance; Give you increase in wealth and sons; and bestow on you gardens and bestow on you rivers (of flowing water)."
(Nuh; 71:10-12)

451

"And O my people! Ask forgiveness of your Lord, and turn to Him (in repentance): He will send you the skies pouring abundant rain, and add strength to your strength: so turn you not back in sin!" (Al-Hud; 11:52)

"But ask forgiveness of your Lord, and turn unto Him (in repentance): For my Lord is indeed full of mercy and loving-kindness." (Al-Hud; 11:90)

Umar who recited these verses concludes his speech as follows:

"Then, ask for forgiveness of your wrongdoings and sins from your Lord, repent sincerely, and turn towards Allah." (Baihaqi, al-*Sunan al-Kubra*, III, 351-351)

Then, leaving sins and asking for forgiveness is a key that opens the Heavens. When people leave sins and make up with their almighty Lord, the doors of heaven will open and all sorts of mercy will shower us.

❁

Once four people came to Hasan al-Basri and each one of them complained from different things: drought, poverty, one from lack of his kids, and another one from infertility of his fields. This great friend of Allah recommended asking for forgiveness to each one of them.

Those who were with him said:

"Master, even though these people were troubled with different things, you recommended the same thing to all of them?"

Then, Hasan al-Basri responded them by reciting the verses 10-12 of Chapter Nuh (71), just like Umar (r.a.) did. (Aynî, *Umdat al-Qari*, XXII, 277; Ibn Hajar, *Fath al-Bari*, XI, 98)

❁

In our sixth hadith, it is stated that people will not be subjected to divine torment as long as they ask for forgiveness. As asking for forgiveness is a shield against worldly torments, it is also a salvation from eternal torment. It is trust and safety.

In our seventh hadith, people with many istighfars (asking for forgiveness) in their books of deeds are given the good news and called "How happy they are!" This is because, as stated in another noble hadith:

"Istighfar shines like light in the book of deeds. (Suyutî, *Jaami*, no: 3056)

Then, we need to keep on asking for forgiveness with sincerity and whole-heartedly. If asking for forgiveness is done only by the tongue, then it may not be seen in the book of deeds on the Day of Judgment. For this reason, the heart and soul need to participate in asking for forgiveness.

In our eighth hadith, the Messenger of Allah teaches a supplication for asking for forgiveness which includes every kind of prayer and repentance. Due to its importance, he names it as **"Sayyid al-Istigfhar:" the Master of istighfars**. Reciting this istighfar every day by making it one of our habitual recitations is a means for abundance in this world and in the hereafter. It is the renewal of the promise and contract that we gave in past eternity. Thus, how nice a deed it would be to recite and help everyone memorize such virtuous supplications and asking for forgiveness, just like our ancestors did. Muslims are in need of such direction from their leaders.[244]

Let us remind that a person should not be heedless to commit a sin by trusting in repentance and asking for forgiveness. A person who commits a sin by saying "Allah forgives" may not be saved from it and can go further. Or before he gets a chance to repent, he may face death when repentance is not accepted.

Our Exalted Lord warns us as follows:

"…Verily, the promise of Allah is true: let not then this present life deceive you, nor let the chief Deceiver deceive you about Allah." (Luqman; 31:33) Also see. (Al-Fatir; 35:5)

It is also true that not committing a sin is superior to being forgiven. Even though a sinner repents and his sin is forgiven, he loses many things. How nicely Mawlana Jalaladdin Rumi expresses this:

"True, there is forgiveness. However, even though he is forgiven, a thief would be happy to have saved his life. Otherwise, would it be possible for a thief to be a Wizir (Deputy King) or the Minister of Treasury?" (*Masnawi*, c. V, verse no: 3153-3154)

---

244. There are many narrations on the virtues of supplications like those recited after the ritual prayers and those recited at the location of the imam such as "Huwallahulladhi" ve "Amana'r-rasulu" in the morning, evening, and night prayers. It is very difficult for our people to know these. However, our scholars have turned this into regularity and had our people gain a good habit. In this way, people from all levels are performing a good deed by taking the advice of scholars even though they may not know the narrations regarding its virtue.

6. Piety (Taqwa)

٢٠٠. عَنْ أَبِي ذَرٍّ رَضِيَ اللهُ عَنْهُ قَالَ: قَالَ لِي رَسُولُ اللهِ صَلَّى اللهُ عَلَيْهِ وَسَلَّمَ:

«اِتَّقِ اللهَ حَيْثُمَا كُنْتَ وَأَتْبِعِ السَّيِّئَةَ الْحَسَنَةَ تَمْحُهَا وَخَالِقِ النَّاسَ بِخُلُقٍ حَسَنٍ».

200. Abu Dharr (r.a.) says:

The Messenger of Allah (pbuh) told me as follows:

"Wherever and however you are, be afraid of Allah! If you commit a bad deed, do a good deed right after that so that it would nullify and destroy that result of the evil act. Treat people with nice manners!" (Tirmidhi, Birr, 55/1987)

❀

٢٠١. عَنْ عَطِيَّةَ السَّعْدِيِّ رَضِيَ اللهُ عَنْهُ قَالَ: قَالَ رَسُولُ اللهِ صَلَّى اللهُ عَلَيْهِ وَسَلَّمَ:

«لَا يَبْلُغُ الْعَبْدُ أَنْ يَكُونَ مِنَ الْمُتَّقِينَ حَتَّى يَدَعَ مَا لَا بَأْسَ بِهِ حَذَرًا لِمَا بِهِ الْبَأْسُ».

201. As narrated from Atiyya b. Sadi‘ (r.a.), Allah's Messenger (pbuh) said:

"A servant of Allah cannot reach the degree of pious believers (muttaqin) unless he stays away from such things that are not harmful just because of his fear to commit a sin." (Tirmidhi, Qiyamah, 19/2451. Also see Ibn Majah, Zuhd, 24)

❀

٢٠٢. عَنْ أَبِي ذَرٍّ رَضِيَ اللهُ عَنْهُ قَالَ: قَالَ رَسُولُ اللهِ صَلَّى اللهُ عَلَيْهِ وَسَلَّمَ:

«إِنِّي لَأَعْرِفُ كَلِمَةً -وَقَالَ عُثْمَانُ آيَةً- لَوْ أَخَذَ النَّاسُ كُلُّهُمْ بِهَا لَكَفَتْهُمْ» قَالُوا:

«يَا رَسُولَ اللهِ، أَيَّةُ آيَةٍ؟» قَالَ:

(وَمَنْ يَتَّقِ اللهَ يَجْعَلْ لَهُ مَخْرَجًا).

202. Abu Dharr (r.a.) narrates:

"One day the Messenger of Allah said:

'I know such a verse that if all people acted in accordance with it, it would be sufficient for all of them.'

The Noble Companions asked:

'O the Messenger of Allah which verse is it?'

The Messenger of Allah recited:

"And for those who fear Allah, He (ever) prepares a way out…"[245] (Ibn Majah, Zuhd, 24)

۲۰۳. عَنْ سَعْدِ بْنِ أَبِي وَقَّاصٍ رَضِيَ اللهُ عَنْهُ قَالَ: سَمِعْتُ رَسُولَ اللهِ صَلَّى اللهُ عَلَيْهِ وَسَلَّمَ يَقُولُ:

«إِنَّ اللهَ يُحِبُّ الْعَبْدَ التَّقِيَّ الْغَنِيَّ الْخَفِيَّ».

203. Sa'd b. Abu Waqqas (r.a.) narrated that "I heard Allah's Messenger (pbuh) as saying:

"Allah loves the servant who is God-conscious and is free from want and is hidden (from the view of people)." (Muslim, Kitab al-Zuhd wa al-Raqa'iq, 11)

---

245. Al-Talaq; 65:2.

٢٠٤. عَنْ أَبِي هُرَيْرَةَ رَضِيَ اللّٰهُ عَنْهُ قِيلَ:

«يَا رَسُولَ اللّٰهِ مَنْ أَكْرَمُ النَّاسِ؟» قَالَ:

«أَتْقَاهُمْ ...».

204. Abu Huraira (r.a.) narrated:

Some people asked the Prophet:

"O Messenger of Allah! Who is the most honorable amongst the people?"

The Messenger of Allah (pbuh) replied:

"The most honorable among them is the one who is the most Allah-fearing." (Bukhari, Anbiya, 8, 14, 19; Manaqib, 1; Tafsir, 12/2; Muslim, Fadail, 168)

❧

٢٠٥. عَنْ أَبِي أُمَامَةَ رَضِيَ اللّٰهُ عَنْهُ يَقُولُ: سَمِعْتُ رَسُولَ اللّٰهِ صَلَّى اللّٰهُ عَلَيْهِ وَسَلَّمَ يَخْطُبُ فِي حَجَّةِ الْوَدَاعِ فَقَالَ:

«اِتَّقُوا اللّٰهَ رَبَّكُمْ وَصَلُّوا خَمْسَكُمْ وَصُومُوا شَهْرَكُمْ وَأَدُّوا زَكَاةَ أَمْوَالِكُمْ وَأَطِيعُوا ذَا أَمْرِكُمْ تَدْخُلُوا جَنَّةَ رَبِّكُمْ».

205. Abu Umama (r.a.) says: I listened to the Messenger of Allah (pbuh) in the Farewell Sermon while he was speaking to people. He said the following:

"Be pious towards Allah who is your Lord! Pray five times a day. Fast during the month of Ramadhan. Pay the mandatory Alms (zakat) rightfully out of your wealth. Obey your rulers! (In this case) you would (directly) go to your Lord's Heaven." (Tirmidhi, Jum'a, 80/616)

❧

٢٠٦. عَنْ عَدِيِّ بْنِ حَاتِمٍ رَضِيَ اللّٰهُ عَنْهُ قَالَ: سَمِعْتُ رَسُولَ اللّٰهِ صَلَّى اللّٰهُ عَلَيْهِ وَسَلَّمَ يَقُولُ:

«مَنْ حَلَفَ عَلَى يَمِينٍ ثُمَّ رَأَى أَتْقَى لِلهِ مِنْهَا فَلْيَأْتِ التَّقْوَى».

206. 'Adi b. Hatim reported Allah's Messenger (pbuh) as saying:

"He who took an oath, but he found something else better than that, should do that which is better and break his oath." (Muslim, Aiman 15)

❀

٢٠٧. عَنْ زَيْدِ بْنِ أَرْقَمَ رَضِيَ اللهُ عَنْهُ قَالَ: كَانَ رَسُولُ اللهِ صَلَّى اللهُ عَلَيْهِ وَسَلَّمَ يَقُولُ:

«اَللّهُمَّ آتِ نَفْسِي تَقْوَاهَا وَزَكِّهَا أَنْتَ خَيْرُ مَنْ زَكَّاهَا أَنْتَ وَلِيُّهَا وَمَوْلَاهَا».

207. Zaid b. Arkam (r.a.) reported: The Messenger of Allah (pbuh) used to supplicate:

"...O Allah, grant to my soul the sense of righteousness and purify it, for Thou art the Best Purifier thereof. You are the Protecting Friend thereof, and Guardian thereof." (Muslim, Kitab Al-Dhikr, 73)

Explanations:

Taqwa (piety) means to stay away, protect, hesitate, keep away from things that are disliked, to protect oneself from dangers, and to place a bar between himself and the things that he is afraid of. Piety means to carefully protect oneself from the things that can hurt and cause pain in the Hereafter by seeking refuge in the protection and trust of Allah and to hold on to righteous deeds by staying away from sins.

The lower limit of piety is to protect oneself from disbelief and associating partners with Allah. Its mid level is to leave great and lesser sins, and the upper level is to protect the heart from all kinds of negative thoughts and to turn away from everything (masiwa) other than Allah. There is no limit or end for this state of piety. For each pious person, there is always a higher rank that he can rise up to. This spiritual journey continues until death.

One of the higher ranks of piety is to obey Allah in whatever way, in no way to rebel to Him, to always remember Him and always to be thankful and never to be ungrateful to bounties from Allah.

A person's piety is assessed by his keeping away from prohibitions rather than his acts of worship.

One day Umar (r.a.) asked Ubai b. Qa'b what piety is. Ubai (r.a.) said to him:

"Did you ever walk on a path with thorny plants on the side, O Umar?"

When Umar (r.a.) responded:

"Yes, I did." This time Ubai (r.a.) asked:

"So, what did you do?" Umar (r.a.) responded:

"I raised my clothes and paid utmost attention for the thorns not to harm me." Upon this, Ubai bin Qa'b (r.a.) said:

"There you go, this is piety." (Ibn Kathir, *Tafsir*, I, 42)

Just as a person walks carefully, diligently, and alert in a thorny field in order not to get harmed, a believer should act with similar care and accuracy in his religious life in order not to touch the prohibited and disliked things. God-fearingness or piety is the state that makes us obey Allah's commands and prohibitions in order not to lose His love and contentment and not to attract His Wrath. It is placing this state of submission as a curtain between us and those that are feared. For this reason, piety (taqwa) can be shortly interpreted as "Fearing from Allah" and "Revering Him."

Piety necessitates to be respectful to Allah and to be continuously alert, careful, and conscious when alone, with people, in times of trials and turbulences, in wealth as well as in poverty, in short in every state.

Maimun b. Mahran said:

"So long as a servant of Allah does not hold himself accountable just like he watches around and holds other people accountable thinking 'from where he finds his sustenance,' he can never reach the level of Muttaqi (pious)." (Tirmidhi, Qiyamah, 25/2459)

Almighty Allah cites the attributes of his servants who are pious (righteous) as follows:

• To have faith in Allah, the hereafter, angels, books, and prophets,

• To spend in charity for the kin, for orphans, for the needy, for the wayfarer, for those who ask, and for the slaves from the good and liked part of one's possessions because of the love or Allah.

• To perform the ritual prayer

• To give the mandatory alms (zakat)

• To keep one's promise when an agreement is made

• To be patient in pain (or suffering) and adversity, illness, and war. (Al-Baqarah; 2:177)

• To spend for the sake of Allah, whether in prosperity, or in poverty;

• To restrain anger,

• To pardon (all) men,

• To remember Allah, repent and ask for forgiveness whenever he commits a sin,

• Never insist in doing wrong deeds knowingly and willingly (Al-i Imran; 3:134-135)

As it can be seen, piety is one of the essential principals of religion. There is no higher state in religion than piety. It is also the only criterion that determines the honor and rank of a servant in the sight of Allah.

Indeed the statement of Allah **"Verily the most honored of you in the sight of Allah is (he who is) the most righteous of you"**[246] expresses this truth. So, piety is the most important means for the servant to gain spiritual stations and finally to reach the friendship of Allah.

Indeed in a noble verse it is said that:

"Allah is the Protector of the Righteous." (Al-Jasiyah; 45:19)

---

246. Al Hujurat; 49:13.

Piety is the most important sustenance for the Hereafter. It saves a person from eternal torment, makes him reach the heaven and Allah's consent.

Almighty Allah says the following:

"And take a provision (with you) for the journey, but the best of provisions is right conduct. So fear Me, O you that are wise." (Al-Baqarah; 2:197)

In our first hadith, it is emphasized that piety needs to encompass all aspects of life. Wherever and in whatever state a person is, he needs to know Allah as being with him and even closer than his jugular vein. In case he commits a sin due to falling into heedlessness, he should immediately pull himself together, and, after repenting and asking for forgiveness, should do a good deed as expiation for his sin. In this case, his wrongdoing will be erased and he will become all pure again.

Indeed, the life of a believer should pass with this kind of struggle to erase evil deeds and make good deeds victorious. A believer should spend all his effort in protecting himself from Allah's torment and achieving His contentment.

Indeed, Almighty Allah commands His servants as follows:

"O you who believe! Fear Allah as He should be feared, and die not except in a state of Islam." (Al-i Imran; 3:102)

"So fear Allah as much as you can; listen and obey and spend in charity for the benefit of your own soul and those saved from the covetousness of their own souls, they are the ones that achieve prosperity." (Al-Taghabun; 64:16)

How examplary the following example is, which reflects the spiritual state of a believer who fears Allah even in lonely places and he had opportunities:

Abdullah ibn Umar (r.aanhuma) was out somewhere near Medina. A table was spread to eat. At that instance, a sheep sheppard stopped by and greeted them.

Ibn Umar (r.anhuma) said

"Come O sheppard, let's eat,"

The Sheppard responded:

"I am fasting."

Ibn Umar said with awe:

"Are you fasting in this severe and suffocating heat? In addition, you are shepparding sheep in this state."

Afterwards, in order to measure the sense of piety and loyalty of the sheppard he proposed:

"Why don't you sell us a sheep from this flock? We can pay you its price, and give you from its meat sufficient for you to break your fast in sunset. He responded:

"I don't have a flock, these sheep belong to my master."

Ibn Umar (r.a.) said:

"You can say you lost it, how will your master know?"

The shepard turned his face away from him, raised his finger towards the sky and said:

"Where is Allah?"

Ibn Umar (r.a.) was very much touched by this piety state of the shepard. He continued repeating the words of the shepard to himself as "The shepard said 'Where is Allah', The shepard said 'Where is Allah.'"

When he arrived at Medina, he sent a messenger to the master of the shepard, and he purchased the flock and the shepard. He emancipated the shepard who was a slave and donated the flock to him. (Ibn Athir, *Usd al-Ghaba*, III, 341)

The Messenger of Allah (pbuh) has shown us the way in order to reach the state of piety that our Exalted Lord wants us to reach. As expressed **in our second hadith,** this way, which is extremely easy and short, is to keep away from even some permissible things that are close to harmful and doubtful things due to the fear of falling into harmful things.

Almighty Allah commands as follows:

"... Those are limits (set by) Allah. Approach not near thereto. Thus does Allah make clear His Signs to men: that they may learn self-restraint" (Al-Baqarah; 2:187)

In order never to fall into sin, the believer should have a sincere intention and should be as careful as possible. He should stay away from certain permissible things that he does not need or that would be wasteful. He should act carefully, thinking that every bounty has to be accounted for. One should know that it is a more foresightful act to use something in the way of good rather than to be accountable for it.

The soundest dress that protects one from the hot and cold of the eternal life is not to approach to the borders of harmful thing. Allah the Almighty called this the "Dress of Piety (Raiment of Righteousness)." This dress not only protects a person from embarrassment in the spiritual world, but also helps him look beautiful and ornamented thee.

How nicely our Exalted Lord speaks:

"O you Children of Adam! We have bestowed raiment upon you to cover your shame, as well as to be an adornment to you. But the raiment of righteousness, that is the best. Such are among the Signs of Allah, that they may receive admonition!" (Al-Araf; 7:26)

After stating the necessity of dressing for the body, Allah the Almighty emphasizes that in fact one should pay attention to the dress of the spirit. It protects the person from harm in the endless world, protects from embarrassing things, and adorns him in the best fashion.

Our second hadith explains that in order to achieve piety one should have determination and spend effort. Umar says the following to point out this fact:

"A person who does not try to protect himself from sin is not allowed to attain piety." (Bukhari, *al-Adab al-Mufrad,* no: 371)

Anas b. Malik (r.a.) explains Umar's effort in this respect as follows:

"I heard Umar b. Khattab's voice. I went to him immediately. At that time, someone had entered the garden. There was a wall between us. I heard him say as follows in the garden:

"O Umar b. Khattab, the ruler of believers! Look: be careful, be careful! By Allah, either you have piety for Allah or He torments you." (Muwatta, Kalam, 24)

Indeed, Umar reached the level of pious people (al-muttaqin) by continuously prompting himself with warnings of piety and with his piety became ever famous. May Allah bless him.

Piety, which is hard to attain, is such a blessing that it is enough for all people both in this world and in the Hereafter. **In our third hadith,** the Messenger of Allah (pbuh) informed us that if people acted upon a certain verse it would sufficient for all of them and recited the following noble verse:

"…Such is the admonition given to him who believes in Allah and the Last Day. And for those who fear Allah, He (ever) prepares a way out."[247]

In the following verses, Almighty Allah cites the bounties that He will favor upon people of piety as follows:

"And He provides for him from (sources) he never could imagine." (Al-Talaq; 65:3)

"…and for those who fear Allah, He will make their path easy. That is the Command of Allah, which He has sent down to you: and if any one fears Allah, He will remove his ills, from him, and will enlarge his reward." (Al-Talaq; 65:4-5)

As it can be seen, Almighty Allah repeats being a person of piety many times due to its importance.

One day the Messenger of Allah (pbuh) said:

"O people! If you take being pious towards Allah as commerce, your bounties will arrive to you even without having capital and making commerce." (Haythami, VII, 125) and then he recited the second verse of the aforementioned Chapter Talaq (65).

These expressions of the Prophet never mean "do not work." In contrast, it means "If you work honestly, Allah saves you from troubles, makes your job easier, gives you bounties from unexpected places, accepts your work for sustenance as worship by forgiving your sins, and favors you with a lot of rewards." On the other hand, bounty does not only mean things to eat and drink. Material or spiritual, all kinds of sustenance are bounties. Peace of mind, being able to taste, family bliss, being able to worship Allah, being able to prepare for the

---

247. Al-Talaq; 65:2.

Hereafter, seeing the marriage of one's kids, health, wellness are all bounties. So, the pious people are provided with such material and spiritual bounties.

There is one more favor of Almighty Allah to His pious servants, and it is also very important.

It is said in a noble verse:

"O you who believe! If you fear Allah, He will grant you a criterion (to judge between right and wrong), remove from you (all) evil (that may afflict) you, and forgive you: for Allah is the Lord of grace unbounded." (Al-Anfal; 8:29)

Thanks to the ability and understanding that are favored upon him due to his precision against the commands and prohibitions of Allah, the servant of Allah can separate right from wrong and achieves bliss in both worlds. Even in the most difficult or negative circumstances, he finds a way out and transforms all of his works into good.

The rewards of such a life that is lived upon such piety are bounties such as:

• To achieve the praise,[248] friendship,[249] help against enemies,[250] love[251] of Almighty Allah.

• To achieve honor in the sight of Allah (Al-Hujurat; 49:13)

• To have our conduct made whole and sound and our sins forgiven (Al-Ahzab; 33:70-71)

• To be saved from the sorrow of the Hereafter and to be received with glad tidings in the moment of death (Yunus; 10:63)

• To be removed far from the Hellfire[252] and to achieve endless bliss in Heaven.[253]

---

248. Al-i Imran; 3:186
249. Yunus; 10:62.
250. Al-i Imran; 3:120.
251. Al-i Imran; 3:76; at Tawba; 9:4.
252. Al-Layl; 92:17.
253. Al-i Imran; 3:133.

The Hereafter, in the sight of our Lord is for the righteous (pious).[254] They are in a position of security there.[255] The gardens, springs, the rivers, cool shades and all kinds of bounties are prepared for them.[256]

Almighty Allah speaks as follows:

"As to the Righteous, they will be in the midst of Gardens and Rivers, in an Assembly of Truth, in the Presence of a Sovereign Omnipotent." (Al-Qamar; 54:54-55)

Could there be a greater achievement than this? May our Lord bestow it upon all of us Amin!

In our fourth hadith, on the other hand, we are informed that Allah loves His servants who live a pious life. In the noble verses it is said that:

"Verily Allah loves those who act aright." (Al-i Imran; 3:76)

"Allah is with those who restrain themselves." (Al-Baqarah; 2:194, At-Tawbah; 9:36, Al-Nahl; 16:128)

Allah's love for one of His servants and His being with him is a bounty whose value is so high that it cannot be appreciated. Indeed, Almighty Allah gives the glad tidings that He will give these unmatched bounties to pious people.

A pious believer would be a person of charity, and would be precise in his worship, and hurts no one. He would stay away carefully from violations of other people's rights. Since he is an amicable person, everyone likes him and he likes everyone. Such a servant is liked by Almighty Allah and the Prophet, and other servants.

Indeed our Master the Pride of Universe (pbuh) says:

"For sure my friends are only the God-fearing." (Abu Dawud, Kitab Al-Fitan Wa Al-Malahim, 1/4242)

"The closest ones to me among the people are the pious for Allah whoever and wherever they are." (Ahmad, V, 235; Haythami, IX, 22)

---

254. Al-Zuhruf; 43:35.
255. Al-Duhan; 44:51.
256. Al-Rad; 13:35; Al-Duhan; 44:51-55; Al-Hijr; 15:45; Al-Zariyat; 51:15; Al-Tur; 52:17; Al-Qamar; 54;54; Al-Qalam; 68:34; Al Mursalat; 77:41; An-Naba; 78:31-36.

This is because such people are the most noble, righteous, and valuable among the creation. Indeed, **in our fifth hadith,** when people asked the Prophet who the most superior among the people are, he responded as *"The most pious ones."*

The differences among people such as race, color, nation, tribe, wealth, and property are determined by Almighty Allah due to many kinds of wisdom. People have no choice on them. So, these are not things that one should truly take pride in. The only honor that will cause a human to be praised in the sight of God is the state of piety that he obtained through great effort.

It is said in the Noble Qur'an:

"O mankind! We created you from a single (pair) of a male and a female, and made you into nations and tribes, that you may know each other (not that you may despise (each other). Verily the most honored of you in the sight of Allah is (he who is) the most righteous of you. And Allah has full knowledge and is well acquainted (with all things)." (Al-Hujurat; 49:13)

The following event which is the reason for the revelation of this verse and which shows how honorable the pious people are in the sight of both Allah and His Messenger is very exemplary:

One day the Messenger of Allah (pbuh) stopped by in one of the markets of the Medina. In the market a black slave was being sold by auction. The slave was saying:

"I have one condition for the person who will be my owner."

One of the potential owners said:

"What is your condition?"

The slave said:

"He will not prevent me from praying behind the Messenger of Allah in obligatory prayers."

The man accepted this condition and purchased the slave.

The Messenger of Allah (pbuh) would always see this slave coming to the obligatory prayers. One day, he again looked for him but could not see him. He asked the slave's owner, *"Where is your slave?"* He said:

"O Messenger of Allah (pbuh), he got malaria."

The Messenger of Allah (pbuh) said to his companions:

"Let's go and visit him."

"They got up and paid a get-well visit to the slave. A few days later the Messenger of Allah (pbuh) asked to the slave's owner:

"How is your slave?"

He responded:

"O Messenger of Allah! He is close to death."

Upon this, Allah's Messenger (pbuh) went to the slave and arrived just before he passed away. When the slave passed away, the Messenger of Allah (pbuh) personally handled his last ritual bath, shrouding, and burying.

The Noble Companions were surprised by his. The Immigrants (Muhajirun) said:

"We left our land, property, and family and migrated here, none of us has seen the esteem that this slave has received from the Messenger of Allah (pbuh), neither in our life nor in our death.

The Helpers (Ansar) thought:

"We gave refuge to the Messenger of Allah (pbuh), helped him, and supported him with our property and lives, but he preferred and Ethiopian slave over us. Upon this the aforementioned 13th verse of the chapter Al Hujurat (49:13) was revealed. (Wahidi, pp. 411-412)

Our Master the Pride of universe told Abu Dhar at another time that piety is the only measure of value and honor in the sight of Allah:

"Look! You are superior neither to red nor to black. You can be superior to them only by piety." (Ahmad, V, 158)

For this reason, the Messenger of Allah (pbuh) used to recommend piety to his companions and his followers at every opportunity. For example, he always recommended piety in his sermons to his companions.[257]

To a companion who came to him and asked:

---

257. For example see Abu Dawud, Sunnah, 5; Tirmidhi, Ilm, 16; Ibn-i Majah, Muqaddimah, 6.

"O Messenger of Allah (pbuh), I am going on a trip please advise me." He said

"The most necessary thing for you is to be pious towards Allah…" (Tirmidhi, Daawat, 45/3445)

To those who came to him asking "What is the most significant thing that would make one go to Heaven?" he again recommended piety and good manners. (Tirmidhi, Birr, 62/2004; Ibn Majah, Zuhd, 29)

Also, when he was passing away his last words have been on piety.

In our sixth hadith, we also see and advice that shows how important piety is.

"He who took an oath, but he found something else better than that, should do that which is better and break his oath." (Muslim, Aiman 15)

In fact, taking a vow is binding and one needs to keep it. A person who turns away from his vow needs to fulfill some kind of expiation (kaffarah) as punishment.[258] Even though taking an oath has such significance in Islam, breaking an oath and doing the action closer to piety is advised by the Prophet (pbuh) when it comes to matters related to piety.

In this respect, how teaching the following event is:

A beggar came to Adi b. Hatimm (r.a.) and begged him to give him the price of a slave, or some portion of the price of the slave. He (Adi) said:

"Currently, I have nothing to give you except my coat-of-mail and helmet. I will, however, write to my family to give that to you, but he did not agree to that.

Thereupon Adi was enraged, and said:

"By Allah, I will not give you anything." The person (then) agreed to accept Adi's offer, whereupon Adi (r.a.) said:

---

258. **The expiation (kaffarah) for taking an oath,** if one can afford it, is to free a Muslim or non-Muslim slave or she-slave. Those who cannot afford this should moderately dress ten poor people, if they are unable to do that, they should feed 10 poor people in the morning and evening, and if they are also unable to do that, they should fast for three days in sequence. The monetary compensation should be given to the poor, giving it to mosques and other similar institutions are not permissible.

"By Allah, had I not heard Allah's Messenger (pbuh) saying: *"He who took an oath, but then found something more pious in the sight of Allah, he should (break the oath) and do that which is more pious,"* I would not have broken my oath (and thus paid you anything)." (Muslim, Kitab al-Aiman, 15, 19; Imara, 13. Also see. Bukhari, Ahkam, 5, 6; Kitab al-Aiman, 1; Kaffarat, 10)

Piety comes first among the characteristics to be asked from Allah the Almighty. For this reason, as it can be seen **in our eight hadith** and in other narrations, the Messenger of Allah (pbuh) had always asked for piety from Almighty Allah. He said in his supplications:

"O Allah. I beg of You the right guidance, piety, chastity and freedom from want." (Muslim, Kitab Al-Dhikr, 72; Tirmidhi, Daawat, 72; Ibn Majah, Dua, 2)

When he was going on a trip he used to say:

"O Allah! We pray from you goodness and piety in this trip and that you allow us to do deeds that would please you." (Muslim, Kitab Al-Hajj, 425; Abu Dawud, Jihad, 72; Tirmidhi, Daawat, 45-46)

Let us too ask for piety from our Exalted Lord and try to be a pious believer.

7. To Leave Certain Desires and Passions

٢٠٨. عَنْ أَبِي هُرَيْرَةَ رَضِيَ اللهُ عَنْهُ أَنَّ رَسُولَ اللهِ صَلَّى اللهُ عَلَيْهِ وَسَلَّمَ قَالَ:

«حُجِبَتِ النَّارُ بِالشَّهَوَاتِ وَحُجِبَتِ الْجَنَّةُ بِالْمَكَارِهِ».

208. Abu Huraira (r.a.) narrated that the Messenger of Allah (pbuh) said:

"The (Hell) Fire is surrounded by all kinds of desires and passions, while Paradise is surrounded by all kinds of disliked undesirable things." (Bukhari, al-Riqaq, 28; Muslim, Jannah, 1. Also see. Abu Dawud, Sunnah, 22; Tirmidhi, Jannah, 21; Nasai, Aiman, 3)

٢٠٩. عَنْ أَبِي هُرَيْرَةَ رَضِيَ اللهُ عَنْهُ أَنَّ رَسُولَ اللهِ صَلَّى اللهُ عَلَيْهِ وَسَلَّمَ قَالَ:

«لَمَّا خَلَقَ اللهُ الْجَنَّةَ قَالَ لِجِبْرِيلَ: اذْهَبْ فَانْظُرْ إِلَيْهَا فَذَهَبَ فَنَظَرَ إِلَيْهَا ثُمَّ جَاءَ فَقَالَ: أَيْ رَبِّ وَعِزَّتِكَ لَا يَسْمَعُ بِهَا أَحَدٌ إِلَّا دَخَلَهَا ثُمَّ حَفَّهَا بِالْمَكَارِهِ ثُمَّ قَالَ: يَا جِبْرِيلُ اذْهَبْ فَانْظُرْ إِلَيْهَا فَذَهَبَ فَنَظَرَ إِلَيْهَا ثُمَّ جَاءَ فَقَالَ: أَيْ رَبِّ وَعِزَّتِكَ لَقَدْ خَشِيتُ أَنْ لَا يَدْخُلَهَا أَحَدٌ قَالَ فَلَمَّا خَلَقَ اللهُ النَّارَ قَالَ: يَا جِبْرِيلُ اذْهَبْ فَانْظُرْ إِلَيْهَا فَذَهَبَ فَنَظَرَ إِلَيْهَا ثُمَّ جَاءَ فَقَالَ: أَيْ رَبِّ وَعِزَّتِكَ لَا يَسْمَعُ بِهَا أَحَدٌ فَيَدْخُلَهَا فَحَفَّهَا بِالشَّهَوَاتِ ثُمَّ قَالَ: يَا جِبْرِيلُ اذْهَبْ فَانْظُرْ إِلَيْهَا فَذَهَبَ فَنَظَرَ إِلَيْهَا ثُمَّ جَاءَ فَقَالَ: أَيْ رَبِّ وَعِزَّتِكَ لَقَدْ خَشِيتُ أَنْ لَا يَبْقَى أَحَدٌ إِلَّا دَخَلَهَا».

209. Abu Huraira (r.a.) narrated that the Messenger of Allah (pbuh) said:

When Allah created Paradise, He said to Gabriel:

"Go and look at it!" He went and looked at it, then came and said:

"O my Lord! By Your might, no one who hears of it will fail to enter it."

Allah then surrounded it with disagreeable things, and said:

"Go and look at it, Gabriel!"

He went and looked at it, then came and said:

"O my Lord! By Your might, I am afraid that no one will enter it."

When Allah created Hell, He said:

"Go and look at it, Gabriel!"

He went and looked at it, then came and said:

"O my Lord! By Your might, no one who hears of it will enter it!"

Allah then surrounded it with desirable things and said:

"Go and look at it, Gabriel!"

He went, looked at it, then came and said:

"O my Lord! By Your might and power, I am afraid that no one will remain who does not enter it." (Abu Dawud, Kitab Al-Sunnah, 21-22/4744; Tirmidhi, Jannah, 21)

۲۱۰. عَنْ أَبِي بَرْزَةَ رَضِيَ اللهُ عَنْهُ عَنِ النَّبِيِّ صَلَّى اللهُ عَلَيْهِ وَسَلَّمَ قَالَ:

«إِنَّ مِمَّا أَخْشَى عَلَيْكُمْ شَهَوَاتِ الْغَيِّ فِي بُطُونِكُمْ وَفُرُوجِكُمْ وَمُضِلَّاتِ الْهَوَى».

210. Abu Barza (r.a.) narrated that the Noble Prophet (pbuh) said as follows:

"One of the things that I fear most about you is strong desires that lead you to excess in the matters of your stomachs and chastity, another one is the possibility that your desires and passions to lead you to fall into heresy." (Ahmad, IV, 420, 423; Haythami, I, 188; Abu Nuaym, *Hilya*, II, 32)

۲۱۱. عَنْ أَبِي مَالِكٍ رَضِيَ اللهُ عَنْهُ قَالَ: قَالُوا:

«يَا رَسُولَ اللهِ! حَدِّثْنَا بِكَلِمَةٍ نَقُولُهَا إِذَا أَصْبَحْنَا وَأَمْسَيْنَا وَاضْطَجَعْنَا» فَأَمَرَهُمْ أَنْ يَقُولُوا:

«اللَّهُمَّ فَاطِرَ السَّمَوَاتِ وَالْأَرْضِ عَالِمَ الْغَيْبِ وَالشَّهَادَةِ أَنْتَ رَبُّ كُلِّ شَيْءٍ وَالْمَلَائِكَةُ يَشْهَدُونَ أَنَّكَ لَا إِلٰهَ إِلَّا أَنْتَ فَإِنَّا نَعُوذُ بِكَ مِنْ شَرِّ

471

أَنْفُسِنَا وَمِنْ شَرِّ الشَّيْطَانِ الرَّجِيمِ وَشِرْكِهِ وَأَنْ نَقْتَرِفَ سُوءًا عَلَى أَنْفُسِنَا
أَوْ نَجُرَّهُ إِلَى مُسْلِمٍ)).

211. Abu Malik al-Ash'ari (r.a.) narrated:

The Companions of the Prophet (pbuh) said to him:

"Tell us a supplication which we repeat in the morning, evening and when we rise:

The Messenger of Allah (pbuh) commended them to say:

"O Allah! Creator of Heavens and Earth; Knower of all that is hidden and open; You are the Lord of everything; the angels testify that there is no god but You, for we seek refuge in You from the evil within ourselves, from the evil of the Devil accused and from the evil of his suggestion about partnership with Allah, and that we earn sin for ourselves or drag it to a Muslim." (Abu Dawud, Kitab Al-Adab, 100-101/5083)

Explanations:

Almighty Allah has created humans prone towards both good and evil. He taught humans both mischief and piety. In everything, He has stated its evil and goodness, what is good and bad, what is beneficial and harmful by saying things like "This is evil, bad, and sinful, it would lead yourself to mischief, so don't do it! This, on the other hand, leads to piety, goodness and obedience, and protection from evil, so do it!" So, He directed us and stated that we should keep away from one and do the other. (Al-Shams; 91:7-8)

In addition, Almighty Allah had clearly stated right and wrong and established criteria called prohibited and permissible by sending prophets and books. Then, in order to test humans who He gave intellect, understanding, and self-control capacity, He left them alone with their choice between these two paths.

In a verse it is said:

"And shown him the two paths?" (Al-Balad; 90:10)

However, also, with the deception of Satan, the carnal self of humans tend towards the prohibited rather than the permissible. The prohibited and unacceptable seem to him as more beautiful and attractive. The carnal self dislikes the difficulties of worships, good deeds, and charities. It tends towards things that come easy such as, leisure, entertainment, and personal benefits. These are called the passions and desires.

Desire (*hawa*) has meanings such as wants, passion, tendency, descending just like that of a falcon, fall, be destroyed, that a cup is empty, fruitless, and valueless. It is used to mean more for the tendency of the carnal self towards the bad desires prohibited by the intellect and religion; and also for deviating from the honesty, truth, and virtue and tending towards pleasure and personal benefits. So, staying away from passion and desires is one of the most important attributes of a believer. This is because such desires are the catastrophe of the intellect.

Even if a person advances to the highest levels of sainthood, he is still face to face with the tricks, whispers (causing baseless anxiety), and traps of the worldly attractions, carnal self, and Satan. As a matter of fact, the value of being a servant to Allah is becoming a pious person by defeating the attractive deceptions of this mortal world and as a result tending towards Allah.

Since humans came to this world for the test of servanthood to Allah, their mission is to struggle with the passions and desires of the carnal self until the moment of death and to direct it towards worship and good deeds.

However, the struggle with the desires of the carnal self is not an easy matter. For this reason, it is named by the Messenger of Allah (pbuh) as "the Great Struggle (Jihad)."

According to Jabir's (r.a.) narration, the Messenger of Allah (pbuh) said to the veterans returning from a difficult expedition:

"You have come in the best fashion. You have returned from the lesser jihad to the greater (or greatest) jihad."

They asked:

"What is greater (the greatest) jihad?"

The Messenger of Allah (pbuh) responded:

"It is the struggle of the slave of God with his desires." (Baihaqi, *al-Zuhd al-Kabir*, p. 198/374; Suyuti, *Jami*, II, 73/6107)

Also, the Prophet has praised those who struggle against their desires and passions as:

"(The true) mujahid is the person who struggles against his carnal self." (Tirmidhi, Fadail al-Jihad, 2/1621; Ahmad, VI, 20)

This is because while military jihad is obligatory on the community in general (fard kifayah), jihad with the carnal self is obligatory on everyone.

Ibrahim b. Adham said:

"The most intense jihad is the one with desires. Whoever denies his carnal self and his desires finds refuge from the world and its troubles. He will be protected from its torment and problems and have achieved peace." (Abu Nuaym, *Hilya,* VIII, 18)

Almighty Allah has informed us repeatedly with the strongest type of vows that those who discipline their carnal self and improve it with piety and those who enlighten it will achieve the true salvation. (Al-Shams; 91:1-9)

Disciplining the self is to purify it from spiritual blemishes such as disbelief, ignorance, evil feelings, false beliefs, bad habits, and desires and passions.

Those deceptive people who do not protect their carnal selves and lower it and bury it to darkness will be truly harmed and sorry by causing their soul to spoil. Following several vows Almighty Allah took one after another, He has informed us about this matter. (Al-Shams; 91:1-10)

This is because, an undisciplined carnal self left alone and free will cause its owner to deviate by being buried in unlimited lust and desire, and it drags him to catastrophe both in this world and in the Hereafter.

A person who follows the desires of his carnal self is a foolish and weak person. His carnal self both causes him to make mistakes and gives him false hopes that he can be saved in the Hereafter. On the other hand, the weak person who follows his desires somehow never wants to understand that there could be no such thing as both rebelling to Allah in this world and entering into Paradise in the Hereafter. He falsely consoles himself that his heart is pure and that Allah will treat him with mercy. We take these from the following noble hadith of the Prophet (pbuh):

"Smart person is the one who has disciplined his carnal self and who works for the life after death. Weak person is the one who subjects his carnal self to his

desires and keeps on asking from Allah (and sees this as sufficient)." (Tirmidhi, Qi-yamah 25/2459. Also see Ibn Majah, Zuhd 31; Ahmad, IV, 124; Hakim, IV, 251)

When a person obeys the desires of his carnal self, he moves away from purifying his soul with virtuous things and gives it to evil deeds and bad manners. Finally, he buries his soul in material by rotting it with bestial purposes and evil and dark feelings and hence makes it deserve to be thrown into hell-fire.

For this reason, the friends of Allah have seen the passions and desires of the carnal self as one of the biggest dangers for their spiritual and moral lives. This is because the Prophet has mentioned *"the desire that is followed"* among the things that cause distraction. (Munawi, *Faid al-Qadir*, III, 404/3471)

Mujahid, one of the great scholars of the Successors, said as follows:

"I am not sure which one of these two favors of Allah is greater: that He led me to the true path of Islam or that He protected me from the desires of my carnal self" (Darimi, Muqaddima, 30)

Also, Harith al-Muhasibi says:

"Whatever comes to you from Satan, who is your enemy, comes via the desires of your carnal self." (*al-Riaya*, p. 325)

One needs to be extremely alert and careful against the passions and desires of the carnal self. Otherwise, a person can be deceived, tricked by it, and falls into one of its countless traps.

Some of the warnings of Mawlana Jalaladdin Rumi in his *Mathnawi* are as follows:

"A person with a carnal soul is like Pharaoh, and his body is his Moses: he keeps running (to and fro) outside, asking, "Where is my enemy? His fleshly soul (is) luxuriating in the house, which is his body, (while) he gnaws his hand in rancour against some one else." (Mathnawi, II, v. 774-75)

"O son, if you seek (to know) the form of the self, read the story of Hell with its seven gates." (Mathnawi, I, v. 779)

"What you call carnal soul is a triagonal thorn: however you may place it, it will pierce, and how will you escape from its stab? Set the thorn on fire with

renunciation of sensual passion, and cling to the righteous friend." (Mathnawi, III, v. 375-76)

"The scoundrel carnal self tries to lead you to a worldly gain. For how long will you continue to busy yourself with such temporary worldly gain? Enough already that you have spent so much time on it."

"Even though the carnal self gives you fresh promises about goodness and righteousness he violates those promises and repentances thousands of times. Even if life gives you a term of a thousand years, your carnal self will find a new excuse every day." (Mathnawi, II, v. 2279-80)

"If that scoundrel carnal self asks from you righteous deeds that are noble and sacred that is, deeds that will provide you with spiritual benefits, do not be deceived! Behind this demand, there would be a trick of that enemy carnal self." (Mathnawi, II, v. 2274)

"The fleshly soul hath glorification of God (on its tongue), and the Qur'an in its right hand; (but) in its sleeve (it hath) dagger and sword." (Mathnawi, III, v. 2554)

"Be careful! You have ridden in chase of a deer and have made yourself the prey of a hog! In other words, you become a slave to your carnal self while you are trying to walk in the path of Allah." (Mathnawi, VI, v. 3684)

"All people except those who got drunk with the love of Allah are like children. None except those who have freed themselves from passions and desires have reached the age of adolescence."

"You, O prayerless man, have put the polisher of the heart (or Reason) in bonds and have loosed the two hands of passions and desires. If bonds be put on sensuality, the hand of the polisher (Reason) will be untied. A piece of iron that became a mirror of the Unseen - all the forms (of the Unseen) would be shot into it." (Mathnawi, VI, v. 2476-78)

As it is repeatedly expressed by the friends of Allah, passions and desires are the worst traps of Satan. The people who are drifted by them do not usually even understand that they are in error. They get consumed in them so much that they never even think of asking for forgiveness for their sins and turning to Allah.

Imam Awzai narrates:

Satan, the leader of the devils, said to his friends:

"From which way do you approach the Sons of Adam and deceive them?"

They said:

"We approach them from all sides with all things."

Upon this, Satan asked:

"All right, can you approach them through the path of asking for forgiveness?"

They said:

"Alas! Unfortunately, that is too difficult." Asking for forgiveness is done together with the word of acknowledging the oneness of God (la ilaha illallah)."

Satan said:

"I will spread such a thing among them that they will not ask for forgiveness for it!" and spread the passions and desires (of the carnal self) among people. (Darimi, Muqaddima, 30)

People who disregard the divine warnings and follow Satan and the desires which are attractive and pleasing to the carnal self will face the torment of Hell after briefly enjoying the worldly pleasures. This is because they have willingly and knowingly fallen into the trap of the carnal soul expressed **in our first hadith**.

As a requirement of the divine test, passions and desires are spread to the paths to Hell. Those who run after them will at the end see that Malik, the gate keeper of Hell, is waiting for them. The road to Heaven, on the other hand, is full of things that are considered as thorns and obstacles by the carnal self. In order to walk through that road, one needs to perform the acts of worship, live in accordance with the virtues, and make sacrifices that the carnal self does not like at all. The human carnal self, on the other hand, does not want to endure these difficulties. However, the real bliss is to endure those temporary difficulties and open those curtains. Indeed, struggle and fight with the carnal self step in right there.

If the carnal self is left alone, it follows the things that it likes without thinking where they end. However, one should never forget that "poison is presented in a golden cup." Those who act only by looking at the outside appearance of things will eventually face their miserable end. Those who sweetly scratch a wound on their body will soon notice that it turns into a large one which gives them a lot of pain.

The statement in our hadith "Hell is surrounded by the wants and lustful desires of the carnal self" shows that the drifting of people to Hell is mostly the result of their following the passions and desires of their carnal self. Since carnal self tends towards lustful desires, Gabriel (pbuh) states his fears **in our second hadith** that a great majority of humans will be drifted to Hell.

The expression in the hadith that "Heaven is surrounded by difficulties" states that entering there is possible only by following Allah's commands, staying away from His prohibitions, resisting the passions and desires of the carnal self, and enduring all the difficulties that will be faced in this path.

Since it is not the easy to conduct all of these fully and correctly, Gabriel (pbuh) has feared that humans will not be able to enter there.

The commands and prohibitions of Allah are difficult for the carnal self but they are like capital for the eternal bliss to the soul. Indeed, Abdurrahman b. Awf (r.a.) says:

"Islam has brought commands that were not pleasing to the carnal self. We found the best of the best in these difficult commands that our carnal selves disliked. For example, we had emigrated by exiting Mecca with the Messenger of Allah (pbuh). With the emigration that was hard on our carnal souls, superiority and victory were granted to us (the paths of victory were opened).

Again, we unwillingly went to Badr accompanying the Messenger of Allah thinking that we were almost being driven to death. Allah the Exalted describes our situation at that moment as follows:

"Just as your Lord ordered you out of your house in truth, even though a party among the Believers disliked it, disputing with you concerning the truth after it was made manifest, as if they were being driven to death and they (actually) saw it." (Al-Anfal; 8:5-6)

At the end, Almighty Allah favored us with dominance and victory in Badr.

<u>In short, we always reached the best favors thanks to the commands that were difficult upon our carnal self.</u> (Haythami, VII, 26-27)

Almighty Allah gives the following glad tidings to his servants who leave their desires and live a pious life:

"And for such as had entertained the fear of standing before their Lord's (tribunal) and had restrained (their) soul from lower desires, their abode will be the Garden." (An-Naziat; 79:40-41)

With his deep mercy to his followers, the Messenger of Allah (pbuh) warned them in order to to save them from Hell and go to Heaven. Indeed, **in our third hadith,** the Messenger of Allah (pbuh) states that the greatest of worries that he has for his nation are passions and desires.

It is definite that a person who does not struggle with his carnal self and agrees with all of its desires will eventually turn to wrong paths. This is because desires are the greatest reasons for falling into heresy according to the Noble Qur'an. Almighty Allah commands the Messenger of Allah (pbuh) as follows:

"Say: "I am forbidden to worship those - others than Allah - whom you call upon." Say: "I will not follow your wain desires: If I did, I would stray from the path, and be not of the company of those who receive guidance." (Al-An'am; 6:56)

In another verse, it is stated that none are more astray than those who follow their own desires:

"But if they hearken not to you, know that they only follow their own lusts: and who is more astray than one who follow his own lusts, devoid of guidance from Allah for Allah guides not people given to wrong-doing." (Qasas; 28:50)

This is because either the person will obey the commands of Allah or follow the desires of the carnal self. Doing them simultaneously is impossible. How nicely the poet expresses this:

With two *qibla* one cannot go straight on the path of *tawhid*,

Either the consent of the Friend or the desires of the carnal self will prevail.

It is not possible to get the carnal self fully satisfied and leave wrongdoings by itself. As one allows it to taste its desires, it asks for more and greater. How nicely Mawlana Jalaladdin Rumi describes this:

"Fiery lust is not diminished by indulging it: it is diminished, without any escape (inevitably), by leaving it (ungratified). So long as thou art laying faggots on a fire, how will the fire be extinguished by a carrier of faggots?" (*Mathnawi*, I, 3703-4)

In time, the rampant carnal self asks for so many things that if they are done, neither the individual's, nor the societies', nor the universe's order can stand. This is because the carnal soul always thinks of the pleasuring and entertaining aspects of things and never bothers with whether it is right or wrong.

Almighty Allah speaks as follows:

"If the Truth had been in accord with their desires, truly the heavens and the earth, and all beings therein would have been in confusion and corruption! Nay, We have sent them their admonition, but they turn away from their admonition." (Al-Muminun; 23:71)

It would also be appropriate here to point out the grave danger of the people who would like to understand and interpret the Qur'an according to their own desires.

Those who follow their passion and desires fall into the great heresy of prioritizing their desires before all and adopting them as their gods. While they hold onto none of Allah's commands, they want to realize all kinds of passions and desires that they have. Almighty Allah criticizes such people with a heavy style and speaks as follows:

"Do you see such the one as takes for his god his own passion (or impulse)? Could you be a disposer of affairs for him? Or do you think thou that most of them listen or understand? They are only like cattle; nay, they are worse astray in Path." (Al-Furqan; 25:43-44, Al-Jasiyah; 45:23)

Those who follow their desires pretend not to have heard the verses of Allah and do not take lessons from the signs of His power in this universe. Since their carnal selves are pleased by swimming in heedlessness, they never want to wake up. Since they do all these even though they are bestowed with intellect and they know the truth, they fall into lower levels than animals. (Al-Araf; 7:179; (Al-Furqan; 25:43-44)

The Messenger of Allah (pbuh) expresses as follows how great an evil it is to adopt desires as deity;

"According to Allah, there is no more serious and worse false deity among the deities that are worshipped under the sky than the desires that are followed." (Haythami, I, 188)

A person conducts all the sins and wrongdoings when he follows the desires of the carnal self. So, there is not any person worse than the one who follows his passions and desires as if he adopts them as deity. In a noble hadith, the wrongdoings that leaving the Qur'an and Sunnah (the traditions of the Prophet) and following the desires bring and the evilness of the people who commṣt them are listed as follows:

"*How bad is a slave of Allah who forgets Allah the Greatest and the Most Exalted by drifting in empty dreams and boasting! How bad is a slave who is tyrant and violates others' rights by forgetting Allah the Compeller! How bad is a slave who laughs and plays in heedlessness and forgets the decay in graves! How bad is a slave who goes excessive and rampant and forgets his beginning and end. How bad is a slave who looks religious and deceives people and runs after worldly benefits! How bad is a slave who corrupts his religion with doubtful things!* How bad is a slave who is drifted to rebellious acts due to his greed and ambition! How bad is a slave who falls into despicableness due to his excessive desires and wants towards worldly wealth!*"* (Tirmidhi, Qiyamah, 17/2448; Hakim, IV, 351/7885; Haythami, X, 234)

The Messenger of Allah (pbuh) also expressed that he is distant from those following their desires, and they are also distant from him. (Haythami, VII, 22)

When it is carefully analyzed, it can be inferred from the hadith that all of the attributes listed here emerge due to being subject of one's desires. For this reason, the Messenger of Allah (pbuh) was worried about his followers who were the subjects of their desires and he said:

"*For my followers, I am most worried that they listen to their carnal desires.*" (See Haythami, I, 187; Suyuti, I, 12)

In various verses of the Noble Qur'an, following those who are subjects of their desires is also strictly forbidden. That is because acting this way drags one to disaster as well. The thing that Muslims should do is to act upon knowledge rather than accepting the leadership of those who are the followers of their own desires. Since the source of knowledge is divine revelations, revelation and human desires are contradictory and opposite of each other. It is expressed in a noble verse:

"Never will the Jews or the Christians be satisfied with you unless thou follow their form of religion. Say: "The Guidance of Allah, that is the (only) Guidance." Were you to follow their desires after the knowledge which has reached you, then would you find neither Protector nor helper against Allah." (Al-Baqarah; 2:120)

"Say: "O people of the Book! exceed not in your religion the bounds (of what is proper), trespassing beyond the truth, nor follow the vain desires of people who went wrong in times gone by, who misled many, and strayed (themselves) from the even way." (Al-Maidah; 5:77)

For this reason, the Messenger of Allah (pbuh) advised us to take refuge in Allah often from the evils of the carnal self. **In our forth hadith,** when one of the Companions of the Messenger of Allah (pbuh) asked "How should we pray in the morning, evening, and when we go to sleep?" he taught them a prayer and first of all said *"We take refuge in You my Lord from the evils of our carnal selves."*

Again the Messenger of Allah (pbuh) said in one of his sermon prayers:

"We take refuge from the evils within ourselves." (Abu Dawud, Kitab Al-Nikah, 31-32/2118; Tirmidhi, Kitab Al-Nikah, 17/1105; Nasai, Jum'a, 14)

The Messenger of Allah said to Husain, one of his Companions:

"If you convert to Islam, I will teach you two benefitial sentences" and after he became Muslim, he taught him the following prayer:

"O Lord, show me the best and most true one and protect me from the evils of my carnal self!" (Tirmidhi, Daawat, 69/3483)

Therefore, the era of the Messenger of Allah became a time period in which people stayed away from the fancies and desires of the carnal self. Ibn Mas'ud (r.a.) compared that exemplary era and following ones and warned someone saying:

"You live in a time period when canonists (of Islamic jurisprudence) are many and ignorant readers are few, when more weight is given to the judgments of the Qur'an than its recitation, when people who ask for something are few and people who give are many, when the prayers are performed long and sermons are kept short, and when good deeds are preferred over wants and desires. There will be a time period when canonists will be few and ignorant readers will be many, people will pay attention to the recitation of the letters and the words of the Qur'an but will not pay attention to practicing the commands in the Qur'an, there will be many people who will ask for something but few people who will give, they will keep the performance of the prayer short but the sermon long, and their wants and desires will be preferred over their good deeds." (*Muwatta*, Qasr al-Salat, 88; Bukhari, *al-Adab al-mufrad*, no: 789)

May Our Almighty Lord protect us from the evils of our carnal selves and from being the slaves of their wishes and desires! May Allah make us among His servants who abandon his desires and look for the content of the Friend!

Amin!.

8. Not to be fooled by Satan

٢١٢. عَنْ عَبْدِ اللهِ بْنِ مَسْعُودٍ رَضِيَ اللهُ عَنْهُ قَالَ: قَالَ رَسُولُ اللهِ صَلَّى اللهُ عَلَيْهِ وَسَلَّمَ:

«إِنَّ لِلشَّيْطَانِ لَمَّةً بِابْنِ آدَمَ وَلِلْمَلَكِ لَمَّةً فَأَمَّا لَمَّةُ الشَّيْطَانِ فَإِيعَادٌ بِالشَّرِّ وَتَكْذِيبٌ بِالْحَقِّ وَأَمَّا لَمَّةُ الْمَلَكِ فَإِيعَادٌ بِالْخَيْرِ وَتَصْدِيقٌ بِالْحَقِّ فَمَنْ وَجَدَ ذَلِكَ فَلْيَعْلَمْ أَنَّهُ مِنَ اللهِ فَلْيَحْمَدِ اللهَ وَمَنْ وَجَدَ الْأُخْرَى فَلْيَتَعَوَّذْ بِاللهِ مِنَ الشَّيْطَانِ الرَّجِيمِ» ثُمَّ قَرَأَ:

(اَلشَّيْطَانُ يَعِدُكُمُ الْفَقْرَ وَيَأْمُرُكُمْ بِالْفَحْشَاءِ).

212. Abdullah b. Mas'ud (r.a.) narrated: The Messenger of Allah (pbuh) said:

"Surely Satan and angels can have a guiding influence upon the hearts of humans. Satan's influence is guiding towards the wrong deeds and to deny the truth and the angels' influence is towards the good deeds and to acknowledge the

truth. Those who feel the influence towards the good deeds should acknowledge that this is from Allah and thank Him. Those who sense a feeling that encourages him towards wrong deeds should take refuge in Almighty Allah from the evils of the expelled Satan."

Then the Messenger of Allah (pbuh) recited the following verse from the Noble Qur'an:

"The Evil one threatens you with poverty and bids you to conduct un-seemly." (Al-Baqarah; 2:268) (Tirmidhi, Tafsir, 2/2988)

❁

٢١٣. عَنْ عَلِيِّ بْنِ الْحُسَيْنِ رَضِيَ اللهُ عَنْهُمَا أَنَّ صَفِيَّةَ زَوْجَ النَّبِيِّ صَلَّى اللهُ عَلَيْهِ وَسَلَّمَ أَخْبَرَتْهُ: كَانَ النَّبِيُّ صَلَّى اللهُ عَلَيْهِ وَسَلَّمَ فِي الْمَسْجِدِ وَعِنْدَهُ أَزْوَاجُهُ فَرُحْنَ فَقَالَ لِصَفِيَّةَ بِنْتِ حُيَيٍّ:

«لَا تَعْجَلِي حَتَّى أَنْصَرِف مَعَكِ» وَكَانَ بَيْتُهَا فِي دَارِ أُسَامَةَ فَخَرَجَ النَّبِيُّ صَلَّى اللهُ عَلَيْهِ وَسَلَّمَ مَعَهَا فَلَقِيَهُ رَجُلَانِ مِنَ الْأَنْصَارِ فَنَظَرَا إِلَى النَّبِيِّ صَلَّى اللهُ عَلَيْهِ وَسَلَّمَ ثُمَّ أَجَازَا وَقَالَ لَهُمَا النَّبِيُّ صَلَّى اللهُ عَلَيْهِ وَسَلَّمَ:

«تَعَالَيَا إِنَّهَا صَفِيَّةُ بِنْتُ حُيَيٍّ» قَالَا:

«سُبْحَانَ اللهِ يَا رَسُولَ اللهِ» قَالَ:

«إِنَّ الشَّيْطَانَ يَجْرِي مِنَ الْإِنْسَانِ مَجْرَى الدَّمِ وَإِنِّي خَشِيتُ أَنْ يُلْقِيَ فِي أَنْفُسِكُمَا شَيْئًا».

213. Ali b. al-Husain narrated from Safiya (r.anha), the respected wife of the Prophet:

The wives of the Prophet were with him in the mosque (while he was in retreat (itikaf)) and after a while they wanted to depart. The Prophet (pbuh) said to Safiya bint Huyai:

"Don't hurry, for I shall accompany you."

That is because her home was a little far and it was later given to Usama b. Zaid. The Prophet (pbuh) went out to accompany her. In the meantime two Ansari men met him and they looked at the Prophet and (upon seeing that his family was with him) passed by quickly.

The Prophet said to them:

"Come here. She is (my wife) Safiya bint Huyai."

They replied:

"Subhan Allah, (How dare we think of evil) O Allah's Apostle! (We never expect anything bad from you)."

The Messenger of Allah (pbuh) said:

"Satan circulates in the human being as blood circulates in the body, and I was afraid lest Satan might insert an evil thought in your minds." (Bukhari, I'tikaf, 11. Also see Bukhari, Bad'u'l-halk, 11; Ahkam, 21; Muslim, Salam, 23-25; Abu Dawud, Sawm, 79; Adab, 81; Ibn Majah, Siyam, 65)

۲۱٤. عَنْ عَبْدِ اللهِ رَضِيَ اللهُ عَنْهُ قَالَ: خَطَّ رَسُولُ اللهِ صَلَّى اللهُ عَلَيْهِ وَسَلَّمَ خَطًّا بِيَدِهِ ثُمَّ قَالَ:

«هٰذَا سَبِيلُ اللهِ مُسْتَقِيمًا» قَالَ ثُمَّ خَطَّ عَنْ يَمِينِهِ وَشِمَالِهِ ثُمَّ قَالَ:

«هٰذِهِ السُّبُلُ وَلَيْسَ مِنْهَا سَبِيلٌ إِلَّا عَلَيْهِ شَيْطَانٌ يَدْعُو إِلَيْهِ» ثُمَّ قَرَأَ:

(وَأَنَّ هٰذَا صِرَاطِي مُسْتَقِيمًا فَاتَّبِعُوهُ وَلَا تَتَّبِعُوا السُّبُلَ فَتَفَرَّقَ بِكُمْ عَنْ سَبِيلِهِ ذٰلِكُمْ وَصَّيكُمْ بِهِ لَعَلَّكُمْ تَتَّقُونَ).

214. Abdullah b. Mas'ud (r.a.) said:

The Messenger of Allah (pbuh) drew a line and said:

"This is the true (straight) path of Allah."

Then he drew other lines to the left and to the right sides of the first one and said:

"These are some other paths. There is Satan on each one of these paths to call you to follow these paths."

Then he recited the following verse of Allah the Almighty:

"Verily, this is My way, leading straight: follow it: follow not (other) paths: they will scatter you about from His (great) path: thus He commands you that you may be righteous." (Al-An'am; 6:153) (Ahmad, I, 465, 435; III, 397. Also see Ibn Majah, Muqaddima, 1; Darimi, Muqaddima, 23; Hakim, II, 349/3241)

٢١٥. عَنْ أَبِي هُرَيْرَةَ رَضِيَ اللهُ عَنْهُ أَنَّ النَّبِيَّ صَلَّى اللهُ عَلَيْهِ وَسَلَّمَ قَالَ:

«إِذَا نُودِيَ لِلصَّلَاةِ أَدْبَرَ الشَّيْطَانُ لَهُ ضُرَاطٌ حَتَّى لَا يَسْمَعَ التَّأْذِينَ فَإِذَا قُضِيَ التَّأْذِينُ أَقْبَلَ حَتَّى إِذَا ثُوِّبَ بِالصَّلَاةِ أَدْبَرَ حَتَّى إِذَا قُضِيَ التَّثْوِيبُ أَقْبَلَ حَتَّى يَخْطُرَ بَيْنَ الْمَرْءِ وَنَفْسِهِ يَقُولُ لَهُ: اذْكُرْ كَذَا وَاذْكُرْ كَذَا لِمَا لَمْ يَكُنْ يَذْكُرُ مِنْ قَبْلُ حَتَّى يَظَلَّ الرَّجُلُ مَا يَدْرِي كَمْ صَلَّى».

215. Abu Huraira (r.a.) reported the Messenger of Allah (pbuh) as saying:

"When the call to prayer is made, Satan runs back and breaks wind so as not to hear the call being made, and when the call is finished. He turns round when Iqama is proclaimed he turns his back, and when it is finished he turns round to distract a man, saying: Remember such and such; remember such and such, referring to something the man did not have in his mind, with the result that he does

not know how much he has prayed." (Muslim, Salah, 19. Also see Bukhari, Adhan, 4; Amal fi al-Salat, 18; Sahw, 6; Bad' al-khalk, 11; Abu Dawud, Salat, 31; Nasai, Adhan, 20, 30)

❀

٢١٦. عَنْ جَابِرٍ رَضِيَ اللهُ عَنْهُ قَالَ: سَمِعْتُ النَّبِيَّ صَلَّى اللهُ عَلَيْهِ
وَسَلَّمَ يَقُولُ:

«إِنَّ الشَّيْطَانَ قَدْ أَيِسَ أَنْ يَعْبُدَهُ الْمُصَلُّونَ فِي جَزِيرَةِ الْعَرَبِ وَلَكِنْ
فِي التَّحْرِيشِ بَيْنَهُمْ».

216. Jabir (r.a.) reported: I heard the Prophet (pbuh) saying:

"*Satan abandoned hope that Muslims in the Arabian Peninsula to worship him. However, Satan will work on to set them against each other and rift them.*" (Muslim, Munafiqin, 65. Also see. Tirmidhi, Birr, 25/1937; Fitan, 2/2159; Ahmad, III, 313, 354, 384)

❀

٢١٧. عَنْ حُذَيْفَةَ رَضِيَ اللهُ عَنْهُ قَالَ: كُنَّا إِذَا حَضَرْنَا مَعَ النَّبِيّ
صَلَّى اللهُ عَلَيْهِ وَسَلَّمَ طَعَامًا لَمْ نَضَعْ أَيْدِينَا حَتَّى يَبْدَأَ رَسُولُ اللهِ صَلَّى
اللهُ عَلَيْهِ وَسَلَّمَ فَيَضَعَ يَدَهُ وَإِنَّا حَضَرْنَا مَعَهُ مَرَّةً طَعَامًا فَجَاءَتْ جَارِيَةٌ
كَأَنَّهَا تُدْفَعُ فَذَهَبَتْ لِتَضَعَ يَدَهَا فِي الطَّعَامِ فَأَخَذَ رَسُولُ اللهِ صَلَّى اللهُ
عَلَيْهِ وَسَلَّمَ بِيَدِهَا ثُمَّ جَاءَ أَعْرَابِيٌّ كَأَنَّمَا يُدْفَعُ فَأَخَذَ بِيَدِهِ فَقَالَ رَسُولُ
اللهِ صَلَّى اللهُ عَلَيْهِ وَسَلَّمَ:

«إِنَّ الشَّيْطَانَ يَسْتَحِلُّ الطَّعَامَ أَنْ لَا يُذْكَرَ اسْمُ اللهِ عَلَيْهِ وَإِنَّهُ جَاءَ
بِهَذِهِ الْجَارِيَةِ لِيَسْتَحِلَّ بِهَا فَأَخَذْتُ بِيَدِهَا فَجَاءَ بِهَذَا الْأَعْرَابِيِّ لِيَسْتَحِلَّ
بِهِ فَأَخَذْتُ بِيَدِهِ وَالَّذِي نَفْسِي بِيَدِهِ إِنَّ يَدَهُ فِي يَدِي مَعَ يَدِهَا».

487

217. Hudhaifa (r.a.) reported:

When we attended a dinner along with the Messenger of Allah (pbuh) we would not lay our hands on the food until Allah's Messenger (pbuh) had laid his hand and commenced eating (the food). Once we went with him to a dinner when a girl came in a rush as it someone had been pursuing her. She was about to lay her hand on the food, when Allah's Messenger (pbuh) caught her hand. Then a desert Arab came there (in a rush) as if someone had been pursuing him. He (the Holy Prophet) caught his hand; and then Allah's Messenger (pbuh) said:

"Satan considers that food lawful on which Allah's name is not mentioned. He had brought this girl so that the food might be made lawful for him and I caught her hand. And he had brought a desert Arab so that (the food) might be lawful for him. So I caught his hand. By Allah, in Whose hand is my life, it was (Satan's) hand that was in my hand along with her hand." (Muslim, Kitab Al-Ashriba, 102. Also see Abu Dawud, At`ima, 15/3766; Ahmad, V, 382, 397; Hakim, IV, 121/7088)

Explanations:

When Almighty Allah created the man and wanted angels to prostrate to him, all of the angels followed the command of Allah except the arrogant Satan and **"He said, "Shall I bow down to one whom Thou didst create from clay?"** (Al-Isra; 17:61)

Satan made a wrong comparison by thinking that he himself is created from fire but man is created from clay and therefore he thought that he is superior to man. (Al-Araf; 7:12)

Since Allah the Almighty does not like arrogance, He expelled Satan from His mercy and His Paradise. Allah degraded Satan as punishment comparable to Satan's arrogance. Allah let Satan know that He will curse him until the Day of Judgment.

Satan who rebelled due to his arrogance and pride did not think of asking for forgiveness due to the same reason and asked for some time from Allah. He dreamed of saving himself from death by living until the Day of Resurrection. Allah the Almighty gave him some time until the Day of Judgment as part of the testing in this world. Allah wished to distinguish and reveal those who believe in the hereafter and those who suspect. (Al-Saba; 34:21)

Upon this, Satan swore that he will trick up sins and try everything to misguide humans and approach them from everywhere:

"Then will I assault them from before them and behind them, from their right and their left: Nor will you find, in most of them, gratitude (for your mercies)." (Al-Araf; 7:17)

However, He let us know that the servants who found salvation are exceptions since Satan's power is not enough for them.

Almighty Allah many times warned Satan and his followers by scaring them with Hell. (See Al-Araf; 7:11-18; Al-Hijr; 15:30-44; Sad; 38:71-85)

Later, our Almighty Lord placed the first human Adam and our mother Eve to Paradise. Allah let them take from all of the blessings as much as they want but He forbade them to approach to one tree. At that moment, the testing of mankind has started. Satan got took action and got closer to them with many tricks. Satan took many vows, told lies, made false promises, said "I want good for you," gave advices, misguided them, and finally deceived them.

This is told in verses of the Noble Qur'an as:

"Then began Satan to whisper suggestions to them, bringing openly before their minds all their shame that was hidden from them (before): he said: "Your Lord only forbade you this tree, lest you should become angels or such beings as live forever." And he swore to them both, that he was their sincere adviser. So by deceit he brought about their fall: when they tasted of the tree, their shame became manifest to them, and they began to sew together the leaves of the garden over their bodies. And their Lord called unto them: "Did I not forbid you that tree, and tell you that Satan was an avowed enemy unto you?"" (Al-Araf; 7:20-22)

Satan deceived man by taking advantage of his greed and desire to be eternal. Therefore, we must be careful about these feelings.

When they rose against the Divine Command by following Satan, Allah the Almighty ordered them out of His Paradise and sent them to Earth, the world of difficulties, as enemies to each other. Therefore, the testing and the troubles of humankind have started. (Al-Baqarah; 2:36, Al-Araf; 7:24)

Allah tells this happening to humans for us to take a lesson and warns us as:

"Behold! We said to the angels, "Bow down to Adam": They bowed down except Iblis. He was one of the Jinns, and he broke the Command of his Lord. Will you then take him and his progeny as protectors rather than Me? And they are enemies to you! Evil would be the exchange for the wrong-doers!" (Al-Kahf; 18:50)

"O you Children of Adam! Let not Satan seduce you, in the same manner as He got your parents out of the Garden…" (Al-Araf; 7:27)

"O people! Eat of what is on earth, Lawful and good; and do not follow the footsteps of the evil one, for he is to you an avowed enemy." (Al-Baqarah; 2:168)

"Whoever, forsaking Allah, takes Satan for a friend, hath of a surety suffered a loss that is manifest. Satan makes them promises, and creates in them false desires; but Satan's promises are nothing but deception." (An-Nisa; 4:119-120)

"He did lead me astray from the Message (of Allah) after it had come to me! Ah! The Evil One is but a traitor to man!" (Al-Furqan; 25:29)

"About the (Evil One) it is decreed that whoever turns to him for friendship, him will he lead astray, and he will guide him to the Penalty of the Fire." (Al-Hajj; 22:4)

Allah the Exalted talks about the intentions and the tricks of Satan in the Qur'an and explains them in detail, and He asks His servants:

"…What! Would you then take him and his offspring for friends rather than Me, and they are your enemies? Evil is (this) change for the unjust." (Kahf; 18:50)

After all these warnings of our Almighty Lord, it would be expected that man would use his intelligence and be aware of the tricks of Satan. It would be expected that he would not be fooled by the suggestions of Satan and would not follow his orders. It would be wished that he would notice the tricks and traps of Satan soon and save both himself and his brothers. However, it did not happen. Most humans followed their eternal enemy despite of all these warnings. They got be fooled by the easy traps of Satan and followed him step by step. There were even times where people got more evil than Satan himself. They even left Satan open-mouthed with astonishment and got away from them by making Satan say "I am far from you, I am afraid of Allah the Lord of all universes." (Al-Hashr; 59:16) (Al-Anfal; 8:48)

Almighty Allah reproaches His servants as:

"And on them did Satan prove true his idea, and they followed him, all but a party that believed. But he had no authority over them, except that We might test the man who believes in the Hereafter from him who is in doubt concerning it: and your Lord does watch over all things." (Al-Saba; 34:20-21)

As a matter of fact, Satan cannot drag people to sinful acts by holding from their hands. He can only whisper into their ears. On the other hand, angels give inspirations to humans, too. As a matter of fact, in our first hadith, it is expressed that both Satan and angels can influence humans and Satan calls them to evil deeds and angels call them to good ones. When someone starts to be carried away by feelings and thoughts that distract him towards the wrong way, he must understand that this comes from Satan and must take refuge in Allah right away.

If a person acts fairly, he can easily sense whether the thoughts inspired in his heart is coming from Satan or the angels. That is because Satan always suggests impudicity, shamelessness and bad manners.[259] On the other hand, angels suggest goodness, benevolence, and preparation for the Hereafter. At this point, a person should try to pass the test by preferring goodness.

On the other hand Satan makes wrong deeds look attractive to people.[260] When the carnal self gets carried away by this attraction, it becomes easier for them to fall into the traps. Therefore it is necessary for a person to be aware of these dangers at all times.

For the suggestions of Satan, Allah advised:

"And if (at any time) an incitement to discord is made to you by the Evil One, seek refuge in Allah. He is the One Who hears and knows all things." (Al-Fussilat; 41:36)

For this reason, a person should take refuge in Allah from his carnal self, Satan, and from the evil of other creatures by remembering Allah and praying to Him at all times.

259. Al-Nur; 24:21.
260. Al-An'am; 6:43.

In our second hadith, we are informed that Satan circulates in the human being as blood circulates in the body, in other words Satan has a chance to deceive and influence human beings and will work hard to do this and won't miss any opportunity. However, this does not mean that Satan can do whatever he wishes to do. While Almighty Allah has given him some time and permission for the purpose of testing, He has not given him unlimited power. As a matter of fact, his traps are very weak.[261] However, since carnal self is attracted to sinful acts, people fall into these traps by themselves. Satan only invites to sinful acts by making them look attractive and people usually fall into them knowingly.

In our hadith, it is wished to express that Satan never stays unemployed but whispers suggestions at every chance. For this reason, one must be careful and alert to this humans' eternal enemy. A believer should avoid deeds that others may misinterpret and be careful not to be present in implacable positions. On the other hand, he himself as well should avoid bringing someone under suspicion due to some acts right away and should not come to conclusion before understanding the truth of the matter. One must explain the truth about the things that can be misinterpreted and should be careful about them. The Messenger of Allah (pbuh) taught us a very nice way and method on this issue.

In our third hadith, the Messenger of Allah (pbuh) explained Allah's straight path and other ways that distract people from the true way by drawing lines on the ground. In this way, he not only clearly and explicitly explained the issue to us but he also taught us a very nice method of teaching.

There is only one right way. This way is the way of tawhid (oneness of God) that unifies and does not dispel its followers. The other ways deviate from this way more or less and drag people to wrong directions. The Messenger of Allah (pbuh) informed us that there is Satan at the entrance of each of these paths and invites people to these paths.

Satan makes the right way look difficult and unpleasant but the other ways appealing and attractive. All paths except the straight one, various religions, schools of thoughts, innovations, and deviances separate believers from the way of Allah by dividing up them into sects and groups.

---

261. Al-Nisa; 4:76.

Therefore the thing that believers should do is not to be the subjects of their desires but to search for the contentment of the Friend and stay on the right path.

In our forth hadith, we are informed that Satan deceives people about worships and he especially whispers things into our ears while praying. When humans worship Allah, Satan becomes furious, burns with pain and does whatever he can to keep people away from worshipping. If he cannot succeed in his efforts, he tries to empty the inside of the worships. He turns worships into some mere physical acts which are far from awe, love, and sincerity.

In our hadith, it is told that when Satan hears adhan and iqamah, he runs away with a fear and terror.[262] However, since Satan's job is to misguide people and lead them away from the straight path, he comes back. In the end, by whispering some worldly thoughts into the ears of the person in prayer, he makes the heart of the performer distant from the prayer and even makes him forget how many rakahs (units of a prayer) that he has performed. The solution to this problem is to try not to think about other things and remember that while praying one is in the presence of Allah.

Satan works hard to prevent people from doing any good deed. In this regard the Prophet (pbuh) said:

"There are two qualities or characteristics which will not be returned by any Muslim without his entering Paradise. While they are easy, those who act upon them are few. One should say:

"Glory be to Allah" ten times after every prayer, "Praise be to Allah" ten times and "Allah is Most Great" ten times. That is a hundred and fifty on the tongue,

---

262. There are various reasons why Satan runs away upon hearing the adhan (call to prayer):
  1. He runs away since he fears from the magnificence of adhan. That is because adhan is a call that mentions all of the principles of the religion. Intrinsically, Satan hates this.
  2. Adhan is an invitation to prayer and congregation. Prayer is the worship that gets humans closest to Allah, and its most important element is prostration. Satan was expelled from the mercy of Allah since he did not obey the command of Allah which was to prostrate himself before Adam. When Muslims gather for congregation and head for worship and prostration, Satan abandons his hope of deceiving them and runs away from adhan and iqamah (call for actual start of prayer) with sorrow.
  3. Everything that hears the voice of adhan will testify for the muazzin. Satan does not want the benefit of any believer. Therefore, by running away he tries to save himself from the good deed of testifying for them, which he never likes. (See. M. Yaşar Kandemir and et al. *Riyazu's-salihin*, V, 187)

but one thousand and five hundred on the scale. When he goes to bed, he should say:

"Allah is Most Great" thirty-four times, "Praise be to Allah" thirty-three times, and "Glory be to Allah thirty-three times," for that is a hundred on the tongue and a thousand on the scale. (He said:)

I saw the Messenger of Allah (sallallahu 'alaihi wa sallam) counting them on his hand. The people asked:

"O Messenger of Allah! How is it that while they are easy, those who act upon them are few?" He replied:

"The Devil comes to one of you when he goes to bed and he makes him sleep, before he utters them, and he comes to him while he is engaged in prayer and calls a need to his mind before he utters them." (Tirmidhi, Daawat, 25/3410; Abu Dawud, Kitab Al-Adab, 99-100/5065; Nasai, Sahw, 90)

In our fifth hadith, we are informed that Satan deceives people in their social lives and sets them against each other and seeds hostility and enmity plants among them.

The word "irritation" used in our hadith means to express all kinds of acts that cause enmity, anarchy, and unrest. These are the works of Satan and his followers. For this reason, one must act consciously when facing any irritation and corruption that is contrary to the religious brotherhood and avoid making Satan happy. That is because every kind of huff, disconnection, enmity, and disorder among Muslims is something evil that Satan wishes for and gets happy about. In these situations one must act carefully and try to sustain the friendship of brotherhood. Those who offend each should make peace with each other no later than three days and everyone should apologize for the mistakes done and Muslims should approach to each other with tolerance.

The following story is very exemplary to explain how Satan works hard to turn two Muslims against each other and what we should do to prevent this:

While the Apostle of Allah (pbuh) was sitting with some of his companions, a man reviled Abu Bakr and insulted him. But Abu Bakr remained silent. He insulted him a second time, but Abu Bakr controlled himself. He insulted him once more and Abu Bakr gave him the response he deserves.

Then the Apostle of Allah (pbuh) got up. Abu Bakr said:

"Were you angry with me, O Apostle of Allah?"

The Messenger of Allah (pbuh) said:

"No." Then he continued:

"However, an angel had come down from Heaven and he had been rejecting what he had said to you. When you took revenge, the angel left and a devil came down. I cannot sit in a place where the devil comes." (Abu Dawud, Kitab Al-Adab, 41/4896)

In our sixth hadith, we are told about how Satan works to deceive people in their daily lives. Satan fights humans with his soldiers and warriors and wants to be partners to them in their eating, drinking, sleeping, entering into their houses, earning money, and raising children.

The Messenger of Allah (pbuh) said in his another saying:

"The Satan is present with any one of you in everything he does; he is present even when he eats food; so if any one of you drops a mouthful he should pick it up and remove any of the filth on it, and then eat it, and should not leave it for the Satan." (Muslim, Kitab Al-Ashriba, 133-135)

Satans wish to enter into houses, to spend the night there, to use the blessings of the house, to deceive the people in the house and to make them commit sins. The thing which can prevent this is to recite basmala (or to say "in the name of Allah") when we are entering into a house. When someone does this, Satan hears it and sadly tells his followers that they cannot enter into this house that night. Also, they wait for the meal time thinking that they can benefit from it. If basmala is not recited before eating in that house, Satans eat from the food and take the blessings of the food away. Not remembering Allah is like a food and nourishment to Satans and causes them to gain power. Then they start to deceive the people of the house. If they recite basmala before eating, Satans would understand that they will not get any benefit from them and leave the house.

Satan wants to be partner in people's works. This partnership starts when someone leaves the house with some bad intentions and thoughts. This is explained in a noble hadith as:

"There would be two flags in the hands of everyone when they leave their houses; one of them would be in the hands of angel and the other one in the

hands of Satan. If the person leaves the house for something that Allah loves and consistent with His contentment, then the angel follows him with the flag until he returns to his house. If the person leaves the house for something that angers Allah, then Satan follows him with the flag in his hands. That person would be under the flag of Satan until he returns his house." (Ahmad, II, 323)

Almighty Allah informs us about the deceptions of Satan about wealth and children as:

"He said: "Tell me. This is the one whom You have honored above me! If You will but respite me to the Day of Judgment, I will surely bring his descendants under my sway - all but a few!" (Allah) said: "Go your way; if any of them follow you, verily Hell will be the recompense of you (all) an ample recompense. Lead to destruction those whom you can among them, with your (seductive) voice; make assaults on them with your cavalry and your infantry; mutually share with them wealth and children; and make promises to them." But Satan promises them nothing but deceit. As for My servants, no authority shall you have over them:" Enough is your Lord for a Disposer of affairs." (Al-Isra; 17:62-65)

Overlooking mistakes and sinful acts by finding excuses in personal, social, and business life is all caused by Satan's deception and empty promises. People surrender to sinful acts for reasons such as wishing to earn more, to be better, or to advance their condition. However, one must never forget that carnal self and Satan have a finger in these things. A believer should hold on to the rope of sincerity and piety and search to find them in order to gain the protection and the help of Allah.

The Messenger of Allah (pbuh) warned believers about their acts as:

"If anything (in the form of trouble) comes to you, don't say: If I had not done that, it would not have happened so and so, but say: Allah did that what He had ordained to do and your "if" opens the (gate) for the Satan." (Muslim, Kitab al-Qadar, 34. Also see Ibn Majah, Muqaddima, 10)

If humans show weakness, anxiety and they do not show submission to their fate and do not trust in Allah, then they may show hesitations in their deeds and may act in ways that contradict having faith such as nonacquiescence, rebelling to fate, and denying the existence of Allah. This only makes Satan happy.

The Messenger of Allah (pbuh) gives the following advice in order to emphasize the importance of solidarity and unity against Satan:

"Satan is a wolf among humans. Just like the wolf that hunts the sheep that wanders away from the herd. Don't get divide up into groups. Don't abandon congregations, social gatherings, and prayer rooms." (Ahmad, II, 400; V, 335; Hakim, I, 73/59)

"Satan whispers into the ears of people when they are alone or with someone else. If there are three people, he would not come close to them." (*Muwatta'*, Isti'dhan, 36)

As a matter of fact, Satan cannot harm anyone who does not have ill-intentions. That is because **"feeble indeed is the cunning of Satan."**[263] The thing that makes him powerful is the desires and ambitions of people. As a matter of fact, the Messenger of Allah (pbuh) said:

"As long as a judge is just, Almighty Allah is with him (helps him). When he becomes unjust, Allah leaves him and Satan comes close to him and never leaves him alone." (Tirmidhi, Ahkam, 4/1330)

It is understood from the sayings of the Prophet (pbuh) and verses of the Qur'an that Allah did not leave devils unconstrained and so they have to obey some rules. It is seen that Satans have permission to be partner in the works of those who forget to remember Allah and who have ill-natured intentions. However, it is impossible for Satan to benefit from neither houses nor works of those whose hearts are awake, who always remember Allah, who enter their houses and start eating in the name of Allah, and who obey the commands of Allah.

Almighty Allah treats with mercy and grace and protects His servants from the tricks of Satan those who do their best to be pious and especially sincere. It is said in the noble Qur'an:

"Were it not for the Grace and Mercy of Allah unto you, all but a few of you would have fallen into the clutches of Satan." (Al-Nisa; 4:83)

"No authority has he over those who believe and put their trust in their Lord. His authority is over those only, who take him as patron and who join partners with Allah." (Al-Nahl; 16:99-100)

---

263. Al-Nisa; 4:76.

Our Almighty Lord taught us the following prayer for the protection from Satan:

$$\text{وَقُلْ رَبِّ اَعُوذُ بِكَ مِنْ هَمَزَاتِ الشَّيَاطِينِ.}$$
$$\text{وَاَعُوذُ بِكَ رَبِّ اَنْ يَحْضُرُونِ}$$

"And say: O my Lord! I seek refuge with Thee from the suggestions of the Evil Ones. And I seek refuge with You O my Lord! Lest they should come near me." (Al-Muminun; 23:97-98)

In summary, every act that makes Satan happy is against human salvation. That is because Satan's goal and pleasure is to harm people both materially and spiritually. Therefore, one must disappoint Satan and must not be fooled by his tricks by seeking refuge in Allah and remembering Him at all times.

G. CALLING TO ISLAM AND SERVING IN THE WAY OF ALLAH

1. The Responsibility of Calling to Islam

٢١٨. عَنْ عَبْدِ اللهِ بْنِ عَمْرٍو رَضِيَ اللهُ عَنْهُ أَنَّ النَّبِيَّ صَلَّى اللهُ عَلَيْهِ وَسَلَّم قَالَ:

«بَلِّغُوا عَنِّي وَلَوْ آيَةً».

218. Abdullah b. Amr (r.a.) narrated that the Messenger of Allah (pbuh) said:

"Even if it is one verse from me, make it available to others!.." (Bukhari, Anbiya 50; Tirmidhi, Ilm, 13/2669; Darimi, Muqaddima, 46; Ahmad, II, 159, 202, 214)

❈

٢١٩. عَنْ عَبْدِ اللهِ بْنِ مَسْعُودٍ رَضِيَ اللهُ عَنْهُ قَالَ: سَمِعْتُ رَسُولَ اللهِ صَلَّى اللهُ عَلَيْهِ وَسَلَّمَ يَقُولُ:

«إِنَّكُمْ مَنْصُورُونَ وَمُصِيبُونَ وَمَفْتُوحٌ لَكُمْ فَمَنْ أَدْرَكَ ذٰلِكَ مِنْكُمْ فَلْيَتَّقِ اللهَ وَلْيَأْمُرْ بِالْمَعْرُوفِ وَلْيَنْهَ عَنِ الْمُنْكَرِ وَمَنْ كَذَبَ عَلَيَّ مُتَعَمِّدًا فَلْيَتَبَوَّأْ مَقْعَدَهُ مِنَ النَّارِ».

219. Abdullah b. Mas'ud (r.a.) said: I heard the Messenger of Allah (pbuh) say:

"You will receive help and overcome your enemies, will gain war-booty and will conquer many places. Whoever reaches this time period should be scared of Al-

lah, command goodness, and forbid wrong. Whoever tells a lie knowingly giving My Name should prepare a place in Hell." (Tirmidhi, Fitan, 70/2257; Ahmad, I, 401, 436)

❀

٢٢٠. عَنْ أَبِى سَعِيدٍ الْخُدْرِيّ رَضِيَ اللهُ عَنْهُ قَالَ: سَمِعْتُ رَسُولَ
اللهِ صَلَّى اللهُ عَلَيْهِ وَسَلَّمَ يَقُولُ:

«مَنْ رَأَى مِنْكُمْ مُنْكَرًا فَلْيُغَيِّرْهُ بِيَدِهِ فَإِنْ لَمْ يَسْتَطِعْ فَبِلِسَانِهِ فَإِنْ لَمْ
يَسْتَطِعْ فَبِقَلْبِهِ وَذٰلِكَ أَضْعَفُ الْإِيمَانِ».

220. Abu Sa'id al-Khudri (r.a.) narrated: "I heard the Messenger of Allah (pbuh) saying:

"He who amongst you sees something abominable should modify it with the help of his hand; and if he is not strong enough to do it, then he should do it with his tongue, and if he is not strong enough to do it, (even) then he should (abhor it) from his heart, and that is the least of faith." (Muslim, Iman, 78. Also see. Tirmidhi, Fitan, 11; Nasai, Iman, 17)

❀

٢٢١. عَنِ النُّعْمَانَ بْنِ بَشِيرٍ رَضِيَ اللهُ عَنْهُمَا عَنِ النَّبِيّ صَلَّى اللهُ
عَلَيْهِ وَسَلَّمَ قَالَ:

«مَثَلُ الْقَائِمِ فِى حُدُودِ اللهِ وَالْوَاقِعِ فِيهَا كَمَثَلِ قَوْمٍ اسْتَهَمُوا عَلَى
سَفِينَةٍ فَأَصَابَ بَعْضُهُمْ أَعْلَاهَا وَبَعْضُهُمْ أَسْفَلَهَا فَكَانَ الَّذِينَ فِي أَسْفَلِهَا
إِذَا اسْتَقَوْا مِنَ الْمَاءِ مَرُّوا عَلَى مَنْ فَوْقَهُمْ فَقَالُوا: لَوْ أَنَّا خَرَقْنَا فِي
نَصِيبِنَا خَرْقًا وَلَمْ نُؤْذِ مَنْ فَوْقَنَا فَإِنْ يَتْرُكُوهُمْ وَمَا أَرَادُوا هَلَكُوا جَمِيعًا
وَإِنْ أَخَذُوا عَلَى أَيْدِيهِمْ نَجَوْا وَنَجَوْا جَمِيعًا».

221. It is narrated from An-Nu'man bin Bashir that the Messenger of Allah (pbuh) said:

"*The example of the person abiding by Allah's order and restrictions in comparison to those who violate them is like the example of those persons who drew lots for their seats in a boat. Some of them got seats in the upper part, and the others in the lower. When the latter needed water, they had to go up to bring water (and that troubled the others), so they said:*

"*Let us make a hole in our share of the ship (and get water) saving those who are above us from troubling them.*"

So, if the people in the upper part left the others do what they had suggested, all the people of the ship would be destroyed, but if they prevented them, both parties would be safe." (Bukhari, Shirkat, 6; Shahadat, 30. Also see Tirmidhi, Fitan, 12)

❁

٢٢٢. عَنْ حُذَيْفَةَ رَضِيَ اللهُ عَنْهُ عَنِ النَّبِيِّ صَلَّى اللهُ عَلَيْهِ وَسَلَّمَ قَالَ:

«وَالَّذِي نَفْسِي بِيَدِهِ لَتَأْمُرُنَّ بِالْمَعْرُوفِ وَلَتَنْهَوُنَّ عَنِ الْمُنْكَرِ أَوْ لَيُوشِكَنَّ اللهُ أَنْ يَبْعَثَ عَلَيْكُمْ عِقَابًا مِنْهُ ثُمَّ تَدْعُونَهُ فَلَا يُسْتَجَابُ لَكُمْ».

222. It is narrated from Hudaifa (r.a.) that the Messenger of Allah (pbuh) said:

"*I swear to Allah who holds my life in His hand, you either command goodness and forbid evil or Allah will send a punishment on you soon, and then you would pray Allah but your prayers would not be answered.*" (Tirmidhi, Fitan, 9/2169)

❁

٢٢٣. قَالَ أَبُو بَكْرٍ رَضِيَ اللهُ عَنْهُ بَعْدَ أَنْ حَمِدَ اللهَ وَأَثْنَى عَلَيْهِ:

يَا أَيُّهَا النَّاسُ إِنَّكُمْ تَقْرَءُونَ هَذِهِ الْآيَةَ وَتَضَعُونَهَا عَلَى غَيْرِ مَوَاضِعِهَا:

(عَلَيْكُمْ اَنْفُسَكُمْ لَا يَضُرُّكُمْ مَنْ ضَلَّ اِذَا اهْتَدَيْتُمْ)

قَالَ عَنْ خَالِدٍ وَإِنَّا سَمِعْنَا النَّبِيَّ صَلَّى اللّٰهُ عَلَيْهِ وَسَلَّمَ يَقُولُ:

«إِنَّ النَّاسَ إِذَا رَأَوُا الظَّالِمَ فَلَمْ يَأْخُذُوا عَلَى يَدَيْهِ أَوْشَكَ أَنْ يَعُمَّهُمُ اللّٰهُ بِعِقَابٍ» وَقَالَ عَمْرٌو عَنْ هُشَيْمٍ: وَإِنِّي سَمِعْتُ رَسُولَ اللّٰهِ صَلَّى اللّٰهُ عَلَيْهِ وَسَلَّمَ يَقُولُ:

«مَا مِنْ قَوْمٍ يُعْمَلُ فِيهِمْ بِالْمَعَاصِي ثُمَّ يَقْدِرُونَ عَلَى أَنْ يُغَيِّرُوا ثُمَّ لَا يُغَيِّرُوا إِلَّا يُوشِكُ أَنْ يَعُمَّهُمُ اللّٰهُ مِنْهُ بِعِقَابٍ».

223. One day Abu Bakr (r.a.) said the following after completing his supplication:

"You people recite the following verse but don't quite get it correctly:

"Guard your own souls: If you follow (right) guidance, no hurt can come to you from those who stray…" (Al-Maidah; 5:105)

As a matter of fact, we heard the Prophet (pbuh) say:

"When the people see a wrongdoer and do not prevent him, Allah will soon punish them all."

The narrator Amr narrated from Hushaim that he heard Abu Bakr saying:

"I heard the Prophet (pbuh) saying:

"If acts of disobedience are done among any people and do not change them though they are able to do so, Allah will soon punish them all." (Abu Dawud, Kitab Al-Malahim, 17/4338; Tirmidhi, Fitan, 8; Tafsir, 5/17; Ibn Majah, Fitan, 20; Ahmad, I, 2, 7, 9)

۲۲٤. عَنْ أَبِي سَعِيدٍ رَضِيَ اللّٰهُ عَنْهُ قَالَ: قَالَ رَسُولُ اللّٰهِ صَلَّى اللّٰهُ عَلَيْهِ وَسَلَّمَ:

«لَا يَحْقِرْ أَحَدُكُمْ نَفْسَهُ» قَالُوا:

«يَا رَسُولَ اللهِ! كَيْفَ يَحْقِرُ أَحَدُنَا نَفْسَهُ؟» قَالَ:

«يَرَى أَمْرًا، لِلهِ عَلَيْهِ فِيهِ مَقَالٌ ثُمَّ لَا يَقُولُ فِيهِ فَيَقُولُ اللهُ عَزَّ وَجَلَّ
لَهُ يَوْمَ الْقِيَامَةِ: مَا مَنَعَكَ أَنْ تَقُولَ فِي كَذَا وَكَذَا فَيَقُولُ: خَشْيَةُ النَّاسِ
فَيَقُولُ: فَإِيَّايَ كُنْتَ أَحَقَّ أَنْ تَخْشَى».

224. Abu Said (r.a.) said: The Messenger of Allah (pbuh) said:

"No one should be so humble as to make himself despicable!"

The Companions of the Messenger of Allah (pbuh) said:

"O Messenger of Allah! How could anyone among us make himself look despicable?"

The Messenger of Allah (pbuh) said:

"A person faces with something and does not say anything despite the fact that he must say something about it for the sake of Allah. Allah the Exalted says to him on the Day of Judgment:

"What was the thing that stopped you from saying anything in such and such situations?"

He answers:

"I was scared of others!"

Allah the Exalted says:

"Should you not have feared from Me?" (Ibn Majah, Fitan, 20; Ahmad, III, 30, 91)

Explanations:

Allah the Exalted has made Muslims responsible from each other as brothers and sisters in Islam, from the society that they live in, and from the condition that the whole world is into. The Messenger of Allah (pbuh) informed us that each of us is responsible just like the shepherd in front of the herd, and therefore we are responsible for the people that depend on us, our positions, and duties.[264] In other words, everyone, from the president to laymen, must protect his dependents, his position, and his surroundings from material and ethical disasters.

For this reason, a Muslim should not only think of himself but also try to lead others to good deeds and protect them from wrongdoings. Namely, a Muslims should be in an effort to save himself first and then the whole humanity.

Allah the Exalted says:

"The Believers, men and women, are protectors one of another: they enjoin what is just, and forbid what is evil…" (At-Tawbah; 9:71)

"You are the best of peoples, evolved for mankind, enjoining what is right, forbidding what is wrong…" (Al-i Imran; 3:110)

For this reason, enjoining the good and forbidding the evil, namely, suggesting the good and explaining why evil is bad and trying to prevent wrongdoings of those who we are responsible for is an important religious duty. Almighty Allah declares in the Noble Qur'an that believers are responsible for each other. This responsibility which is also known as "Tabligh (Delivering the message of Islam)" and "Da'wah (Invitation to Islam)" is one of the most important duties in Islam and the essence of the religion. The order of Islam becomes perfect by this and the name of Allah gets exalted mainly by this way. Even though everyone is responsible to do this duty as much as they can, Muslim leaders and scholars have more responsibility.

Allah the Exalted says:

"(They are) those who, if We establish them in the land, establish regular prayer and give regular charity, enjoin the right and forbid wrong: with Allah rests the end (and decision) of (all) affairs." (Al-Hajj; 22:41)

The duty of the society, beginning from its leaders, is to raise scholars who will teach what is good and right to others. That is because while there are simple facts that everyone can know, there are also issues that not everyone can understand which requires proper education. It is not right for those who

---

264. Bukhari, Jum'a, 11; Istiqraz, 20; Itk, 17, 19; Wasaya, 9; Nikah, 81, 90; Ahkam, 1; Muslim, Imara, 20; Abu Dawud, Imara, 1, 13; Tirmidhi, Jihad, 27.

do not have the proper knowledge to correct these issues. They must be left to experts. For this reason, our Almighty Lord says:

"Let there arise out of you a band of people inviting to all that is good, enjoining what is right, and forbidding what is wrong: They are the ones to attain felicity." (Al-i Imran; 3:104)

It is understood from this noble verse that it is *fard al-kifayah* to organize a group that fulfills the responsibility of inviting people to goodness. The followers of Islam must train a group that can fulfill this responsibility. Unless this responsibility is fulfilled, all Muslims would be guilty.

The Messenger of Allah (pbuh) paid so much attention to this task that when he received the allegiance of his noble companions, he set as a condition to give advice to all Muslims and act sincerely. Jarir b. Abdullah (r.a.) narrated:

"I gave the oath of allegiance to the Prophet to perform prayers perfectly, to pay zakat, and to advise goodness to every Muslim." (Bukhari, Iman, 42; Mawakit, 3; Zakat, 2; Muslim, Iman, 97-98; Nasai, Bay'ah, 6, 17)

Ubada b. al-Samit (r.a.) narrated:

"We gave the oath of allegiance to Allah's Apostle that we would listen to and obey him both at the time when we were active and at the time when we were tired and that we would not fight against the ruler or disobey him unless they openly do something considered disbelief, and **would stand firm for the truth or say the truth wherever we might be, and in the Way of Allah we would not be afraid of the blame of the blamers.**" (Bukhari, Ahkam, 42; Muslim, Imara, 41; Nasai, Bay'ah, 1, 2, 3; Ibn Majah, Jihad, 41)

To those who told that they had to sit on the corners of the streets because of their jobs, the Messenger of Allah (pbuh) told that they have to command what is good and right and dissuade from what is bad. (See Bukhari, Mazalim, 22; Isti'dhan, 2; Muslim, Libas, 114; Abu Dawud, Adab, 12)

All these prove the importance of announcing and inviting to what is good and right, enjoining the good, and forbidding the evil.

Our first hadith indicates that every Muslim should fulfill the responsibility of inviting others to Islam and teach Islamic knowledge even if it is one verse of the noble Qur'an or one hadith. Every Muslim can have some knowledge that those who are not close to Islam may not know. Therefore, a Muslim should teach the facts he knows about Islam to others.

In our second hadith, the Messenger of Allah (pbuh) gave the good news that Muslims will overcome their enemies, will get wealthy by receiving war-booty, and gain power by widening their lands. However, Allah's Messenger (pbuh) worried about something at this point which was: When people experience prosperity and gain power, their fancy for this world would increase and their religious values may get weak. Then, they may ignore their responsibility of inviting others to Islam.

As a matter of fact, the Messenger of Allah (pbuh) said in one of his hadiths:

"Unless two kinds of drunkenness appear in you, you would continue to be on the right path: The drunkenness of ignorance and fanatic love of the world. While you command what is right and good and prevent what is bad and fight in the way of Allah, when the love of this world appear, you turn into people who do not command what is good and who do not prevent what is bad and abandon fighting in the way of Allah. That day, those who talk about the noble Qur'an and Sunnah and those who try to explain them are like the first ones to convert to Islam among the Ansar and al-Muhajirun." (Haythami, VII, 271; Abu Nuaym, *Hilya*, VIII, 49)

The Messenger of Allah (pbuh) invited Muslims to fear Allah and explain Islam to others by words and actions by drawing our attention to the fact that being pious is extra important in times where everyone is like drunk from the love of this world. In such time periods, supporting and encouraging what is good and preventing what is bad are some of the most important responsibilities of believers. The difficulty of accomplishing this duty is obvious. However, for sure its rewards are comparable to its difficulty. As a matter of fact, the Messenger of Allah (pbuh) gave the good news that those who explain Islam and invite people to good deeds earn divine rewards as much as the first ones who converted to Islam among Ansar and al-Muhajirun.

However, those who call others to Islam should satisfy some requirements and they should be very careful in their acts. It is not right for those who do not know the religion to cause confusion with their inaccurate or wrong statements. Those who talk about the religion should not say wrong things about the Messenger of Allah (pbuh). Whoever attributes to the Messenger of Allah (pbuh) the things that he did not say or do, would push himself into Hell. As a matter of fact, in our hadith there is a harsh warning that "they should prepare their place in Hell." This expression also has the meaning of cursing for those who lie about the Messenger of Allah (pbuh) and teasing the ignorant ones who throw themselves into the Fire.

It is understood that those who know the religion should fulfill the responsibility of commanding what is good and right and preventing what is bad and wrong. However, if the matter is something that everybody knows, every Muslim can interfere properly. If the commands and preventions are about detailed subjects, only scholars should fulfill this responsibility. They too could command and prevent the issues on which there is common consensus but stay away from controversial issues.

Those who fulfill the responsibility of commanding what is good and preventing what is bad should know the method in Islam of inviting people to religion. As a matter of fact, to abide by common principles such as being nice and polite, having a soft way of talking, approaching to people with mercy are very crucial.

In our third hadith, it is pointed out that Muslims should never overlook anything that is bad. When a Muslim sees something abominable or sinful, he should try to modify it with the help of his hands, if he cannot do that he should do it with his words, if he cannot do this either, he should at least try to do it with his heart. By disliking them from their hearts, those who cannot do anything about bad deeds can at least control their hearts and save themselves from considering bad things permissible eventually. On the other hand, one should try to prevent bad things from happening by praying to Allah from his heart. This is the lowest level of faith. Those who even cannot do this would endanger their faith. Their hearts would start to look like the hearts of sinners.

It is said in a Noble hadith:

"Never was there one among the prophets who had not disciples who followed his direction and followed his ways. Then there came after them their successors who said whatever they did not practice, and practiced whatever they were not commanded to do. He who strove against them with his hand was a believer: he who strove against them with his tongue was a believer, and he who strove against them with his heart was a believer and beyond that there is no faith even to the extent of a mustard seed." (Muslim, Iman, 80)

The state of the heart when facing wrongdoings is very important. In order to show this, the Messenger of Allah (pbuh) said:

"When sin is committed on earth, he who sees it and disapproves of it (assuming that he cannot do anything else) will be taken like one who was not present (and therefore he is saved from the evil of the sin), but he who is not present and approves of it (when he hears it) will be like someone who sees it and will be harmed accordingly." (Abu Dawud, Kitab al-Malahim, 17/4345)

Another attention drawing hadith that explains how the state of the heart should be when facing wrongdoings is as follows:

"Allah inspired one of His angels as:

"Turn that city upside down upon his people!"

The angel said:

"There is a servant of You among them who did not rebel You even for a blink of an eye."

Almighty Allah said:

"Turn that city upside down upon him too as well as the others! That is because his face haven't change (didn't hate them for the sake of Allah) even once (upon seeing their evil deeds.)" (Haythami, VII, 270)

In our forth hadith, the importance of announcing Islam to others and calling them to Islam and the fact that, when abandoned, the whole community will be harmed is explained with a nice example.

Due to the mistakes and sins that evil people do, discord occurs in the land and sea.[265] Almighty Allah sends troubles and calamities on bad people. It harms the world which is like a ship that everyone sails on it. If Muslims do not prevent those bad things from happening, everyone who lives in this world gets harmed. However, when Muslims spread goodness and clear off wrongdoings, then both Muslims and everyone else can be save from the great punishment.

Almighty Allah says:

---

265. Al-Rum; 30:41.

"…We rescued those who forbade Evil; but We visited the wrong-doers with a grievous punishment because they were given to transgression." (Al-Araf; 7:165)

In other words, trying to prevent wrongdoings saves everyone. Abandoning the responsibility of announcing Islam to others causes getting a share from the punishment of oppressors.

Our fifth hadith informs us about the sad consequences of over-looking wrongdoings. Increase in sins angers Almighty Allah, and in order to sober up His servants, He lets them taste some punishments of the Hereafter in this world for what they had done. By this, He wants His servants to find the right path by understanding their mistakes. This harms everyone both good and bad. Those good people who did not prevent wrongdoings would receive punishment for their acts as well. They start praying when others are in trouble but since it is too late, their prayers would not be accepted.

Drought, scarcity, natural disasters, oppression of the cruel and bad people, discord among Muslims, and similar troubles are common fates of people. They cause destruction, collapse, and annihilation. Societies that abandon or ignore the responsibility of commanding what is good and prohibit what is bad deserve these kinds of troubles.

The Messenger of Allah (pbuh) explained the fact that social corruption starts with abandoning the responsibility of announcing and inviting others to Islam through an example from the Children of Israel:

"The first defect that permeated the Israelites was that a man (of them) met another man and said:

"O so-and-so, fear Allah, and abandon what you are doing, for it is not lawful for you!" He then met him the next day and that did not prevent him from eating with him, drinking with him and sitting with him. When they did so, Allah mingled their hearts with each other.

He then recited the verse:

"Curses were pronounced on those among the Children of Israel who rejected faith, by the tongue of David and of Jesus the son of Mary: because they disobeyed and persisted in excesses. Nor did they (usually) forbid one another the iniquities which they committed: evil indeed were the deeds which they did. Thou seest many of them turning in friendship to the un-

believers. Evil indeed are (the works) which their souls have sent forward before them (with the result), that Allah's wrath is on them, and in torment will they abide. If only they had believed in Allah, in the Messenger, and in what has been revealed to him, never would they have taken them for friends and protectors, but most of them are rebellious wrong-doers." (Al-Maidah; 5:78-81)

Then the Messenger of Allah (pbuh) said:

"By no means, I swear by Allah, you must enjoin what is good and prohibit what is evil, prevent the wrongdoer, bend him into conformity with what is right, and restrict him to what is right." (See Abu Dawud, Kitab Al-Malahim, 17/4336; Tirmidhi, Tafsir 5/6, 7; Baihaqi, *al-Sunan al-Kubra,* X, 93)

In our sixth hadith, a misinterpreted verse is mentioned by those who do not want to see this danger coming:

"O you who believe! Guard your own souls: If you follow (right) guid-ance, no hurt can come to you from those who stray." (Al-Maidah; 5:105)

This verse, which is sometimes misinterpreted as "you correct yourself, others are none of your business," actually invites Muslims to perfectly fulfill all their responsibilities. The responsibility to enjoin the good is among them as well. When Muslims do their part, they would waiver from their liability and save themselves from being called to account for their share of others' mistakes. That is because no one can be accountable for others' mistakes.[266] However if they ignore the responsibility of enjoining the good, then they face with the threat mentioned in the hadith narrated by Abu Bakr. If they do not prevent the wrongdoings performed in their presence while they can, Allah the Al-mighty certainly sends a common punishment on them.

The people of Sabt are one of the best examples of this:

The people of Sabt from the children of Israel used to live in the town called Eyle by the shore of the Red Sea. While they were supposed to drop ev-erything and worship on Saturdays, they would go fishing instead on that day. That is because on Saturdays, many fish used to appear in the sea. Fish did this since they knew that people do not fish on that day, and they did not appear so many on other days. This society became furious and acted in defiance of Al-

---

266. al-Fatir; 35:18.

lah's commands due to their desire to go fishing on Saturday upon seeing them coming like this, and they started to catch them.

After a while, the society divided up into two groups:

1. Those who broke the rules and commit sin

2. Pious and benevolent ones. However, those who practice the religion were in the minority and could not influence and stop others.

Then, those who are good also divided up into two groups:

1. Those who worked hard, tried everything, got up, took pains and advised wrong doers in order to bring them to the right path but then stopped and gave way to despair. After a while, those people abandoned their responsibility of enjoining the good.

2. Those are the Muslims who continued to give sermons and advices to disobedient people by enduring all kinds of troubles and difficulties without giving away to despair. The number of this self-sacrificing people was few.

Those who abandoned enjoining the good by giving away to despair told them:

"Why do you flounder? Why do you advise in vain? Those sinners will not listen to your advices, don't you see how many times we've told them? They don't listen." Those few righteous people did not pay attention to these discouraging suggestions and continued by thinking of being accountable in the Hereafter.

The following verse of Qur'an expresses this as:

"When some of them said: "Why do you preach to a people whom Allah will destroy or visit with a terrible punishment?" said the preachers:" To discharge our duty to your Lord, and perchance they may fear Him." (Al-Araf; 7:164)

Then those who continued to enjoin the good set a wall which parted them from the others in order to protect themselves from the punishment that will come to others. When they did not heard any voice from the other side of the wall, they saw that all the people turned into monkeys overnight!.. Even those who were saved from the torment did not recognize their relatives, the relatives who turned into monkeys recognized them. Those miserable people who faced with the torment stroll around their relatives crestfallenly for some time. When their relatives asked:

"Didn't we dissuade you from sins by warning you?" they used to nod their heads with tearful eyes.

Three days later, all of the rebellious people who were turned into monkeys died.

Some of the scholars of the Qur'anic exegesis said:

"Those who did not fish on the forbidden day but kept silent without prohibiting or warning those who disobeyed the command are turned into monkeys with them." In this case, the verse is one of the most intense warnings about those who do not forbid what is evil.

Almighty Allah says:

"So We made it an example to their own time and to their posterity, and a lesson to those who fear Allah." (Al-Baqarah; 2:66)

When the Children of Israel worshipped the calf, Moses (pbuh) feared that those Muslims who did not stray from the right path but did not try hard to prevent this evil from happening would be perished as well, and he took refuge in Allah as:

"… would You destroy us for the deeds of the foolish ones among us?" (Al-Araf; 7:155)

The following hadith implies the same meaning:

"Allah the Exalted does not punish innocents for the sins of the community but with an exception for those who witness that sins are committed among them but do not prevent them despite the fact that they can." (Ahmad, V, 192)

In our seventh hadith, we are reminded that one should not abstain from the responsibility of enjoining the good due to fear of others or by forgetting. We are informed that acting this way will put one into a belittling and despicable position.

Almighty Allah shows His messengers as examples about this and says:

"(It is the practice of those) who preach the Messages of Allah, and fear Him, and fear none but Allah. And enough is Allah to call (men) to account." (Al-Ahzab; 33:39)

Again in the Noble Qur'an it is proudly declared that the distinguished people who love Allah and are loved by Allah are gentle and humble to believers; proud, honorable, rigorous, brave, and confident to non-believers, who can sacrifice everything in the way of Allah and who work hard and who do not fear any critic, who serve Islam ignoring the condemnation of others and seek not the consent of others but the consent of Allah. (Al-Maidah; 5:54)

Almighty Allah charged believers for correcting improper actions that they see contrary to Islam. A believer who sees that something that is prohibited by the religion is done is liable to Allah for announcing what is right and should try to stop them from the wrongdoing. If he keeps silent due to fear from condemnation of others or that something may happen to him, Almighty Allah will ask him on the Day of Judgment why he did not enjoin the good. When the faulty believer expresses that he feared others, Almighty Allah will remind him that a believer should fear Allah before everything else. For sure, a Muslim who puts himself into this situation did nothing else but making himself disgraced.[267]

Abu Said al-Hudri (r.a.) said:

The Messenger of Allah (pbuh) stood up and preached to people. Among his words, there were:

"Be careful! The fear felt towards others should not make one stop from telling the things that he knows are right!"

Abu Said (r.a.) cried after narrating this hadith and regretted that:

"I swear to Allah, we've seen things in this world but couldn't say anything due to our fear." (Tirmidhi, Fitan, 26/2191; Ibn Majah, Fitan, 20; Ahmad, III, 5)

---

267. Truly, to be embarrassed in front of all people in the Hereafter is much heavier and worse compared to the shame in this world. Indeed, the Messenger of Allah (pbuh) said:
"O people! Whoever has violated the right of someone should pay it back and never hesitate thinking he will be ashamed in this world! You should know well that the shame in this world fares really light compared to that of the Hereafter." (Ibn Sa'd, II, 255; Ibn Athir, al-Kamil, II, 319; Tabari, Tarih, III, 189-190)

As Almighty Allah will hold accoutable the believers who ignore the responsibility of enjoining the good, those who are left with their sins and have not been warned will get a hold of them as well.

Abu Huraira narrated:

We used to hear the following fact among the noble companions of the Messenger: On the Day of Judgment, a man gets held off by someone he does not know of and the man gets shocked and asks:

"What do you want from me? I do not even know you!"

The man who gets a hold of him proceeds against him as:

"When we were in the world, you used to see me doing wrong and evil things but did not warn and stop me." (Munziri, *at-Targhib wa al-tarhib*, III, 164/3506; Rudani, *Jam' al-fawaid*, V, 384)

We should also say that when enjoining the good and forbidding the evil, one must not cause some things to get worse. If correcting wrongdoings with one's hands or words will cause something worse such as getting him or someone else killed, he should prefer to hate that evil from the heart. That is because risking one's life knowingly is not considered permissible in our religion.

2. The Virtue of Delivering the Message of Islam and Calling Others to It

٢٢٥. عَنْ سَهْلِ بنِ سَعْدٍ رَضِيَ اللهُ عَنْهُ أَنَّ النَّبِيَّ صَلَّى اللهُ عَلَيْهِ وَسَلَّم قَالَ لِعَلِيٍّ رَضِيَ اللهُ عَنْهُ:

«فَوَاللهِ لَأَنْ يَهْدِيَ اللهُ بِكَ رَجُلاً وَاحِداً خَيْرٌ لَكَ مِنْ حُمْرِ النَّعَمِ».

225. Sahl b. Sad (r.a.) narrated that the Messenger of Allah (pbuh) said to Ali:

"I swear to Allah that it is better for you that Allah makes one find the true path through you than having red camels which is the best worldly possession." (Bukhari, Ashab al-Nabi, 9; Maghazi, 38; Muslim, Fadail al-Sahaba, 34; Abu Dawud, Ilm, 10/3661)

٢٢٦. عَنْ عَبْدِ اللهِ بْنِ مَسْعُودٍ رَضِيَ اللهُ عَنْهُ عَنِ النَّبِيِّ صَلَّى اللهُ عَلَيْهِ وَسَلَّمَ قَالَ:

«نَضَّرَ اللهُ امْرَأً سَمِعَ مَقَالَتِي فَوَعَاهَا وَحَفِظَهَا وَبَلَّغَهَا فَرُبَّ حَامِلِ فِقْهٍ إِلَى مَنْ هُوَ أَفْقَهُ مِنْهُ».

226. It is narrated from Abdullah b. Mas'ud that the Noble Prophet (pbuh) said:

"May Allah make blameless the face of those who hear my words and clearly understand and memorize them! There are many knowledgeable persons who transmit it to a person who has a better understanding." (Tirmidhi, Ilm, 7/2685)

٢٢٧. عَنْ أَبِي هُرَيْرَةَ رَضِيَ اللهُ عَنْهُ أَنَّ رَسُولَ اللهِ صَلَّى اللهُ عَلَيْهِ وَسَلَّمَ قَالَ:

«مَنْ دَعَا إِلَى هُدًى كَانَ لَهُ مِنَ الْأَجْرِ مِثْلُ أُجُورِ مَنْ تَبِعَهُ لَا يَنْقُصُ ذٰلِكَ مِنْ أُجُورِهِمْ شَيْئًا وَمَنْ دَعَا إِلَى ضَلَالَةٍ كَانَ عَلَيْهِ مِنَ الْإِثْمِ مِثْلُ آثَامِ مَنْ تَبِعَهُ لَا يَنْقُصُ ذٰلِكَ مِنْ آثَامِهِمْ شَيْئًا».

227. It is narrated from Abu Huraira (r.a.) that the Messenger of Allah (pbuh) said:

"He who called (people) to righteousness, there would be reward (assured) for him like the rewards of those who adhered to it, without their rewards being diminished in any respect. And he who called (people) to error, he shall have to carry (the burden) of its sin, like those who committed it, without their sins being diminished in any respect." (Muslim, Kitab Al-'Ilm, 16. Also see Abu Dawud, Sunnah, 6; Tirmidhi, Kitab Al-'Ilm, 15; Ibn Majah, Muqaddimah, 14)

Explanations:

The fact that Almighty Allah made believers responsible for calling others to Islam shows that He loves His servants a lot and He is very merciful to them. Our Almighty Lord wants everyone to benefit from the divine blessings and benedictions by finding the right path. For this reason, He promised great rewards to those believers who serve for the realization of this aim.

In order to express the virtue of the responsibility of calling others to Islam, it is enough to remind that it is one of the characteristics of the prophets. As a matter of fact, having the attributes of loyalty, trust, smartness, and innocence is an obligation for prophets for them to accomplish their duty of announcing and calling to the true religion.

When Almighty Allah declares the characteristics of the beloved people, He says:

"…They rehearse the Signs of Allah all night long, and they prostrate themselves in adoration. They believe in Allah and the Last Day; they enjoin what is right, and forbid what is wrong; and they hasten (in emulation) in (all) good works: They are in the ranks of the righteous." (Al-i Imran; 3:113-114)

Almighty Allah mentions in the Noble Qur'an the believers whose wealth and lives He purchased in exchange for Paradise. He gives glad tidings to these subjects who He praised to all humanity and informs us that this is indeed a great benefit. After stating that these beloved servants have altruistically struggled (jihad) in the way o Allah, Almighty Allah lists some of their attributes as follows: **"Those that turn (to Allah) in repentance; that serve Him, and praise Him; that wander in devotion to the cause of Allah; that bow down and prostrate themselves in prayer; that enjoin good and forbid evil; and observe the limit set by Allah. (These do rejoice). So proclaim the glad tidings to the Believers."** (At-Tawbah; 9:112)

Also, Luqman (pbuh) advised his son that announcing and calling to Islam is one of the most important affairs and that he should bear with patient constancy whatever difficulty he may face. (Luqman; 31:17)

In our first hadith, the Messenger of Allah (pbuh) informed us by swearing that being a means for someone's finding the true path as a result of fulfilling the duty of calling to Islam has a value that is greater than the most valuable worldly material goods.

The Messenger of Allah (pbuh) told this statement to Ali (r.a.) when he gave him the flag to send him to conquer the Fort of Khaiber. So, rewards and gifts for being a means for removing the barriers between people and Islam and for them to meet the truth is so superior and valuable that it cannot be compared with any worldly material good. This is because everything in this world, even this world itself, is temporary and ends like a summer cloud. However, faith and being on the true path are eternal and their rewards and compensation will be sufficient to make us whole in the Hereafter. If not dealt with appropriately, the worldly benefits can cause one to be dragged to rampageousness, heresy, and at the end to Hell. Being on the true path, on the other hand, makes one achieve bliss in this world and in the hereafter, and allows one to eternal life in Paradise.

The "red camels" mentioned in the hadith were one of the most important signs of being wealthy among the Arabs of that era. It is possible to think of this as different material goods for different regions. The Messenger of Allah (pbuh) mentioned red camels as an example to the virtue of calling to Islam.

In our second hadith, the Messenger of Allah (pbuh) prays for those who hear his words and transmits them to others and says *"May Allah brighten your face."* How great an accomplishment it is for a believer to deserve this beautiful prayer of the Prophet (pbuh).

Allah the Almighty also praises his servants who fulfill their duties of calling to Islam. Indeed, it is said in a noble verse that:

"Who is better in speech than one who calls (men) to Allah, works righteousness, and says, "I am of those who bow in Islam"?" (Al-Fussilat; 41:33)

In the rest of our hadith, the Messenger of Allah (pbuh) touches upon one of the wisdoms of calling to Islam. A person who hears, reads, and even memorizes a verse may not duly understand it. A person who transmits his knowledge to others may also have transferred the truths to others with better understanding and intellect. In turn, this transfer causes knowledge to be utilized better. As expressed **in our third hadith,** Almighty Allah gives the same reward to the person who transmits the knowledge as the person who acts upon it and conducts good deeds utilizing the knowledge. Thus, both parties end up wining.

Anas (r.a.) tells us an event that shows the virtue of calling to Islam:

One day the Messenger of Allah (pbuh) had said:

"Shall I inform you of some people? They are neither prophets nor martyrs. However, on the Day of Judgment both prophets and martyrs admire their rank in the sight of Allah. They sit on pillows made of light and everyone knows them."

We asked "Who are they, O Messenger of Allah?"

The Messenger of Allah (pbuh) responded:

"They are those who make Allah love His servants and who make His servants love Allah. They walk around the Earth by desiring goodness for people and giving advice."

We asked:

"O Messenger of Allah! It is easy to understand making His servants love Allah, but how is it possible to make Allah love His servants?"

In response, the Messenger of Allah (pbuh) said:

"They enjoin people what Allah loves and forbid people that He dislikes. When people obey them, Allah -the Mighty and the Magnificent- loves them." (Baihaqi, *Shuab*, I, 367; Ali al-Muttaqi, III, 685-686)

The goal of the Prophet here is to declare the rewards in this world and in the Hereafter of those people who call to Islam. Otherwise, one should not think by just looking at the literal meaning of this narration that there is a higher rank than that of prophethood. This is true because prophets and martyrs have already sacrificed their lives for the purpose of inviting people to Islam.

It is also necessary here to touch upon another important matter: the necessity of fully complying with good manners, appropriate styles and methods when delivering the message of Islam to people. Almighty Allah commands us to invite to His path with wisdom, sagacity, and beautiful preaching. In case it becomes obligatory to struggle with tongue or hand, this should also be done justly and in the best fashion. (Al-Yusuf; 12:108; Al-Ankabut; 29:46) (Al-Nahl; 16:125)

When a Muslim enjoins the good he should treat others with love and kindness because doing everything in the best fashion only befits him.

Almighty Allah speaks as follows:

"Nor can goodness and Evil be equal. Repel (Evil) with what is better: Then will he between whom and you was hatred become as it were your friend and intimate!" (Al-Fussilat; 41:34)

Almighty Allah points out those words spoken mildly have a better chance of being taken into account. (Taha; 20:44)

Acts that are harsh and rude would cause people to hate. For this reason, it is necessary to ask mildness and tolerance from Allah's mercy.

Almighty Allah speaks to the Prophet (pbuh):

"It is part of the Mercy of Allah that you do deal gently with them were you severe or harsh-hearted, they would have broken away from about you: so pass over (Their faults), and ask for (Allah's) forgiveness for them; and consult them in affairs (of moment). Then, when you have taken a decision put your trust in Allah. For Allah loves those who put their trust (in Him)." (Al-i Imran; 3:159)

The most important and influential one among the methods of inviting people to the Truth is to show the truths by living them. It is both easier and also more influential to teach something by personally practicing it. As a matter of fact, people who do opposite of what they said will face a difficult account in the Day of Judgment because they erred even though they knew.

The Messenger of Allah (pbuh) says:

"On the night of Isra (Mi'raj), I saw some people whose lips were being slit with scissors of fire. I asked

'O Gabriel who are these people?'

He replied

'They are the khatibs (preachers) who command people to do good deeds while forgetting themselves. Don't you realize and think?"[268] (Ahmad, III, 231, 120, 180, 239; Baihaqi, *Shuab,* II, 283. Also see Bukhari, Bad'u'l-halk, 10; Fitan, 17; Muslim, Zuhd, 51)

It is important and necessary for those who fulfill the responsibility of enjoining the good and forbidding the evil to practice it first themselves in

---

268. In this narration is refered to the following noble verse:
"Do you enjoin right conduct on the people, and forget (to practice it) yourselves, and yet you study the Scripture? Will you not understand?" (Al Baqara; 2:44)

order for their words to be taken seriously but it is not a must. Even if a person cannot put what is right into practice, he should not stay away from telling it to others. By this, those people first enjoin the good and forbid the evil to themselves and then wish the same thing for others and we wish that eventually they too put what they know into practice.

Anas (r.a.) narrated:

We asked:

"O the Messenger of Allah! Shouldn't we command what is right unless we practice it and forbid the evil unless we abandon it?"

The Messenger of Allah (pbuh) said:

"Even if you cannot perform it perfectly command the good and even if you cannot stay away from it completely forbid the evil!" (Haythami, VII, 277)

However, this can never be an acceptable state. This is a temporary permission to indicate the importance of calling to Islam. One must start practicing soon the good deeds that he commands others to do. Otherwise, his situation in the Hereafter will be miserable.[269]

3. The Love of Serving Islam

a. Being a Key to Goodness

٢٢٨. عَنْ أَنَسِ بْنِ مَالِكٍ رَضِيَ اللهُ عَنْهُ قَالَ: قَالَ رَسُولُ اللهِ صَلَّى اللهُ عَلَيْهِ وَسَلَّمَ:

«إِنَّ مِنَ النَّاسِ مَفَاتِيحَ لِلْخَيْرِ مَغَالِيقَ لِلشَّرِّ وَإِنَّ مِنَ النَّاسِ مَفَاتِيحَ لِلشَّرِّ مَغَالِيقَ لِلْخَيْرِ فَطُوبَى لِمَنْ جَعَلَ اللهُ مَفَاتِيحَ الْخَيْرِ عَلَى يَدَيْهِ وَوَيْلٌ لِمَنْ جَعَلَ اللهُ مَفَاتِيحَ الشَّرِّ عَلَى يَدَيْهِ».

---

269. For methods of calling to Islam and details see Osman Nûri Topbaş, *Hazret-i Muhammed Mustafâ*, Istanbul 2005, I, 260-281; Ömer Çelik, Mustafa Öztürk, Murat Kaya, *Üsve-i Hasene*, Istanbul 2004, II, 15-144.

228. Anas b. Malik (r.a.) narrated: The Messenger of Allah (pbuh) said:

"There are people who are keys to what is good and locks to what is evil. There are also others who are keys to what is evil and locks to what is good. How happy are those to whom Allah has given them to be the keys of the good! Woe to those to whom Allah has given to be the keys of the evil!" (Ibn Majah, Muqaddima, 19; Baihaqi, *Shuab,* I, 455)

✿

٢٢٩. عَنْ أَبِي مُوسَى رَضِيَ اللهُ عَنْهُ قَالَ: كَانَ رَسُولُ اللهِ صَلَّى اللهُ عَلَيْهِ وَسَلَّمَ إِذَا جَاءَهُ السَّائِلُ أَوْ طُلِبَتْ إِلَيْهِ حَاجَةٌ قَالَ:

«اِشْفَعُوا تُؤْجَرُوا وَيَقْضِي اللهُ عَلَى لِسَانِ نَبِيِّهِ صَلَّى اللهُ عَلَيْهِ وَسَلَّمَ مَا شَاءَ».

229. Abu Musa al-Ash'ari (r.a.) narrated: Whenever a beggar came to Allah's Apostle (pbuh) or he was asked for something, he used to say (to his companions):

"Help and recommend him and you will receive the reward for it; and Allah will bring about what He wills through His Prophet's tongue." (Bukhari, Zakat, 21; Adab, 36, 37; Tawheed, 31; Muslim, Birr, 145. Also see. Abu Dawud, Adab, 116-117/5131; Tirmidhi, Ilm, 14/2672)

✿

٢٣٠. عَنْ أَبِي مَسْعُودٍ الْأَنْصَارِيّ رَضِيَ اللهُ عَنْهُ قَالَ: جَاءَ رَجُلٌ إِلَى النَّبِيِّ صَلَّى اللهُ عَلَيْهِ وَسَلَّمَ فَقَالَ:

«إِنِّي أُبْدِعَ بِي فَاحْمِلْنِي» فَقَالَ:

«مَا عِنْدِي» فَقَالَ رَجُلٌ:

((يَا رَسُولَ اللهِ أَنَا أَدُلُّهُ عَلَى مَنْ يَحْمِلُهُ)) فَقَالَ رَسُولُ اللهِ صَلَّى اللهُ عَلَيْهِ وَسَلَّمَ:

((مَنْ دَلَّ عَلَى خَيْرٍ فَلَهُ مِثْلُ أَجْرِ فَاعِلِهِ)).

230. Abu Mas'ud al-Ansari (r.a.) narrated:

A man came to the Messenger of Allah (pbuh) and said:

"My riding beast has been killed, so can you give me some animal to ride upon?"

The Messenger of Allah (pbuh) said:

"I have none with me."

A man who was present there said:

"Messenger of Allah, I can guide him to someone who will provide him with a riding beast."

Upon this, the Messenger of Allah (pbuh) said:

"One who guides to something good has a reward similar to that of its doer."
(Muslim, Kitab Al-Imara, 133. Also see. Abu Dawud, Adab, 115; Tirmidhi, Ilm, 14)

Explanations:

Being keys to the good and locks to the evil has a side to both calling others to Islam and also serving Islam. Both of them are the most virtuous deeds, which are rewarding and ensuring the contentment of Allah.

As one can earn divine rewards from his own good deeds, one can also earn rewards from others' good deeds. It is not possible to perform every good deed personally. Sometimes this is the result of lack of time and sometimes the lack of human capacity. In these situations, an intelligent believer can earn divine rewards as if he personally performs good deeds by leading and guiding people to do that good by using his intelligence, words, pen, knowledge, power, position, and wealth.

On the other hand, both the ways to goodness and to evil exist and will always continue to exist in this world. The believers have the responsibility of opening the doors of goodness and closing the doors of evil. For this reason, they always have to be the leaders of good deeds in this world and should strain never to allow the evil.

On the other hand, unfortunately, there will be people who are the keys to the evil and who lock the good. For sure, they will have the burden of evils that they cause.

Almighty Allah says:

"Whoever recommends and helps a good cause becomes a partner therein: And whoever recommends and helps an evil cause, shares in its burden: And Allah has power over all things." (An-Nisa; 4:85)

In this situation, the thing to be done is to increase the number of those who are keys to the good and decrease the number of those who are keys the evil.

In our first hadith, the Messenger of Allah (pbuh) said *"How happy!"* to those who are the keys to the good. The expression *"Woe to you!"* for those unfortunate who are the keys to the evil and locks to the good.

In another narration, the Prophet (pbuh) said:

"This goodness (that I brought to you) is comparable to a treasure. There are keys to this treasure. How happy is whom Allah made a key to the good and a lock to the evil! Woe to those whom Allah made a key to the evil and lock to the good!" (Ibn Majah, Muqaddimah, 19)

The good are the things that Allah is content with and the evil are the things that Allah hates and forbids. When Allah is content with one of His servants, the sign of this is to make him a key to the good. When this type of person is seen, he reminds good deeds; when he comes, the good comes with him; when he speaks, he speaks of the good; when he thinks, he thinks of goodness; he always has good feelings and intentions and helps people who want to do good. This type of person who always wants goodness to overcome the evil is a source of goodness for those who are around him. A person who is a key to the evil, since all he does is evil, he always speaks of evil, thinks of evil, plans evil things, helps evil, and brings evil wherever he goes. This type of person who wants evil to spread is a source of pain to those around him. For this reason, being with the first type of person is happiness and being with the second type of person is brigandage.

Prophets are the leaders of being keys to the good. Almighty Allah says about them:

"And We made them leaders, guiding (men) by Our Command..." (Al-Anbiya; 21:73)

All Muslims should be guides to what is good and right by taking prophets as an example. Even, they should pray as:

"And those who pray, "Our Lord! Grant unto us wives and offspring who will be the comfort of our eyes, and give us (the grace) to lead the righteous."[270]

Since a person who guides to good deeds earns divine rewards as if he personally performed them, guiding pious people is a good deed that is very rewarding and beneficial.

In our second hadith, the Messenger of Allah (pbuh) advised being means to all kinds of goodness, especially solving the problems of the needy. The Messenger of Allah (pbuh) said in another hadith:

"Sometimes a person asks for something from me. I would delay satisfying his needs so that you can intercede and help him in getting what he wants and earn divine rewards! Yes, intercede needy in satisfying his need so you can earn divine rewards from it." (Nasai, Zakat, 65)

On the one side there are many needy people and organizations who should receive goodness and help, who struggle in despair and lack of means, and on the other side there are many good people who want to help and try to find those who are really in need. Leading and becoming a mediator to them is a huge responsibility on Muslims and also an opportunity to gain divine rewards. For example, foundations that bring together the needy with the wealthy people are the most significant institutions serving this purpose.

The Messenger of Allah (pbuh) gave the good news to the Muslims who become means to goodness:

---

270. Al-Furqan; 25:74.

"There are some servants of Allah whom He created to satisfy the needs of the needy. People run to these good people for their needs. These are the people who are safe from the anger of Allah." (Haythami, VIII, 192)

In our third hadith, we see an example of becoming a means to a good deed. A man who needs a mount came to the exalted presence of the Prophet. At that moment, there was nothing with the Messenger of Allah. However, there was a Muslim on the other side who could help him with this. One of the Noble Companions of the Messenger who knew about this Muslim brought them together and became a means for a good deed to happen. Upon this, the Messenger of Allah (pbuh) said:

"One who guides to something good has a reward similar to that of its doer."

Another similar incident is as follows:

A young man from the Aslam tribe said:

"O Messenger of Allah, I wish to fight (in the way of Allah) but I don't have anything to equip myself with for fighting."

The Messenger of Allah (pbuh) said:

"Go to so and so, for he had equipped himself (for fighting) but he fell ill."

So, he (the young man) went to him and said:

The Messenger of Allah (pbuh) sends you his greetings and says that you should give me the equipage that you have provided yourself with.

The man said (to his wife or maidservant):

"Dear, give him the equipage I have collected for myself and do not withhold anything from him. Do not withhold anything from him so that you may be blessed therein." (Muslim, Kitab Al-Imara, 134)

Thanks to this one good deed, three people earned divine rewards and none of their rewards are diminished. These are; the Noble Companion of the Messenger who intended to do something good but could not do due to his illness, the young man who performed the good deed by getting the military equipment from him, and the Messenger of Allah (pbuh) who brought them together...

That is to say, encouraging and becoming means to goodness is as important as performing the goodness. As a matter of fact, the Messenger of Allah (pbuh) encouraged his companions to give alms and to do good deeds in every opportunity and often advised them in this direction.

For example, Jabir (r.a.) narrated:

"My maternal aunt was divorced, and she intended to pluck her dates. A person scolded her for having come out (during the period of 'Idda). She came and told about what happened to Allah's Prophet (pbuh) and he said:

"Certainly you can pluck (dates) from your palm trees, for perhaps you may give charity or do an act of kindness." (Muslim, Kitab Al-Talaq, 55; Abu Dawud, Kitab Al-Talaq, 39-41/2297; Nasai, Kitab Al-Talaq, 70; Ibn Majah, Kitab Al-Talaq, 9)

Also, the Messenger of Allah (pbuh) finally said to a noble companion who came and asked him various questions:

"Doing good deed is always better for you." (Abu Dawud, Kitab Al-Buyu, 60/3476)

The prayer that the Messenger of Allah advised to recite when visiting the ill is one of the best examples showing that he always suggested goodness:

"O Allah, cure Your servant, who may then wreak havoc on an enemy for Your sake, or walk at a funeral for Your sake, or join congregation for a prayer." (Abu Dawud, Funerals (Kitab Al-Jana'iz) 8/3107)

By praying in this fashion, the Messenger of Allah (pbuh) suggests the ill to perform good deeds such as fighting in the way of Allah, attend a funeral, and regularly join the congregation for a prayer when he gets well. In this way, the ill Muslim understands the value of his health and the fact that he should utilize these blessings to earn the eternal happiness. He pursues good deeds more passionately when he gets well.

b. Pursuing Good Deeds

٢٣١. عَنْ أَبِي هُرَيْرَةَ رَضِيَ اللهُ عَنْهُ أَنَّ رَسُولَ اللهِ صَلَّى اللهُ عَلَيْهِ وَسَلَّمَ قَالَ:

«بَادِرُوا بِالْأَعْمَالِ فِتَنًا كَقِطَعِ اللَّيْلِ الْمُظْلِمِ يُصْبِحُ الرَّجُلُ مُؤْمِنًا وَيُمْسِي كَافِرًا أَوْ يُمْسِي مُؤْمِنًا وَيُصْبِحُ كَافِرًا يَبِيعُ دِينَهُ بِعَرَضٍ مِنَ الدُّنْيَا».

231. It is narrated from Abu Huraira (r.a.) that the Messenger of Allah (pbuh) said:

"Be prompt in doing good deeds (before you are overtaken) by turbulence which would be like a part of the dark night. During (that stormy period) a man would be a Muslim in the morning and an unbeliever in the evening or he would be a believer in the evening and an unbeliever in the morning, and would sell his faith for worldly goods." (Muslim, Kitab Al Iman, 186. Also see. Tirmidhi, Fitan, 30; Zuhd, 3; Ibn Majah, Iqamah, 78; Ahmad, II, 303, 372, 523)

❁

٢٣٢. عَنْ أَبِي هُرَيْرَةَ رَضِيَ اللهُ عَنْهُ أَنَّ رَسُولَ اللهِ صَلَّى اللهُ عَلَيْهِ وَسَلَّمَ قَالَ:

«بَادِرُوا بِالْأَعْمَالِ سَبْعًا هَلْ تَنْتَظِرُونَ إِلَّا فَقْرًا مُنْسِيًا أَوْ غِنًى مُطْغِيًا أَوْ مَرَضًا مُفْسِدًا أَوْ هَرَمًا مُفَنِّدًا أَوْ مَوْتًا مُجْهِزًا أَوِ الدَّجَّالَ فَشَرُّ غَائِبٍ يُنْتَظَرُ أَوِ السَّاعَةَ فَالسَّاعَةُ أَدْهَى وَأَمَرُّ».

232. It is narrated from Abu Huraira (r.a.) that the Messenger of Allah (pbuh) said:

"Hasten to do good deeds before you are overtaken by one of the seven afflictions." Then (giving a warning) he said,

"Are you waiting for

1. Such poverty which will make you unmindful of devotion; or

2. Prosperity which will make you corrupt, or

3. Disease as will disable you, or

527

4. Such senility as will make you mentally unstable, or

5. Sudden death, or

6. Al-Dajjal (Anti-Christ) who is the worst expected absent, or

7. The Hour, and the Hour will be most grievous and most bitter". (Tirmidhi, Zuhd, 3/2306)

۞

٢٣٣. عَنْ عَمْرِو بْنِ عَبَسَةَ رَضِيَ اللهُ عَنْهُ أَنَّ رَسُولَ اللهِ صَلَّى اللهُ عَلَيْهِ وَسَلَّمَ قَالَ:

«مَنْ شَابَ شَيْبَةً فِي سَبِيلِ اللهِ كَانَتْ لَهُ نُورًا يَوْمَ الْقِيَامَةِ».

233. It is narrated from Amr b. Abase (r.a.) that the Messenger of Allah (pbuh) said:

"Whosoever's single strand turns gray in the path of Allah, it becomes a divine light (nur) on the Day of Judgment for him." (Tirmidhi, Fadail al-Jihad, 9/1635; Nasai, Jihad, 26/3140; Ahmad, IV, 113)

۞

٢٣٤. عَنْ جَابِرِ بْنِ عَبْدِ اللهِ رَضِيَ اللهُ عَنْهُ قَالَ: قَالَ رَجُلٌ لِلنَّبِيِّ صَلَّى اللهُ عَلَيْهِ وَسَلَّمَ يَوْمَ أُحُدٍ:

«أَرَأَيْتَ إِنْ قُتِلْتُ فَأَيْنَ أَنَا؟» قَالَ:

«فِي الْجَنَّةِ» فَأَلْقَى تَمَرَاتٍ فِي يَدِهِ ثُمَّ قَاتَلَ حَتَّى قُتِلَ.

234. Jabir bin Abdullah (r.a.) narrated:

On the day of the battle of Uhud, a man came to the Prophet and asked:

"Can you tell me where I will be if I should get martyred?"

The Prophet (pbuh) replied:

"In Paradise."

The man threw away some dates he was carrying in his hand, and fought till he was martyred. (Bukhari, Al-Maghazi, 17; Muslim, Imara, 143. Also see. Nasai, Jihad, 31)

۲۳٥. عَنْ أَبِي سَعِيدٍ الْخُدْرِيِّ رَضِيَ اللهُ عَنْهُ أَنَّ رَسُولَ اللهِ صَلَّى اللهُ عَلَيْهِ وَسَلَّمَ رَأَى فِي أَصْحَابِهِ تَأَخُّرًا فَقَالَ لَهُمْ:

((تَقَدَّمُوا فَأْتَمُّوا بِي وَلْيَأْتَمَّ بِكُمْ مَنْ بَعْدَكُمْ لَا يَزَالُ قَوْمٌ يَتَأَخَّرُونَ حَتَّى يُؤَخِّرَهُمُ اللهُ)).

235. Abu Sa'id al-Khudri (r.a.) reported that the Messenger of Allah (pbuh) saw (a tendency) among his Companions to go to the back (in congregation), so he said to them:

"Come forward and follow my lead, and let those who come after you follow your lead. People will continue to keep back till Allah will put them at the back." (Muslim, Salat, 130. Also see Abu Dawud, Salat, 97; Nasai, Imamah, 17; Ibn Majah, Iqamah, 45; Ahmad, III, 34)

Explanations:

Humans as the travelers for the Hereafter and responsible from the general state of the world will be happy as much as they fill their lives, which passes by as quick as a wink, with good deeds and benefactions. The rewards that Almighty Allah gives for the good deeds are unimaginably magnificent. For this reason, when Muslims see the blessings of Allah in the Hereafter and the rewards that He gives for the good deeds performed in the world, they consider their good deeds very few and regret that they did not perform more good deeds. As the Messenger of Allah informed us "even if a person lives a life full of struggles, in other words, even if he endures all kinds of troubles in order to worship, obey Allah, and serve in the way of Allah from the day he is born until the day that he dies due to his old age, on the Day of Judgment, all he has done will seem very few to him and he will wish that he could have done more." (Ahmad, IV, 185; Baihaqi, *Shuab*, I, 479; Haythami, I, 51; X, 225, 358)

The real benefit of all good deeds is for those who perform the deed. Even if it seems that those who benefit from good deeds are the recipients, the final benefit and the spiritual gain is for the performer.

It is said in noble verses that:

"If any one does a righteous deed, it ensures to the benefit of his own soul." (Al-Jasiyah; 45:15)

"It is not required of you (O Messenger., to set them on the right path, but Allah sets on the right path whom He pleases. Whatever of good you give benefits your own souls, and you shall only do so seeking the "Face" of Allah. Whatever good you give, shall be rendered back to you, and you shall not be dealt with unjustly." (Al-Baqarah; 2:272)

Also, no goodness can get loss. Almighty Allah records everything and will appear before us on the Day of Judgment. As a matter of fact, it is said in a noble Qur'an:

"And whatever you do that is good, (Allah) knows it well." (Al-Baqarah; 2:215)

"And be steadfast in prayer and regular in charity: And whatever good you send forth for your souls before you, you shall find it with Allah, for Allah sees well all that you do." (Al-Baqarah; 2:110)

For this reason, a believer should perform good deeds and pursue beneficial works in this world as much as he can. Good traits such as making good use of time, benefitting from the opportunities, searching for the opportunities of good deeds, and hurrying about these acts should be signs of a believer who sincerely believes in Allah and the Day of Judgment. That is because Almighty Allah advised His servants to behave this way and He says:

"...then strive together (as in a race) towards all that is good." (Al-Baqarah; 2:148)

"They believe in Allah and the Last Day; they enjoin what is right, and forbid what is wrong; and they hasten (in emulation) in (all) good works: They are in the ranks of the righteous." (Al-i Imran; 3:114)

In our first hadith, the Messenger of Allah (pbuh) advised that one must not show negligence and hurry in doing good deeds while there are opportunities. As a matter of fact, time not always ticks away the same. There comes a time where circumstances can change, unrest can occur, and some deeds which can be performed easily cannot be performed. The social disturbances can darken the society so much so that people may not discern between the good and the evil. Everyone starts fighting for their lives; they would not want to be busy neither with the religion nor withthe faith; and faith, the most valuable fortune of humans, can lose its value in the eyes of people. Since many of them may not know what they are doing and due to their lack of Islamic knowledge, they may be Muslims in the morning but unbelievers in the evening or Muslims in the evening but unbelievers in the morning. This may be caused by the lack of Islamic education or most of the time by giving up everything for the worldly benefits. At that point, some people may trade their faith and religion for a small benefit in this world.

In times like this when the world is in a slippery slope, the strongest handle that a believer should grasp in order to protect his faith is the performance of good deeds. In extraordinary times when disorder, corruption, cruelty and abasement are present, arming oneself with good deeds protects and strengthens one's faith.

In another narration, it is expressed that *"those whom Allah has blessed with knowledge"* can protect their faith in times of disorder. (Darimi, Muqaddimah, 32)

Doing good deeds are not only prevented by great discords. There are also other reasons that prevent people from performing good deeds. **In our second hadith,** the Messenger of Allah (pbuh) advised us that one must pursue good deeds that make us gain the consent of Allah and divine rewards before these kinds of disorders take place.

For example, a person can be poor at any time. When people struggle with poverty, they would not think of doing good deeds. As a matter of fact, most of the good deeds are done with financial means. Those who lose their wealth miss out these opportunities. Yet, the doors of possibilities for doing good deeds are not completely closed for them. As long as they want, there are countless ways of doing good deeds. However, being poor makes the performance of some important good deeds impossible.

On the other hand, one can be wealthy when he was poor but this may cause him to pursue good deeds. As a matter of fact, when his financial possibilities advance, he may get rampageous by losing his control over the carnal self, he may become greedy, and the love of this world invades his heart and makes him forget the Hereafter.

For this reason, one must be thankful for his situation and search for the ways of doing good deeds. Poor should not wait to become rich and rich should not wait to become old. That is because a person can get sick at any age. God forbid, a young person who becomes seriously ill loses the opportunity of serving in the way of Allah. A sick person whose enjoyment of the life and power of his body is gone must busy himself mostly with his health problems. No matter how much he wants, his opportunities to perform good deeds decrease.

While a healthy person keeps postponing doing good deeds, he may realize that the old-age has arrived. Then, he may not have the power of performing the good deeds that he has been putting off. As a matter of fact, since his intelligence and apprehension may start to show the sings of old-age, he may even not be able to think of doing good deeds for the Hereafter. Even if he thinks, since he may have speech problems, he may not express himself clearly.

The heaviest one of those is the death. It is impossible to know when one will die. While a person is busy in ignorance, a sudden death changes everything. After passing away from this world of opportunities to win the hereafter, no matter how hard he wants, he cannot perform anything. When facing with the fright and torments of the Day of Judgment, he wants to come back and pursue and perform good deeds, but in vain indeed... The test of humans ends there. He will be alone with whatever he has done before.

At the end of the hadith, the Messenger of Allah (pbuh) referred to the following noble verse of the Qur'an in order to make one feel the horror of the Day of Judgment where those who did not pursue good deeds will burn with the fires of regret:

"Nay, the Hour (of Judgment) is the time promised them (for their full recompense): And that Hour will be most grievous and most bitter." (Al-Qamar; 54:46)

As a result, a Muslim should not wait for anything to perform good deeds. As the Prophet expressed in one of his sermons, one should pay attention to this warning:

"O people! Repent to Allah before you die! Embark upon good deeds before you become occupied with some troubles and hardships! Try to give Allah His due

upon you by remembering Him a lot and by giving much sadaqah (charity) both secretly and openly so that you will be endowed bounties by Allah, receive help and get ameliorated!" (Ibn Majah, Iqamah, 78)

Such serious warnings of the Prophet on doing good deeds fast and without delay shows that people have a great weakness in this respect and so that this matter is extremely important.

On the Day of Judgment, great rewards await the believers who were able to overcome this weakness without being defeated by their carnal self. Indeed, **in our third hadith**, we are given the glad tidings that even the smallest of efforts in the way of Allah will shine like a light on the Day of Judgment, will light up his way to Heaven, and will save him from the intense troubles of the Day of Judgment. So, a Muslim should make each hair strand on his head turn gray while running for services in the way of Allah.

In our fourth hadith, a companion is teaching how to run around for good deeds by personally practicing himself. This companion who learned that he will obtain Heaven in exchange for the deed that he will conduct had accepted the word of the Prophet with certain faith and had run to jihad upon hearing it and had not even waited to eat the dates in his hand.

A similar event took place in the Battle of Badr. In Badr, the Messenger of Allah (pbuh) had encouraged his companions for jihad and reminded them of Heaven. And when the enemy had come quite close, he commanded:

"Come on, stand up for Heaven, which is as large as the skies and the Earth."

Upon this, Umair b. Humam (r.a.) jumped in and said:

"O the Messenger of Allah (pbuh)! Did you say 'the Heaven as large as the skies and the Earth?'

The Messenger of Allah (pbuh) responded

"Yes." Umair said:

"How nice, how beautiful!"

When the Messenger of Allah (pbuh) asked:

"Why did you say so?" He said:

"O the Messenger of Allah (pbuh), I did not say this for anything but only to be one from the people of Heaven."

In order to enter the struggle (jihad) strong, Umair took out a few dates from his bag and started to eat them. However, he could not be patient for the delay any longer and said:

"If I live until I finish eating these dates, this indeed will be a long life. If I sit down until they finish, I will have shown undue ambition towards the world" and threw away the dates in his hand and drew the sword and fought with the enemy. Finally, he achieved the degree of martyrdom. (See Bukhari, Al-Maghazi, 17; Muslim, Imarah, 145; *Muwatta,* Jihad 42)

Indeed, pursuing good deeds like this means running to the forgiveness and Heaven of Allah and racing for the contentment of Allah. Only the pious servants of Allah can accomplish this.

Almighty Allah says the following:

"Be quick in the race for forgiveness from your Lord, and for a Garden whose width is that (of the whole) of the heavens and of the earth, prepared for the righteous!" (Al-i Imran; 3:133)

Pursuing good deeds and doing the good thing at the very first opportunity had become the distinguishing sign of the Noble Companions. The reason that Abu Bekr was called 'Abu Bakr' was because he was the first person in all kinds of good deeds. Even when the Companions were over the age of eighty, they used to work in the way of Allah like a young person's excitement. Abu Zibyan narrates an example about this:

Abu Ayyub al Ansari (r.a.) had joined a military expedition launched against the Romans. He got sick on the way. When his death was approaching he said the following:

"If I die, then take me forward with you! Carry me as far as you can in the Roman lands. When you meet the enemy lines and can't move any further, bury me there under your feet!" (See Ahmad, V, 419, 416)

At that time, Abu Ayyub al Ansari (r.a.) was over 80 years old and this was his second expedition to Istanbul.

According to a narration from Ali (r.a.), the Prophet's uncle Abbas (r.anhuma) had asked for the purpose of hurrying in doing good deeds if he could give his zakat (obligatory alms) before one year is completed. The Messenger of Allah (pbuh) gave him permission this respect. (Abu Dawud, Zakat, 22/1624; Tirmidhi, Zakat, 37/678; Ibn Majah, Zakat, 7; Ahmad, I, 104; Daarimi, Zakat, 12)

Indeed noble companions used to pursue such good deeds with their lives and wealth and hurry in conducting good deeds.

In our fifth hadith, the harm of staying back from good deeds is explained. The Messenger of Allah (pbuh) had warned his companions who were lining up at the back while praying in the mosque or sitting down during conversations. He advised them to come closer to the imam as much as possible, to follow his moves and to hear his words as best as they can, and to pass on what they learn from him to the next generation. Some commentators have understood this saying of the Prophet (pbuh) as:

"You learn from me the rules of Islam, then, the ones who come after can learn from you, and the ones who come after them learn from them… let it continue like this until the Day of Judgment!"

The punishment of staying distant from good deeds and sources of knowledge is the sign of Allah's leaving that person spiritually backward. Indeed, the Messenger of Allah (pbuh) spoke as follows:

"Be present during the sermon and be close to the imam because by continuing to be further and further away, a person will be in the back even if he enters the Heaven. " (Abu Dawud, Salat 232/1108; Ahmad, V, 11; Hakim, I, 427)

In other words, the people who stay back without an excuse in righteous deeds, such as sitting in the back while listening to the Friday sermon, will gain and enter Heaven with difficulty and after everyone else, even if they earn it. Their rank in the Heaven would also be low.

Another noble hadith on this matter is as follows:

"If a person sits in a mosque at a place where he can see and listen to the imam, listens carefully, and does not speak, then there are two times the rewards. If the person ends up sitting at a far place where he cannot listen but keeps silent and quiet …" (Abu Dawud, Salat 209/1051)

As it can be seen, compensation and rewards decrease as one move away from the source of insight.

c. The Ease of Performing Good Deeds

٢٣٦. عَنْ أَبِي هُرَيْرَةَ رَضِيَ اللهُ عَنْهُ قَالَ: قَالَ رَسُولِ اللهِ صَلَّى اللهُ
عَلَيْهِ وَسَلَّمَ:

«الْإِيمَانُ بِضْعٌ وَسَبْعُونَ أَوْ بِضْعٌ وَسِتُّونَ شُعْبَةً فَأَفْضَلُهَا قَوْلُ لَا إِلٰهَ
إِلَّا اللهُ وَأَدْنَاهَا إِمَاطَةُ الْأَذَى عَنِ الطَّرِيقِ وَالْحَيَاءُ شُعْبَةٌ مِنَ الْإِيمَانِ».

236. Abu Huraira (r.a.) narrated: The Messenger of Allah (pbuh) said:

"Faith has over seventy branches or over sixty branches, the most excellent of which is the declaration that there is no god but Allah, and the humblest of which is the removal of what is injurious from the path: and modesty is a branch of faith." (Muslim, Iman, 58. Also see Bukhari, Iman, 3; Abu Dawud, Sunnah, 14; Nasai, Iman, 16; Tirmidhi, Birr, 80; Iman, 16; Ibn Majah, Muqaddima, 9)

٢٣٧. عَنْ أَبِي هُرَيْرَةَ رَضِيَ اللهُ عَنْهُ عَنِ النَّبِيِّ صَلَّى اللهُ عَلَيْهِ وَسَلَّمَ
قَالَ:

«يَا نِسَاءَ الْمُسْلِمَاتِ لَا تَحْقِرَنَّ جَارَةٌ لِجَارَتِهَا وَلَوْ فِرْسِنَ شَاةٍ».

237. Abu Huraira (r.a.) narrated that the Messenger of Allah (pbuh) said:

"O Muslim women, none of you should consider even a sheep's trotter too insignificant to give to her neighbor." (Bukhari, Hibat, 1; Adab, 30; Muslim, Zakat, 90. Also see. Tirmidhi, Wala, 6)

❀

٢٣٨. عَنْ أَبِي هُرَيْرَةَ رَضِيَ اللهُ عَنْهُ عَنِ النَّبِيِّ صَلَّى اللهُ عَلَيْهِ وَسَلَّمَ
قَالَ:

«كُلُّ سُلَامَى عَلَيْهِ صَدَقَةٌ كُلَّ يَوْمٍ يُعِينُ الرَّجُلَ فِي دَابَّتِهِ يُحَامِلُهُ عَلَيْهَا أَوْ يَرْفَعُ عَلَيْهَا مَتَاعَهُ صَدَقَةٌ وَالْكَلِمَةُ الطَّيِّبَةُ وَكُلُّ خَطْوَةٍ يَمْشِيهَا إِلَى الصَّلَاةِ صَدَقَةٌ وَدَلُّ الطَّرِيقِ صَدَقَةٌ ».

238. Abu Huraira (r.a.) narrated that the Messenger of Allah (pbuh) said:

"There is a (compulsory) almsgiving to be given for every joint of the human body (as a sign of gratitude to Allah) everyday. To help a man concerning his riding animal by helping him to ride it or by lifting his luggage on to it, is regarded as almsgiving, and (saying) a good word is also almsgiving, and every step taken on one's way to offer the compulsory prayer (in the mosque) is also almsgiving and to show the way when asked is also almsgiving." (Bukhari, Jihad, 72. Also see Muslim, Zakat, 56; Abu Dawud, Tatawwu', 12; Adab, 160)

۲۳۹. عَنْ أَبِي ذَرٍّ رَضِيَ اللهُ عَنْهُ عَنِ النَّبِيِّ صَلَّى اللهُ عَلَيْهِ وَسَلَّمَ أَنَّهُ قَالَ:

«يُصْبِحُ عَلَى كُلِّ سُلَامَى مِنْ أَحَدِكُمْ صَدَقَةٌ فَكُلُّ تَسْبِيحَةٍ صَدَقَةٌ وَكُلُّ تَحْمِيدَةٍ صَدَقَةٌ وَكُلُّ تَهْلِيلَةٍ صَدَقَةٌ وَكُلُّ تَكْبِيرَةٍ صَدَقَةٌ وَأَمْرٌ بِالْمَعْرُوفِ صَدَقَةٌ وَنَهْيٌ عَنِ الْمُنْكَرِ صَدَقَةٌ وَيُجْزِئُ مِنْ ذٰلِكَ رَكْعَتَانِ يَرْكَعُهُمَا مِنَ الضُّحَى».

239. Abu Dhar (r.a.) narrated that the Messenger of Allah (pbuh) said:

"Almsgiving is due on every joint of a person, every day the sun rises. In every declaration of the glorification of Allah there is a almsgiving, and every Takbir (i.e. saying Allah-O-Akbar) is a almsgiving, and every praise of His (saying al-Hamdu Lillah) is a almsgiving and every declaration that He is One (La illha ill-Allah) is a almsgiving, and enjoining of good is a almsgiving, and forbidding of that which is evil is a almsgiving. Performing two rakah of Duha (mid-morning)

prayer includes all." (Muslim, Musafirin, 84; Zakat, 56. Also see Bukhari, Sulh, 11; Jihad, 72; 128; Abu Dawud, Tatawwu', 12; Adab, 160)

❁

٢٤٠. عَنْ جَابِرٍ رَضِيَ اللهُ عَنْهُ قَالَ: قَالَ رَسُولُ اللهِ صَلَّى اللهُ عَلَيْهِ وَسَلَّمَ:

«مَا مِنْ مُسْلِمٍ يَغْرِسُ غَرْسًا إِلَّا كَانَ مَا أُكِلَ مِنْهُ لَهُ صَدَقَةً وَمَا سُرِقَ مِنْهُ لَهُ صَدَقَةٌ وَمَا أَكَلَ السَّبُعُ مِنْهُ فَهُوَ لَهُ صَدَقَةٌ وَمَا أَكَلَتِ الطَّيْرُ فَهُوَ لَهُ صَدَقَةٌ وَلَا يَرْزَؤُهُ أَحَدٌ إِلَّا كَانَ لَهُ صَدَقَةٌ».

240. Jabir (r.a.) narrated: The Messenger of Allah (pbuh) said:

"*If a Muslim plants a tree (or a plant), that part of its produce consumed by men will be as almsgiving for him. Any fruit stolen from the tree will also be as almsgiving for him. That which the birds eat will also be as almsgiving for him. Any of its produce which people may eat thus diminishing it, will be as almsgiving for the Muslims who planted it.*" (Muslim, Musakaat, 7)

❁

٢٤١. عَنْ أَبِي هُرَيْرَةَ رَضِيَ اللهُ عَنْهُ أَنَّ رَسُولَ اللهِ صَلَّى اللهُ عَلَيْهِ وَسَلَّمَ قَالَ:

«بَيْنَمَا رَجُلٌ يَمْشِي بِطَرِيقٍ وَجَدَ غُصْنَ شَوْكٍ عَلَى الطَّرِيقِ فَأَخَّرَهُ فَشَكَرَ اللهُ لَهُ فَغَفَرَ لَهُ».

241. Abu Huraira (r.a.) narrated that the Messenger of Allah (pbuh) said:

"*While a man was walking on a road, he saw a thorny branch and removed it from the way and Allah became pleased by his action and forgave him for that.*" (Bukhari, Adhan, 32; Mazalim, 28; Muslim, Birr, 127; Imara, 164)

❁

٢٤٢. عَنْ أَبِي مُوسَى الْأَشْعَرِيِّ رَضِيَ اللهُ عَنْهُ عَنِ النَّبِيِّ صَلَّى اللهُ عَلَيْهِ وَسَلَّمَ قَالَ:«عَلَى كُلِّ مُسْلِمٍ صَدَقَةٌ» فَقَالُوا: «يَا نَبِيَّ اللهِ فَمَنْ لَمْ يَجِدْ» قَالَ: «يَعْمَلُ بِيَدِهِ فَيَنْفَعُ نَفْسَهُ وَيَتَصَدَّقُ» قَالُوا: «فَإِنْ لَمْ يَجِدْ» قَالَ:«يُعِينُ ذَا الْحَاجَةِ الْمَلْهُوفَ» قَالُوا:«فَإِنْ لَمْ يَجِدْ» قَالَ: «فَلْيَعْمَلْ بِالْمَعْرُوفِ وَلْيُمْسِكْ عَنِ الشَّرِّ فَإِنَّهَا لَهُ صَدَقَةٌ».

242. Abu Musa al-Ash'ari (r.a.) narrated that the Messenger of Allah (pbuh) said:

"Every Muslim should give sadaqa and do good deeds."

The Companions asked:

"O the Prophet of Allah! What if someone has nothing to give what should he do?"

The Messenger of Allah (pbuh) said:

"He should get work and earn something with his hand and give sadaqa (help himself and others)."

They said:

"And if someone is unable to do that?"

He said:

"He should help someone in need." They said:

"What if he cannot find anyone?"

He said:

"He should do good and refrain from evil. That is sadaqa for him." (Bukhari, Zakat, 30; Adab, 33; Muslim, Zakat, 55)

۞

٢٤٣. عَنْ أَبِي ذَرٍّ رَضِيَ اللهُ عَنْهُ قَالَ: قَالَ لِي النَّبِيُّ صَلَّى اللهُ عَلَيْهِ وَسَلَّمَ:

«لَا تَحْقِرَنَّ مِنَ الْمَعْرُوفِ شَيْئًا وَلَوْ أَنْ تَلْقَى أَخَاكَ بِوَجْهٍ طَلْقٍ».

243. Abu Dharr (r.a.) narrated: The Messenger of Allah (pbuh) said:

"Don't consider anything insignificant out of good things even if it is that you meet your brother with a cheerful countenance." (Muslim, Birr, 144. Also see Abu Dawud, Libas, 24; Tirmidhi, At'ima, 30)

Explanations:

Almighty Allah, who continuously commands His servants to do good deeds, whether big or small, in order for them to achieve eternal bliss, has made it extremely easy for them to do good deeds and earn rewards as a result of His endless favors. As it can be seen **in our first hadith**, from the smallest to the biggest, there are many kinds of good deeds. There is definitely a kind of good deed that a person at any level can do. Even simple acts that people do not pay attention such as removing a stone that discomforts those walking on a path are considered good deeds and believers earn rewards for them.

On the other hand, small or big, all good deeds are related to faith. It is not possible to do a healthy and essential good deed without belief in Allah and the thought of pleasing Him. When one acts with this intention, even the feelings, words, and actions of a person which look like they have no relationship with worship also are counted among the good and beneficial deeds. The continuation of the feelings of doing good deeds depends on having faith in Allah and the Hereafter. This is because faith in Allah and the Hereafter causes a person to have spiritual pleasure from the good and beneficiary deeds that he does and leads him to continuously do good deeds.

Indeed, the Messenger of Allah (pbuh) responded to one of his companions who asked "What is faith?" as:

"If a good deed that you performed pleases you and a bad deed saddens you, then you are a believer!" (Ahmad, V, 252, 255; Haythami, I, 86)

This saying of the Prophet is sufficient to show how rooted and encompassing the ideal of good and beneficial is in Islam.

In our second hadith, the Messenger of Allah (pbuh) told that it is necessary to do every good deed without belittling any of them, and in order for this principle to be better understood he gave an example: Muslims should not stay back from doing good deeds even if it is presenting a hoof of sheep. Starting with women, all Muslims should set aside laziness, miserliness, and showing off and should be in an effort to do good deeds as much as they are able to. This is because the Messenger of Allah (pbuh) says the following:

"Never belittle even the smallest of good deeds! If one of you cannot find anything to do, he should meet his brother with a smiling face! If you purchase meat or cook a pot of food, then add a little extra water and present from it to your neighbor." (Tirmidhi, At'ima, 30/1833)

In our third hadith, it is pointed out that doing good deeds is necessary for a person and that the individual should thank for each bounty that Allah favored by doing good and beneficial deeds. A person should thank Allah everyday for He granted health to every joint and bone in his body, and he is obliged to show his gratitude in the form of good and beneficial deeds. This is because there is an inconvenience for each bounty and every bounty necessitates thanking Allah. Health, on the other hand, is the beginning of everything and is a great treasure. Performing the thanks of health is also not difficult at all. Almighty Allah has accepted as almsgiving and good deed to help someone to get on its ride, to help someone load his ride, to say a nice word, every step to the mosque when going for a prayer, and to give directions to a stranger.

In another narration, *"establishing justice among people (or two individuals)"* and *"removing of harmful things from the pathway"* are also added to the lists of almsgiving. (Bukhari, Sulh, 11; Jihad 72, 128; Muslim, Zakat, 56)

All of these are easy things that almost anyone can do. However, when conducted with a sincere intention, they help us please Allah.

Our fourth hadith shows that there are easier ways of conducting good and beneficial deeds that will please Allah. The Messenger of Allah (pbuh) informs us that all recitations of "Subhanallah (Glory be to Allah)," "Alhamdulillah (All Praise be to Allah)," "La ilaaha illallah (There is no god but God)," and "Allahu akbar (Allah is Greater)" are considered almsgiving. That is, giving a material good is not absolutely necessary for something to be considered as sadaqah and beneficial deeds. Poor people with not much wealth can also conduct a lot of good deeds by their hands, tongues, and smiles. However, those who have wealth and resources cannot fulfill their responsibilities just by these deeds because everyone's responsibility is commensurate with the bounties that they are bestowed with.

In addition to these deeds, advising the good and forbidding the evil are also accepted as sadaqah. The obligatory and supererogatory worships, Friday prayer, listening to the sermon, utilizing the noble month of Ramadan… are all among the good and beneficial acts. All of these good and beneficial acts both increase the degrees of believers and are expiation for their minor sins.

In our fifth hadith, we are informed how even the smallest of good deeds that is done with sincerity is a gateway for abundant rewards. Anything that is used from a tree or plant that a Muslim planted by people or animals who eat from it, by kids who take from it, and by being cut or broken is separately counted as sadaqa as long as its products are utilized. As seeds are made from that tree or plant and new products are produced, the new ones are also included in the same rule and the rule of sadaqah continues like this.

In other words, there is no need for a good believer to be sorry. If Allah gives abundance to his wealth, then he donates from it and earns divine rewards; if something occurs and his wealth is destroyed, then this situation is also considered sadaqa and he still earns rewards. Then, a believer should do as much good as he can. He should do good and "throw it to the sea"[271] and should wholeheartedly believe that it will never be lost.

Before the Messenger of Allah (pbuh) declared it, people did not even know that animals could be the subject of good deeds. As the Messenger of Allah (pbuh) taught humanity all the beauties, he also taught us that all living beings, plants, and even non-living beings are subject to good deeds.

One day the Messenger of Allah (pbuh) said the following:

"While a man was walking he felt thirsty and went down a well and drank water from it. On coming out of it, he saw a dog panting and eating mud because of excessive thirst. The man said, 'This (dog) is suffering from the same problem as that of mine. So he (went down the well), filled his shoe with water, caught hold of it with his teeth and climbed up and watered the dog. Allah thanked him for his (good) deed and forgave him."

The Noble Companions asked:

---

271. *Translator's note:* A Turkish proverb indicating that even if the person to whom help is extended does not appreciate the help, God knows about it and gives rewards for it.

"O Allah's Apostle! Is there a reward for us in serving (the) animals?"

The Messenger of Allah (pbuh) said:

"Yes, there is a reward for serving any animate!" (Bukhari, Musakat, 9; Mazalim, 23; Adab, 27; Muslim, Salam, 153; Abu Dawud, Jihad, 44; Ibn Majah, Adab, 8)

In our sixth hadith, how good deeds that are considered minor such as removing a thorny branch from a road help us earn great rewards is expressed. The greatest reward is to achieve the contentment of Allah. Almighty Allah is also extremely pleased that something that could harm His servants is moved to the side of the road. It is also easy to see this in the following narration:

The Messenger of Allah (pbuh) said the following:

"A person while walking along the path saw the branches of a tree lying there. He said: By Allah, I shall remove these from this road so that these may not do harm to the Muslims, and he was admitted to Paradise." (Muslim, Birr, 128)

In our seventh hadith, it is seen that there is no excuse to stay away from good and beneficial deeds. A person who cannot find anything to give as sadaqa carries some load on his back, earns two portions of food and leaves one with his family and gives the other as sadaqa. If he cannot do these, he helps someone in difficulty by using his intellect, words, and physical power. If he cannot even do these, he displays good manners to people and stays back from committing evil. The effort of a believer not to hurt anyone is also a good and beneficial act for himself.

The Messenger of Allah (pbuh) advises people who cannot perform any good deed to still do good deeds by at least smiling to people. Namely, there is no excuse to stay back from good deeds. As long as one is alive, any person can do good deeds. There is no person who can't do this. So, even if Muslims cannot find any other opportunities, they could do good deeds by smiling at their brothers in religion.

The Messenger of Allah (pbuh) says the following in another narration:

"Every good deed is sadaqah. Even greeting your brother with a smiling face and pouring water into your brother's cup from your bucket is considered sadaqa." (Tirmidhi, Birr, 45/1970)

543

So, as long as there are good intentions and sincerity, each word and deed of a believer is sadaqa (almsgiving) and benefaction. This is a great blessing of Allah.

Then, since a Muslim never sees any sin as minor, he should also never see any good as minor. This is because the good small deeds that are neglected due to belittling cause great losses at the end. A Muslim should act with a sincere intention and turn all of his words and actions into good deeds and benefactions.

4. Struggle (Jihad) in the Way of Allah

٢٤٤. عَنْ أَنَسٍ رَضِيَ اللهُ عَنْهُ أَنَّ النَّبِيّ صَلَّى اللهُ عَلَيْهِ وَسَلَّمَ قَالَ:

«جَاهِدُوا الْمُشْرِكِينَ بِأَمْوَالِكُمْ وَأَنْفُسِكُمْ وَأَلْسِنَتِكُمْ».

244. Anas narrated that the Messenger of Allah (pbuh) said:

"Use your property, your bodies, and your tongues in striving against the polytheists!" (Abu Dawud, Jihad, 17/2504; Nasai, Jihad, 1, 48)

❀

٢٤٥. عَنْ أَنَسِ بْنِ مَالِكٍ رَضِيَ اللهُ عَنْهُ عَنِ النَّبِيّ صَلَّى اللهُ عَلَيْهِ وَسَلَّمَ:

«لَرَوْحَةٌ فِي سَبِيلِ اللهِ أَوْ غَدْوَةٌ خَيْرٌ مِنَ الدُّنْيَا وَمَا فِيهَا».

245. Anas b. Malik (r.a.) narrated that the Messenger of Allah (pbuh) said:

"...a morning's or an evening's journey which a slave (person) travels in Allah's Cause is better than the world and whatever is on its surface." (Bukhari, Jihad, 6)

❀

٢٤٦. عَنِ ابْنِ عَبَّاسٍ رَضِيَ اللهُ عَنْهُ قَالَ: بَعَثَ النَّبِيُّ صَلَّى اللهُ عَلَيْهِ وَسَلَّمَ عَبْدَ اللهِ بْنَ رَوَاحَةَ فِي سَرِيَّةٍ فَوَافَقَ ذٰلِكَ يَوْمَ الْجُمُعَةِ فَغَدَا أَصْحَابُهُ فَقَالَ ((أَتَخَلَّفُ فَأُصَلِّي مَعَ رَسُولِ اللهِ صَلَّى اللهُ عَلَيْهِ وَسَلَّمَ ثُمَّ أَلْحَقُهُمْ)) فَلَمَّا صَلَّى مَعَ النَّبِيِّ صَلَّى اللهُ عَلَيْهِ وَسَلَّمَ رَآهُ فَقَالَ:

((مَا مَنَعَكَ أَنْ تَغْدُوَ مَعَ أَصْحَابِكَ؟)) فَقَالَ:

((أَرَدْتُ أَنْ أُصَلِّيَ مَعَكَ ثُمَّ أَلْحَقَهُمْ)) قَالَ:

((لَوْ أَنْفَقْتَ مَا فِي الْأَرْضِ جَمِيعًا مَا أَدْرَكْتَ فَضْلَ غَدْوَتِهِمْ)).

246. Ibn Abbas (r.a.) narrated: The Messenger of Allah (pbuh) sent Abdullah b. Rawaha (r.a.) for a military expedition. This took place on Friday. His friends departed in the morning and he thought "Let me lag behind so that I can pray with the Messenger of Allah (pbuh)." When he performed the prayer with the Noble Prophet (pbuh), the Messenger saw him and asked:

"Why didn't you go with your friends in the morning?"

Abdullah b. Rawaha said:

"I wanted to join you in prayer and then catch up with them."

The Messenger of Allah (pbuh) said:

"Even if you donate everything on this world, you would not gain the rewards that they would by departing early." (Tirmidhi, Jum'a, 28/527; Ahmad, I, 224, 256. Also see. Ahmad, III, 438; Baihaki, *al-Sunan al-kubra*, III, 187)

⁕

٢٤٧. عَنْ أَبِي هُرَيْرَةَ رَضِيَ اللهُ عَنْهُ قَالَ: جَاءَ رَجُلٌ إِلَى رَسُولِ اللهِ صَلَّى اللهُ عَلَيْهِ وَسَلَّمَ فَقَالَ:

«دُلَّنِي عَلَى عَمَلٍ يَعْدِلُ الْجِهَادَ» قَالَ:

«لَا أَجِدُهُ قَالَ هَلْ تَسْتَطِيعُ إِذَا خَرَجَ الْمُجَاهِدُ أَنْ تَدْخُلَ مَسْجِدَكَ
فَتَقُومَ وَلَا تَفْتُرَ وَتَصُومَ وَلَا تُفْطِرَ» قَالَ:

«وَمَنْ يَسْتَطِيعُ ذٰلِكَ».

247. Abu Huraira (r.a.) narrated: A person came to the Messenger of Allah (pbuh) and said:

"What deed could be an equivalent of Jihad in the way of Allah, the Almighty and Exalted?

The Messenger of Allah (pbuh) replied:

"I do not know such a deed" and continued:

"One who goes out for Jihad is like a person who keeps fasts, stands in prayer (constantly), (obeying) Allah's (behests contained in) the verses (of the Qur'an), and does not exhibit any lassitude in fasting and prayer until the Mujahid returns from Jihad in the way of Allah, the Exalted. Would you have the strength to do that deed?"

The man said:

"Who would have the strength to do that deed?" (Bukhari, Jihad, 1; Nasai, Jihad, 17. Also see Muslim, Kitab Al-Imara, 110; Tirmidhi, Fadail al-jihad, 1; Ahmad, II, 344, 423)

❀

٢٤٨. عَنْ سَلْمَانَ رَضِيَ اللهُ عَنْهُ قَالَ: سَمِعْتُ رَسُولَ اللهِ صَلَّى اللهُ
عَلَيْهِ وَسَلَّمَ يَقُولُ:

«رِبَاطُ يَوْمٍ وَلَيْلَةٍ خَيْرٌ مِنْ صِيَامِ شَهْرٍ وَقِيَامِهِ وَإِنْ مَاتَ عَلَيْهِ
عَمَلُهُ الَّذِي كَانَ يَعْمَلُهُ وَأُجْرِيَ عَلَيْهِ رِزْقُهُ وَأَمِنَ الْفَتَّانَ».

248. Salman (r.a.) narrated: I heard the Messenger of Allah (pbuh) say:

"Keeping watch for a day and a night is better (in point of reward) than fasting for a whole month and standing in prayer every night. If a person dies (while, performing this duty), his (meritorious) activity will continue and he will go on receiving his reward for it perpetually and will be saved from the torture of the grave." (Muslim, Kitab Al-Imara, 163. Also see. Tirmidhi, Fadail al-jihad, 2; Nasai, jihad, 39; Ibn Majah, Jihad, 7)

۲٤۹. عَنِ ابْنِ الْخَصَاصِيَةِ رَضِيَ اللهُ عَنْهُ قَالَ: أَتَيْتُ النَّبِيَّ صَلَّى اللهُ عَلَيْهِ وَسَلَّمَ لِأُبَايِعَهُ قَالَ فَاشْتَرَطَ عَلَيَّ شَهَادَةَ أَنْ لَا إِلَهَ إِلَّا اللهُ وَأَنَّ مُحَمَّدًا عَبْدُهُ وَرَسُولُهُ وَأَنْ أُقِيمَ الصَّلَاةَ وَأَنْ أُوَدِّيَ الزَّكَاةَ وَأَنْ أَحُجَّ حَجَّةَ الْإِسْلَامِ وَأَنْ أَصُومَ شَهْرَ رَمَضَانَ وَأَنْ أُجَاهِدَ فِي سَبِيلِ اللهِ فَقُلْتُ:

«يَا رَسُولَ اللهِ أَمَّا اثْنَتَانِ فَوَاللهِ مَا أُطِيقُهُمَا الْجِهَادُ وَالصَّدَقَةُ فَإِنَّهُمْ زَعَمُوا أَنَّهُ مَنْ وَلَّى الدُّبُرَ فَقَدْ بَاءَ بِغَضَبٍ مِنَ اللهِ فَأَخَافُ إِنْ حَضَرَتْ تِلْكَ جَشِعَتْ نَفْسِي وَكَرِهَتِ الْمَوْتَ وَالصَّدَقَةُ فَوَاللهِ مَا لِي إِلَّا غُنَيْمَةٌ وَعَشْرُ ذَوْدٍ هُنَّ رَسْلُ أَهْلِي وَحَمُولَتُهُمْ» قَالَ فَقَبَضَ رَسُولُ اللهِ صَلَّى اللهُ عَلَيْهِ وَسَلَّمَ يَدَهُ ثُمَّ حَرَّكَ يَدَهُ ثُمَّ قَالَ:

«فَلَا جِهَادَ وَلَا صَدَقَةَ فَلِمَ تَدْخُلُ الْجَنَّةَ إِذًا» قَالَ قُلْتُ:

«يَا رَسُولَ اللهِ أَنَا أُبَايِعُكَ» قَالَ فَبَايَعْتُ عَلَيْهِنَّ كُلِّهِنَّ.

249. Bashir b. Hasasiyye (r.a.) said:

I came to pledge allegiance to the Noble Prophet. He put forth the condition that I have to testify that there is no god but Allah and the Messenger is

His servant and the Prophet, to perform regular prayers, to give Islamic poor-due, to perform Pilgrimage (Hajj), to fast during the month of Ramadan, and perform jihad in the way of Allah.

I said to him:

"O the Messenger of Allah! I swear to Allah that I cannot perform two of these. These are the Jihad and Sadaqah (charity). Muslims say that those who run away from the frontage returns by getting the anger of Allah.[272] I fear that my carnal self may get scared from dying.

When it comes to sadaqah (charity), I swear to Allah that I do not have anything else than a small sheep herd and ten camels. They are the source of livelihood of family and mounts.

The Messenger of Allah (pbuh) clenched and waived his hand saying:

"No Jihad, no sadaqah (charity), how are you going to go to Paradise?!"

I said right away:

"O the Messenger of Allah, I pledge allegiance to you!" and pledged upon all the conditions that he proposed. (Ahmad, V, 224; Ibn Kathir, *Tafsir*, II, 306, [from the interpretation of Al-Anfal; 8:16)

٢٥٠. عَنْ أَبِي هُرَيْرَةَ رَضِيَ اللهُ عَنْهُ قَالَ: قَالَ رَسُولُ اللهِ صَلَّى اللهُ عَلَيْهِ وَسَلَّمَ:

((إِنَّ فِي الْجَنَّةِ مِائَةَ دَرَجَةٍ أَعَدَّهَا اللهُ لِلْمُجَاهِدِينَ فِي سَبِيلِ اللهِ مَا بَيْنَ الدَّرَجَتَيْنِ كَمَا بَيْنَ السَّمَاءِ وَالْأَرْضِ فَإِذَا سَأَلْتُمُ اللهَ فَاسْأَلُوهُ الْفِرْدَوْسَ فَإِنَّهُ أَوْسَطُ الْجَنَّةِ وَأَعْلَى الْجَنَّةِ)).

250. Abu Huraira (r.a.) narrated: The Messenger of Allah (pbuh) said:

---

272. Here, the companion was minding the following noble verse:
"If any do turn his back to them on such a day - unless it be in a stratagem of war, or to retreat to a troop (of his own)- he draws on himself the wrath of Allah, and his abode is Hell,- an evil refuge (indeed)!" (al-Anfal; 8:16)

"Paradise has one-hundred levels which Allah has reserved for the Mujahidin who fight in His Cause, and the distance between each of two levels is like the distance between the Heaven and the Earth. So, when you ask Allah (for something), ask for Al-firdaws which is the best and highest level of Paradise." (Bukhari, Jihâd, 4; Tawhîd, 22. See also Nasai, Jihad, 18; Ahmad, II, 335, 339)

Explanations:

Jihad comes from the Arabic root "jahd" which means to exert and make an effort, to utilize all the possibilities in order to succeed in something. In technical terms, it means "to learn commands of the religion and live by them and to teach others, to enjoin the good and forbid the evil, to call others to Islam, to be at war with the carnal self and the external enemies." Jihad can be made by various means such as heart, tongue, hands, wealth, life, and weapons.

As it can be seen, jihad has a wide range of meanings that cover all kinds of deeds of learning Islam and helping to protect and ensure its continuation. For this reason, considering jihad consisting of solely battle is not only incorrect representation of the truth but also is a faulty and wrong understanding of the meaning of Jihad given in the Qur'an and Sunnah.

In this situation, any effort and struggle to exalt the religion of Allah, that is, "*'ila-i kalimatullah*," is jihad. A person first believes in Allah, then learns his religion, and then tries to take his religion to other people in an appropriate style. He struggles with those who object this, again, within the rules brought by religion. Namely, he tries to remove all the barriers between Islam and humans. This is because the only goal of jihad is to provide opportunities for those who want to accept the religion without any imposition, with their own will, and discretion and to prepare the basis for those who want to learn the necessities of their religion and to live what they learned.

Jihad aims to purify the Earth from all kinds of oppression and polytheism and to establish justice, compassion, and mercy there. This means not just Muslims, but all humanity, living beings, and even non-living beings are under protection. The real difference between the life-granting jihad of Muslims and the war of oppressors who loot everything is seen here.

For this reason, the foundation of the building of Islam is considered as faith and its peak and highest dome is accepted as "jihad." The Messenger of Allah (pbuh) said:

549

"Jihad is the peak of Islam." (Tirmidhi, Iman 8; Ibn Majah, Fitan 22; Ahmad, V, 245-246)

Deeming jihad as superior to all virtuous deeds is because it is a means to establish the hegemony of Allah's will on Earth and it helps people achieve salvation both in this world and in the hereafter. Both the religion and the order of the world are dependent upon it, so each step that serves this purpose has a great value.[273]

The Noble Companions who properly understood the virtue of jihad have pursued one jihad after another. There are many companions who left their own lands and emigrated to faraway places that they have never known and who never came back in order for those people to become Muslims and to teach them Islam even though their ages were very advanced.

In this regard how exemplary the following narration is:

Harith b. Hisham and Suhail b. Amr were with Umar (r. anhum). They sat so that Umar was between them. After a while the first Emigrants started to come. As each emigrant came Umar (r.a.) used to move them to the side as "Make room O Suhail! Move forward a little and let them sit O Harith!" Then, the Helpers started to come. Umar again told Suhail and Harith to make room for the newly arriving Helpers so that they ended up at the end of the congregation. When they exited from Umar's presence, Harith (r.a.) said to Suhail:

"Have you seen what Umar did to us?"

Suhail (r.a.) responded:

"We have no right to blame him. We should blame ourselves. We caused this to ourselves. The people who he respected ran to Islam immediately when they were called and accepted without delay. We, on the other hand, acted slowly and stayed back."

When people scattered around from the presence of Umar, Harith and Suhail visited him again and asked:

"O the Ruler of Believers! We saw what you did today. But we also know that it is us who caused this to happen. However, is there a way to compensate for this mistake?" Umar (r.a.) said:

---

273. For details on jihad see Ahmet Özel-Bekir Topaloğlu, "Cihad", *Diyanet İslâm Ansiklopedisi*, VII, 527-534.

"This can be the only way to compensate for this" and pointed towards the war fronts towards direction of the Roman Empire.

Upon this, they went out for jihad to Damascus and never came back until they reach the rank of martyrdom. (See Ali al-Muttaqi, XIV, 67/37953; Hakim, III, 318/5227)

Almighty Allah speaks as follows:

"Not equal are those believers who sit (at home) and receive no hurt, and those who strive and fight in the cause of Allah with their goods and their persons. Allah has granted a grade higher to those who strive and fight with their goods and persons than to those who sit (at home). Unto all (in Faith) Allah has promised good: But those who strive and fight He has distinguished above those who sit (at home) by a special reward, ranks specially bestowed by Him, and Forgiveness and Mercy. For Allah is Oft-forgiving, Most Merciful." (An-Nisa; 4:95-96)

Indeed, the Noble Companions and the righteous believers who came after them have all pursued jihad in order to achieve the reward, superiority, forgiveness, and mercy of Almighty Allah, they had never sat down and remained at where they are. This is because the Messenger of Allah (pbuh) commanded them to struggle in the way of Allah with all their property, lives, tongues, that is, with all their capacities.

In our first hadith, the Messenger of Allah (pbuh) shows us how broad the meaning of jihad is. Namely, jihad can be done by wealth, lives, and tongues.

Almighty Allah vows that He will give many times more to his servants who participate in jihad with their wealth. The Messenger of Allah (pbuh) gives the related glad tidings as follows:

"Seven hundred times the reward is given to those who spend their wealth in the way of Allah." (Tirmidhi, Fadail al-jihad, 4. Also see Nasai, Jihad, 45)

"But the Messenger, and those who believe with him, strive and fight with their wealth and their persons: for them are (all) good things: and it is they who will prosper." (Al-Tawbah; 9:88)

"O you who believe! Shall I lead you to a bargain that will save you from a grievous Penalty? That you believe in Allah and His Messenger, and

that you strive (your utmost) in the Cause of Allah, with your property and your persons: That will be best for you, if you but knew!" (Al-Saff; 61:10-11)

When asked who the most virtuous person is, *the Messenger of Allah (pbuh)* again said:

"The believer who struggles in the way of Allah with his life and property." (Bukhari, Jihad, 2; Muslim, Kitab Al-Imara, 122)

When it comes to jihad with tongue, it is also very important. Jihad with forces like language, paper, pen, culture, and economics has gained more importance especially in our day. The Noble Qur'an named calling to Islam, which is very important in carrying the divine message to humanity, "the Great Jihad (strive with utmost strenuousness)."

In the noble verse it is said:

"Therefore listen not to the unbelievers, but strive against them with the utmost strenuousness, with the (Qur'an)." (Al-Furqan; 25:52)

The "utmost strenuousness" in the verse is doing everything possible to spread and exalt Islam, and to mobilize all resources and capacities for this cause.

The Messenger of Allah (pbuh) said the following about those who speak of things that they do not do and do things that they were not commanded:

"...He who strove against them with his hand was a believer: he who strove against them with his tongue was a believer, and he who strove against them with his heart was a believer and beyond that there is no faith even to the extent of a mustard seed." (Muslim, Iman, 80)

The usage of the term jihad (strive) by the Prophet is worthy of attention. Then, enjoining the good and forbidding the evil with tongue is also jihad. If one does not have the strength to do this, then hating from the heart and praying is also jihad. However, this understanding never means to neglect, belittle, or give up the jihad in the war front. It only shows that the mentality that considers jihad something that can only be done with the hand and at the war front is incomplete. This is because it may not always be necessary to fight on the war front. Moreover, some accomplishments are obtained outside the war front. No doubt there are many ways and methods to spread the religion of Allah and to take Islam to people. Even the army that will fight in the war front can only be formed by calling to Islam and training.

The jihad with tongue in our hadith is also understood as activities such as encouraging the warriors to fight with the enemy, saying words or reciting poems that increase their courage and state the virtue of jihad. Indeed, when the verses that decry the poets who deal with invalidity and poetry in this context, Qa'b b. Malik (r.a.), one of the famous poets, came to the Prophet and asked:

"As you know, Allah the Exalted has revealed some verses on poetry, what do you command in this regard?" The Messenger of Allah (pbuh) sad to him:

"The believer strives (jihad) with his sword and tongue. I swear by Allah in Whose Hand my soul is the words that you throw to the enemy with your tongue are just like arrows, it divides and destroys them." (See Ahmad, III, 456; VI, 387)

In the same manner, to announce the bad ends of the disbelievers and unbelievers, to put forth with evidence their heresy and invalidity are also jihad with the tongue. Namely, all kinds of verbal service for Islam are considered jihad with tongue.

Almighty Allah has informed us that he loves his servants who fight in the direction of the sake of Allah and are never afraid of the reproaches of such people who find fault, and He also testified that such servants also love Him. This indeed is a great favor from Allah. (Al-Maidah; 5:54)

While the meaning of jihad (striving, struggling in the way of Allah) is very broad due to its difficulty and the necessity of putting one' life at stake the physical jihad has been accepted as the most virtuous. When all the possibilities for peace are exhausted or when enemy attacks, war may become necessary as a last resort. In this situation, going on an expedition by risking everything is of course the most virtuous righteous deed. Indeed, **in our second hadith**, we are informed that walking a little in the morning or in the evening for this purpose is better for a Muslim than the world and all there is in it. Due to the superiority of this effort in the way of Allah, Almighty Allah has decreed as virtuous the steps are when returning from jihad as the steps taken going for jihad.

All military moves, the morning and evening training activities, which are important for the military, and even stepping somewhere that would anger the disbelievers are from the acts that are considered rewarding and are included in the content of our hadith.

Almighty Allah speaks as follows:

"It was not fitting for the people of Medina and the Bedouin Arabs of the neighborhood, to refuse to follow Allah's Messenger, nor to prefer their own lives to his: because nothing could they suffer or do, but was reckoned to their credit as a deed of righteousness,- whether they suffered thirst, or fatigue, or hunger, in the cause of Allah, or trod paths to raise the ire of the Unbelievers, or received any injury whatever from an enemy: for Allah suffers not the reward to be lost of those who do good." (Al-Tawbah; 9:120)

However, jihad needs to be done only for the sake of Allah. Indeed questions like the following were directed to the Prophet:

"O the Messenger of Allah (pbuh)! Some people fight so that they can obtain war booty (spoils of war), others fight so that they can be famous, others fight so that they show off as heroes and prove the superiority of their race, and some people fight because of their anger. Now who among these are in the way of Allah?"

The Prophet (pbuh) said:

"Only he who fights that Allah's Word (i.e. Islam) should be superior fights in Allah's Cause." (See Bukhari, Jihad, 15; Muslim, Imara, 149-151)

In our third hadith, we are informed that hurrying in jihad and being early in this way even for a few hours is better than performing a prayer with the Messenger of Allah (pbuh) or than donating everything on this world. When the Messenger of Allah (pbuh) saw that Abdullah bin Rawaha that he has sent to a military expedition got behind from his friends due to his desire to pray with the Messenger of Allah, he said:

"Even if you donate everything in this world, you would not gain the rewards that they would by departing early."

Again one day, the Messenger of Allah (pbuh) sent some of his noble companions to a military expedition. One of them stayed back. He said to his family:

"I stayed back thinking 'let me perform the Salat al-Zuhr with the Messenger of Allah and then say goodbye to him'. He also said that 'the Messenger can pray for me so that prayer can be intercessor for me on the Day of Judgment."

This person approached our Noble Prophet after the prayer and greeted him.

The Messenger of Allah (pbuh) said:

"Do you know by how much your friends got in front of you?"

The companion said:

"Yes, they have got ahead of me as much as it can be traveled since the morning."

Upon this, the Messenger of Allah (pbuh) said:

"I swear to Allah who holds my carnal self in His hands that they have got ahead of you in terms of virtue as much as the distance between the east and the west." (Ahmad, III, 438)

This is to say that the steps taken and the seconds spent in the way of Allah are so valuable. As a matter of fact, it is impossible to find another worship that is better and more virtuous than jihad in terms of its goal and hardships. Indeed, **in our forth hadith,** the Messenger of Allah (pbuh) said the following to a person who asked if there is worship same in virtue as jihad:

"I don't know such a deed (that is equivalent to Jihad)!"

According to the narration in the Muslim, this question was repeated two or three times and the Messenger of Allah (pbuh) answered in each time:

"You cannot find a deed that is equivalent to it!" Then he said:

"One who goes out for Jihad is like a person who keeps fasts, stands in prayer (constantly), (obeying) Allah's (behests contained in) the verses (of the Qur'an), and does not exhibit any lassitude in fasting and prayer until the Mujahid returns from Jihad in the way of Allah, the Exalted." (Muslim, Kitab Al-Imara, 110. Also see Tirmidhi, Fadail al-jihad, 1; Nasai, Jihad, 17)

When the noble companion who asked the question heard what the Prophet had said, he had to confess that no one can do that.

Not only jihad but everything that is related to it is also virtuous. As a matter of fact, **in our fifth hadith** it is told about the virtue of being on duty (e.g. protecting the border etc.)

The word "Ribat" mentioned in the hadith (in the original text) means to be ready and wait to prevent the attack of the enemy and depend in the way of Allah. The same term is used for the border that is formed between unbelievers and Muslims in order to protect the believers. The posts located at the border between a Muslim country and a country of non-believers is also called "ribat." The soldiers who are on duty in these places are called "murabit."

We see from the original text of the following noble verse that feeding a horse and making them ready for jihad is also called ribat:

"Against them make ready your strength to the utmost of your power, including steeds of war, to strike terror into (the hearts of) the enemies, of Allah and your enemies, and others besides, whom ye may not know, but whom Allah doth know. Whatever you shall spend in the cause of Allah, shall be repaid unto you, and you shall not be treated unjustly." (Al-Anfal; 8:60)

Based on this verse, our scholars expressed that it is one of the most important duties of Muslims to have all the weapons that are necessary for the time, and producing war weapons and equipment and making them ready for use. Therefore, every act and preparation that is related to jihad is a good deed and included in the good news of the hadith.

As per the first meaning of ribat, a person who is on duty at the border gains rewards that are equivalent to fasting during the day and conducting miscellaneous acts of worship in the night. If the person passes away during this duty, the righteous deed that he was performing transforms into an everlasting reward (sadaqah jaria) and he earns divine rewards until the Day of Judgment. Since he passed away during a duty related to jihad, he is considered a martyr, and he immediately starts to benefit from the bounties of the Paradise. He is saved right away from the hardships of the grave, which is the most passage for humans, and questions of the angels.[274]

---

274. Indeed the grave is a great source of fear and anxiety for humans. Indeed the Messenger of Allah (pbuh) said:
"The grave is the first of the stages of the Hereafter; whoever is saved from it, what comes afterwards will be easier for him, but if he is not saved from it, what comes afterwards will be worse (more difficult and intense) for him. ... I have never seen any scene that was as frightening and scary as the grave." (Ahmad, I, 63-64)

Indeed, ribat is a virtuous deed that saves one from the horrific scenes of the grave. This is because it is a hard and difficult service in order to protect people's religion, life, property, honor, and chastity.

In our sixth hadith, we are informed that jihad with property and life is the most important worship that is a means to entering Heaven. The Messenger of Allah (pbuh) has proposed some conditions to the companion who came to pledge allegiance to him. When the companion said that he would fear the anger of Allah in case he leaves jihad because he would fear for his life and also he would not be able to give sadaqah from his wealth which is sufficient only for his family, the Messenger of Allah (pbuh) clenched and shook his fist and said:

"There is neither striving nor almsgiving, then how will you enter the Paradise?"

Allah knows the best but maybe the Prophet (pbuh) wanted to show by clenching his fist that what prevents one from jihad and sadaqah is miserliness that clenches a person like an iron shield.

So, jihad and sadaqah, are two means to practice the religion and to earn the Heaven. This is because striving in the way of Allah through ones wealth and life is the beginning of the matter and the peak of the religion. When jihad and sadaqah disappears from the scene, the religion weakens and mischief covers the world. Indeed, in one of the hadith of the Messenger of Allah (pbuh), which he starts by saying *"There will come such a time upon people that..."* and where he describes the times where religiousness weakens, he informs us that people will see jihad as loss and zakat as a difficult loan that is hard to handle and pay back. (Ali al-Muttaqi, III, 236/6322)

For this reason, the companion has not been late to realize the seriousness of the matter upon the Prophet's meaningful question and has participated in the jihads by immediately accepting all the conditions and pledging allegiance. Indeed, in our sources it is stated that that person has participated in the conquest of Madain at the time of Umar. (Ibn Asaakir, *Tarihu Dimashq*, X, 308)

Jihad does not just help a person enter the Heaven also helps the person reach the highest ranks. **In our seventh hadith,** we are informed that there are one hundred grades in Heaven for the martyrs and that the distance between each of them are as far as the distance between the Earth and the Sky. In our hadith, there is also an indicator that the mujahedeen (strivers) are going to be placed in the Heaven of Firdaows, the highest rank in Heaven.

The Messenger of Allah (pbuh) says the following:

"Nobody who enters Paradise likes to go back to the world even if he got everything on the earth, except a Mujahid who wishes to return to the world so that he may be martyred ten times because of the dignity he receives (from Allah)." (Bukhari, Jihad, 21; Muslim, Imara, 109. Also see. Tirmidhi, Fadail al-jihad, 13, 25)

As jihad and being mujahidin are so virtuous, those who leave jihad also correspondingly burden themselves very heavily and end up risking themselves.

The Messenger of Allah (pbuh) says the following:

"He who does not join the warlike expedition (jihad), or equip, or looks well after a warrior's family when he is away, will be smitten by Allah with a sudden calamity before the Day of Resurrection" (Abu Dawud, Jihad, 17/2503. Also see Ibn Majah, Jihad, 5)

"When you transact via i'nah[275] method, when you hold on to the tails of oxen, when you prefer farming and leave jihad, Allah will bestow upon you such a despicableness that it won't be removed until you go back to your religion." (Abu Dawud, Kitab Al-Buyu, 54/3462)

The purpose of saying 'holding on to the tails of oxen and preferring farming…' is to be busy with worldly affairs when it is necessary to do jihad. This situation is nothing but the heedlessness of one's risking oneself with his own hands. The following narration that shows this contains lots of lessons to take:

In the time of Umayyads, the army of Abdurrahman, the son of Khalid b. Walid (r.a.), had departed in order to achieve the glad tidings and praise of the Messenger of Allah regarding the conquest of Istanbul. Abu Ayyub Al Ansari (r.a.) was also in that army. When the Romans were fighting while their back was towards the city walls, a person from the Ansar rode his horse to the middle of the Romans.

---

275. I'nah is sales transaction where a person sells a good with installments at a certain price but purchases back the same good with a price that is lower than the price he charges when he sells with no installments. Such a transaction has not been found permissible because it contains a doubt that it could be interest. (H. Yunus Apaydın, "İne", *Diyanet İslâm Ansiklopedisi*, XXII, 283-284)

Recalling the verse **"...make not your own hands contribute to (your) destruction...** (Al Baqara, 2:195)," the believers who saw this said:

"*La ilaaha illallah*! Look at him! He is recklessly risking his life!"

Upon his Abu Ayyub Al Ansari said the following:

"O believers! That verse was revealed about us, the Helpers (Ansaar). When Almighty Allah helped His Prophet and had his religion prevail we had said, 'From now on, we should stay and be busy with our property.' Upon his Almighty Allah revealed the following verse to His Messenger:

"And spend of your substance in the cause of Allah, and make not your own hands contribute to (your) destruction; but do good; for Allah loves those who do good."[276]

The purpose of 'make not your own hands contribute to (your) destruction; but do good' in this verse is that you should not leave aside and neglect jihad by busying yourself with worldly goods such as gardens and fields."

Abu Ayyub al-Ansari did not leave jihad even though he was over the age of eighty. He continued to strive in the way of Allah until he was martyred and buried in Istanbul. (See Abu Dawud, Jihad, 22/2512; Tirmidhi, Tafsir, 2/2972)

CR

---

276. Al-Baqara, 2:195.

BIBLIOGRAPHY

Abdurrazzaq b. Hammam, *Musannaf,* I-XI, Beirut, 1970.

Abdülaziz Çaviş, *Anglikan Kilisesine Cevap,* simplified by Süleymân Ateş, Ankara 1974.

Ahmad b. Abdullah bin Muhammad al-Tabari, *al-Riyad al-Nadra,* Beirut, 1996.

Ahmad b. Hanbal, *al-Musnad,* I-VI, Istanbul 1992;

az-Zuhd, n.p., n.d.

Ali al-Qari, Abu al-Hasan Nuraddin Ali bin Sultan Muhammad, *Mirqat al-Mafatih sharhu Mishkat al-Masabih,* I-XI, (Beirut: Dar al-Fikr) 1992.

Ali al-Muttaqi, Alauddin Ali b. Abdulmalik, *Kanz al-ummal fi sunan al-aqwal wa al-af'al,* I-XVI, Beirut 1985.

Alusi, Shihabuddin Sayyid Mahmud, *Ruh al-Ma'ani fi tafsir al-Qur'an al-'Azim,* I-XXX, (Beirut: Dar ihya al-Turath al-'Arabi), n.d.

Ayni, Abu Muhammad Badruddin Mahmud bin Ahmad bin Musa al-Hanafî, *Umdat al-Qari sharhu Sahih al-Bukhari,* I-XXV, (Beirut: Idarat al-Taba'at al-Muniriyye) n.d.

Azimabadi, Abu al-Tayyib Shams al-Haq Muhammad b. Amir Ali, *Awn al-Ma'bud Sharhu Sunan Abu Dawud,* I-XVI, (Beirut: Daru'l-Kutubi'l-Ilmiyya) 1998.

Babanzade Ahmad Naîm - Kâmil Mîras, *Sahih-i Buhari Muhtasari Tecrid-i Sarih Tercümesi ve Şerhi,* I-XIII, Ankara, 1993.

Baghdadi, Abu Bakr Ahmad bin Ali, *Tarihu Baghdad,* I-XIV, Beirut, n.d.

Balazuri, Abu al-Abbas Ahmad bin Yahya, *Ansab al-Ashraf,* Egypt, 1959.

Baihaqi, Abu Bakr Ahmad b. al-Husain, *al-Sunan al-Kubra,* I-X, Dar al-Fikr, n.d.;

Shuabu'l-iman, I-IX, Beirut, 1990.

ez-Zuhdu'l-kabeer, Kuwait 1983.

Bukhari, Abu Abdillah Muhammad bin Ismail, *al-Jami al-Sahih,* I-VIII, Istanbul, 1992;

al-Adabu'l-mufrad, Beirut 1989.

Daraqutni, Abu al-Hasan Ali bin Umar, *Sunan,* I-IV, Beirut 1986.

Darimi, Abu Muhammad Abdullah b. Abdurrahman, *Sunan al-Darimi,* I-II, Istanbul 1992.

Dailami, Abu Shuja' Shiruya b. Shahridar, *Al-Firdaws bi-Ma'sur al-Hitab,* Beirut, 1986.

İzzet Derveze, *et-Tefsîru'l Hadis,* I-VII, Istanbul 1998.

Diyarbakri, Husain b. Muhammad, *Tarih al-Khamis,* I-II, Beirut n.d.

Abu Dawud, Sulaiman bin Ash'as al-Sijistani, *Sunanu Abu Dawud,* I-V, Istanbul 1992.

Abu Nuaym, Ahmad b. Abdillah, *Hilyat al-Awliya,* I-X, Beirut 1967.

Elmalılı, M. Hamdi Yazır, *Hak Dîni Kur'ân Dili,* I-X, Istanbul 1971.

Fariduddin Attar, *Tadhkirat al-Awliya,* Tehran 1372.

Ghazali, Abu Hamid Muhammad, *Ihyau Ulum al-Din,* I-VI, Beirut 1990.

Hadimi, *Majmuat al-Rasail,* (Istanbul: Dar al-Tiba'at al-Amira) 1304.

Hakim, Abu Abdillah Muhammad b. Abdillah al-Naisaburi, *Al-Mustadrak ala' al-Sahihain,* I-V, Beirut 1990.

Halabi, Abu al-Faraj Ali b. Ibrahim, *Insan al-Uyun,* I-III, Egypt 1964.

Harith al-Muhasibi, *Al-Riaya li-Huquqillah,* Beirut 1985.

Hatib al-Baghdadi, Abu Bakr al-Hatib b. Ali bin Thabit, *Al-Faqih wa al-mutafaqqih,* Beirut 1395;

Tarihu Baghdad wa Madaniyyat al-Salam, I-XIV, (Beirut: Dar al-Kutub al-Arabi).

Haydar Hatipoğlu, *Sünenü Ibni Maceh Tercemesi ve Şerhi,* I-X, Istanbul 1982-1983.

Hayreddin Karaman, item "Cuma", *Diyanet İslâm Ansiklopedisi*, VIII, 87;

İslâm'ın Işığında Günün Meseleleri (Today's Issues in the Light of Islam), I-III, Istanbul 1982.

Haythami, Hafız Nuraddin Ali b. Abi Bakr, *Majma' al-Zawaid wa manba' al-Fawaid*, I-X, Beirut 1988.

Ibn Abdilbar, Abu Umar Yusuf b. Abdullah b. Muhammad, *al-Istiab fi Marifat al-Ashab*, I-IV, Cairo, n.d.;

Istidhkar, Beirut 2000.

Ibn al-Arabi, Abu Abdillah Muhyiddin Muhammad b. Ali, *al-Futuhat al-Makkiyya*, I-XIV, ed. Uthman Ismail Yahya, Ibrahim Madkur, (Cairo: al-Hay'at al-Misriyyat al-Amma li'l-Kitab), 1978.

Ibn Asakir, Abu Qasim Ali b. Hasan, *Tarihu Dimashk*, n.d.

Ibn al-Jawzi, *Sifat al-Safwa*, I-IV, Beirut 1979.

Manaqibu Amir al-Mu'minin Umar b. Khattab, ed. Ali Muhammad Umar, Cairo 1997.

Ibn Abi al-Dunya, Abu Bakir Abdullah, *Mawsuat Rasaili Ibn Abi al-Dunya*, Beirut 1993.

Ibn Abi Shayba, Abu Bakr Abdullah b. Muhammad, *al-Musannaf*, I-IX, ed. Said Muhammad al-Lahham, Beirut 1989.

Ibn al-Athir, Abu al-Hasan Ali b. Muhammad, *al-Kamil fi al-Tarikh*, I-XIII, Beirut 1979-1982;

Usd al-Ghaba, I-VII, Cairo 1970.

Ibn Hajar al-Askalani, Shihabuddin Ahmad b. Ali, *Fath al-Bari sharhi Sahih al-Bukhari*, I-XXVIII, Dar al-Fikr, Fuat Abdulbaqi publication, n.d.;

Al-Isaba fi tamyiz al-Sahaba, Egypt 1379;

Talkhis al-Khabir, I-IV, al-Madinat al-Munawwara, 1964;

Munabbihat, Istanbul 1960.

Ibn Hibban, Abu Hatim al-Busti, *Sahihu Ibn Hibban*, I-XVIII, Beirut, 1993.

Ibn Hisham, Abu Muhammad Abdulmalik bin Hisham, *Sirat al-Nabi,* I-IV, (Beirut: Dâru'l-Fikr), 1937.

Ibn Huzaima, Abu Bakr Muhammad b. Ishaq, *Sahihu Ibn Huzayma,* I-IV, Beirut, 1970.

Ibn Ishaq, Muhammad b. Ishaq b. Yasar, *Siratu Ibn Ishaq (Kitab al-mubtadai wa al-mab'asi wa al-maghazi),* Konya 1981.

İbn-i Kayyım el-Cevziyye, Muhammed Ebî Bekir, *Zadu'l-mead,* I-VI, Kuveyt, 1991.

Ibn Kathir, Imaduddin Abu al-Fida, *Tafsiru Qur'an al-Azim,* I-IV, Beirut 1988;

al-Bidaya wa al-Nihaya, I-XV, Cairo 1993.

Ibn Majah, Abu Abdillah Muhammad b. Yazid al-Qazvini, *Sunanu Ibn Majah,* I-II, Istanbul 1992.

Ibn Sa'd, Muhammad, *al-Tabakat al-Kubra,* I-IX, (Beirut: Daru Sadr).

Ibn Sayyidinnas, *Uyun al-Athar fi funun al-Maghazi wa al-shamail wa al-Siyar,* I-II, Beirut 1992.

Ibrâhim Canan, *Hadis Ansiklopedisi,* I-XVIII, Istanbul, n.d.

Imam Malik b. Anas, *Muwatta',* I-II, Istanbul 1992.

Ismail Lütfi Çakan, *Hadislerle Gerçekler,* Istanbul 2003.

Kadı Iyaz, Abu al-Fadl Iyaz b. Musa b. Iyaz al-Yahsubi, *Al-Shifa bi ta'rifi huquq al-Mustafa,* (Istanbul: Halil Efendi Matbaası), 1290.

Qasimi, Muhammad Jamaladdin, *Mahasin al-Ta'wil* (pub. Muhammed Fuad Abdulbaqi), I-XVII, (Cairo: Daru Ihya al-Kutub al-'Arabiyya), n.d.

Qastallani, Abu al-Abbas Ahmad bin Muhammad, *al-Mawahib al-Ladunniyya,* I-II, Egypt 1281.

Qattani, Muhammad Abdu al-Hayy, *Nizam al-hukumat al-Nabawiyya (al-Taratib al-Idariyya),* Beirut 1996.

Qurtubi, Abu Abdillah Muhammad b. Ahmad, *al-Jami li-Ahkam al-Qur'an,* I-XX, Beirut 1985.

Kushayri, Abu al-Qasim Abdulkarim b. Hawazin, *al-Risalat al-Kushayriyya,* Cairo 1966.

Mawlana Jalaladdin al-Rumi, *Mathnawi-yi Ma'nawi;*

Divan-ı Kabir, Ankara 2000.

Mubarakfuri, Abu al-Ala Abdurrahman, *Tuhfat al-Ahwazi bi sharhi Jami' al-Tirmidhi,* Cairo, n.d.

Muhammad Ilyas Abdulghani, *Tarihu Makkat al-Mukarrama Qadiman wa Hadithan,* al-Madinat al-Munawwara, 2001.

Muhammad Nur Suwaid, *Peygamberimizin Sünnetinde Çocuk Eğitimi,* trans. into Turkish by Zekeriya Güler, Konya 1994.

Munawi, Muhammad Abdurrauf, *Fayd al-Qadir sharh al-Jami al-Saghir,* I- VI, Beirut 1994.

Munziri, *at-Targhib wa al-tarhib,* Beirut 1417.

Muslim, Abu al-Husain b. Hajjaj al-Qushairi, *al-Jami' al-Sahih* (thk. Muhammad Fuad Abdulbaqi), I-III, Istanbul, 1992.

M. Yaşar Kandemir, İsmâil Lütfi Çakan, Râşit Küçük, *Riyazu's-Salihin -Tercüme ve Şerh,* I-VIII, Istanbul 2001.

Necati Yeniel -Hüseyin Kayapınar, *Sunen-i Abu Dawud Terceme ve Şerhi,* Istanbul 1988.

Nasai, Abu Abdirrahman Ahmad b. Shuayb, *Sunan al-Nasai,* I-VIII, Istanbul 1992.

Nawawi, Abu Zakariyya Yahya b. Sharaf, *Sharhu Sahih-i Muslim,* I-XVIII, Egypt 1981.

Ömer Çelik, *Kur'an'a Göre Kur'an-ı Kerim ve Muhatapları,* Istanbul 1997, (Unpublished Ph.D. dissertation at the Institute of Political Science at Marmara University).

Rudani, *Jam' al-Fawaid,* translated by Naim Erdoğan, Istanbul n.d.

Said Baktash, *Fadl al-Hajar al-Aswad wa Maqami Ibrahim,* Beirut 1420.

Saharanfuri, Halil Ahmad, *Bazl al-majhud fi Halli Abu Dawud,* I-X, Beirut 1973.

Sarraj, *al-Luma',* Cairo 1960.

Suyuti, Abu al-Fadl Jalaladdin Abdurrahman b. Abu Bakr, *al-Jami al-Saghir,* Egypt 1306;

Lubab al-Nuqul, Beirut 2006;

Tarih al-Khulafa, Egypt 1969.

Shah Waliyyullah Dihlawi, *Hujjatullah al-Baligha,* I-II, thk. Muhammad Sharif Sukkar, Beirut 1990.

Shaih Sadi Shirazi, *Bostan,* translated by Kilisli Rıfat Bilge, Istanbul 1995.

Taberânî, el-Hâfız Ebu'l-Kâsım Süleyman bin Ahmad, *al-Mu'jamu'l-Kabir,* I-XXV, 1983.

Tabari, Abu Jafar Muhammad b. Jarir, *Jami al-Bayan an ta'wil ay al-Qur'an,* I-XXX Beirut 1995;

Tarih, I-XI, Egypt, n.d.

Tirmidhi, Abu Isa, Muhammad b. Isa, *Sunan al-Tirmidhi,* I-V, Istanbul 1992.

Wahidi, Imam Abu al-Hasan Ali b. Ahmad, *Asbabu nuzul al-Qur'an,* thk: Kemal Basyuni Zaghlul, Beirut 1990.

Waqidi, Abu Abdillah Muhammad b. Umar, *Maghazi,* I-III, Beirut, 1989; Egypt 1948.

Zekeriya Güler, *40 Hadiste Kadın ve Aile (Women and Family in 40 Hadith),* Konya 2004.

Hadis Günlüğü (Hadith Diary), Konya 2006.

Zamahshari, Abu al-Qasim Jarullah Mahmud b. Umar b. Muhammad, *Tafsir al-Kashshaf an haqaiq al-Tanzil wa uyun al-Aqawil fi wujuh al-Ta'wil,* I-VI, ed. Muhammad Mursi Amir, Cairo 1988.